# The Carolingian Revolution

UTRECHT STUDIES IN MEDIEVAL LITERACY

48

UTRECHT STUDIES IN MEDIEVAL LITERACY

General Editor

Marco Mostert (Universiteit Utrecht)

Editorial Board

Gerd Althoff (Westfälische-Wilhelms-Universität Münster)
Michael Clanchy (University of London)
Erik Kwakkel (Universiteit Leiden)
Mayke de Jong (Universiteit Utrecht)
Rosamond McKitterick (University of Cambridge)
Arpád Orbán (Universiteit Utrecht)
Francesco Stella (Università degli Studi di Siena)
Richard H. Rouse (UCLA)

THE CAROLINGIAN REVOLUTION

UNCONVENTIONAL APPROACHES TO MEDIEVAL LATIN LITERATURE I

Francesco Stella

BREPOLS

British Library Cataloguing in Publication Data

A catalogue record for this book is available from the British Library

The preparation of this volume benefitted from support of the
University of Siena, Department DFCLAM.

© 2020 – Brepols Publishers n.v., Turnhout, Belgium

All rights reserved. No part of this publication may be reproduced, stored in a retrieval system, or transmitted, in any form or by any means, electronic, mechanical, photocopying, recording, or otherwise, without the prior permission of the publisher.

D/2020/0095/371

ISBN 978-2-503-58799-8

e-ISBN 978-2-503-58800-1

DOI 10.1484/M.USML-EB.5.119333

ISSN 2034-9416

eISSN 2294-8317

Printed in the EU on acid-free paper

Quicumque hos versus legeritis, imperfectum meum videant oculi vestri et vos imperfecti mei supplementum estote.

Baldricus

In memory of my Parents

Laetitiam habentes renovationis, facta vetera fugiamus.
   Hrabanus Maurus, *De rerum natura*, ed. in: PL 111, col. 588B (*De Universo*).

Ad quod sane principium innovationis revocamur.
   Paschasius Radbertus, *In Lamentationes Ieremiae*, ed. in: PL 120, col. 1254D.

Renovatur autem sensus noster per exercitia sapientiae.
   Smaragdus S. Michaelis, *Collectiones in epistolas et evangelia*, ed. in: PL 102, col. 76B, and Hrabanus Maurus, *Enarrationes in Epistolas B. Pauli*, ed. in: PL 111, col. 1543D, from Origen, *In Ep. ad Romanos*, ed. in: PG 14, cols. 1206-1207.

Ut veterum renovet studiosa mente sophiam.
   Alcuin, *Carmina*, 2, 21.

Novus semper innovatur et quotidie, si dici potest, ipsa novitas innovanda est, ut numquam sit quando haec innovatio non augescat.
   Sedulius Scotus, *Collectanea in omnes Pauli Epistolas*, ed. in: PL 103, col. 60A, from Origen, *In ep. ad Romanos*, ed. in: PG 14, col. 1042A.

Illud innovantis semper vitalis virtutis.
   Iohannes Scotus Eriugena, *Expositiones super Ierarchiam caelestem S. Dionysii*, ed. in: PL 122, col. 260C.

Contents

Acknowledgements	xiii
Abbreviations	xv
List of Illustrations	xvii

Introduction   1

1. Intercultural Imitation in Christian Latin Poetry as a Path to the Medieval Poetics of Alterity   9

2. The Women of the Old Testament in Early Medieval Poetry: Judith and the Others

    The Canon of Biblical Heroines in One Verse – The Model of Avitus – The Intercultural Foresight of Dracontius: Pagan and Christian Heroines – The Other Judiths, from Aldhelm to Milo – Instances in the Carolingian Age – Exegetical Sources and Later Developments – Other Biblical Heroines   29

3. *Ad Supplementum Sensus*: Hermeneutic Plurality and Increase in Meaning in Biblical Poetics from the Middle Ages to Derrida

    The End of Exclusion – Medieval Precursors – Ineffability and Allegory – The Legitimacy of a Heteronomous Aesthetic   53

4. A Repressed Beauty: Biblical Poetics and the Legitimisation of Poetry in Medieval Culture

> The Exclusion of Poetry from the Medieval Cultural System – Foundations of a Possible Legitimisation: The Symbolism of Eriugena and Chartres – The Anomaly of Biblical Poetry – Exegetical Poetry and the Rhetoric of Otherness (The *modus symbolicus*) – Double-Level Poetics – Technicalities of Exegetical Beauty – Multifigurality – Poetry about the Exegetical Process – Implicit Poetics and Explicit Theories   73

5. *Reticere nefas*: The Poetics of Communication in the Carolingian Age

> The Poetry of Writing – The Poetry of Scripture – The Invocation of the Reader and the Circle of Communication – Relational Poetry   97

6. A Lexical Journey through Alcuin's Poetry

> Witnesses and Judgements – The Editions – Tradition and Innovation in Poetic Genres and Themes: A Lexical Journey (The Historical-Hagiographical Poem: *Regnum* and *pietas* – Epigraphical Poetry: *Domus*, *viator* – Lyrical poetry)   121

7. Some Linguistic Features of Popular Songs in Medieval and Modern Times

> The Ritual Aspect – Anisosyllabism – Music-Text Relationship – Alterations of Accentuation – Combined Presence of Archaisms and Linguistic Vulgarisms – Development of an Internal Tradition – Plurality of Versions   147

8. *Versus ad picturas* in the Carolingian Age

> History of the Genre – The Carolingian Era and the Problem of Images – Carolingian Typologies – The Cycles of the Great Bibles of Tours – Appendix: Vivian's Bible, Poetic Captions (Selection)   175

Contents xi

9. Verse Historiography in the Carolingian Era: The Political Typology of the Ingelheim Paintings

    The Studies – The Political Use of Biblical References - The Poeta Saxo – Ermold – The Biblical Cycle – The Cycle of Power – The Meaning of the Paintings   209

10. The Sense of Time in Carolingian Poetry: *Horologium nocturnum* and the Christian Zodiac in Pacificus of Verona

    The Inscription of Verona – The *Horologium Nocturnum* – Avranches – Chartres – Vatican – Paris 12117 and the Link with the Astrolabe – Sense of Time and Stellar Observation in the Middle Ages – Computistical Verse – Appendix: Pacificus's Epitaph   233

11. Everyday Life in the Literary Inscriptions of the Carolingian Monastery

    The Matter of Poetic Epigraphy – Carolingian Monastic Epigraphy: Saint-Riquier – Epitaphs – Vestments and Furniture – Locales – The Role of Alcuin   261

12. New Forms of Verse Collections in the Carolingian Laboratory

    Late Antiquity – The Carolingian Ages: Authors' Collections – Local Collections – Epigraphical Collections – Biblical Anthologies – Poetic Anthologies – Appendix   285

13. The Modern Success and Medieval Marginality of Modoin of Autun's *Karolus Magnus et Leo Papa*

    The Meaning of Anonymity – *Karolus Magnus et Leo Papa (KMLP)* – Editions and Studies – The Problem of Dating and Completeness – The Author – New Developments in the Research – Hypotheses about the Author – Medieval Authority – Appendix   305

14. A 'Post-Colonial' Approach to Medieval Latin Literature?

    Carolingian Cases – Extensions - Second Language Analysis   339

Bibliography

    Sources – Literature　　　　　　　　　　　　　　　　351

Indices

    Manuscripts – Websites – General Index　　　　　395

Acknowledgements

Chapter One was published as "Intercultural imitation in Christian Latin poetry as a way to the medieval poetics of alterity", in: *Latinitas Perennis*, 1, *The Continuity of Latin Literature*, ed. I. PAPY and W. VERBAAL (Leiden: Brill, 2006), pp. 31-52. Chapter Two appears in *The Early Middle Ages*, ed. F.E. Consolino and J. Herren (Atlanta: SBP Press, 2020). Chapter Three was published in Italian in the proceedings of the Florence conference *La Scrittura Infinita: Bibbia e poesia in età medievale e umanistica* (Florence, SISMEL 2001), pp. 31-46. Chapter Four was published in *Retelling the Bible: Literary, Historical, and Social Contexts*, ed. L. DOLEŽALOVA and T. VISI (Frankfurt am Main: Peter Lang, 2011), pp. 303-323. An Italian version of Chapter Five was published in the proceedings of *Comunicazione e significazione nell'alto medioevo* (Spoleto: CISAM, 2005), pp. 615-652. A first version of Chapter Six was published in German as "Alkuins Dichtung", in: *Alkuin von York und die geistige Grundlegung Europas*, ed. E. TREMP and K. SCHMUKI (Saint Gall: Verlag am Klosterhof, 2010), pp. 107-128. Chapter Seven was a paper presented under invitation to a 2011 Columbus (Ohio) conference in honour of Charles Atkinson. An Italian version of Chapter Eight appeared in *Text, Bild und Ritual in der mittelalterlichen Gesellschaft (8.-11. Jh.)*, ed. P. CARMASSI and Ch. WINTERER (Florence: SISMEL 2014), pp. 177-200. A French version of Chapter Nine was published in *La typologie biblique comme forme de pensée dans l'historiographie médiévale – Biblical Typology as a Mode of Thinking in Medieval Historiography*, ed. M. KRETSCHMER (Turnhout: Brepols, 2014), pp. 25-52. A version of Chapter Ten was published in the proceedings of *Le Sens du Temps – The Sense of Time: Actes du VIIe Congrès du Comité International de Latin Médiéval – Proceedings of the VIIth Conference of the International Medieval Latin Committee (Lyon, 10-13. 09.2014)*, ed. P. BOURGAIN and J.-Y. TILLIETTE (Geneva: Droz, 2017), pp.

193-218. Chapter Eleven is a new version of a paper published in *Le Scritture dai Monasteri: Atti del II seminario internazionale di studio 'I monasteri nell'alto medioevo', Rome, 9-10 May 2002*, ed. F. DE RUBEIS and W. POHL (Rome, 2003), pp. 123-144. A first version of Chapter Twelve was presented at a seminar organised at Ghent University by the research network Interfaces within the framework of the Centre for Medieval Literature. An Italian version of Chapter Thirteen has been published in *Filologia Mediolatina* 23 (2016), pp. 23-58. A different version of Chapter Fourteen came out in *Colonial – Post-Colonial: Writing as Memory in Literature*, ed. I. MATA (Lisbon: Edições Colibri, 2013), pp. 13-23. Changes have been made in every chapter.

There is nothing more inadequate than the book's expressions of gratitude: if they were to be complete, they should include hundreds of people and institutions. To adapt the cliché, I limit myself to thank, among many others, the scholars (too many to name them here) who involved me in interdisciplinary projects, thereby stimulating my interest in different approaches to early medieval Latin culture, and the ones who helped me in editing such a magmatic matter: Matthew Fox and Helen Glave for individual translations, Erin Brady for thoroughly reviewing (and sometimes translating) many chapters, Graeme Boone for correcting the musical paper, Inocencia Mata for reading the 'postcolonial' contribution, Judith Herrin and Sarah Bairstow for translating the essay on Biblical women, Lucie Doležalová for editing the paper about biblical hermeneutics, my friend Alessandro Barchiesi for all his precious suggestions on the whole book, and Marco Mostert for accepting this work in the series he directs and for his reading tips; obviously any errors and imperfections remain my responsibility.

Abbreviations

AASS	*Acta sanctorum quotquot toto orbe coluntur ...*, ed. J. BOLLANDUS, red. G. HENSCHENIUS *et al.*, 1- (Antwerpen etc., 1643-).
AASS OSB	*Acta sanctorum ordinis Sancti Benedicti*, ed. J. MABILLON, 9 vols. (Paris, 1668-1701).
CCSM	*Corpus Christianorum Series Latina: Continuatio Mediaevalis*, 1- (Turnhout, 1966-).
CCSL	*Corpus Christianorum Series Latina*, 1- (Turnhout, 1954-).
CRM	*Corpus Rhythmorum Musicum saec. IV-IX*, 1- (Florence, 2007-).
CSEL	*Corpus Scriptorum Ecclesiasticorum Latinorum*, 1- (Vienna, 1866-).
MGH	*Monumenta Germaniae Historica*
AA	*Auctores Antiquissimi*, 15 vols. (Berlin, 1877-1919).
Capitularia	*Capitularia regum Francorum*, ed. A. BORETIUS and V. KRAUSE, 2 vols. (Hanover, 1883-1887).
Concilia	*Concilia*, 3 vols. (Hanover and Leipzig, 1893-1984).
Epp	*Epistolae (in Quarto)*, vols. 1-8.1 (Berlin, 1887-1939).
PP	*Poetae Latini medii aevi*, 1- (Berlin, etc., 1881-).
SRG in usum scholarum	*Scriptores rerum Germanicarum in usum scholarum separatim editi*, 63 vols. (Hanover and Leipzig, 1841-1987).
SRG Nova Series	*Scriptores rerum Germanicarum: Nova Series*, vols. 1-13, 15 (Berlin etc., 1922-1990).
SRM	*Scriptores rerum Merovingicarum*, 7 vols. (Hanover and Leipzig, 1884-1951).
SS	*Scriptores (in Folio)* 30 vols.; *(in Quarto)* vols. 31-34 (Hanover, 1826-1980).

LDM	*Lexikon des Mittelalters*, 9 vols. and *Registerband* (Munich etc., 1977-1999).
PC	F. STELLA, *La poesia carolingia* (Florence, 1995).
PG	*Patrologiae cursus completus ... Series Graeca*, ed. J.P. MIGNE, 161 vols. (Paris, 1857-1936).
PL	*Patrologiae cursus completus ... Series Latina*, ed. J.P. MIGNE, 221 vols. (Paris, 1841-1864).
PLAC 1	*Poetae Latini aevi Carolini* 1, ed. E. DÜMMLER (Berlin, 1881 = MGH PP 1).
PLAC 2	*Poetae Latini aevi Carolini* 2, ed. E. DÜMMLER (Berlin, 1884 = MGH PP 2).
PLAC 3	*Poetae Latini aevi Carolini* 3, ed. L. TRAUBE (Berlin, 1886-1896 = MGH PP 3).
PLAC 4.1	*Poetae Latini aevi Carolini* 4.1, ed. P. VON WINTERFELD (Berlin, 1899 = MGH PP 4.1).
PLAC 4.2	*Poetae Latini aevi Carolini* 4.2 [*Rhythmi aevi Merovingici et Carolini*], ed. K. STRECKER (Berlin, 1954 = MGH PP 4.2).
PLAC 4.3	*Poetae Latini aevi Carolini* 4.3 [*Supplementa*], ed. K. STRECKER (Berlin, 1954 = MGH PP 4.3).
PLAC 5.1-2	*Die Ottonenzeit*, ed. K. STRECKER with N. FICKERMANN (Leipzig, 1937-1939 = MGH PP 5.1-2).
PLAC 5.3	[*Ergänzungen, Nachträge, Register*], ed. G. SILAGI with B. BISCHOFF (Leipzig, 1979 = MGH PP 5.3).
PLAC 6.1	*Nachträge zu den Poetae aevi Carolini*, 1, ed. K. STRECKER with O. SCHUMANN (Munich, 1951 = MGH PP 6.1).
Poetria Nova 2	*Poetria Nova: A CD-ROM of Medieval Latin Poetry (650-1250 A.D., with a Gateway to Classical and Late Antique Texts*, ed. P. MASTANDREA and L. TESSAROLO (Florence, 2010).
SC	*Sources Chrétiennes*, 1- (Paris, 1942-).

List of Illustrations

Fig. 1	*Septem artes liberales* from the *Hortus deliciarum* by Herrad from Landsberg (*c.* 1180). Cf. O. GILLEN, *Herrad von Landsberg, Hortus Deliciarum* (Neustadt, 1979).	74
Fig. 2	*Ante saecula*, as preserved in MS Naples, Biblioteca Nationale, IV. G. 68, f. 207r (from *CRM*).	161
Fig. 3	*Gloriam Deo*, as preserved in MS Rome, Biblioteca Angelica 123, f. 188v (from *CRM*).	161
Fig. 4	*Avis haec magna*, from MS Berne, Burgerbibliothek 455, f. 13v (from *CRM*).	163
Fig. 5	*O tu qui servas*, strophe 1, line 4. MS Modena, Archivio storico diocesano, O.1.4, f. 154v (from *CRM*).	163
Fig. 6	Out-of-sync timing in *Dolcenera* by Fabrizio De André, as transcribed by Errico Pavese.	164
Fig. 7	*Homo quidam*, as it occurs in MS London, British Library, Add. 19768, MS Fulda, Hessische Landesbibliothek, Aa 62, and MS Vienna, Österreichische Nationalbibliothek, lat. 1888; transcription of Sam Barrett (from *CRM*).	165
Fig. 8	MS Paris, Bibliothèque nationale de France, latin 1, f. 2r.	187
Fig. 9	MS London, British Library, Add. 10546, f. 5v.	191
Fig. 10	MS Paris, Bibliothèque nationale de France, latin 1, f. 27v.	193
Fig. 11	MS Paris, Bibliothèque nationale de France, latin 1, f. 215v.	196
Fig. 12	MS Paris, Bibliothèque nationale de France, latin 1, f. 329v.	198
Fig. 13	MS Paris, Bibliothèque nationale de France, latin 1, f. 415v.	200
Fig. 14	MS Paris, Bibliothèque nationale de France, latin 1, f. 423v.	203
Fig. 15	MS Paris, Bibliothèque nationale de France, latin 1, ff. 1v-2r.	204
Fig. 16	Ingelheim, isometric representation of the remains of the palace, with indication of the building periods. After <http://www.kaiserpfalz-ingelheim.de>.	220

Fig. 17	Ingelheim, reconstruction of the Aula Regia. After <http://www.kaiserpfalz-ingelheim.de>.	221
Fig. 18	MS Venice, Biblioteca Nazionale Marciana, lat. VII. 22 (= 2760) (s. XII-XIII), f. 1r, photo F. STELLA.	234
Fig. 19	Pacificus's Epitaphs in Verona (photo C. SAVINI).	236
Fig. 20	MS Avranches, Bibliothèque Municipale, 235, f. 32v (detail).	241
Fig. 21	Detail of MS Chartres, Bibliothèque Municipale, 214 (now lost), in WIESENBACH 1993.	243
Fig. 22	MS Vatican, Biblioteca Apostolica Vaticana, Vat. lat. 644, f. 76r.	244
Fig. 23	MS Cava dei Terreni, Archivio e Biblioteca della Badia, 3, f. 203r.	245
Fig. 24	MS Paris, Bibliothèque nationale de France, latin 12117 f. 423v (detail).	246
Fig. 25	Night clock (s. XVI) with Zodiac. Museo della Scienza Galileo Galilei, Florence.	248
Fig. 26	Saint-Riquier. Engraving of 1612 after a (now destroyed) miniature of the eleventh century.	266
Fig. 27	MS Zurich, Zentralbibliothek Ms C 78, f. 103v (after <http://e-codices.ch/de/searchresult/list/one/zbz/C0078>).	329
Fig. 28	MS Zurich, Zentralbibliothek C 78, f. 104r (after <http://e-codices.ch/de/searchresult/list/one/zbz/C0078>).	329
Fig. 29	MS Zurich, Zentralbibliothek C 78, f. 107v (after <http://e-codices.ch/de/searchresult/list/one/zbz/C0078>).	329
Fig. 30	MS Zurich, Zentralbibliothek C 78, f. 110r (after <http://e-codices.ch/de/searchresult/list/one/zbz/C0078>).	330
Fig. 31	MS Zurich, Zentralbibliothek C 78, f. 113r (after <http://e-codices.ch/de/searchresult/list/one/zbz/C0078>).	330
Fig. 32	MS Zurich, Zentralbibliothek C 78, f. 114v (after <http://e-codices.ch/de/searchresult/list/one/zbz/C0078>).	330

Introduction

Medieval studies are undergoing a profound transformation, but despite medieval Latin being by far the richest in texts of all the medieval languages, its literature continues to be one of the least studied. This is because it is a supranational literature, whose language does not coincide with the language of a modern country. Consequently, it is not protected in university systems, and in the European and American schools where Latin is still studied what prevails is the classicist paradigm imposed from the eighteenth century on. In Italy, this model was standardised first through the school reform promoted in 1859 by Gabrio Casati, and later by the influential programmes of Giovanni Gentile and Giuseppe Bottai in the Fascist age. According to this model, the history of Latin ends in the fourth or fifth century, if not with Apuleius. Wherever medieval Latin literature is studied it is almost always in the service of national cultures, with each country favouring authors born on its own territory. And yet Latin was, before English, the most widespread language of culture in the world for a very long period that ranged from the year 500 to the nineteenth century: Medieval Latin was a global language and a textual heritage that for millennia hosted complex ways of thinking, scientific innovations, and fascinating forms of art and literature from Ireland to Japan, from Mexico to North Africa.

In recent years, a new attention to medieval Latin writings has emerged, albeit in an unsystematic and sporadic way, due to the pressure of the interest in the national identity of individual European countries or regions and the diffusion of narratives, even on screen, inspired by the medieval era, by its varied customs and figures. Hardly any of the viewers of the TV series *Vikings*, when inquiring about the Viking destruction of Lindisfarne, will have noticed that the sources of the records are not Anglo-Saxon chronicles, which dedicate only a few lines to the event, but a long elegy by Alcuin of York and his letters to Abbot Hygbald, as well as the *Historiae* of Simeon of Durham, all in Latin. Yet this general resurgence of interest in medieval narratives has had some positive effects also on the research on medieval Latin literature. Within this immense field, which includes over 18,000 authors from what today corresponds to over thirty-five countries for ten centuries, there are nuclei that always remain in the spotlight due to the prominence of a few historical figures. Among these is the Carolingian age, and in particular its first generation, the period that gave rise to one of the giants of history and, regardless of our judgment about it, of European identity: Charlemagne. A book is published on this figure every month in every western language, and the expression 'Carolingian Renaissance' is still used to refer to the time of his rule, due to the hypothetical recovery of classical readings (according to an old model, now outdated) and, I would say above all, to the innovations and standardisations that were introduced in those years and that changed the face of European culture. These include the idea that a heterogeneous political area should be governed according to a uniform cultural and linguistic strategy, and that this strategy should be developed in continuous confrontation with the best international minds and be integrated into the highest forms of socialisation possible (known as the *schola palatina*); the idea, related to the first and so current that it is now the basis of applications from network theory to epistolography,[1] of a *cultural network* understood as a web of people and centres of production and transcription in contact with each other and with other hubs, which multiplies the circulation of cultural developments and their communication power; the idea (*Admonitio generalis*) of a school programme (with related didactic tools) common to the whole kingdom or empire, based in turn on the idea, still revolutionary today, that correct behaviour derives from a correct way of thinking, and a correct way of thinking depends on the correct and profound knowledge of the language in which it is expressed (*Epistola de litteris colendis*); the idea of a script (the *carolina*, or Caroline minuscule) and a language (Alcuin's *De ortographia*) that are common and understandable in every region, associated with the idea that communication is the guarantee of identity of a people and of individual persons (as Poeta Saxo states in book V of the *Gesta Karoli Magni*), but also of every element of a culture: including music, which before this time was not written down (Notker of Saint Gall); the idea, on the trail of Au-

---

[1] Cf. the work of Mary Garrison, e.g. M. GARRISON, "Send more socks: On mentality and the preservation context of medieval letters", in: *New Approaches to Medieval Communication*, ed. M. MOSTERT (Turnhout, 1999: *Utrecht Studies in Medieval Literacy* 1), pp. 69-99.

gustan politics, that a state needs an intellectual class that is both autonomous and collaborative (Jonas of Orléans, Paulinus of Aquileia, Sedulius Scotus); the idea that works of art should not be the object of worship and therefore its subjects and its modes of representation are free, because they have an exclusively aesthetic purpose and, by way of aesthetics, a pedagogical one (Theodulf's – or Alcuin's – *Opus Caroli*); the idea that communities, monastic or urban, are historical and historiographical subjects like and even more than people or individuals (*Gesta episcoporum Mettensium, De sanctis Euboricensis ecclesiae*, monastic collections of poems like the *Carmina Centulensia*, etc.); the idea that Latin, adopted as a global language, can subsume oral elements of popular cultures, disguising them while saving them (*Conflictus, Aenigmata*, symbologies), but that every language is worth writing (*Sequence of Eulalia, Serment de Strasbourg, Evangelienbuch* of Otfrid, Charles's Germanic grammar); the idea that, thanks to trust in writing as communication and memory, we can tackle complex scientific and theological problems in a socialised form (see the *Karolingische Enzyklopädie*, edited by Arno Borst in 2006;[2] debate on predestination under Charles the Bald, circular investigations about astronomical phenomena); the idea that every aspect and object of life, history, and sacred text has more than one meaning and that this exegetical turn is destined for a multiplication of meanings over time (Hrabanus, Theodulf, Angelomus, Smaragdus), which deeply influenced the development of poetry; and finally, just to stop a potentially infinite list, the ideas that God is not (only) male, that sin is punishment of itself, that authority is inferior to reason, that figurative language is the only one capable of describing God, and, following Augustine, that the universe is like a text that expresses God (John Scotus Eriugena). Most of these ideas are transmitted in the capitularies, in exegetical treatises, and in an enormous epistolary heritage, but also in a poetic corpus of over 110,000 lines. Indeed, as Paul Lehmann wrote in 1954,[3] if there is any reason to call this era a 'Renaissance' also from the point of view of artistic merit, it is above all its poetry which was considered the peak of stylistic expression and a guarantee of the duration of memory. Like any literature, according to Theodor Adorno, the Carolingian one is a privileged and almost always unique way of accessing 'deep' history – that is, the perceptions, emo-

[2] *Schriften zur Komputistik im Frankenreich von 712 bis 818*, ed. A. BORST, 1 (Hanover, 2006: MGH *Quellen zur Geistesgeschichte des Mittelalters* 21.1).
[3] P. LEHMANN, "Das Problem der karolingischen Renaissance", in: *I problemi della civiltà carolingia* (Spoleto, 1954: *Settimana di studio del Centro Italiano di Studi sull'Alto Medioevo* 1), pp. 309-358.

tions, points of view, and external and internal landscapes of those who lived through the historical events. Nonetheless, when they are not speaking of great personalities (such as Einhard in the *Vita Karoli*), Carolingian poetry and literature are the *grands négligés* of the extraordinary attention usually paid to the Carolingian world. In the companions to medieval culture that we like publishing today, the period's poetry, unless it is cited as a mere source, is conspicuously absent, often confined to inadequate summaries or scholastic clichés dating back to the nineteenth century.

Of course, this book cannot fill such a glaring gap. Its goal is only to collect, in English, some essays on Carolingian poetry, written from 1988 to 2018 and sometimes printed in publications not easily available, about some 'lateral' aspects – thus labelled because undervalued – of this Renaissance, explored through methods not usually applied to this literature: interdisciplinary, intercultural, intermedial, statistical, digital. In doing so, it proposes the concept of a cultural movement that was not only powerful and full of lasting influence (just think of Caroline miniscule, which, through the *littera antiqua* and its recovery in modern prints, was developed into the Times New Roman font that we use today), but revolutionary in its many aims, ambitions, and achievements, often marginalised if compared to official Carolingian 'discourse'.

The contributions, which will ideally be complemented by two volumes of Carolingian essays in Italian (one comprising more philological and linguistic studies, the other including essays on hagiographical rewritings, the emergence of subjectivity, and other topics not addressed here), do not all exclusively concern the Carolingian age but sometimes explore its remote foundations or its follow-up in later cultures. This is true for the chapter (first written for conferences in Rhetymno and Brussels) on the layers of Roman patterns and biblical content in late antique Christian epic, the basis of Carolingian didactic literature, which sometimes places strikingly different cultures (the Greco-Roman and the biblical) in dialogue with each other, as would happen again in the Carolingian age; or in the two essays on biblical hermeneutics (from conferences in Florence and Prague), which constitute the necessary premise of meaning and cult of the book and writing documented in the chapter on paratextual poetry in this volume's companion volume in *Utrecht Studies in Medieval Literacy*, entitled *Digital Philology and Quantitative Criticism of Medieval Literature*.

This ideology of writing is responsible for another of the most powerful innovations of Carolingian culture: exegetical poetry, where theological methods of interpreting the Bible become the driving force of a new type of poetic elaboration, whose subjects are not so much the facts and characters of the Bible but the intellectual processes that serve to decrypt their meaning. Something similar could be said about the research on female characters in biblical epic, which also appeared in Italian, Spanish, and German on the initiative of Franca Ela Consolino and Judith Herrin, in which the Carolingian period is placed on a continuum between late antique creativity and the full Middle Ages. The chapter on song, presented at a Columbus (OH) conference for Charles Atkinson, is a side result of the *Corpus Rythmorum Musicum* project that explores another of the explosive novelties of the Carolingian revolution, musical writing; it analyses linguistic phenomena, in the musical relationship between text and accentuation, which occur in examples of popular poetry that can be as distant from each other as Latin music rhythms and twentieth-century Italian song-writing.

The project also includes a contribution on poetic anthologies, a product of two seminars in Ghent and Hamburg, which classifies the many types of poetic collections and rediscovers the innovative effect of some of the primary impulses of the Carolingian age: the osmosis between scholastic culture and popular culture and the creation of local intellectual communities, mostly around the monastic centres, which intertwined, in a new blend of historical background, school register, diaristic anecdotes and interpersonal messages.

Under the aegis of intermediarism, which, by subordinating itself to writing, governs medieval culture, there is also the study, presented at two seminars, in Zurich and Saint-Andrews, on poetic inscriptions as a privileged testimony of access to everyday settings and, comparably, the study on the hermeneutic relationship between poetic captions and illustrations of manuscripts, from a seminar at Villa Vigoni. Another examination of the crucial connection between text and image is the proposal (read as a paper during a conference in Lyon and as a lecture in Vienna) to interpret an astronomical poem by Pacificus of Verona – whose work we are preparing for the Italian National Edition – in connection with the invention of the night clock and with the Christianisation of the Zodiac, another intercultural operation made necessary by the period's need for ideological conversion from paganism to Christianity.

Two final chapters, which connect this book with its companion volume on the application of information technology – and therefore quantitative research – to the criticism of medieval Latin literature, conclude the selection. The first is an essay on the author of the poem *Karolus Magnus et Leo papa*. This explores a research path typical of a scholar of my generation, combining traditional techniques of reading the manuscript and its codicological aspects with intertextual investigations enhanced by the use of electronic archives (such as *Poetria Nova*) and statistical techniques, in this case on the metrical and lexical phenomena that characterise the style of the possible authors.

The final chapter derives from a seminar at the charming Les Treilles Foundation, organised by the Interfaces network; it was published in Lisbon in a booklet that is no longer available. It proposes the adoption of a postcolonial point of view about medieval Latin literature, which was always an expression of authors who are non-native Latin speakers, and the consequent application of methods and categories of studies on Second Language Acquisition for the interpretation of its texts. Here, too, the Carolingian environment, which arose from the encounter and interaction of intellectuals of different origins, cultures, and mother tongues, is the first and most striking example of the idea's possible application. The final chapter of book two, concerning the digital *Eurasian Latin Archive* and therefore the Latin texts from East Asia, is in some way a computer-assisted accomplishment of this same approach.

Latin passages are usually translated or paraphrased where needed. Unless stated otherwise, translations are made by the author. In some cases, when the contents of a Latin phrase are less important than the philological or linguistic reasons for which they have been adduced, in line with the practice of Medieval Latin studies, no reference has been made to an edition. These cases are limited to the Bible, the Latin classics, and those authors and anonymous texts for which editions are listed in the "Quellenverzeichnis" of the *Mittellateinisches Wörterbuch* and the *Clavis clavium*.[4] The bibliographical status of the contributions generally reflects that of their original creation, as a comprehensive update in light of subsequent studies would alter the relationship with the text and would have required profound changes that risked distorting the perception of the research context. Some minimal bibliographical updates have been added at the end of the chapters in square brackets. Limited repetitions and some small overlaps between different chapters have sometimes been unavoidable except by fundamentally modifying their original form, which would have made the line of argument incomprehensible. Despite this, I hope

---

[4] Conveniently available online at <http://woerterbuchnetz.de/cgi-bin/WBNetz/wbgui_py?sigle=MLW&lemid=NA00001&mode=Vernetzung&hitlist=&patternlist=&mainmode=Quellenverzeichnis> and <https://clavis.brepols.net/clacla/Default.aspx>.

Introduction

that this collection of seemingly eccentric and admittedly somewhat centrifugal proposals can resist the conventions that often seem to dominate medieval Latin studies, maintaining a kind of propulsive force and sharing a multiform, unpredictable love for an age that has never ceased to remind us of the joy of innovation.

The original title of this book was to be *The Carolingian Laboratory*. The publisher has chosen differently, but there is no doubt that the formal, scientific, artistic, graphical, philosophical, theological and literary laboratories of the short age of Charlemagne and his immediate successors have had a momentum and has produced revolutionary effects in many areas of culture and political management, whose scope has not yet been adequately explored.

Chapter 1

Intercultural Imitation in Christian Latin Poetry as a Path to the Medieval Poetics of Alterity

For some years, trends in neo-historicism have been renewing the issue of 'continuity and change' with regard to literary history: the age-old question, raised in 1992 by David Perkins in *Is Literary History Possible?*,[1] also elicits new answers in the field of ancient literatures. As far as the history of Latin texts is concerned, the problem of the relationship between epochs has to be taken into consideration according to these critical perspectives. A traditional periodisation, depending on studies in institutional history, imposed the three labels of classic, medieval, and humanistic, which in recent times have often been called into question. A very sophisticated debate about this subject started in the seventies, inspired by the philosophical paradigms of Blumenberg, Kuhn, and Luhmann,[2] and it evoked some important contributions on late antique and medieval culture.[3] Multiple periodisations, asynchronic cultural

---

[1] The best witness in this sense is *Littérature et histoire*, ed. C. JOUHAUD (= *Annales E.S.C.* 49.2 (1994)).

[2] See S. MÜLLER, "Paradigmenwechsel und Epochenwandel: Zur Struktur wissenschaftshistorischer und geschichtlicher Mobilität bei Thomas S. Kuhn, Hans Blumenberg und Hans Freyer", *Saeculum* 32 (1981), pp. 1-30; H. BLUMENBERG, *Die Legitimität der Neuzeit* (Frankfurt am Main, 1966); N. LUHMANN, "Das Problem der Epochenbildung und die Evolutionstheorie", in: *Epochenschwellen und Epochenstrukturen im Diskurs der Literatur- und Sprachtheorie*, ed. H.U. GUMBERT and U. LINK-HEER (Frankfurt am Main, 1985), pp. 11-33. See also H.R. JAUSS, *Literaturgeschichte als Provokation der Literaturwissenschaft* (Konstanz, 1967); trans. A. VÀRVARO, *Perché la storia della letteratura?* (Naples, 1970).

[3] *Kontinuität – Diskontinuität in der Geisteswissenschaft*, ed. H. TRÜMPY (Darmstadt, 1973); *Kulturbruch oder Kulturkontinuität im Übergang von der Antike zum Mittelalter*, ed. P.E. HUBINGER (Darmstadt, 1968); *Zur Frage der Periodengrenze zwischen Altertum und Mittelalter*,

series, and deep differences between the way historical ages are viewed by modern or contemporary eyes are by now taken for granted, at least among scholars, although they are not yet part of the collective consciousness.

One of the most innovative contributions of recent literary theories to the historiography of antique literature is likely the assumption that interference among cultures can also be a criterion for literary analysis. This intuition, already elaborated by Momigliano,[4] is now widespread in historiographical publications, even though it is not yet widely accepted in literary interpretations. If it is true, as the Russian critics have long been emphasising, that "it is not possible for a culture to progress without an external stream of texts", and that every external contribution "is a factor of acceleration in literary development",[5] then it might become possible to contemplate a literary history that is finally free from the romantic and colonial concept of the 'source'. This approach would create more flexible landscapes, based on Jaussian and Bachtinian concepts of creative reception and retroaction, interference and polyphony, responsivity and exotopy. A literature such as Latin literature, which Rémi Brague recently claimed to be founded on a constitutive "secondariness",[6] is effectively well suited to this kind of analysis.

---

ed. P.E. HUBINGER (Darmstadt, 1969); R. WENDOR, *Zeit und Kultur: Geschichte des Zeitbewusstseins in Europa* (Opladen, 1980²); H. VON PETRIKOVITS, *Der diachorische Aspekt der Kontinuität von der Spätantike zum frühen Mittelalter* (Göttingen, 1982: *Nachrichten der Akademie der Wissenschaften in Göttingen, Philologisch-Historische Klasse*); A. CAMERON, *Continuity and Change in Sixth-Century Byzantium* (London, 1981); and the excellent miscellany *Epochenschwelle und Epochenbewusstsein*, ed. R. HERZOG and R. KOSELLECK (Munich, 1987). For more recent publications, see: *Continuity and Change: The Harvest of Late Medieval and Reformation History: Essays Presented to Heiko A. Oberman on His 70th Birthday*, ed. R.J. BAST and A.C. GOW (Leiden and Boston, 2000); and *Kontinuität – Wandel: kulturwissenschaftliche Versuche über ein schwieriges Verhältnis*, ed. N. LANGREITER (Vienna, 2002).

[4] A. MOMIGLIANO, *Alien Wisdom: The Limits of Hellenization* (Cambridge, 1975).

[5] V.M. Žirmunskij, quoted in J. LOTMAN, "Una teoria del rapporto reciproco fra le culture", in: ID., *La semiosfera: L'asimmetria e il dialogo nelle strutture pensanti* (Venice, 1985), pp. 113-130, at p. 114. On this issue and on the application of this approach to the classic and medieval literatures I have proposed some comments in F. STELLA, "Eteroglossia del testo e comparazione interculturale", in *Interculturalità: Antropologia Religioni Letteratura* (= *Testimonianze* 384-385 (1995) pp. 99-122; reprinted in: *Semicerchio: Rivista di poesia comparata* 14 (1996), pp. 2-14, and as ID., "Antichità Europee", in: *Letteratura comparata*, ed. A. GNISCI (Milan, 2002), pp. 31-61; a Spanish version in: *Introducción a la literatura comparada* (Barcelona, 2002), pp. 71-127.

[6] R. BRAGUE, *Il futuro dell'Occidente: Nel modello romano la salvezza dell'Europa*, trans. A. SOLDATI and A.M. LORUSSO (Milan, 2005).

Since Erich Auerbach's *Mimesis* of 1946,[7] it has become common knowledge in the field of literary criticism that different narrative models and different tools of artistic and poetic expression correspond to diverse cultures or world views. His famous comparison of the episode of Ulysses' scar and the sacrifice of Isaac[8] highlighted the radical difference between two descriptive worlds and stimulated a deeper (because implicitly comparative) analysis of the cultural influences upon the literary technique of Antiquity. Important works have developed the parallel study of biblical narrative on the one hand,[9] and Homeric and post-Homeric narrative strategies on the other.[10] It is only recently, however, that energy dedicated to comparative intercultural research has permitted an examination of the *intersections* of the two stylistic modes. I am referring specifically to experimental works – from Nonnos of Panopolis to Eliot and Péguy through Juvencus, Sedulius, Avitus, and Arator – which propose solutions to the problem that lies embedded between the second and fourth centuries: how to create a code adapted to Jewish expressions, using tools belonging to the western tradition, in other words Greek and above all Latin.

An initial solution, and one that has remained theoretical, was that of demonstrating the two styles to be incompatible. At times Jerome and Augustine sustained this approach; Tertullian did so with a certain radical violence. European classicism of the post-seventeen-hundreds voiced this very same thesis. An identical position was likewise clearly enunciated, in 1948, almost in the same year that *Mimesis* appeared, by Ernst Robert Curtius in his *European Literature and the Latin Middle Ages*.[11] But the social impracticability of such a drastic division of the two cultures had already brought about the theory's

---

[7] E. AUERBACH, *Mimesis: Dargestellte Wirklichkeit in der abendländischen Literatur* (Berne, 1946).

[8] In my opinion Segal's criticisms are partial and unjustified. See C. SEGAL, "Classics and comparative culture", *Materiali e discussioni* 19 (1984), pp. 9-21. A discussion of the argument can be found in STELLA, "Antichità europee", at p. 39.

[9] Think of what are by now classic texts such as R. ALTER, *The Art of Biblical Narrative* (New York, 1981) or *The Literary Guide to the Bible*, ed. R. ALTER and F. KERMODE (Cambridge, MA, 1987). A panorama of these studies can be found in: R. CESERANI, "Brevi appunti sulla riscoperta della Bibbia come grande testo letterario", in: *La Scrittura infinita: Bibbia e poesia in età romantica e contemporanea*, ed. F. STELLA (Florence, 1999), pp. 19-38, and in Chapter Three below.

[10] U. HÖLSCHER, *Die Odyssee: Epos zwischen Märchen und Roman* (Munich, 1988).

[11] E.R. CURTIUS, *Europäische Literatur und lateinisches Mittelalter* (Berne, 1948).

abandonment, as early as the fourth century, with the exception of occasional medieval reappearances.

A second solution, also minimally pursued, was manifested in poetry through the process of making a Latin calque of the biblical, specifically psalmic, style. This is the solution, for example, found in the text of the Papyrus Barcinonensis published in 1968 by Roca-Puig, the so-called *Psalmus Responsorius*, and likewise in the hymns of Marius Victorinus. Yet the distance that separated this response from the sophisticated expectations of the cultured Roman audience would bring about its failure.

The third solution, that which would give rise to the "third poetic cycle of western literature"[12] beside the Homeric and Carolingian-Arthurian ones, is represented by biblical poetry. Relatively early on, the writings of Proba, Juvencus, Cyprian, Sedulius, Dracontius, Avitus, Arator, and others constituted a canon that would dominate medieval and even humanist circles, and would later reach its apex in counter-reformation religious culture, only to vanish during the Enlightenment. This was a literary thread that, after being implicated in the discredit connected with the classicist preconception of late imperial decadence, has now for some time been embraced by the explosive interest in this period and its literature. One reason for the revived curiosity in Christian poetry of late Antiquity is, in fact, none other than the interaction of emerging cultures, including Germanic but above all biblical-Semitic, with Greco-Roman civilisation and its established modes of expression. Consequently, much research has been dedicated to the exploration of the role played by imitation of the Augustan poets or the post-Vergilian epic by the *Bibeldichter*, but nearly always under a viewpoint of *Quellenforschung*, of recognition of the reuse and reconstruction of hypothetical intertexts.[13] This flourishing of studies created a space which makes possible a study of the compositional techniques of the Christian poets in intercultural terms. Starting from this perspective, the old question of imitative connections and of imitative or intertextual typologies can be explored from new, previously unexamined angles. As Mikhail Bakhtin stated, if the dialogic exchange at the heart of every proposition necessarily assumes the traits of an intercultural exchange, then the creative understanding that observes and reuses tradition from an external

---

[12] As expressed by R. HERZOG, *Die Bibelepik der lateinischen Spätantike: Geschichte einer erbaulichen Gattung* (Munich, 1975).

[13] For such questions, see *La Scrittura infinita*.

point of view is the most powerful tool available for grasping a culture's heritage in order to gain access to its true communicative potential.[14]

What problems arise from the study of imitative technique between the post-Vergilian legacy and biblical re-writing? A first issue, and one thoroughly examined by German scholars such as Herzog and Thraede with his disciples – who also institutionalised a specific terminology not easily translatable in either Italian or English – concerns the functions and the operative modalities of the revival of pagan epic.

While Thraede's categories – contraposition, substitutive transposition, opposing imitation, and spiritualising inclusion – should be subscribed in their schematic simplicity, they also reflect a cultural itinerary of passage from direct juxtaposition to gradual integration, more than they describe a specific compositional poetic process.[15] A more subtle approach is that of Reinhart

---

[14] Three privileged perspectives can be discerned for further investigation on intertextuality as intercultural phenomenon: the relations of Greece with the Orient, masterfully explored in M. WEST, *The East Face of Helicon: West Asiatic Elements in Greek Poetry and Myth* (Oxford, 1997). The relations of Rome with Greece have been studied by Momigliano and his successors; cf. the recent miscellany *Rezeption und Identität: die kulturelle Auseinandersetzung Roms mit Griechenland als europäisches Paradigma*, ed. G. VOGT-SPIRA and B. ROMMEL (Stuttgart 1999). A panorama of these scholarly perspectives can be found in STELLA, "Antichità Europee". For a more recent application of Bakhtin's method to ancient literatures, see *Bakhtin and the Classics*, ed. R.B. BRANHAM (Evanston, IL, 2002).

[15] K. THRAEDE, "Epos", in: *Reallexikon für Antike und Christentum: Sachwörterbuch zur Auseinandersetzung des Christentums mit der antiken Welt* 5 (Stuttgart, 1960), pp. 1034-1041. The phases of the interpretative process for pre-Christian elements in theological literature are as follows (*ibid.*, pp. 1006-1014):

– Antithesis and recognition, above all referring to the mythology initially rejected *en bloc* but then adopted as a moral example (Aeneas as a model for the Christian) or as a list of proverbial phrases (Lucan, VII. 819 "*caelo tegitur, qui non habet urnam*");

– transposition, above all begun by Lactantius: he interprets epic deeds and locution in a Christian sense, such as the hymn to Epicurus in Lucretius, in *Divinae institutiones* VII. 27, 6 or "*Iovis omnia plena*" (*Aeneid* 6, 724). Two methods are discussed: on the one hand spiritualisation or generalisation, and on the other hand transposition of concepts and ambivalent formulae;

– interpolation: Christian interpolation, as Traube defined it: "*prolem sancta de coniuge natam*" (Ovid, *Metamorphoses* 15, 835) became "*de virgine natam*" in a manuscript from the thirteenth century;

– contamination: for example, *Eclogue* 3, 60 and *Aeneid* 6, 726-727 juxtaposes *Iuppiter* and *spiritus*, according to a method previously studied by H. HAGENDAHL, "Methods of citation in postclassical Latin", *Eranos* 45 (1947), pp. 114-128, or more specifically concerning a biblical (Matthew 10, 41: "*Qui recipit prophetam in nomine prophetae, mercedem prophetae accipiet: et qui recipit iustum in nomine iusti, mercedem iusti accipiet*") and a pagan passage (*Aeneid* 6, 661-664: "*Quique sacerdotes casti, dum vita manebat,/quique pii vates et Phoebo digna*

Herzog, who in 1975 applied the *formgeschichtliche* readings of the Konstanz school to the foundational period of the Christian poetic language. His reconstruction, which takes up dozens of pages in his *Bibelepik*, examines all stages of the imitative process, whether in prose or poetry, thus providing a framework that is extremely analytical but not exempt from the overlapping or reintroducing, into different categories, of forms which were actually analogous or barely distinct from one another. It gradually becomes clear that this process can be recognised as an "inclusion of the not-accepted" ("*Einschluss des nicht Akzeptierten*",[16] the acceptance of foreign bodies through correction, cutting, or dissolving; usurpation without modification, decontextual neutralisation ("*tum vero manifesta fides*", *Aeneid* 2, 309; Juvencus 4, 754), actualisation of metaphor (that is, a return to its literal meaning: "*tabe peresos*" in *Aeneid* 6, 442, said of love, is taken literally by Juvencus 1, 440), until the extreme case of a double neutralisation: "*eripit a femine gladium, quem veste tegebat*", which contaminates (conflates) *Aeneid* 10, 788 and 6, 406, had already been created by Ausonius *Cupido cruciatus* 10 (*Imminutio*) l. 15 and by Luxorius in the erotic sense, but is recovered, or reworked by Cyprian the poet (*Iudices* 178) in the literal sense.

With a finesse equal to the tortured complexity of his German, Herzog enters unexplored territory: on the one hand, the explanation of the Bible through epic quotations, and on the other, the retroaction of the 'foreign bodies' of classical paganism upon the formulation of the content of the new Christian literary culture.[17] One has only to think of the account of the subterranean world and in general of the hereafter, whether heaven or hell, but also of the influx of elegiac language in the description of female biblical characters and specifically of the erotic language in the expression of *amor dei* examined by Schmid in *Tityrus christianus*.[18]

---

locuti,/inventas aut qui vitam excoluere per artis / omnibus his nivea cinguntur tempora vitta"), as occurs in Augustine, *Civitas Dei* 21, 27.

[16] HERZOG, *Die Bibelepik der lateinischen Spätantike*, p. 193.

[17] The minimal pattern he identified is, for example, the reuse of linguistic ready-made phrases, from those of a proverbial nature to the repertory of scenes, such as 'the danger of death', 'the lord and the knight', 'the armour of gold', or epic epithets, above all in the paraphrasing of the historical books of the Bible known as the *Heptateuch*. On the other hand, the anti-pagan poetic citations previously described by Thraede have demonstrative functions.

[18] W. SCHMID, "Tityrus christianus", *Rheinisches Museum* 96 (1953), pp. 101-165, reprinted in: *Europäische Bukolik und Georgik*, ed. K. GAMBER (Darmstadt, 1976), pp. 44-121. F. STELLA, "La poesia biblica come problema interculturale: Saggi sulle creazioni di Eva", *Semicerchio: Rivista di poesia comparata* 20-21 (1999), pp. 28-32.

To cite Mikhail Bakhtin once more: "In language there no longer exists any neutral word or form ... every word and every form is imbued with intentions".[19] In fact, imitative dynamics configure not only a process of elaboration of codes, but a real intervention that moulds cultural content. Herzog documented the process of Romanisation that marked certain elements of the evangelical narrative in the Vergilian cento of Proba or in Cyprian's *Heptateuchos*, the paraphrasis of the first seven books of the Old Testament. Jesus's position at the banquet is reclining (4, 410), and Joshua's enemies are killed on the cross instead of on a tree (Joshua 357-358): "Immediately, they were fixed on the cross, hanging there bloodless until the falling of black night".[20] The Palestinian landscape is reinterpreted following patterns of epic Roman expression by Juvencus 1, 130 (John in the desert): "From now on the boy led always a life hidden in remote valleys".[21] Or by Cyprian in Exodus 637 (the expedition of Israel into the desert, presented as a grassy steppe): "Nothing but grasses waving with the winds' blowing".[22] Finally, the earthly paradise is described using terminology peculiar to the Roman palace (Genesis 50, 54). In the same fashion Adam and Eve's relationship, in both Dracontius's *De laudibus Dei* and Marius Victor's *Alethia* (1, 385-398), is immediately configured as a conjugal union in terms that represent the Roman legal reality (such as the equality between spouses and the joining of wills) more than the Semitic reality.

Likewise remarkable, but less evident, is the negation of specifically Hebrew traits in a synthetic paraphrase such as the epic type of Juvencus or, less frequently, through the substitution with codifications more customary to the reader, or at least to the expressive code of the Roman epic – for example the concrete form of eschatology interpreted in the abstract spiritual sense of Juvencus 1, 314 – or with the selection of only the common traits shared with Christian culture (for instance, in Juvencus 1, 117 ff., the *Benedictus*, the Old Testament references are eliminated). These phenomena are labelled as *Romanisierung* and *Entjudaisierung*, 'Romanisation' and 'de-Judaisation'.

---

[19] M. BAKHTIN, *Slovo v romane* (1934-1935) partially published in *Voprosy literatury* 6 (1972), then in: ID., *Voprosy literatury i estetiki* (Moscow, 1975), trans. C. STRADA JANOVIČ, *Estetica e romanzo* (Turin, 1979), pp. 67-230 ("La parola nel romanzo"), at p. 101.
[20] Ps.-Cyprian, *Ioshua* 357-358: "*Ilicet exsangues crucibus figuntur in altis / Pendentes, donec sese nox reddidit atra.*".
[21] Juvencus, 1, 130: "*Exhinc secretis in vallibus abdita semper / vita fuit puero*".
[22] Ps.-Cyrian, *Exodus* 637: "*Nil praeter undantes ventorum flatibus herbas*".

In 1999,[23] I proposed analogous observations about the process of Romanisation of the legal framework in the description by the biblical poets of the union and unity of the first couple, the elegiac *descriptio puellae* of Eve, and the interpretation of the episode of Adam's rib through the use of elements of the Narcissus legend as a mirroring motive.

The necessity of cultural interaction also exerts a structural influence on compositional technique, on imitative processes and on the topical repertoire, and it is necessary to have a fuller understanding of these influences in order to reach a fuller comprehension of the texts and, more generally, of the mechanisms at work in every attempt to translate one culture into the language of another. This process is visible on two levels: the first has been dubbed "*innerchristliche Traditionsbildung*" by German scholars, and comes into being by way of the "*sekundäre Imitation innerhalb der christlichen Spätantike*".[24] Until now, this phenomenon has still received little scholarly attention because of the prevalent interest in classical sources. It remains, however, at the basis of the mechanics of allusion in a secondary or tertiary tradition such as the Latin-Christian one.

A prime example is found in an excerpt from the poem *De laudibus Dei* by Dracontius, "the much underrated poet" who "emerges as an impressively creative writer" to be "the most talented poet in fifth-century Africa".[25] The poem praises God's greatness first with the account of Genesis and incarnation, and then by linking together stories of biblical and Roman legends as moral examples. Line 2, 24 *"imperii per saecla tui sine fine manentis"* is at first glance an obvious borrowing from Vergil *Aeneid* 1, 270 *"imperium sine fine dedi"*. However, we must realise firstly that, as Servius *ad Aeneidem* 6, 847 tells us, this constitutes already a *locus rhetoricus* in the pagan school, and secondly, that a long-standing tradition exists of patristic citations of the verse and of poetic *Kontrastimitationen* that effectively transfer the empire to Christ: Prudentius, *Contra Symmachum* 1, 542: *"Christus (…) imperium sine fine docet"* and Sedulius, *Carmen Paschale* 2, 55: *"imperium sine fine manet"*. The *manentis* of Dracontius's verse demonstrates that the model here is not Vergil but Sedulius. In Dracontius's poem the term assumes various connotations of theological twists and turns, because the lexeme *manere* refers to a series of poetic formulations of eternity upon which Dracontius makes subtle and re-

---

[23] STELLA, "La poesia biblica", pp. 28-32.
[24] HERZOG, *Bibelepik*, p. 207 n. 177.
[25] D.F. BRIGHT, *The Miniature Epic in Vandal Africa* (Norman and London 1987), p. IX.

fined variations, in relation to the Augustinian treatment of the theme. However, it is important to notice that the intertextual relationship is located between and hinges on the two Christian poets, while the Vergilian model is at the head of this chain, as a kind of starting archetype.

The second level is the imposition and use of a functional hierarchy among biblical and classical influences. The former being the true motive behind the act of writing, they are ranked first, while the latter are placed in a secondary position, as a repertoire of elements required for the formation of a new code. Line 610 of Dracontius's second book: "*Christus enim datus est nobis spes una salutis*" is considered a reuse of Lucan 2, 113 "*Spes una salutis / oscula pollutae fixisse trementia dextrae*" and 5, 636 "*Spes una salutis / quod tanta mundi nondum periere ruina*",[26] itself later taken up by Silius *Punica* 15, 402: "*ducibus spes una salutis, / si socias iungant vires*". The existing commentaries on *De laudibus Dei*, particularly that of Moussy-Camus in the Les Belles Lettres edition (1985), stop at this point, in the tradition of the best *Quellenforschung*, taking into account that Dracontius demonstrates an astounding grasp of classical and post-classical epic. I believe rather that to evaluate even a simple expression of periods this late we should fan out the different converging and intersecting inspirations, and search the realm of biblical culture and the Christian tradition. We can thus detect with relative certainty that the original subtext is the line in *Isaiah* 9, 6 which in fact announces the arrival of the Son of God as salvation: "*parvulus enim natus est nobis, filius datus est nobis*", a text interpreted Christologically in exegesis as well as in the liturgy.[27] Other Christian texts could be invoked as co-texts of the biblical revival (Acts 27, 20 "*spes omnis salutis nostrae*"), and the syntagm returns twice in Commodianus, the wild bard of Christian Africa (*Apologeticum* or *Carmen de duobus populis* 303 and 310), in which it refers to the hope in eternal life. But in Christian poetry there is a wide range of cases with *spes* and *salus* as references to God or Christ.[28] Thus the choice depends on the context; in this case, the hymnal excerpt is replete with Christian references: the convergence with Lucan therefore constitutes a revival of an epic utterance already invested, both in its singular elements and in its complex semantics, with Christian valences. It seems

---

[26] Perhaps preceded by *Ciris* 295 (apostrophe to Britomartis).
[27] *Messale Romano* (Turin and Rome, 1933) p. 175: *Introitus* to the third Christmas Mass.
[28] F. STELLA, "Per una teoria dell'imitazione poetica cristiana: Saggio di analisi sulle *Laudes Dei* di Draconzio", *Invigilata Lucernis* 7-8 (1985-1986), pp. 193-224, esp. pp. 215-216.

to me that we can no longer speak of the *interpretatio christiana* of the classics, but of Christian terms in a juncture that connects them in a manner both effective and legitimised by tradition.

An exemplary example of the incongruity that this composite model could create is provided by Dracontius in 3, 626: "*Eripe me his, invicte, malis in corpore sanum*", where the conflation of the famous call of Palinurus (*Aeneid* 6, 365) and the likewise proverbial hemistich of Juvenal 10, 356 must be considered against the background of an entire series of re-workings of Vergilian verse already attempted by Christian poetry: first of all by Proba, who in her Vergilian cento authorises Christian use of the formula (515: "*Eripe me his, inuicte, malis. Quid denique restat, / Quidue sequens tantos possim superare labores?*"), and later by Cyprian, *Genesis* 1032: "*Eripe me his, inuicte, malis et specula fratris / Infracto placidus quam primum decute ferro*", where it is spoken by Jacob (Genesis 32, 11). The patristic history of this expression was already partially reconstructed by Courcelle,[29] and is largely founded on the frequency of psalmic incipits with "*eripe me*".[30] It is therefore reasonable to wonder if the process might not be exactly the opposite of what has been hypothesised: in a context of prayer, replete with psalmic echoes, the appeal "*eripe me*" activated the memory of the Vergilian verse, which itself bears a Christian depth, even in patristic prose. What remains to be noted is the fact that the Vergilian revival imports with it the semblance of a certain contextual impropriety: the use of the adjective *invicte*. The epithet is not only alien to Dracontian usage, although it belongs to biblical usage,[31] but the passage does not even justify a military metaphor because Dracontius is referring to a helpful, peaceful God, *boethós*, not to a God victorious over his enemies. Yet, when thinking of the Vergilian context, it is possible to identify a certain relevance: in the *Aeneid*, *invictus* signifies 'invincible by fate', referring to Aeneas, and therefore disposed to help those in disgrace who implore pity. As such, we would be looking not at an integrative allusion, but rather at a reflexive one, in keeping with Conte's terminology. A similar allusion presupposes an informed reading aimed at identifying the resonances and justifications of the intertext. I think that in Christian poetry this form of allusion is active only in polemical contexts, that is only – to employ Thraede's terminology – as a *Kontrastimi-*

---

[29] P. COURCELLE, "Les pères de l'Église devant les enfers virgiliens", *Archives d'histoire doctinale et littéraire du moyen âge* 30 (1955), pp. 5-74, at p. 18 n. 2.

[30] Psalms 30, 16; 58, 2 f.; 68, 15 and 19; 70, 2 and 4; 118, 153 and 170; 139, 2; 142, 9; 143, 7.

[31] *Thesaurus Linguae Latinae*, 1- (Leipzig, 1900-), 7.2 (1979), col. 187, l. 65 f., e.g. Sirach 18, 1: "*Deus solus iustificabitur et manet invictus rex in aeternum*".

tation. In this case, Dracontius simply allowed himself to be led along by the usual mechanism of reuse of Christian terms in accordance with traditional epic models, and *invicte* can be defined as an intertextual remnant, a category which Herzog dubbed 'surplus'. This excess obviously exerts a retroaction upon the image of God, which emerges from the verses of Dracontius: an image that consequently appears the more garishly military and warlike, the less the context requires it. In my opinion, this incongruity is influenced by the fact that the prayer to the liberator God in this poem is a macro-metaphor of the prayer to the Vandal king, imploring him to free the poet from his imprisonment. But here I am venturing too far astray into the field of psycho-philology, and even in katabasis one should not exceed certain limits.

This creative disconnection triggered by intertextual excesses can also be detected in the sphere of intertextual models, for instance that of the poetic topoi. An example of the latter, the most topical topos of epic poetry, would be that of the 'hundred mouths', the most common metaphorisation of an *affectatio modestiae* studied by Curtius, and one already the subject of detailed analyses by Pascucci, Courcelle, Barchiesi, and Hinds:[32] in the field of Christian studies, Klaus Thraede dedicated ponderous theoretical essays that draw upon a vigorous discourse among German scholars, as demonstrated by more than one miscellany devoted to *Toposforschung*.[33]

In the third book of his *De laudibus Dei*, Dracontius justifies his own inadequacies to praise God with what Wolfgang Kirsch has dubbed a "*geniale Idee*":[34] to appeal not to subjective incapacity, but rather to objective impossi-

---

[32] P. COURCELLE, "Le cliché virgilien des cent bouches", *Revue des Études Latines* 33 (1955), pp. 231-240; G. PASCUCCI, "Ennio, Ann. 561-562 V. e un tipico procedimento di auxesis nella poesia latina", in: ID., *Scritti scelti* 2 (Florence, 1983), pp. 575-597 (originally published in 1959); A. BARCHIESI, "Cento bocche: Narratività e valutazione nello studio dell'epica romana", in: *Reges et proelia: Orizzonti e atteggiamenti dell'epica antica, Pavia 17 marzo 1994* (Como, 1994), pp. 45-71; S. HINDS, *Allusion and Intertext: Dynamics of Appropriation in Roman Poetry* (Cambridge, 1998), pp. 34-47. Excellent development in L. EDMUNDS, *Intertextuality and the Reading of Roman Poetry* (Baltimore, MD, 2001). The method of *Quellenforschung* still dominates in the contributions to *La poesia tardoantica e medievale: Atti del I convegno internazionale di studi, Macerata 4-5 maggio 1998*, ed. M. SALVADORE (Alessandria, 2001).

[33] K. THRAEDE, "Untersuchungen zur Ursprung und zur Geschichte der christlichen Poesie", *Jahrbuch für Antike und Christentum* 4 (1961), pp. 108-127; 5 (1962), pp. 125-157; 6 (1963), pp. 101-111; and, on the general topic, O. PÖGGELER, "Dichtungstheorie und Toposforschung", in: *Toposforschung*, ed. M. BÄUMER (Darmstadt, 1973), pp. 22-135, and W. VEIT, "Toposforschung: Ein Forschungsbericht", in: *Toposforschung*, pp. 136-210.

[34] F. STELLA, "Fra retorica e innografia: Sul genere letterario delle 'Laudes Dei' di Dra-

bility, the linguistic incompatibility between God and the systems of rhetorical encomium (*laus*, in its rhetorically restricted sense) too closely tied to contemporary dynamics to be able to face the eternal being. But the cliché of the hundred mouths does not appear in the passage under consideration. It surfaces elsewhere in the third book, in a *confessio* that takes up a large part of it. In lines 565-591 the poet writes:

> We are criminals, we do not deserve generosity,
> And I am the first to be considered more than a sinner.
> In fact, when will I confess every crime, along with
> the heart and the flesh? *Not even if I had a voice of iron*
> *or as many mouths as there are teeth that whiten on the bone, arose in me*
> *or I possessed as many tongues as hairs I combed on my head,*
> *I will succeed in exhausting the number of crimes without deceit,*
> *It will be enough to admit being guilty of every offence.*
> That which your commandments forbid, I alone will admit to committing,
> I will not deny having done all that which horrifies you.
> (...)
> So I confess with a guilt and pitiful soul
> full grave evil, committing more than only one crime;
> *because the number of my crimes is greater than the grains*
> *of sand on the shore and my evils outnumber the sea's waves*
> I cannot believe that Noah's flood could have punished more crimes
>
> Than those which now weigh upon me.
> The rivers of crime and the storms hit and toss me
> and the seething wave of sins has covered me;
> the water's flows submerge me with surges of guilt and blame
> until the wave has reached my soul, grave watery horror.[35]

---

conzio", *Philologus* 132 (1988), pp. 213-245.

[35] Dracontius, *De laudibus Dei* (ed. F. VOLLMER in: *MGH AA* 14 (Berlin, 1905), pp. 23-113), 3, 565-591: (565) "*Gens scelerata sumus, nil de pietate merentes, / Quorum primus ego plus quam peccator habendus. / Quando fatebor enim scelerum simul omne, reatum / Pectoris et carnis? Non si mihi ferrea uox sit, / Ora tot exsurgant quot dentes ossibus albent /* (570) *Aut mihi sint linguae quantos caput omne capillos / Pectinat, explebo numerum sine fraude fidelem, / Sed satis est dixisse reum sub crimine cuncto; / Quod tua iussa uetant, solus peccasse fatebor, / Omne quod horrescis non me fecisse negabo.* (...) (581) *Ergo ego confiteor miseranda mente reatum / Plenum, grande malum, non uno crimine partum; / Nam scelus omne meum numeros superabit harenae /* (585) *Littoris et pelagi uincent mala nostra liquores. / Non puto diluuium tantos punisse reatus / Quantos ipse gero culparum pondere pressus. / Flumina me scelerum rapiunt quatiuntque procellae / Et peccatorum torrens simul obruit unda; /* (590) *Me delictorum*

Intercultural Imitation in Christian Latin Poetry

Only a few decades earlier, Sedulius in his *Carmen Paschale* had given his own version of the topos (1, 99-102):

The ancestor's belief and the venerable
forefathers' original witness is proved, and in no epoch should they be abolished:
through time the signs of your power remain firm and strong.
To my strength I barely trust the task of briefly recounting them
with audacious display of exposition, and entering the extensive wood
I just try to touch a few branches.

Because even if one hundred voices should open and roar with iron voices
and a hundred sounds may emanate from the human breast
this would exhaust all the deeds which even the parched sand
cannot number nor the bright stars of the heavens either?[36]

We will not analyse these two passages in detail. I would merely point out the alien element that in both modifies not only the choice of imagery but also the very structure of the cliché. An important innovation is the introduction of the image of innumerability: in the preceding history of the topos the concept of number, the 'ground' of the metaphor upon which the argument is based, is implicit in the various *omnia* or *cuncta* or *tot* that since Vergil have represented the song's unreachable objective. The Christians render it explicit first by naming it (*numeris* in l. 102 of Sedulius, *numeros* in l. 584 of Dracontius), and, secondly, by introducing an image of innumerability: the stars in the sky and the sand in the sea, which in themselves constitute a topical metaphor at least since Catullus 7.[37] This secondary imagery carries with it a biblical valence that in turn impregnates these allusions with rather complex exegetical resonances, which we will not examine here (just think of the uncountable offspring of Abraham: Genesis 13, 6; 15, 5; 22, 17; 26, 4; 28, 14). It is only in Sedulius that sand and stars come to be associated with the topos of modesty, particularly the

meserunt fluctibus amnes, / Vsque animam uenit unda meam, grauis horror aquarum".

[36] Sedulius, *Carmen Paschale* (ed. J. HUEMER (Vienna, 1885: CSEL 10), pp. 1-154), 1, 99-102: "*Indicio est antiqua fides et cana priorum / Testis origo patrum, nullisque abolenda per aeuum / (95) Temporibus constant uirtutum signa tuarum. / Ex quibus audaci perstringere pauca relatu / Vix animis committo meis, siluamque patentem / Ingrediens aliquos nitor contingere ramos. / Nam centum licet ora mouens uox ferrea clamet / (100) Centenosque sonos humanum pectus anhelet, / Cuncta quis expediet, quorum nec lucida caeli / Sidera nec bibulae numeris aequantur harenae?*"

[37] E.S. MCCARTNEY, "Vivid ways of indicating uncountable numbers", *Classical Philology* 55 (1960), pp. 79-89.

version of the hundred mouths, and Dracontius constitutes the second link in a new Christian chain. In Dracontius the impetus to increase, which according to Pascucci establishes one of the rules for the development of this topos, acts differently by multiplying the mouth and tongue metaphors, which are then separated from one another to become independent metaphors, while still remaining connected. But anxiety about increasing these elements triggers nasty tricks: in fact, Dracontius's mouths number "*quot dentes ossibus albent*", that is – still using Vergil (*Aeneid* 12, 36) – as many as there are teeth. Normally, a human mouth has less than one hundred teeth.

Compared to the progressive *auxesis* of Homer's one hundred mouths or the future one thousand of the Carolingian Theodulf, Dracontius's application implies a clumsy jump backwards. And as if that weren't enough: the tongues, in contrast, and evidently in a monstrous body in which there is no homology between mouth and tongue, number as many as the combable hairs on one's head. Dracontius is in fact the first and only Latin poet to use the verb *pectinare* twice. But it is precisely this innovation, which we could easily attribute to the baroque passion for multiplying metaphors, that actually has a biblical justification. Moreover, it can be understood only when we consider Psalms 39, 13, as did Faustino Arevalo, the first Dracontius editor and commentator from the late seventeen hundreds: "[My evils] are more than the hairs of mine head".[38]

In these verses, Dracontius is actually confessing his own faults and expressing the very impossibility of counting them, and in this way he needs the model of intonation offered by the penitential Psalms, which for centuries provided the model for the prayerful *confessio*. That the Psalms would indeed be the subtext for the passage is confirmed by the choice of the imagery of innumerability instituted by Sedulius. Whereas Sedulius speaks of sand and stars, Dracontius only mentions sand, and immediately links it to the successive metaphor of waves, also used as an illustration of the innumerability of his faults. In this instance, the metaphoric ground comes once more from Psalm 68: "(…) for the waters are come in unto my soul (…) I am come into deep waters, where the floods overflow me".[39]

---

[38] Translation according to the King James version (= Psalm 40, 12). Psalm 39, 13: "*Multiplicate sunt [iniquitates] super capillos capitis mei*" (*iuxta Hebraeos* version: "*plures factae sunt quam capilli capitis mei*").

[39] Translation according to the King James version (= Psalm 69, 1-2). Psalm 68, 2-3: "*Intraverunt aquae usque ad animam meam (...) Veni in altitudinem maris et tempestas demersit me*". Also Psalm 17, 5: "*Torrentes iniquitatis conturbaverunt me*".

Dracontius extends the aquatic metaphor at length, in accordance with his tendency for prolixity and his predilection for chains of metaphors. And the fact that *"mala nostra"* is an expression favoured by Ovid, especially in the poems of exile,[40] only confirms the process by which a cultural repertoire (the biblical one) functions as a hierarchically superior arch-text, while the classics function as a formulaic reserve;[41] it is the former that activates the latter.[42] The relationship between the two is not always balanced, or to put it more aptly: it is not always possible to identify a semantic compatibility between the two codes, and the fissure between these two systems paves the way for the 'betrayal' perpetrated by the Christian epic, to the damage of the biblical system. In the work of the African poet a further mechanism is added to this scheme, one constantly charged with meaning due to its very position as hinge between the two cultures: the penchant for extended imagery, for increased articulation and multiple levels such as those I attempted to study in a previous essay.[43] In many passages this process involves the images' exegetical meaning, their projection into an ulterior dimension – divine or moral, or metaphysical, or eschatological.

A poetics of alterity gradually develops, perpetually shifting within a network of meaning in which each element can refer to another, in a cycle of significations whereby they unendingly dodge the restriction of a unique definition. If it is true, as has been written, that in the classical topos a kind of suspension of the referential discourse is activated,[44] then the Christian poets'

---

[40] In the *Tristia*, in the *Epistulae ex Ponto*, and in the *Heroides*.

[41] The example of Dracontius, however violent his intervention in the elastic but fragile topos structure might be, was followed by others. In the Carolingian era Alcuin of York took it up again in a prose letter (39), and in the Ottonian period Heriger of Lobbes, *Vita Ursmari*, ed. K. STRECKER, in: *PLAC* 5, pp. 178-210, vv. 773 ff.) imitated it with little variations in order to express the indescribability of Saint Ursmar's merits, including the teeth and the combable hair.

[42] M. ROBERTS also observes in *The Jeweled Style: Poetry and Poetics in Late Antiquity* (Ithaca and London, 1989), p. 143, that "Christian literature may include descriptive passages in the manner of its secular counterparts, but they must be read according to a different code".

[43] F. STELLA, "Ristrutturazione topica ed estensione metaforica nella poesia cristiana: Da spunti draconziani", *Wiener Studien* 102 (1989), pp. 213-245. Many suggestions in this regard are to be found in the masterful M. ROBERTS, *Biblical Epic and Rhetorical Paraphrase in Late Antiquity* (Liverpool, 1985) p. 157: "At times the opportunity to incorporate a poetic reminiscence seems to have been the main motive for the expanded syntactical structure", and p. 206: "The details that are chosen for ecphrastic amplification from the biblical text are those which evoke reminiscences of pagane epic or lend themselves readily to the mannered treatment favoured by contemporary taste". Further steps in this direction are taken by G. MALSBARY, "Epic exegesis and the use of Vergil in the early biblical poets", *Florilegium* 7 (1985), pp. 53-83.

[44] BARCHIESI, *Cento bocche*, p. 48.

need to recover the link with a *new* system of reference gives a new motivation even to the most basic compositional choices. This is the historic moment in which the inertial weight of the topos is exhausted, and in turn is recharged by completely new mental categories. In practice, this reactivation occurs thanks to the interaction with an entire complex of texts – biblical and patristic – perceived as superior, in terms of both morals and content, to those that transmitted the verbal elements of the topos. These poets construe a structural diphony that would always guarantee a double reading of every single verse: it is the embryo of the *modus allegoricus* that would dominate medieval poetry, and which originates from the need to connect different cultural systems and apparently incompatible modes of expression; but also, more trivially, from the need to relate stories separated by centuries, such as those of Isaiah and of Christ, of Eve and of Mary.

In his sophisticated monograph on the skills of late antique literature, *The Jeweled Style*, Michael Roberts described certain cases of "spiritual reading of visual experience" as examples of a specific aspect of the Christian aesthetic. The aesthetic theories of J. Elsner go in the same direction.[45] Yet we can probably go beyond the statement that "Christian piety and secular literary preferences are woven together in a seamless web that manifests that unproblematic assimilation of the two traditions in the poet's own creative imagination".[46] Jakobson has demonstrated that the *Kreuzung der Gattungen*, the crossover of genres and styles, is an illusion on the part of the reader accustomed to certain reading traditions:[47] in each text, elements deriving from different genres are not ordered on the same level, but rather according to hierarchies that designate a new configuration which cannot be reduced to the sheer sum of the elements.

We are looking at the signs of a rebuilding of the poetic code, which configures a different type of continuity of Latin literature. And if it is worth it, as Jauss proposed, to attempt a poetic history of the invisible from late An-

---

[45] J. ELSNER, "Late antique art: The problem of the concept and the cumulative aesthetic", in: *Approaching Late Antiquity: The Transformation from Early to Late Empire*, ed. S. SWAIN and M. EDWARDS (Oxford, 2004), pp. 271-304.

[46] ROBERTS, *The Jeweled Style*, p. 147.

[47] The usual notion of *mélange des genres* is still familiar to P.A. DEPROOST, "L'épopée biblique en langue latine: Essai de définition d'un genre littéraire", *Latomus* 56 (1997), pp. 15-39; see K. POLLMANN, "Das lateinische Epos in der Spätantike", in: *Von Göttern und Menschen erzählen: Formkonstanzen und Funktionswandeln vormoderner Epik*, ed. J. RÜPKE (Stuttgart, 2001), pp. 93-129. Sound critiques of this notion by A. BARCHIESI, "The crossing", in: *Texts, Ideas and the Classics*, ed. S.J. HARRISON (Oxford, 2001), pp. 142-163.

tiquity to Baudelaire, it might also be interesting to reconstruct the dynamics that have been used to express the invisible with the language of the visible.

The fundamental mechanism is obviously the one which was most profoundly defined in medieval times by John Scotus Eriugena and Alain de Lille, and amply studied by Auerbach and by De Lubac, above and beyond an infinite number of recent studies.[48] The *modus symbolicus* was not adopted as an occasional and ornamental figure but as a constant structural orientation and perspective. Just as Jauss's intuition theorised a poetic history of the invisible, it was not so different, from the point of view of mental categories, from the type of perception of nature and of spiritual life that would be reintroduced by Baudelaire in the poetry of the nineteenth century, and which today, with technical terms which are unlike those of allegory but substantially faithful to them, could be defined as "the assumption of alterity in the same poetry's creation", a visual or polyphonic dialogue based on the permanent multiplicity of every narrative line, every meaning, every significance.[49]

---

[48] A survey in F. STELLA, *Poesia e teologia: L'Occidente latino tra IV e VIII secolo* (Milan, 2001), esp. the Introduction, and J.D. DAWSON, *Christian Figural Reading and the Fashioning of Identity* (Berkeley, CA, 2002).

[49] A remarkable example can be found in the *Actus Apostolorum* by Arator (ed. A.P. MCKINLAY (Vienna, 1951: CSEL 72)): the encounter between Peter and Simon the Magician, which finishes with a diatribe against the latter, who claims that he can buy spiritual skills. In I. 643-671 Arator announces his resort to the allegory: "*Haec de voce sacrae lux est manifesta figurae*", and starts recounting, as a 'cameo' inside the main plot, the story of Noah's ark, typus of the Church ("*Ecclesiae speciem praestabat machina quondam / temporibus constructa Noe, quae sola recepit / omne genus clausisque ferens baptismatis instar*" – "The mechanism once built by Noah represented the beauty of the Church, the only one to receive each species in the likeness of baptism and to bring them all in an enclosed space"): an explanation which apparently was neither necessary to the economy of the primary narration nor to the economy of the subsequent simile, and therefore bombastic, alienating, and poetic. The dove and the raven break away from the ark: the latter, a predator, is not satisfied and comes back without good results; the former, more unselfish, comes back with the olive branch, a symbol of the love that always bears fruits (secondary allegory). Both fly over the swells: the example demonstrates that without individual endowments baptism is not sufficient (secondary tropology): "*non ergo saluti / sufficit unda lavans nisi sit sine felle columba / qui generatur aquis*" ("therefore, for salvation the purifying water is not enough, if you are not a dove devoid of poison that is reborn from the water"). The same happens to Simon the Magician: in this figure, compared to the raven, the spiral of the symbologies finds its semiotic centre, its primary referent: "*Simon hic baptismatis undam / contingerat, sed corvus erat sua lucra requirens, / quae numquam meruere Deum, qui limine templi / vendentes arcere solet*" ("Simon had touched the wave of the baptism, but he was a raven that was looking for his own gain and he could not deserve God, who throws salesmen out of the temple"). Peter, on the contrary, is the dove: "*Petrus ad ista vocat, qui filius esse*

To the *allegoria in verbis* that is possible in all poetry, we may add the *allegoria in factis* in biblical poetry, which derives from the Christian Bible's historical dimension, not only acting within the correspondence of the two Testaments but also within its many historical interpretations. For this literature, therefore, exegesis represents something more than what simile represented in classical poetry: the transition to another dimension of reality, the correlation with a different code of meaning. In fact, it introduces the perception of a *permanent* co-presence of the alterity in the script, of a plurality of aspects and senses.

The communicative situation is also different: the 'bi-univocity' of the habitual communicative rapport between author and addressee in Christian poetry is replaced by a type of *semiotic triangulation* between author, God, and audience, with which a theologian could audaciously make an analogy to the circular communication between the three figures of the Holy Trinity. God acts as the permanent addressee, as is seen in a hymn or in confession; and yet he functions at the same time as co-author, or main author, or source of inspiration; and, simultaneously, he is the object of the narration, as in biblical poetry, or in the varieties of its theological extensions.

It seems clear that the triangle of Christian communication can be translated on a poetic level as a triangle of codes of meaning. These consist of the biblical source, the repertoire of classical poetry, and finally the tradition of Christian poetry. A member of this trio that nonetheless maintains its own

columbae / dicitur ore Dei meritoque hac matre creatus / ecclesiae sublimat opus; de munere prolis / nomen habet genetrix, quod Spiritus eligit almus, / alitis innocuae dignatus imagine cerni" ("Peter (…) is called son of the dove by the voice of God and, rightly created by this mother, upholds the work of the Church; as his mother's offspring, he receives the gift of her name – elected by the Holy Ghost which deigned to present itself in the image of an innocent bird"). Here the spiral folds up: Peter is an example of love that bears peace, like the dove, but like the dove he is also the apex of activity of the Church (with the twofold meaning that Peter – the pope – is at the summit of the Church and that supreme love is the summit of the Church).

In this example the fusion of the hermeneutic and poetic strategies – what has been called (Angelucci) "the emotion of the interdimensional passage" – is perfected, and bestows a textual meaning on every single one of its aesthetically autonomous elements, which were originally products of intellectual elaboration. The typological dimension of the story merges with the allegorical one (due to the moral aspect) and the sacramental one (due to the Church), and all three spin a semiotic triangle that reaches its peak in the final coincidence of the references. In Arator the repertoire of the figurants of the Holy Scripture becomes a code of the imaginary, where, for the first time in poetical history, the signifiers become at the same moment the bearers of significance (the *signifiant* works simultaneously as the *signifié*), in a fusion of contexts inconceivable in other cultural situations, and rarely mastered to such a degree even in medieval times.

autonomy, the latter is the first ring of mediation between the other two elements, composed of *centones*, of Juvencus's *Evangeliorum libri*, and subsequently of the authors who became part of this canon-in-progress.

Chapter 2

The Women of the Old Testament in Early Medieval Poetry: Judith and the Others

The Canon of the Biblical Heroines in One Verse

Medieval Christian culture was much less reluctant to place value on women than classical culture had been, but it strictly selected the contexts and values in which women would become symbols and representations. That selection was based on the needs of the social system in which cultural expressions gradually came to operate – above all, those of the moral world, which was considered the carrier of such expressions.

The canon of exemplary biblical women, who were a model for virtuous behaviours or symbols of religious life, was established rather early in the patristic tradition. We find a trace of it in Jerome's *Epistola* 65, written for the virgin Principia in the form of an explanation of Psalm 44, interpreted as an epithalamium for Christ and the Church. In it, Jerome emphasises the indispensability of a series of female figures in the success of the sacred people throughout history, and Augustine returns to the list in a condensed form in *De natura et gratia.* 26, writing on the women who, like Mary, not only lived without sin but also lived in accordance with justice. In the poetic tradition, this canon, which is mentioned in other documentary sources, is condensed into a brief list quoted in a verse of the short poem *De virginitate* by Venantius Fortunatus (530-607), which came to enjoy a certain success.[1] Composed in

---

[1] In fact, we find it again cited as a famous reference in the text of the blessing of Judith, daughter of Charles the Bald and wife of Aethelwulf, King of Wessex, as quoted by Hincmar of Reims in his *Coronationes Regiae* (ed. in: PL 125, cols. 803-818, at col. 811): "*Despondeo te uni*

Poitiers in 567, when Agnes, the adopted daughter of Queen Radegund, was named abbess, it has been described by Maria I. Campanale as a "mystic epithalamium", in that it blends the *de virginitate* genre (praise and encouragement for virginal living), previously tackled by Ambrose, Jerome, and Avitus, and the *epithalamium* ('wedding poem') genre, adapted to the theme of the mystical marriage between consecrated virgins and Christ.[2] According to Campanale, the four-hundred-hexameter poem is organised into an *exordium* ('introduction'), based on the description of the blessed souls in heaven, a *perì gamou* ('celebration of marriage'), a *laus sponsae* ('praise of the bride'), and an epilogue, and each part includes a series of exempla. Among these, within the praise of the bride, there is an emphasis on the *felix virginitas* ('happy' or 'fecund virginity') of Mary, who was honoured with the generation of her Lord, a condition that cannot be equalled even by the most famous women of the Bible: "Though Sarah, Rebecca, Rachel, Esther, Judith, Anna, and Naomi rise up to the stars, they were not worthy of generating the father of the world" ("*Sarra Rebecca Rachel Hester Iudith Anna Noemi / quamvis praecipue culmen ad astra levent, / nulla tamen meruit mundi generare parentem*"; *Virg.* 99-101). The biblical women, listed with the *accumulatio* or *articulus*, which we know to be one of Venantius's most beloved rhetorical figures, are presented as a sort of *a minori* example, which Campanale defines as "a model of non-preferability".[3] This position is later corrected or integrated into other sections, where some of the women cited are invoked as positive individual examples.[4]

Venantius's verse, however, presented a list of excellent women inferior only to Mary, a list that the poet's stylistic authority establishes as a model of expression for later writers. The first of these is found in the work of the monk Agius of Corvey, who composed a dialogue-based *consolatio* for the death of Abbess Hathumoda in 876, drawing widely on the biblical exemplum, which

---

viro virginem castam, atque pudicam futuram conjugem, ut sanctae mulieres fuere viris suis, Sara, Rebecca, Rachel, Esther, Iudith, Anna, Noemi, favente auctore et sanctificatore nuptiarum, Iesu Christo Domino nostro".

[2] M.I. CAMPANALE, "Il *De Virginitate* di Venanzio Fortunato (*carm.* 8, 3 Leo): Un epitalamio mistico", *Invigilata Lucernis* 2 (1980), pp. 75-128. In addition to Ambrose's *De virginitate* and *De virginibus*, Campanale recalls Jerome's *Epist.* 22 and 130; Augustine's *De sancta virginitate*; Gregory of Nazianzus's *Parteníes épainos, hypothékai parthénois* (MIGNE, PG 37); and Gregory of Nyssa's *Perì parthenías*; see CAMPANALE, "*De Virginitate*", p. 75, n. 1.

[3] CAMPANALE, "*De virginitate*", p. 122.

[4] Judith, for instance, in Venantius Fortunatus, *Virg.* 304: "*hoc etiam recolens, quid possit parcior usus: / sobrietas Iudith vincere sola facit*".

he unimaginatively understood as a list of famous figures who are also dead.[5] And after a series of prophets and fathers, he adds female names for the sake of equality (*Virg.* 299-300): "*Sara, Rebecca, Rachel, Debora, Noemi, Ruth et Anna, / Holda, Susanna, Iudith et simul Hester obit*".[6] – Agius's list closely follows that of Venantius for the first hemistich of verse 299, but he varies the second – "*Esther Iudith Anna Noemi*" – moving the first two heroines to the following verse and replacing them with Ruth and Deborah, and adding Huldah, prophetess of 2 Kings 22, and Susanna, the beautiful wife of Joachim, who was harassed by two elders while bathing in her garden and was later defended against their accusations by Daniel (Daniel 13).

This variation may demonstrate that Agius's source was not directly Venantius, or not just him, but that Venantius was helpful to Agius, lending his source a brilliant and widely accepted poetic arrangement. In the history of medieval Latin poetry, it seems that Huldah is cited by only one other poet, another Carolingian, a few decades prior to Agius: Walahfrid Strabo of Reichenau. His work, *De imagine Tetrici*, an enigmatic, short, allegorical poem in 268 verses on the court of Louis the Pious, was written when the statue of Theoderic was transported from Ravenna to Aachen.[7] In his poem, he pauses to praise the queen and empress Judith, who had been Louis's second wife since 818, comparing her to the fair Rachel who loved Benjamin just as Judith loved little Charles, the later Emperor Charles the Bald, who appears to have been Walahfrid's pupil. The poet emphasises the significance of her name, matching her "valour and religious spirit" ("*at Iudith virtute refert et religione*"; v. 193) with that of the biblical heroine, who beheaded the Assyrian invader, freeing and saving her fellow citizens. He also recalls an unusual characteristic of the queen: the ability to play an instrument ("Judith strummed the instrument with the sweet-sounding plectrum" – "*organa dulcisono percurrit pectine Iudith*"; *Virg.* 198).[8] This aspect allows the poet a comparison with the prophetess Miriam, who in Exodus 15, 20 plays the drums ("a timbrel in her hand" – "*tympanum in manu sua*"; see *Imag. Tetr.* 197: "Miriam beat the

---

[5] On Agius, see F. STELLA, *La poesia carolingia* (Florence, 1995), pp. 93-94, 310-321, 479-481.

[6] *PLAC* 3, p. 378.

[7] See M. HERREN, "The *De imagine Tetrici* of Walahfrid Strabo: Edition and translation", *Journal of Medieval Latin* 1 (1991), pp. 118-139.

[8] The editor, Dümmler, connects this verse to Judith 16, 1-2 – the Song of Praise – "*cantate Domino meo in cymbalis*", but this may perhaps refer to Judith the empress and not to the biblical heroine.

rough-sounding skin of the timbrels" – "*tympana raucisona pulsavit pelle Maria*"). He seizes the chance for further hyperbole in writing that, if Sappho and Huldah were there (2 Kings 22, 14), Judith would even be able to compose metric poetry and issue prophecies, adding the habitual praise for a woman "despite" being a woman – "In fact, whatever the limits of your sex may have detracted has been compensated by a life dedicated to spiritual practice" ("*quicquid enim tibimet sexus subtraxit egestas / reddidit ingeniis culta atque exercita vita*") – followed by praise in the form of a list (fruitfulness, learning, kindness, strength of spirit, and eloquence) and good wishes for her life and afterlife.

This poetic list of biblical women was taken up again three centuries later by the poet Marbod of Rennes (1035-1123), schoolmaster at Angers, who, in his famed *Liber decem capitulorum* on the ten subjects of Christian culture, dedicated the fourth chapter to women (*De matrona*). In it, he overturns all the anti-female prejudice common to the misogynist literature of the Middle Ages, although he also contributes to it in other texts. He, too, emphasises that Mary was not the only one to raise the prestige and importance of women, but in addition to her, we read that many women were endowed with manly merit at times superior to that of men, and through their strength they received due glory. He lists Sarah, Rebecca, Rachel, Esther, Judith, Anna, and Naomi, comparing them to the seven stars. He pauses to praise Judith, Esther, and Ruth individually, dedicating a few verses to each of them.[9] This time, the form of

---

[9] Marbod of Rennes, *Liber decem capitulorum*, ed. W. BULST (Heidelberg, 1947: *Editiones Heidelbergenses* 8), vv. 79-97: "And however, with this exception, since the conception of Mary appears a unique event, we read that more than a few women have had a manly mind, or have even exceeded men, and with a strong spirit have received the just reward together with the glory that they deserved. We read that Sarah, Rebecca, Rachel, Esther, Judith, Anna, and Naomi, whom the generations of old held to be like the seven stars, were equal to men or exceeded them. For Judith achieved an excellent endeavor, which none of the men had dared undertake, returning after having killed Holofernes, and the salvation granted to the city of Bethulia by a woman kept away the enemy, driven out from every other city, out of fear. Everlasting fame honors Queen Esther, who, married to the tyrant like a lamb to a cruel wolf, risking her life, was unafraid of crossing that threshold from which none who passed through it without permission returned, and in defense of her people put her own safety at stake, and turned the edict of death intended for her people against the enemy. I speak not of Ruth, who, accompanying alone her chaste mother-in-law, deserved to give royal blood to her children, while she fled her country and parents because of her faith" ("*hoc tamen excepto quoniam res unica constat, / non paucas legimus mentes gessisse virorum, / aut etiam superare viros, et pectore forti / dignam mercedem merita cum laude tulisse. / Sara, Rebecca, Rachel, Esther, Iudith, Anna, Noemi, / sidera ceu septem quas saecula prisca tulerunt, / aequiparasse viros, aut exsuperasse leguntur. / nam Iudith egregium facinus, quod nemo virorum / ausus erat, gessit, caeso rediens Holoferne, / Bethuliaeque salus*

the verse repeats Venantius's model without variations, and Marbod's contribution is limited to the *amplificatio* of information on three of the main figures, later finishing this portrait of female virtues with saintly or pagan exempla such as Lucretia, Thrasea, and Alcestis.

The Model of Avitus

While Venantius provided a model in verse for the canon of biblical heroines, the poetic textual model for *De virginitate* is the eponymous book by Alcimus Avitus, archbishop of Vienne from 494 to 523; he also wrote the poem *De spiritalis historiae gestis*, five books on sacred history from the creation to the crossing of the Red Sea, which soon became a textbook in medieval schools. After writing the poem, and thus after 506-507, Avitus sent Bishop Apollinaris, upon the latter's request, a short book on the "religion of our relatives" or "on the virgins in our family," written for his sister Fuscina, who had become a nun. The topic employed by Avitus is not structured according to the exempla, as in Venantius, but follows the reasoning found in the treatises of the church fathers, especially Augustine's *De sancta virginitate*. The main comparison is, of course, with Mary, offering the opportunity for an extensive description. After this excerpt, Avitus urges the reader to combat, quoting as examples the famed women he had come across in his readings: "In fact, for some time now the glory of your sex has often been known through reading" (*"nam gloria dudum / sexus ista tui nota est tibi saepe legendo"*; *Virg.* 340-341).

He begins with Deborah, who spurred the Israelite army on against the Canaanites led by general Sisera – whose gigantic body he describes, a fact extraneous to the Bible and perhaps derived from the *conflatio* with Goliath – and predicted their defeat. He continues with Jael, who is not named and who stabs Sisera in her tent, thus celebrating a "female ... victory" (*"femineus ... triumphus"*; *Virg.* 362). He then digresses on the personified representation of virginity as described by Prudentius, explicitly quoted, and how it is glorified

urbi data per mulierem, / urbibus a reliquis pulsum deterruit hostem. / Esther reginam commendat fama perennis, / quae velut agna lupo crudeli nupta tyranno / non timuit, capitis discrimine, limen inire, / quod non exibat quisquis non iussus inisset, / opposuitque suam propria pro gente salutem, / edictumque necis populi conuertit in hostes. / Ruth taceo quae sola socrum comitata pudicam, / ad regale genus meruit transfundere prolem, / dum fidei causa patriam fugit atque parentes").

throughout the Holy Scriptures; he rapidly retraces this theme from Ruth through the prophetic books to Esther and Judith, briefly summarising Judith's undertaking of false seduction and murder: "How could one forget Esther and the lies of the chaste Judith, in which the satrap is aroused by the trickery of her painted face and the woman continues to avoid his obscene bed and suppresses his furious gaze by cutting off his head?" (*Virg.* 391-394).[10] After this consideration of the heroine, the biblical *percursio* continues to the end of the New Testament, culminating in praise of reading sacred texts and its effect on individual behaviour, repeating the tale of the wise and the foolish virgins (Matthew 25) and its commentaries in an already varied thematic context.

Another example surfaces only in verses 513-514, and it concerns a martyr: the well-known legend of Eugenia of Rome, who refused to be married and thus hid in a monastery disguised as a man, where she was discovered when a woman fell in love with her, believing her to be a man. When rejected, the woman denounced Eugenia, forcing her to reveal herself. Immediately thereafter, Avitus identifies exemplary virginity in the story of Joseph, who is sold by his brothers and who resists the advances of Potiphar's wife: Potiphar's wife is not even named as a character in a story known to all.

The next reference is to Susanna (*Virg.* 549-551), who fled from attacks by two elders: "After him, who will ever celebrate with sufficient praise Susanna, who one time, at a delicate age, defeated the desires and mad conspiracy of the elders?" ("*Susannam post hunc dignis quis laudibus umquam / excolat, infirmis quondam quae vicit in annis / improba vota senum coniuratosque furores?*"). Her story, like that of Judith, is not passed down in the Hebrew Bible but only in Greek (Daniel 13 LXX), and it is told with a certain narrative flavour owing to differentiation of the characters and psychological analysis otherwise absent or only roughly sketched in other *exempla*. One can easily imagine the episode of the two judges who walk away but then soon find themselves in the same place, both consumed by the desire to see Susanna, the one having already declared it, the other until then unsuspected of it. Avitus also dramatises the dissent of Susanna, who is uncertain as to how to respond to the harassment of the two. Daniel's intervention to save her, by consulting the two elders separately and thus discovering the truth, is an opportunity for a further digression on the history that awaited the prophet after his emergence onto the sacred

---

[10] Alcimus Avitus, *De virginitate*: "*Virg.*: *Hester quid memorem et castae mendacia Iudith, / ornati cum fraude Satraps accenditur oris, / cum manet illudens obscenum femina lectum / desectoque feros compescit vertice visus?*" (ed. R. PEIPER (Hanover, 1883: MGH AA 6.2, p. 286)).

stage. The short poem closes with the glorification of virgins, first to enter the kingdom of heaven, and the final example of Martha and Mary, the latter of whom keeping the best part for herself, as Avitus's sister had done by choosing to enter a convent.[11]

The Intercultural Foresight of Dracontius: Biblical and Pagan Heroines

Dracontius of Carthage was the first poet to make extensive use of female exempla, an aspect of his work that until now has been little observed by scholars.[12] He authored a collection of *Romulea* (short poems on 'Roman' subjects) recounting episodes of myth; a Christian poem, *De laudibus Dei*, largely composed of biblical paraphrases and doctrinal and moral exposition; and a *Satisfactio* to the Vandal king, which requested the author's release from prison.

The third book of *De laudibus Dei* begins with a laudatory hymn to omnipotence and divine generosity, which are contrasted with human greed, represented by the episode in the gospels of the rich man and Lazarus. Its central part (*Laud. Dei* 76-530), symbolically addressed to non-Christian readers, includes a series of examples of moral behaviour, closing with a second hymn followed by a confession of individual sins and a concluding prayer. The exem-

---

[11] This contribution had already been written (in 2010) when Avitus's *De virginitate* (or, rather, the *De consolatoria castitatis laude*) was published in the edition Alcimus Avitus [Avit de Vienne], *Éloge consolatoire de la chasteté (sur la virginité)*, ed. N. HECQUET-NOTI (Paris, 2011: SC 546), which I was unable to use.

[12] The bibliography on Dracontius through 1996 has been collected and discussed by L. CASTAGNA, *Studi draconziani (1912-1996)* (Naples, 1997). A number of works have been published in recent years (up to 2011), of which two also examine the *De laudibus Dei*: M. DE GAETANO, *Scuola e potere in Draconzio* (Alessandria, 2009); G. SANTINI, *Inter iura poeta: Ricerche sul lessico giuridico in Draconzio* (Rome, 2006). I have written on Dracontius several times, particularly in articles; see F. STELLA, "Fra retorica e innografia: Sul genere letterario delle 'Laudes Dei' di Draconzio," *Philologus* 132 (1988), pp. 213-245; ID., "Ristrutturazione topica ed estensione metaforica nella poesia cristiana: Da spunti draconziani," *Wiener Studien* 102 (1989), pp. 213-245; ID., "Per una teoria dell'imitazione poetica cristiana: Saggio di analisi sulle *Laudes Dei* di Draconzio," *Invigilata Lucernis* 7-8 (1985-1986), pp. 193-224; ID., "Innovazioni lessicali delle *Laudes Dei* di Draconzio fra latinità tardo-antica e medievale," *Invigilata Lucernis* 21 (1999), pp. 417-444; ID., "Epiteti di Dio in Draconzio fra tradizione classica e cristiana", *Civiltà Classica e Cristiani* 8 (1987), pp. 601-633; ID., "Variazioni stemmatiche e note testuali alle *Laudes Dei* di Draconzio: Con edizione del florilegio Paris, *B.N.*, Lat. 8093, f. 15ᵛ (sec. VIII-IX)," *Filologia Mediolatina* 3 (1996), pp. 1-34.

pla thus have a demonstrative function as models of morality even in pagan history, following the pattern of Tertullian's *Ad martyras* (4, 2-3) and, above all, Augustine's *De civitate Dei* (5, 12-13). The first part of the poem features stories of personal or family sacrifices, to be compared with that of Abraham for Isaac, such as Menoeceus; Codrus; Leonidas; the Philaeni; Lucius Junius Brutus; Verginius (though he is not named explicitly), who killed his daughter Verginia to prevent her from being dishonored by Appius Claudius; Manlius Torquatus, who had his son killed for disobeying military orders; Scaevola; Curtiu; and Regulus. These are followed by the stories of the sacrificial loyalty of two cities, Saguntum and Numantia, after which Dracontius announces with his usual wordiness – but also with the ideological openness that we have recognised in other aspects of his poem – his wish to balance his survey with a series of female exempla:[13]

> Lest anyone by chance believe that these words are dedicated only to men, and that woman is as an inert sex, weak with her fragile body, terrified by the weight of fame, and fearful of pursuing it beyond life at the cost of heroic suffering, having refused the countless eternal gifts of God, I will add that even a wicked woman can offer material for the highest consideration: nothing in the world is bolder than she when caught at fault; they draw courage from their very crime, and wrath provides women with an unstoppable force. Thus from that very place whence are they capable of drawing inspiration for their mad wickedness may they gather honest feelings around their heart and do what befits their dignity, what the reputation of their modesty demands, and what may aid them in attaining the glory of their future life. (*Laud. Dei* 3, 468-479)[14]

---

[13] In an unpublished chapter of my degree thesis, *L'epica di Draconzio fra tradizione classica e Cristiana* (PhD diss., Università di Firenze, 1986), supervised by Rosa La Macchia and Rita Pierini, I dedicated a few dozen pages to observations on the ideology of harmony between the natural elements and social classes; to Dracontius's celebration of the role of women in marriage and in the community; to his theory on the overthrowing of the classes and the new relationship between Romans and Barbarians; and to his theology of forgiveness, the grace / free will dialectic, and his idea of evil, which reveal a nonchalantly modern Augustinianism capable of engaging in dialogue with the classical poetic tradition so as to resemanticise it in the face of completely new problems and ideals.

[14] Dracontius, *Laudes Dei* 3, 468-479: "*sed ne forte viris tantum data verba putentur / et quasi sexus iners, fragili sub corpore mollis / laudis onus metuens, ne sit sibi fama superstes / tormentis quaesita suis, aeterna recuset / plurima dona Dei, laudis mala femina summae / materiem retinere potest: audacius illis / deprensis nihil est, animos de crimine sumunt / datque nimis grandem mulieribus ira furorem. / unde igitur furiale nefas assumere possunt / inde pios animi rapiant sub pectore motus / et faciant quod honesta decet, quod fama pudoris / exigit et vitae prodest sub laude futurae*". Reproduced here, with some changes, is the translation in

The introduction to the female exempla thus paints an anthropological picture true to the misogyny at the heart of ancient culture and in fact based on the verses of Juvenal: "Nothing is bolder than they when they are discovered: they draw courage and wrath from their own guilt" (*"nihil est audacius illis / deprensis: iram atque animos de crimine sumunt"*; *Sat.* 6, 284-285); "They show courage in the foul deeds they dare to commit" (*"fortem animum praestant rebus quas turpiter audent"*; 6, 97). Women are capable of grand gestures, and it is right to attribute proper importance to them, but – the poet would seem to say – the energy they employ in these undertakings is simply the underside of the violence that they ordinarily express in committing evil (*mala femina*). Reading between the lines of this excerpt of *De laudibus Dei* in the light of Juvenal, but also in the light of the fact that nearly all the (male) examples adopted up to this point are *exempla scelerum*, enables us, however, to propose the hypothesis that here Dracontius is actually attempting to correct the negative topos inherited from Juvenal, whose terms he reuses but reversing their sense, though without arriving at a purely positive or neutral connotation of women's nature.[15]

The first example adopted in *Laud. Dei* 3, 480-495 is that of the very chaste Judith, who "pretended to love Holofernes, and, penetrating the general's camp, a fearful place even for men, generated true glory from a simulated crime [the betrayal of her people]".[16] The term used by Dracontius to define her character is *virago*, which, according to Claude Moussy, takes on the meaning here of 'heroine' or, more literally, 'woman warrior', as Ovid had done in reference to Minerva in *Metamorphoses* 2, 765 ("a woman formidable in war"; *"belli metuenda virago"*) and as Dracontius would do when referring to Clytemnestra in *Orest. trag.* 752 or to Medea in *Rom.* 10, 12, and 62. Judith thus takes on a specifically warlike connotation. There follows a depiction of the military camp, which constitutes a work of compositional skill marked by references to Statius, *Thebais* 4, 321 and by expressions extolling female courage as superior to that of men: "the assault of men is not so great a force" (*"et quod tanta manus non est aggressa virorum"*; *Laud. Dei* 3, 486) or "woman alone" (*"femina sola"*; 3, 487); then comes the tale of the decapitation and

---

Blossii Aemili Dracontii, De laudibus Dei libri tres, ed. F. CORSARO (Catania, 1962), p. 159.

[15] The observation that the examples are all *exempla scelerum* belongs to Claude MOUSSY; see the comment in his edition of Dracontius: *Réparation*, part 3 of *Louanges de Dieu*, vol. 2 of the *Oeuvres* (Paris, 1988), p. 102.

[16] "*Iudith Holofernem castissima finxit amare / et ibimet peperit de ficto crimine laudem / contra ducis metuenda viris ingressa virago*".

display of the head to the Hebrew notables and to her city, which gave Judith both freedom and victory. The episode concludes with a hymnodic ending that reiterates the femininity of her undertaking against a courageous male commander: "The bold and courageous commander dies at the dagger of a woman" ("*femineo mucrone perit dux fortis et audax*"; v. 478). He was crushed not by battle but by the hope of pleasure ("*promissa voluptas*"; v. 492), and yet "the pleasure was hoped for but not consummated" ("*sperata licet, non est perfecta libido*"; v. 493); typical of Dracontius, he does not resist the temptation of the paradox, emphasising the punishment for a crime of adultery not yet committed. Also typical of Dracontius is the sophisticated reuse of a thematic intertext such as Paulinus of Nola's (355-431) *carmen* 26, in which Judith was cited within a series of examples of victory achieved without weapons but through the protection of God:

> The wily Judith with her chaste cunning deceived and mocked Holofernes, who had terrorised mighty people far and wide. She remained inviolate in that lewd bed, and then fled from the barbarians' camp victorious after slaughtering their leader.

> *terrentem magnos late populos Holofernem*
> *arte pudicitiae deceptum callida Judith*
> *risit, in impuro quae non pulluta cubili*
> *barbara truncato victrix duce castra fugavit* (26, 165).[17]

Paulinus brings out the derisory aspect of the episode, leading to the contrast *impuro-polluta* later exploited by Dracontius and emphasising the heroine's warrior-like virtues less than her cunning, which on the contrary finds no importance in Dracontius's portrayal.[18]

The other examples adopted in the *De laudibus Dei*, however, are drawn from Roman history and pagan mythology: Semiramis, Tomyris, Evadne, Dido, and Lucretia, women who vary greatly and are exponents of virtues or abilities that are often contradictory but who are equally courageous and determined. The moral that the poet draws from them in verses 524-530 is that "a thousand types [*exempla*] of crimes everywhere are attributed to this or that woman: they

---

[17] Translation from *The Poems of St. Paulinus of Nola*, trans. P.G. WALSH (New York, 1975), pp. 259-260.

[18] Paulinus of Nola also cites Judith in *Carm.* 28, another *natalicium* for Felix, which, describing the paintings in the basilica of Nola, mentions the depiction of the heroine in a tableau dedicated to women: "*ast aliam sexus minor obtinet, inclita Iudith, / qua simul et regina potens depingitur Esther*" (28, 26-27).

committed them either because they were influenced by the mirage of a bit of glory, or certainly out of devotion, but to a vain deity" ("*Milia femineis numerantur ubique catervis / exempla scelerum: modicae vel laudis amore / aut certe fecere pie pro numine vano*"). Following this is a comparison between legendary gods and the true God, who is later praised with another lengthy hymnodic discourse. This conclusion / transition seems to confirm that Dracontius bases his material on a rhetorical inventory and treats it as such – namely, an inventory of crimes perpetrated for glory. This perpetration of crimes for glorious purposes has positive connotations because it is presented in the anthropological preface as one of the objectives to which women must not feel inadequate; they are, in any case (*certe*), crimes for a good cause (*pie*), committed for a noble aim, though at times – in all cases except for Judith – in the name of a pagan deity. The biblical narratives become intertwined with the exemplary materials of the rhetoricians and poets in the wake of Augustine's *De civitate Dei*, but without any further cultural contrast.

The Other Judiths, from Aldhelm to Milo

Naturally, Paulinus of Nola, Dracontius, and Avitus were not the first to write poetry about Judith. Before them, Prudentius had mentioned her in his *Psychomachia* (here in H.J. Thomson's archaic style):

> "Shalt thou, O troubler of mankind, have been able to resume thy strength and grow warm again with the breath of life that was extinguished in thee, after the severed head of Holofernes soaked his Assyrian chamber with his lustful blood, and the unbending Judith, spurning the lecherous captain's jeweled couch, checked his unclean passion with the sword, and woman as she was, won a famous victory over the foe with no trembling hand, maintaining my cause with boldness heaven-inspired?" But perhaps a woman still fighting under the shade of the law had not force enough, though in so doing she prefigured our times, in which the real power [Christ] has passed into earthly bodies to sever the great head by the hands of feeble agents? (58-69)[19]

---

[19] Prudentius, *Psychomachia*, ed. in: Prudentius, *Carmina*, ed. M.P. CUNNINGHAM (Turnhout, 1966: CCSL 126), pp. 149-181, 58-69: "*tene, o vexatrix hominum, potuisse resumptis / viribus extincti capitis recalescere flatu, / Assyrium postquam thalamum ceruix Olofernis / caesa cupidineo madefactum sanguine lauit / gemmantemque torum moechi ducis aspera Judith / spreuit et incestos compescuit ense furores, / famosum mulier referens ex hoste tropaeum / non trepidante manu, vindex mea caelitus audax. / at fortasse parum fortis matrona sub umbra / legis*

The episode is recalled within a discussion on *Pudicitia* toward the *Libido* that she defeated, and the context leads the poet, in a passage of concentrated strength, to force or constrain the meaning of the episode into a particular area. It is shifted onto the level of sexual mores, raising Judith to a symbol of virtue, avenger of the attempted adultery rather than a symbol of courage, and makes her into a typological figure that hints at the present time, in which the authentic virtue (of Christ) has been made flesh in an earthly body to cut off the great head of the enemy through the work of feeble servants (*infirmos*).

Sidonius Apollinaris (430-486) had also spoken of her in his *carmen* 16, in which he invites his zither and his spirit to sing no longer of pagan deities but of the God who penetrated the breast of Miriam and helped "the hand of Judith as it smote the neck of Holophernes, when the trunk was laid prostrate with the throat cut through and the strong blow gloriously disguised the weak sex" ("*quique manum Iudith ferientem colla Olophernis / Iuuisti exciso iacuit cum gutture truncus / et fragilis valido latuit bene sexus in ictu*"; 16, 11-13).[20] Thus the episode is one of the elements of a biblical aretalogy, which includes other episodes, but it is noted not just for its usual contrast between strength and femininity but for its emphasis on divine intervention rather than the heroine's initiative. This aspect is imposed by the hymnodic context, in which the subject must topically remain the 'you' of that God who is being celebrated, and thus each event must be presented in the light of the external agent.

The next appearance – besides Venantius, who, in addition to the mnemonic verse of the female canon, quickly cites Judith in verse 304 of the same poem, *De virginitate* – is found in the third poetic *De virginitate* of the Latin tradition, that of Aldhelm of Malmesbury (639-709), excluding simple mentions in lists of biblical books, which are not considered in this essay. This metric reduction of the prose *De laude virginitatis* is dedicated to the monastic community of Barking and is, in any case, much more extensive than the precedents of Avitus and Venantius.[21] In fact, it occupies 2,904 hexameters dedi-

---

adhuc pugnans, dum tempora nostra figurat, / vera quibus virtus terrena in corpora fluxit, / grande per infirmos caput excisura ministros". Translation by H.J. Thomson in: *Prudentius*, 1 (Cambridge, MA, 1949: *Loeb Classical Library*), p. 283.

[20] Translation by W.B. ANDERSON, in: Sidonius, *Poems* (Cambridge, MA, 1936: *Loeb Classical Library*), p. 243.

[21] The comprehensive edition is *Aldhelmi opera*, ed. R. EHWALD (Berlin, 1913-1919: *MGH AA* 15). For a critical review of the prose treatise (with an edition of the glosses), see Aldhelm of Malmesbury, *Prosa de virginitate cum glosa Latina atque Anglosaxonica*, ed. S. GWARA (Turnhout, 2001: *CCSL* 124). For a translation, see *Aldhelm: The Poetic Works*, ed. and trans. M. LAPIDGE and J.L. ROSIER (Cambridge, 1985). The most significant study of Aldhelm as a poet (up

cated to explaining the doctrine on the matter (that is, virginity), composing a sort of themed bibliography in verse and a history of martyrial and institutional virginity, especially in monastic and church institutions. It is also replete with biblical references and exempla; those drawn from the Bible are explained in the last part of the text within a kind of *psychomachia* from Nabal to Joseph to Judith. To the latter, in the Anglo-Latin poet's redundant and rather empty style, he dedicates a brief narrative and exegetical elaboration:

> What can be said of Judith, born of noble stock, who with her pure body disdained the king's brothel and with her heart trod on unholy, lustful relations with the pagan? Through this endeavour her chaste satchel brought the bloodied trophy to her fellow citizens who had run the risk of death, keeping her modesty intact with a devout mind, and thus chaste purity triumphantly disdained the vice of the flesh, guilty of immoral stain, and she resisted the attack with the arrows of combatant virginity to prevent the filthy poison of the brothel from creeping into her delicate members, reaching her innermost organs.[22]

Aldhelm employs strong terms to glorify her rejection of relations with the pagan king and the display of the severed, bloody head as the triumph of chastity, and he portrays the battle as spiritual combat (*"virgineis ... sagittis"*) and highlights the contrast between the woman and the poison of a corrupt sexuality (*postribulum*, used twice). Here we sense the influence of Prudentius's model, with the allegorisation and radical abstraction of Judith's character, whose feminine aspect becomes secondary, though there is some allusion to it in the *fibras fragiles* of line 2570, almost as if to echo the expressions of Sidonius or Dracontius.

---

to 2011) remains A. ORCHARD, *The Poetic Art of Aldhelm* (Cambridge, 1994), while on the *De virginitate*, see G.T. DEMPSEY, "Aldhelm of Malmesbury's social theology: The barbaric heroic ideal christianised", *Peritia* 15 (2001), pp. 58-80; E. PETTIT, "Holiness and masculinity in Aldhelm's opus geminatum De Virginitate", in: *Holiness and Masculinity in the Middle Ages*, ed. P.H. CULLUM and K.J. LEWIS (Cardiff, 2004), pp. 8-23.

[22] Aldhelm of Malmesbury, *Laud. virg.* 2560-2570: "*quid referam Iudith generosa stirpe creatam / prostibulum regis temnentem corpore puro / et stuprum sceleris calcantem corde profanum? / civibus idcirco mortis discrimina passis / casta cruentatum gestauit bulga tropeum / seruans integrum deuota mente pudorem. / sic vitium carnis polluta sorde nocentis / integritas almo contemnit casta triumpho / aemula virgineis proturbans bella sagittis, / lurida prostibuli ne possit serpere virus / in fibras fragiles succensis torre medullis*"; trans. M. LAPIDGE and M. ROSIER.

Instances in the Carolingian Age

The popularity of Prudentius is confirmed in part by the reuse of his expression *"castae mendacia"*, from the above-cited *Psychomachia*. We find it again in the *titulus* of Wigbod 1, 8, 2, 23, *"Esther quid memorem et castae mendacia Iudith?"*, within a summary of biblical books composed in the proto-Carolingian era, the late eighth century, by recovering passages from Eugenius and Avitus.[23] Even in the fully Carolingian era, the heroine is mentioned above all in biblical *percursiones* (today, we might say parades), such as that in *carmen* 41 by Theodulf, Bishop of Orléans († c. 821). This was transmitted in the early Middle Ages as a metric introduction to complete scriptural codices – "We find then the story of a woman famed for her undertaking, Judith, under whose blows fell unchaste madness" (*"scribitur insignis Iudith mox femina facti / incestus cecidit qua feriente furor"*) – and in very similar terms in *carmen* 21 – "With her sword Judith drove back unchaste madness, but she did not succeed in driving back you, unjust scourge of death" (*"incestos Iudith compescuit ense furores, / te non compescit, mortis iniqua lues"*; 21, 71-72). These occur within a series of examples of famous figures who did not escape death, whose consoling topic we have already seen in previous examples. Here, a faint allusion to female characterisation reemerges and accompanies the praise of chastity, or rather the punishment of lust. In the next generation, Walahfrid Strabo, as we have seen, would again invoke the biblical Judith to celebrate the imperial Judith, praised for her *virtus* and *religio* as was her namesake.

The other instances in this era come from the monk and schoolmaster Milo of Saint-Amand († 871/872), author of a poem in two books, *De sobrietate*, which has been studied very little in relation to its value and originality. This poem adapts the distant model of Prudentius's *Psychomachia* to deal with moral subjects using an exegetical method – that is, by commenting on biblical references. In the first book, he dedicates a long passage to Judith, which is the most extensive in Latin poetry (Milo, *Sobr.* 16, 331-393 (sixty-three verses)).[24] It is dominated by psychological matters as much as moral ones, carefully describing the details of the scene, absolutely unusual in a doctrinal work,

---

[23] *Versus libris saeculi VIII adiectis*, ed. E. DÜMMLER, in: *PLAC* 1, p. 96; later updated by L. MUNZI, "Compilazione e riuso in età carolingia: Il prologo poetico di Wigbodo", *Romano-Barbarica* 12 (1992-1993), pp. 189-210.

[24] Milo of Sint-Amand, *Carmen de Sobrietate*, 16, 331-393 (ed. L. TRAUBE, in: *PLAC* 3, pp. 625-627).

which the author presents as a chronicle of the *historica ratio* – that is, the literal narration rather than the spiritual, typological, or tropological meaning – trusting that this order of the events is governed by divine providence. Certainly, the heroine is repeatedly described as *casta*, as would occur when he refers to her in another episode, verse 476: "your pure acting praises you, Judith, and makes you blessed" ("*acta pudicitiae te, Iudith, laude bearunt*"). We are also reminded of the *sobrietas* that permits her to be included in the gallery of examples in the poem, for after her husband's death, she kept to her room alone (or, rather, "with her sister, moderation"; "*cum sobrietate sorore*"), fasting in her beauty and her propriety and thus becoming, in an innovation of religious imagination, a model of salvation for widows. Declaring that he will skip over the details of her story, which the poet knows is familiar to all, he focusses on the simulated offer of adultery made by the "*castissima foemina*" and imagines the expression of Holofernes upon seeing the woman, a vision of dignity before his coarse, surly eyes, the expression of a shaken soul and of lust set ablaze. Death enters through the large windows and takes him prisoner; the luxury and pleasures of the banquet only hasten the end, and the wine that has been drunk will only serve to soften the pain of the blows.[25] The incipit of the epilogue, which makes use of Virgilian expressions, requalifies the protagonist as an example of moral virtue, but immediately after the epithet *bellatrix*, in an accumulation of virtues ("*virtutibus associatis*"), it brings out once more the warrior aspect that had been obscured by the writers after Dracontius. The passage lingers at length on colourful details: the refined clothing, the luxurious backdrop of the Assyrian banquet, the chronology of Judith's stay at court (here five days, as opposed to four in the biblical account), the trunk without a head or a name, its display to the Hebrews and the Assyrians on the walls at dawn. The episode is immediately followed by that of Jael, introduced in the form of a comparison.[26] Her moderation (the *sobrietas* recalled in verse 391),

---

[25] The reference to entering through large windows might cause one to think of Judith's eyes, but this is actually a reference, correctly identified by the editor, Ludwig Traube, to the image in Jer 9, 21: "*quia ascendit mors per fenestras nostras, ingressa est domos nostras*". A characteristic of Milo's craft is cross-referencing biblical passages (through reciprocal intrascriptural references) to deepen the meaning of the text further while strengthening its expressiveness in an unexpected manner.

[26] Milo, *Sobr.* 16, 386-393: "*sic Iahel, uxor Aber, Sisaram post bella fugacem, / quae male nongentis falcatis curribus egit / qui dum poscit aquas, lac accipit - hospita amico / asperior solito clauo terebrauit acuto / pertractans in fronte locum; mors iuncta sopori est. / sobrietas ductrix lac praebuit atque reatum / sacrilegi pugnax audaci perculit ulna / femineasque manus fabrorum malleus auxit* ("so Jael, Haber's wife, a meaner guest than usual with her friend, stuck

which is the constant theme of each of the poem's stories, perhaps lay in the exegetical interpretation of Jael as enemy of the prince of vices (Sisara, as in Hrabanus Maurus, *In Iudices*, 1, 12)[27] or in the strength with which she succeeded in stabbing the temple of general Sisera with a sharp nail, demonstrating courage, combativeness, and boldness. Behind the characters, the Moderation that had offered the milk armed the woman with a hammer, punishing the sacrilegious commander for his offense.

The next story (*Sobr.* 17) is that of Esther, in a sequence that apparently recalls Venantius's exempla of female heroism, here forcibly adapted to fit examples of moderation.[28] Esther is one such example due to her fasting, probably a reference to a detail just barely hinted at in the Bible (Esther 2, 15), the moderation with which Esther had preferred not to use all the resources that the king had provided to those seeking to be queen or the fast that she had undertaken when she decided to go before King Xerxes and beg for mercy for the Jews, whom Haman had wished to persecute. The source is probably Ambrose, who in *De Helia et ieiunia* 9 had specified that "with her fast Judith beheaded Holofernes, and by the same method Esther freed her people, to whom the drunken Haman paid the penalty for his wrongdoing" ("*Iudith ieiunans Holophernem obtruncat, iisdem artibus populum suum liberat Esther, cui poenas ebrius Aman exsolvit*"). Here the interpretation is so forced as to deny that her beauty was the reason for the king's choice ("*non sua forma suasit*"). But most of the verses dedicated to this character focus on the conspiracy of Haman, whose fate on the fifty-cubit-high gallows (Esther 5, 14) is depicted as a reversal, to his detriment, of the fate that he had initiated for the Jews and is dramatised by the detail of his ten sons witnessing his death, sons who are actually only named in the Bible much later on as victims of the Jews' retalia-

---

a sharp nail in the forehead, feeling her to find the right place, of Sisara, fleeting after the battle, who ran towards evil with ninety wagons: while asking water, he receives milk. Death was combined with sleep. The leading Moderation offered milk and, combative, brought down the guilt of the sacrilege with a bold arm and a smith's hammer gave power to the woman's hands").

[27] Ed. in: *PL* 108, col. 1134A.

[28] Milo, *Sobr.* 17, 394-410: *Hester reginam jejunia sobria regi / fecerunt gratam, quam non sua forma suasit / terribili feritate suo se offerre marito: / lamentum gemitus luctus suspiria saccus / verterunt urnam cunctasque ex ordine sortes. / haec humilis deiecit Aman regina superbum, / sub rege Asuero populus quem cunctus honorans / orabat genibus telluris in aequore flexis, / extulit et ligno iam spe meliore leuatum, / quod quinquagenis cubitis altum ipse pararat / Mardocheo humili; finis fuit iste superbo. / spectauere decem pendentem in stipite nati, / quod genitor passus, passuri sorte reatus. / sic cadit in foueam commenti fraudibus instans; / inlaqueatur enim, nodos qui nectit iniquos. / sic ruit ascendens ventosa superbia fastum; / invidia occumbit, genitrix quae facta diabli est*".

tion (Esth 9:12). Here the moral crux of the story is presented as the reversal of arrogance and treachery, which turn against those guilty of such sins, and the starting point of *sobrietas* is nothing more than a narrative pretense. In fact, Milo resumes the story of Judith in the second book ("we mocked the infamous Holofernes, whom the chaste Judith beheaded" – "*risimus infandum quem Judith casta Holofernem / truncavit*"; verses 200-201) to contrast it – by setting it in the role of a monument to chastity – against the dramatic nature of another severed head, that of John the Baptist, beheaded by the "monkey dancer of the prophet" ("*saltatrix simia vatis*"), which in turn sets off a tirade against carnal lust, richly embellished with biblical exempla.

In the same period, Judith appears several times as a character in the rhythmic version of the *Cena Cypriani*, drafted by the deacon Johannes Hymmonides around 876 for the festivities connected to Emperor Charles the Bald's visit to Rome, a work which has been the object of recent critical attention.[29] As we know, in this scriptural masquerade composed in prose between the end of the fourth and the beginning of the fifth centuries, each of the characters appears as an invitee to the wedding banquet of King Joel in Cana and is portrayed with an adjective or a gesture recalling his or her role in the Bible. Judith is here presented as a "victor" and as "chaste", combining the two most frequent connotations with which she was associated in late antique literature, but also as the lead dancer and as an example of beauty and elegance in her hair and clothing.[30]

A few decades earlier in rhythmic literature, however, Judith had received the honour of a short poem dedicated entirely to the events of her life, evidence of the popularity of her story, of which the rhythmic text was probably a recited version. This is the Strecker III rhythmic poem, passed down in its entirety, alongside many other examples of this genre, in MS Verona, Biblioteca Capitolare XC (85), and in part in other contemporary manuscripts (ninth to tenth century) – MS Paris, Bibliothèque nationale de France, latin 1154, MS Brussels, Bibliothèque Royale, 8860-67, and MS Verona, Biblioteca Capitolare

---

[29] Among many titles, see, e.g. Hrabanus Maurus and Johannes Hymonides, *La Cena di Cipriano*, ed. E. ROSATI and F. MOSETTI CASARETTO (Alessandria, 2002) and L. DOLEŽALOVA, *Reception and its Varieties: Reading, Re-Writing, and Understanding "Cena Cypriani" in the Middle Ages* (Trier, 2007).

[30] Johannes Hymonides, *Cena Cypr.* 2, 34: "*Iudith victrix Oloferni offert opertorium*"; 2, 150: "*Lazarus sepultus umbram, Iudit* casta *soleam*"; 2, 259: "*Iudith sericum seruabat* casta *coopertorium*"; 2, 199: "*choreas Iudith ducebat et Iubal psalterium*"; 2, 247: "*Bersabeth crines decoros et Iudith conopeum*".

88 (83) – fifty stanzas of three catalectic trochaic septenarius or fifteen-syllable lines. Unfortunately, most of these (stanzas 13-44) are illegible, given the scrawl in which the version of MS Verona XC was written. Here, as far as one can decipher, Judith – in any case, also celebrated as a woman – is above all a symbol of the victory over pagan peoples, as the text closes with a wish for victory similar to that in the Bible story: "But they praised Judith of all women: may that God that then defeated the Assyrian troops through the strength of her courage and her heroic arm bring the pagan peoples who do not believe in the Lord to ruin" ("*Iudith vero inter omnes laudauerunt feminas. / ille deus, qui percussit tunc castra Assyrii / in virtute preualenti et in forti brachio, / perdat gentes paganorum incredulas domino*"). At the time, it was thought that the text could be placed in the context of the Carolingian wars against the Saxons, or rather – given its probable northern Italian origins – against the Muslims (793) or the Avars (796). Another clue is the exegetic interest in the book of Judith, favoured by the presence of an empress of that name, to whom Hrabanus Maurus dedicated his commentary of the Bible text in the 830s. But the warlike atmosphere renders the first dating more likely. The course of the tale retraces that of the biblical book, recalled in quick strokes for a readership already familiar with the story, but with the desire to contextualise it in chronological terms ("it was in the thirteenth year of the reign" – "*anno tertio in regno cum esset et decimo*") instead of portraying a character and to stay as true as possible to the source, which is just barely adapted to rhythmic requirements. The story is transformed indirectly into a sort of epic, with the repetition of epithets for the same characters (such as "Holefernes ... head of the army" – "*Olofernus ... princeps militiae*") or recurring words and phrases such as "many nations" ("*multas gentes*"), "against the nations" ("*contra gentes*"), "with his God" ("*deo suo*"), and "sword" ("*gladius*"), with a patina of clericalisation that emerges when compared with the source: in stanza 48, the rhythmic poem uses "churches" ("*ecclesiis*") while the original text has "people" ("*populus*").[31] The result is the equivalent of a fifteenth-century popular *cantare* on knights or paladins, concentrating on essential elements and select scenes of the story and almost completely closed to any chance of exegesis or symbolism other than a superficial contrast between Christians and unbelievers, and it is probably a Latin precursor of this folkloric and literary genre.

---

[31] For an analysis of these recurring terms, see F. STELLA, *Poesia carolingia latina a tema biblico* (Spoleto, 1993), pp. 332-335.

Exegetical Success and Later Developments

The figure of Judith is presented in different ways in the forms of early medieval cultural expression beyond Latin poetry: the thesis of Cécile Coussy documents her above all in iconography, but Old English literature presents another, unfortunately mutilated poem on Judith, preserved in the famous MS London, British Library, Cotton Vitellius A. XV that also holds *Beowulf*.[32] The most significant trace is without a doubt the commentary – the first ever dedicated in the Latin West to this book of the Bible – that Hrabanus Maurus, abbot of Fulda and later archbishop of Mainz (d. 856), devoted to it and that has been discussed in a recent critical edition.[33] The commentary was composed around 834, when Hrabanus Maurus was still abbot of Fulda, and is dedicated to the empress Judith, as attested by the preface in verse and the *carmen figuratum* accompanying it. Along with the commentary to the book of Esther, with which it is usually associated in the many manuscripts preserving it, the poem was revised and rededicated to the empress Ermengarde, wife of Lothair I, a few years later (around 840).[34] As Adele Simonetti has noted, this commentary is not very systematic, owing to the lack of direct sources on which to base it, and it is founded on two fundamental meanings: the literal and allegorical. The exegete explains this in the double preface published as poem No. 4 by Ernst Dümmler in *Poetae Latini aevi Carolini*. In his prose dedication (edited in: *PL* 109, col. 539), Hrabanus Maurus clearly presents his comments on Judith and Esther, associated with the gift for the queen, as a model of behaviour to imitate for "virtue and zeal in good works" ("*virtutes ac studium in bono opere*"), all the more so because the empress shares the name of the one and the regal dignity of the other. He specifies, however, that both characters are allegorical figures (although further on he uses the term 'type', *typus*) of the Church, even though Judith is in any case a "*castitatis exemplar*". The qualifying point of their exemplary nature lies – as in the rhythmic poem, and only there – in the

---

[32] C. COUSSY, *La figure de Judith dans l'Occident médiéval (Vᵉ-XVᵉ siècles)*, 2 vols. (Limoges, 2004). Unfortunately, it appears that the book, published in two volumes (with additional iconography), is not available in Italian libraries and is also absent from the Bibliothèque Nationale in Paris and the Bodleian Library at Oxford University. Stacy S. Klein analyses the context of the Old English poem in a chapter of S.S. KLEIN, *Ruling Women: Queenship and Gender in Anglo-Saxon Literature* (Notre Dame, 2006).

[33] Hrabanus Maurus, *Commentario al Libro di Giuditta*, ed. A. SIMONETTI (Florence, 2008).

[34] On the interpretative success of the book of Esther, see E.L. DATURI, *Représentations d'Esther entre écritures et images* (Berne, 2004), who, however, does not consider the Latin poetic sources.

fact that both defeated spiritual enemies with strength and physical enemies with the maturity of wisdom. In the same way, if the empress Judith, who had already proven her ability to conquer her enemies, had persevered in this behaviour, she would have easily overcome all her opponents.[35] Thus what emerges is a purely war-related and anti-pagan interpretation, which seems peculiar to the second generation of Carolingians.

The dedication in verse, which is composed of thirty-five mesostich hexameters in hymnodic style and end in a generic, long-winded prayer requesting that God protect the queen, was published with the first edition of the commentary, but was actually composed for the second (for Ermengarde). The second, in twenty hexameters, addresses Ermengarde directly, urging her not to disdain the "commissioned work" ("*opus commissum*") and the "sent song" ("*carmen missum*") of her devoted servant. It then praises the recipient and proposes to her the noble example of the heroine Judith ("pray, accept Judith as a noble model for all: in fact, you will imitate her at the same time in your mind and by your hand" – "*accipe, quaeso, Judith exemplar nobile cunctis, / mente manuque simul atque hanc imitabere rite*"; verses 10-11). He thus acknowledges the moral and political aspect of the biblical model because it will render her welcome to Christ in heaven and prevent the enemy (a sign that seems to coincide with that of the rhythmic poem) from saying so much as *puppup*, an onomatopoeic word perhaps referring to children's talk. This word seems to be found exclusively in Aldhelm ("*regales vastans caulas bis dicere puppup*"; *De virg.* 20), and Hrabanus Maurus reuses it in his *De laudibus sanctae crucis* 2, 21. The content of this dedication is similar to the one for Ermengarde in his commentary on the book of Esther, a "queen whose wisdom and steadiness of mind and victory over her enemies offer all Christians a most noble model, so that they may follow divine law and, maintaining a firm hope in the goodness of

---

[35] Ed. in: *PL* 109, col. 539: "*sanctarum mulierum quas sacra Scriptura commemorat, virtutes ac studium in bono opere imitari, non frustra arbitratus sum quarumdam illarum historiam, allegorico sensu ad sanctae Ecclesiae mysterium a nobis translatam, vestro nomini dicare atque transmittere, Iudith videlicet, atque Esther: quarum unam coaequatis nomine, alteram dignitate. quae quidem ob insigne meritum virtutis, tam viris, quam etiam feminis sunt imitabiles, eo quod spiritales hostes animi vigore, et corporales consilii maturitate vicerunt. Sic et vestra nunc laudabilis prudentia, quae jam hostes suos non parva ex parte vicerat, si in bono coepto perseverare atque semetipsam semper meliorare contenderit, cunctos adversarios suos feliciter superabit*". Isidore of Seville, *Allegoriae*. 22 (ed. in: *PL* 83, col. 116A), presents the same interpretation, which was standard throughout the Middle Ages: "*Iudith et Esther typum Ecclesiae gestant, hostes fidei puniunt, ac populum Dei ab interitu eruunt*" ("Judith and Esther are symbols of the Church: they punish the enemies of faith and free the people of God from ruin").

God, have faith in the possibility of being freed from all enemies".[36] The similarity of both topic and expressions confirms the parallelism and the quasi-equivalence that the two biblical figures enjoyed in this period. Hrabanus Maurus adds in the verse preface that the queen, like Esther, is urged to take care of her people, raising them up in every manner. Indeed, beauty and strength fade, and as day becomes night and the leaves and flowers fall, so Ermengarde – whom the poet salutes from his bed, where he lies ill – will be "a guest of a short time" ("*parvi temporis hospes*"). In this dedication, of a more personal and reasoned kind, in which Hrabanus Maurus reuses expressions such as "O, powerful queen" ("*o regina potens*"), which Venantius Fortunatus had dedicated to Radegund, Esther is set forth as an example of wisdom, tenacity, and success in her hope in God and obedience to the law. These qualities ensure her effectiveness in the fight against her enemies, but above all, unlike Judith, she is a model queen, a woman to whom power offered the condition and the opportunity to do good.[37]

Mentions of Judith after the ninth century are relatively few, but they seem to emphasise a specific typification of the figure: the strong and victorious woman, a model for other women in power, treated in an identical way as Esther, who, however, was much less popular in poetry.[38]

---

[36] Hrabanus Maurus, *Carm.* 4 (ed. E. Dümmler, in: *PLAC*, 2, pp. 167-168): "*expositionem libri Hester reginae ... cuius prudentia et constantia mentis victoriaque de hostibus nobilissimum quibusque fidelibus praebet exemplum, ut divinam legem servantes et spem firmam in dei bonitate habentes confidant se de universis inimicis liberandos*".

[37] Hrabanus Maurus's relationship with these empresses has been studied through biblical models by M.B. DE JONG, "The empire as ecclesia: Hrabanus Maurus and biblical *Historia* for rulers," in: *The Uses of the Past in the Early Middle Ages*, ed. Y. HEN and M. INNES (Cambridge, 2000), pp. 191-226.

[38] If we exclude mentions of Esther in lists of biblical books, she is only quoted in two passages by Paulinus of Nola (*Carm.* 26, 95 and 28, 27), which later surface together with other biblical heroines in Marbod's *Liber decem capitolorum*, and obviously in Petrus Riga's *Aurora* and John of Garland's *Epithalamium virginis*. Aelfric had produced an English version of the book of Esther; see M. CLAYTON, "Aelfric's *Esther*: A *speculum reginae*?", in: *Text and Gloss: Studies in Insular Learning and Literature Presented to Joseph Donovan Pheifer*, ed. H. CONRAD-O'BRIAIN, V.J. SCATTERGOOD, and A.M. D'ARCY (Dublin, 1999), pp. 89-101. Carolingian political treatises had made her a paradigm of equality in royalty, as documented by F.-R. ERKENS, "*Sicut Esther Regina*: Die westfränkische Königin als *consors regni*", *Francia* 20 (1993), pp. 15-38. This tendency revealed a continuity in the post-Carolingian period, becoming a topos, as documented by L.L. HUNEYCUTT, "Intercession and the high-medieval queen: The Esther topos", in: *Power of the Weak: Studies on Medieval Women*, ed. J. CARPENTER and S.-B. MACLEAN (Urbana, IL, 1995), pp. 126-146. Discussion of Esther in later periods is found in B. FRANKE, *Assuerus und Esther am Burgunderhof: Zur Rezeption des Buches Esther in den*

In tenth- to thirteenth-century poetry, Judith returns as an example in the *Scolasticus* by Walther of Speyer (*c.* 963-1027), who dedicated verses to her that sung of military undertakings but placed them in a passage devoted to controlling one's instincts, thus indirectly praising her for her chastity.[39] Similarly, the twelfth-century *Vita Eduardi* dedicates some verses to the wedding of Edward the Confessor and his queen Edith, celebrating the king's piety, writing that he had entrusted himself to God, who inspired the victories of Joseph, Judith, and Susannah in chastity, resuming the exemplary sequence that we have seen at work in the poets of late Antiquity. But the relationship to the model becomes more pertinent in the *Vita Mathildis* by Donizo of Canossa as a model of virile opposition to the kings (2, 798-799). After the eleventh century, the exemplum emerges again, primarily in specifically biblical poems such as the *De ordine mundi* attributed to Hildebert of Lavardin (1056-1133), who broadly elaborated on Judith, or the excerpt already mentioned in the *Liber decem capitulorum* by Marbod of Rennes (1035-1123). The citations remain rather numerous (Bernard of Morlaix, Walter of Châtillon, John of Garland, and others), proving the popularity of the figure, who would later dominate Renaissance and Baroque iconography. Perhaps more varied is her success in exegesis, which saw the emergence of interpretations only hinted at in the early Middle Ages: the devotion to Mary sustained by Cistercian culture, for example, led Helinand of Froidmont (ca. 1160-1230) to consider Judith a type of the Virgin rather than the Church, while John of Salisbury (1120-1180) in his *Policraticus* makes her an example of "*pia simulatio*" – that which the early medieval poets had defined "*castae mendacia Iudith*" – within a debate on ethical / political methodology.[40] The etymological interpretations of the

---

Niederlanden (1450-1530) (Berlin, 1998), while reinterpretations of her in late medieval mysticism have been gathered in L. GNÄDINGER, "Esther: Eine Skizze," *Zeitschrift für deutsche Philologie* 113 (1994), pp. 31-62.

[39] Walther of Speyer, *Scolasticus*, 4, 87-88: "*Anne oblita tibi pudibundae foedera Judith / non hoc pacta modo? quae postquam legis in umbra / marcida sopiti transfixit colla tyranni, / cartallum festina suum ceruice recisa / te pereunte domum victrix reditura grauauit / incolumisque suam duce me repedauit in urbem*" ("Did you forget that the pacts of the modest Judith were not entered into in this way? After, in the shadow of the Jewish law, she pierced the rotten neck of the tamed tyrant and cut off his head, she victoriously hastened to load his basket, while you died, and under my guidance he returned unharmed to the city").

[40] On Judith as a type of the Virgin, see A.T. THAYER, "Judith and Mary: Hélinand's sermon for the Assumption", in: *Medieval Sermon and Society: Cloister, City, University: Proceedings of International Symposia at Kalamazoo and New York*, ed. J. HAMESSE *et al.* (Louvain-la-Neuve, 1998), pp. 63-75. Judith has been discussed as an example of *pia simulatio* by M.L. COLISH, "Rethinking lying in the twelfth century," in: *Virtue and Ethics in the Twelfth Century*, ed. I.P.

figures' names, however, do not seem to have had cultural impact: based on Jerome, they repropose Hrabanus Maurus's *De natura rerum*, in which Judith is associated with "praise or confessing" ("*laudans vel confitens*") and with Esther "hiding" ("*absconsa*"; 3, 1).

Other Biblical Heroines

The example of Judith – and, in part, Esther and other Old Testament heroines – has provided us with a guide for exploring the presence of biblical women in Latin and other poetry of the early Middle Ages, including moral interpretations and political adaptations, but above all in the contextualisations that, the various poetic frameworks required, each time produced a new variation on the meaning attributed to the figure. These instances should be compared with the hundreds of mentions in exegesis, letters, chronicles, and hagiography in order to obtain a reliable picture of the cultural meaning and social impact of characters who are so forcefully projected into mythology. But even limiting our study to poetic literature, what emerges vividly are both the constants of a moral and ideological exemplariness and the wealth of human nuances and adaptations for the intended readers; the poets skillfully bring these out in different frameworks and contexts, starting with the biblical tale, along with its less visible details, some even reconstructed by narrating their verisimilitude.

And Judith is clearly not the only case, though perhaps she is the one that offers the greatest continuity and variety of reuses. A more extensive but never exhaustive analysis would require us to retrace the poetic rewritings of episodes regarding Sarah's late fertility, celebrated in the so-called biblical epic by Marius Victor and Cyprianus Gallus, before the revivals of the tenth century brought back the late Carolingian era and Matthew of Vendôme (late twelfth century) made her one of the characters in his *Tobias*. The prophetess Anna, mother of Samuel, makes a shy appearance in some poems by Walahfrid Strabo and Milo of Saint-Amand, but she would only later take on an important role, in the paraphrases of the book of Kings that proliferated in the twelfth century (especially the *In libros Regum* by Hildebert of Lavardin) and in other biblical poetry of the same period and of the following century (such as, again, *Tobias* and the *Epithalamium Virginis*). Naomi is cited just three times before the

BEJCZY and R.G. NEWHAUSER (Leiden, 2005), pp. 155-173.

twelfth century. Rachel (and her counterpart Leah) was widely celebrated by the poet Cyprianus in his *Genesis* and in the best Carolingian hymns and sequences (before Abelard), and she was also present in much poetry of the twelfth century, well beyond the religious sphere. Rebecca, mother of Isaac, is perhaps the first biblical woman of the Old Testament documented in Latin poetry (in Commodian, Hilarius, Ambrose, and Paulinus of Nola, then in Cyprianus the poet and Arator). Deborah only just surfaced in the Carolingian age and under Matilda.

Limits of space prevent such an investigation, but it could produce important information on the representation of biblical women in an early Middle Ages in which the written documentation, especially if sung in liturgy or rhythmic poetry, often had a much greater actual circulation than the iconography that influences us so deeply today. Our impression, which we hope may serve as a suggestion for a monograph, is that these instances are structured around a few but very specific theoretical and political core ideas: trust in God, even beyond the limits of nature and one's strength; ability to exceed males despite their uncertainty and fearfulness; warrior-like and regal exemplariness; chastity for the purposes of achieving success as well as fertility despite all expectations – in other words, exceptional qualities serving as the distinctive mark of short narrative or lyrical cycles that were soon firmly established around select exegetical / ideological motifs. Beauty is limited to being an instrument for achievement, as with Esther or Judith, or an element that can only be interpreted on an allegorical level, as with Rachel. The bride of the Song of Solomon is entirely absent in early medieval Latin poetry, and poems dedicated solely to Susanna and Jezebel only appear in the twelfth century. The picture clearly needs to be completed, including an investigation of femininity in the New Testament, which brings qualities of gentleness, tenderness, even sensuality, and emotional and spiritual union with a person or a message, all of which are extraneous or marginal to the Old Testament and, in part, to the early Middle Ages. The early centuries evidently favour sharp hues and simple contrasts and extol women's abilities in sexual self-control, combativeness, and the empowerment of communities. These abilities are better suited to the needs and therefore the values of the intellectual class, with its ecclesiastical background and its political points of reference. But every text of any depth manages to soften the unyielding, monumental quality of these models, shedding a different light on them and thus providing us with some glimmer of alternative and complementary interpretations awaiting our attention.

Chapter 3

Ad Supplementum Sensus: Hermeneutic Plurality and Increase in Meaning in Biblical Poetics from the Middle Ages to Derrida

The End of Exclusion

The tradition of biblical poetry, from Juvencus to Tasso, to Milton, Blake, Klopstock, and Péguy, is undoubtedly one of the main pillars of European literature, a more or less karstic river that runs throughout its lifetime. However, the reductionisms encountered in Catholic apologetics and antireligious humanism – prejudices that Italian society institutionalised in a juxtaposition of repercussions, even political ones, that is now finally understood as meaningless – have contributed to the suppression of such poetry to the point of disavowing its continuity and legitimacy as a literary phenomenon. The most savage chapters of this lengthy discrimination, widely discussed in recent volumes,[1] bear famous names such as Tasso,[2] Marvell,[3] Kierkegaard,[4] Lewis,[5] Auden,[6] and Curtius.[7]

---

[1] S. PRICKETT, *Words and 'The Word': Language, Poetics and Biblical Interpretation* (Cambridge, 1986), studies both the history of discrimination and the thread of critical resistance that brings us from John Dennis, Robert Lowth, and Coleridge to Vico, Herder, von Humboldt, Matthew Arnold, and Newman. On medieval studies see the introductory pages by R. HERZOG, *Bibelepik: Geschichte einer erbaulichen Gattung* (Munich, 1975).

[2] In the first of his *Discourses on the Art of Poetry*, Torquato Tasso argues for the poetic inalterability of biblical narration, while having himself attempted an experiment in conjunction with "*Il mondo creato*": "the epic poet will not dare reach his hand toward histories of the first kind [i.e. religious histories]; rather, he will leave them, in their pure and simple truth, for the pious, because invention here is not permitted" (in L.F. RHU, *The Genesis of Tasso's Narrative Theory: English Translations of the Early Poetics and a Comparative Study of Their Significance*

After this long-term suppression, it was only beginning in the seventies – as Roland Barthes[8] was developing his structuralist analyses of biblical passages and Paul Ricoeur[9] was formulating hermeneutic theories on the affinity between poetic and religious language – that a first reconsideration of the literary weight of the Bible was also launched in late antique and medieval studies, in the spheres of Latin, Germanic philology, and the novel. The points of greatest awareness within this revival are perhaps found in Max Wehrli's essay "*Sacra poesis*", in the brilliant and complex contributions by the late Reinhart Herzog, in Michael Roberts's rhetorical reconstruction, and in the clear examinations by Dieter Kartschoke and Klaus Thraede (with his students Flieger and Fichtner).[10] In Italy there was above all a growth in interest, following Curtius,

---

(Detroit, 1993), pp. 99-153, at p. 105).

[3] Andrew Marvell, in a poem on *Paradise Lost*, expresses fear "That he would ruin (for I saw him strong) / The sacred truth to fable and old song". According to Harold Bloom, who was inspired by these lines to create the title of his *Ruin the Sacred Truths* (H. BLOOM, *Ruin the Sacred Truths: Poetry and Belief from the Bible to the Present* (Cambridge, MA, etc., 1989)), this is the task of any accomplished poet.

[4] "... only pastoral ignorance can hit upon the idea of praising [Saint Paul] aesthetically".

[5] In his essay "Is theology poetry?", C.S. Lewis, while sharing an involved sensibility for theological culture, attacks from a Christian viewpoint the critics disposed to invoke poetics as an instrument of biblical exegesis.

[6] "To a Christian, unfortunately, both art and science are secular activities and therefore small beer": this view is quoted in PRICKETT, *Words and the Word*, as are the two before.

[7] This assertion from E.R. CURTIUS, *Europäische Literatur und lateinisches Mittelalter* (Berne, 1948), trans. *European Literature and the Latin Middle Ages* (London, 1953), p. 462, is well known: "Throughout its existence – from Juvencus to Klopstock – the Biblical epic was a hybrid with an inner lack of truth, a genre faux. The Christian story of salvation, as the Bible presents it, admits no transformation into pseudo-antique form. Not only does it thereby lose its powerful, unique, authoritative expression, but it is falsified by the genre borrowed from antique Classicism and by the concomitant linguistic and metrical conventions. That the Biblical epic could nevertheless enjoy such great popularity is explained only by the need for an ecclesiastical literature which could be matched with and opposed to antique literature. So a compromise solution was reached".

[8] R. BARTHES, "La lutte avec l'ange: Analyse textuelle de Genèse 32. 23-33", in: ID., *Analyse structurale et exégèse biblique: Essais d'interprétation* (Neuchâtel, 1971), pp. 27-39.

[9] P. RICOEUR, *Biblical Hermeneutics* (Missoula, 1975).

[10] M. WEHRLI, "Sacra Poesis: Bibelepik als europäische Tradition", in: ID., *Formen mittelalterlicher Erzählung* (Zurich and Freiburg im Breisgau, 1969), pp. 51-71; HERZOG, *Bibelepik*; D. KARTSCHOKE, *Bibeldichtung: Studien zur Geschichte der epischen Bibelparaphrase von Juvencus bis Otfrid von Weissenburg* (Munich, 1975); M. ROBERTS, *Biblical Epic and Rhetorical Paraphrase in Late Antiquity* (Liverpool, 1985); K. THRAEDE, "Untersuchungen zum Ursprung und zur Geschichte der christlichen Poesie", *Jahrbuch für Antike und Christentum* 4 (1961), pp. 108-127, and second part, *ibid.* 5 (1962), pp. 125-157; M. FLIEGER, *Interpretationen zum*

in the matter of the relationship between poetry and theology, in particular in the late medieval and pre-humanistic period, as an opportunity for the definitive recognition of the sacredness of poetry, even profane, which Peter von Moos called "the key development in the literary theory of the modern age".[11] Evidence of this in Italy are books such as those by Mésoniat and Ronconi[12] and the considerable literature that originated from the analysis of the debate between poetry and theology in Mussato, Petrarch, Dante, Boccaccio, and Salutati. But this special attention, as I understand it, maintained a particular focus on the humanistic outlet and the theologisation and sanctification of poetry *tout court*, which were perceived as inevitable in retrospect, instead of on a possible new assessment of poetry with theological or biblical content.[13] In a book from 1993,[14] I attempted to address, on a philological basis, the problem of Carolingian poetics as a hermeneutic poetics and to put forward proposals about the aesthetic consequences of this approach. However, despite this special focus, this book did not explicitly tackle the matter of the literary *status* of a genre, biblical poetry, which had enormous and elusive dimensions in the Middle Ages:[15] as we know, many works, even important ones, are still unpublished. Slowly but surely the very first editions are being published of authors ranging from Severus of Malaga in the sixth century to Andreas Sunesen by Ebbesen-Mortensen (1985-1988), Hildebert's *Carmina minora*, edited by Scott, Rigg, and Baker (*Medieval Studies* 1985), Munari's Matthew of Vendôme (1982), the anonymous *De creatione mundi* submitted in 1991 to *Medi-*

Bibeldichter Iuvencus (Stuttgart, 1993); R. FICHTNER, *Taufe und Versuchung Jesu in den Evangeliorum libri quatuor des Bibeldichter Juvencus* (Stuttgart and Leipzig, 1994). I put forward an overview of the genre in F. STELLA, *La trasmissione letteraria: la poesia*, in: *La Bibbia nel Medioevo*, ed. G. CREMASCOLI and C. LEONARDI (Bologna, 1996), pp. 40-63.

[11] P. VON MOOS, "La retorica del Medioevo", in: *Lo spazio letterario del Medioevo*, 1, *Il medioevo latino*, ed. G. CAVALLO, C. LEONARDI and E. MENESTÒ, 3 vols. (Rome, 1992-1994), 2, *La circolazione del testo*, pp. 231-272, at p. 251.

[12] C. MÉSONIAT, *Poetica Theologia: La «Lucula noctis» di Giovanni Dominici e le dispute letterarie tra '300 e '400* (Rome, 1984); G. RONCONI, *Le origini delle dispute umanistiche sulla poesia (Mussato e Petrarca)* (Rome, 1976).

[13] According to the hypothesis, also expressed by Mésoniat, that Christian art actually sets itself out as an organic extension of the Bible, in an echoing that may be unintentional of Novalis's words, "and could the Bible not continue still?".

[14] F. STELLA, *La poesia carolingia latina a tema biblico* (Spoleto, 1993).

[15] Nor does P.-A. DEPROOST, "L'épopée biblique en langue latine: Essai de définition d'un genre littéraire", *Latomus* 56.1 (1997), pp. 15-39, bring a conclusive contribution to the table.: it does not go beyond the definition of the *mutation* of the traditional epic, even recycling an empty category like the *mélange des genres*, long since dealt with by formalist criticism, which shows the inability of the term itself to grasp the specific nature of new genres.

eval Studies, and Laurence of Durham, being prepared by Susanne Daub, as well as many others on which we cannot linger here.[16]

More than ten years later, the Italian – and especially the international – cultural panorama was further transformed, offering the study of the Bible as a literary structure and an element of literary tradition a space to which it had not had access before then (what Lukács wrote in his monumental work on aesthetics springs to mind here: "right when the religious vision of the world breaks down, is drained away, art is tied to religious factors to a greater degree than has been the case for centuries"[17]). While the theological sphere was revisited by authoritative impulses to reaffirm the biblical aesthetic,[18] the success of the deconstructionist tendency in French, English, and Anglo-American literary criticism had immediate effects on the revaluation of the relationship between the Bible and poetry: Frank Kermode's impressive analyses[19] reactivated the study of the Bible as a literary structure also in Italy, according to an interpretative method that finds a famously like-minded precedent in the prologue of Peter Abelard's *Commentary on the Letter to the Romans*: "*omnis scriptura divina, more orationis rhetoricae, aut docere intendit aut movere*" ("every divine scripture, in the same way as a rhetorical speech, wants to teach or to move").[20] Because, as Von Moos wrote, to Abelard and his school, "of all the liberal arts only rhetoric prepares the horizon of understanding for the multiple linguistic approaches of the ineffable".[21] Exceptionally interesting

---

[16] Alexander of Ashby has been edited as Alexandri Essebiensis *Opera poetica*, ed. G. DINKOVA-BRUUN (Turnhout, 2004: CCCM 188A).

[17] G. LUKÁCS, *Estetica*, Italian trans. (Turin, 1970), p. 1561.

[18] After K. RAHNER, "Priest and poet", in: *The Word: Readings in Theology*, ed. R.A.F. MACKENZIE (New York, 1964), pp. 3-26 and U. VON BALTHASAR, *Gloria: Una estetica teologica* (Milan, 1975); H. KÜNG and W. JENSEN, *Dichtung und Religion: Pascal, Gryphius, Lessing, Hölderlin, Novalis, Kierkegaard, Dostojewski, Kafka* (Munich and Zurich, 1988²); F. BURCH BROWN, *Religious Aesthetics: A Theological Study of Making and Meaning* (Basingstoke and London, 1990); R. HARRIES, *Art and the Beauty of God* (London and New York, 1993).

[19] *The Literary Guide to the Bible*, ed. R. ALTER and F. KERMODE (Cambridge, MA, 1987); see also D. NORTON, *A History of the Bible as Literature*, 2 vols. (Cambridge, 1993), and the rich overview of L. RYKEN, "Literature and the Bible", in: *Oxford Companion to the Bible*, ed. B.M. METZGER and M.D. COOGAN (New York and Oxford, 1993), pp. 438-463. The awareness of this connection is developed by B.D. INGRAFFIA, *Postmodern Theory and Biblical Theology: Vanquishing God's Shadow* (Cambridge, 1995). Evidence of the renewal in interest is also found in *La Bible et la littérature: Actes du colloque internationale de Metz*, ed. P.-M. BEAUDE (Paris, 1987), which Anna Dolfi referred me to, and P. BOITANI, *Ri-scritture* Bologna, 1997).

[20] Prologue to the commentary of the *Epistola* to the Romans in: Petrus Abaelardus, *Opera theologica*, 1, ed. E.M. BUYTAERT (Turnhout 1969: CCCM 11), pp. 41-44.

[21] VON MOOS, "La retorica del Medioevo", p. 262.

essays such as Stephen Prickett's "Words and 'the Word': Language, poetics and biblical interpretation" (1986) and the miscellany *Reading the Text: Biblical Criticism and Literary Theory*, which he edited in 1991,[22] have documented the importance of the impetus that biblical science has given to literary theory and poetic practice. According to Prickett, "to discuss biblical hermeneutics in the light of poetic theory is not to apply an alien concept, but to restore a wholeness of approach that has been disastrously fragmented over the past hundred and fifty years",[23] in this way echoing Northrop Frye, who in *Words with Power* urged literary criticism to recognise its mythical-religious roots. Onto this landscape Prickett successfully grafts the concept of the analogy between poetic and religious language proposed by Ricoeur in *The Rule of Metaphor* and *Biblical Hermeneutics*. Along this path, the recovery of romantic poetics is revealed crucial; not by chance it is also the subject of the renewed attentions of the deconstructionist school of Yale, from Paul de Man to the recent work of Geoffrey Hartman.[24] Only partly justified caution and a certain avoidance of the historicism dominant in our country have almost suppressed the circulation of such studies in Italy not limited to literary fashion. It is no coincidence that one of the most important Italian contributions on the subject, Sergio Givone's article "Poesia e interpretazione della Bibbia" (1988) starts from a reflection on the proto-romantic *Biblische Betrachtungen*, in which Georg Hamann (1758) establishes the analogy between interpreting the Bible as an extension of the poetic act that produced it and writing poetry as a recognition of the presence in profane language of the divine word *sub contraria specie*.[25]

Leading back to this romantic premise[26] in a nihilistic key – which some have called, following Bloom, "American gnosticism"[27] – in different ways is

---

[22] *Reading the Text: Biblical Criticism and Literary Theory*, ed. S. PRICKETT (Oxford and Cambridge, MA, 1991).

[23] In his opinion, the entire debate over translation and literary criticism for topics such as the nature of the text and relationships with the reader, in its major trends, can be traced back to biblical-ecclesiastical matters that a slavish acceptance of Kantian aesthetics then clouded until recently.

[24] E.g. *Midrash and Literature*, ed. G. HARTMAN and S. BUDICK (New Haven, 1986).

[25] S. GIVONE, "Poesia e interpretazione della Bibbia", *Annali di Storia dell'Esegesi* 3 (1988), pp. 7-17, at p. 8.

[26] Keep in mind the development of romantic aesthetics on the work of art as a symbol, an allegorical expression of the infinite that is never adequate. For Schlegel, as we know, Romantic poetry is progressive because it "should forever be becoming and never perfected".

[27] I refer to the excellent essay by W. SITI, "An American gnosis: Appunti su critica e religione in margine all'opera di Harold Bloom", *Rivista di Letteratura Italiana* 3 (1985), pp.

the provocative *Ruin the Sacred Truths: Poetry and Belief from the Bible to the Present*, also by Bloom,[28] and the lesser known but perhaps more stimulating collection of Anglo-Hungarian studies *Literary Theory and Biblical Hermeneutics* (1992), edited by Tibor Fabiny,[29] which uses a rich variety of information to tackle the problem of the interaction between the reception of the Bible and the renewal of literary criticism. It makes particular reference to the concept of *réfiguration* in Ricoeur, but also to the extraordinary affinity that is found between the idea of a Scripture that expands on itself teleologically through progressive (in other words cataphoric, at least in the Christian interpretation of the two Testaments) narrative structure and the need, illustrated by Jacques Derrida in *Writing and Difference*, to interpret Western cultural tradition as a constant rewriting of signs that never find appropriate referents, in a "perennially incomplete state of sense that exists in the absence of all meaning". In the book, republished by Einaudi in 1990, the French philosopher begins from the premise that language precludes totalisation to uphold the image of Scripture as a field of infinite substitutions in the closure of a finite ensemble,[30] in a continuous game that is defined using the term 'supplementarity', taken ironically from the much admired and criticised Lévi-Strauss. 'Supplement' as the addition of sense to a signifier that lacks and will always lack a complete, comprehensive meaning.

147-170.

[28] BLOOM, *Ruin the Sacred Truths*; trans. *Rovinare le sacre verità: Poesia e fede dalla Bibbia a oggi* (Milan, 1992).

[29] *Literary Theory and Biblical Hermeneutics: Proceedings of the International Conference: 'Reading Scripture – Literary Criticism and Biblical Hermeneutics': Pannonhalma, Hungary, 4th-6th July 1991*, ed. T. FABINY (Szeged, 1992).

[30] J. DERRIDA, *L'écriture et la différence* (Paris, 1967); trans. (Turin, 1990^2); VON MOOS, "La retorica del Medioevo", p. 270, applies a similar concept to the biblical interpretation of Abelard: "what was once closed once and for all over time produces a growing richness of interpretation and thus serves as a lasting stimulus of labour of the spirit: *labor facit cariora*". Lukács had already observed that it is that same closure of the text that produces an 'intensively infinite totality' (LUKÁCS, *Estetica*, p.612).

Medieval Precursors

A scholar of medieval literature might be led, without any desire for undue updates, to compare these deconstructionist reflections with the methodological premises of the medieval exegetes, starting from the concept of the sacredness of writing as a word that encompasses its own subject in itself.[31] Beginning, as we must, with Augustine: but not so much with the *De doctrina christiana,* which as we know is the official manual of Christian semiology, as with the exegetical part of the *Confessions*. Set aside for the reader of contemporary hermeneutics in book 12 are phrases of extraordinary audacity (and normative phrases, as it is Augustine) on the 'opening' of the biblical text, on the "*diversitas sententiarum verarum*" with regard to Moses' interpretations of *Genesis*.

> 42. *Ita cum alius dixerit "Hoc sensit, quod ego", et alius: "Immo illud, quod ego", religiosius me arbitror dicere: cur non utrumque potius, si utrumque verum est, et si quid tertium est et si quid quartum et si quid omnino aliud verum quispiam in his verbis videt, cur non illa omnia vidisse credatur, per quem Deus unus sacras litteras vera et diversa visuris multorum sensibus temperavit? (...) Sensit ille omnino in his verbis atque cogitavit, cum ea scriberet, quidquid hic veri potuimus invenire et quidquid nos non potuimus aut nondum potuimus et tamen in eis inveniri potest. (43) (...) Si quid homo minus vidit, numquid et spiritum tuum bonum, quid deducet me in terram rectam, latere potuit, quidquid eras in eis verbis tu ipse revelaturus legentibus posteris, etiamsi ille, per quem dicta sunt, unam fortassis ex multis versi sententiam cogitavit?*
> (...) *Si hoc dixero, quod sensit minister tuus, recte atque optime: id enim conari me oportet; quod si assecutus non fuero, id tamen dicam, quod mihi per eius verba tua veritas dicere voluerit, quae illi quoque dicit quod voluit.*

Thus, when one man says, "Moses meant what I mean", and another, "No, he meant what I mean", I that I speak more faithfully when I say, "Why could he not have meant both if both opinions are true?" And if there should be still a third truth or a fourth one, and if anyone should seek a truth quite different in those words, why would it not be right to believe that Moses saw all these different truths, since through him the one God has tempered the Holy Scriptures to the understanding of many different people, who should see truths in it even if they are different? (...) Surely when he was writing these words, he saw fully and understood all the truth

---

[31] The equivalency between holy Scripture and human writing at least in (Ps.-?) Dante, *Epistola a Cangrande,* and *Convivio* (MÉSONIAT, *Poetica Theologia,* pp. 67-68).

we have been able to find in them, and also much besides that we have not been able to discern, or are not yet able to find out, though it is there in them still to be found. (43) (...) if any man sees anything less, can anything lie hid from 'thy good Spirit' who shall 'lead me into the land of uprightness', which thou thyself, through those words, wast revealing to future readers, even though he through whom they were spoken fixed on only one among the many interpretations that might have been found? (...) This is the faith of my confession, that if I could say what thy servant meant, that is truest and best, and for that I must strive. Yet if I do not succeed, may it be that I shall say at least what thy Truth wished to say to me through its words, just as it said what it wished to Moses. (trans. Outler[32])

With this approach, Augustine[33] authoritatively establishes the indefinite hermeneutic opening of Scripture, the exegetical creativity that the Scripture grants to any interpreter, beyond what we might think we can determine in a particular, and therefore transient, communicative situation.[34] As it is for Augustine so for Derrida, too, "the meaning of the meaning (...) is infinite implication, the indefinite referral of signifier to signifier (...) its force is a certain pure and infinite equivocality which gives signified meaning no respite, no rest, but engages it in its own *economy* so that it always signifies again and differs".[35] Both texts seem to presume that what Derrida calls the "identity in itself" of writing, an objective and absolute meaning, does not exist.

Reflections on this doctrine are obviously found across the Middle Ages, and in the Carolingian era a particularly significant text appeared: Hrabanus Maurus's *De clericorum institutione*. In the third book, chapter 7, *De modo*

---

[32] <https://www.ourladyswarriors.org/saints/augcon12.htm>.

[33] B. DE MARGERIE, *Introduction à l'histoire de l'exégèse*, 3, *Saint Augustin* (Paris, 1983), chapter 2, esp. pp. 61 ff., briefly addresses this matter, while trying to limit the scope of Augustine's "*étonnante affirmation*" – which, according to Pierre Benoit, was even in 1947 not yet accepted "*par le sentiment commun de la tradition chrétienne*" – by invoking the De doctrina christiana 3, 27 and 38: "*ce qu'Augustin refuse Hrabanus (...) c'est un sens littéral unique au point d'être exclusif de tout autre compatible avec lui*" (p. 69). For this exegetic approach, De Margerie coins the definition 'unipluralism', accepting a plurality of *secondary* meanings.

[34] With respect to poetry, the connection is later found in Coluccio Salutati, in a passage of the *De laboribus Herculis* (B.L. ULLMAN, *The Humanism of Coluccio Salutati* (Padua, 1963), p. 46) that is much more quoted that the Augustinian one: "*Quis audeat affirmare quod, quisquis ille fuerit qui semel aliquid ipsorum exponens attigerit, reliquos quibus illud idem relictum sit a iure atque facultate expositionis excludat?*" ("Who would dare to say that whoever is the one who once achieved the goal in his explanation, this excludes others to whom the same question is proposed by the right to explain it?").

[35] DERRIDA, *L'écriture et la différence*; trans. *Writing and Difference*, trans. A. BASS (Chicago, 1978), p. 362.

legendi Sacras scripturas, ff. he addresses biblical hermeneutics, and in chapter 15 he explains "*Quod non sit periculum varius intellectus in eisdem Scripturae verbis, si sensus ipse congruat veritati*" ("That the variety of interpretation of the same words of Scripture is not a risk, if the meaning corresponds to the truth"). Obviously Hrabanus, a systematic soul, nonetheless tries to introduce a criterion for exegetical reliability, also implied in the passage from the *Confessiones* cited above: coherence with other parts of the biblical text, in other words, consistency with the system as a whole. Each meaning was laid down by the Spirit, and up to this point we are moving within a framework consistent with the traditional image of systemicity that we associate with the abbey of Fulda. But right after that, the most extreme case is also recognised:

> *Ubi autem talis sensus eruitur, cuius incertum certis sanctarum scripturarum testimoniis non possit aperiri, restat ut ratione reddita manifestius appareat, etiam si ille cuius verba intelligere quaerimus, eum forte non sensit.*

> Where then such a meaning emerges, that its uncertainty cannot be resolved with certain testimonies of the holy Scriptures, the fact remains that it manifests itself more clearly through reasoning, even if the one whose words we try to understand perhaps did not think it.[36]

It is therefore legitimate to infer the meaning, which has proven to be inaccessible through the usual internal comparisons, attempting to identify it with the use of an individual rationale, even if it was not a meaning intended by the compiler of the Scriptures. It therefore becomes legitimate to create new meanings, according to the supplementary procedure of which the desconstructionists speak. But Augustine, and Hrabanus after him, does not contradict himself, adding: "*Sed haec consuetudo periculosa est*".[37]

This is in any case the path that, once we move beyond the dogmatic trepidation of the Carolingians, would lead to Abelard's *Sic et non*. Although it was applied mainly to the language of the Holy Fathers, when it addresses the problem of biblical polysemy manages to stipulate, once again quoting Augustine,

---

[36] Hrabanus Maurus, *De clericorum institutione*, ed. in: PL 107, 392A, from Augustine, *De doctrina christiana*, ed. in: PL 34, col. 80.

[37] The oscillation between hermeneutic openness and references to dogma is studied by P.C. BORI, *L'interpretazione infinita: L'ermeneutica cristiana antica e le sue trasformazioni* (Bologna, 1987).

Contra Faustum 11, 5: "the reader or listener is free in this case to sanction what pleases him or attack what troubles him".[38]

Along the way, we find William of Saint-Thierry, who writes in the *Expositio in Epistolam ad Romanos*:[39]

> *ut omnia quae intersunt quasi ad supplementum sensus interposita sint; sed, dum vitant obscuritatem perplexitatis interpositarum rationum, maiorem sensus incurrunt involutionem.*

> *as everything in between [in the text of the letter] is interposed so as to integrate meaning; but while they avoid the obscurity of the intertwining of interposed arguments, they incur a greater involution of meaning.*

Derrida's further meaning is anticipated by this author almost word for word, and in Latin the meaning of *supplementum* (with the original sense of *supplere* as 'to make full again by filling the gaps') is more fully grasped as 'completion', 'achievement', which surfaces in an expression often repeated by the medieval exegetes of Saint Paul. This frequent phrase, "*evangelia supplementum legis*", admirably summarises – if we keep in mind the hermeneutic sense of *supplementum* – the biblical, or bi-testamentary, root of hermeneutic medieval culture.

Tibor Fabiny seems to be thinking along the same lines when he reintroduces the fruitfulness of the concept of *sensus plenior*, a term that he attributes to an invention by Fernandez in 1925 – later theorised by Raymond Brown with reference to Antiochian exegesis. This progressive fullness finds a critical-literary expression in Frye:

> This "something new" is not necessarily something we have overlooked before, but may come rather from a new context in our experience. The implication is that when we start to read, some kind of dialectical process begins to unfold, so that any given understanding of what we read is one of a series of phases or stages of comprehension.[40]

Frye clearly distinguishes himself from Derrida by tracing plurality back to the context of a continuity. But in this case, too, it is possible to find patristic and

---

[38] Cf. A. MINNIS, *Medieval Theory of Authorship* (London, 1984; 1988²), p. 97.
[39] William of Saint-Thierry, *Expositio in Epistolam ad Romanos*, ed. in: PL 180, col. 592.
[40] N. FRYE, *The Great Code: The Bible and Literature* (New York, 1982), p. 220.

Ad Supplementum Sensus

medieval antecedents, terminologically speaking. Augustine already speaks of *sensus plenior* in his *Enarrationes in Psalmos* 25,[41] although I find chapter 16 of Philip of Harvengt's *Commentaria in Cantica Canticorum*[42] even more noteworthy. On the subject of the biblical expression "*aliquantulum imperfecta*" he notes:

> *nec in ea* sensus plenior *invenitur, si non ad inveniendum foris aliquid subauditur? Quid autem verius, quid certius velit ipsa quae loquitur subaudire, facile, ut arbitror, non potest ad liquidum inveniri, ab his praecipue quos constat mentis caligine praepediri, nec sibi Scripturarum occulta merentur aperiri, quia ego tenuis intellectu, meritis non abundo,* supplementum *verbi huius ipse mihi et non alius sic abscondo, ut et loquentem non arguam et eius verbum sensu devio non infirmem, dum si quis illic dixero, magis coniiciam quam affirmem.*

and there is no fuller meaning in it unless something is added to find it out. In fact, what she who speaks would like to express truer and more certain cannot be easily found clearly, especially by those who are known to be obstructed by the fog of the mind, and the mysteries of the Scriptures do not deserve to be revealed because I, of slender intellect, do not abound with merits, and the integration of this word I hide from myself and not from another, so as not to accuse the speaker and not weaken his word with an improper meaning, while, if I say something, it will be more a conjecture than a statement.

The comparisons put forward, and so far not discussed, except for the usual Abelard, in the few works on medieval Latin literary criticism (I am thinking especially of those by Minnis), seem to show a certain similarity of approach in thinkers so ostensibly remote, in the conviction that "grace can only be that which is missing",[43] and therefore writing, whether religious or not, is only a simulacrum, a substitute for an entity that is always deferrable, always renewable in the reworking of the interpreter, who becomes at once the secondary producer, recreator, and continuer. There is therefore no objective meaning, only the individual enucleation of a truth that is always within the interpreter, and therefore limited to him. Obviously, the difference lies between the Augustinian faith in an ultimate guarantee of all the truths of all the interpreters – emulated by Frye's faith in a continuous meaning – and the disenchanted

---

[41] Augustine, *Enarrationes in Psalmos*, ed. in: PL 37, col. 1571D.
[42] Premonstratensian abbot who lived between 1100 and 1183, a correspondent of Saint Bernard.
[43] DERRIDA, *L'écriture et la différence*; trans. *Writing and Difference*, p. 15.

Derridian belief in the absence of any guarantee, but at a certain level this difference does not affect the hermeneutic system. Then Prickett is not only right when he writes that "the deconstructive modes of analysis associated with Derrida are more closely rooted in the twentieth-century philosophical problems of theology and the Bible than many of his followers seem to realize",[44] but perhaps those same problems have even older roots than Prickett himself thinks.

Ineffability and Allegory

A poetic instrument of this infinite signification is what the other great deconstructionist Paul de Man, in *Blindness and Insight* and in *Allegories of Reading*, called 'allegory', in the now-established sense that it has overlap with 'symbol', in other words a 'surplus of meaning' of the text with respect to what is said, a distance of the sign from its own origin. Within the gap of this difference, allegory, rejecting any nostalgia or desire to coincide, establishes its own language. The desire for correspondence, or confusion between linguistic and natural reality, between referential and phenomenal elements, is what the deconstructionsts call ideology.[45] The neoplatonic assumption of the unattainability of divine truths (nihilistically taken to the extreme in the assumption of their nonexistence, though equivalent in terms of articulation) brings together, conceptually and irrefutably, this neo-romanticism of disillusion and the hermeneutic culture of the neoplatonic medieval period. This is the final outcome of a very rich thread, which begins as we have seen with Augustine's Platonism and continues in the apophatic theology of Dionysius the pseudo-Areopagite and John Scotus Eriugena to resurface successful with the school of Chartres: as for Eriugena "*nihil digne de Deo dicitur*" ("nothing worthy can be said of God") and "*signa proprie de Deo dici non posse*" ("signs cannot be expressed about God in a proper sense"), and therefore one must inevitably "*praedicare de Deo translative*" ("speak about God in metaphorical language") by images (*De praedestinatione* IX), also for the *Regulae Theologicae* of the

[44] PRICKETT, *Reading the Text*, p. 9.
[45] De Man writes, following from the just quoted Derrida, that the interpretation of a sign is not a meaning but another sign (P. DE MAN, *Allegories of Reading: Figural Language in Rousseau, Nietzsche, Rilke and Proust* (New Haven, 1979); trans. *Allegorie della critica. Strategie della decostruzione nella critica americana*, ed. M. AJAZZI MANCINI and F. BAGATTI, (Naples, 1987), p. 9).

Chartrain Alain de Lille (chapter 10) "*omnis praedicatio de Creatore facta, copulata est atque coniuncta*" ("every statement about God implicitly contains much more than what it explicitly declares"), and in the summa *Quoniam homines,* published only in a periodical by Glorieux in 1953,[46] "*transnominatio locum habet in divinis, sed non denominatio*" ("in the discourse on divinity there is no room for denomination, but only for the figurative"). We cannot speak of God if not through metaphor, and each time that we speak of God, we must allude to a double meaning, we use a simultaneity of plural meanings. This typology of production of meaning, explored in a logical-dialectical key in Gillian Evans's brilliant book *The Language and Logic of the Bible*,[47] would produce veritable treatises on the simile in biblical language, such as the second homily on psalm 132 from another Chartrain-Bernardian abbot, Arnold of Bonneval (twelfth century). Here the "*similitudo, maxime theologiae familiaris*" is analysed in terms of its forms and functions, among which that of 'necessity' is used to express meanings that are located "*supra rationem*". In this sense, Arnold even speaks of a "*sacramentum similitudinis*" ("a sacred mystery of simile").[48] We are now deep into that identification of metaphor as language – or rather, metalanguage (Von Moos) – common to theology and poetry, and in particular to the Bible and poetry, which eventually culminates in Ricoeur's *Biblical Hermeneutics,* where the philosopher – analysing the evangelical parables almost as suggested by an anonymous *declaratio* in response to one of Mussato's letters[49] – identifies in the metaphor the strategy of the discourse, which, thanks to its semantic impertinence, opens up a new relation of meaning: a function of poetic language, and of its use in the religious language that is its counterpart, is the weakening of the first-degree reference of ordinary language to make possible the second-degree reference through which the metaphor redescribes the world, insinuating the moment of the 'even more' that constitutes the ownership of religious discourse and, ethically and

---

[46] Alain de Lille, *Quoniam homines*, ed. P. GLORIEUX, "La somme 'Quoniam homines' d'Alain de Lille", *Archives d'Histoire Doctrinale et Littéraire du Moyen Âge* 20 (1953), pp. 113-369.

[47] G. EVANS, *The Language and Logic of the Bible: The Earlier Middle Ages* (Cambridge, 1984).

[48] Arnold of Bonneval, *Commentarius in Psalmum CXXXII*, ed. in: PL 189, col. 1573C.

[49] Reader of Albertino Mussato (maybe Castellano of Bassano and Guizzardo of Bologna): "*Poetica scientia theorica est, cum quis super veritatem aliquam fabulam fingit, sicut faciebat Dominus noster Iesus Christus in parabolis*" ("Poetics is a theoretical science, when someone creates a story about a truth, as did our Lord Jesus Christ in the parables"), ed. in: *Il pensiero pedagogico dell'umanesimo*, ed. E. GARIN (Florence, 1958), p. 14.

politically speaking, of prophetic impetus. As we know, for centuries this was the main argument for the analogy between poetry and holy Scripture, which has always been contrasted with the stricter but more naive Thomistic distinction between allegory of literal meaning, or *allegoria in verbis*, and allegory of content, or *allegoria in factis*.[50] It now risks becoming, especially in Harold Bloom's fascinating provocations, an argument for a reduction of religion to literature, or, if we prefer, an elevation of literature to religion that radicalises the sanctification of poetry and of the poet already dominant from Blake on in European romanticism. In the twelfth century the subject became a variation of the topos of the ineffability of God, which had had its first poetic attestation already in Dracontius, at the end of the fifth century. One extremely knowing literary attestation is the biblical poem *Tobias*, by Matthew of Vendôme, who in the doxological epilogue addresses God with an *affectatio modestiae* in terms of exegetical theory: "*Te laus nulla canit quia significatio vocum / deficit auctorem significare suum; / de virtute tua vocum penuria cogit / nos quasi vagitu deficiente loqui*" ("No praise sings you because the semantics of words cannot mean their creator; the scarcity of terms on your power compels us to speak almost with a cry that disappears").[51]

The transition from biblical poetics to biblical poetry was not at all immediate, as we might think. Even Von Moos, in his contribution to the third volume of the *Spazio letterario del Medioevo latino*, admits that since Abelard's apology of the Bible's literary aesthetics no direct path has led to literary production: Abelard defends the Bible's poetic force but at the same time repeats Platonic anathemas against lying poets.[52] The only function of an 'allegorical' poem is the intellectual stimulation to *inquisitio veritatis*, which is the same function (but not the same cause) that John Scotus Eriugena assigned to the metaphorical fabric of theology. Perhaps it is also because of this that much medieval autoreception of biblical poetry tends to introduce even the more narrative paraphrases, such as those of Juvencus and Sedulius, as allegorical

---

[50] Thomas Aquinas, *Summa Theologiae*, Ia I, 10: "these senses are not multiplied because one word signifies several things; but because the things signified by the words can be themselves types of other things"(<https://archive.org/stream/summatheologicao011thom/summatheologicao011thom_djvu.txt>).

[51] It is interesting to observe how in Dracontius ineffability is theorised in terms of panegyrist Cassiodorian rhetoric (see F. STELLA, "Tra retorica e innografia", *Philologus* 132 (1989), pp. 258-274), while in Matthew it takes on the appropriate guise of medieval Apophatic poetics.

[52] Peter Abelard, *Theologia Christiana*, book 2, Conclusion.

works: thus Giovanni Dominici, who also recommended reading them, in *Lucula noctis* speaks of late antique biblical paraphrases such as "*carmina sub tegumento sacram exprimentia veritatem*" ("poems that express sacred truth under cover").[53]

The Legitimacy of a Heteronomous Aesthetic

The problem is whether it is or was viable to incorporate a language, the Bible's, with which poetic function already goes hand in hand – open as such to unlimited rewriting – into a language, like that of the Western epic from Homer to Péguy, whose poetic force is concentrated on narrative elements on the one hand, and rhythmic-musical ones on the other. It was a necessary step the first time, in late Antiquity, in order to allow the intercultural translation of biblical – that is, Semitic-Hellenistic – content to the language of classical poetry. And it was felt necessary a second time at the time of the chronological convergence of literary classicism and Gregorian reform between the eleventh and twelfth centuries, and a third time after the success of the humanistic revival, to attempt a homologous but this time no longer intercultural operation, in a classicised style, or the "metrical rhetoricisation" (Herzog) of the spiritual proclamation: what Herzog cursorily called "the kitsch outcome of poeticisation as act of faith".[54] This was the misstep of the genre stigmatised by Curtius: to have attempted a disguise and not a translation. But I believe that it was incorrect of Curtius to have projected the failure of the classicist operation back to the late antique transition. And in this sense the similar judgments of Auerbach ("*das frühe christliche Mittelater hatte weder eine Tragödie noch ein großes Epos*"), Golega ("hybrid"), Süß ("attack on the spirit of the story"), Heinze ("an omnipotent god is wholly unusable as a character in an epic poem"),[55] which repeat the age-old condemnation of the contradictory Torquato Tasso,[56] passively comply with a critical cliché that tends to confuse a relative model – the classical-humanistic one – with an aesthetic criterion.[57]

---

[53] Giovanni Dominici, *Lucula noctis*, 10, 89-102, ed. E. HUNT (Notre Dame, 1960).
[54] HERZOG, *Die Bibelepik*, p. LIX.
[55] These passages are found in HERZOG, *Die Bibelepik*, p. xlv; translations mine.
[56] Quoted *supra*, note 2.
[57] There still remains the problem of an explanation for the success of this literary genre. It is superfluous to remember that – although the immense and largely unexplored manuscript fortune of Juvencus, Sedulius, and Proba, and then of the still unpublished compendium of

The main question, once the humanistic and positivistic cages have been dispelled, is a historical-critical one. It is the one asked lucidly by Herzog in 1975: do forms of an aesthetical heteronomous experience (which thus finds its criterion not in itself but in external values, be they ethical, or religious, or otherwise) exist? Following the references to Germanic and Roman production in Brinkmann and Wehrli, although without theoretical knowledge, medieval Latin explorations on the Carolingian era have also highlighted some interesting findings in this regard: biblical reenactment as an anonymous tale – that is, a story without a protagonist – in the paraphrases of Florus of Lyon; the lyricisation of exegesis in Wandalbert of Prüm's Pherecratean verses; the metrification of the typological correspondence in Hrabanus's epanaleptic distich, in imitation of Sedulius's *Collatio*; the meta-symbolisation of Sigfried of Corbie, who outlines the *Song of Songs* by oscillating between the images of the letter and those of its allegorical explanation, both treated as expressive code; the refined semiological metaphors of Hrabanus Marus, Ingobert, and Paulus Alvarus; the bucolic *mise en abyme* of Audrad of Sens, in whose *Fons vitae* the biblical search for personal salvation alludes to one's own search for intiatic happiness; and finally the progressive metamorphisms of symbolic images in the London Evangeliary (Hrabanus again!)[58] create elements of an entirely new formal catalogue that is deeply rooted in biblical exegesis and which the new critical assumptions of our time allow us to rediscover with increased awareness.[59]

Alexander of Villedieu and Petrus Riga *Aurora* and their French and Germanic parallels, is easily (but not exclusively) brought back to the need of epic texts with Christian content for scholastic instruction – cases such as Sannazaro's *De partu virginis*, Du Bartas's *Sepmaine* and Marino's *The Slaughter of the Innocents*, Million's *Paradise Lost*, Blake's *Songs of Experience*, *Books of Thel*, and *Marriage of Heaven and Hell*, Vittorio Alfieri's *Saul*, Péguy's *Eva*, and many works, particularly in English and Anglo-American literature, considered to be artistically successful attempts of poetic rewriting of the Bible, are often recognised as true masterpieces of their respective literatures.

[58] For information on these texts and a related bibliography see Stella, *La poesia carolingia latina a tema biblico*.

[59] It was in these very years that in the USA there was a wish to reconstruct a Christian neo-aesthetics based on the anti-aesthetics of Paul de Man that rejected the idea of aesthetic experience as an unfinished phenomenon (Kant, *Critique of Judgment* (1790), section XVI), proposing a para-aesthetic – as they called it – that was concerned with the reciprocal contamination of aesthetics and non-aesthetics. On that basis it could become easier to carry out an unbiased evaluation of heteronomous aesthetics, from the all-encompassing aesthetics of Christianity, Islam, and communism to specific aesthetics such as futurism.

Ad Supplementum Sensus   69

I believe that Auerbach's intuition about the exegesis that became a "general method of comprehending reality" in Christian culture,[60] an intuition also investigated separately by Claudio Leonardi,[61] finds a revolutionary kind of expression in medieval and also baroque poetry, by entrusting the exegetical relationship with a function analogous to that of the simile in classical poetry and to the symbol in modern poetry: the encounter between different levels of reality or history, the exchange between different codices, the refiguration – in Ricoeur's words – of an unprecedented sense of the links between facts, times, and things, and between all this and past and present readers. It is not a humanistic and romantic equalisation between polysemic poetry and progressive revelation, but the conversion of semiotic or interpretative processes into poetic forms (semiological metaphors, exegetical hierarchies of images, metric parallelisms, narrative interruptions, figural metamorphoses).[62]

All the same, in addition to the unknowability of as yet unpublished texts, the idea of reassessment also poses many problems: in medieval biblical poetry, the output of new forms stimulated by the biblical hypotext in fact almost never manages to express awareness of this dependence.[63] When it does happen – for example in Matthew of Vendôme's *Tobias* – it is rather to deny literary status to a metrification of biblical content that is limited to declaring purely didactic, utilitarian goals:

vera loquens non pingo metrum, ne picta supellex / Carminis incurrat ambitionis onus. / vernans metaphoris, epythetis fabula, nugis / ebria, venatur credulitatis opem. / Vera negant pingi, quia vera relatio nescit, / nescit adulari floridiore sono.[64]

---

[60] E. AUERBACH, *Mimesis: Dargestellte Wirklichkeit in der abendländischen Literatur* (Bern, 1959); trans. *Mimesis: The Representation of Reality in Western Literature*, trans. W.R. TRASK (Princeton, NJ, 1953), p. 16.

[61] C. LEONARDI, "L'intellettuale nell'Altomedioevo", in: *Il comportamento intellettuale nella società antica* (Genoa, 1980), pp. 119-139.

[62] The seeds of a new poetry in which images are not only used to express another interpretation of reality but are created to poetically represent the mechanisms of interpretative processes: milk and solid food (the Paulines), *proelium* hermeneutics, the textual forest, the harvest field, the sea of various depths, body and shadow, the sound of waterfalls, wheels.

[63] Carolingian allusions are rare; one example is the passage in which Hrabanus speaks of polysemy and multiple representivity of biblical images such as *ars nova* (see *infra*).

[64] Matthew of Vendôme, *Tobias*, ll. 2161 ff., ed. in: *Mathei Vindocinensis Opera*, ed. F. MUNARI (Rome, 1977).

while expressing truth I do not paint verse, so that the painted embellishment of poetry does not take on the weight of ambiguity. The drunken story of epithets and futility, flourishing with metaphors, hunts for credibility. Truth does not admit to being colored, because the authentic story does not admit to be flattered by a richer sound.

The heteronomous influence on the aesthetic product is turned into a negation of its aesthetic specificity: the heteronomous aesthetic experience therefore produces new forms – the exploration of which is one of the goals of this conference – but does so reluctantly, denying itself. It is nonetheless true that it performs aesthetic functions: only it does so unintentionally. It thus ends up paradoxically confirming the omnipotence of the autonomous aesthetic, in terms of poetic theory, even over aesthetics that actually escape it. This is not as surprising as in Matthew of Vendôme, when Horatian poetics had already regained its centrality. But it is a problem that recurs in different forms and at different times: the *accessus* to Sedulius that introduce him[65] as an epic poet because he recounts the heroic feats of a king, the *summus rex*, end up legitimising the system of classical genres that biblical poetry had played a role in disintegrating; Hugo von Trimberg's definition of biblical poems as "theology in verse" justifies their confessional element but at the same time stresses their aesthetic distance. Even the organisation of many biblical epics from late Antiquity in proto-Carolingian codices, where the poems in verse are alternated with exegetic works or biblical books, attests to a reception limited to dependence on and contiguity with the Bible. Thus we observe an irremediable discrepancy between an implicit poetics, *in re* – a revolutionary poetics founded on the exegetic relationship – and an explicit one, founded on the recognised scholastic tradition, incapable of grasping the originality of biblical-poetic production – which not coincidentally Hrabanus calls *ars nova*[66] – in an appropriate aesthetic framework. That discrepancy has continued until today, and the insufficiency of both Curtius's position and Jauss's more advanced idea of a poetic history of the invisible prove this. Only today is hermeneutic renewal creating the conditions for the reconstruction of these identities.

---

[65] *Accessus ad auctores: Bernard d'Utrecht, Conrad d'Hirsau: Dialogus super auctores*, ed. R.B.C. HUYGENS (Leiden, 1970), p. 29.

[66] In *carmen* 3, 16, the foreword in verse to the commentary on the Books of Kings: the *mysticus ordo*, i.e. biblical narrative, *indicat*, here the achievements of the redeemer *arte nova*.

[Recently I returned to the subject in F. STELLA, "Condanna e difesa della poesia: Dalla Scolastica all'Umanesimo", in: *Figure del pensiero medievale*, 6, *La via moderna: XIV e inizi del XV secolo* (Milan, 2010), pp. 251-328, 350-357, after reading a significant though underestimated monograph by C.C. GREENFIELD, *Humanistic and Scholastic Poetics, 1250-1550* (London and Toronto, 1981), and in "Théologie de la poésie entre Scolastique et Humanisme: Le statut de la poésie biblique", in: *Poetry, Bible and Theology from Late Antiquity to the Middle Ages*, ed. M. CUTINO (Berlin etc., 2020), pp. 473-494.]

Chapter 4

A Repressed Beauty: Biblical Poetics and the Legitimisation of Poetry in Medieval Culture

The Exclusion of Poetry from the Medieval Cultural System

In the renowned miniature illustrating folio 32r of the lost manuscript of the *Hortus Deliciarum* (Fig. 1)[1] we see a corolla of niches inscribed within a circle, which illustrates the array of relations among the arts and disciplines of the medieval cultural system. At the centre of the circle reigns Wisdom, *Philosophia*, seated on a throne beneath which Socrates and Plato converse and write, while seven chapels radially arranged in a sunburst pattern frame the seven liberal arts. Outside of the circle, below it, dressed in flowing tunics, are the figures of four scribes, or writers, characterised by a malevolent inspirer: a black bird, the devil, who suggests in their ears the contents of their burning writings. The legend explains that they are the "*poetae, vel magi, spiriti immundo instincti*" ("poets, or magicians, inspired by filthy spirits"). And among the chairs is an inscription: "*Isti, immundis spiritibus inspirati, scribunt artem magicam et poetriam id est fabulosa commenta*" ("They, inspired by filthy spirits, write magic or poetic arts, that is, fabulous fictions"). The poets, or less probably the codifiers of the art of poetry (*poetica*), are therefore perpetrators of evil and are likened to magicians as the producers of an alien reality, a

---

[1] Masterpiece of Herrade of Landsberg, the twelfth-century abbess of Hohenbourg in Alsace. Editions of the nineteenth-century reproduction by O. GILLEN, *Herrad von Landsberg, Hortus Deliciarum* (Neustadt, 1979) and by R. GREEN, *Herrad of Hohenbourg, "Hortus deliciarum"*, 1, *Commentary*, 2, *Reconstruction* (Leiden, 1979); the images are commented on by G. CAMES, *Allégories et symboles dans l'Hortus deliciarum* (Leiden, 1971).

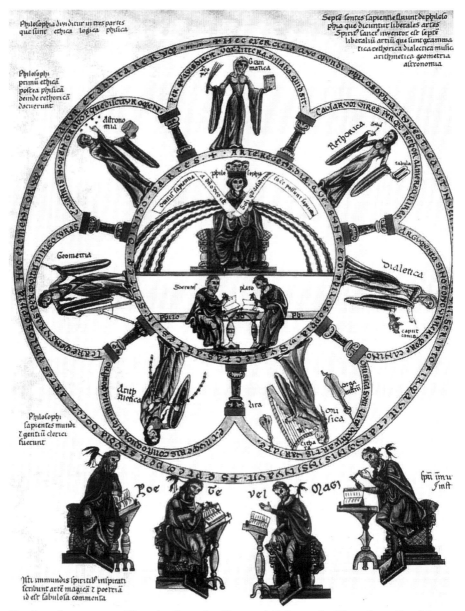

Fig. 1   *Septem artes liberales* from the *Hortus deliciarum* by Herrad von Landsberg (*c.* 1180), image in the public domain. cf. O. GILLEN, *Herrad von Landsberg, Hortus Deliciarum* (Neustadt, 1979).

fiction of the human mind; like magicians, they are excluded from the system of knowledge and relegated outside its borders.[2] In this iconic attitude, the criterion of inclusion and hence of value is the *level of reality* that art teaches us to describe or understand: a level that is clearly scarce in works of poetic invention, which, according to an old tradition, dating back at least to Plato, are distinguished from all other activities by their fabulous and mythical, or at any rate unrealistic, content. A century later, Thomas Aquinas would classify poetry as "*infima inter omnes doctrinas*",[3] on the basis of the low degree of truth that it is capable of transmitting: "*minumum continet veritatis*".[4] He follows the schemes of Albertus Magnus who writes "*Poeticus modus infirmior est inter modos philosophiae*".[5] The *Decretum Gratiani*, in the meantime, seems to forbid the clergy from cultivating poetry.[6]

As we know, the nature of the relationship radically changed beginning with the Paduan poet Albertinus Mussato (1261-1329), who took up the neo-Platonic ideas elaborated by John Scotus Eriugena and the School of Chartres[7] in order to legitimise an equivalence between poetry and theology (epistles 4,

---

[2] See L. GOMPE, "Figmenta poetarum", in: *Literatur und Sprache im europäischen Mittelalter: Festschrift für Karl Langosch* (Darmstadt, 1973), pp. 53-62; P. VERDIER, "L'iconographie des arts libéraux dans l'art du Moyen Âge jusqu'à la fin du quinzième siècle", in: *Arts libéraux et philosophie au Moyen Âge: Actes du quatrième congrès international de philosophie médiévale Université de Montréal, Montréal, Canada, 27 août-2 septembre 1967* (Montréal and Paris, 1969), pp. 305-355; I. PAGANI, "La critica letteraria", in: *Lo spazio letterario del Medioevo*, 1, *Il medioevo latino*, ed. G. CAVALLO, C. LEONARDI and E. MENESTÒ, 3 vols. (Rome, 1992-1994), 3, *La circolazione del testo*, pp. 113-162, esp. p. 151.

[3] Thomas Aquinas, *Summa Theologiae*, Ia, q. 1, a. 9, obj. 4. A complete anthology of Aquinas's testimonia on this topic has been gathered in the paper STELLA, "Poésie biblique", quoted in F. STELLA, *Poesia e teologia III. Condanna e difesa della poesia dalla Scolastica all'Umanesimo* (Milan, 2010), pp. 251-328, 352-357.

[4] Thomas Aquinas, *Scriptum super sententiis*, pr., 1, 5; qc. 3 co.

[5] See *infra*, n. 14.

[6] *Decretum Gratiani*, *Distinctio* 37. The title of this *distinctio*, founded on the *Sententiae* of Isidore, is *Quare prohibetur Christianus poetica figmenta legere*. The prohibition against reading poems was not imposed on just the clerics (although the *distinctio* is devoted to the formation of the clerics) but on every Christian for this reason: "Thanks to the attraction of the histories they [the poems] excite the mind to the passions too much, because they don't celebrate only the demons but they accept with pleasure their words". And yet Gratian responds (*pars V*) that for a priest the worst is ignorance, because it puts the guidance of a soul into the hands of another. The subtle consequence is that, in effect, the danger that comes from giving up the reading of poetry (that is, of classical poetry) is greater than the danger that comes from the reading of its most lascivious parts.

[7] On this point, see the synthesis by M. LEMOINE, *Intorno a Chartres: Naturalismo platonico nella tradizione cristiana del XII secolo*, Italian trans. (Milan, 1998).

7 and 18),[8] an equivalence that attributed to poetry a value in itself and even a position of pre-eminence in the cultural system. Even though it was fiercely opposed by Thomist intellectuals, this formulation was adopted by Petrarch[9] and Boccaccio.[10] Thus the path was cleared for the sacralisation of poetry that led from the self-conscious humanism of Coluccio Salutati[11] and Scaliger[12] through connected but distinct mediations to William Blake and Novalis, which is to say up through the conception of poetry belonging to romanticism and to part of today's world (I think especially of the remarks by Paul de Man or Paul Ricoeur about the likeness of religious and poetic discourse).

This well-known development has already been widely studied, following the seminal work of Ernst Robert Curtius.[13] Here it will be sufficient to mention that the principal argument on which the defense of the sacrality of poetry was based in these authors is not so much poetry's power to serve as the vehicle for moral contents, which is in any case widely recognised, but the fact that poetry works like the Bible: on the one hand it produces *fabulae* with symbolic value that transcend the mere traces of historical narration, and on the other hand it makes use of figurative methods, divided by the rhetorical tradition into various types of symbolism and allegory which essentially coincide with those identified in the Bible by exegetes and which permit the expression of truths otherwise irreducible to a linguistic form.

---

[8] Albertino Mussato, *Écérinide: Épîtres métriques sur la poésie: Songe*, ed. J.-F. CHEVALIER (Paris, 2000).

[9] Francesco Petrarca, *Epistolae familiares*, 10, 4, 1: "*parum abest quin dicam theologiam esse poeticam de deo*".

[10] Giovanni Boccacio, *Genealogie deorum gentilium*, libro XIV.

[11] He defends his position in Coluccio Salutati, *De laboribus Hercolis*; for Ullman's 1951 edition (Zurich, 1951), see <http://www.bibliotecaitaliana.it/xtf/view?docId=bibit000478/bibit000478.xml> (accessed August 2020).

[12] Josephus Justus Scaliger, *Declamatio contra poetices calumniatores* (1600). For the Leiden edition, see <http://www.uni-mannheim.de/mateo/itali/scaliger2/jpg/s409.html> (accessed August 2010).

[13] E.R. CURTIUS, *Europäische Literatur und lateinisches Mittelalter* (Berne, 1948); trans. *Letteratura europea e medioevo latino* (Florence, 1992). See also *supra*, Chapter Four.

Foundations of a Possible Legitimisation: The Symbolism of Eriugena and Chartres

The pre-humanistic legitimisation does not emerge, as we might think, from a revival of classicist positions or from influences external to the medieval cultural system, but rather – since the idea is to ennoble poetry precisely in relation to this system that tended to exclude it – establishes its arguments *within* this system. The theological and linguistical foundations of this legitimisation, that some scholars (such as Curtius) ascribe to developments of the late Middle Ages, such as Alexander of Hales[14] and Gentile da Cingoli,[15] prove on the contrary to remount to a more ancient stream: the negative or apophatic theology produced by Denys the Areopagite, known in the West through the translations of Hilduin, abbot of Saint-Denis (827), John Scotus Eriugena (860-862) and John the Saracen (twelfth century; the version used by Thomas Aquinas).

The theological and linguistic assumption from which Dionysius began, was the total inexpressibility of God, and the consequent inadequacy of human language to describe divinity and the absolute. The practical consequence of this condition was the need to speak of God through images and metaphors, as outlined by John Scotus in his *De praedestinatione*. The apophatic premise – the unspeakability of God – necessarily leads discourse on the supreme to a symbolic or allegorical style of speech. In this obligatory turn to figural and symbolic procedures, we thus find theology coinciding, at least on the level of its communicative code, with the methods of poetic composition as defined by the tradition of allegorical interpretation. Again, it was John Scotus who first elaborated on the consequences in a famous passage commenting on Dionysus's *Celestial Hierarchy*:

> As the art of poetry presents a moral or natural doctrine through invented stories and allegorical similitudes, with the aim of engaging the human soul (this is in fact

---

[14] CURTIUS, *Letteratura europea*, pp. 248-249: Alexander Halensis, *Summa theologiae*, I. 1, ed. Collegium S. Bonaventurae (Quaracchi, 1924), 1, p. 7; Albertus Magnus, *Summa theologiae* I. q. 5, membrum 1, in: *Beati Alberti Magni, Ratisbonensis episcopi, Ordinis Praedicatorum, Opera quae hactenus haberi potuerunt*, ed. T. TURCO et al., 21 vols. (Lyon, 1651), 17, p. 13a.

[15] CURTIUS, *Letteratura europea*, p. 250 and n. 34; M. GRABMANN, *Gentile da Cingoli, ein italienischer Aristoteleserklärer aus der Zeit Dantes* (*Sitzungsberichte der Bayerischen Akademie der Wissenschaften*, 1940), p. 62 (on the *modi tractandi* listed by Dante in the *Epistola a Cangrande*).

typical of the epic poets, who celebrate the deeds and actions of heroes through symbols): thus theology, like a poetess, adapts the sacred Scripture for the use of our soul, in order to lead it back with fictitious fantasies to the perfect knowledge of intelligible reality, as from a state of imperfect childhood to a kind of interior maturity.[16]

Here Eriugena explicitly establishes an analogy between the procedures of theological reflection and those of poetic composition, beginning with their shared need for a *figured narrativity*: he thus pins down the mainstay of all future legitimisations of poetic truth as an instrument of knowledge not unworthy of Christian culture. Nevertheless, from this assertion it does not follow that poetic activity as such is justified, let alone ennobled. In the same commentary on the *Celestial Hierarchy*, Eriugena also develops a strictly theological path toward the legitimisation of the arts: if reality is indeed a theophany, and each thing is a manifestation of God and an instrument of revelation, then even works of art become "*manuductiones ad Deum*", the means of elevation to divinity and knowledge. Still, among all these arts John actually only cited music and the plastic arts.

Analogously, when Anselm of Laon and Abelard later developed their rhetorical and stylistic analysis of the Bible, which had precursors in the treatises of Bede and of the Carolingian age,[17] the defense of biblical aesthetics did not lead to the acceptance of poetry as a justified art in medieval Christian culture through an analogy of its compositional mechanisms to those of the Bible.[18] Rather, Abelard, despite being a refined poet himself, in this respect

---

[16] Iohannes Scotus Eriugena, *Super Ier. Cael. Sancti Dionysii*, ed. in: PL 122, col. 146B-C: "*Quemadmodum ars poetica per fictas fabulas allegoricas que similitudines moralem doctrinam physicam componit ad humanorum animorum exercitationem (hoc enim proprium est heroicorum poetarum, qui virorum fortium facta et mores figurate laudant): ita theologia, veluti quaedam poetria, sanctam Scripturam fictis imaginationibus ad consultum nostri animi et reductionem a corporalibus sensibus exterioribus, veluti ex quadam imperfecta pueritia, in rerum intellegibilium perfectam cognitionem, tamquam in quadam interioris hominis grandaevitatem, conformat*". Cfr. Dyonisus, *De praedestinatione*, IX, ed. in: PL 122, col. 390B.

[17] J. CHATILLON, "La Bible dans les écoles du XIIe siècle", in: *Le Moyen Âge et la Bible*, ed. P. RICHÉ and G. LOBRICHON (Paris, 1984), pp. 163-197, at p. 167.

[18] This process begins to surface in the production of Chartres and in the theories of the school of Saint Victor, which come close to a belief in the universal pansemiosis of Eriugenian Platonism. Bernard of Chartres acknowledges the function of the poets' *introductoria* towards philosophy, quoting the Macrobian image of the *cunae nutricum*. Alain expresses the conscience of the value of the poetic activity as inspiration which comes, according to the later Boccaccian formula, *ex sinu Dei*. Richard of Saint Victor developed the idea from the premise that every visible thing is the shadow and sign of an invisible reality, resulting in "*operatio industriae (id*

repeats the Platonic denunciations of the deceptive poets in his theoretical elaborations.[19]

Eriugena's position proved extraordinarily fertile, even before its pre-humanistic revival, in the culture of the school of Chartres. Accepting the need for a symbolic discourse about God, the school claimed a communicative power for poetry in which (according to Alain de Lille and William of Conches[20]), alongside the *"suavitas"* of the literal meaning and *"instructio moralis"*, the *"acutior allegorie subtilitas"* stands for a secret intended for those able to elevate themselves beyond the apparently inappropriate images to the contemplation of supra-celestial forms.[21] This legitimisation also authorised the adoption of verse for philosophical works, as in Alain de Lille and Bernard Sylvester.

In the late medieval period, however, the analogical theory – before its vigorous humanistic revival – became gradually weaker, even independently from the scholastic reaction. Prior to the flowering of troubadour poetry, which invested the courts with a new prestige, John of Salisbury, who was probably trained at the school of Chartres and who defended the didactic usefulness of poetry in his *Metalogicon* I, 17 (*c.* 1159),[22] discredited poetry's claim to be as ennobled as philosophy based precisely on an affinity with biblical polysemy. According to him, only Scripture could sustain true allegorical meaning. Profane authors, who wrote according to their own, or to a figural meaning, had to compose works that could still be comprehensible in and of themselves. An essential affinity, *ante litteram*, existed in the Thomist argument that irreversibly distinguished figurative language, present only in the Bible, from the *sensus parabolicus* that was also possible in human writing but which still re-

---

est artis) in quantum imitatur naturam in tantum in se gestet invisibilium vel futurorum umbram" ("the activity of work, i.e. of art, carries within itself the shadow of invisible and future things as it imitates nature"). And yet, even this opening, very important in itself, does not lead to an explicit legitimization of poetry because it remains restricted inside the generic sanctification of human creativity and in a poetics of realism otherwise marginalized in the medieval era.

[19] Peter Abelard, *Theologia Christiana*, II, 24, in: Petrus Abaelardus, *Opera theologica* 2, ed. E.M. BUYTAERT (Turnhout, 1969: CCCM 12), pp. 192-193.

[20] Alain de Lille, *Theologicae Regulae* and *Quoniam homines*, ed. P. GLORIEUX, in: *Archives d'histoire doctrinale et littéraire du Moyen Âge* 20 (1953), pp. 119-359; cf. E. JEAUNEAU, "L'usage de la notion d'integumentum à travers les gloses de Guillaume de Conches", *Archives d'histoire doctrinale et littéraire du Moyen Âge* 32 (1957), pp. 35-100.

[21] PAGANI, "La critica letteraria", p. 155.

[22] John of Salisbury, *Metalogicon*, I. 17, ed. C.Ch.J. WEBB (Oxford, 1929), pp. 42, 32 ff.: however, he only confirms the subordinated position of the grammar in order to avoid its autonomy and therefore excludes it from the system of the *artes*.

mained within the *sensus literalis*, that is, within the intention of the writer. The Bible, on the other hand, contains ulterior meanings *unforeseen* by its human compilers, and it is in this inexhaustibility of the meanings of its *res*, as well as of its *verba*, that its unattainable sacredness lies.[23]

Naturally, the issues are not as schematic as we are forced to represent them: even in the Aristotelian revival that led to the inevitable Thomist responses, there was still more room for the incursions on poetry, for example in Averroes or in Domenicus Gundisalvus. But what prevails beyond every discussion is the condemnation culminated in *quaestio* 9 of the first part of Thomas's *Summa Theologiae*.

The Anomaly of Biblical Poetry

These and other documents seem to confirm therefore that, even if early medieval theology elaborated the foundations of an expressive analogy between the Bible and poetry, and of a sacredness of poetic activity, the theorisation most specifically related to poetry did not subsequently develop these premises and remained the victim of a devaluing of poetry that was already latent in the derivation of *carmen* from *carere mente*. We read this in Isidore of Seville, who, in his *Sententiae* III, 13, arrives at the famous conclusion: "*Ideo prohibetur Christianus figmenta legere poetarum, quia per oblectamenta inanium fabularum mentem excitant ad incentiva libidinum*" ("Therefore the Christian is forbidden to read the inventions of poets, because the attractions of futile stories excite the mind to the stimuli of the passions").[24]

---

[23] Thomas Aquinas, *Quodlibet* VII. q. 6, a. 3 (16), ed. in: Sancti Thomae de Aquino *Opera omnia* 25, *Quaestiones de quolibet*, 1 (Rome and Paris, 1996), p. 32: "*in nulla scientia humana industria humana inventa, proprie loquendo, potest inveniri nisi literalis sensus: sed solum in illa Scriptura*"; ID., *Summa Theologiae*, parte I. q. 1, a. 3, ad tertiam: "*sensus parabolicus sub litterali continetur*" (<https://archive.org/stream/summatheologicao011thom/summatheologicao011thom_djvu.txt>), ed. R. SPIAZZI (Turin, 1956), digital edn. R. BUSA, *Corpus Thomisticum*, printed in: *S. Thomae Aquinatis Opera omnia*, ed. R. BUSA (Stuttgart and Bad Cannstatt, 1980), p. 480.

[24] Cf. Isidorus Hispalensis, *Etymologiae* I. 39 (*De metris*): "*Carmen vocatur quidquid pedibus continetur; cui datum nomen existimant, seu quod carptim pronuntiaretur (unde hodie lanam quam purgantes discerpunt, carminare dicimus), seu quod qui illa canerent carere mente existimabantur*" (ed. in: PL 82, col. 118B).

A Repressed Beauty 81

The revaluing of the *modus symbolicus*[25] carried out by neo-Platonic theologians was not enough to reclaim an autonomous value for poetry.[26] If the problem consisted of the mythological, or at any rate fictitious, content attributed to all poetic compositions – the "*minimum continet veritatis*"[27] – then the theoretical solution could be produced by a poetry that would draw its content from Truth itself, that is, from the Bible. This poetry – biblical poetry – existed from the end of the fourth century (following Greek precursors, of which most traces have been lost), when the first Vergilian centos began to be composed with a Christian theme. Hence, the first Latin poem with a fully biblical theme, the *Evangeliorum libri* by Juvencus, appeared in the age of Constantine. It is the progenitor of an immense tradition of poetic works that were inspired by the Bible, and which the medieval scholastic system accepted into the canon: Sedulius, Marius Victor, Dracontius, Avitus, Arator. This tradition of works on the divine epic reached Milton, Klopstock, Blake, and continued to nourish the poetry of our times, if not our literary canons, as we have discussed in the 50 papers of a conference about "the unending Scripture" in Florence in 1997 regarding the books of Kartschoke, Herzog and many others.[28] The classicist and renaissance model dominant in Western culture has long obscured its continuity and importance, as is witnessed by the opinions of Jerome,[29] Petrarch,[30]

---

[25] The expression is from St. Thomas: *Super Sententias [Petri Lombardi]*, Prol. 1, q. 1, a. 5 ad 3, ed. S. Tommaso d'Aquino, *Commento alle Sentenze di Pietro Lombardo* (Bologna, 2001), p. 154 (based on the 1856-1858 edition of Parma; also ed. R. BUSA (Stuttgart-Bad Cannstatt, 1980), p. 3: "*Ad tertium dicendum, quod poetica scientia est de his quae propter defectum veritatis non possunt a ratione capi; unde oportet quod quasi quibusdam similitudinibus ratio seducatur: theologia autem est de his quae sunt supra rationem; et ideo modus symbolicus utrique communis est, cum neutra rationi proportionetur*".

[26] The concept of poetics as an autonomous subject, Curtius writes in CURTIUS, *Letteratura europea e medioevo latino*, p. 167, was lost for a thousand years.

[27] Thomas Aquinas, *Super Sententias* I Prol. q. 1 a. 5, ad 3, ed. in: S. Thomae Aquinatis *Opera omnia*, ed. R. BUSA, 1 (Stuttgart-Bad Cannstatt, 1980), cit. p. 3: "*Praeterea, scientiarum maxime differentium non debet esse unus modus. Sed poetica, quae minimum continet veritatis, maxime differt ab ista scientia, quae est verissima. Ergo, cum illa procedat per metaphoricas locutiones, modus huius scientiae non debet esse talis*".

[28] Proceedings published in: *La Scrittura infinita: Bibbia e poesia in età romantica e contemporanea*, ed. F. STELLA (Florence, 1999), and in: *La Scrittura infinita: Bibbia e poesia in età medievale e umanistica*, ed. F. STELLA (Florence, 2001).

[29] I recall the assessment on Proba and Jerome, *Ep*. 53, 7, in: Hieronymus, *Epistolae*, ed. I. HILBERG, 3 vols. (Vienna, 1910-1912: CSEL 54-56), 1, pp. 456-457, on the incompatibility between Vergil and the Christian contents: "*Taceo de meis similibus, qui si forte ad scripturas sanctas post saeculares litteras venerint (...) sed ad sensum suum incongrua aptant testimonia, quasi grande sit et non vitiosissimum dicendi genus depravare sententias et ad voluntatem suam*

and Curtius, who consider biblical poetry and above all the biblical epic as a structural anomaly, a *genre faux* incompatible with the literary system of the Occident.[31] Nevertheless, in recent decades the change of interpretive paradigms and the spread of new critical tools, such as Northrop Frye's literary archetypes, Jaussian hermeneutics, and Ricoeur's studies of metaphor, the allegoricism of the deconstructionists, and currently intercultural dialogue, allow us to approach this subject with an attitude free of critical, idealist, and classicist prejudices, which in recent decades has so severely limited our understanding of medieval and modern literature. Even the few attempts at a history of medieval aesthetics, such as those by Hans Hermann Glunz, Edgard De Bruyne, Władysław Tatarkiewicz, Clive Staples Lewis and Hennig Brinkmann, who had begun to reconstruct the artistic conceptions of the medievals that were not based on models external to this period, were long ignored (and still are in common opinion), with the exception of Umberto Eco's handbook, *Art and Beauty in the Middle Ages*. Recent research on this subject has produced two kinds of acquisitions in particular: the exploration of a method of poetic composition structured by analogy with biblical exegesis, and the discovery of a poetic genre whose object is not so much the Bible as a reservoir of contents, but rather exegesis itself as an intellectual process and mental journey.

Exegetical Poetry and the Rhetoric of Otherness

The adoption of biblical rather than historical, mythological, or naturalistic content was not without consequences for the purposes of compositional structure – at least from Auerbach on,[32] even without drawing on the analyses recently advanced by Alter, Kermode, Ceserani, Boitani,[33] and others, the major

---

scripturam trahere repugnantem (...) *Puerilia sunt haec et circulatorum ludo similia, docere, quod ignores, immo, et cum Clitomacho loquar, nec hoc quidem scire, quod nescias*".

[30] I refer to Petrarch, *Ecloga* X, in: *Il Bucolicon Carmen e i suoi commenti inediti*, ed. A. AVENA (Padua, 1906), p. 152, where he defines the biblical poetry as "*fragilis vox*"; cf. Amarcius, *Satire* 3, 270-271, in: Sextus Amarcius, *Sermones*, ed. K. MANITIUS (Weimar, 1969), p. 136: "*Alcimus Arator Sedulius atque Iuvencus / non bene tornatis opponunt regia vasis*".

[31] I refer to the definition of "*verfehlte Gattung*" in CURTIUS, *Letteratura europea e medioevo latino*, analysed by K. SMOLAK, "Die Bibeldichtung als 'verfehlte Gattung'", in: *La Scrittura infinita: Bibbia e poesia in età medievale e umanistica*, pp. 14-29.

[32] AUERBACH, *Mimesis*, chapter 1.

[33] Literature in R. CESERANI, "Brevi appunti sulla riscoperta della Bibbia come grande testo

ity of scholars recognising that biblical storytelling introduces essential changes into the narrative field, the web of elements to be considered and the stylistic registers admitted, the construction of the landscape, the hierarchy of perspectives in play, as well as the values that stem from them. Many efforts have been made to investigate the effects of these alterations in the literary corpus of the Bible itself, though almost no one has explored their effects in works that were inspired by the Bible, and that one must reckon with other immanent poetics and habitual rhetorics tinged with another mode of composition. Even an approximate series of examples may give some idea of the tradition of forms and models with which these productions have experimented.

The modus symbolicus

The fundamental mechanism is naturally the one identified by Eriugena and Alain de Lille: the adoption of the *modus symbolicus* not as an occasional and decorative figure but as a constant perspective and structural orientation. As Jauss has intuited, we are not far, from the point of view of mental categories, from the perception of nature and interiority that would be reintroduced by Baudelaire in the poetry of the nineteenth century, and that today, in terminology not technically 'allegorical' but essentially identical, might be defined as the adoption of the dimension of otherness in the very genesis of poetry, a dialogic or polyphonic view based on the permanent multiplicity of every narrative thread, every signified, every signifier. A kind of inherent secondariness distinguishes every manifestation of this new genre. Exegesis – the body of commentary and explanations that identifies the system of connections and meanings between the various parts of the Bible and their key spiritual values – therefore represents a parallel dimension for this literature, something more than what similitude represented in classical poetry: the movement toward another dimension of reality, a different code of expression. In fact, it introduces into writing a perception of the permanent coexistence of otherness, of a plurality of aspects and meanings.

Not all authors were aware of the revolutionary potential of this mechanism, nor were all the authors who were aware of it able to control its effects or to make its theoretical claims explicit. The least effective ones, obviously,

letterario", in: *La Scrittura infinita: Bibbia e poesia in età romantica e contemporanea*, pp. 19-38; P. BOITANI, *Ri-Scritture* (Bologna, 1997).

were those who claimed to overcome the laws of classical poetics in a hypertext like that of the Bible that was radically opposed to them: this often occurred during moments of classical revival, as in Florus of Lyon's literal paraphrasing of the Gospel in the Carolingian age, or in the biblical poems of Marbod of Rennes and Hildebert of Lavardin in the twelfth century, and as later occurs in the Renaissance and the eighteenth century. However, in the macroforms of literature almost no one was able to evade some general tendencies such as, for example, the inclination towards a type of open structure – a *carmen perpetuum* of the Ovidian kind, hence at its core anti-classical – in which elements of the past return with new significance and current events prefigure the future in a circularity of meanings that inevitably characterises every biblical poet aware of his exegetical function.

Double-Level Poetics

The consequences of this position appear in many characteristics of the compositional technique: most of them arise from the fact that every rewriting of the Bible can refer to the globality of the cultural system in all of its expressions. One example is the *cyclical arrangement* of narrations: in this way the ultimate meaning of an episode is anticipated by its introduction and is then taken up again after its conclusion; in this type frequently the story is reduced to the elements that are used for exegesis, except for those with a purely narrative function, to the detriment of historical readability, which is clearly felt to be secondary, and in favour of a moral characterisation that is conceived as the primary goal. A second case is the intrusion of iconographic techniques of description in the body of the text. In Carolingian biblical poetry, for example, the lines introducing the disciple John simply labels him as *accubitor*, translated as "reclining at the table",[34] a neologistic epithet referring to the gospel

---

[34] *Accubito* was already in use by Sedulius (*Carmen Paschale*, praef. 2, ed. J. HUEMER, *Sedulii Opera omnia* ... (Vienna, 1885: CSEL 10), p. 14) and Pomponius Porphyrius (commentary to Horace, *Ep*. 1, 18, 10, ed. in: *Acronis et Porphyrii Commentarii in Q. Horatium Flaccum*, ed. F. HAUTHAL, 2 vols. (Berlin, 1864; reprinted Amsterdam, 1966), 2, p. 483), while *accubitor* is found in a Christian inscription (*Inscriptiones christianae urbis Romae septimo saeculo antiquiores*, 2, *Pars prima: Series codicum in quibus veteres inscriptiones christianae praesertim urbis Romae sive solae sive ethnicis admixtae descriptae sunte ante saeculum* XVI, ed. J.-B. DE ROSSI (Rome, 1888), p. 258) related to John, and in Aldhelm, *Virg.* 461 and *De metr*., 65, (ed. EHWALD pp. 234 and 372 respectively). It is also found in another inscription attributed to Hrabanus Maurus, *Carmina*, 51, II. 2, ed. E. DÜMMLER, in: PLAC 2, p. 216: "*accubitor domini ipse*

verse that describes him as seated near Jesus at the Last Supper and "leaning" on his chest (John 13, 25). This epithet became an iconographical cliché in many miniatures and depictions beginning in the early medieval period.[35] A third example refers to the metrical effect of the exegetical dimension. In the *Collatio* by Sedulius,[36] a poet of the fifth century, the second hymn was written in epanaleptic couplets so that the first half of the first line (hexameter) had to be the same as the second half of the second line (pentameter). Sedulius structures this scheme, which is present in rare examples from Ovid and of the *Anthologia Latina*, based on a typological criterion: every couplet refers to an episode or element of the Old Testament that has a counterpart in the New Testament or an interpretation in doctrine. The common element in the two lines, which is repeated, might be defined as the *tenor* of the comparison; the other two contextualise the element in the respective fields.

Unius ob meritum cuncti periere minores:
salvantur cuncti unius ob meritum.

The common element here is the responsibility of one alone that falls on everyone: the first line refers to Adam, the second to Christ. The figures are not named. In a circle of readers prepared by their own biblical-theological culture, the functional echo is enough to re-evoke and arrange them according to an implicit signification. Typological epanalepsis is a technical and intellectual virtuosity that arose in the ninth century at the hands of Hrabanus Maurus, the Carolingian teacher, abbot of Fulda, and archbishop of Mainz, who imitated and expanded the *Collatio* in his *carmen* 16.[37]

Biblical poetry appears, even in its most modest form, as a *fragment of a global discourse*, and of an all-encompassing knowledge – iconic, juridical, educational, exegetical, or moral – which is presupposed and echoed, even unconsciously: what in classical Antiquity or other cultural systems characterises the great epic poems, an expression of a culture shared by a broad collectivity rather than an individuality, returns in the Middle Ages as a feature of all

---

Iohannes adest", and in a preface to a gospel book (ed. K. STRECKER, in: *PLAC* 4, pp. 928-929), while Alcuin uses *recubus* (*Carmen* 69, 167).

[35] Some remarks on this subject can be found in F. STELLA, *La poesia carolingia latina a tema biblico* (Spoleto, 1993), in the chapter "Le strutture espressive", pp. 518-557 (paragraph "Codici stilistici").

[36] The text can still be read in the edition by I. HUEMER, *Sedulii Opera omnia*, pp. 155-162.

[37] Ed. E. DÜMMLER, in: *PLAC* 2, pp. 178-181.

biblical poetry and permeates its code of expression. To this must be added the influence of the internal tradition, that is to say the works of biblical poetry, whose intertextual echoes it soon becomes quite difficult to avoid, so much so that while it is natural that a Latin poet of the twelfth century might allude both to the Bible and to its late antique and Carolingian poetic interpretations, even Milton in the seventeenth century cannot help but look back to the poem of Avitus, which dates to the sixth century.

Technicalities of Exegetical Beauty

Stylistically, the most well-rounded results appear in the *De spiritalis historiae gestis* by Alcimus Avitus, who, with great awareness, takes a step farther in defining the aesthetic involvement in the theological subject matter: as he declares in lines 12-18 of the fifth book, describing the crossing of the Red Sea, the explosion of meaning produced by an exterior wrapping teeming with possibilities is a guarantee of greater beauty compared to the already considerable beauty of the narrative surface, of a kind of creative ulteriority.[38] Alexander Arweiler has analysed the poem in this way,[39] and identifies an entire series of mechanisms through which the theologisation of poetry, and the poeticisation of theology, are produced. Some of the most influential are: 1) the exegetical modification of semantics;[40] 2) the choice of terms influenced by exegetical sources that interpret the same biblical referent; 3) allusions to previous instances of poetic exegesis, which reveal the development of a tradition already felt as such at the beginning of the sixth century, especially in relation

---

[38] *Alcimii Ecdicii Aviti Viennensis episcopi Opera quae supersunt*, ed. R. PEIPER (Berlin, 1883: MGH AA 6.2), p. 255. The transition is described as a "*celeberrima ... scriptorum series, in cuius pondere sacro / causarum mage pignus erat pulchramque relatu / pulchrior exuperat praemissae forma salutis, / historiis quae magna satis maiorque figuris / conceptam gravido peperit de tegmine vitam*" ("very famous story of the writings in whose sacred weight the facts had greater value: beautiful to narrate, but more beautiful emerges the symbol of the salvation sent, which is already great in history and greater in figures, and has generated from the pregnant envelope the life that was conceived").

[39] A. ARWEILER, *Die Imitation antiker und spätantiker Literatur in der Dichtung "De spiritalis historiae gestis" des Alcimus Avitus: Mit einem Kommentar zu Avit. Carm. 4, 429-540 und 5, 526-703* (Berlin, 1999).

[40] As in 1, 57-58: "*et nostram, celso donatus honore, /induat interius formonsa in mente figuram*" ("and with great honour clothes our beautiful spirit within with our figure") where *formonsa*, that is 'beautiful', refers more to the exegetical sense of *forma* = 'figure' than its original meaning of 'beauty'.

to Prudentius;[41] 4) exegetical interpolations, which compensate for the scarcity of epic similes by providing a metahistorical and moral term of comparison;[42] 5) homiletic formulas,[43] the 'parenthetical' and absorbing use of the first person plural which presents sacred history and its meanings as a collective heritage, or the hymnodic prayers that are typical of both genres;[44] 6) the grouping of episodes not connected by a narrative thread but by a thematic one.[45] Thus, an entire technique of thematic connections develops based on the use of recurring semantic fields and their internal echoes, which gives rise to a terminology of temptation, of desperation, repentance, etc.: a true vocabulary of poetic theology.

All this leads in turn to a series of consequences for the relationship with language and with models – even classical ones – and at the same time opens up important new possibilities.

Multifigurality

The process of adopting exegesis, with its various theological implications, as the principal criterion of poetic composition has its most forceful model in *De actibus apostolorum* by the subdeacon Arator, who in recent years has received growing attention from critics. Written in two books and comprising

---

[41] These allusions are not limited to the reuse of phrases, to stylistic emulation, or the imitation of analogous passages, but sometimes establish a true dialogue with the model, even to the point of confuting the precursor.

[42] In 1, 165-167, the blood and water gushing from the rib of Christ, the second Adam, represent martyrdom and baptism ("*qui vivum populis iam tum spondente lavacrum / fluxit martyrium et sanguinis unda*"), as was widely illustrated by Jerome in his *Tractatus in psalmos* II. 88 (ed. G. MORIN, in: Hieromymus, *Tractatus sive homiliae in Psalmos – in Marci evangelium – Alia varia argumenta*, ed. G. MORIN, B. CAPELLE, and J. FRAIPONT (Turnhout, 1958: CCSL 78), p. 407).

[43] These introduce into poetry transitional expressions that were widespread in sermons, such as *namque legis* or *scriptura ait*, or they offer up their favorite hermeneutic methods, such as the multiple exegesis of the same figure (e.g., the *lignum* in Avitus, *De spiritalis historiae gestis*, 3, 362-364).

[44] In general, these interpolations end up strengthening the recourse to those styles that were considered common to poetic and homiletic-exegetical language, such as parallelism.

[45] As according to Dracontius in *De laudibus Dei*, and as is confirmed by the titles of particular books by Dracontius or Avitus in manuscripts, florilegia, or medieval literary histories (of the Isidorian variety); the books of Avitus are entitled: *De mundi initio, De originali peccato, De diluvio mundi, De transitu Maris Rubri*.

2,336 hexameters, the poem was read in April 544 to Pope Vigilius, who may have commissioned it to implant a sense of the centrality of the Church and of the Roman see in a work of poetry. Thus, Arator's work represents the first epic mythologisation (later re-attempted in the tenth century, with less success, by Flodoard of Reims in *De triumphis Christi*).

Many recent studies[46] have highlighted in Arator not only a dense exegetical texture and the purpose of exalting the historical and meta-historical role of the Church, but also in particular the translation of this ideological strategy into a kind of archmetaphor of baptism that informs the poem's entire composition through a triple mechanism: the amplification of passages with a clear baptismal theme (such as the episode of the Pentecost or the baptism of Simon Magus), making explicit passages which were only implicitly baptismal, and the interpolation of allusions to baptism (in the narrative or in the corresponding exegesis) into passages clearly lacking this theme. The pervasiveness of the baptismal archetype was converted at the level of the metaphorical signifier into a predominating water symbolism, but it is also an example of a compositional practice that reduces the boundaries between narration and pertinent interpretation, allowing figural allusions to abound at every level no longer according to the habitual typological correspondences between episodes, but between elements of one episode and elements of another. Thus a continuous and unforeseeable interweaving is produced that leaves behind the double-level Sedulian and Avitian poetics and inaugurates the coexistence of a figural plurality: it escapes, therefore, the need for interpretation in order to use the wedges of the theological imaginary with the overriding aim of constructing a new poetic imaginary. Exegesis was not restricted to its use as a hermeneutical method; it became a language (typological, Christological, anagogical) and a global message (ecclesiological, sacramental, tropological).

---

[46] See especially R. HILLIER, *Arator on the Acts of the Apostles: A Baptismal Commentary* (Oxford, 1993); P. ANGELUCCI, *La tecnica poetica di Aratore* (Rome, 1990); ID., *Centralità della chiesa e primato romano in Aratore* (Rome, 1990); I. BUREAU, *Lettre et sens mystique dans l'"Historia Apostolorum" d'Arator: Exégèse et épopée* (Paris, 1997); J. SCHWIND, *Arator-Studien* (Göttingen, 1990); and ID., *Sprachliche und Exegetische Beobachtungen zu Arator* (Stuttgart, 1995).

Poetry about the Exegetical Process

Another subgenre of biblical poetry also exists, in which the relationship between poetry and exegesis is developed from a methodological rather than a narrative point of view – that is, poetry about exegesis as an intellectual process. "The Intellectualism of the Philosophy of the Art" is a chapter from De Bruyne's *Esthétique du Moyen Âge*, but what has never been studied is the *poetic* application of this principle, which subordinates every artistic production to an intellectual criterion, to an ideological or religious end, to a philosophical idea. Indeed, until recently it was branded as non-poetry, and with an obscurantism that has harmed the reputation of even Dante himself. But if we read the texts of the poetry of exegesis without prejudice, we see that they offer the reader a new beauty, and the transformation of the intoxication of the spiritual quest that the medieval age, more than any other, felt to be the summit of human realisation, even to the point of mythologising it in the legend of the Grail. This is a theme that appears in the *metra* of Boethius's *Consolatio Philosophiae*. But more than any others, the Carolingian poets developed a repertory of semiological metaphors, one of the innovations produced by the exegetical genre, that is, images of the relationship of signification, metaphors of polysemy: from the Pauline metaphors of the body in the Old Testament that project their New Testament shadow, or of milk suited for the smaller and unlearned, and of meat for solid spiritual food fit to more capable interpreters,[47] to the image of the Old Testament shell that conceals the evangelical or Christological pearl up to hermeneutical combat, to the forest to be explored, to the sea that has many levels of depth and appearance, to the concentric wheels of Ezekiel and Gregory and the depths of the cataracts of the two Testaments, a symbol taken from Psalm 42 and interpreted by Ps.-Jerome as a figure for the relationship between the two parts of Scripture. All this creates a new imaginary, partly derived from the range of overused symbols, partly from the codification of examples already used in the Bible itself, partly elaborated by poets – an expressive code that contributes to the transformation of theology into a creative mechanism.[48]

---

[47] C. VIRCILLO FRANKLIN, "Words as food: Figuring the Bible in the early Middle Ages", in: *Comunicare e significare nell'alto medioevo*, 2 vols. (Spoleto, 2005: *Settimane di studio della Fondazione Centro italiano di Studi sull'alto medioevo* 52), 2, pp. 733-764.

[48] In BORI, *L'interpretazione infinita* and SPITZ, *Die Metaphorik des geistigen Schriftsinn*, both authors are concerned with these images of the exegetical relationship in prose exegetical literature, but the application to poetry, which involves resorting to models and styles derived

This poetic practice continues undisturbed, frequently and slowly repeated though continually enriched, throughout the entire medieval period, often not as an autonomous genre but concealed as a subject of the verse prefaces to biblical codices, or in ecclesiastical epigraphs, or in theological poems. One exemplary instance is the eleventh-century *De doctrina spiritualis* by Othlo of St. Emmeram, who dedicates the twelfth chapter to *De spirituali Scripturae Sacrae intelligentia*, insisting on the importance of the spiritual meaning of the Bible, beginning with the recognition of a kind of pansemiosis, as Umberto Eco has called it,[49] of creation: "*mystice signatur quicquid famulatur / tam nota librorum quam cuncta creatio rerum*" ("everything that belongs to the world is a sign of a spiritual reality, both the letters of books and the whole of creation"). He exemplifies this type of relationship with an exegetical image: straw and grain, metaphors of the body and the spirit that are hidden together, and live together beneath the pressure and the covering of the other, since the grain can renew itself protected by the straw and hope to reach maturity and then be purified by the grinding of earthly suffering.[50] This image, developed at length with poetic force, then gives way to another – that of the mirror which exists within each of us, preventing us from seeing reality directly, but bearing a trace of it like a seal on wax, which is an image of the image: this is why God speaks to us *parabolatim*.

---

from classical poetry, establishes another dynamic, initiating an intertextual relationship with the poetic tradition that becomes an intercultural dialogue between the Christian and the classical use of the same image. For more on this process in Medieval Latin poetry, see STELLA, *Poesia carolingia latina a tema biblico*, and *La Scrittura infinita: Bibbia e poesia in età medievale e umanistica*.

[49] U. ECO, *Arte e bellezza nell'estetica medievale* (Milan, 1988), pp. 75-79.

[50] "*Exemplum quoddam satis enarrabile ponam: / ecce vides nasci paleas cum germine grani; / attamen unius pressura aliud moderatur. / Nunquid cum paleis comedi frumenta parabis? / Quod patet atteritur, ut quod latet hinc renovetur. / Sic, quia per paleas carnalis vita notatur, / et grani titulis signatur spiritualis: / spiritus ergo intra patulae latet abdita carnis / quolibet ut granum sub visceribus palearum*" (Otloh of St. Emmeram, *De doctrina spirituali*, ed. in: PL 146, cols. 29-434, at col. 271C). On this topic, see H. SCHAUWECKER, *Otloh von St. Emmeram: Ein Beitrag zur Bildugs- und Frömmigkeitsgeschichte des 11. Jahrhunderts* (Munich, 1964).

Implicit Poetics and Explicit Theories

This dual poetic and intellectual project seems to presuppose a refined knowledge of the role that poetic form can play in an exegetical literature: in the prologue of the *Spiritalis Doctrina* by Othlo of St. Emmeram, a figure filled with a disquiet that Gustav Vinay defined as neurotic, we see in fact a long reflection on the meaning of the choice of poetry. First, he dismisses all possible accusations of ambition and then suggests the usefulness of addressing his doctrinal compendium not only to the lovers of prose but also to those enamoured of poetry, who probably increased in number with the spread of the liberal arts. He then confesses that he is, all in all, more versed in metre than in the *dictamen* of prose, and that he has not been able to change his style, except in regards to the demands of someone to whom he alludes (someone addressed to him as able to write in verse); however, he only accepts those demands with some resistance. Hence he proclaims that he will commit himself, banishing mental torpor, not to suffocate the "*divina rusticitas*", the "sacred roughness", with "*pretioso famine*", the "precious style", or with the degree of worldly culture inevitably connected with the adoption of poetry. The versification of sacred Scripture, or at any rate of religious subject matter, was apparently felt to be a sin, albeit one that qualified as venial. The novelty of exegetical poetry was *not* considered as an experiment of faith or a cultural innovation – categories that are in any case foreign to the medieval mind – but as a technical undertaking full of doctrinal dangers.

Two centuries later, in the third quarter of the twelfth century, Matthew of Vendôme gave his pupils one of the most successful biblical poems of the entire medieval period, *Tobias*,[51] which in 1,113 elegiac couplets relates the famous biblical tale in a sparkling style, setting it in a lively chivalric context with a broad array of exegetical, doctrinal, and moral interpolations. With this work, Matthew joined those who were concerned with the biblical text on the philological or exegetical level. But in the epilogue, as we mentioned in the previous chapter, he declares with modesty that he reserves all honour for the subject rather than the author[52] – and shortly afterward he enquires about the

---

[51] Ed. in: *Mathei Vindocinensis Opera*, 2, *Piramus et Tisbe – Epistulae – Tobias*, ed. F. MUNARI (Rome, 1982).

[52] Vv. 2129-2131, ed. MUNARI, p. 250: "*Nullus ad auctorem fiat respectus, honore / thematis sacrum festivat opus, non auctor, honestas / materie celebria materiata iuvat*" ("No respect is due to the author, the sacrality of the subject is celebrated by the work, not by the author, and it is the dignity of the matter that helps to honour the description of such matter").

relationship between the sacredness of the subject and the faithfulness of the poetic instrument, concluding that when the subject is the truth, it is not permissible to embellish it with rhetorical frills out of literary ambition. The truth does not allow itself to be praised with pleasing sounds. The only way to move beyond the letter of the text is through a spiritual interpretation of it, which vivifies it by combining it with a new meaning: "The letter must not deceive: it kills those who read it improperly, while the aroma of the spirit gives it life. The prostituted letter turns its path to any suitor, attaching itself to a spouse-meaning; when the voice commits the sin of adultery with an ancient meaning (…) one single sound wavers among many significations". Matthew thus played on the polysemy of the biblical text, but he did not see – as Avitus had – a path between this and the aesthetic embellishment of the poetic texture. Rather, as he concludes in his final prayer to God, "no praise is able to sing of you, since the sound of the voice cannot succeed in signifying its own creator: the misery of words in relation to your majesty forces us to speak as in a faint whimper".[53] He returns therefore to the subject of the unspeakability of the divine, but without drawing any consequences that would authorise it to be replaced with poetic symbolism.

The majority of the evidence gives the impression that to a large degree the medievals, essentially indifferent to the literary problem as a question of value, were not able to elaborate a heteronomous aesthetic, that is to say, an aesthetic that takes its criterion from other orders of values – religious or theological – external to aesthetics, in a mechanism typical of ideologically universal, or totalitarian, if you will, systems, such as the Islamic or the socialist aesthetic. The new poetic implemented *de facto* in biblical or exegetical poetry was not sufficiently appreciated either in the theoretical elaborations or in the declarations of the biblical poets themselves: it was not perceived as a novelty capable of re-determining the system of values attributed to the various genres of writing, and that was still based on the old opposition between pagan stylistics and Christian morality: in many places and many manuscripts, these poetic works are grouped together with prose exegetical works, and considered mere "metri-

---

[53] Vv. 2217-2220, ed. MUNARI, p. 254: "*Te laus nulla canit quia significatio vocum / deficit auctorem significare suum; / de virtute tua vocum penuria cogit / nos quasi vagitu deficiente loqui*".

cal theology":[54] with this gesture, they are ennobled in their religious dignity, but denied any aesthetic relevance.

Sporadic signs still exist, however, of a methodological questioning that gripped the medieval observers most aware of this latent contradiction.[55] In the twelfth-century *Dialogus super auctores*, Conrad of Hirsau proposes some insights on this question that deserve to be noted: the chapter on Sedulius, in fact, is able to portray the fundamental difference in which Sedulius's poetry is interested, and Christian poetry in general. In fact, when a teacher presented a disciple with the introduction to Sedulius after the scholastic poets whom he had already expounded (Cato, Aesop, Avianus), the student stopped him and pointed out a discrepancy: "if the fabulous stories of the poets, with which you dealt, referred to a moral aim, doubtless they have some significance: in fact, the poets never refer their stories to human behaviours, except through a secondary meaning".[56] And the teacher responds:

> You have not understood. On the one hand you have the poems and popular sayings without any weight, transient as a faint sound, and an entirely different thing is divine discourse, which is eternal and founded on spiritual interpretation: and words, rather than simple, bare letters, are in some way signs of a hidden meaning, but are absolutely dissimilar from the immutable and eternal word. (...) The litera-

---

[54] The definition is witnessed in Emo, a Frisian monk of the thirteenth century, referring to the *Aurora* of Peter Riga, the most important biblical poet of the Latin Middle Ages, in: *Emonis et Menkonis Werumensium chronicon, Continuatio*, ed. L. WEILAND, in: *[Chronica aevi Suevici]*, ed. G.H. PERTZ *et al.* (Hanover, 1874: MGH SS 23), pp. 465-572, at p. 524. The same expression has been used by R. HERZOG, *Bibeldichtung* 1 (Munich, 1975).

[55] As early as the Carolingian age, some sign of the consciousness of the methodological innovation that was beginning to come into effect emerged: in the verse preface to his commentary on Kings (ed. E. DÜMMLER, in: PLAC 1, p. 164). Hrabanus Maurus emphasises that in the biblical book in question the *mysticus ordo* (that is the biblical narration) here *indicat* the deeds of Christ the redeemer, and thus has a typological significance, and this kind of signification is defined as an *ars nova*, with an unexpected admiration in a conservative spirit such as that of Hrabanus, who many times in his works took care to note that he did not invent or added anything to the authority of the Fathers, since, as Umberto Eco has written, "medieval culture has a sense of innovation, but is engaged in concealing it beneath the pretense of repetition (the opposite of modern culture, which pretends to be innovating even when it is repeating)" (ECO, *Arte e bellezza*, p. 5). We see, therefore, something revolutionary in the intellectual process of exegesis, even if this intuition does not produce any references to its poetic application, not even when, as here, it is expressed in verse.

[56] Conrad of Hirsau, *Dialogus super auctores*, ed. in: *Accessus ad auctores*, ed. R.B.C. HUYGENS (Leiden, 1970), p. 88: "*Si fabulosa figmenta poetarum, de quibus agas, ad morum finem sunt relata, proculdubio sunt aliquid significantia: numquam enim ad mores hominum fabulas suas poetae referrent, nisi per eas aliquid significarent*".

ture of any language, therefore, is of one kind, whether it speaks out of faith in truth or whether it comes from a series of falsehoods, but they are distinguished by their disparity in signification.[57]

Conrad thus poses the problem and gives a tentative theoretical solution at a level that we would not have expected in such an early era: he expresses a lucid awareness of the identity in literary genre between poetry with moral, albeit pagan, content, and poetry of Christian content, explaining the specific difference between them in the distinct semiotic method adopted by the two subgenres. That is to say, he captures the innovation that I have been trying to bring to light in this chapter. Two centuries afterward, an anonymous reader of the poet Albertinus Mussato, in a *declaratio*[58] on his debate with Giovanni Dominici from Mantua, the Dominican enemy of the humanistic conception of sacred poetry, summed up the problem by dividing poetics into a theoretical science – one that operates when a story is constructed about truth, similar to the constructions used by Jesus in the parables – and a practical poetics, when works or actions are described in verse with another meaning, as was done by

---

[57] Conrad of Hirsau, *Dialogus super auctores*, ed. HUYGENS, pp. 89-91 (*super Sedulium*): "*Magister—Minus hoc intellexisse videris, de quo levi questione moveris. Aliud enim sunt poemata et in his vulgaria proverbia nihil ponderis habentia, utpote quasi sonus levis transeuntia, aliud divina eloquia, quae fundata et aeterna sunt spiritali intelligentia ; et verba, immo literae simplices et nudae, signa quaedam sensus latentis sunt, sed verbo immutabili et aeterno longe dissimilia sunt : putasne, cum caelum et terra transibunt, hesopicae fabulae durabunt ? Verum verba domini non transibunt. Genus quidem unum est in literis quarumcumque linguarum, sive loquantur ad fidem veritatis seu promantur serie falsitatis, sed quadam differentiae specie diversificantur ex inequalitate significationis. (…) Quicquid in homine, licet perfido et impio, veritatis umquam inveniri potuit, eius fuit qui hominem creavit et homini dedit quod homo per se non habuit. Sunt igitur in literatura seculari verborum quidem signa aliquid significantia, sed spiritali intelligentiae minime compendentia nec ad veritatis rationem expressiva. Adtendamus igitur Sedulium in literis ewangelicis sedulum, hominem vernantis periciae, fructum scientiae suae dispertientem ecclesiae. Qui videns suo tempore in disciplinis scolaribus gentilium librorum nenias teri et literas ecclesiasticas prorsus a studentibus negligi, ad communem utilitatem convertens calamum metrice resolvit evangelium, parvulorum primordia sic imbuens, ut infuso veritatis poculo falsitatis amodo non delectarentur absinthio: quicquid enim tenera aetas primis imbiberit annis, artius retinet ad fructum vitae provectioris*".

[58] "*Poetica scientia theorica est, cum quis super veritatem aliquam fabulam fingit, sicut faciebat Dominus noster Iesus Christus in Parabolis. Poetica vero practica est, quum quis dicta vel acta sunt super alia significatione in metro describit, ut illi Arator et Sedulius*" ("Poetics is a theoretical science, when someone creates a story about the truth, as did our Lord Jesus Christ in the parables. On the other hand, poetics is a practical science when someone recounts in metric form discourses or actions with a second meaning, such as Arator and Sedulius"), ed. in: *Il pensiero pedagogico dell'umanesimo*, ed. E. GARIN (Florence, 1958), p. 14.

Arator and Sedulius. Even Giovanni Dominici credits Prudentius and Sedulius as the authors of poems "*sub tegumento sacram exprimentia veritatem*", though the contents of their biblical poems usually do not have *tegumentum*, that is a mythological veil or screen, but narrate the biblical deeds directly.[59] And yet these hints are not enough to valorise the cultural dignity of poetry as a literary genre. Poetry as a genre is *intrinsically* profane and hence foreign to the Christian cultural system. Exegetical poetry therefore represents a problem of theoretical systematisation for the medieval structure of the arts, for the same reason that it represents a problem, usually repressed, for modern literary criticism: the degree of structural innovation absolutely irreducible to the canons and to the rhetorical grids of classical poetry – that is to say, of what was and has been for centuries the only recognised poetic tradition studied and valued in the West. The richness of expressive possibilities which this poetry has given rise to, and which derives from its coexistence with the dimension of

[59] Giovanni Dominici, *Lucula noctis*, X. 89-102, taken up by Boccaccio, *Genealogie deorum gentilium*, XIV, 22, 8-9, ed. V. ZACCARIA, in: *Tutte le opere di Giovanni Boccaccio*, 7, 2 vols. (Milan, 1998), p. 1504: "*Item plures ex nostris poetae fuere qui sub tegminibus fictionum suarum Christianae religionis devotosque sensus commendavere: ut Dantes noster, dato materno sermone, animarum triplicem statum post hanc vitam describit; et illustris Petrarcha in suis Buccolicis, sub velamine pastoralis eloquii, divine Trinitatis laudes irasque in calcantes ignavia Petri naviculam mira descriptione notavit. Hos ultra vigent Prudentii atque Sedulii carmina sub tegumento sacram exprimentia veritatem. Arator quoque sacerdos et Ecclesiae cardo heroico carmine Apostolica gesta cantando more poetico designavit. Iuvencus quidem insuper, Yspanus solo et religione Christianus, sub cortice hominis, leonis, bovis, et aquilae Redemptoris nostri actus omnes etiam fingendo composuit*" ("in the same way many of ours were poets who exposed, under the veil of invented stories, the profound meanings of the Christian religion, as our Dante in his mother tongue describes the triple state of souls after this life, and the illustrious Petrarch in his Bucolic expresses with extraordinary description the praises of the divine Trinity and the wrath against those who trample Peter's ship out of cowardice, under the veil of a pastoral discourse. In addition to these, the poems of Prudentius and Sedulius which expose the sacred Truth under allegory are important. Even the priest Arator, cardinal of the Church, poetically recounted the apostolic deeds in epic yardstick. And then the Hispanic Juvencus, a Christian of homeland and religion, narratively composed all the acts of our Redeemer under the figures of man, lion, ox and eagle"); cf. Giovanni Dominici, *Lucula noctis*, XLV 45, 133-137: "*Si delectat poetas legere (…) propter dulcedinem metri et eloquii venustatem (…) legantur primo Torquatus, buccolicum Petrache Dantisve, Prudentii, Sedulii, Aratoris, Iuvencii*" ("If you like reading poets (...) for the sweetness of the meter and the beauty of style (...) read them first: Torquatus, the Bucolics of Petrarch, Dante, Prudentius, Sedulius, Arator, Juvencus"). He adds Alain de Lille and Peter Riga to these authors, thus associating biblical poets with philosophical poets. [A more recent discussion, which nevertheless overlooks the relevant literature, can be found in A. PIACENTINI, "Riflessioni a partire da un recente libro sulla biblioteca e le Ecloghe di Dante", *Rivista di Studi Danteschi* 15 (2015), pp. 144-165, at pp. 160-165. The book under review is L. GARGAN, *Dante, la sua biblioteca e lo Studio di Bologna* (Rome and Padua, 2014).]

absolute otherness, is a heritage that the Latin Middle Ages shares with other medieval literatures and that is worthwhile recovering both for these reasons and for its role as a precursor to the great European symbolist movement.

Chapter 5

Reticere nefas: The Poetics of Communication in the Carolingian Age[1]

In the 6,843 titles of the precious bibliography compiled by Marco Mostert on communication in the Middle Ages, none addresses Carolingian Latin poetry specifically.[2] And yet, even before the term 'communication' assumed the critical importance in medieval studies that is given to it today, Gustavo Vinay in his famous essay on the Carolingians lucidly individuated in the "revision of the channels of communication"[3] between the élite and peripheral centres of power the principal operation that the court circle had to project: to propose a new "politico-religious programme" one needed to rearticulate with clarity the language necessary for the definition of a common expressive standard.

The restoration of a level of communication that conformed to the necessity of comprehension and execution of biblical, liturgical, juridical, and scholastic texts was – as is known – the watchword around which the entire cultural panorama was being organised. But poetry, too, takes on the reconquest of communication as a myth on which it is possible to found an interpretation of the cultural process in action and at the same time its own legitimisation. The poetic register represents the instrument in which this self-consciousness

---

[1] Translated by Matthew Fox.
[2] M. Mostert, *A Bibliography of Works on Medieval Communication* (Turnhout, 2012: *Utrecht Studies in Medieval Literacy* 2), an extended edition of ID., "A bibliography of works on medieval communication", in: *New Approaches to Medieval Communication*, ed. M. Mostert (Turnhout, 1999: *Utrecht Studies in Medieval Literacy* 1), pp. 193-318, which numbered 1580 items.
[3] G. Vinay, *Alto medioevo: Conversazioni e no* (Naples, 1978), p. 179.

reaches its very apex and the point of greatest technical and social prestige. In this sense, the more than 3,200 pages of surviving Carolingian poetry, which even in their impressiveness are only ruins of a monument of European culture for the most part lost, make up a clear reflection of the myth of written communication, the laboratory for the elaboration of an imaginary of symbols able to communicate at different levels and in different times.

In Carolingian verses, Charlemagne is not only the king who subdued Bavarians and Lombards and who converted the Saxons, nor is he even simply the sovereign Maecenas who protects and solicits and pays poets and intellectuals: Charlemagne is the king who declared war on errors in texts, as the famous poetic *subscriptiones* of the copyists of Saint Gall Winitharius and Jacob recite,[4] but he is above all the king who brought writing where it did not exist before, and with this he gave the word to peoples that did not have it. The Saxon Poet writes about it with pride in the fifth book of the so-called *Annales de gestis Caroli Magni*,[5] where he asks himself to whom, if not to Charles, one should give the merit of the *scintillula* that inspired his *scripturae*, from the moment his Saxon parents not only did not know the teachings of the faith, but were also completely ignorant of letters: this dignity, *honestas*, was given to the Saxons by Charles and through this dignity the hope of an eternal life. In the gift of writing and reading not only is the self-consciousness of the intellectual class expressed, but also an irreplaceable instrument of definitive moral and social redemption is offered. The propagation of writing, which involved in the processes of civilisation peoples still confined to the temporariness of oral expression, becomes one of the points that qualifies the literary image of the emperor, one of the original virtues of his poetic aretologies[6].

---

[4] W. WATTENBACH, *Das Schriftwesen im Mittelalter* (Leipzig, 1896; reprint Graz, 1958), p. 327. Winithar: "*Qui sternit per bella truces fortissimus heros, / Rex Carolus, nulli cordis fulgore secundus, / Non passus sentes mendarum serpere libris, / En, bene correxit studio sublimis in omni*" (MS Vienna, Österreichische Nationalbibliothek 743 (s. VIII), f. 78v), in: *Versus libris saeculi VIII adiectis*, ed. E. DÜMMLER, in: *PLAC* 1, pp. 89-90. The other manuscript, MS Zurich, Zentralbibliothek C 78 (s. IX, or. Saint Gall), presents Iacob's verses on f. 57v: "*Inclitus invictum Christi virtute tropheum / Qui regit, haec fieri Karlus rex namque modestus / mandat ut in seclis rutilet sophisma futuris. / Legit enim famulus stilo anomoque Iacobus*", ed. *ibid.*, pp. 97-98, vv. 17-20. See the translations of these passages in this books companion volume, *Digital Philology and Quantitative Criticism*, p. 43. I am sorry for the partial overlap of the contents.

[5] Written 888-891, ed. P. VON WINTERFELD, in: *PLAC* 4.1, pp. 1-71. See Poeta Saxo, *Le gesta dell'imperatore Carlo Magno*, ed. A. ISOLA (Milan, 1988).

[6] A trace in *Karolus Magnus et Leo papa*; see *De Karolo rege et Leone papa*, ed. L.E. VON PADBERG (Paderborn, 1999) and F. STELLA, "Autore e attribuzioni del '*Karolus Magnus et Leo papa*'", in: *Am Vorabend der Kaiserkrönung: Das Epos "Karolus Magnus et Leo papa" und der*

The Poetry of Writing

1. A first field of exploration, for some aspects already familiar to readers and followers of Wattenbach,[7] is that which we would call the poetry of writing, scripture with a lower-case *s*. The references to the act of writing – in some ways self-referential –, to its support, to the graphic materials, and to the situations of reading and composition pullulate in the entire Carolingian poetic corpus, despite its immensity, as a sign of a very lucid self-consciousness of the author as the agent of a gesture that confers on him a privileged statute and inserts him into a vital circuit in which all the propulsive processes of the Carolingian epoch take place, save that of the military. The occurrences of *codex, liber, libellus, volumen, scriba, scriptio,* and *scriptura, scribere,* and *inscribere, pingere* and *compingere, legere, relegere, perlegere, recitare, lector, sermo, lingua, eloquium, penna* with its variants *pinnula, stilus, calamus,* and *canna, fistula, arundo,* and *avena,* but above all *carta* and *cartula, pagina, litterae* and *litterulae, apex* and *titulus,* not to mention *carmina, versus, versiculi, cantus* and *cantiones,* fill whole tables for those who have undertaken specific research projects on the texts of this period. This is because the Carolingians did not limit themselves to writing poetry on poetry like every epoch has done. In the Carolingian age there is a verifiable and systematic process of poetisation of that which Gérard Genette defined as "thresholds", that is the set of epigraphs, prefaces, dedications, afterwards, invitations to reading, *argumenta*, and comments that accompany the Carolingian text and that this epoch often expresses in verse. In fact, in contrast to what Genette writes,[8] who places the autonomous development of these thresholds after the invention of the printing press, the Carolingian epoch is precisely the one which institutionalises these apparatuses and make of them a privileged place of para-textual communication, to the point of favouring the evolution of new genres. The preface to the Bible generates the *Versus de bibliotheca*, and like-

---

Papstbesuch in Paderborn 799, ed. P. GODMAN, J. JARNUT, and P. JOHANEK (Berlin, 2002), pp. 19-33 (a revised English version in the present volume, pp. 305-337).

[7] Especially Guglielmo Cavallo, who quotes some texts in G. CAVALLO, "Scrivere leggere memorizzare le sacre scritture", in: *Morfologie sociali e culturali in Europa fra tarda antichità e alto medioevo*, 2 vols. (Spoleto, 1998: *Settimane di Studio del Centro Italiano di Studi sull'Alto Medioevo* 45), 2, pp. 987-1008, in particular pp. 994-995 and 1000.

[8] G. GENETTE, *Seuils* (Paris, 1987); trans.: *Soglie: I dintorni del testo* (Turin, 1989). On this subject, see *Digital Philology and Quantitative Criticism*, Chapter Two. Some passages have been repeated in part.

wise the metrical colophon, the dedications, the signatures, and the verses on the *artes*, and the riddles about writing, while the envoy to one's own *carta*, which will be transmitted up to the *dolce stil novo*, takes on the vivacity of a subgenre with its constant factors and its emulative variations.

2. But the Carolingians do more: they emphasise to a mythic level the material, graphic operation, with which the Carolingian intellectual reconquers his centrality.

The impulse comes from far away, from the presuppositions of the Cassiodorean ideology and from Anglo-Latin culture, which acts as incubator for many elements of the Carolingian Renaissance. This is demonstrated by the insular riddles on letters, pen, and ink that all blend in the prospective of writing as instrument for the acquisition of spiritual wealth. Especially in the collection of Lorsch, ascribable perhaps to the ambient of Boniface,[9] the ulterior level is that which founds and justifies even the most banal gestures and instruments: not only is the pen a beautiful girl that cries dark tears, covering white fields with black traces, but this is the track that leads to the shining courts of a heaven that is flowered with stars[10] in the same way in which the ink – that was once wood and thus forest together with water and thus river – announces with its black figures the kingdoms of light together with horrific hell, so that he who reads may know and may avoid it.[11] As in the panegyric of the Saxon Poet, the connection between writing and salvation is that on which from the beginning is founded the supplemental value of the gesture of writing.

3. The trend finds developments again and again in the successive generations. The epigraph, catalogued as number 94 of the poetic corpus of Alcuin,[12] entitled *De scribis* and recorded later in the *scriptorium* of Fulda,[13] invites one not to interfere with frivolous conversations about the act of transcription of a

---

[9] The *Aenigmata Anglica* or *Laureshamensia* are transmitted in MS Vatican, Pal. Lat. 1753 (s. X, or. Lorsch), and are edited by F. GLORIE in: *CCSL* 133 (Turnhout, 1968), pp. 347-358.

[10] Text No. 19 of the anthology *La poesia carolingia*, ed. F. STELLA (Florence, 1995); ed. GLORIE, p. 355.

[11] *La poesia carolingia*, No. 20; ed. GLORIE, p. 358: "*Nascimur albenti loco sed nigrae sorores; / Tres unito simul nos creant ictu parentes. / Multimoda nobis facies et nomina multa, / Meritum que dispar uox et diuersa sonandi. / Numquam sine nostra nos domo detenet ullus,/ Nec una responsum dat sine pari roganti*". A precedent is riddle 30 of the *Appendix Eusebiana*.

[12] Ed. in: *Poetae Latini aevi Carolini* 1, cit., p. 320 (after the editions of Quercetanus and Brower). On the evidence from Fulda, see WATTENBACH, *Schriftwesen*, p. 432; H. KUSCH, *Einführung in das lateinische Mittelalter*, 1, *Dichtung* (Darmstadt, 1957), p. 48.

[13] Vv. 1-6, 11 and 12: see WATTENBACH, *Schriftwesen*. Further literature in: *Clavis des auteurs latins du Moyen Âge: Territoire français 735-987*, 2, *Alcuin*, ed. M.-H. JULLIEN and L. PERELMAN (Turnhout, 1999), p. 417.

holy or patristic book, in order to stop the hand from following the tongue in error. It invites one to procure correct manuscripts, which place the pen of he who flies on the correct path, which scrupulously distinguish *cola* and *commata* and place every single period where it must, so that the "*lector in ecclesia*" might not find himself reading false messages or fall into a sudden silence. The work of the scribe is "important" ("*egregius*"), and it will not be lacking in collecting its compensation. In the end, Alcuin concludes, it is always better than hoeing in the vineyards.[14] But not, as we could think, because hoeing is more difficult, but because caring for the vines is an act that projects before it the horizon of physical satisfaction, the "belly", while the scribe is at the service of the soul. Also in the preface to the Bible given to Charlemagne, probably in the Christmas of 801,[15] Alcuin – initially addressing the "*populorum turba*" that must pray for the emperor – later dedicates several verses to advice for the church reader. He exhorts him to know how to distinguish clearly with his voice the concepts, titles, phrases, and clauses in order to make the intonation resound in his chant and to allow the people to follow along with him. The *lector in ecclesia*, who defines the social horizon present for Alcuin's poetic production, seems to be, then, the supplemental addressee of these poems. The *lector* indicates not so much the illustrious official recipient of the text, nor the generic reader implicit in the composition itself, but – coinciding with the second of the minor orders – a kind of mediator of communication, the performer, material or vocal, of the indications of sense expressed by the text, the drive belt between the writing of the author and the public fruition of its results.

---

[14] Here appears a contrast that in Alcuin is revealed as topical, that between textual commitment and wine: at other times, he regrets having lost his own pupils, who fled the school to pursue the pleasures of alcohol; even in the inscriptions, perhaps for St. Peter in Salzburg, he proposes to the *viator*, who is at the crossroads between tavern and library, the alternative "*aut potare merum aut discere libros, elige quod placeat*" ("drink wine or learn by reading books, choose what you like"), with the malicious addition that to drink one must pay while culture is free: "*gratis quod quaeris habebis*" (Alcuin, *Carmina*, ed. E. DÜMMLER, in: *Poetae Latini aevi Carolini* 1, pp. 169-351, No. 111).

[15] Alcuin, *Carmina*, No. 68, pp. 287-292, and H. QUENTIN, *Biblia sacra iuxta vulgatam versionem*, 1, *Librum Genesis* (Rome, 1926), pp. 44-51; a commentary in STELLA, *La poesia carolingia latina a tema biblico*, pp. 39-54. Similar recommendations can be found in Alcuin, *Epistolae*, ed. E. DÜMMLER, in: *Epistolae Karolini Aevi*, 4, ed. E. DÜMMLER, E. PERELS, *et al.* (Berlin, 1902-1925: *MGH EPP* 4), pp. 18-481, *Ep.* 172.

4. In this vein is song 21, composed by Hrabanus Maurus for Eigil,[16] his predecessor at the abbey of Fulda. It is an epigraph that premises the sylloge of *tituli* composed between 819 and 821 for churches founded by Eigil, and it exalts the material act of transcribing a biblical codex, a humble labour and modest act on the intellectual level, as the most important labor that a man can do. Because writing makes the fingers happy – even if, as we know, the *versus scribarum*[17] often recount a less enthusiastic experience – as well as the eyes. It directs the mind to the profound meanings of the divine words. No human work is immune from the assault of time passing, from the destiny of its senescence: only letters are exempt from the end, push away death, renew time spent. God taught it, when he chose the writing on stone (Exodus 31, 18) to give his people a law that finally conferred to it an identity. What is, what has been, and what will be, letters know and they say it to the world. Only that which is written assumes its degree of reality, only writing is able to restore life to that which has passed. In this kind of dedication Hrabanus expresses the self-consciousness of the ideology that upholds the immense effort of spreading literacy in the Carolingian culture, its method of acquiring control over reality by naming it, the material substance of its propulsive power.

5. Hrabanus takes the subject up again in his other poetic texts as well, such as song 38 for Atto, his successor at Fulda. It is a kind of comparative eulogy in which the prerogatives of writing emerge thanks to a comparison with painting – a comparison that, as we know, is at the centre of the theological and intellectual debate of the epoch.[18] Atto seems to prefer figurative art, but Hrabanus invites him to not underestimate the labour of transcription, because the letter is worth more than a empty image and it confers to the spirit a greater dignity than the painting that represents not the reality of things but their figurative representation. The inexplicit supposition is, that writing possesses a greater degree of reality in virtue of the multiplicity of levels of sense and of the multiplicity of corporal senses involved. Writing is indeed the rule

---

[16] Abbot from 818 to 822. F. RÄDLE, "Eigil", in: *LdM* 3, coll. 1725-1726. Text in *La poesia carolingia*, No. 39, pp. 266-269 and 457.

[17] Just an example: *Carmina Centulensia*, ed. L. TRAUBE, in: *PLAC* 3, pp. 265-368, No. 16, p. 298: "*Scribentis labor ignaris nimium levis extat, / Sed durus sat manet atque gravis*" ("The fatigue of the writer appears very light for those who do not know it, but instead remains hard and heavy").

[18] D. APPLEBY, "Instruction and inspiration through images in the Carolingian period", in: *Word, Image, Number: Communication in the Middle Ages*, ed. J.J. CONTRENI and S. CASCIANI (Florence, 2002), pp. 85-111. Updated literature in *Digital Philology and Quantitative Criticism*, Chapter Two.

of salvation and it is more useful, easier, even more fitting to pleasure, more complete in the communication of the concept, and better able to being preserved in the minds of men since it involves more senses: hearing, the word, vision, while painting gives consolation only to the eyes.

Nam pictura tibi cum omni sit gratior arte,
Scribendi ingrate non spernas posco laborem.
Psallendi nisum, studium curamque legendi,
Plus quia gramma valet quam uana in imagine forma,
5 *Plusque animae decoris praestat quam falsa colorum*
Pictura ostentans rerum non rite figuras.
Nam scriptura pia norma est perfecta salutis,
Et magis in rebus ualet, et magis utilis omni est,
Promptior est gustu, sensu perfectior atque
10 *Sensibus humanis, facilis magis arte tenenda.*
Auribus haec seruit, labris, obtutibus atque,
Illa oculis tantum pauca solamina praestat.
Haec facie uerum monstrat, et famine uerum,
Et sensu uerum, iucunda et tempore multo est,
15 *Illa recens pascit uisum, grauat atque uetusta,*
Deficiet propere ueri et non fide sequestra est.
(...)[19]

In fact, although painting is more pleasing to you than any art, I ask you not to despise the ungrateful effort of writing, the effort to chant, the commitment and care to read, because a single letter is worth more than the empty figure of an image, and gives the soul greater beauty that the false color painting, which does not adequately show the shapes of things.

In fact, writing is the perfect norm of salvation and in reality it has greater value and is more useful than anything, more immediate than taste and more complete in the [spiritual] sense and for the senses of man, and easier in practical implementation: it serves the ears, the lips and the view, while that [painting] offers only a little comfort to the eyes.

This shows the face and the language and the meaning of the truth and is pleasant for a long time, that nourishes just the immediate sight, but as it gets older, it gets heavier, quickly lacks the true and does not transmit faith.

---

[19] Hrabanus Maurus, *Carmina*, ed. E. DÜMMLER, in: *Poetae Latini aevi Carolini* 2, No. 38, pp. 196-197. Revised edition by H. HAEFELE, "*Decerpsi pollice flores*: Aus Hrabans Vermischten Gedichten", in: *Tradition und Wertung: Festschrift Franz Brunhölzl zum 65. Geburtstag*, ed. G. BERNT, F. RÄDLE, and G. SILAGI (Sigmaringen, 1989), pp. 59-74, at pp. 68-71.

From the verses of Hrabanus, as from those of other Carolingian authors, emerges a concept of writing as a multimedia code that today we are no longer able to share but that reveals itself indispensable to understanding this epoch – not only for the *carmina figurata*.[20] The truth of writing is in its appearance, in its sound, in its meaning, and in its duration, while painting would suffer from a kind of perishability and especially a greater degree of distance from the truth and certainty of faith.[21]

6. The mythologising of writing and reading, which is different from the sacralisation and from the metaphorisation of the book documented in part by Curtius, Keller, and others,[22] becomes in this way a permanent cult of the materials and gestures of writing, bibliophilia and bibliomania. In evidence of this are not only the extremely high frequency of terms quoted in the Carolingian corpus, but also the single passages in which this physical attachment is expressed and, I would say, the quasi-dramatisation of the verses themselves. In the famous preface to the Bible of Le Puy,[23] Theodulf exhorts the reader (selected here as an intelligent reader[24]) to a frequent meditation, day and night,

---

[20] See the comments on this text in APPLEBY, "Instruction", pp. 99-100, and D. GANZ, "*Pando quod ignoro*: In search of Carolingian artistic experience", in: *Intellectual Life in the Middle Ages: Essays Presented to Margaret Gibson*, ed. L. SMITH and B. WARD (London, 1992), pp. 25-32. Appleby interprets the text as an expression of the "strict subordination of matter and physical sensation to spirits and intellectual perception": to us it seems instead that the text of Hrabanus exceeds the dichotomy physical-spiritual that we are used to expect in texts of this culture, and emphasises s also the multimediality of alphabetic communication, which involves not only the intellect but also the senses, because it is also voice and sound, one of the manifestations of his superiority.

[21] He adduces then, as is his method, even if with some logical forcing, a historical topic that we find in *De rerum naturis* and which is partly drawn from Isidore (19, 16, 2): in fact, painting was invented by the Egyptians, colouring the silhouettes of shadows, but the meaning of 'Egypt' is "*angustans tribulatio*", that is – he explains himself – vain effort, which in an allegorical sense indicates the lust for greed, while the law of God was carved in stone by letters, and this confirms the superiority of writing over other forms of communication.

[22] E.R. CURTIUS, *Europäische Literatur und lateinisches Mittelalter* (Berne, 1948), pp. 306-352; H. KELLER, "Vom heiligen Buch zur Buchführung: Lebensfunktionen der Schrift im Mittelalter", *Frühmittelalterliche Studien* 26 (1992), pp. 1-31. A precious summary of knowledge in this regard in M.C. FERRARI, *Il "Liber sanctae crucis" di Rabano Mauro: Testo – immagine – contesto* (Berne etc., 1999), pp. 250-262; see also the paragraph in MOSTERT, *A Bibliography*, on the magic of writing (pp. 495-499).

[23] Theodulf of Orléans, *Carmina*, ed. E. DÜMMLER, in: PLAC 1, pp. 445-581, No. 41, pp. 532-538, and H. QUENTIN, *Biblia sacra iuxta vulgatam versionem*, 1, pp. 52-60. Analysis of the text and information about the manuscripts in STELLA, *La poesia carolingia latina a tema biblico*, pp. 54-68.

[24] Verse 246, p. 538: "*lector, cui fulvum mentis acumen inest*".

Reticere nefas: The Poetics of Communication in the Carolingian Age 105

to be enacted by carrying with him and in him, spiritually and physically, the biblical codex: "*hanc gere corde, manu, proprio non desit ab ore, / tuque aliorum actus, corrigat illa tuos*" ("keep it in your heart, in your hand, not far from your mouth and you correct thanks to it the actions of others, it corrects yours"). The concrete proximity must be such that the manuscript be carried even to bed, and the physical engagement, which should not be neglected, of hugging a complete edition of the Bible generates a kind of affective familiarity accompanied and almost confirmed by the participation of the whole body – including the neck, folded arms, and knees: "*Haec in parte thori sedeat, hanc lumina cernant, / hanc colla, hanc genua, hanc brachia curva vehant*" ("It sits in a part of your bed, your eyes see it, your neck, your knees, your bent arms folded"). The codex had to lie at the head of the bed even in the time when even a learned reader gives himself up to snoring ("*solito dum tempore stertis*", v. 225), because as soon as sleep passes, there is the codex that keeps us company in our insomnia. The words of Ivan Illich on Hugh of Saint Victor come to mind: "reading a man-made book is an obstetric operation. Far from being an act of abstraction, reading is an act of incarnation. Reading is a somatic, bodily act of assisting birth, which bears witness to the sense created by all the things encountered by the pilgrim in his voyage through the pages".[25]

For these generations the reconquest of a full capacity of expression and a network of recipients capable of giving meaning and prestige to the activity of text production, it results in a real cult; it gives rise to a lexicon of the imagination, and communication constitutes a field of exercise and constant emulation among the poets of several generations. The metaphor of writing as navigation, already canonised by the prologues of Christian poems, finds favour with scribes of all levels, from anonymous copyists to illustrious intellectuals;[26] the idea of biblical writing, as a forest of meanings shows as multi-faceted, extremely sophisticated variations. The purple of the gospel of Gottschalk[27] associates red with martyrdom (an image that will re-occur in Calderón), the white

---

[25] I. ILLICH, *In the Vineyard of the Text: A Commentary to Hugh's* Didascalion (Chicago, 1993), trans. *Nella vigna del testo: Per una etologia della lettura* (Milan, 1994), p. 130.

[26] Alcuin, *Nauta rudis pelagi*, ed. in: *La poesia carolingia*, No. 37, pp. 266-267 and commentary.

[27] MS Paris, Bibliothèque nationale de France, n.a.l. 1203 (AD 781-783), edited among the *Versus libris saeculi VIII adiectis*, ed. E. DÜMMLER, in: *PLAC* 1, pp. 94-95; cf. B. BRENK, "Schriftlichkeit und Bildlichkeit in der Hofschule Karls d. Gr.", in: *Testo e immagine nell'alto medioevo*, 2 vols. (Spoleto, 1994: *Settimane di Studio del Centro Italiano di Studi sull'Alto Medioevo* 41), 2, pp. 631-691, at pp. 640-647.

blond of the gold letters with the virginity of the blessed, and silver with the life of the married. The *Regula fidei* by Paulinus of Aquileia,[28] in a desire to prepare the reader ("*karissime frater*") for the acerbity of his style, invokes understanding for the spring buds not yet flowered, which hide bunches within them of grapes to grow in their time, but also for the heads of ears of wheat that float in the wind bristling with spikes pungent, remembering to keep in mind not what they do see but the sweetness of the flavours they announce, and that they are obtained only by beating the ears of corn and pressing the grapes with the feet. The repertoire of this poetic allegorisation of writing and text could easily continue, because all Carolingian poetry, and to some extent even the prefaces of prose works, harbours an infinite metaphorical arsenal on this topic that varies and enhances the one transmitted by late antique rhetoric. If the latter, as a consequence of the debate with paganism, was focussed on the problem of expressive levels and the ability to adapt the old style to the new material, after the Merovingian decline the gaze focusses on the appearance of the communicative material and the need for illuminating its spiritual and even theological value. From the first to the second Carolingian generation one perceives indeed a slip from the first to the second point: with the culture of Louis the Pious and Charles the Bald poetry on codices and inks continues to be written, but it becomes a variation of commonplaces, while that on the significant power of the text gradually takes on more and more breath and incisiveness.

7. In this cultural climate, even the preface to a grammatical treatise becomes a field of poetic virtuosity, such as the comment on Donatus, written in the early 800s by the Hispanic Smaragdus before he became abbot of Saint-Mihiel-sur-Meuse.[29] Here one finds a taste, even if an awkward one, for poetic transfiguration of linguistic elements, a taste that exceeds by far the necessity of the occasion. The unusual terms and obsolete genres are compared to the power of rowers, which diminishes with time, like a ship that crosses the seas of grammar, while the participle – which sums up in itself verbal and nominal values – is like a sea that receives rivers from many different valleys, and conjugation is a metaphor of peace and harmony, with all its musical implications, just as the imperative is a knight who holds back a horse and drives the chariot.

---

[28] It is transmitted in MS Paris, Bibliothèque nationale de France, latin 2846 (s. X), MS Vatican, Reg. lat. 192 (s. IX), and MS London, British Library, Harley 3091 (s. X), and edited in D. NORBERG, *L'oeuvre poétique de Paulin d'Aquilée* (Stockholm, 1975), pp. 95-96.

[29] Before the year 809. Smaragdus of Saint-Mihiel, *Liber in partibus Donati*, ed. B. LÖFSTEDT, L. HOLTZ, and A. KIBRE Turnhout, 1986: CCCM 68).

The adverb is the integration of sense that serves the verb and follows it like a servant does his master, like a servant-girl ready to clean the feet of her lady. While the lady, the verb, extends her long arms through immense books, the maidservant tries to satisfy her by following her everywhere or by holding her feet in her lap when she is sitting on the throne.

> *Sic sibimet pariter sensus subplendo ministrant,*
> *Vt pars diuitior sit tribuente pari.*
> 15 *Haec tamen ut domino supplex assecula uerbo*
> *Adiacet, ut famula tergere docta pedes.*
> *Illa sedet solio regali culmine pollens,*
> *Illius in gremio continet ista pedes.*
> *Illa per inmensos extendit brachia libros,*
> 20 *Ista satis faciens currit ubique sequens.*

This potent baroque imagery, in appearance disproportionate to such a technical subject, is not comprehensible if not within a culture that elevates the reconquest of communication to the supreme objective of its civil mission. This verb-lady with immense arms makes the grandiose image of the giant Harthgrepa come to mind, she who in the Danish sagas sung by Saxo Grammaticus in the twelfth century extends her body and leads it back to pleasure, and who represents, in the learned interpretation that is superimposed, the "metaphoric power of Grammar"[30] capable of incessant *amplificationes* and *abbreviationes*: "at will I change my form, adopting now one principal now another: I raise my neck to the stars / and I near the supreme Thunderer obliquely, or I fall / into human form again, detaching my head from heaven / to make it touch the earth. In such a way I easily transform my body / in different shapes and my appearance passes from one mood to another" (from the translation of L. Koch).

I vi 3

> *Nam sequor alternas diverso schemate formas*
> *arbitrio variata meo; nunc sidera cervix*
> *aequat et excelso rapitur vicina Tonanti,*
> *rursus in humanum ruit inclinata vigore,*

---

[30] L. KOCH, "Introduzione" to Sassone Grammatico, *Gesta dei re e degli eroi danesi* (Turin, 1993), p. LVII.

contiguumque polo caput in tellure refigit.
Sic levis in varios transmuto corpora flexus
ambiguis conspecta modis: nunc colligit angens
stricti membra rigor, nunc gratia corporis alti
explicat et summas tribuit contingere nubes

8. In Smaragdus as in the other authors, language – which serves to understand Scripture – is an instrument of pragmatism that allows for the transmission from correct comprehension to correct behaviour, and thus to the happiness that this certainty opens. And that the centre of this idolatry is language as communication, is confirmed by the last preface, regarding precisely interjection, the expression of that which today one calls non-verbal communication. Exclamation cannot be converted into verbal meaning, cannot be translated into *minium* on a page. It carries one to the shining face that it has inside, and there is not a letter than can make it resound. "*Muta sonat reboans et sine voce boans*". And yet, he says, those little signs transmit something of what the heart feels, pacifying or wild, festive or bitter, melancholic or fearful. Here the extra-verbal sign is able to make what was hidden in the soul emerge from matter.

9. The paradoxical capacity of writing to be a vehicle even of non-verbal communication confronts the challenge of the relationship with other artistic languages especially in the infinite series of texts that describe or interpret images, multiple examples of that iconological writing to which the Centro Italiano di Studi sull'Alto Medioevo at Spoleto dedicated a wonderful week in 1993.[31] But this reaches its point of greatest virtuosity in the effort to describe the monastic language of mute communication, which invests song 16 of the versatile Theodulf of Orleans, more attracted – compared to his rival Alcuin – by the hermeneutics of signs than by their material reality, more by the power of stratification of sense than by the taste for personal relation.[32] The exercise,

---

[31] *Testo e immagine nell'Alto medioevo*, 2 vols. (Spoleto, 1994: *Settimane di Studi* 41).

[32] In this group of poems, Theodulf comments in a sophisticated manner the parable of the seed and the fruit of Matthew 13, 8, which, according to current exegesis, referred to the three degrees of fructification of the three orders of Christians, married widows, and virgins (or martyrs), in ascending order of perfection. This explanation generates two different semiotic interpretations of playful register: the second of these relates to the ancient monastic code of 'silent' communication (cf. MOSTERT, *A Bibliography*, p. 138, Nos. 1621-1630), in which to every social order corresponds a sign made with the thumb and forefinger of the left hand: if the two fingers touch each other on the top there is the number 30, and this soft touch represents the sweets kisses of the marital state; the thumb pressed by the curved index indicates 60, the *angor* that oppresses widows like caste doves when they groan. Finally, the joining of the two fingers in the right forms a circle that signifies 100, "*venustatis typus*" ("figure of beauty") which

which we will not take up in detail, seems close to certain enigmatic moments in Theodulf, like the enchanted and mysterious little poem about the battle of the birds, but also and more importantly close to the semiotic obsession that dominates Carolingian poetry and that derives it from the assumption of biblical exegesis as the vertex of intellectual preparation.

The Poetry of Scripture

1. This figural obsession is evident in all its creative potential in biblical poems, that is, those poems that introduce or dedicate editions of the Bible or that paraphrase it and comment on aspects or episodes of it. Theodulf exponentially multiplies the exegetical coefficient of poetry. On the level of the message of redemption, in his *carmen* 41 holy Scripture is at the crossroads of the two Testaments, it is food that satisfies the soul but that generates hunger for justice, a drink that quenches thirst, a trumpet of a terrible sound that beckons the human race to heaven, a light that dispels darkness, a law brighter than the stars and whiter than snow, a wine that cures, an oil that soothes, a river to fish in. All commonplaces that will later be taken advantage of by his imitators. Where Theodulf is innovative, is in the presentation of holy Scripture as potentiality of sense, differentiated according to the preparation of the readers like the food and milk of Pauline memory. For Theodulf this reading is a true hermeneutic conflict ("*proelium*"), a dense forest, "*silva dumosa*", in which the reader opens a way and traces a path by means of trying and retrying, but it is also a daily labour, "*lanae studium*". It is a field to harvest. In his imitator, Paulus Alvarus, a Jew of Cordoba with a disturbing and inelegant geniality, Scripture is a sea of different depths, calm on the surface but rumbling where it is lowest, an aquamarine that purifies, coal that burns through its tropological sense, evergreen emerald,[33] just as in the Bible of Count Vivian for Charles the Bald the New Testament body is followed by the Old Testament shadow, in the footsteps of Saint Paul.[34] One arrives at the highest degree of satisfaction of the imagery when Ingobert, scribe-author of the Bible of San Paolo Fuori-le-Mura, describes Scripture as the voice of the cataract where the abyss screams and

---

indicates saints and virgins, warning to despise the sinister and transient realities and to seek the future goods of the right ones.

[33] *Carmen* 8, ed. L. TRAUBE, in: *PLAC* 3, pp. 131-132. Gems to be referred to the exegesis of Revelations 21, 12 and Exodus 28, 9 f.

[34] *Bibliothecarum et psalteriorum versus*, ed. L. TRAUBE, in: *PLAC* 3, pp. 243-248.

with a fluttering of wings calls another abyss, a place where hope and fear unite and the clement judge is heard with a sure response. Here Ingobert, through the term *abyssus*, crosses Genesis 1, 2, "*et tenebrae super faciem abyssi et spiritus Dei ferebatur super aquas*", with Psalm 41, 8, "*abyssus abyssum invocat in voce cataractarum tuarum*",[35] which in the patristic interpretation referred back to the typological foundation of the relationship between the two Testaments[36].

2. The imagery of different places of the Bible – waterfalls, abysses, and wings – is, in a way, set together in order to produce a new poetic meaning that would represent exactly that ever-renewed power of the mechanism of meaning. Already in Theodulf, in fact, the superiority of holy Scripture compared to pagan texts is not so much due to a greater moral authenticity as much as it is to the plurality of levels of communication: "*quumque has in cunctis vincat, fandi ordine vincit / quod sermone uno multa notanda docet*" (vv. 161-162: "although it is superior in all, it stands out particularly for the levels of enunciation, because in a same discourse it teaches many important contents"). The variety of levels is not only in regard to the habitual bipolarity between letter and spirit, here synthesised by the terms *narratio* and *mysteria*, but to the co-presence of different dimensions of signified realities ("*magna et maiora*", "*vilis actus*" and "*Deus*"), of times as historical succession (*praeteritum* and *futurum*), or of times as moral projection (*acta* and *agenda*, *facta* and *facienda*), grammatical translation of the duplicity between *relatio* and *praedicatio* (v. 170), referent and meaning[37]. We are at a point of exemplary condensation of that hermeneutic behaviour that – as Leonardi wrote[38] – specif

---

[35] "A whirlpool draws the other, roaring over your waterfalls", a cry of nostalgia by Levites away from God and exiled to the sources of the Jordan, where the waves are a symbol of pain. See *Bibliothecarum et psalteriorum versus*, ed. TRAUBE, in: *PLAC* 3, No. 6, pp. 257-259.

[36] Ps.-Hieronymus, *Sermo in Psalmum XLI ad neophitos*, ed. in: *pl* 40, col. 1206C: "*clamemus ad Dominum, et profunda scripturarum ipsius de aliis scripturarum testimoniis interpretemur. Quicquid in abysso Veteris Testamenti non possumus invenire, hoc de absconso Novi Testamenti solvimus in voce catactarum Dei, hoc est Prophetarum ipsius et Apostolorum, omnia excelsa Domini, et fluctus ipsius, et impetus fluminis qui laetificant civitatem Dei, super nos transierunt in Christo*". Similar expressions in Cassiodore, *Expositio in Psalmos*, 41, 8: "*duabus enim abyssis duo testamenta significat, id est novum et vetus, quae se utraque mutua attestatione confirmant*" (ed. in: *PL* 70, col. 304C).

[37] This line is maintained and developed by the imitators of Theodulf: for Angelomus of Luxeuil, for example, this semiological attention exceeds the possibilities of communication of languages: there is no Greek, Hebrew or Latin that could express what the Bible (in this case, Genesis) contains in its lap.

[38] C. LEONARDI, "L'intellettuale nell'Alto medioevo", in: *Il comportamento intellettuale*

ically marks out the Carolingian intellectual and conditions profoundly the poetic creation. This happens even in its expressive structures, as the epenalectic *Collatio* demonstrates where Hrabanus Maurus, in the footsteps of Sedulius, plays on the different exegetical meanings that one hemistich assumes in two successive verses, one linked to the Old Testament and one to the New Testament.

The Invocation of the Reader and the Circle of Communication

1. The propulsive push of this interest in the processes of signification leads biblical poetry outside of its own perimeter to recuperate the implicit communicative instance in every poetic act. This is clearly revealed in the preface written by Paulus Alvarus for the Bible of Leovigildus cited above. In the concluding passage, in fact, Alvarus[39] addresses the reader of "every time", that we later understand to be the reader of posterity, and invites him to remember that he too must die, exactly like – in that time – the author will die. This form, as eccentric as it is in the genre *Versus de bibliotheca*, is understandable if seen in its relationship with the formulary of epitaphs, which often set up the invocation of the reader – or *viator* – with this *memento*, meant to create a kind of familiarity.[40] But Alvarus goes beyond this. He continues by

---

nella società antica (Genua, 1980), pp. 119-139, reprinted in ID., *Medioevo Latino: La cultura dell'Europa cristiana* (Florence, 2004), pp. 3-21.

[39] *Carmen* IX. Text, with translation and commentary, in STELLA, *La poesia carolingia*, pp. 437-439.

[40] See Paulus Alvarus, *Carmina*, No. VIII, *Item lamentum metricum proprium* (transmitted in MS Cordoba, Archicanon (s. X), used in the edion of FLOREZ of 1753, and transcribed in a further Cordovan copy of the s. XVII), ed. L. TRAUBE, in: *PLAC* 3, p. 131 (also in *Corpus Scriptorum Muzarabicorum*, ed. I. GIL (Madrid, 1973)): "*Tu, lector, relegens redde nunc praemia vocis / Et lacrimas domino fundens hec cantu resulta: / "Cunctipotens genitor (...) Albarum solita semper pietate guberna. (...) Ergo, age, rumpe moras et our fine quiesce*". The scheme derives from a kind of adaptation to the locus by the signature of formulas typical of the epitaph: cfr. the self-epitaph of Alcuin, *carmen* 123: "*Hic, rogo, pauxillum ueniens subsiste uiator / Et mea scrutare pectore dicta tuo, / Vt tua deque meis agnoscas fata figuris: / Vertitur o species, ut mea, sicque tua. / Quod nunc es fueram, famosus in orbe, uiator, / Et quod nunc ego sum, tumque futurum eris*"; Theodulf's epitaph for Pope Adrian (Theodulf, *Carmina*, 26, 39 f.): "*Hos apices quicumque legis, te nosce futurum / Hoc quod hic est, omnis hoc caro pergit iter*"; and Walahfrid's Strabo's epitaph for Abbot Wolfhart (Walahfrid Strabo, *Carmina*, ed. E. DÜMMLER, in: *PLAC* 2, pp. 267-423, No. 70, p. 410): "*Hic lector, subsiste parum, lege verba sepulti, / ut tua praecauus fata videre queas. / Es quod eram; quod sum liquido es, mihi crede, futurus*".

inviting the reader – since he too must die – to stop putting it off and not waste more time, to do it immediately so that he might join the author in the beyond and tell him how things are going in the world:

> Alvarus is he who re-echoes in verses / in the long centuries: he returned to dust / from the dust that he was, but his tongue / sounds. You who in some other time / read, reader, our verses, / remember you will be our companion through death; / break, I beg you, the hesitations / of your life, and closed in your tomb / tell us, among the spirits of the dead / how much salvation remains to our dear ones, / and reports the news about / the world, through the obscure places / who is happy and who cries, good or evil or in between, / what plots – now – the world / with cruel ability, / what error threatens the living and what useless / battle renews who denies the true, / what empty honour now digs into the hearts / of kings, and what ephemeral luxuries / certainly entertain them; / because if you squeeze them between your fingers / like rapid water they flee.

150   *Albarus hec metrice longa per secla reboat*
       Et cinis in cinerem uersus - set lingua resonat.
       Tu qui legis nostra quoquum<que> tempore, lector,
       Te recole nobis socium per morte futurum:
       Rumpe moras uite, queso, tumbaque retrusus
155   *Quanta salus nostris maneat narrare sub umbras,*
       Nuntium ut mundi referas, per sedes opacas
       Quis bene quis male quis medie gaudetque gemetque,
       Quid mundus sceua fallens nunc arte refingit,
       Qui maneat uibis herror quantaque rebellis
160   *Hec uera refutans pugna consurgat inhanis,*
       Qualis honorque cauus regia nunc corda deleret,
       Que sint delicias fluxe liquideque caduce
       Que dum stringuntur digitis, ut limfa refugunt.[41]

2. In this way the poet goes beyond the convention that imposed on the genre of the 'Preface to the Scriptures' a generic or 'hidden' author, as is often the case in high medieval literature, and above all required a dialectic reader, always oscillating between the aristocratic or ecclesiastical addressee that had commissioned the manuscript or edition, and that God who always remains the

---

[41] Text, translation, and commentary in STELLA, *La poesia carolingia* (1995), pp. 216-223, 437-439; critical edition in: *Corpus Scriptorum Muzarabicorum*, ed. I. GIL (Madrid, 1973), p. 354.

centre of prayer for every Christian poetic act. With an invention unique in non-epigraphic Carolingian poetry, he addresses himself directly to the ideal reader, outside of time, and he invites the reader to die so that he can renew the dialogue with the author, so that the reader can reactivate the circle of communication with the world that the author has left behind. Death deprived him of the possibility of receiving messages from the world but not of communicating with the reader still living in the world. The poetic text is not an instrument of survival in virtue of its technical merits, or in virtue of the power of poetry, very often exalted in court panegyrics from Exul Hibernicus onwards. It finds its power especially and only in being an instrument of communication between two personal entities, above the social contingencies, whose statute is defined by the act of poetic communication, which thus becomes circular. An analogue invocation can be read, many centuries later, in the verses of Walt Whitman, founder of American poetry (1819-1892): "Camerado, this is no book, / Who touches this touches a man, / (Is it night? are we here together alone?) / It is I you hold and who holds you, / I spring from the pages into your arms – decease calls me forth".

3. What assures the duration of a poetic text is the intervention of the reader who reactivates its communicative potential, thus resuscitating the author for the umpteenth time.

If Alvarus's is an extreme case, the invocation of the reader is, all the same, a resource frequently used in this literature, so much so that on the level of lexical statistics Carolingian poetry is configured as that in which, more than any other, the relationship with a real or ideal addressee is explicit, involving him in his different titles in the circle of communication that the text intends to activate.[42]

A case we can remember is the *planctus* written in 874 by Agius of Corvey for the death of Hatumoda, abbess of Gandersheim,[43] structured as a dialogue

---

[42] The percentages of the recurrence of *lector*, elaborated through *Poetria Nova*, are: Paul the Deacon 3 occurrences (2.86%), Alcuin 35 (8.35%), *Tituli metrici* 15 (20.04%), Angilbert 4 (20.30%), Bernowin 3 (12.71%), Hibernicus Exul 10 (29.41%), Rhabanus Maurus 17 (5.91%), Alvarus 4 (12.40%), Milo 17 (6.04%), Wandalbert of Prüm 7 (6.70%), Cyprian of Cordoba 4 (34.81%), *Carmina bibliothecarum* (11.56%), *Carmina Centulensia* 24 (15.24%), Ubaldus 4 (20.60%), *Carmina librorum suppl.* 4 (31.01%): except for the titles of the Ottonian *tituli librarii* (with low occurrences in an absolute sense but high percentages) no other poet will ever exceed 3% percentage except Petrus Riga, and in very many poets postdating the ninth century the term *lector* will not appear at all. See on that *Digital Philology and Quantitative Criticism*, Chapter Two.

[43] Ed. L. TRAUBE, in: *PLAC* 3, pp. 372-388; P. VON MOOS, *Consolatio: Studien zur mittel-*

between the poet and the sisters of the deceased: an unprecedented dialogic *consolatio* crossed by an authentic current humanism, and masterfully analysed by Von Moos, who begins with a brief preface from the appearance of a narration in medias res (*"Cum praesens ego supremis fortasse fuissem ..."*), which recalls the occasion and explains to repeat here in verse what he had said in that moment crying, to console the nuns satisfying this desire, and only at the end (vv. 17-18) an allocution is revealed to the reader, who is explicitly invited to participate in crying through reading: *"Tu modo me, lector, cum his adverte loquentem / Et te cum our participa gemitu"*.

4. This performatory instance, which requires on the part of the reader a competence of a second-degree communication of the text, no longer from author to reader but from performer to listeners, is dominant, as one might expect, in genres more open to a public use, such as many rhythmic songs and epigraphs. Daniel Jacob, following the suggestions of Paul Zumthor concerning high medieval rhythmic poetry, used the category of the "immediate communicative"[44] in order to surpass, on a linguistico-pragmatic level, the difficulties of definition for texts in which one can neither document orality nor even speak *tout court* of written communication. In connection with the definitions of rhythm that – all the way from Marius Victorinus – spoke of *"motus corporis"*[45] and especially of *"iudicium aurium"*, many elements have been recognised: from the mnemotechnic realisations to the use of rhyme, that would confirm a use and oral diffusion of texts, even in the field of "elaborated orality".[46] The presence of versions put to music, which we are publishing in the *Corpus Rhythmicum musicum*[47] and that regard even rhythmic poems of a scholastic and secular tradition, confirms this hypothesis, as do the numerous *incipit* in *Audite* that recur in the Corpus modelling themselves on Psalm 48, 1,

---

lateinischen Trostliteratur über den Tod und zum Problem der christlichen Trauer, 4 vols. (Munich, 1971-1972), 1, pp. 146-184; STELLA, *La poesia carolingia* (1995), pp. 93, 310-321, 479-481.

[44] D. JACOB, "Poésie rythmique et 'traditions discursives'", in: *Poetry of the Early Medieval Europe: Manuscripts, Language and Music of the Rhythmical Latin texts: III Euroconference for the Digital Edition of the "Corpus Rhythmorum", Munich 2-4 november 2000*, ed. E. D'ANGELO and F. STELLA (Florence, 2003), pp. 267-289, at p. 283. The term was first used by P. KOCH and W. OESTERREICHER, "Langage parlé et langage écrit", in: *Lexikon der Romanistischen Linguistik*, ed. G. HOLTUS *et al.*, 8 vols. (Tübingen, 2001-2005), 1.2, pp. 584-627.

[45] Marius Victorinus, *Ars grammatica*, ed. in: *Grammatici Latini*, ed. H. KEIL, 8 vols. (Leipzig, 1857-1870), 6, p. 41: *"differt autem rhythmus a metro, quod metrum in verbis, rhythmus in modulatione ac motu corporis sit"*.

[46] D. JACOB, "Poésie rythmique", p. 283.

[47] <www.corimu.unisi.it>.

with incessant exhortations to song. In *rhythmus* 42 on the death and resurrection of Christ, written in a monastic milieu[48] for an Easter of the seventh or eighth century and transcribed in two manuscripts of Saint Gall following models from Corbie, it is reminded (str. 22) that "*Ymnorum sonus modulantur clerici / ad aulam*[49] *regis et potentes personae, / procul exclusit saeculares fabulas*" ("Clerics modulate the sounds of hymns in the halls of the king and the powerful; secular fairy tales are excluded"), identifying, then, para-theatrical preparation in a court of the secular aristocracy of a Merovingian or proto-Carolingian epoch and documenting the vein that leads up to the rhythmic version of the *Cena Cipriani* of John the Deacon. Thus the biblical narrative *rhythmi* composed by Paulinus of Aquileia for private masses or solemn occasions, designed openly as substitutes for pagan recitations, or the *epithalamium* of an aristocratic couple from the ninth century (*Laudes dulces fluant*),[50] configure, with a high probability, a public recitation of rhythmic compositions that further transform the relationship with the reader-performer, already present in the work of Alcuin, into a specific module of composition that requires a formulary of its own, recitative schemes absent in quantitative poetry, and a stylistic level that is as non exclusive as possible. I do not know if it is possible, as Jacob hypothesises, to see directly, in this distinction between communicative distance of written expression (even metric) and immediacy of the rhythmic register, the antagonism between "*une culture scolaire – qui, parfois, a l'air de tourner dans l'élitaire et corporatiste – et un besoin d'expression et de communication immédiate et intuitive*".[51] Certainly, rhythmic poetry presupposes a kind of textual transmission that is oral as well, a recited reading and a participatory hearing; from this point of view it represents only the extreme level of a scale of relations between addresser and addressee that in the Carolingian age requires a degree of proximity together with a degree of multi-

---

[48] *Audite omnes canticum mirabile*, ed. in: *Rhythmi syllogae Sangellensis*, ed. K. STRECKER, in: *PLAC* 4.2, pp. 447-613, at pp. 565-569, Strophe 21: "*Xristum laudemus, exultemus odie, / Paschalem diem celebremus plurimi, / Sobria sistant nostraque convivia; / Pauperum cutis contegentes clamida, / Abbati iuncti simul et neophitae*".

[49] *Ibid.*, p. 569. "*convenitis ad aulam*" also in *rhythmus* 85, *Hanc quicumque devoti*, 1, 1 (ed. in: *Rhythmi ex variis codicibus collecti*, ed. K. STRECKER in: *PLAC* 4.2, p. 639) which later (str. 2, 1) is glossed with "*sacris aedibus*".

[50] *Rhythmus* 96 (ed. in: *Rhythmi ex variis codicibus collecti*, ed. K. STRECKER, in: *PLAC* 4.2, pp. 655-656) transmitted in MS Darmstadt, Hessische Landes- und Hochschulbibliothek, 3303 (fragm. Wimpfense s. IX), str. 7: "'*Benedicat Christi manu' et devoti dicite*".

[51] JACOB, "Poésie rythmique", p. 286.

plicity certainly greater than in the modern age, and perhaps also greater than in other medieval epochs.

Relational Poetry

1. The idea that one gets in reading these texts is that the exaltation of writing and the necessity of a continual interactive relationship with the reader do not derive from an extension of the role of the Bible to ordinary situations of daily and poetic communication, but reflect rather a kind of power of relation that the setting up of the channels of communication had conferred on an entire class of cultural operators – not to use the term 'intellectuals' that in this sense is both excessive and limitative. The novelty, in fact, is not only in the acquisition or reacquisition of a competence ever possessed, as comes to light in the passage cited from the Saxon Poet, or one diminished and degraded in time, as the *Admonitio generalis* and in general the emphasis on the scholastic institution both highlight. It is in the sensation of a power that consents an expansion and recognition of each other as the sharing of one's own literary, ideological, and institutional creativity, matured through the sharing of a code of communication. In *The Making of Textual Culture* Martin Irvine entitled a paragraph "Carolingian Renaissance and the Power of *Grammatica*",[52] connecting the Carolingian government's necessity of legislation and of official communication to the increase in grammatical studies and texts. But the political aspect, as important as it may be, is only one part of the problem.

2. The factor of the extension of the Carolingian civilisation, that which will resist the dislocation and the fragmentation of the centres of power, is the multiplication of the contact points in the network of cultural production and communication: episcopal seats, monasteries, noble and imperial courts, secular and parochial schools, private preceptors and palatine academies, public churches and private oratories, civil inscriptions and abbatial signs (in the sense of sign-boards, signages, street signs, etc.), monastic refectories and Easter representations. Differently from how Auerbach perceived the situation, who spoke of a disappearance of the non-professional public from late Antiquity to Humanism, the Carolingian reform is based, instead, substantially on

---

[52] M. IRVINE, *The Making of Textual Culture: "Grammatica" and Literary Theory, 350-1100* (Cambridge, 1994).

Reticere nefas: The Poetics of Communication in the Carolingian Age 117

the creation and the expansion of this network, which will resist until the modern age, that is until the rebirth of an audience that is also literary.

3. The presence of a real addressee, of a concrete commission (it is unimportant if official or implicit), is a factor that redetermines from its bases the entire system of literary communication – poetic communication in particular. In this sense the epistolary typology, even in verse, is no longer only a specific genre that broadens until it becomes, as Godman wrote, a vehicle of intellectual debate[53]. It becomes a kind of universal attitude of all Carolingian poetry. The very model of the epistle, that is, the text addressed to a known and aware addressee and signed by the sender with a salutation, becomes a constant guideline and a generalised interpellation. This impulse toward poetry as communication is born precisely from the necessity of keeping alive the consciousness of the fact that what unites and renders valuable authors and addressees, producers and public, is the possession of a common competence, the sharing of instruments, materials and codes of communication, and above all the certainty of a real reader, an interested and reactive addressee who is also interchangeable with any of the other infinite points in this dense network. It is also a network of human relations and personal passions, in which the need of texts is the need of another. This is evidenced by the cult of friendship that in the Carolingian civilisation accompanies and utilises the homologous cult of writing, and to which some attention has been dedicated. Even a cold intellectual as Florus of Lyon is willing to acknowledge that "*sermo ligat mentes, (...) ut specimen cordis pagina pulchra daret*" ("language unites souls, (...) so that the beautiful page represents the beauty of the heart").[54]

4. In this direction, a kind of overall rotation of the system of literary genres towards interlocution is verified; not only the creation of, but rather the triumph of a true para-textual poetry: prefaces, dedications, invitations, insults, merrymaking, weeping, celebrations, thanksgivings, but also a slipping of the eclogue and of the *planctus* towards a regular dialectic structure, of prayer as a discourse with God, of the lyric as an epistle to a concrete addressee, of the epitaph as a dialogue with the passer-by, and of the very Bible as a place of double flux of communication. In the preface to the Psalter for Gisla, his (spiritual) daughter, Theodulf writes that through the reading-prayer-song of this

---

[53] "An ostensibly medium of intellettual debate" (P. GODMAN, *Poetry of the Carolingian Renaissance* (Oxford, 1985), p. 10).

[54] Florus of Lyon, *Carmina*, ed. E. DÜMMLER, in: *PLAC* 2, pp. 509-566, No. 23, pp. 550-551, to Vulfinus of Orléans, vv. 2 and 27.

book "*ipsa deo loqueris, et deus ipsi tibi*" (v. 18):[55] "you speak to God and God to you", and the same concept is taken up again in the Bible of Vivian.

5. Much evidence of this need and of this feast of poetic communication is offered by the monastic epigraph in verse, of which Alcuin's poetic corpus, that of Hrabanus Maurus, and the *Carmina Centulensia*, but also other minor textual collections, have left us an imposing testimony explored only by the rapid panorama of Bernt.[56] As John Contreni had observed on the basis of literary documentation, and as has been noted recently by John Mitchell on the basis of archeological documentation,[57] a Carolingian monastery presented itself as literally covered with inscriptions, captions, warnings, indications, explanations, and epitaphs in an measure unimaginable for us. And a large part of these inscriptions were in verse, of which the compilations cited have preserved many examples. They concern churches and paintings, cult objects and paraments, garments and sashes, dining and bathing, litters and flywhisks, lanterns and street signs, hospices for the poor and guestrooms for the noble, fruit bowls and pantries, herbaria and lecterns, scriptoria and beds, oratories and dormitories, bell towers and chapels. There is no corner of inhabited space nor a second of daily life – as the famous inscription of Alcuin "*in latrinio*" demonstrates – that escapes the confrontation with writing, that is subtracted from the necessity of finding its authentication in a text that defines its function and essence in the recognised and shared code, the only one able to individuate, together with its visible role, the utility or the meaning it assumes in the spiritual dimension.

6. The true sin of the Carolingian epoch, judging from the poetic evidence, is silence. As the poetic version of the romance of Apollonius of Tyre recites, it too presented in MS Ghent, Centrale Bibliotheek der Rijksuniversiteit, 169, in the form of a dialogue between a *Strabo* and a *Saxo*, "*Est reticere nefas*", "to be silent is a crime", from the moment when we have been given the ability to express ourselves.[58] Silence is a "*torpor gravis*". And even if we are not in possession of the most sophisticated levels of the instruments of communication, we must write and speak. In presenting his poetic version of the *Vita*

---

[55] Theodulf, *Carmina*, 43, pp. 541-542, on the basis of the Sirmond edition.

[56] G. BERNT, *Das lateinische Epigramm im Übergang von der Spätantike zum frühen Mittelalter* (Munich, 1968), pp. 295-305.

[57] J. MITCHELL, "Literacy displayed: The use of the inscriptions at the monastery of San Vincenzo al Volturno in the early ninth century", in: *The Uses of Literacy in Early Medieval Europe*, ed. R. MCKITTERICK (Cambridge, 1990; reprint 1992), pp. 186-225, at p. 192.

[58] *Gesta Apollonii*, ed. E. DÜMMLER, in: *PLAC* 2, pp. 483-506.

Amandi to his master Aiminus, Milo of Saint-Amand leaves behind the cliché of the *affectatio modestiae*, writing that he is not afraid of his own "*rusticitas, quia rusticatio, ut quidam ait, ab altissimo creata est*" ("roughness, because rusticity, as someone says, has been creatd by the Most High"). The "*quidam*", in a purposeful misinterpretation of the Bible, is the author of the Book of Ecclesiasticus.[59] The answer of the enthusiastic and witty Aiminus is that even if "*nemo poeta in patria*", one can still not avoid the obligation of communication: "*noli solus bonum commune possidere velle*" ("do not want to own a common good yourself"). This is the only currency that can multiply itself in use, the only one that, if it is dispersed, grows and gives back what it gave, but it is also the only gift that punishes who hides it and prizes with an eternal payoff he who distributes it to others.[60]

In Alcuin's poetry, and that of all the authors who depend on him, there are only two forces that can induce one to desperation, even within the framework of a Christian humanism: the force of time that passes, that is the consciousness of the irreversibility of a lost season, and the absence of communication. If in song 17 to Paulinus of Aquileia he gives us a brilliant painting of the physical happiness that he acquires in reading a friendly text, "*quo se divertit laetus relegentis ocellus*" ("on which the happy wink of the reader dwells"), and if in 66 he confirms that he likes "*dulces gustare loquelas*" ("enjoy pleasant speeches"), in song 32 to one of his students, perhaps Modoin of Autun, the *reduplicatio* that animates the verse is a sign of a lacerating loss: "*Nunc tua lingua tacet, cur tua lingua tacet?*" ("Now your tongue is silent, why is your tongue silent?"). And the same cry for an answer that is not there is found in song 60, "*carmina cur taceat?*" ("why doesn't he compose poems?"). The scenario of the ruin of poetry on the lost monastery of his youth is represented by the heavy silence, by the absence of the voices of a time. The entire poetic collection of letters between Walahfrid Strabo and Gottschalk the Saxon, like that between Notker and Hartmann, transmits to us the warmth of a message

---

[59] Milo of Saint-Amand, *Vita S. Amandi*, 7, 16, ed. L. TRAUBE, in: *PLAC* 3, pp. 561-609, at p. 566: "*non oderis laboriosa opera et rusticationem creatam ab altissimo*".

[60] *Epistula Milonis levitae ad venerabilem patrem Haiminum Christi sacerdotem directa*, ed. *ibid.*, pp. 566-567: "*(...) Rusticitati autem meae veniam date, necesse est, quia rusticatio, ut quidam ait, ab altissimo creata est. Et quamvis difficilioribus uti potuerim aliquibus in locis verborum ambagibus, ne id facerem sum prohibitus, quia etiam credidi futurum opus istud gratius, si omnium fratrum pateret auditibus. (...) Rescriptum Haimini (...) Novimus siquidem (...) nullum poetam acceptum esse in patria sua (...) Noli tamen, obsecro, ab incoepto desistere; noli desidiae aut inerti otio succumbere; noli gratiam, quae tibi adiacet, negligere; (...) noli, quod gratis accepisti, aliis denegare; noli solus bonum commune possidere velle (...)*".

awaited as a sun that dissipates the clouds of the court fog, the "*nebulae palatinae*", and that warmth arrives to him as rest to a tired man, as mother's milk to a lamb, as rain to arid fields, or as the sun to the window of a prisoner.

7. For this reason a profound sadness is produced from passing a long time without receiving communications from him with whom was shared one's youth and poverty, the fear that – as Aiminus will write to Milo – the hand of a friend would save and hide its riches. Gottschalk, perhaps just at this request, writes a sweet song to ask if he can save himself from that which Paschasius Radbertus called the "*officium linguae*" ("the duty of language").[61] "*O Cur iubes canere*", he implores: "why do you order me to sing?" My condition of exile and privation does not allow me to, as for the Hebrew people in Babylon it was not permitted to sing. But in the end the communicative pressure imposes itself: "*quia vis omnimode, canam*" ("since you want it anyway, I'll sing"). He accepts song, even if he displaces the addressee: he no longer writes to his friend, but for the friend to Christ, who in all Christian poetry acts as the permanent super-addressee of a colloquium that is always between more than two interlocutors.[62]

This impulse to communicate that models every poem in the form of an epistle, will influence in the long term the system of the medieval lyric, which up to Petrarch presents itself as an evolution of an *ars dictandi* penetrated to the root by the function of the addressee and so thought of as a real dialogue among absents, as a compensation for a lack. All medieval poetry will share the belonging to a rhetoric of communication that is generated by concrete social dynamics and that sees in the Carolingian age its founding season, the epoch of textuality elevated to self-purpose and to a degree of value, of writing and reading in the concreteness of their communicative dimension as myths of the imaginary and horizons of consciousness and even of happiness.

The hope is that a poetic civilisation that verified its identity in the will to communicate itself will not find its limits of knowability in the silence of posterity.

---

[61] Paschasius Radbertus, *Ecloga duarum sanctimonialium*, v. 5, ed. L. TRAUBE, in: *PLAC* 3, pp. 45-51, at p. 45.

[62] *Die Gedichte des Gottschalk von Orbais*, ed. M.-L. WEBER (Frankfurt am Main, etc., 1992), pp. 147-151; Latin text with Italian translation and commentay in STELLA, *La poesia carolingia* (1995), pp. 166-171 and 407-411.

Chapter 6

A Lexical Journey through Alcuin's Poetry

Witnesses and Judgements

In all historical reconstructions of Carolingian culture, poetry always occupies the same place: the last one. Since the time of Paul Lehmann[1] it has been repeated that the most solid justification for the definition of the Carolingian Renaissance is none other than poetic production, and yet the most recent overviews of cultural development between the eighth and ninth centuries[2] ignore poetry or assign it only to the residual pages of summaries dedicated above all to theological treatises, historiographical chronicles, rhetorical and grammatical compendia, sermons, hagiographical texts, capitularies, and exegetical sequences. This also seems to be the case when it comes to Alcuin: there are many volumes on the greatest of the Carolingian intellectuals, but none of these is dedicated to his poetry.[3] Not only that: in many of these books[4]

---

[1] P. LEHMANN, "Das Problem der karolingischen Renaissance", in: *I problemi della civiltà carolingia* (Spoleto, 1954: *Settimane di Studio del Centro Italiano di Studi sull'Alto Medioevo* 1), pp. 309-358, reprinted in ID., *Erforschung des Mittelalters: Ausgewählte Abhandlungen und Aufsätze*, 5 vols. (Leipzig and Stuttgart, 1941-1962), 2, pp. 109-138, at p.130.

[2] Just a couple of examples: J. CONTRENI, "Carolingian Renaissance: Education and literary culture", in: *The New Cambridge Medieval History*, 2, *c. 700-c. 900*, ed. R. MCKITTERICK (Cambridge, 1995), pp. 709-757; P. BROWN, *The Rise of Western Christendom: Triumph and Diversity 200-1000 AD* (Malden, MA, etc., 1996).

[3] The dissertation of M.B. GARRISON, *Alcuin's World through his Letters and Verse* (PhD, University of Cambridge, 1995), is unpublished; it can be consulted at Cambridge University Library. The same goes for the thesis of H.-D. BURGHARDT, *Philologische Untersuchungen zu den Gedichten Alkuins* (Diss. Phil. Heidelberg, 1960), which can be consulted in the Bayerische Staatsbibliothek at Munich.

there is not even one chapter that addresses his poetry. The only monograph that made it the main subject of research, Burghardt's thesis, has never been really printed, although it can be consulted in typewritten form in a few libraries. Even the Alcuinian conference in Tours 2004 included only one report on his poetry, out of 28 contributions.

Is this a matter of the limited sensitivity of our era to poetry, and to medieval poetry in general? Or does this marginalisation correspond to the effectively accessory role of poetry in early medieval culture? Certainly, the predominance in medieval studies of the historical and religious paradigm over the literary one has always entailed a prevalent, if not exclusive, attention for writings that more directly and extensively help to reconstruct the historical and historic-cultural overview of an era. It has even led to reading the written witnesses of the Middle Ages with more of a documentary focus than a critical-aesthetic one. But we should ask ourselves why this does not occur for pictorial and architectural witnesses from the same period. In the case of Alcuin, the writer's closeness to the monumental figure of Charlemagne has directed research on his intellectual activity towards the historical and ideological dimension. Many of the books on Alcuin are actually books about Charlemagne. Even excellent volumes on Carolingian poetry are unable to escape this pole of attraction, which acts as a measure of the interest and value of the research, and are consequently conditioned by it.

On the other hand, this *conventio ad excludendum* is shared by the medieval period itself. Not in the sense that Alcuin's poems were not read. As we shall see, individually or in blocks sorted by literary genre, they were read – indeed more often than we think. And not even in the sense that they were not imitated: the Alcuinian model, taken up directly or indirectly, was used in a poetic and an epigraphic context for centuries. Rather, they were undervalued in the sense that they were not mentioned as an important part of his intellectual biography, of his status as Master. Of the dozens of medieval and humanistic *testimonia* gathered by Frobenius and Migne in their edition of Alcuin, almost none of them concern his poems. Alcuin is a "*philosophus, scholasticus, deliciosus Caroli, maximus librarius, sanctissimus e doctissimus magister*" ("philosopher, scholar, favourite of Charlemagne, the greatest librarian, very

---

[4] Even Donald Bullough's recent, masterful posthumous overview (D. BULLOUGH, *Alcuin: Achievement and Reputation: Being Part of the Ford Lectures Delivered in Oxford in Hilary Term 1980* (Leiden and Boston, 2004)), which studies the cultural influence of Alcuin through the examination of the manuscript tradition, completely neglects to treat his poetry, which nonetheless takes up a fifth of the entire inventory of Alcuinian manuscripts preserved.

saintly and learned master"), as well as someone who "*scientia litterarum praepollet*" ("stands out in literary knowledge"), to the extent that in the humanistic age a legend was circulated of an Alcuinian foundation of the University of Paris as the result of a *translatio studiorum* from Athens to Rome and from Rome to Paris; but he is never a poet.[5] Only in the Carolingian era do we find Theodulf, bishop of Orléans and rival of Alcuin, praising him as "*Flaccus nostrorum gloria vatum*" ("Flaccus [nickname for Alcuin], glory of our poets";1, 131 ff.).[6] Moduin, later bishop of Autun, who may have been his pupil, mentions Alcuin's as an example of a successful poetic career, awarded with concrete rewards to which he also aspires.[7] Lupus of Ferrières explicitly quotes a line of his from a moral poem, while Amalarius of Metz and Hariulf of St. Riquier remember his poetic-liturgical creations, such as antiphons and hymns.[8] That is all, as far as we can tell. The fame of the English monk as exegete, rhetorician, grammarian, and theologian remains unchanged over the

---

[5] Helinand, quoted in the *Speculum historiale* of Vincent of Beauvais, chapter XXIII, 173 (no critical edition; see the editions of the *Speculum maius*, of which the *Speculum historiale* forms part, published in Strasbourg, 1473-1476 or Douai, 1624): "*Alchuinus, scientia vitaque praeclarus, qui et sapientiae studium de Roma Parisiis transtulit, quod illuc quondam a Graecia translatum fuerat a Romanis*"; Donato Acciaioli, *Vita Caroli Magni*, ed. W. STROBL (Berlin, 2019): "*Albinum cui postea Alcuino cognomen fuit, eruditissimum summumque philosophum, a quo non solum studium sapientiae, set etiam praecepta oratorio artemque disserendi accepit: cuius opera tunc primum Parrhisiense gymnasium a Carolo institutum tradunt*"; cf. Polydore Vergil, *Historia Anglica*, lib. V (Basel, 1570), p. 106 (which also establishes a parallel with Gorgias of Leontini, who went to Athens as an ambassador just as Alcuin would have come to France bound to Offa); see also John Leland, *Commentarii de scriptoribus Britannicis*, ed. A. HALL (Oxford, 1709) 88: "*haec fuit Academia Parisiorum origo*"; John Bale, *Scriptorum illustrium maioris Brytanniae catalogus*, 2 vols. (Basel, 1557-1559), 2, which repeats the parallel with Gorgias. For references to these texts, see MIGNE, *PL* 100, cols. 121B ff., *De beato Alcuino Caroli Magni praeceptore Testimonia veterum et quorundam recentiorum scriptorum*.

[6] Theodulf of Orléans, *Carmina*, ed. E. DÜMMLER, in: *PLAC* 1, pp. 445-581, No. 1, vv. 131 ff., p. 486: "*Qui potis est lyrico multa boare pede, / Quique sophista potest est, quique poeta melodus, / Quique potens sensu, quique potens opera est*".

[7] Modoin, *Ecloga* I, vv. 87-88, ed. E. DÜMMLER, in: *PLAC* 1, pp. 384-391, at p. 387: "*Ni Flaccus calamo modulari carmina nosset, / non tot praesentis tenuisset praemia vitae*". Cfr. A. EBENBAUER, "Nasos Ekloge", *Mittellateinisches Jahrbuch* 11 (1976), pp. 13-27, and R. GREEN, "Modoin's Eclogues and the Paderborn Epic", *Mittellateinisches Jahrbuch* 16 (1981), pp. 43-53, together with my commentary in *La poesia carolingia latina*, ed. F. STELLA (Florence, 1995), pp. 386-390.

[8] Hariulfus Alenburgensis, *Chronicon Centulense*, ed. in: *PL* 174, col. 1249B: "*Antiphonas quoque et responsoria vel hymnos de eodem sancto composuit, ut magni patris festivitas nihil minus congrui officii habere videretur. Ubi notandum est, quod quodam in hymno ipsum sanctum Richarium laudando alloquens dicit: 'Tu struxisti coenobium / in loco prope Argubium / et aliud in Centulo / ambo perenni merito'*".

centuries, but his poetic works are not mentioned, not even by the *Vita Alcuini* – and in the twelfth century Thiofrid of Echternach, as Michele Ferrari has shown, recalls Alcuin's poetic hagiography only to criticise its metrical quality.[9] It is not until Johannes Trithemius (1462-1516) that Alcuin is called "*carmine excellens et prosa*" ("excellent both in poetry and prose"), and only in the *Scriptores Britannici* of the English theologian John Bale (1557-1559) does the list of his work include a "*Carminum ad diversos liber unus*". The *Patrologia Latina* records many Alcuinian quotations, which reach their peak with the 1100 instances of Alcuin in Peter Lombard's *Commentarius in Psalmos*; but none of these seems to concern his poetic work.

It is clear that Alcuin's fame as a theologian and rhetorician ended up overshadowing his poetic production and building up a canon of values that has conditioned studies until today. But it is undeniable that the Middle Ages, as we know, had a conception of poetry as a noble and highly expressive form that lacked practical authority. It was valorised only by its content, only ever important as a vehicle of information that was nonetheless less about the author than the educational utility of the subject matter.

Yet, in the handbook of medieval Latin literature released in Italy under Claudio Leonardi's direction, Michael Lapidge, after listing Alcuin's treatises, exegetical studies, and hagiographic works, writes:[10] "all these texts certainly guarantee Alcuin a prestigious place in the history of Western pedagogy, but this author would like to draw the contemporary reader's attention to him as a poet". He further adds, "Alcuin's poems speak to us directly across the centuries and it is not incorrect to consider them perhaps the greatest literary work of the Carolingian renaissance".[11] Other scholars, from Raby and Waddell to Peter Godman, had occasionally extolled the interest and value of Alcuinian poetry,[12] and the role of founder that Alcuin played also as a poet. But this

---

[9] M.C. FERRARI, "'Dum profluit est lutulentus': Thiofrido, Alcuino e la metrica della 'Vita S. Willibrordi'", in: *Gli umanesimi medievali: Atti del II Congresso dell' 'Internationales Mittellateinerkomitee', Firenze, Certosa del Galluzzo, 11-15 settembre 1993*, ed. C. LEONARDI (Florence, 1998), pp. 129-140.

[10] M. LAPIDGE , "Il secolo VIII", in: *Letteratura latina medievale*, ed. C. LEONARDI (Florence, 2003; reprinted 2004), pp. 41-73, at p. 66.

[11] *Ibid.*, p. 70.

[12] F.J.E. RABY, *A History of Christian Latin Poetry* (Oxford, 1924), p. 162: 'On the whole, Alcuin was a mediocre poet. His real talent lay elsewhere'; G. VINAY, *Alto Medioevo Latino: Conversazioni e no* (Naples, 1978), pp. 252-253 (about the *Conflictus*): "Sentiment is not specified by place or time and can be expressed through allusions, but in the Carolingian age even sentiment is a risk, and Alcuin must resort to too many things, from winter to spring to the

judgment by Lapidge, so clear and absolute, refutes a long marginalisation and warrants explanation. Essentially, it tells us that Alcuin's poetry can be considered a manifestation at the highest level of an activity that many have declared non-existent, in its pure state, in the Middle Ages: literature.

cuckoo, to speak at once of a simple affection and of an overly complex existential situation, and he becomes generic: in this way, too, his limitation is typical"; and p. 253: "The poet of the first, according to experts, is in any case not Alcuin, a good-natured amateur, but Theodulf ...". S. VIARRE, "Les Carmina d'Alcuin et la réception de la tradition chrétienne dans les formes antiques", in: *Lateinische Kultur im VIII. Jahrhundert*, (St. Ottilien, 1989), pp. 217-241: "Alcuin is not a genuine inspired poet". She remarks "on the one hand a composition teeming with plays on words and their rhythms, on the other an extremely sophisticated practice of mixing genres". According to Viarre, Alcuin accentuates the repetitions of words and simplifies procedures when dealing with texts that form groups and whose cohesion he wishes to highlight. His style is defined as "*figé*" (p. 240). His poetry is a poetry of communication. He writes with the simplicity of a kind of spiritual advisor, but also, clearly, with real pleasure. Intellectual, psychological, and poetic coherence: aesthetics of the sets. On p. 237 Viarre comments on Alcuin's search for an original poetic expression by the mixing, to different degrees, of classical tools and reminiscences with references to the Psalms, long compound words, renewed images, very pronounced alliterations: "a new harmony (...) searching for a discrete and coherent expression" (p. 240). D. SCHALLER, "Alkuin", in: *Die deutsche Literatur des Mittelalters: Verfasserlexikon*, 2nd edn., ed. K. RUH *et al.*, 1- (Berlin and New York,1977-), 1, cols. 241-243, *at* cols. 241-242, rightly remarks: "*Alkuins poetisches Oeuvre ist das umfänglichste erhaltene der karolingischen Literatur und wird nach seinem geistigen Rang nur von dem Theodulfs übertroffen*"; P. GODMAN, *Poetry of the Carolingian Renaissance* (London, 1985), pp. 16-22, and p. 6: "one of the most versatile and influential of early Carolingian poetry". M. GARRISON, "Alcuin, 'Carmen IX' and Hrabanus, 'Ad Bonosum': A teacher and his pupil write consolation", in: *Poetry and Philosophy in the Middle Ages: A Festschrift for Peter Dronke*, ed. J. MARENBON (Leiden, Boston, and Cologne, 2001), pp. 63-78, at pp. 65-66: "Latin verse was the privileged koiné of this new world. To be able to address a friend or potential patron in classical quantitative feet displayed the formal mastery of the *trivium*. At the same time, verse was also the medium where the personal met the political – the appropriate form for expressions of panegyric, friendship, flattery and consolation, and occasionally satire and homesickness. It is easy enough to lose sight of the remarkable novelty and suddenness of the Carolingian cultivation of quantitative metre. In the middle of the eighth century, it appeared that no one at the papal court had been capable of composing quantitative verse". She highlights that the climax of the first volume of *Poetae* is an outpouring of Franks and Saxons – the first cohort of whom was familiar with Alcuin or studied with him. "Thus here too Alcuin stands as the head of a tradition but one that has been maligned as monotonously conformist. A by-way rather than a highroad of cultural history? [footnote 19 at p. 67:] Hence perhaps the demise of larger Alcuin-poetic collections after the tenth century, when memory of Alcuin was faded".

The Editions

Modern printed editions propose a varying number of poems, for the most part short, under Alcuin's name; in the most recent edition, published in 1881 by Ernst Dümmler in the *Poetae Latini aevi Carolini* of the *Monumenta Germaniae Historica*, the total reaches 124 pieces. Many of them, especially those concerning inscriptions, are composed of multiple units aggregated according to where they were composed or published. We can say that the individual poetic components number over 300, varying widely by genre and type. The first publication in print was edited by André Du Chesne (Duchesne), Latinised as Andrea Quercetanus, in 1617, and included 272 poems, almost all drawn from a Saint-Bertin manuscript – now lost but certainly old, perhaps from the ninth century, and probably transcribed in an abbey connected to Alcuin's school, such as Tours or Salzburg. There are a few additions from texts that Quercetanus drew from editions of other authors and that he attributed to Alcuin. Two centuries and a half later, in 1777, Frobenius Forster published an edition of 283 poems based on Quercetanus's edition, only partially accepting his selections and modifying them both by moving texts and sections of text and with deletions and additions, drawn from a Regensburg manuscript that originally came from Salzburg, dating from the ninth century and now lost. This edition was taken up again, with some modifications, in Migne's *Patrologia Latina*, vol. 101. The Dümmler edition, strongly criticised by Traube[13] and Burghardt, added new texts from many other manuscripts and incorporated groups of poems according to thematic criteria, reducing the total number, as already mentioned, to 124. From then on the attribution of several texts changed, and Burghardt's thesis proposes a further organisation of the corpus into about 30 groups, but this hypothesis has not led to a new edition and remains only theoretical.[14] The fact remains that in 2020 we can read the larger, albeit incomplete, corpus of poems by Alcuin only in an edition from 139 years ago; though certainly a commendable work, it is based on a partial and now surpassed list of manuscripts, and weakened by the presence of inauthentic

---

[13] L. TRAUBE, *Karolingische Dichtungen* (Berlin, 1888).
[14] The *Clavis des auteurs latins du Moyen Âge*, 2, *Alcuin,* ed. M.-H. JULLIEN and L. PERELMAN (Turnhout, 1999), provides accurate information on the critical situation of each individual text, with a bibliography updated to 1998 and indication of unknown manuscripts, drawn from the register of the Institut de Recherche et d'Historie des Textes (IRHT) in Paris, also searchable on the database *In principio* (access through <http://apps.brepolis.net/BrepolisPortal/default.aspx>).

texts and groupings that are not always reliable. It should also be added, however, that individual texts, such as the poem on the Church of York or the eclogues, can be read in recent, well annotated editions, and it is better to avoid the risks of a monolithic consideration of the author rather than the text. The criticism of the late twentieth century should eventually have become accustomed to taking the texts into consideration, rather than authors in bulk. And this was exactly what was done in the Middle Ages. Of the approximately 45 manuscripts mentioned in the Dümmler edition, not one transmits Alcuin's complete poetic corpus, but only individual texts or blocks of text that are usually homogenous or similar for their theme, destination, geographical location, or another reason. Almost complete collections, perhaps derived from an author's copy, were those handed down in the manuscripts of Saint-Bertin[15] and Salzburg, used by Du Chesne and Frobenius and later lost. Here we cannot carry out a review just of the main Alcuinian codices, for which see the essay published by Dümmler in the *Neues Archiv*,[16] but it can be said that most of the poems were witnessed in unique manuscripts or in traditions limited to four or five codices. The exceptions are the *Praecepta*, a collection of moral teachings expressed in single lines (monostichs) that are proverbial in nature, which Dümmler published based on ten manuscripts and a *pro manuscripto* print, to which we can now add another six; the *Conflictus veris et hiemis*, which Dümmler based on fifteen manuscripts but for which at least another 45 were later indicated; the prefaces to exegetical commentaries or rhetorical-grammatical handbooks, which naturally follow the tradition of the treatises, and for which today we are usually aware of many more manuscripts than those known to Dümmler;[17] Alcuin's epitaph, if it is to be considered a self-epitaph, is transmitted by at least eleven codices, of which only six were known to Dümmler,

---

[15] This was an anthology of proto-Carolingian poetry that also included poetry by Aldhelm, Bede, Paul the Deacon, Fardulf, Angilbert, Laurentius Scotus, and anonymous texts from the eighth century.

[16] E. DÜMMLER, "Die handschriftliche Überlieferung der lateinischen Dichtungen aus der Zeit der Karolinger", *Neues Archiv* 5 (1879), pp. 89-159, at pp. 118-139.

[17] In his edition of the first part of the preface to the homilies commentary *Fulmina qui metuat* Dümmler uses, beside Quercetanus's print, also two manuscripts (MS Valenciennes, Bibliothèque Municipale 149, and MS Munich, Bayerische Staatsbibliothek Clm. 14478), while F.S. D'IMPERIO, in her doctoral dissertation *Alcuino di York, Expositio in Ecclesiasten: Studio della tradizione manoscritta* (Florence, 2004), signals six more manuscripts (MS Douai, Bibliothèque Municipale 302, MS Paris, Bibliothèque Sainte-Geneviève 80, MS Kremsmünster, Stiftsbibliothek 14614, MSS Göttweig, Stiftsbibliothek 429 and 430, and MS Munich, Bayerische Staatsbibliothek Clm.14614).

and the sequence for Saint Michael, of uncertain authorship, also present in several hymnals and reported in seven codices that are new with respect to MS Trier, Stadtbibliothek 1285, with neumes, the only used by Dümmler.

Despite being unable to carry out precise calculations, if we include the poetic dedications and the prefaces to books in prose, all these indications of new witnesses in the repertories of recent decades make the number of manuscripts that hand down Alcuin's poetry total more than 140. When we consider that the total number of Alcuin's manuscripts of Bullough's census comes to 500, we understand that Alcuin's poetry experienced, especially in some of his texts, an extremely significant transmission, especially in the central medieval period – that is, until the eleventh century – only to then disappear in the age of the universities and later to reappear in the humanistic age. Of course, there were probably few codices that handed down his entire corpus, perhaps two or three, and they are now lost; all the others are presented not as editions of Alcuin's work but as collections of epigraphs, of exegetic texts with metrical prefaces, of Bibles with poetic dedications, of letters with greetings in verse, of Anglo-Latin or Carolingian anthologies that contained, among other things, *also* poems by Alcuin. But this does not mean that in the Middle Ages Alcuin's poetry was not read, only that Alcuin was not read out of interest in the biographical and intellectual personality of the author – a concept that moreover was unknown at this time, as Zumthor and others have shown. Alcuin was read, among others due to the contribution that he had made to diverse thematic and formal literary spheres, to moral and theological questions, such as the model for dedicatory poetry or the collection of proverbial verse, the invention of the poetic *tenso* and riddles. But he was read. And not only would it be a glaring historical error, contradicted by 140 manuscripts, to support the idea that Alcuin's poetry was not known, but it is also probably a cultural error to think in general terms about poetry (or prose) by an author rather than in terms, more viable historically and formally speaking, of individual texts or groups of poetic texts. This is obviously not an attribution of literary value: there is no sense in judging the value of a work by the number of copies read. This did not make sense in the medieval period just as it never has in the modern and certainly not in the contemporary one. Today, however, as Lapidge says, it is precisely Alcuin's poems, perhaps even those least transcribed and read in the Middle Ages, which can help us to grasp better his personality as a writer and his creativeness.

The same can be said, although it is more difficult to demonstrate, for the imitations, revivals, and variations attested not by manuscripts but by intertextual relationships. A master's poetry lives above all in its imitations, revivals, and in reworkings by pupils and readers. In this sense it is important to recognise that much of Hrabanus Maurus's poetry, from the *carmina figurata* to the epigrams and the hymns, hinges on Alcuin's, especially in the genres structured as book and monastic epigraphs. This kind of affinity is clearly felt also in the poetic collections of Saint-Riquier; likewise, the *Streitgedicht* rediscovered by Alcuin would be revived by Sedulius Scotus, just as the poetic epistolary formulae, initial and final greetings, and signature would be taken up by all the continuators of the genre. The same is true for the epitaph, also thanks to the fact that the best Alcuinian examples, the epitaph for Pope Hadrian and the one for Alcuin himself, would remain publicly displayed for centuries, and still are, in Rome and Verona (in its reworking by Pacificus). For subgenres such as the prefaces to bibles or biblical commentaries, his influence even became structural: in this area the Alcuinian formulations are, to use a term from *Formgeschichte, traditionbildend*. But in general those of us who are working on the features of the medieval Latin poetic style stumble every day on authors – from Florus of Lyon to Audradus of Sens, from Micon of Saint-Riquier to Thiofrid of Echternach to Ottonian poetic hagiographers – who at least until the twelfth century took up phrases or clausulae invented or recreated by Alcuin.

Tradition and Innovation in Poetical Genres and Themes: A Lexical Journey

The Historical-Hagiographical Poem: Regnum *and* pietas

What kind of poetry are Alcuin's poems? My research has led me to focus on several specific genres, such as biblical poetry, lyrical poetry, and epigraphic poetry, but the organisers of the Saint Gall conference of 2004 had asked me to prepare a general presentation of Alcuinian poetry, and so I will try to summarise the general trends, which will unavoidably remain rather generic. We will be guided by an exploration of the main genres under discussion, along with the key words that emerged from a statistical analysis I conducted on the lexicon of Alcuinian poetry.

We shall begin with *rex* and *pius*, which regard one of the first poetic texts by Alcuin. When he was still in England, probably between 780 and 782[18] or even before,[19] he wrote a poem of 1657 hexameters. It was entitled *Versus de patribus regibus et sanctis Euboricensis ecclesiae* by its editors on the basis of the final lines,[20] which Alcuin added in a second phase, while the declaration of intentions in the protasis, after the invocation of the religious muses, speaks of "*laudes patriae*" ("praise of the homeland"; 16), and "*veteres cunae praeclarae Euboricae urbis*" ("ancient cradles of the illustrious town of York; 17): these actually concern, before the Church of York, the history of the English people and church (1-1214), and only in the last 447 lines that of York, making them the subject of an ecclesiastical epos that is also the historical portrait of a country. A debt of *pietas* towards the place of his own educational formation, which was also one of the symbolic places for the formation of early medieval England: a historical novel in verse that ends as an autobiographical one,[21] a gallery of characters that ends with, after his master Aelbert, the writer himself, who was Aelbert's successor at the school of York. Alcuin progressed with the history of the Church of York in a way parallel to what Paul the Deacon, or someone on his behalf, was doing in those years with the *Gesta episcoporum Mettensium*, a second example of an ecclesiastical epos in verse, and thus launched an attempt that was somehow lucky enough to produce the necessary innovations for giving the Christian Middle Ages an epic that was not the scholastic, sterile one of political panegyric, attempted for example by Hibernicus Exul or by *Karolus Magnus et Leo papa*. Alcuin instinctively produced, inspired by elements of Anglo-Latin poetry and historiography, an operation with a high awareness of the relationship between literary forms and the demands of social communication. But his poem reveals a political understanding much more complex than Paul the Deacon's. The predominant terms here are *regnum* and *rex*,[22] in reference both to the various Anglo-Saxon kings and to the God

---

[18] But it was thought that the final part (ll. 1596-1657) was composed during his second stay in England (790-793). The text was transmitted by two codices from Reims, now lost, and by a copy from the seventeenth century kept in Cambridge (MS Cambridge, Trinity College, O.2.26).

[19] According to D. BULLOUGH, "Hagiography as patriotism: Alcuin's 'York Poem' and early Northumbrian vitae sanctorum" in: *Hagiographie, cultures et sociétés IVe-XIIe siècles* (Paris, 1981), pp. 339-359, it should be dated to the end of the 770s, with later changes.

[20] Vv. 1653-1654: "*Haec idcirco cui propriis de patribus atque / Regibus et sanctis ruralia carmina scripsi*".

[21] Vv. 1601-1602: "*Ergo fuit quidam iuvenis nutritus in urbe / Euborica*".

[22] With 22 occurrences it is, after *pius* (25), the most frequent meaningful (i.e. not 'empty') term in the poem.

who was the model for their government, along with *pius*, the qualification of the saintly bishop or saintly king. The poem on York is therefore Christian history in the sense that his model, Bede, uses:[23] a history of saintly men in connection with power, and a history of powers, supported by their even thaumaturgical sanctity, which follow each other in connection with the Church.[24] The narrative scheme, which follows in parallel the succession of political and ecclesiastical power and then describes the relationship between the two, sees its model of perfection in the two brothers Egbert and Aelbert, one a bishop and the other a king, "*fortis hic, ille pius*" (1281), who, both powerful, "*rex et praesul concordi iure regebant*" ("the king and the prelate ruled in agreement 1277). In this scheme we can already glimpse the embryo of the Carolingian ideology of which Alcuin would be the main developer. The gallery of personalities ends with the panegyric and enthusiastic portrait of his own master Aelbert, of his teaching programme, and of the library of York that he, dying, entrusted to Alcuin and, in a seemingly minor episode, the prophetic visions of one of his schoolmates and one of his pupils. It therefore ends, between books and fellow students, in the celebration of the scholastic environment and the didactic research activity that would inspire Alcuin's best verse until his final days, revealing the intimately and openly autobiographical nature of the Alcuinian poetic gesture. The poem therefore contains all the source nuclei of Alcuin's poetry, and demonstrates awareness of them through the recurring call to his muse, *Thalia*, his poetic flute (*fistula*), and his youth in York, and each call introduces and illustrates changes in subject or editing of topics or compositional criteria that reveal a very mindful, although still imperfect, awareness of the need for a balance between content and form: the peaks of this self-awareness are the passage dedicated to epicising his own source, namely the venerable Bede (ll. 1287-1317), and the one in which Alcuin names himself as Aelberth's assistant, his successor and heir to the library, and as witness of the last two episodes. Alcuin's poetry was therefore born mature, and not even at a formal and expressive level can we glimpse qualities that would be refined in later texts, although this stability suggests that Alcuin polished and corrected his youthful text in his final years.

---

[23] Following, in order of frequency, are *corpore* (21), *meritis* (21), *tempore* (20) (*tempora* (11)), *statim* and *nunc* (19), *subito* (18), *salutis* and *annis* (17), *semper* (16), *praesul* (16), *Christi* (15), and, among others, *magister* (11).

[24] The interrelation of the Church and the king began with Gregory's mission, but developed internally especially with Bishop Wilfrid (vv. 577 ff.), in connection with King Ecgfrith.

To us classicists and moderns, accustomed to unified epics and more loyal to Vergil than to Ovid, this could seem like an effort that is well-crafted but lacking in inspiration or potentiality. There is no heroic figure or precise event on which to build the narration, such as the life of Saint Cuthbert, already successfully told by Bede. It is true that the histories of the good King Oswald and the good King Ecgfrith take up hundreds of lines, that women also have an eminent representative in the virgin queen Æthelthryth (Adaltrude), and also that the necessary figure of evil is briefly represented by the enemy pagan King Penda, who opposes Oswi. Nor does it lack a great vision of the afterlife like that of Dryhthelm, which takes up the middle of the poem (ll. 876-1007). But compared to the main model, Bede's *Historia ecclesiastica*, Alcuin finds neither a superior unity nor the spiritual dimension that poetry could guarantee, nor the epic passage of an authentically Vergilian way of writing, driven by an openly informative *intentio*: this is shown by the fact that when he describes the figure of Æthelthryth, who could have the charm needed to shape a great character, he stops, remembering that she has already been celebrated in one of Bede's hymns, to which there is no point in adding another.[25] Too tied to a diligent annalistic demand, he does not have the courage to focus on more evocative scenarios, such as the missions of Scotland or Friesland might have been, or on figures such as the two martyrs with the name same, Ewald, different in hair colour, one white and the other black (1045), but united by death; nor to develop the more disturbing settings, such as the magic, otherworldly ones of the history of Imma, which would lead to the success of the Arthurian romances based on the same ground. Thus the poem on the Church of York remain, above all, the hagiography of a people and a place, that of Alcuin's youth and first school,[26] but it is precisely through this that they represent a brilliant intuition. The poem on York establishes the new real medieval epos, the hagiographical one, the transformation of the personal panegyric into the institutional panegyric, which far exceeds its explicitly didactic, utilitarian intentions[27] and produces, as Godman wrote, "the first major narrative poem on

---

[25] However, there is a new figure in Bosa, a bishop who organised an important ecclesiastical reform, for whom Alcuin provides information and evaluations that far exceed the few words dedicated to the character by Bede (*Historia Ecclesiastica Gentis Anglorum*, IV. 12 and 23; V. 3, ed. B. COLGRAVE and R.A.B. MYNORS (Oxford, 1969), pp. 370, 408, 460).

[26] Even before that of York a school appeared upon the death of Wilfrid, mourned by the "*discipuli socii*" (v. 620).

[27] Cf. vv. 786 ("*aestimo quod multis prodesse legentibus ista*") and 877 ("*proderit aeterna multis*").

a historical subject in the extant Latin literature of the medieval West".[28] At the same time, it also demonstrates the maturation of all the driving centres of Alcuin's intellectual activity, namely the parallel relationship between civil and ecclesiastical power, the centrality of the scholastic setting in his creative universe, his fierce love of books and studying and, poetically speaking, the high rate of personalisation of his writing, and the projection into the past of ideal perfections that are no longer attainable. The work nonetheless remained little known, because a good part of the information that it provided was already found in Bede's widely circulated *Historia ecclesiastica*, and also because, Alcuin not having yet entered Charles's court, its tradition was likely limited to England.

The structural link between history and autobiography is found in the other poem dedicated to a monastery, the elegy of 240 lines, in couplets, sent by Alcuin to the abbot of the English monastery of Lindisfarne, destroyed by the Danes in 793. He structured it as a lament on the transience of things – that is, on an extratemporal and spiritual level that allows the acceptance of the feeling of a tragedy, as the destruction of the monastery must have been, framing it within the sphere of a divine setting. The poem, whose transmission is now limited to two manuscripts from Reims,[29] is parallel to the letters than Alcuin wrote, commenting on the same event, to Abbot Higbald. However, while the letters focus on practical problems and concrete solutions, the poem draws inspiration from the tragedy to identify a reason for it, and draws its beauty precisely from the contradiction that would always be peculiar to Alcuin: the contrast between the strong sensitivity to the beauty of things and of times that are lost, and the awareness that they are destined to be lost and that it is in fact right that they are lost, because they are things and times limited by their earthly nature and therefore inferior to heavenly goods.

Qui iacet in lecto quondam certabat in arvis/cum cervis, quoniam fessa senectus adest. / (...) / Longa dies oculos atra caligine claudit / solivagos athomos quae numerare solet. / Dextera quae gladios, quae fortia tela vibrabat / nunc tremit

---

[28] Ed. in: *The Bishops, Kings and Saints of York*, ed. P. GODMAN (Oxford, 1982), p. LXXXVIII. A far-reaching analysis of Alcuin's contribution to the history of literary genres in W. KIRSCH, "Alkuins York-Gedicht (C. 1) als Kunstwerk", in: *Gli umanesimi medievali*, ed. C. LEONARDI (Florence, 1998), pp. 283-295. A more torough analysis in Mary Garrison's unprinted dissertation (M. GARRISON, *Alcuin's World through his Letters and Verse*, University of Cambridge, Christ's College and Corpus Christi College, 1995 [to be found on <academia.edu>]).

[29] MS London, British Library, Harley 3685, and the source of Quercetanus's edition.

atque ori porrigit aegre cibos. / Clarior ecce tuba subito vox faucibus haesit, / auribus adpositis murmura clausa ciet. / (...) marcescit tota iuventus, / iam perit atque cadit corporis omne decus / et pellis tantum vacua vix ossibus haeret, / nec cognoscit homo propria membra senex. / Quod fuit alter erit, iam nec erit ipse quod ipse: / fur erit ipse suus temporibus variis.[30]

He who once rested joyful in purple / will barely cover his inert limbs with a threadbare cloth. / The long day ends with dark mist in the eyes, / which before counted the passage of solitary stars. / The hand that shook heavy arms and swords / now trembles and cannot feed the mouth. / Now the voice, once clearer than a trumpet, fades in the throat, / gives sighs and whispers that strain the ears. / But what else should I sing? All youth rots, / each bodily pride is already lost and falls away, / and empty skin barely adheres to bones, / nor does the old man still recognise his body. / What has been will be different, no longer what it was before: / it is the thief of itself in the past.

These lines sufficiently emphasise that the decay of places and of powers is felt by Alcuin through the sense of physical senescence; the age of history is his own age, the time that passes and leaves behind ruins is, it seems, above all the time of the man who is writing. In this way Alcuin reveals a classical ability to lyricise history, which allows him to invent a poetic form of biblical lamentation, as Paulinus's on Aquileia and Hildebert's on Rome would also be, creating a sort of personal epyllion capable of linking the perception of history through the example of an event, the religious projection of its meaning, and the individual understanding of this tension. A tell-tale of this is, in my opinion, the high frequency of the term *mundus*, which, contrary to what would be expected from a pious Carolingian abbot, clearly exceeds that of the alternative *caelum*. Just as *corpus* clearly trumps both *anima* and *spiritus*.[31]

A similar process involving the creation of a setting that went beyond the biographical is also the *Vita metrica* of Willibrord, commissioned between 792 and 797 by Beornrad, archbishop of Sens and abbot of the monastery of Echternach, of which Willibrord had been the founder, and composed by Alcuin as the second book of a hagiographical corpus that also included a first book in prose to be read to his fellow monks.[32] Divided into 34 chapters of rather un

---

[30] Vv. 101-116, ed. DÜMMLER, in: *PLAC* 1, pp. 231-232.

[31] Although here the lexical alternative is instead *mens*, which actually recurs more frequently than *corpus*.

[32] See I DEUG-SU, *L'opera agiografica di Alcuino* (Spoleto, 1983), for historical-literary data on his hagiography in prose; C. VEYRARD-COSME *L'oeuvre hagiographique en prose*

equal length, with a total of 471 lines, all hexameters except for the two final chapters on the blessed Wilgisus, Willibrord's father, it adopts the path of a scholastic epyllion, divided as it is into events and episodes that are also very slight, which once again implies an autobiographical undercurrent: lines XXXIII, 3-5, *"fecunda Britannia mater / Patria Scottorum clara magistra fuit, / Francia sed felix rapuit"* ("the fertile mother country Britannia was an illustrious teacher of the Scots, but happy France kidnapped them"), could easily be adapted for Alcuin himself, who in the final lines – where Alcuin often likes to place his own 'signature' – calls himself *"carmiger indoctus"* ("ignorant composer of poetry").[33]

With this poem Alcuin instead performs the transposition of the *opus geminum*, in the tradition that links Sedulius to Bede, to genuine hagiography, once again capturing a social demand: the request for a more aesthetically and linguistical advanced level for hagiography, which was at risk of limiting itself to the popular and monastic genre. And it also constitutes an experiment in the literary valorisation even of oral sources, which Alcuin would use in other poetic genres as well. The limitation remains that of the link to a prose source that the poem does not intend to substitute but simply to complement: in chapter 13 Alcuin clearly writes that the description of miracles will be swift and summary, given that it is possible to refer the reader to the life in prose.[34] And so the biography is resolved in a series of detached episodes, of 15-20 lines each, enlivened only by the final chapter, the elegy on Wilgisus, Willibrord's father, which with its 84 lines begins to possess its own narrative unity. Despite this limitation, the operation was successful because it became a model for many other Carolingian and Ottonian versifications, from Milo's *Vita Amandi* to the many biographies in verse from the tenth century published in the fifth volume of the *Poetae*.

---

d'Alcuin: Vitae Willibrordi, Vedasti, Richarii: *Edition, traduction, études narratologiques* (Florence, 2003), for an edition and analysis of his metrical hagiography.

[33] It is handed down in three manuscripts: MS Stuttgart, Württembergische Landesbibliothek, G 38 (from Weingarten; s. IX); MS Saint Gall, Stiftsbibliothek 565 (s. XI); and MS Alençon, Bibliothèque Municipale 14 (s. XI). Fragments in MS Vienna, Österreichische Staatsbibliothek, lat. 808 (s. IX; "codex Z").

[34] "*Plurima perque suum fecit miracula servum, / Quae nunc non libuit versu percurrere cuncta, / sed strictim quaedam properanti tangere plectro, / et gestis titulos paucis praefigere musis, / ad prosamque meum lectorem mittere primam: / illic inveniet iam plenius omnia gesta / pontificis magni, studium, documenta magistri, / progeniem, vitam, mores, mentemque benignam, / devotumque deo semper cor omnibus horis, / legibus in sacris meditans noctesque diesque*".

Epigraphic Poetry: Domus, viator

A similar ability, typical of great intellectuals but also of great writers, to grasp the heart of the demands of the society surrounding them and also to shape them, is demonstrated by Alcuin in what we might consider his other great far-reaching work, although it is composed of myriad lyrical pieces: the 197 inscriptions which Dümmler published, almost always based on Quercetanus, regrouping them into 31 blocks, which in his edition occupy number 86 to 117, to which several epigraphs published in earlier blocks must be added.[35]

Until now scholars have focussed – once again – only on the epigraphs that have value as historical documents – that is, above all, the epitaph for Pope Hadrian I and the one for himself, later imitated in many other epitaphs, both Carolingian and not. I have dedicated too many pages to the dedicatory and prefatory epigrams to bibles and biblical commentaries, for it to be necessary to return to them once again. On all the rest there are only a few good pages by Günter Bernt[36] and two exploratory contributions, including the excellent report by Cecile Treffort at the 2004 conference in Tours.[37] Yet in my opinion it is an impressive corpus that follows in the wake of distinguished precedents, from Paulinus of Nola's epigraphs for Cimitile to those by Damasus and Venantius Fortunatus. Alcuin surpassed them with the same spirit with which he made a name for himself compared to other Carolingian intellectuals: the ability to write impressive amounts that contained subtle, sensitive distinctions between places, between one commissioner and another, and the density of the network of relationships that allowed him to contribute to monasterial signage throughout Europe. Indeed he wrote, often on express request, as documented by several letters,[38] epitaphs, notices, signs, instructions, and various inscrip-

---

[35] Such as No. 64 *Fornax*.

[36] See F. STELLA, "Epigrafia letteraria e topografia della vita quotidiana dei monasteri carolingi", in: *Le scritture dei monasteri: Atti del II seminario internazionale di studio 'I monasteri nell'alto medioevo': Roma 9-10 maggio 2002*, ed. F. DE RUBEIS and W. POHL (Rome, 2003), pp. 123-144; on Alcuin pp. 131 ff. An English translation is provided in Chapter Eleven.

[37] C. TREFFORT, "La place d'Alcuin dans la rédaction épigraphique carolingienne", *Annales de Bretagne et des pays de l'Ouest* 111.3 (2004), pp. 353-360.

[38] Letter to the brothers of Saint-Vaast, No. 295, ed. in: *Alcuini sive Albini Epistolae*, ed. E. DÜMMLER, in: *Epistolae Karolini aevi* 1, ed. E. DÜMMLER *et al.* (Berlin, 1895: MGH EPP 4), pp. 1-481, at pp. 454-455: "*Sicut domni abbatis vestraeque suavissima caritas demandavit, versus per singulos titulos aecclesiarum et altaria singula dictavimus, et utinam tam rationabiliter quam libenter, quia vestrae sanctitatis iussio me compellit citato dictare sermone*" etc.; Letter to Radon, No. 74, pp. 115-117, at p. 116: "*Sicut magno labore domum dei optime habes ornatam et largissimis donis decoratam*"; and the marginal annotation on ff. 85 and 87 of

tions for Saint-Amand, Saint-Vaast, Saint-Denis, Tours and Corméry, Metz, Saint-Avold, Nouaillé (in Vienne), Sankt Peter of Salzburg, Cologne, Jumièges, Rome, Gorze, and for other churches whose identification cannot be verified: "a great work that circulated models of poetic and epigraphic communication that would exert its influence over many genres for some time".[39] I cannot linger over the details here, but I must focus your attention on several innovative aspects. These texts, seemingly repetitive and serial, are primarily dedicated to the celebration of restorations or consecrations of ecclesiastical buildings and to the celebration of spaces, of furnishings, or of works of art contained within them, rather than to the exaltation of the client. They therefore certainly compose a kind of prosopography of the artistic-architectural patronage of the Carolingian revival, which could have its own historic-cultural interest. But they also give rise to their own kind of emotionality because they represent a joining link between the literary schemes inherited or innovated by Alcuin and the daily reality that surrounded him and that he wanted to encircle and underpin his writings: Alcuin's gaze caresses gates, altars covered with precious metals, *pallia* hung on walls and lamps, paraments, and crosses, portraying the decoration that in his opinion should give dignity to the offering of faith and to the institution that transmits it. But his epigraphic lines also introduce us to less frequented corners: the washtub where Alcuin bathed speaks in first person in *carmen* 92, playing with riddle conventions but in an elegiac tone on the ambivalence between water that once, when it was a river, carried wooden boats and is now in turn poured into a wooden container, and closing with a call to the *puer* not to look at what the hand of the first man is covering. A little miniature summation of what Alcuin's short poetry offers: an inclination towards jest and irony; a predilection for puzzle devices tied to didactic practices; an elegiac tone, namely a tendency to emphasise the transformation of things over the passage of time; and the usual diplopic ability to keep in parallel both the loving vision of earthly reality and the biblical and moral landscape. In the same register is the famous epigraph *In latrinio*, which – perhaps based on a lost Latin translation of an epigram by Agathias – urges the reader to abstain from the sin of gluttony to avoid its unpleasant consequences,

---

MS Douai, Bibliothèque municipale 753 (s. XII), reported by E. DÜMMLER in: *Monumenta Alcuiniana*, ed. W. WATTENBACH and E. DÜMMLER (Berlin, 1873: *Bibliotheca Rerum Germanicarum* 6), pp. 308-309, No. 1 of his edition.

[39] STELLA, "Epigrafia letteraria", p. 132 (see Chapter Eleven). The literary fortune of the Alcuinian epigraphic formulary is well documented by TREFFORT, "La place d'Alcuin dans la rédaction épigraphique carolingienne".

the same argument touched on in letter 65 to Dado.[40] Here the emphasis does not fall on the grotesque, but on the naturalness with which Alcuin addresses every aspect of reality, investing it with his Christian culture, understood as hermeneutic openness, by reading a transcendent meaning into all aspects of existence, even the most humble and vulgar, and by using this interpretation to rebuilt a moral style or behaviour. The inscription of Fleury (105 II) on the "*clocca cocorum*", the serving (or cook's) bell or *Speiseglocke*, is similar in spirit. The choice between stomach and spirit is moreover a leitmotif of Alcuinian lyric, and not only the epigraphic kind. It is also present, for example, in the entertaining *carmen* 111, inserted in the block of inscriptions for Sankt Peter of Salzburg but perhaps not belonging to it: here Alcuin informs the *viator* passing "*per stratam*" that he is at a crossroads between the tavern and the library, and the choice is between "*potare merum*" or "*sacros discere libros*" ("drinking wine" or "reading holy books"). "*Elige quod placeat*" ("choose whichever you like"). But know that if you wish to drink you will have to pay, while if you wish to learn you will spend nothing: "*gratis quod quaeris habebis*". We are perhaps looking at a monastic complex like that of Saint-Riquier, where the 2500 individual houses were gathered into neighbourhoods specialised according to activity, and among these there was also a "*vicus cauponum*",[41] a "tavern neighbourhood". In a negative or positive sense, the alimentary *Bildfeld* is always present in Alcuin's imagination: *cibus* and *potus* are terms used by him, in epigraphs and in letters in verse, more than by almost any other Latin poet in history. And what brings Alcuin closer to the humanism that we have been suspecting of him is none other than his ability to consider the fleshly aspect of life as inferior to the spiritual one – not contemptible in itself, rather actually worthy of mention and song, with a glance that is capable of irony but absolutely distant from the ascetic, forlorn austerity that is seen later in the medieval period.

Number 112 – which invites the cold wanderer to warm himself in a house protected by the cross, a house where the door is always open – also guides us on the one hand to an understanding of monastic realities that to us are sometimes abstract, such as the calefactory, the *pisalis*, also present on the plan of Saint Gall, and on the other explores the range of emotional reactions to places

---

[40] Ed. in: *Alcuini sive Albini Epistolae*, p. 108. Text, Italian translation, and commentary in *La poesia carolingia*, ed. F. STELLA, pp. 266-267 and 456-457.
[41] STELLA, "Epigrafia letteraria", p. 137; P. RICHÉ *La vie quotidienne dans l'empire carolingienne* (Paris, 1973), trans. *La vita quotidiana nell'impero carolingio* (Rome, 1994). p. 59.

and gestures, opening us to the feeling of the everyday that for the early medieval period would almost completely escape us, if not for these windows that were so overlooked until now. As a whole, Alcuin's poetic epigraphy opens up windows for us onto the private spaces of monastic life, taverns and washtubs, kitchens and toilets, which we are not accustomed to associating with noble Carolingian imagery; it helps us to reconstruct the link between the material conditions of life and their echoes on the spiritual plane and in individual attitudes. Inscription 6 of series 104 shows how consistent this is with Alcuin's spiritual world: dedicated to the hermitage of Corméry near Tours, where the poet contrasts his cell in the forest hermitage to the *"nova culmina"*, the new houses that are arising in important cities, *"urbes egregiae"*, already sung of in ancient books but in the process of expansion or renovation in the years of the first Carolingian impetus. And he praises the peace of that cloister where sacred studies flourish, and where the mysterious words of the ancients are contemplated: in city schools – and this seems like a landscape from the twelfth century – they sell countless lies, but here they do religious research, and this is done using a *"famen pacificum"*, a word of peace, where even the tone of communication becomes the sign of an alternative kind of life that is radical and perfect. The big cities are dominated by drunkenness, which drowns intelligence, and the servant barely manages to bring his master home in his arms – a painting worthy of Bruegel – but in the forest hermitage the evening sees long fasts, and only holy foods feed the hearts of scholars.

Lyrical Poetry

Cella, iuventus: *The Monastery and the Past*

The extreme coherence of Alcuin's poetic world leads us to compare this epigraph with Alcuin's famous ode to his *cella*, which Waddell called "the loveliest" lyric in the medieval period, Alcuin's farewell to an unspecified monastery, perhaps the one where he spent his youth, his *"sacra iuventus"*, and which he sought to find again first in York, then in Aachen, and then in Corméry. There was a time when scholars expressed doubts about the authenticity of this text. The most recent criticism, except for Brunhölzl, believes it to be Alcuin's work.[42] And its comparison with the epigraph that we have just read

---

[42] Text, Italian translation, and commentary in my anthology, *La poesia carolingia*, ed. F.

reveals the same existential and linguistic universe, the same positive terminology (*sophia*, *sacri libri*), and above all the same tone of voice in each text: "*pacificis sonuit vocibus atque animis*" in the abandoned monastery, a mark of an irrecoverable age, and "*famine pacifico*" in the epigraph of Corméry. It is the formulation of a monastic ideal deeply rooted in a rural context and in the model of a community of studies, a school, the small sacred city that finds one of its most unsuspected expressions in the affection with which the poetic inscriptions guide us through the spaces of that way of life. In his ode to the cell Alcuin manages to link the monastic ideal to the poetic model of the *locus amoenus*, but as in the poem on York and the one on Lindisfarne, he declines this description in the past, giving the entire description a nostalgic tone of irrecoverable loss that is typical of his poetry. The memory of the monastery is the memory of the school that it hosted, where young men's voices and poems used to resonate, and where a dismal silence now reigns. The memory of the monastery is the memory of a lost youth, which no medieval writer ever sacralised with the same sweetness as Alcuin: the phrase "*sacra iuventus*" appears two times in the poet's texts, and the reader is given the impression that it refers not only to the monastic – that is, consecrated – state of the young scholars, but also to the feeling of sacredness of youth, given that it is irrecoverable. The nucleus of the *carmen*, and perhaps of all Alcuinian poetry, is in line 31: "Why do we seek our unhappiness, loving you, fleeting and vanishing world?" ("*Nos miseri cur te fugitivum, mundus, amamus?*"). We have already seen how fond of the term *mundus* Alcuin is, statistically speaking. Here the use of the second person for *mundus* reveals the implicit affection for it. Love of terrestrial life is in vain, and leads to unhappiness. But it is not weaker because of this. This love is not negated, not even when its nullity is being stated. All the best poetry by Alcuin, from the epigraphs to the lyric on the nightingale, owes its artistry to this contradiction between the security of the moral pronouncement and the melancholy of the elegiac tone that denies it, to the conflicting coexistence of the two truths and two distinct levels of expression: one given, in semiotic terms, by denotation, the other by connotation. Once again the qualities of Alcuin's poetry are drawn with simple clarity within the very same text: the retrospective glimpse into the juxtaposition of past and present, the conciliation and tension between the moral world and earthly reality, the myth of the school and poetry as a place of happiness, the marked sensitivity to daily

STELLA, pp. 364-369 and 503-506.

realities, the ability to personalise each context and thought, and the lightness of melancholy and jest.

Magister, amicus: The Myth of School and Friendship

But every one of the features recalled here takes on a thousand faces, builds on itself until it becomes a constellation of Alcuin's imagery and therefore of his poetic repertoire. The school, for example, is the real myth of Carolingian literary production: the place of personal and political socialisation, the place where friendships and loves are contracted, the instrument with which competence and concrete power are acquired, the laboratory for the development of legal and religious directives that hold their influence over the whole kingdom and empire, and therefore the observatory from which to control all that moves. In the lyric to the cell of York the school is *hortus conclusus* and a place of transmission of knowledge, while in the poem on the saints of York it is also a place of transmission of power. But in a famous series of lyrics on the cuckoo the school is the group of teachers and students among whom strong friendships that border on love – interpreted by some also in a homoerotic sense – are born. The figure that symbolises this situation is the cuckoo: a beloved scholar, who, after proving his poetic abilities, disappears from the school and ruins his life in court revelries. And Alcuin pleads for his return and laments his absence repeatedly. But always with paternal benevolence, with a willingness to welcome his return but also a resignation to confining the experience to memory. In these poems the school becomes a nest, just like the nightingale's nest and the nest that represents Giovanni Pascoli's family home centuries later, and so the pupils become birds, just as birds were the souls of the poets in Celtic imagery and birds are the costumes of court intellectuals in several later poems by Alcuin himself and Theodulf, where ravens are contrasted with swans; but the pupils are also sons, *nati*, of a master, *pater*: these roles also enhance the familiar imagery that in the Alcuinian universe links the cell to the royal palace, so much so that in *carmen* 26 Charles's great hall is celebrated as the palace that hosts many schools and many masters, of medicine, poetry, writing, priesthood, song, and astronomy: "*iam tenet ordo suum proprie nunc quisque magistrum*" ("now each group already has its own teacher"). These poems, which often conceal individuals with biblical or classical nicknames but sometimes mention them explicitly, sketch out an authentic prosopography of the Carolingian school, which coincides in part with the one that emerges from the rich epistolary but surpasses it by adding a formalised language that comes from the past and putting that language in contact with acquired poetic heritage, both learned and popular. Just think of the figure of the cuckoo, which also appears in the letters but in poetry makes the entire landscape of Vergilian bucolic grow around it – shepherds with classical Greek-style names and pleasant landscapes and unhappy loves and hopes entrusted to poetry and dialogue structure –, but at the same time the dialogical alternation, which reaches perfection in the *conflictus* between spring and winter, where the cuckoo is the symbol of victory and activates recalls of probable folkloric origin that Alcuin is able to graft onto the classical repertoire in a natural way.[43]

Dulcis amor, vox *and* sonus

In turn the glue of this scholastic community, friendship, becomes the central theme of a good part of the remaining Alcuinian lyrical poetry, even in the poems that do not refer to pupils, such as the notes to Paulinus of Aquileia, or to the Bishop Arno, who was his pupil, or to Richard of Lorsch (31), or to Angilbert, another former pupil who had a successful career. And built on top of this secondary trait of the 'school' archiseme is a subset of images and formulae: the expression sometimes borders on erotic language ("*dulcis amor, lacrimis absentem plangis amicum*" ("sweet love, you mourn the absent friend"; 55, 1,1); "*vestrum faciat quoque cernere vultum*" ("and let you show your face"; 55, 3, 5-6), and sometimes alludes to theological language, when the affection is a three-way relationship between Christ and the two friends ("*Tres olim fuimus, iunxit quod spiritus unus*" – "Once upon a time there were three that a unique spirit united"; 57, 45), a relationship that is in turn an earthly image of the Trinity, in a dizzying short-circuit between theological abstraction and vocabulary of spiritual friendship that goes back to Venantius Fortunatus, but with a skilful result in its simplicity and strength. The closed nature of the *hortus conclusus* is also revealed in the repetitive seriality of the phrase,

---

[43] In *carmen* 42, ed. E. DÜMMLER, in: *PLAC* 1, pp. 253-254, he likewise makes use of the Vergilian figure of Entellus, the old boxer who during the games for Anchises defeats the young champion Dares, to identify himself in the old master who does not accept the plagiaristic techniques of the up-and-coming boxers, and each morning wakes up to tell the young men about the flowers gathered in the fields of antiquity.

which always recurs in the same formulae and modules. *Dulcis amor*, a rather unusual expression in classical poetry, is used by Alcuin more than any other Latin poet[44] until the elegiac comedy and the *Carmina Burana*. In the same way, often linked to scholastic and poetic practice is Alcuin's insistence on oral and musical communication, the use of the terms *vox* and *sonus* and associated verbs, the connotation of the school and the monastery not so much as a place of meditation and prayer but as a place where things, voices, and thoughts ring out: although *carmina* appears 35 times and *carmen-carmine* 37, there are 41 instances of *voce* and *vox* and no fewer than 97 of *ore*.

The sphere of the attraction of friendship even allowed Alcuin to recover, perhaps unwittingly, a genre that was much practised in the classical period and that was able to acquire meaning as an everyday practice in the cultural mobility of the Carolingian world: the *propemptikón*, the farewell wish for a safe journey. Alcuin wrote several of these, from *carmen* 44 to Witto, his disciple who went to Roma with Arno in 798, to 52 "*Angelus e caelo veniens comitetur euntem*" and 53 "*Curre viam frater*", proposing what was almost a Christianisation of the genre and also a link of the same to his lyric on friendship. The centrality of the theme *amicitia* in Alcuin is confirmed by lexical statistics: *amicus* and *amor* are among the most frequent terms in his poems. This centrality is such because his poetry is a writing of communication, which is enhanced through the possibility of conveying greetings, wishes, or invitations to a real addressee, and which in its compositional process always keeps its communicative nature in mind: today in Romance philology[45] we tend to emphasise, contrary to the formalistic and structuralist trends of past decades, the dialogic moment of poetic writing, the communicative function that all poetic documents seem to have in the time of Romance origins. This tendency was not born in the thirteenth century but found its roots in the 'relational' setup of all Carolingian poetry: the Carolingians always knew whom they were writing to, and why, and this pragmatic social arrangement deeply conditioned the very structure of poetry. This is particularly clear in Alcuin, who more than all his contemporaries exalted the relational nature of poetry, in this way uniting it with the epistolary sphere, of which Alcuin was also – as we have heard – a master of his time. This feature allowed Alcuin to conceive of each composition as a message and also as a social contribution: from the history of York conceived as a continuity with his own master and past to monastic epigraphs

---

[44] The *iunctura* only Catullus 66, 6 and Statius, *Theb.* 2, 399, then Sedulius and Dracontius.
[45] C. GIUNTA, *Versi a un destinatario* (Bologna, 2002).

in constant dialogue with the reader and the client, to book inscriptions in an almost mutual relationship between book and client or book and dedicatee, all the way to lyrical poetry, always permeated by this epistolary setup, of a relationship between two friends or between master and pupil. Many formal features are revealed to be consistent with this pattern: the urging of the *carta* or *cartula* to go to the recipient to bring him greetings or communications, the call to the *lector*, the use of the second person, the final signature that Alcuin used more than other poets and that has allowed the authentication of almost all the poems that remain: all elements that in Alcuin's poetry are statistically much more frequent that in poetry by other writers from the same period, and that ushered in poetic customs destined to last. This has led me to point out Alcuin as one of the inventors of paratextual poetry, in the sense that Genette used, which is a typical sign of Carolingian culture. Here, too, Alcuin's vocabulary does not disappoint: not only is he the Latin poet who most often uses the term *lector*, but in his verse the imperative *dic* is frequent, with percentages equal to or greater than those of theatrical texts such as Plautus or Terence or of heavily dialogical poems such as the *Ruodlieb*. *Propemptikón,* friendship, dialogicity, and irony reached peak fusion in *carmen* 4, which in his masterful study of the *Vortrags- und Zirkulardichtung* Schaller classifies as an itinerant epistle: a journey from England through Utrecht, Cologne, Echternach, the court, Mainz, and Speyer to Saint-Denis as a fluvial itinerary from one friend to another, represented through the poet's urging of the *cartula*, an internal and fictitious addressee, to bring greetings to all the real addressees, one by one, moving from solemn homage to jest, and urging the *carta*, the song, to avoid the enticements of beautiful landscapes, of castles and palaces, of cities and fields in flower in order to complete its mission and return to the peacefulness of its author when spring gives him new inspiration. The *carmen's* models are probably Venantius's farewell in the *Vita Martini*, which ideally crosses all of Europe, and the journey of the *libellus* in Sidonius Apollinaris's *carmen* 24. But Alcuin's relational sensitivity is able to transform a formal scheme into a journey through geography and Carolingian prosopography. And although this was the first time that a Latin poem began with the call to the *carta* that would later have so much success ("*cartula, perge cito pelagi trans aequora cursu*"; "leaflet, quickly cross the sea's surface with your run"), a few years later the model was imitated by Angilbert in *carmen* 2: "*cartula, curre modo per sacra palatia David*" ("leaflet, run early for the sacred palaces of David [i.e. Charles]"). But it was the leap from Europe to the royal palace that signalled the end of the propulsive Carolingian impetus and the seed of decline.

It is an impossible task to give an overview of Alcuin's poetry in just a few pages. But these examples will have contributed to illustrating how he managed, in each of the fields and genres to which he dedicated himself, to make innovative contributions that were often determinative for future development: the poeticisation of the contrast; the versification of ecclesiastical history; the bucolic contextualisation of the poetry of friendship; the recovery of the propemptikón; the creation of an epigraphic formulary for the most disparate everyday and cultural situations; the transformation of the scholastic riddle and the animal *fabula* in lyrical poetry; the invention of a poetry that was not a 'school' poetry but that dealt *with* the school as a social and human place, and the choice of poetry as the instrument of communication of that school; and the interpretation of the Carolingian cultural revolution as a multiplication of points of communication and a circulation of the ability to entrust the processes of the acquisition of knowledge to writing.[46]

But even if we limit ourselves to examining the many cases already specified, it seems clear that Alcuin succeeded at what is the sole task of the great poet: to create a world of one's own that is new, unique, and unrepeatable, which transforms the key words, needs, and obsessions of a time and a culture into myth. The technical and expressive quality of his lines is not always original and is typically not inelegant, because his genius is clearly systematic, not analytic, and his language is powerful and precise, but poor; however, the specifically literary operation at which Alcuin succeeded was in creating a small fictional, symbolic universe that transferred the neuralgic elements of Carolingian society to an enduring language, a poetic and textual background, and in his ability to interpret the social demands of his era through the structuring or restructuring of poetic forms. Alcuin did not create great poetic monuments, but he did create effective models, because he understood which forms his era needed, and so he invented or reinvented the institutional history poem, the hagiographical poem, the scholastic bucolic, the circular lyric, the epigraph of the everyday, and the paratextual poem. But in these models, he revealed a

---

[46] Were the attribution of *carmen* 120, *Summi regis archangele*, ed. DÜMMLER, pp. 348-349, not debated, despite the evidence of the codices that assign it to Alcuin, we could even speak of Alcuin, also the author of rhythmic poems, as the inventor of the poetic sequence, which Notker of Saint Gall was to master in the following century.

weakness: he left behind not only instructions for others but traces of his private world, of his fears and fragilities, of his delusions. And today it is these very imperfections that bring him closer to us. Still *magister*, still *amicus*.

Chapter 7

Some Linguistic Features of Popular Songs in Medieval and Modern Times

Theories on the nature and origins of syllabotonic and rhythmical versification, both medieval and modern, have followed one another and overlapped over the years without ever reaching a shared conclusion, as similarly happened with theories on the development of the Romance languages out of Vulgar Latin. The diversity of hypotheses is due in part to the heterogeneity of the sources considered by different scholars. If, for instance, we regard the *versus quadrati* of the popular Roman tradition, passed down through later quotations, as the earliest examples of this versification, the explanation must lie in popular oral tradition, as Gaston Paris claimed in 1866;[1] if we go by the coincidence of accent / ictus, as Schlicher did in 1900,[2] we can attribute rhythmical evolution to causes which are purely linguistic; if we consider the *Psalmus responsorius* of the Barcelona Papyrus or St. Augustine's *Psalmus contra Donatistas*, which professedly mimics Punic songs familiar to the Carthaginian population, we might arrive at a Biblical-Semitic model like that suggested by Wilhelm Meyer;[3] if we analyse poetry set to pre-existing music, we might deduce that the placing of the stress is dictated by the melody, as suggested by

---

[1] G. PARIS, "Lettre à Léon Gautier sur la versification latine rythmique", *Bibliothèque de l'École des Chartes* 27 (1866), pp. 578-610.

[2] J.J. SCHLICHER, *The Origin of Rhythmical Verse in Late Latin* (PhD diss., University of Chicago, 1900).

[3] W. MEYER, "Anfang und Ursprung der lateinischen und griechischen rythmischen Dichtung", in: ID., *Gesammelte Abhandlungen zur mittellateinischen Rythmik*, 3 vols. (Berlin, 1905-1936), 2, pp. 1-202.

Vroom;[4] if we take Fulgentius's *Psalmu*s, we can hypothesise a rhythmical reworking of rhymed prose such as that suggested by Nicolau;[5] if we consider the Latin rhythmical hymns of the seventh-century Mozarabic tradition or the eighth- and ninth-century Frankish tradition, the explanation of the transposition or imitation of metrical systems put forward by Dag Norberg[6] and Michail Gasparov[7] appears well founded; if we go by linguistic considerations, we have to postulate the perfect coincidence of accent and ictus, as does Pulgram;[8] if we assemble the claims of grammarians or early medieval music theorists, other hypotheses can be formulated according to whatever aspects we wish to emphasise. Analysing some alternative hypotheses in 1994, Avalle,[9] using both early and late medieval sources, seemed to lean towards an acceptance of the arguments of Gaston Paris, while Pascale Bourgain,[10] using more or less the same sources in 2000, revealed some alleged inconsistencies in the Latin theoretical tradition.

Thus, in the absence of strict agreement on methods and sources, the problem seems almost insurmountable. The *Corpus Rhythmorum Musicum* project (*CRM*), which publishes early medieval *rhythmus* verse set to music, aims to supply not only philological, metrical, and linguistic material, but also new documentation and statistics for approaching the problem itself, based as it is on each transcribed and catalogued manuscript witness and not only on the critically reconstructed text. The textual base developed thus far (the first vol-

[4] H.B. VROOM, *Le Psaume abécédaire de saint Augustin et la poésie latine rythmique* (Nijmegen, 1933).

[5] M.G. NICOLAU, "Les deux sources de la versification latine accentuelle", *Archivum Latinitatis Medii Aevi* 9 (1934), pp. 55-87.

[6] D. NORBERG, *La Poésie latine rythmique du Haut Moyen Âge* (Stockholm, 1954); ID., *Introduction à la versification latine médiévale* (Stockholm, 1958), trans. G.C. ROTI and J. DE LA CHAPELLE SKUBLY, ed. J.M. ZIOLKOWSKI, *An Introduction to the Study of Medieval Latin Versification* (Washington, DC, 2004); ID., "Mètre et rythme entre le bas-empire et le haut moyen âge", in: *La cultura in Italia fra tardo antico e alto Medioevo: Atti del convegno tenuto a Roma, Consiglio nazionale delle ricerche, dal 12 al 16 novembre 1979*, 2 vols. (Rome, 1981), 1, pp. 357-372.

[7] M.L. GASPAROV, *Storia del verso europeo*, trans. S. GARZONIO (Bologna, 1993).

[8] E. PULGRAM, "Latin-Romance metrics: A linguistic view", in: *Metrik und Medienwechsel – Metrics and Media*, ed. H.L.C. TRISTRAM (Tübingen, 1991), pp. 53-80.

[9] A. D'ARCO SILVIO AVALLE, "Dalla metrica alla ritmica", in: *Lo spazio letterario del Medioevo*, 1, *Il medioevo latino*, 1, *La produzione*, ed. G. CAVALLO, C. LEONARDI, and E. MENESTÒ (Rome, 1992), pp. 391-476.

[10] P. BOURGAIN, "Les théories du passage du mètre au rythme d'après les textes", in: *Poesia dell'alto Medioevo europeo: Manoscritti, lingua e musica dei ritmi latini*, ed. F. STELLA (Florence, 2000), pp. 25-42.

ume and the CD-ROM, 2007) is too scant to offer reliable conclusions: twenty-eight poems set to music, in about 140 different textual versions from 80 different witnesses.[11] Nevertheless, this edition has, for the first time, supplied comparative text / music data that allow the advancement of new hypotheses. New methods, however, can emerge both from an analysis of the definitions of rhythm not yet included or not rightly appreciated in the scholarly debate, as well as from comparison, as yet unexplored, with rhythmical production in music of the modern (twentieth- and twenty-first-century) period.

In my opinion, the debate of the last century was led astray by the comparison, considered implicit and inevitable, with quantitative classical metre. The assumption put forward, but not demonstrated, was that new forms of verse constituted the development and transformation of quantitative ones. This was probably true in the case of forms such as the so-called rhythmical hexameter, found mostly in rare Lombard epigraphs, or the pseudo-Sapphic strophe documented by Peter Stotz in a few dozen texts.[12] But both are learned or, at any rate, scholastic procedures, conducted by *maestri* and grammarians (such as Paulinus of Aquileia) in experiments that are relatively peripheral with respect to mainstream early medieval production. The classicist position emerges clearly with Dag Norberg, who, convinced that "*un poème rhythmique est cependant un poème où l'ancien système est remplacé par un nouveau*",[13] draws up the famous five paths to creation of rhythmical verse:[14]

1 imitation of the structure of classical verse;
2 imitation of the ictus;
3 imitation of the number of syllables;
4 imitation of the number of words;
5 imitation of the quantity.

Each case is necessarily the result of imitating elements of quantitative verse. This position, repeated in many classicist analyses, is partly the consequence of historical prejudice, sadly still widespread, according to which the cultural artifacts of the Middle Ages develop mainly from creations of the classical

---

[11] *Corpus Rhythmorum Musicum saec. IV-IX*, 1, *Songs in Non-Liturgical Sources*, 1, *Lyrics*, ed. F. STELLA, S. BARRETT, *et al.* (Florence, 2007), <www.corimu.unisi.it>.

[12] P. STOTZ, *Sonderformen der sapphischen Dichtung: Ein Beitrag zur Erforschung der sapphischen Dichtung des lateinischen Mittelalters* (Munich, 1982).

[13] NORBERG, *Introduction à la versification latine médiévale*, p. 94; trans. *An Introduction*, p. 88.

[14] NORBERG, *Introduction à la versification*, pp. 94-135; trans. *An Introduction*, pp. 88-129.

period. And yet, in this case, the oldest sources[15] seem clearly to exclude a classical matrix: Servius (fourth century) explains the Virgilian *phrase "versibus incomptis ludunt"* by recalling rhythmically composed popular verse: "that is, with poetry composed in Saturnian metre, which only the popular poets compose rhythmically".[16]

In his *Retractationes*, St. Augustine explains that in 393 he composed his *Psalmus contra Donatistas* in verses of 16 syllables of 8+8 with caesura and monorhyme in -*e*. This was a polemical song against heretics, *"psalmum qui eis cantaretur"*, that is a song to the Donatists themselves, destined to reach *"ad ipsius humillimi vulgi et omino imperitorum atque idiotarum notitiam"*, that is a popular rather than cultured audience and *"et eorum quantum fieri possit per nos posset inhaerere memoriae"*, thus composed using techniques which favour memorisation. The structure he describes is based on alphabetic strophes, on the refrain (*hypopsalma*), used responsorially (*"quod responderetur"*), and on the *"prooemium causae"*, not in alphabetical order, *"quod nihilominus cantaretur"* – a kind of prologue for singing although, as revealed by the *nihilominus*, usually *not* sung. With this system he avoided the *"necessitas metrica"* which would have obliged him to use words *"quae vulgo minus sunt usitata"*, thus confirming without doubt that his *rhythmus* was intended for a popular audience.[17]

The *Ars Palaemonis*[18] again cites the songs of popular poets.[18] This time there are two new pieces of information: the *"iudicium aurium"* – an acoustic, rather than quantitative-prosodic criterion, which seems to correspond to what

---

[15] M. BURGER, *Recherches sur la structure et l'origine des vers romans* (Genève, 1957), p. 105 n. 1.

[16] Maurus Servius Honoratus, *In Vergilii Georgicon librum secundum commentarius*, ed. in: *Servii Grammatici qui feruntur in Vergilii carmina commentarii* 3.1, *Bucolica et Georgica*, ed. G. THILO (Leipzig, 1887), p. 253 (No. 385): *"id est carminibus Saturnio metro compositis, quod ad rhythmum solum vulgares componere consuerunt"*.

[17] Augustine, *Retractationes* 1, 20, ed. in: PL 32, col. 617: *"Volens etiam causam Donatistarum ad ipsius humillimi vulgi et omnino imperitorum atque idiotarum notitiam pervenire, et eorum quantum fieri posset per nos inhaerere memoriae, Psalmum qui eis cantaretur per Latinas litteras feci, sed usque ad v litteram. Tales autem abecedarios appellant. Tres vero ultimas omisi; sed pro eis novissimum quasi epilogum adiunxi, tamquam eos mater alloqueretur Ecclesia. Hypopsalma etiam, quod responderetur, et prooemium causae, quod nihilominus cantaretur, non sunt in ordine litterarum; earum quippe ordo incipit post prooemium. Ideo autem non aliquo carminis genere id fieri volui, ne me necessitas metrica ad aliqua verba quae vulgo minus sunt usitata compelleret"*.

[18] *Ars Palaemonis de metrica institutione*, ed. in: *Grammatici latini*, 6, *Scriptores artis metricae*, ed. H. KEIL (Leipzig, 1874), pp. 206-215.

Servius defined as "*ad rhythmum*" – and the "*modulatio*", which has often been interpreted in the musical sense of modulation, that is of singing.[20] On the contrary, in classical and late Latin[21] the meaning of *modulatio* was related almost exclusively to rhythm, deriving from *modus*, meaning 'a measure', *modulator* being 'he who gives the rhythm',[22] and then extended to the more general sense of 'singing' or 'composing'.[23]

Between 680 and 690 the Spanish bishop and grammarian Julian of Toledo, in a letter to Modoenus,[24] had advised his aging correspondent to refrain from composing *rhythmi* usually used by the less educated classes: "*rithmis uti, quod plebegis est solitum, ex toto refugiat*".

In the same period, Virgil the Grammarian, supposedly originally of Irish descent but active in Toulouse, devoted several pages of his *Epitome* to versification and included *prosa* among the genres considered. With this example – "*Phoebus surgit, caelum scandit / polo claret, cunctis paret*" – he records two eight-syllable lines with central caesura, clearly rhythmical.[25] The use of *prosa*

---

[17] *Ars Palaemonis*, ed. KEIL, pp. 206-207: "*rhythmus quid est? Verborum modulata compositio non metrica ratione, sed numerosa scansione* [*numerus sanctione* MS Paris, Bibliothèque nationale de France, latin 7559; *numero* Audacis *De Scauri et Palladii libris excerpta*, ed. KEIL, *Grammatici latini*, 7, p. 331; *numeri sanctione* MS Gotha, Forschungs- und Landesbibliothek, Chart A. 117, and the edition *Rhemnius Palaemon de summa grammatices* (Basel, 1527)] *ad iudicium aurium examinata, ut puta veluti sunt cantica poetarum vulgarium. Rhythmus ergo in metro non est? Potest esse. Quid ergo distat a metro? Quod rhythmus per se sine metro esse potest, metrum sine rhythmo esse non potest. Quod liquidius ita definitur, metrum est ratio cum modulatione, rhythmus sine ratione metrica modulatio*".

[20] Today the term *modulation* tends to signify a change of key, metre, or timbre. Cf. BOURGAIN, "Les théories", p. 27: "et la *modulatio*, c'est peut-être plus précisément la mélodie que l'harmonie".

[21] Cf. Seneca, *De ira* 2, 2, 4, ed. *De ira* (Pisa, 1981), p. 57; Quintilian, *Institutiones oratoriae libri duodecim* 1, 10, 22, ed. M. WINTERBOTTOM, 2 vols. (Oxford, 1970), 1, p. 63.

[22] Columella, *De re rustica* 1, praef. 3, ed. R. H. RODGERS (Oxford, 2010), pp. 1-2.

[23] It means: to modulate verses, to sing accompanying oneself on the lyre, to set the verses to music: "*carmina pastoris Siculi modulabor avena*" ("I will modulate my songs on the Sicilian sheperd's reed-pipe"), Virgil, *Eclogues* 10, 51, cf. *The Works of Virgil*, ed. J. CONINGTON, fifth edn., revised by H. NETTLESHIP and F. HAVERFIELD, 2 vols. (London, 1898), 1, p. 122; "*verba sequi fidibus modulanda*" ("to look for words to sing *to my lyre*"), Horace, *Epistulae* 2, 2, 143, cf. Orazio, *Epistole*, ed. M. BECK (Milan, 1997), p. 120.

[24] *Sancti Iuliani Toletanae sedis episcopi Opera* 1, ed. J.N. HILLGARTH, with W. LEVISON and B. BISCHOFF (Turnhout, 1976: CCSL 115), pp. 259-260: "avoid using rhythmical poems, which are common among popular poets".

[25] Virgilius Maro Grammaticus, *Epitomi ed epistole*, IV, ed. G. POLARA (Naples, 1979), pp. 18-19: "*Multas autem metrorum cantilenas propter poetarum rhetorumque voluntatem eorum sectae declarant: quaedam enim prosa, quaedam liniata, quaedam etiam mederia, nonnullaque*

for rhythmical songs is further confirmed by texts from the Lombard area[26] and cannot be completely separated from the primary meaning of the word, which again excludes quantitative-metrical derivations.

These definitions are used with few variations in many medieval treatises, beginning with Bede's celebrated passage in *De arte metrica*, I, 24.[27] With regard to known sources, Bede specifies that the criterion appraised "by ear" is the *number* of syllables, and adds some invaluable information, to wit, that there are not only rhythmical poems composed by popular poets, as we already know from Servius, St. Augustine, the *Ars Palaemonis*, and Julian of Toledo, but also rhythmical poems composed by cultured authors who developed metrical systems rhythmically. This is confirmed by coeval production such as that of Paulinus of Aquileia, but the phenomenon can be verified also in the case of low-level scholastic imitation, such as the hymn to St. Medard composed by King Chilperic in rhythmical septenarius, imitating the trochaic septenarius.[28]

In the following century, in Mozarabic Andalusia, the converted Jew Paulus Alvarus, in his life of the martyr Eulogius, recalls the playful rhythmical poems circulating in his youth but later discarded to prevent them from being passed down to later generations. This link between youth and rhythmical composition had already appeared in the letter from Julian of Toledo two cen-

---

perextensa ponuntur ... . Prosa quidem sunt perbrevia: Phoebus surgit, celum scandit / Polo claret, cunctis paret. Hii duo versus octo metra habent: primum enim metrum Phiebus, secundum surgit et sic per cetera fona, et ita hii duo collecti sedecim pedibus fulciuntur; omnes autem prosi versus per spondeum edi solent".

[26] Cf. *Alfabetum de bonis sacerdotibus prosa compositum,* cited in PLAC 4.2, *Rhythmi aevi Merovingici et Carolini,* ed. K. STRECKER (Berlin, 1914), p. 569 (where *prosa* = 'rythmical verse'), and *"Scripsi per prosa ut oratiunculam",* ibid., p. 731 (*rhythmus* No. 145). Later, *prosa* or *prosula* will be a common label for the poetical-musical form *sequentia* or similar.

[27] Cf. Bede, *Libri II De arte metrica et De schematibus et tropis,* ed. and trans. C.B. KENDALL (Saarbrücken, 1991), pp. 160-163: *"videtur autem rithmus metris esse consimilis, quae est verborum modulata compositio, non metrica ratione, sed numero syllabarum ad iudicium aurium examinata, ut sunt carmina vulgarium poetarum. Et quidem rhythmus per se sine metro esse potest, metrum vero sine rhythmo esse non potest. Quod liquidius ita definitur: metrum est ratio cum modulatione, rhythmus modulatio sine ratione. Plerumque tamen casu quodam invenies etiam rationem in rithmo, non artifici moderatione servata, sed sono et ipsa modulatione ducente, quem vulgares poetae necesse est rustice, docti faciunt docte. Quomodo ad instar iambici metri pulcherrime factus est hymnus ille praeclarus:* Rex aeterne Domine, / rerum creator omnium, / qui eras ante saecula / semper cum Patre Filius*; et alii Ambrosiani non pauci. Item ad formam metri trochaici canunt hymnum de die iudicii per alfabetum:* Apparebit repentina / dies magna Domini, / fur obscura velut nocte / inprovisos occupans".

[28] Cf. D. NORBERG, "La poésie du roi Chilperic", in: ID., *La poésie latine rythmique,* pp. 31-54.

turies earlier, but the lighter meaning of *rhythmus* as a goliardic song for entertainment is found in later passages hitherto unexamined or overlooked by criticism, such as the phrase in sermon 49 attributed to Hugh of Saint Victor, "*rhythmicis quoque dictis nefariis, risibus, et cachinnis domum Dei profanant*" ("they even profane the house of God with wicked rhythmic compositions, laughter and grins"),[29] which leads us to think of the late-Carolingian rhythmical version of the *Cena Cypriani*,[30] professedly composed to be recited in public.

Further confirmation seems to come from Honorius "of Autun", who died in 1151. He finds a western equivalent of the psalms in the *rhythmi* intended for accompaniment by the cithara: "*rhythmi scilicet cantus certo syllabarum numero compositi, fidibus citharae apti*" ("the rhythmi, that is, songs composed with a fixed number of syllables and suitable for the chords of the zither").[31] In seemingly defining *rhythmi* as poetry for singing, and therefore in effect as songs, he picks up on the tradition that associates them "*ad iuducium aurium*", that is, to be read according to a rhythmical pattern recognisable upon listening. In this case, we are probably already in a different cultural climate, in which other numerous and discordant pieces of evidence could be adduced. But even if we limit ourselves to the late-antique period and the early Middle Ages, Aphthonius's claim[32] seems significant: "*differt autem rhythmus a metro, quod metrum in verbis, rhythmus in modulatione ac motu corporis sit*" ("rhythmus differs from metre since metre is rooted in words while *rhythmus* is rooted in the rhythmic pulse and motion of the body").[33] These claims would seem to exclude the derivation of rhythmical verses from classical metre and suggest rather a derivation from prose. However, they also exclude that rhythmical compositions can be read like prose, or prose with final cadence, as metricologists, including Norberg, have long agreed.

Regardless of the specific differences among definitions – differences that have often confused the ideas of modern interpreters looking for apparent con-

---

[29] Hugh of St. Victor (attr.), *Sermo XLIX: In circumcisione Domini*, ed. in: PL 177, col. 1036D. Cf. also Peter Lombard, who, in his *Collectanea in Paulum: Epistola II ad Timotheum*, c. 4, mentions "*rhythmica scurrilitate*" (ed. in: PL 192, col. 379D).

[30] Cf. *Rhythmi aevi Merovingici et Carolini*, ed. STRECKER, pp. 872-900; commentary in F. STELLA, *La poesia carolingia latina* (Florence, 1995), pp. 442-445.

[31] Honorius Augustudonensis, *Expositio in Psalmos*, ed. in: PL 172, col. 269B.

[32] Aelius Festus Aphthonius, *De arte metrica*, ed. in: *Grammatici Latini* 6, ed. KEIL (as part of Marius Victorinus, *Ars grammatica*), at p. 41, line 29.

[33] Frequently this claim is quoted as Marius Victorinus's, because it is printed inside his grammatical treatise.

tradictions – it appears evident from these statements that rhythmical poetry, that is syllabotonic poetry, of the late antique period and the Middle Ages was usually a *song for a less learned audience, created by mainly popular authors, marked by a rhythmical drive, and later applied to dance,* and also for this reason *lends itself to lighter subjects and themes of daily life*, often not scholastic, sometimes comical. Alongside this production came more learned variations or rhythmical versions of quantitative versification. These, however, should not divert our attention from the popular origins of the *genre*, in which there seems to be no evidence of versification imitating quantitative structure. The fact that Pasolini or Umberto Eco occasionally composed songs should not obscure the fact that the overwhelming majority of songs have popular origins and are for popular audiences. Leonard Cohen and Georges Brassens are the exception, rather than the rule. The characteristic of rhythmical verse that emerges from early medieval sources seems initially to have been a simple beat without precise measure,[34] the same defined by Roman Jakobson as a "reiteration of equivalent units";[35] the early *facies* of a rhythmical composition is therefore a text which is apparently prose, characterised by an acoustically sensitive series of rhythmical pulses, probably of an accentual nature, and it is for this reason that rhythmical poetry was conveyed in medieval manuscripts as prose. The genre was later denoted by recurrent identification marks such as the number of syllables, heptasyllabic or octosyllabic, or a combination of these, the fifteen-syllable, which is in fact the most common type of rhythmical verse. Rhyme came shortly afterwards, beginning with the Irish poets and Gottschalk the Saxon.[36]

From this viewpoint, a study of modern popular musical verse,[36] that is song lyrics, can, if used with caution, provide some elements for comparison

---

[34] BOURGAIN, "Les théories", p. 26.

[35] R. JAKOBSON, "Linguistics and poetics," in: *Style in Language*, ed. Th. SEBEOK (Cambridge, MA, 1960), pp. 350-377, at p. 358.. The same idea of perpetual beat (*numerus perpetuus*) is expressed by Augustine in *De musica* II.1 (389); cf. ed. in: PL 32, col. 1099f. Also in Martianus Capella's definition of *rhythmus* in his *De nuptiis Mercurii et philologiae* IX, 967: "*rhythmus igitur est compositio quaedam ex sensibilibus collata temporibus ad aliquem habitum ordinemque conexa. rursum sic definitur: numerus est diversorum modorum ordinata conexio, tempori pro ratione modulationis inserviens, per id quod aut efferenda vox fuerit aut premenda, et qui nos a licentia modulationis ad artem disciplinamque constringat*" (cf. *Les Noces de Philologie et de Mercure*, IX, *L'Harmonie*, ed. and trans. J.-Y. GUILLAUMIN (Paris, 2011), p. 57.

[36] The subject has been studied by F. STELLA, "Gotescalco, la 'scuola' di Reims e l'origine della rima mediolatina", in: *Il verso europeo: Atti del seminario di metrica comparata (4 maggio 1994)*, ed. F. STELLA (Florence, 1995), pp. 159-165.

Some Linguistic Features of Popular Songs 155

which would be useful to a better understanding of the mechanisms of the rhythmical poetry of the early Middle Ages.

Some years ago,[38] in a paper on the texts of an Italian singer-songwriter, I expressed the conviction that song has now absorbed some of the functions that once belonged to poetry: first and foremost, social representativeness, that is the capacity to express collective sensations and concepts, and to permit the identification of a generational group or a social-cultural category through certain linguistic expressions. In addition to these functions, song plays a mediating role between the language of prose and communication, and the metrical structures imposed by music. Song, therefore, constitutes the first formalisation of the collective conscience in 'poetical' structures that are different from those offered by the cinema or the novel.[39] For this reason, I think that in its role of

---

[36] Studies on songs of every era have been marginalised by philology and linguistics compared to the analysis of works more credited at a stylistic level, because of the prestige of the author, or of the autonomy of the artistic identity (not depending on music). As for the Italian tradition, only beginning in the 1970s, after Umberto Eco's famous chapter on the "consumable song" in U. Eco, *Apocalittici e integrati: Comunicazioni di massa e teorie della cultura di massa* (Milan, 1964), did research methods that before had been used exclusively for literary verse begin to be applied to popular songs. This para-academic legitimisation started to find echoes even in the literary field: see on a general level M. Pagnini, *Lingua e musica: Proposta per un'indagine strutturalistico-semiotica* (Bologna, 1974) and F. Bandini, "Una lingua poetica di consumo", in: *Poetica e stile: Saggi su opsis e lexis*, ed. L. Renzi and F. Donadi (Padua, 1976), pp. 191-200; *La lingua cantata: L'italiano nella canzone dagli anni Trenta ad oggi,* ed. G. Borgna and L. Serianni (Rome, 1994), followed two years later by Accademia degli Scrausi, *Versi rock: La lingua della canzone italiana negli anni '80 e '90* (Milan, 1996) and by the collection *Parole in musica: Lingua e poesia nella canzone d'autore italiana*, ed. L. Coveri (Novara, 1996), while the main reference remains G. Borgna, *Storia della canzone italiana*, 2nd edn. (Milan, 1992), improved by P. Jachia in his *La canzone d'autore italiana 1958-1997: Avventure della parola cantata* (Milan, 1998). The first literary journal that included musical LPs and CDs among poetical 'texts' to be reviewed was *Semicerchio: Rivista di poesia comparata*, beginning in 1989, which organised seminars on the topics; the proceedings of one of these (with Ivano Fossati) was published in the volume *Lezioni di poesia*, ed. A. Francini, P.F. Iacuzzi, and F. Stella (Florence, 2000). After that, S. La Via gave a meaningful acceleration to those studies with *Poesia per musica e musica per poesia: Dai trovatori a Paolo Conte* (Rome, 2006), now a standard reference, and on this path the Centro di Studi De André of Siena University accepted the challenge with the papers collected in the proceedings of a 2009 conference, *Il suono e l'inchiostro: Cantautori, saggisti, poeti a confronto*, ed. Centro Studi Fabrizio De André (Milan, 2009). A specific method for analysing popular music as multimedial communication has been developed by Philip Tagg, whose essays have been translated and collected in P. Tagg, *Popular music, da Kojak al Rave: Analisi e interpretazioni*, ed. R. de Agostini and L. Marconi (Bologna, 1994), proposing the category of 'museme' as a unit of musical meaning.

[38] I quote from *Lezioni di poesia*, ed. Francini *et al.*, p. 157.

[39] More and more we find on the walls of our towns phrases from popular songs as

representative of the collective language, the 'cultured' poetic code – which has, at least in Italy, become affected to the point of incommunicability, as well as socially irrelevant – has been replaced in the common conscience by a new code that has formed gradually through the *metrification pressure of popular music on daily prose*. And I imagine that this mechanism occurred also in Latin and then European rhythmical poetry in the early Middle Ages, when the quantitative versification of classical poetry had lost its pronounceability and its audience. At ecclesiastical assemblies, as crowded as rock concerts, appeared hymns using a new poetic language of syllables and accents.

This hypothesis can be indirectly tested in the work on the *Corpus Rhythmorum Musicum*, which provides the first edition, combining text and music, of the oldest medieval songs. The first volume and CD-ROM, following fifty introductory essays presented at three "Euro-Conferences",[40] were published in 2007[41] by an international research group after eight years of work (part of them were moved online in 2011).[42] When I say 'oldest medieval songs', I am referring to the earliest Latin compositions in versification, no longer quantitative but rhythmical, that is syllabotonic (founded on accentual and syllabic criteria). This textual tradition began in the fourth century with the *Psalmus responsorius* of the Barcelona Papyrus, a liturgical composition, and with the *Psalmus contra Donatistas* by St. Augustine, an anti-heretical polemical poem, and achieved its first mature form in the Carolingian era, to reach grandiose dimensions and influence the formation of European, Latin and vernacular, poetry of subsequent centuries. Of this versifying type, which gave rise to modern western poetry, the first part of the *Corpus* collects those poems which also show a musical tradition, that is, those in which, when sung, there are traces in the manuscripts of some code in neumatic notation, whose edition has been realised by Sam Barrett of Cambridge University.

---

immediately recognisable expressions of shared feelings, due to the facility of memorising widespread lyrics. The same process may have influenced the *probationes pennae* that populate the pages of medieval manuscripts.

[40] *Poesia europea dell'alto medioevo latino: Manoscritti, lingua e musica dei ritmi latini IV-IX secolo:. Atti delle Euroconferenze per il Corpus dei ritmi latini (IV-IX sec.), Arezzo 6-7 novembre 1998 e Ravello 9-12 settembre 1999*, ed. F. STELLA (Florence, 2000) and *Poetry of the Early Medieval Europe: Manuscripts, Language and Music of the Rhythmical Latin Texts: III Euroconference for the Digital Edition of the "Corpus of Latin Rhythmical Texts 4th-9th Century"*, ed. E. D'ANGELO and F. STELLA (Florence, 2003).

[41] *Corpus Rhythmorum Musicum saec. IV-IX*, 1, *Songs in Non-Liturgical Sources*, 1, *Lyrics*, ed. F. STELLA, S. BARRETT, *et al.* (Florence, 2007).

[42] At the website <www.corimu.unisi.it>.

This first selection brings together twenty-eight texts in a kind of anthology of the best religious and non-liturgical profane poetry of the *lato sensu* Carolingian period (seventh to ninth century):

... the confessional masterpieces of Paulinus of Aquileia and the dramatic lyrical creations of Gottschalk, the penitential texts such as *Anima nimis* and the *planctus* for historical personalities such as *A solis ortu* for Charlemagne, *Mecum Timavi* for Duke Henry, and *Hug dulce nomen* for the abbot of Charroux, the Angilbert *ritmus* for the Fontenoy battle and the biblical theatricalisations such as *Adam, Arbor, Fuit domini, Tertio in flore*, surreal riddles such as *Audite versus* and pseudo-liturgical allegorisations such as *Avis haec magna*, texts of moral catechism and popular Christmas songs such as *Gratuletur*, which entered the repertoire of secular songs such as the *Carmina Cantabrigiensia*, war and town songs of the local aristocracies such as the Modenese *rhythmus* and eschatological hymns such as *Qui de mortis* that anticipate the *Dies irae* by centuries, or the precursors to the *Ludus de Antichristo* such as the *Quique cupitis*. One has the impression that in this collection the music had selected a kind of laboratory of poetic tendencies – of themes, mode, and expression – that would flourish in the successive centuries, being distilled into a string of pearls that will sometimes be considered the very height of literature of this epoch and whose musical influence can be imagined to have spread much wider than a close circle of *literati*. We are convinced that this genre of rhythmic poetry represents the literary level of a semi-folk poetry that arose – often outside the schools – probably through rhythmical versification of prose, and that the presence of music served in some way to select the examples that were best able to represent the codes that the new poetic communication required.[43]

The edition which has emerged – for some texts it is the very first and for all texts it is the first which is both textual and musical – also comes in a digital version. This is, first of all, because no reconstructive philology exists in the field of antique music. The edition, however, is an interpretation of the scribal version and therefore requires the transcription of each single manuscript. Secondly, the execution of the modern transcriptions of these ancient notations can be enjoyed only on a multimedia instrument: since it was both possible and necessary to use a digital support and a specially created computer environment, we took the opportunity of supplying the user with a total reproduction, both photographic and textual, of all the sources, together with the 'recon-

---

[43] Adapted from my Introduction to the *Corpus*, p. XXVII. Further texts of a different nature (rhythmic hymns, computational music poems) are being published both on the website and in printed volumes (2020, 2021).

structed' textual version, wherever possible, or the various versions produced through philological hypothesis. The lyrics have been catalogued according to paleographical, linguistic, metrical, and musical information, including audio records of the creative modern transcriptions, thus enabling cross referencing, which allows multiple, quite sophisticated examinations of each text as a document of language and versification.

Of course, it would not be correct to define *tout court* the compositions published in the *Corpus Rhythmorum* as 'popular songs'. Certainly those composed by cultured writers such as Gottschalk the Saxon and Paulinus of Aquileia belong to that category of rhythmical poetry which Bede calls "*docta*", and cannot be analysed as evidence of popular production. Some other texts, or some hand-written versions of those texts, are partly scholastic and in any case all seem to share the same linguistic choices which, as demonstrated for Paulinus of Aquileia, the same writers do not adopt in texts of other genres. The Latin of Paulinus's *rhythmi* is different from the Latin in his treatises or metrical verses, just as the Italian of Pasolini's songs is different from that of his poetry. Therefore the genre imposes linguistic specificity, which creates the impression of strong links with the phenomena found by linguists in modern Italian songs. I shall try to list some aspects, whose similarities might form an embryo of linguistic-philological phenomenology that is peculiar to the 'song' type as opposed to the 'poem' type, regardless of time and place.

The Ritual Aspect

With regard to the practical nature of communication, one of the most obvious similarities regards the *ritual aspect* common to both early medieval and modern popular songs, in both televised and live-concert versions. These manifestations clearly take on a role of civil liturgy which in the early medieval *rhythmi* is evident not only in the hymns but also in many genres recorded in the *Corpus Rhythmorum Musicum* I: the *planctus,* for example, for the death of important people, or the paratheatrical versifications that relate biblical episodes in lyrical, semi-dialogue form. Examples include the story of Joseph and his brothers in *Tertio in flore* and the story of Lazarus in *Fuit domini*, both by Paulinus of Aquileia, but also the anonymous *rhythmus* of Adam and Eve; these texts were probably composed[44] for singing (and dancing?) at sacred ceremonies or ecclesiastical assembles as fringe attractions of a non-religious kind. The social, de facto liturgical function conveys and strengthens the feature of collective expression that this 'poetry' takes on and in this performative aspect represents a dynamic tool that is not accessorial but structural, that is, able to bear upon fundamental elements such as theme, rhythm, language, form.

The definition of 'rhythm' (*rhythmus*), which, according to late-Latin and medieval treatises,[45] can be associated with the movement of the body, to be interpreted as *ictu pollicis* rhythm or dance, leads to the development of specific instruments of analysis that are different from those of poetry and music. In one of the Euro-conferences, held in Munich in 2000, that preceded and prepared the edition, Daniel Jacob[46] proposed, based on the studies of Paul Zumthor,[47] the notion of "*oralité elaborée*",[48] which can be applied both to the songs of the early Middle Ages and to modern pop songs.

Acting within this notion are mnemotechnical and formulaic communication processes whose repeatability contribute to social identification, and which Ambrose and Augustine already defined as instruments to edify and entertain the masses. In modern songs, of course, the specific

---

[44] Walahfrid Strabo, *Libellus de exordiis et incrementis quarundam in observationibus ecclesiasticis rerum*, 26, ed. in: PL 114, col. 954C-D; new edn. and trans. A.L. HARTING-CORREA (Leiden, 1996), p. 160, with reference to Paulinus of Aquileia as author of new religious poetry and innovator in liturgy.

[45] Cf. Aphthonius: "*differt autem rhythmus a metro, quod metrum in verbis, rhythmus in modulatione ac motu corporis sit*", cited *supra*, p. 146. The *Ars metrica* of Atilius Fortunatianus (s. IV) has: "*est etiam rhythmus et in corporali motu*", ed. in *Grammatici latini* 6, ed. KEIL, p. 282, l. 20. The *Musica* of Remigius of Auxerre, forming book 9 of his *Commentum in Martianum Capellam*, speaks about *pulsus*: "*pulsus videlicet, nam et ipsi secundum ipsos rhythmos fiunt, et explorantur indicia signa pulsus*" (cf. ed. in: PL 131, col. 939C) and ID., *Commentum in Martianum Capellam*, ed. C.E. LUTZ, 2 vols. (Leiden, 1962-1965), 2, *Libri III-IX*, p. 352, 516.8: "*Rithmus igitur est compositio quaedam ex sensibilibus* [*scil. numeris*] (...) *collata temporibus* (...) *ad aliquem habitum* (...) *ordinemque conexa*", followed by a detailed explanation.

[46] D. JACOB, "Poésie rythmique et 'traditions discursives': Une perspective prototypicaliste sur les genres médiévaux", in: *Poetry of the Early Medieval Europe: Manuscripts, Language, and Music of the Rhythmical Latin Texts*, pp. 267-289.

[47] P. ZUMTHOR, *La Lettre et la voix: De la "littérature" médiévale* (Paris, 1987).

[48] *Ibid.*, p. 283: "*des discours de* distance communicative *se réalisant dans un modèle discursif dépourvu de recours graphiques*".

factor of commercial distribution cannot be ignored, but, when all is said and done, mass production does not change (nay, it enhances) the destination and social functions of such compositions. This can be seen most clearly in the ritual aspect of the rock concert, with its lengthy preparation, mass identification, mystical chanting of phrases drowning out the singer-celebrant, state of exaltation in proportion to the proximity of the celebrant and the altar-stage, and need for repetition. That Italian singers, for example, are now aware of this mechanism is clear from their own lyrics. Eros Ramazzotti mocks the "priestly" function assumed by "serious" singer-songwriters in the seventies and eighties and coins the term *santautore* ('saint-songwriter')[49] as a play of words on *cantautore* ('singer-songwriter').

Anisosyllabism

A feature shared by the song type in its manifestations in different eras is non-isosyllabism, which in the *Corpus Rhythmorum* can be calculated using the electronic research programme. Of the 28 texts in 140 witnesses published in the first volume and o CD-ROM, it is systematically present in six texts and 26 testimonies. This phenomenon is common in older Romance metrics, especially in the less cultured genres and in jester (*giullaresco*) poetry.[50] Obviously, since isosyllabism is not a normal feature of modern songs, they cannot be adduced as witnesses for non-isosyllabic verses. Even when it tends to be the main criterion of the

---

[49] "*e anche tu* santautore / *che dal tuo altare sparavi giù / non sai più cosa dire / le parole sono quasi finite / specialmente quelle finte*" (Eros Ramazzotti, *Non c'è più fantasia*, from the album *Tutte storie* (Sony BMG, 1993)). Before Ramazzotti, the self-consciousness of this sacrality was acknowledged and parodied by Edoardo Bennato in *Cantautore*, released as a single (Ricordi, 1976) and *Sono solo canzonette*, from the album of that name (Ricordi, 1980).

[50] C. DI GIROLAMO, "Regole dell'anisosillabismo", in: ID., *Teoria e prassi della versificazione* (Bologna, 1976; 2nd edn. 1983), pp. 119-135; B. SPAGGIARI, "Parità sillabica a oltranza nella metrica neolatina delle origini", *Metrica* 3 (1982), pp. 15-105; A. BERTONI, "La musicalità della poesia", *Argo: Rivista ufficiale del Collegium Scribarum Histrionumque*, 1, *Musica e poesia* (Nov. 2000: <https://www.argonline.it/argo/argo-n-1/argo-n-1_alberto-bertoni-musicalita-poesia/ >). A complete bibliography on the topics would be impressive.

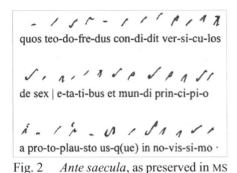

Fig. 2 *Ante saecula*, as preserved in MS Naples, Biblioteca Nationale, IV. G. 68, f. 207r.

single text, it does not exclude hypo- or hypermetre: the *Canzone di Marinella* by the famous Italian singer-songwriter Fabrizio De André is mostly written in hendecasyllables with many exceptions of twelve syllables, as in the first verse: "*Questa di Marinella è la storia vera*". In the same way, *Bocca di Rosa*, which appears to have regular rhythm, oscillates between decasyllable and dodecasyllable.[51]

We need to ask, however, to what extent this feature is influenced by music, not only during performance but also at the time of writing with performance in mind, or rather how much is due to a kind of permanent deviation permitted in the composition of 'low' genres of poetry, or yet again to oscillations of a standard that is still developing. Most likely, in different cases – early medieval poetry for music, early Romance poetry, modern songs – these factors bear influence in different proportions.

Music-Text Relationship

The centrality of performance produces in this genre a complex phenomenology concerning the music-text relationship.

Instances of adapting the melody to the text and vice-versa are evidently normal in songs of every period, and for the Carolingian age they have been analysed, for example by Susan Rankin in the introit *Ad te levavi*[52] and by Sam Barrett[53] in the *Corpus Rhythmorum*. One type of

---

[51] E. Pavese, "Situare lo stile nel suono di De André", in: *Il suono e l'inchiostro: poesia e canzone nell'Italia contemporanea* (Milan, 2009), pp. 221-249, at p. 223, underlines the presence of polyrhythmics and irregular rhythmical nuances in De André's performance.

[52] S. Rankin, "Carolingian Music", in: *Carolingian Culture: Emulation and Innovation*, ed. R. McKitterick (Cambridge, 1994), pp. 274-316.

[53] F. Stella (quoting Barrett's researches), "Ad cantandum carmina: Testo e musica nel

adaptation aims to incorporate redundant syllables, for example in the *rhythmus Ante saecula*, as preserved in MS Naples, Biblioteca Nationale, IV. G. 68, f. 207r (see Fig. 2). In the second strophe, the redundant syllable in the first hemistich of verse 3 is accommodated to the melody by dividing the *pes* (two ascending notes) that had appeared on the fourth syllable of the first strophe into two *virgae* (single notes): *de sex aetatibus et mundi principio* (where the edited text has *de sex aetates*).[54]

The process is also documented, however, in the opposite direction,[55] in the hymn *Gloriam Deo* attributed to the sophisticated proto-Carolingian Lombard poet, Paulinus of Aquileia, as represented in the famous MS Rome, Biblioteca Angelica 123, considered a landmark in the Bologna music school of the eleventh century. In strophe 11, vv. 2-3, where Edoardo D'Angelo's CRM edition (p. 240) has

hodie quia vobis Christus dominus
natus est Bethleem Davidis in oppido,

MS Angelica 123 shows

hodie vobis Christus deus natus est
bethleem • betheleem Davidis in opido.

The word *Bethleem* must be repeated in the text to maintain a certain melodic shape (Fig. 3).[56]

Corpus di ritmi latini musicati", in: *La poesia tardoantica e medievale, IV Convegno internazionale di studi, Perugia, 15-17 novembre 2007*, ed. C. BURINI DE LORENZI and M. DE GAETANO (Alessandria, 2010), pp. 333-354.
   [54] Cf. *Corpus Rhythmorum Musicum*, pp. 104 (Barrett) and 95 (ed. Stella).
   [55] STELLA, "Ad cantandum", p. 347.
   [56] BARRETT, *Corpus Rhythmorum Musicum* 1.1, p. 248.

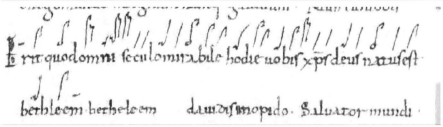

Fig. 3   *Gloriam Deo*, as preserved in MS Rome, Biblioteca Angelica 123, f. 188v.

The notation of *Ante saecula* tends to reflect the melody of the first- and second-verse hemistichs in the first hemistich of the refrain: a textual-musical figure which I believe can also be found in modern songs.[57]

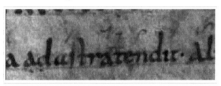

Fig. 4   Addition of a syllable (for musical reasons?) on the first verse of *Avis haec magna*, from MS Berne, Burgerbibliothek 455, f. 13v.

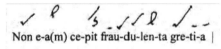

Fig. 5   *O tu qui servas*, strophe 1, line 4. MS Modena, Archivio storico diocesano, O.1.4, f. 154v.

The *rhythmus* of the Modenese sentinels, *O tu qui servas*, famous as a municipal song in the ninth century, shows an attempt to alter the melody in order to articulate *frau-* as a bisyllable[58] in the word *fraudulenta*, and this brings to mind similar cases of modern songs using a three-syllable *gloria* (e.g. *Gloria* by Umberto Tozzi) or *radio* (*Lupo solitario* by Marco Ferradini), two nouns that in modern spoken Italian are commonly pronounced as bisyllables.

The moment when music / text adaptation comes to the fore, of course, is during performance, and this should be explored with specific

---

[57] BARRETT, *Corpus Phytmorum Musicum* 1,1, p. 104. It is well known that neumes do not provide indication regarding rhythmic patterns and drive, but Barrett has demonstrated how in every case an attempt to underline with particular melodic patterns the most pathetic passages of the texts is evident, as happens in the *planctus* for Charlemagne, in the lines where the poet asks for the intercession of St. Columban, patron of the monastery where the author lived. A structural difference with modern songs is the existence of multiple musical settings for every lyric; in modern times this is to be found only for poems set to music and not for songs whose music is born at the same time as the text.

[58] STELLA, "Ad cantandum", p. 350.

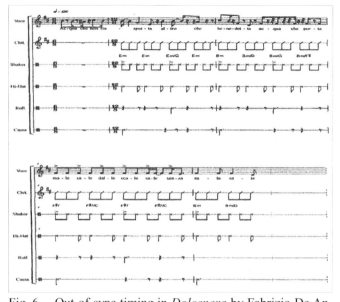

Fig. 6 Out-of-sync timing in *Dolcenera* by Fabrizio De André, as transcribed by Errico Pavese.

tools of analysis. The idiosyncratic performing habits of Italian singer-songwriter De André have been studied: the following table shows the distortions and non-synchronicity between the instrumental and vocal parts and the rhythmic irregularities of the cues of some instruments and the "continual out-of-sync timing" (Fig. 6).[59]

Of special interest for the purpose of historical / literary hypothesis are the cases of adaptation in musical notation to non-isosyllabism, and the symmetry between melodic gesture and accentual structure. In *Homo quidam*,[60] as Sam Barrett has written (cf. Fig. 7),[61]

> The melodic articulation of verse structure can be examined in detail through the close correspondence between the neumes of [MS] London Add. 19768 and the melody of [MS] Fulda [, Hessische Landesbibliothek] Aa 62. What is revealed are ways in which lines with an irregular number of syllables are adapted to a melodic shape that remains the same from the second strophe onwards. In strophes two to six, an association is retained between melodic gestures on odd-numbered syllables and accented syllables of the text. The unaccented upbeats in the third lines of strophes three, four and five are accommodated before the pitch associated with the first syllable.

---

[59] From PAVESE, "Situare lo stile nel suono di De André", p. 236.
[60] STELLA, "Ad cantandum", p. 348.
[61] *Corpus Rhythmorum Musicum* 1.1, p. 290. MS London, British Library, Add. 19768; MS Fulda, Hessische Landesbibliothek, Aa 62.

Some Linguistic Features of Popular Songs 165

Fig. 7   *Homo quidam*, as it occurs in MS London, British Library, Add. 19768, MS Fulda, Hessische Landesbibliothek, Aa 62, and MS Vienna, Österreichische Nationalbibliothek, lat. 1888; transcription of Sam Barrett.

In particular, study of the musical indications of MS Vienna, Österreichische Nationalbibliothek, lat. 1888, seems to confirm that musical stress falls on syllables which would not normally carry word stress but which are in a rhythmically strong position:[62]

> In the first line of the second strophe *c(eleriter)* and *t(enete)* are added to *qui-dam*, indicating that weight is to be accorded to the second syllable rather than the first. This indication runs contrary to the accent pattern of the individual word, but is in accordance with the overall tendency to retain stresses on the melodic figures associated with odd-numbered syllables in the line.[63]

In these cases, the music, which is usually independent of rhythmical structure, offers evidence that challenges the pre-eminence attributed to grammatical or prosodical stress by Norberg. MS Vienna 1888 shows the attempt to make certain melodic elements coincide with rhythmically accented syllables. This was the way of reciting Latin verses that the grammarian Sacerdos found as far back as the third century in Virgilian poetry,[64] and that according to Paul Klopsch[65] is the statistically proven trend of early medieval poetry: the regulating force of the rhythmic beat, which music also tended to recognise as uni-

---

[62] *Corpus Rhythmorum Musicum*, 1.1, p. 290.
[63] STELLA, "Ad cantandum", p. 348.
[64] Marcus Plotius Sacerdos, *Ars Grammatica*, ed. in: *Grammatici Latini* 6, ed. KEIL, p. 448, lines 20-23: "*Hoc tamen scire debemus, quod versus percutientes [id est scandentes] interdum accentus alios pronuntiamus quam per singula verba ponentes:* toro *et* pater *acutum accentum in* to *ponimus et in* pa, *scandendo vero* inde toro pater Aeneas *in* ro *et in* ter". The interpretation of the passage is difficult; it is analysed by BURGER, *Recherches sur la structure*, p. 101 n. 33, and D'ARCO SILVIO AVALLE, "Dalla metrica", pp. 395-396.
[65] P. KLOPSCH, *Einführung in die mittellateinische Verslehre* (Darmstadt, 1972).

form and constant, continues through the whole verse and is not limited to the cadence.[66]

Alterations of Accentuation

The hypothesis of a rhythmical reading of rhythmical verses which, however natural, was, after Norberg, strongly contested by some musicologists and mediolatinists, would seem to be confirmed in the statistical prevalence of strong beats and grammatical stress both in military verses of the first century CE, as reported by Roman historians, as well as by the arrangement found in more mature rhythmic poems from the seventh century onward (starting with the *Apparebit repentina* quoted by Bede). This hypothesis, in fact, would imply the regular recitation of verses even when there is no ictus / accent coincidence. Stefano La Via[67] has devoted an important paragraph to the definition of two permanent trends in the musical interpretation of poetry, one isorhythmical and strophic, and another that he calls non-strophic and therefore independent from isosyllabic verses. But perhaps the dialectic can be still better understood if we appropriate, for the sake of discussion, the medieval musicological terms of *cantus mensuratus* and *cantus planus in campo aperto*.[68] These terms would be redirected to evoke two different interpretations of the same texts set to music, one with accentuation which tends to be regular or isorhythmic on strong metrical beats ('mensural'), and the other with a linguistic accentuation, as required by the rules of the language and not as imposed by the rhythmic scheme adapted to the melodic outline ('open'). These two opposing ways can be found also in modern song and can be seen in different stages in the artistic development of some Italian song-writers. Examples include Lucio Battisti – the leading composer both of mensural songs with lyrics by Mogol, and of *campo aperto* with lyrics by Panella – as well as Baglioni and

---

[66] STELLA, "Ad cantandum", pp. 351-352, from BARRETT, *Corpus Rhythmorum Musicum* 1.1, p. 281.

[67] LA VIA, *Poesia per musica*, pp. 137-146.

[68] *Mensura* normally refers, in later medieval music, to the systematic ordering of rhythmic durations; cf., e.g., Franco of Cologne, *Ars cantus mensurabilis*, ed. G. REANEY and A. GILLES (s.l., 1974). I thank Graeme Boone for this suggestion. *Campo aperto* refers to the lack of written staff lines, and accompanying lack of diastematy, in the earliest musical notations; cf., e.g. W. APEL, *Gregorian Chant* (Bloomington, 1958), p. 118.

Fossati.[69] In English songs, the opposition lies between the metronomic declamation, for example of *Hotel California* by the Eagles, and a freer interpretation of some less commercial pop songs such as *Paint it Black* by the Rolling Stones (1966), when Mick Jagger anticipates the beat in the first bars. Usually the isorhythmical songs achieve the greatest commercial success for the obvious reason that they are easier to remember. However, the mensural way inevitably produces an alteration of word stress to bring it into line with the musical beat. The writer Sandro Veronesi, in his preface to *Versi rock*,[70] one of the first Italian attempts to analyse the language of rock songs, devotes an ironic paragraph to the comical effects of the shifted stress which, as all evidence would seem to suggest, is an indisputable feature of (not only) Italian songs. He quotes examples from the pseudo-folkloric repertoire ("*Urlàno i fedelissimi / E scoppia il cha cha cha*" by Toni Santagata) to the pseudo-cultured one of Battiato ("*furbi contrabbandieri macedonì*", "*dinàstia dei Ming*"), to which I would add the famous *Libèrta* by Ramazzotti. He closed with a quote from a song by Elio e le Storie Tese (*Cateto*) which systematically uses words with the wrong stress for the sake of parody. It is curious that Dag Norberg, too, should describe with scandalised derision the hypothesis that the Latin word *oculi* in St. Augustine's *rhythmus* could be pronounced *ocúli* for the sake of the beat.[71] In my opinion it is just simply what happens in reality, as the popular songs of every region and period show.

In the collection of early medieval songs, examples of such a so-called 'anti-schematic' position are easy to find, if we pursue an ictic rather than grammatical reading of the text: we need go only as far as the first of the readings of the CRM, the planctus *A solis ortu* for Charlemagne, where, if we run through the first verses, we find v. 3, 2 *magnà* ("*Franci, Romani atque cuncti creduli / luctu punguntur et magna molestia*") 5, 2 *interìtum* ("*Iam iam non*

---

[69] See the difference between the early Lucio Battisti (lyrics by Mogol) and the later Battisti (lyrics by Pasquale Panella), the early Ivano Fossati (*La mia banda suona il rock*, RCA 1979) and Fossati post-*Una notte in Italia* (*700 giorni*, CBS 1986), as well as the early vs. later Baglioni (after *La vita è adesso*, CBS 1985).

[70] S. VERONESI, preface to *Versi rock*, p. 15.

[71] Cf. NORBERG, *An Introduction to the Study of Medieval Latin Versification*, trans. ROTI and SKUBLY, ed. ZIOLKOWSKI, p. 82: "[Augustine:] *Propter hoc Dóminus noster voluit nos praemonere / Comparans régnum caelorum retículo misso in mare*. [... Anonymous hymn:] *Óculi somnum capiant, / Cor semper ad te vigilet; / Déxtera tua protegat / Fámulos qui te diligunt*. Strangely enough, certain scholars believe that St. Augustine, in the verses quoted, really followed the accentuation *Domínus, regnúm* and *reticúlo* or that the anonymous author of the hymn read *ocúli, dextéra,* and *famúlos*".

cessant lacrimarum flumina, / nam plangit orbis interitum Karoli") 10, 2 *éxaltét* ("*animam suam exaltet in requiem*"), 17, 2 *illò*, necessary also to compensate for the hiatus ("*precesque funde pro illo ad dominum*"). More than a century ago Johann Huemer recorded similar examples, including *trinìtatis* and *spirìtus*, which he called "*schwebende Betonung*",[72] but the authority of Norberg's opinion against these revelations has prevented them from being properly assessed.

Combined Presence of Archaisms and Linguistic Vulgarisms

The mode of communication in popular poetry produces a linguistic blend that is always artificial, and comparable in different eras. Both early medieval songs and modern pop songs combine an old language and a mutating morphology:[73] a whole series of linguistic phenomena is found in the Latin *rhythmi* of the early Middle Ages much more frequently than in metrical poetry or in other documents. Here we can mention but a few. All these phenomena can now be found, through a search by field on the database, in the texts (and in each individual transcription) of the *CRM*.[74] Some of these alterations have already been noted by experts of Merovingian formulas or Latin *circa romançum* and without a doubt can be classified as vulgarisms or as examples of evolution.

---

[72] J. HUEMER, *Untersuchungen über die ältesten lateinisch-christlichen Rhythmen* (Vienna, 1879), pp. 24ff.

[73] F. STELLA, *La poesia carolingia latina a tema biblico* (Spoleto, 1993). The chapter on rhythmical poetry is at pp. 426-432.

[74] Some selected features: exchange *i/e* (e.g., *gloriose* for *gloriosi* in *A solis ortu* 4, 1 in the version of MS Brussels, Bibliothèque Royale 8860-67, ff. 39r-40r: cf. *Corpus Rhythmorum Musicum* 1.1); falling of final *-t* (especially in north-Italian texts); prosthesis of *e-* before impure *s* (typical of Gallo-Roman and Hispanic areas); *s* for *x* (e.g., *senex* for *senis* in *Tertio in flore* 42, 1 in the version of MS Paris, Bibliothèque nationale de France, latin 1121, ff. 234v-239v: cf. *Corpus Rhythmorum Musicum* 1.1); *g* for *z* and vice versa (*zelo*), *p* for *b*; simplification of the double consonants or of consonantal groups; weakening of final *-m* with subsequent confusion between accusative and ablative; new structuring of the prepositional use of *de, in, a, cum, per, pro*; unique form of the relative pronoun (*qui*); heteroclisy (change of declension: e.g., *Tertio in flore* 17, 3 *oculorum geminum*); heterogenesis (change of gender: e.g., *Tertio in flore* 42, 4 *uterinos soboles*); hypercorrection; extension of the past perfect instead of the perfect, 'prophetical' present (to announce narrative developments); structural re-functionalisation of the present participle (which becomes one of the most frequent forms of subordinate sentence); weakening of other subordinate clauses (consecutive, concessive, etc.); causal value of *nam*, frequency of *dum* in the place of temporal *cum*; adverbial redeterminations (adverbs composed by a group of other adverbs), new locutions, creative neologisms.

Even the analysis conducted on the language of Italian singer-songwriters in the 1980s and 90s frequently shows grammatical changes,[75] to which any of us can easily add examples.[76] The more working-class, street-savvy, or 'transgressive' the musical genre, the more frequently they occur: the ballads sung by Frank Sinatra or Anita Baker are obviously more linguistically regular, from a mainstream-normative standpoint, than the rap of Eminem or 50 Cent. In early medieval songs, a more extreme deformity can be found at a morphological and phonetic level, while modern pop songs usually allow syntactic freedom. In both cases, however, we are dealing with a greater proximity to the spoken word, the adoption of a semi-popular linguistic register which is sensitive to mutations in real time. More analytical observations should be extended to word order and their placement in the 'verse', the result of both metrical and literary influences.[77]

This intentional contiguity with the common language is either flanked or opposed, changing with the writer, by a recovery of elements of traditional poetic language, often trivial and hyperconnoted, which are justified both as a convenient resource in the repertoire of general 'poetese' (standard poetic language) as well as an element of intentional stylistic or parodic enhancement. Examples can be found on opening any page or digital music player, such as

---

[75] L. CEREDA, G. MEACCI, and F. SERAFINI, "Ci ragiono e canto: la canzone d'autore", in: *Versi rock*, pp. 27-143, and other publications by the Accademia degli Scrausi.

[76] E.g., in Eros Ramazzotti, where they individuate the incorrect use of the relative pronoun ("*quello che copiavo*" in the place of "*quello da cui copiavo*") and suspensions or 'project changes', that is, unfinished clauses that change subject irregularly, or the polyvalent *che* ("*in questo sabato d'animale che non sapevo cosa fare*", Ron) and catachretic costructions such as *mi piace di, attraversiamo su* (Concato), besides lexical elements of the spoken language (*sleppare, stressare, casino, sballare*).

[77] The 'Scrausi' documented for example the "*dislocazione a sinistra*" ("move to the left", that is anastrophe) by the pop singer Luca Carboni ("*di persone silenziose / ce ne sono eccome*" from the song and album *Persone silenziose*, BMG Ariola 1989), and of course medieval songs are full of figures of *ordo artificialis* that connotate them as 'poetry', e.g., *Leo ut sevus* (ed. in: PLAC 4.2, ed. STRECKER, p. 589: *rhythmus* No. 58, 11, 1) while they do not avoid the lowest lexical register. In the *Corpus Rhythmorum Musicum*, one of the criteria for statistical analysis of the language was the proximity of the Latin in these songs to proto-Romance, or rather, to a register which is more spontaneous and nearer to those which are now characteristic of the Romance languages: SVO order rather than SOV, the short distance between S and V, the short distance between name and attribute, the frequency of prepositions, etc., calculated according to a numerical grid drawn up by myself and the sociolinguist Michel Banniard. Likewise, a second grid drawn up with the Mediolatinist Peter Stotz records language phenomena that diverged from traditional and, as it were, grammatical use. On this, see *Digital Philology and Quantitative Criticism*, Chapter Six.

"*qui / sotto un mucchio di stelle / qui lo scenario che c'è / è perfetto insieme a te*", by Eros Ramazzotti, who reuses the cliché with a tone of metapoetic awareness that takes the edge off its naivety. In medieval songs, on the other hand, the reuse of late antique cliché (especially by Christian poets such as Sedulius and Prudentius) expects total acquiescence, and is not mitigated by underlying irony. A combination of spoken language, neologisms,[78] stereotypes, residual 'high' language, and innovation (sometimes successful, sometimes clumsy) is constant, and becomes typical in the work of singer-songwriters like Battiato, whose songs are thought to have a kind of "centrifugal structure":[79] they are a mixture of paradox, aphorisms, autobiographical flashes, quotations – cultured and otherwise – assembled and blended together, preserving "the nature of autonomous fragments, devoid of syntactical cohesion and logical consistency".[80] A similar pastiche can be found in fragments of early medieval *rhythmi* as in the Strecker *rhythmus* 25 variation, *De laude dei*, preserved in the eighth-to-ninth century MS Cologne, Erzbischöfliche Diözesan- und Dombibliothek 212,[81] which fuses, in disorderly sequence, quotations from the hymn by Prudentius on Saint Eulalia (*Peristephanon* 3) with references to the story of David and Goliath and the Canticle of Canticles. The clearest examples on a linguistic level, however, are Strecker's *rhythmi* 91-93, from the Merovingian-era MS Lyon, Bibliothèque Municipale 425, which present a vulgarised style, mixing liturgical Latin and proto-French in an extremely early phase, e.g. "*Homnes homo Christianus qui haccepet baptismo / In deo*

---

[78] The neologisms of medieval rhythmical poetry are often a creation by learned authors (such as *balsiger*, *dealis*, *reliquare* of Paulinus of Aquileia, or *salvamen* and *liberamen* of Hrabanus Maurus), but sometimes they are spontaneous inventions by unknown poets, such as *archisedens* (in PLAC 4.2, ed. STRECKER, p. 479: *rhythmus* No. 7, 16, 1) or *previde* (*ibid.*, p. 481: *rhythmus* No. 8, 8, 1), while the much more frequent morphological or semantic neologisms are, on the contrary, relatively unusual among the singer-songwriters.

[79] A sample from *Bandiera bianca* (from Franco Battiato, *La voce del Padrone*, EMI Italiana, 1981): "*Mr. Tamburino non ho voglia di scherzare / Rimettiamoci la maglia, i tempi stanno per cambiare, / siamo figli delle stelle e pronipoti di sua maestà il denaro (...) / Com'è misera la vita negli abusi di potere. / Sul ponte sventola bandiera bianca.* [×4] */ A Beethoven e Sinatra preferisco l'insalata*".

[80] CEREDA, MEACCI, and SERAFINI, "Ci ragiono e canto", pp. 102-103: in the quoted example from Battiato they detect references to Bob Dylan's *Mr. Tambourine Man* and to the 'Risorgimento' song of Arnaldo Fusinato that provided the title for the track, but I would also recognise the title of Alan Sorrenti's song *Figli delle stelle*, with merely phonetic combinations such as *Sinatra - insalata* to highlight the kitsch context. Once again, notwithstanding the grotesque register, the line "*Com'è misera la vita ...*" has become a political catchphrase: its epigraphic reproduction, datable to 2010, can still be read along Via Corridoni in Florence.

[81] PLAC 4.2, ed. STRECKER, p. 524: *rhythmus* No. 25.

devet cogitare, non peccare nemio. / Christi, resuveniad de mi peccatore" etc.[82]

Intentional linguistic and artistic pastiches can of course be found in the plurilingual Romance *descorts* or in the *zagialesca* strophes in Arabic and Spanish. As regards modern Italian songs, the best and most obvious example is found in the lyrics of Pino Daniele in English and Neapolitan, such as "*I say I' sto 'ccà*".[83] But this phenomenon, much studied by world-music researchers, is also present in classical poetry, just in a parodic way.

Development of an Internal Tradition

One of the most interesting aspects of comparative analysis lies in the development of techniques for creating a specific song language through the variation of internal tradition and the growth of genre awareness. In medieval *rhythmi*, a formulaic repertoire is formed on a low paraliturgical base, overlaid with fragments of Christian metrical poetry and biblical echoes. Writers gradually become aware of this series of expressive patterns, this arsenal of cliché, as they begin to quote their predecessors, particularly if they were of the same school (as in the *rhythmi* of Corbie between Theofrid and Siegfried, or in the Verona or Saint Gall schools),[84] although the models are hardly ever actually named. Likewise for modern song: following the first formative decades of the canon, there was a proliferation in the nineties of parody-type references; explicit,[85] as well as implicit and even hidden,[86] sophisticated allusions;[87] and clear references, though without names.[88] The exposure of imitative practice constitutes a tradition, since, as Borges says, every writer creates his own pre-

---

[82] Cf. *rhythmus* No. 92 in *PLAC* 4.2, ed. STRECKER, p. 651.

[83] On these plurilingualisms, see E. CAFFARELLI, G. D'ACUNTI, and A. RICCI, "Neri a metà: Blues, rhythm & blues, funky e fusion", in: *Versi rock*, pp. 251-262.

[84] I believe I have demonstrated such filiations in F. STELLA, "Le raccolte di ritmi precarolingi e la tradizione manoscritta di Paolino d'Aquileia: Nuclei testuali e rapporti di trasmissione", *Studi Medievali*, 3rd sereis, 39 (1998), pp. 809-832.

[85] We have seen it in Battiato.

[86] E.g., to Battisti and Bob Marley in Zucchero, *Donne* (from *Zucchero & the Randy Jackson Band*, Polydor, 1985).

[87] Ivano Fossati lets Lorendana Berté quote (in *Traslocando,*, CBS 1982) his own song entitled *E di nuovo cambio casa* (from *La mia banda suona il rock*, RCA 1979) indebted in turn to Gino Paoli's *La gatta*.

[88] E.g., Concato's *Guido piano*, as quoted by Tiziano Ferro.

decessors, and identifies his language. This procedure is structural in classical poetry, but in popular poetry it appears in moments of growth and artistic fulfilment and comes into play, sometimes in a complex way, with musical allusion.

The growth of a tradition has been physically recorded and formalised through the song book, which is shared by the proto-medieval and contemporary traditions. The whole tradition of early medieval *rhythmi* is defined by the great song books, MS Brussels, Bibliothèque Royale, 8860-67, where music is noted only in the margins of a few pages, and MS Leiden, Universiteitsbibliotheek, Voss. Lat. Q 69, both traceable to the school of Saint Gall; MS Verona, Biblioteca Capitolare, XC (85), the exercise books of a capitular school; MS Paris, Bibliothèque nationale de France, latin 1154, the splendid repertoire of Saint-Martial of Limoges with music.[89] And then the school poetry books, such as the *Carmina Cenomanensia*, the *Carmina Cantabrigensia*, and so on up to the famous *Carmina Burana*, for which the manuscript brings us to the thirteenth century and the text, partially accompanied by music, to the end of the twelfth century. These are different instruments, some produced as a community or school repertoire, others as a record of travelling and court minstrels. This second aspect bears some similarity to songbooks sold today in music shops, which allow amateurs and piano bar singers to learn, perfect, and present their own repertoire in domestic or professional exhibitions. Both types, in fact, offer simple information that is insufficient for knowing how to perform but serves as a reminder, to those who already know the songs, of the melody and rhythms.

Plurality of Versions

In early medieval songs, and also in poetry for music in the later Middle Ages, it is often difficult to reconstruct a unitary *facies* of the original text, because versions of the same text – sometimes so different as to appear irreconcilable – often appear in the sources. This finds an obvious parallel in studio-recorded versions as opposed to live versions of many modern songs, when the lyrics are corrected, integrated, or adapted to new situations and new contents

---

[89] P. BOURGAIN, "Les recueils carolingiens de poésie rythmique", in: *De Tertullien aux Mozarabes: Mélanges offerts à Jacques Fontaine à l'occasion de son 70ᵉ anniversaire*, 2, *Antiquité tardive et christianisme ancien (VIᵉ-IXᵉ siècles)*, ed. L. HOLTZ (Paris, 1992), pp. 117-127.

or 'tidied up', all the versions being legitimate and all traceable to the same composer(s). Sometimes the lyrics published on the covers of LPs and in the booklets accompanying CDs do not match what we actually hear.[90] Similarly, for *A solis ortu,* the funeral *planctus* for the death of Charlemagne, we find at least four different forms of the refrain,[91] and for *Homo quidam*, four different editions of the same text in CRM.[92]

In the same way, the Broadway song *The Man I Love* (lyrics by Ira Gershwin, music by George Gershwin), now an American jazz standard, was originally introduced by a recitative-style 'verse', the word and characteristics ultimately deriving from the early medieval Latin *versus*. It is not sung in the recordings by Gershwin (1934) and Billie Holiday (1939), while in that of Sarah Vaughan (1957), it is. In the same way we can recall the recited prooemium of Augustine's *Psalmus*, and even in Carolingian times the *rhythmus De Lazaro* by Paulinus of Aquileia with incipit *Fuit domini dilectus* was passed down in

---

[90] In a paper on Italian song production (E. DE ANGELIS, "Nota", in: *Il suono e l'inchiostro*, pp. 249-251), Enrico de Angelis underlines the chaos that dominates in transcriptions of contemporary song: starting from the absence of interpunction, always inserted by the editors and never by authors, and continuing with determination of new lines. The sources for reconstructing the lyrics of songs are "extremely heterogeneous and unstable: the author's original draft (obviously, a very rare case); the official SIAE (Società Italiana degli Autori ed Editori) copy, if the text has been deposited (but note that when the titles are deposited, the texts are not necessarily included, and it is not in any event easy to obtain them from the SIAE); the music publisher's copy, if there is one (but the publishers do not always keep them, and when they do, it is not easy to obtain them); transcriptions provided with the published disc; diffuse publications, utterly voluntary and whimsical, on the internet; the lyrics that are presented in musical transcriptions; whatever books may have printed them; transcriptions from listening to a recording". These sources are always precarious and unreliable. De Angelis's conclusion, that only listening can dictate a transcription as close as possible to the original, even if devoid of lines of division and orthography, can be compared to the statements of such medievalist musicologists as Giacomo Baroffio, according to whom (by personal communication) the only possible edition of a musical piece is its performance.

[91] A similar problem surfaces in *Ante saecula,* a kind of resumé of holy history (seventh century) that is transmitted in two versions of more or less contemporaneous composition, but which are completely different in the use of verbal tenses and in orthography: one consistently adopts the perfect tense, the other the past perfect. Which one is the original? We guess that the rougher one is the older, but it is hard to decide if one or both stem from the same author. Cf. STELLA, *Corpus Rhythmorum Musicum* 1.1, pp. 89-102.

[92] Cf. *Corpus Rhythmorumm Musicum*, 1.1, pp. 276-83, where the editor, Francesco Lo Monaco, presents four different versions of the rhythmical poem *Homo quidam,* which recounts the parable of Lazarus and the rich man. Each version is characterised by differing length (presence or absence of some strophes or lines) or readings (single words or hemistichs), or by a refrain.

two versions, one shorter and of a more lyrical-narrative nature, a kind of recited ballad, the other longer, in which the related events are interpreted in the light of the four senses of Scripture. Music accompanies only one of the manuscripts of the first version, but it is possible that also the second was partly sung and partially recited.

The procedures and techniques used in the creation of a popular poetry or song tradition, beginning with the metrical organisation of a prose language, find terms of comparison in various eras, and this could almost suggest the phenomenon's social reproducibility.

As regards both medieval popular poetry and modern song, it is their own *uncertainty* which, for whoever wishes to study them, imposes a historical limit. Created for oral expression, they leave written traces only when collected for the use of schools or professional singers, albeit not in their original form, and certainly with no demonstrable and protected relationship to the original lyrics and music. The commercial distribution and mass production of modern song certainly contribute to a plethora of evidence, but not to greater stability. The spontaneous and occasional forms of quotation in speech or writing and of reuse, as in graffiti, do not guarantee that these forms will endure: in this regard, too, early medieval songs are similar to today's pop songs. Whenever the recording and playback apparatus is superseded – record player, compact disc, mp3 player, iPod, online streaming – many songs not adapted to newer media will be lost. Just as happened with early medieval *rhythmi*, it will then be necessary to conduct a philological study to recover sound, in one of the many forms in which it has entered into the acoustic memory of human lives.

Chapter 8

Versus ad picturas in the Carolingian Age

History of the Genre

The *versus ad picturas* is a term used to indicate the poetic *tituli*, that is, the captions in verse of images, preserved or lost, real or imaginary. The expression derives from a work by Ekkehard IV, a monk of Saint Gall in the eleventh century, who described a cycle of paintings on the Old and New Testaments in 867 hexameters Bishop Aribo had commissioned it from him, after Ekkehard's success at writing *tituli* for a life of Saint Gall,[1] because he was planning on having the frescoes done after the restructuration of the cathedral of Mainz, which had caught fire in 1009. But Aribo died in 1031 and the paintings were never made; so Ekkehard restricted himself to using his compositions, entitled *Versus ad picturas domus domini Moguntine veteris testamenti et novi*, for educational purposes when he returned to the school of Saint Gall. There remains an autograph manuscript,[2] the source of the only modern edition, now a century old and all but impossible to find in libraries, by J. Egli.[3]

Nonetheless, the genre was not invented by Ekkehard. The first instances of it go back to classical Antiquity: in book 5 of his *Descriptio Greciae*, Pausanias speaks of a chest from the sixth century BCE legendarily said to date back to Cypselus, tyrant of Corinth, with mythological scenes explained by epigrams, some of which Pausanias quotes, just as verse was found on frag-

---

[1] Ed. K. STRECKER, with N. FICKERMANN, in: *PLAC* 5.1.2, pp. 540-546.
[2] MS Saint Gall, Stiftsbibliothek 393, pp. 197-238.
[3] *Der Liber benedictionum Ekkeharts IV.: Nebst kleineren Dichtungen aus dem Codex Sangallensis 393*, ed. J. EGLI (St. Gall, 1909).

ments of ceramic representations of Achilles' shield (Rome, Capitoline Museum) or the Iliac tablets (*ibid.*), while we find other metrical *tituli* in the House of the Epigrams in Pompeii. The Greek anthology has preserved others still, from later periods (for example 19 from the first book on the cycle of the temple of Apollo in Cyzicus; second century BCE), while the Christianisation of the genre, which brings us closer to the examples that we wish to discuss, arises in Latin with Paulinus of Nola's inscriptions for the basilica of Primuliacum, requested by Sulpicius Severus (*Epistola* 32), while in *Epistola* 27 he describes to his friend Nicetas when Paulinus is on a virtual tour of Campania, the images of a church dedicated to Saint Felix in Nola, which have been reconstructed by art historians based on Paulinus's descriptions. But the true founder of the genre is the great Christian poet Prudentius, to whom 48 *tituli historiarum*, epigrams with four hexameters, are attributed. These were circulated across the manuscript tradition as the *Dittochaeon*, meaning 'double nourishment', in reference to scenes from the Old and New Testament. Recent research seems convinced that they refer to real images, for which possible models have been sought,[4] but there are no explicit indications of this in the text. Other examples from late Antiquity are the 21 couplets attributed to Saint Ambrose[5] and therefore believed to be connected to the eponymous basilica, the 24 *Tristicha* of Rusticius Elpidius, transmitted in an unknown lost codex that can be reconstructed from G. Fabricius's edition from 1562, and in a difference sequence from the Codex Bertinianus – also now lost but used in 1617 by André Du Chesne (Quercetanus), an editor of the works of Alcuin, which took up most of that codex. Minor series are found in Ps.-Claudian's *Miracula Christi*, in the work of Venantius Fortunatus, especially his inscriptions for ecclesiastical buildings, and in Agnellus's *Liber pontificalis ecclesiae Ravennatis* (ninth century).

With Agnellus, we have already entered the Carolingian era, in which this chapter has the greatest interest: it was in that period that there was a small explosion in the composition of iconographic *tituli*, that would become increasingly frequent with Ekkehard IV, the many bibles and artistic objects of the eleventh and twelfth centuries, the epigrams of Marbod, Baldric, and Hildebert

---

[4] A. ARNULF, *Versus ad picturas: Studien zur Titulusdichtung als Quellengattung der Kunstgeschichte von der Antike bis zum Hochmittelalter* (Munich, 1997), pp. 84-100: "Die Tituli historiarum im Vergleich mit überlieferten Bildzyklen".

[5] S. MERKLE, "Die Ambrosianische Tituli: Eine literarhistorische-archäologische Studie: Mit einer Ausgabe der Tituli als Anhang", *Römische Quartalschrift* 10 (1896), pp. 181-222, at pp. 213 ff.

of Lavardin, and the inscriptions for the abbey church of Fleury in the *Life of Gauzlinus*, in the works of Peter Damian, in the aesthetic-theological reworking of Suger of Saint-Denis, and finally the sacred painting of the fourteenth and fifteenth centuries and in the *Bibliae pauperum*, which would make a popular genre out of these *Versus ad picturas*.

Until some years ago, studies dedicated very little space to this kind of poetry. This was both because art historians did not consider such *tituli* necessary for understanding the artwork, or because they had difficulty interpreting them, and because literary scholars rightly considered them a marginal production, and hard to appreciate in the absence of a figurative context. Not even Julius von Schlosser had used them systematically in his precious collections as Latin sources for art history, except for Rusticius Elpidius and Venantius Fortunatus. I dealt with them amply in a long chapter of my doctoral dissertation,[6] developing the few but well-founded observations set out by Günter Bernt in his work on the history of the epigram.[7] The same year in which that work, completed in 1991, was published, the Spoleto *Settimana di studio* was dedicated to none other than "Text and image", with a series of reports of a very high standard that continue to be points of reference for everyone and which favoured the spread of the text / image theme in current medieval studies.[8] Three years after the publication of the Spoleto conference proceedings, Arnulf Arwed published the first and only monograph on the genre, entitled

---

[6] F. STELLA, *La poesia carolingia latina a tema biblico* (Spoleto, 1993), pp. 147-207: "Tituli iconologici e diversi".

[7] G. BERNT, *Das lateinische Epigramm im Übergang von der Spätantike zum frühen Mittelalter* (Munich, 1968).

[8] I shall cite only, apart from the research on individual texts or manuscripts, *Testo e immagine nell'alto medioevo*, 2 vols. (Spoleto, 1994: *Settimana di studi del Centro italiano di studi sull'alto medioevo* 41); *Die Verschriftlichung der Welt: Bild, Text und Zahl in der Kultur des Mittelalters und der frühen Neuzeit*, ed. H. WENZEL, W. SEIPEL, and G. WUNBERG (Vienna and Milan, 2000); *Testo e immagine nel medioevo germanico: Atti del 26. Convegno dell'Associazione Italiana di Filologia Germanica* [Venice 26-28 May 1999], ed. M.G. SAIBENE and M. BUZZONI (Milan, 2001); *Text – Bild – Kommunikation / Bild – Text – Kommunikation,* ed. E. STRASSNER (Tübingen, 2002); *Medieval Memory: Image and Text,* ed. F. WILLAERT *et al.* (Turnhout, 2004); *Wort – Bild – Text: Studien zur Medialität des Literarischen im Hochmittelalter und früher Neuzeit* (Baden Baden, 2007). In previous years, the topic was addressed in *Text und Bild: Text-Bild-Kommunikationen aus sprachwissenschaftlicer Sicht*, ed. M. MUCKENHAUPT (Tübingen, 1986); *Poesis et pictura: Studien zum Verhältnis von Text und Bild in Handschriften und alten Drucken: Festschrift für Dieter Wüttke zum 60. Geburtstag*, ed. S. FUSSEL and J. KNAPE (Baden Baden, 1989); and *Text und Bild: Aspekte des Zusammenwirkens zweier Kunste im Mittelalter und früher Neuzeit*, ed. C. MEIER-STAUBACH and U. RUBERG (Wiesbaden, 1980).

Versus ad picturas: Studien zur Titulusdichtung als Quellengattung der Kunstgeschichte von der Antike bis zum Hochmittelalter.[9] It addresses the history of this textual typology from its origins until the twelfth century, attempting to assess its continuity, but without keeping in mind the earlier bibliography, especially in non-Germanic languages – not even the Spoleto conference proceedings, which are the most widespread series of medieval studies in the world, and still less the brief but prophetic pages of A. Quacquarelli, who in 1986 was one of the first to speak of a genuine iconological genre.[10] Despite the limits of information and the difficulty of moving through historical-literary terrain, Arnulf's work is precious for the texts under examination because it was the first to reconstruct their history as the expressive codification of an authentic literary genre, even though this recognition runs the opposite risk of isolating the verses for images from other poetic texts produced for the same context but not attributable to images. After all, every work that places itself on the border between different disciplines – in this case medieval art history and medieval Latin philology – inevitably risks a certain lack of contextualisation.

The Carolingian Era and the Problem of Images

In the Carolingian era, this tradition, which largely originated from the practical aims of worship, went through a kind of institutionalisation and cultural re-establishment caused by the problem of images. In fact, as we know, in 787 the restoration of the worship of images by the council of Nicaea led the Western church – the Frankish one in particular – to take on for political contrast a different though not extreme position, reached in the elaboration of the *Libri Carolini*, or rather the *Opus Caroli regis contra Synodum*, which have been much studied in recent years, especially thanks to Ann Freeman, to whom we owe the exemplary edition of 1998[11] that attributed the text to Theodulf, bishop of Orléans. In the *Libri Carolini*, whose real objective was more politi-

---

[9] A. ARNULF, *Versus ad picturas: Studien zur Titulusdichtung als Quellengattung der Kunstgeschichte von der Antike bis zum Hochmittelalter* (Berlin and Munich, 1997).

[10] A. QUACQUARELLI, *Reazione pagana e trasformazione della cultura (fine IV secolo d.C.)* (Bari, 1986), pp. 166-171.

[11] Ed. in: *Opus Caroli regis contra synodum [Libri Carolini]*, ed. A. FREEMAN, with P. MEYVAERT (Munich, 1998: *Concilia aevi Karolini: Supplementum* 1) [Old attribution to Alcuin by L. WALLACH, "Libri Carolini sive Opus Caroli Magni Contra Synodum auctore Alcuino", re-edited in: *Illinois Classical Studies* 42.2 (2017), pp. 319-468].

cal than theological, cultural foundations of an equal, homogenous relationship between images and text were not developed, nor – according to Ann Freeman – did they even contribute to the idea, expressed by Gregory the Great in two letters that have become very popular among art historians, that painting is a kind of writing for the poor and therefore has didactic value.[12] As she writes, "the *Libri Carolini* thus provide little support for the proposition, always ascribed to Gregory, that images might be combined into narrative sequences to form 'Bibles for the poor'", though the *Opus* explicitly quotes such passages from Gregory. In fact, the work fully reflects the dominant position in Carolingian culture, to wit the exaltation of the role of writing that I had the chance to explore in my report in Spoleto in 2005:[13]

> *pictores igitur rerum gestarum historias ad memoriam reducere quodammodo valent, res autem, quae sensibus tantummodo percipiuntur et verbis proferuntur, non a pictoribus, sed a scriptoribus comprehendi et aliorum relatibus demonstrari valent.*

Therefore the painters of the stories of accomplished enterprises somehow manage to bring them back to memory, yet things that are perceived only by the mind and

---

[12] Gregory the Great, *Epistolae*, XI, 10, 47-51, ed. D. NORBERG, 2 vols. (Turnhout, 1982: CSEL 140-140A), 2, p. 875: "*quia picturas imaginum, quae ad aedificationem imperiti populi factae fuerant, ut nescientes litteras ipsam historiam intendentes*". Gregory's statements on the matter of iconoclasm were quoted word for word at the council of Paris in 825 (ed. in: *Concilia aevi Karolini [742-842]*, ed. A. WERMINGHOFF, 2 parts (Hanover and Leipzig, 1906-1908: MGH Conc. 2.1-2), 2, pp. 480 ff.) and were raised in Jonas of Orléans's reply to Claudius of Turin (Jonas of Orléans, *De cultu imaginum*, ed. in: PL 106, col. 310-311). Hadrian I took the Gregorian quotations in good faith in his synodal letter in 785 to Constantine and Irene and in his response to the *Libri Carolini*, which was in line with the Byzantine position (ed. in: *Epistolae selectae pontificum Romanorum Carolo Magno et Ludowico Pio regnantibus scriptae*, ed. K. HAMPE, in: *Epistolae Karolini aevi* 3, ed. E. DÜMMLER, K. HAMPE, *et al.* (Berlin, 1898-1899: MGH Epp. 5), p. 55: "*ut per visibilem vultum ad invisibilem divinitatis maiestatem mens nostra rapiatur spirituali affectu per contemplationem figuratae imagines secundum carnem*". A more conciliatory perspective, which according to Kessler (H.L. KESSLER, "'*facies bibliothecae revelata*': Carolingian art as spiritual seeing", in: *Testo e immagine nell'alto medioevo*, 2 vols. (Spoleto, 1994: Settimane di studio del Centro italiano di studi sull'alto Medioevo 41), 2, pp. 533-594, at p. 544) was integrated into Carolingian culture in the second quarter of the ninth century, e.g. at the council of Paris in 825. To this end, one of the most cited examples was the legend of Constantine.

[13] F. STELLA, "La comunicazione nella poesia carolingia", in: *Comunicazione e significazione nell'alto medioevo*, 2 vols. (Spoleto, 2005: Settimane di studio del Centro italiano di studi sull'alto Medioevo 52), 2, pp. 615-652; here Chapter Five.

are expressed only with words, cannot be understood by the painters, but can be understood by the writers and stories of others.

The same point of view is depicted in the poetry of another of the period's great intellectuals, Hrabanus Maurus,[14] who in *carmen* 38 to Atto, his successor at Fulda, introduces a kind of comparative eulogy in which the prerogatives of writing emerge thanks to a comparison with painting, a comparison that, as we know, is found at the heart of the era's theological and intellectual debate. Atto seems to prefer figurative art, but Hrabanus urges him not to undervalue the work of transcription, because the word is worth more than an empty image, and it confers greater dignity on the soul than does painting, which depicts not the reality of things but their figurative reproduction. The implicit premise is that writing possesses a greater degree of reality in virtue of the multiplicity of levels of meaning and of corporeal senses involved. Writing is in fact a principle of salvation, and it is more useful, easier, even more conducive to pleasure, more complete in its communication of concepts, and more suitable for being preserved in men's minds because it involves more senses (hearing, speaking, and sight). In contrast, painting offers consolation only to the eyes. Emerging from the lines of Hrabanus, as from those of other Carolingian authors, is a conception of writing as a multimedial code that we are no longer able to share today but that proves to be indispensable for understanding this period, and not only for understanding the *carmina figurata*. The truth of writing is in its appearance, in its sound, in its meaning, and in its duration, while painting would suffer from a sort of perishability and especially a greater degree of departure from the truth and from the certainty of faith:

> *Plus quia gramma valet quam vana in imagine forma,*
> *plusque animae decoris praestat quam falsa colorum*
> *pictura ostentans rerum non rite figuras.*
> *Haec facie verum monstrat, et famine verum,*
> *Et sensu verum, iucunda et tempore multo est,*
> *Illa recens pascit visum, gravat atque vetusta,*
> *Deficiet propere veri et non fide sequestra.*[15]

And Hrabanus again gives a demonstration of the method by which to codify the image-text relationship in a place of worship with his epigraph for

---

[14] See Chapter Five.
[15] For a translation, see p. 103.

the *capella Mauri* (*carmen* 61). In it, he invites the reader to kneel down before the image of Christ, explicitly mentioned as an *imago picta* in colour, with an indication of the building's division into one part designated for worship and another for the clergy, and the final invitation to chant psalms in the choir:

> *Omnibus est locuples, qui rebus abundat honestis,*
> *Cui superas Christus diuitias tribuit.*
> *Flecte genu, qui intras, Christum tu et pronus adora,*
> *Cuius imago super picta colore micat.*
> 5 *Lux, uia, uita, salus, sit merces omnibus istic,*
> *Qui Christo reddunt debita uota pie.*
> *En una templum domino hic parte ministro,*
> *Deuotis aliam reddo domum famulis.*
> *Quam dulce et gratum est, fratres perpendite cuncti,*
> 10 *Stare choro, et placidis caelestia psallere uerbis!*

The one who abounds in dignified things, to whom Christ has assigned the riches of heaven, is rich in everything. Bend your knee, you who enter, and, bowing, worship Christ, whose image painted above shines in colour. Light, road, life, salvation, be rewards over there for all those who religiously pay their debts to Christ. Here in a part of the church I administer [the sacraments], another I leave to the devoted servants. Everyone, consider how pleasant and pleasant it is, brothers, to stand in the choir and chant the heavenly truths with words of peace!

Immediately after this, Hrabanus adds a quatrain of typological explanations to the first epigraph: "*Gratia clave aperit quae clausa prophetia condit, / quae lex significat et quae hagiographa figurat; / psallite vos, pueri laeti, et benedicite Christo, / ipse dabit vobis praemia laeta polo*" ("Grace opens with the key what the closed Prophecy hides, what the Law means, and the hagiographical books represent. Chant you boys in happiness and bless Christ, he will give you the rewards of gladness in heaven"). This is a text that cannot be thought of as solely composed for the manuscript version, as the mention of the choir of boys links directly to worship, and also to the boys' expectation of salvation: it is an example of an integrated system of signs that unites text, image, and music, worship, theological conscience, and personal salvation in a coherent code.

That same cultural hierarchy, which did not hesitate to consider the image a kind of second-rate communication, contained within it the premises for the development of iconological poetry. In the *Libri Carolini*,[16] Theodulf proposes an example that is imaginary but drawn from experience: "imagine a woman with her child in her lap: if there is no inscription, how can we know if this represents the Virgin with her Child or Venus with Aeneas, Alcmena with Hercules, or Andromache with Astyanax?". "If there is no inscription" ("*si superscriptio necdum facta sit*"): here, in Theodulf's words, is the seed of an essay on comparative iconology put forward to call attention to the need for text in the understanding of the image. The assumption is that the image's system of communication, even for contemporary viewers, is too generic and too subject to the reuse and polygenesis of motifs to legitimise an unambiguous interpretation, which can only be provided by the word. Because "man can save himself without seeing images, but he cannot save himself without knowledge of God", implying verbal communication.

The council of Paris of 829 called attention to the pedagogical function of images,[17] according to a perspective that was utilitarian and focussed on education, like all Carolingian reform oriented towards the idealisation of schooling, as reflected in many statements by the period's intellectuals. Walahfrid Strabo writes "we often see how simple and unlearned souls, who could scarcely be brought to faith by words, are so touched by a painting of the Passion of Our Lord, or of other miracles, that they avow by their tears that these images are deeply engraved in their hearts".[18]

The mythicisation of the role of writing as an absolute instrument of communication entailed, as one of many consequences, the need for writing to explain images, or sounds, and therefore the multiplication of paratexts accompanying images or objects as a means of integrating images and objects into the Carolingian cultural system, and even more so into the system of theological

---

[16] *Opus Caroli regis contra synodum (Libri Carolini)*, IV, 21 ed. FREEMAN and MEYVAERT, p. 540.

[17] J. HUBERT, J. PORCHER, and W.F. VOLBACH, *L'empire carolingien* (Paris, 1968); trans. *L'impero carolingio* (Milan, 1981), pp. 23 ff. [There is a plentiful later bibliography: we just remind the reader of T. NOBLE, *Images, Iconoclasm, and the Carolingians* (Philadelphia, 2009), and F. STELLA, *Il senso dell'immagine* (Milan, 2020), chapter 2.]

[18] Walahfrid Strabo, *Libellus De exordiis et incrementis quarundam in observationibus ecclesiasticis rerum*, c. 8, ed. in: *Capitularia regum Francorum*, 2, ed. A. BORETIUS and V. KRAUSE (Hanover, 1890-1897), pp. 473-516, at p. 482. Quoted by P. RICHÉ, *Écoles et enseignement dans le Haut Moyen Âge* (Paris, 1979), p. 326; trans. *Le scuole e l'insegnamento nell'Occidente cristiano dalla fine del V secolo alla metà dell'XI secolo* (Rome, 1984), p. 337. An English translation of the same Strabo quotation is found in P. RICHÉ, *The Carolingians: A Family Who Forged Europe*, trans. (Philadelphia, 1993), p. 350.

understanding of the universe, which had to assign every reality a meaning that overcame and transcended it, in this way justifying it. This is why it was mainly in the Carolingian era that the genre of the *Versus ad picturas* was filled with typological explanation, which interpreted a character or an episode from the Old Testament in view of a character or episode from the New Testament, or with tropological explanation that read words and things as signs of moral realities. As Arnulf writes,

> *durch den Ausfall der Tituli des Prudentius und des Rusticus Helpidius als Zeugnisse typologischer Bildprogramme scheint es keinen Hinweis mehr auf ein typologisch gestaltetes spätantikes Bildprogramm aus neu- und alttestamentlichen Bildfolgen in paralleler Anordnung zu geben.*[19]

This, then, is why the unitary configuration of Carolingian culture ended up giving a precise practical and intellectual meaning to the tradition of the *tituli*, and increasing the need for them.

Carolingian Typologies

The Carolingian era, which here we consider limited to the period from the reign of Charlemagne to the empire of Charles the Bald, witnessed a proliferation of the production of *tituli*. As John Mitchell wrote, describing the appearance of the monastery of San Vincenzo al Volturno as implied by archaeological excavations, there was no private or public space in the monastery that was not covered in script, warnings, signs, prayers, or instructions. This is also confirmed for the spaces furnished with images, both externally and in their manuscripts or on objects: there are hundreds of Carolingian poetic epigraphs, which have almost always reached us through manuscripts, about objects of worship, liturgical codices, tombs, walls, doors, clothing, bells, etc. These often consisted of rough texts, as evidenced also by the letters of Paulinus of Nola, who submitted different drafts of *tituli* to Sulpicius Severus to choose from. This was the case, for example, for the epitaph of Pope Hadrian, the subject of a competition between the great poets of the time that gave us both the text of the winner Alcuin, which can still be read at Saint Peter in the Vatican, and that of the loser, or one of the losers, Theodulf of Orléans, transmitted

---

[19] ARNULF, *Versus ad picturas*, p. 334

through manuscripts instead. But its composition was certainly done for a specific occasion – art for art's sake did not yet exist – and in a few rare instances we also have evidence for the actual *tituli* of images as well.

In contrast to what happens for other genres, in this case we have access to texts in very different levels of style:[20] from the *tituli* of Alcuin, Ingobert, and Smaragdus about images in books to those referring to external settings, such as Bernowin's short devotional lines for the gospel cycle at the church of Saint Alyre[21] in Clermont or the talented epigraphs of Sedulius Scotus painted on the sundial or embroidered on the mantle of the empress Ermengarde, to the 'popular' inscriptions of Weissenburg, Saint Gall, and most of all Reichenau-Oberzell, all referring to cycles of biblical episodes whose ties to worship vary widely. They are obviously more direct for epigraphs on display and referring, for example, to saints venerated in a specific place, such as at Reichenau in the church of Sankt Georg, and probably at Saint Gall and Saint Alyre; and they are much more open to interpretation or even tenuous in the cases of luxury bibles that were for display, were ostensory, or were clearly aimed at an educated readership, such as the *tituli librarii* to exegetic works. This typology, which always remains within the framework of text-about-an-image or about the meaning that the image represents, was joined in the Carolingian era by the typology of text-as-image that had arisen in the classical and late antique periods as visual poetry, or figurative *carmina*. In those centuries it found a new flush in the compositions of Joseph Scotus, Eugenius Vulgarius, and especially

[20] Here I quote some sections of STELLA, *La poesia carolingia latina a tema biblico*, integrating and updating them.

[21] Fourth bishop of Clermont, who died in 384 and was buried in the church of Santa Maria ad Sanctos, later called the basilica Sancti Illidii and demolished during the French Revolution. Gregory of Tours speaks of this figure in *Historia Francorum* I, 40. The cycle of five poems over 28 lines in total concerns the annunciation, birth, passion, resurrection, and ascension of Christ, and presents each event with a different stylistic approach: the first has the characters speak and concludes with a prayer in a couplet, and is built around two scenes, the second of which (the encounter with the unborn John) is interposed with the first; the second describes Christmas, alluding to the entire earthly parable of Christ (and implicitly to the whole pictorial cycle), proclaimed at four different times (birth, passion, resurrection, and ascension) by the West, East, South, and North, probably according to the spatial arrangement of the iconographic elements; the third emphasises the value and redemptive efficacy of Christ's death; the two sestinas on resurrection and ascension allude immediately to cultural duty: "*hic pia surgentis veneranda est gloria Christi*" (4, 1), followed by the recall of the three apparitions mentioned in Luke; "*Hic colitur domini veneranda ascensio Christi*" (5,1), followed by an appeal to the reader: "*tu quoque gaudebis, lector, qui talia credis*" (5, 5-6), then announcing the second coming and urging *nos* to charity so that we find ourselves ready for the Judgment. The following *tituli* are about the ecclesiastical building and are unrelated to specific biblical episodes.

Hrabanus Maurus, who with the *De laudibus sanctae crucis* created an extremely successful monument to what I would call the 'iconotextual sign',[22] the painted word, whose fortune would extend over time and even continue today in European literature, and about which much critical literature has been produced – in our field of work consider especially Ulrich Ernst's books and Michele Camillo Ferrari's monograph[23] – but in doing so confirmed the reciprocal need for the two languages, though in hierarchically different positions, where it is always the image that is enhanced by the text.

Its openness to broad and differentiated use, sometimes even barely literate, and its at least virtual dependence on the narrative rhythms of a different language, isolate this genre as a phenomenon characterised by its own specificity. It is nonetheless important not to fall into the typical trap of the few studies in this field, which stop to observe the correspondence of the *tituli* to the related images without considering the entire entity of the textual legacy of a manuscript. For example, to assign the right semantic and ideological value to the verse captions of the miniatures of the Vivian Bible (the name for the first bible of Charles the Bald, MS Paris Bibliothèque nationale de France, latin 1), it is necessary to keep in mind the entire complex of poetic compositions that introduce, dedicate, present, explain, and accompany that edition of the Bible and its images. The goal of observation must be the complete artefact in its entirety, and not only the *titulus / pictura* relationship. This kind of comprehensive analysis was carried out in the monographs dedicated to individual manuscripts, like those of Dutton and Kessler on the Vivian Bible, of Gaehde on the Bible of San Paolo fuori le Mura, and of Köhler on the Moutier-Grandval Bible,[24] but such individual explorations were not linked in a reflection on the poetic *tituli* of biblical cycles, which I believe could lead to findings of some interest.

The momentum of the Carolingian era, which was of a truly impressive intensity, created a custom from sporadic and often random cases and therefore a genre out of them: in fact both the *tituli* of the Bible of Grandval-Moutier, considered the oldest cycle of miniatures with metrical *tituli* known to us, and

---

[22] [After the first presentation of this essay in Italian (2007), L. LOUVEL, *The Poetics of the Iconotext* (Franham and Burlington, Vermont, 2011) was published.]

[23] See the Bibliography.

[24] P.E. DUTTON and H.L. KESSLER, *The Poetry and the Paintings of the First Bible of Charles the Bald* (Ann Arbor, 1997); J.E. GAEHDE, *The Painters of the Carolingian Bible Manuscript of San Paolo Fuori le Mura in Rome* (Ann Arbor, 1993); W. KOHLER, *Die karolingische Miniaturen*, 1, *Die Schule von Tours*; 2, *Die Bilder* (Berlin, 1933).

the Reichenau *tituli*, the oldest example of frescoes with metrical *tituli*, date from this period. But as we know from the only *scriptorium* of Tours from the first half of the ninth century, 18 gospels and another 40 bibles, a dozen of which are traceable to Alcuin's abbacy, were attested either directly or indirectly. A recent development about this production, though from a philological perspective, is owed to Guy Lobrichon.[25] The great innovation of the era, other than the quantitative dimension of production, was the recovery of pandects or complete bibles, of which there were only examples at Vivarium with Cassiodore and then at Wearmouth-Jarrow under Ceolfrith (689-716), a time for which the Amiatine Bible of the Biblioteca Laurenziana in Florence is famously the main literary monument. These bibles, which represent a concrete symbol of Carolingian ideological unity and inspired the papal 'Atlantic' bibles of the eleventh century, are characterised by a set of graphic, codicological, and textual elements. Among them is a series of prologues that in the cases held in the highest regard were written in verse, called the *Versus de Bibliotheca*, or verses on the Bible, to which I dedicated a long study in 1993.[26] These were created from the book epigrams used to indicate the content and author of a codex – such as those composed by Isidore of Seville for his library on a model in turn inspired by Martial, and extended by Eugenius of Toledo – and went so far as to give life to genuine analytical introductions hundreds of lines long, each with a dedication to the addressee, a summary of the biblical books, praise of the virtues of the Bible and its reading, and a concluding prayer. Alcuin and Theodulf composed them, enhancing Eugenius's scheme, and later so did Smaragdus in a grammatical preface, Paulus Alvarus in dedicating a book to the noble Liuvigild, and then the curators of the bibles of Charles the Bald, known as Ingobert and Vivian. The texts are published in De Bruyne's catalogue *Préfaces de la Bible latine* (Namur, 1920), and in different sections of the *Poetae Latini aevi Carolini*: *Bibliothecarum et Psalteriorum versus* (vol. 3), *Versus libris adiecti* (vol. 4), *Verse in Miniaturenhandschriften* (vol. 5), which typically include all the poetic apparatus accompanying bibles, psalters, evangeliaries, or sometimes commentaries on individual books.

---

[25] G. LOBRICHON, "Le texte des bibles alcuiniennes", in: *Alcuin, de York à Tours: Écriture, pouvoir et réseaux dans l'Europe du haut Moyen Âge*, ed. P. DEPREUX and B. JUDIC (Rennes, 2004 = *Annales de Bretagne et des Pays de l'Ouest* 111 (2004)) pp. 209-219. A survey on the subject is M. BASSETTI, "Le Bibbie imperiali d'età carolingia ed ottoniana", in: *Forme e modelli della tradizione manoscritta della Bibbia,* ed. P. CHERUBINI (Vatican City, 2005), pp. 175-265.

[26] The entire first part of STELLA, *Poesia carolingia latina a tema biblico* (pp. 27-113).

Versus ad picturas *in the Carolingian Era*

Fig. 8   MS Paris, Bibliothèque nationale de France, latin 1, f. 2r.

Produced within this apparatus were specialised typologies with specific functions and characterised by their own expressive codes: the quatrains on the evangelists (often reduced to a mere list of names with their related symbols), the lines on the canon tables (such as those of the Irish scholar Aileran or Theodulf's *carmen* 41b), the prefaces to individual books or sections of the Bible (such as Prudentius of Troyes's preface to the Gospels), the mere signatures (such as those of the *Versus Sangallenses*), some of which commonly have an exegetical nature. And each subgenre developed its own internal tradition, with models and imitative processes. All these apparatuses have so far been neglected in favour of the study of image captions, but without realising that almost always, and especially in the great bibles of Tours and Reims, the curator of the textual apparatus was following a complex trail and composing a choral work, albeit one articulated in parts with different functions. Although it is partially true, as Arnulf writes, that there appears to have been no imitation of late antique precedents by the Carolingians, it is nevertheless verifiable that many of the Carolingian *tituli* were imitated or sometimes repeated in their entirety in manuscripts of later generations or from the Ottonian age on. One famous example is the reproduction and development of the *tituli* of the Grandval Bible in the Vivian Bible, as we shall see, but there is also the revival of the Ps.-Alcuinian *carmen* 71, used for an evangeliary from Prüm now in Trier (MS Trier, Stadtbibliothek 23) and for a Wissenburgensis (MS Wolfenbüttel, Herzog Augustbibliothek, Weiss. 26), and in MS Bamberg, Staatsbibliothek, Hist. 161 (E.III.1) from the tenth century, originating from Stavelot: to the extent that Karl Strecker published it in his volume of *Poetae* dedicated to Ottonian *tituli*,[27] without realising that it had already been published by Dümmler as Alcuinian.[28]

The Cycles of the Great Bibles of Tours

This is a subject that has been much discussed in recent literature, especially by Herbert Kessler,[29] following from Köhler, by Rosamond McKitte-

---

[27] "Verse in Miniaturenhandschriften", ed. K. STRECKER, in: *PLAC*, 5.1-2, pp. 415-463, at pp. 452-453.

[28] Alcuin, *Carmina*, *PLAC*, 1, pp. 293-294.

[29] Many titles, among them H.L. KESSLER, *The Illustrated Bibles from Tours* (Princeton, 1977) and ID., *The Cotton Genesis: British Library, Codex Cotton, Otho B. VI* (with K. WEITZMANN) (Princeton, 1986).

rick,[30] and by Arwed, and about which we will limit ourselves to an illustrative literary contextualisation of what is known as the Vivian Bible, to part of what is called the Ingobert Bible, but should be extended to the Codex Aureus of Sankt Emmeram and others.

The Vivian Bible is the first bible of Charles the Bald, number 1 of the fonds latin of the Bibliothèque Nationale de France in Paris, so named after the lay abbot, Vivian, who in 843 had succeeded Adalhard, the second abbot of Tours in the post-Alcuinian period that began with Fridugisus. As we know, it is a literary monument of 423-495 × 345 mm. leaves given to the king, probably on the occasion of the confirmation of the immunity given to the abbey, in a ceremony preemptively depicted in one of the book's miniatures. The codex was then given by the king to the cathedral of Metz, where it remained until 1675, when it was offered to Jean-Baptiste Colbert, the famous minister of Louis XVI. The biblical text is accompanied by a rich apparatus of prefaces, canon tables, indexes, and concordances, and by eight full-page miniatures that depict Jerome, the creation, Moses receiving the commandments, David the psalmist, Christ in Majesty, the conversion of Paul, the Revelation, and the presentation of the manuscript to the king. The first two leaves are taken up by a long dedication in couplets (200 lines) inspired by those of Alcuin and Theodulf (Fig. 8). The text includes the actual dedication, 60 lines long, with the eulogy of the Bible expressed in second person to the king ("*fert quod amas, quod amare velis, quod discere prosit*", l. 3) with a coda of ethical advice, absent in the other bibles, one piece of which is a call to honour the Church and the clergy. The traditional recapitulation of the Bible follows, more streamlined than Alcuin and Theodulf's versions, but with the innovation of a more analytical attention to the Gospels and inclusion of the symbols of the evangelists. A third part (ll. 155-176) presents the exegetical reflection on the relationship between the Testaments, expressed with the Pauline image of a shadow preceding a body,[31] and analysed at different levels of interpretation, according to the disciplines *logica*, *ethica*, and *phisica*, and according to the addressees, whether illiterate, moderately educated, or learned, and attempting a philosophical-theological presentation of the book in which the Creator's wisdom is emphasised, in which the Holy Spirit – in other words, love – acts as an intermediary between the lover and the beloved, and in which God speaks to us

---

[30] R. MCKITTERICK, "Text and image in the Carolingian world", in: *The Uses of Literacy in Early Medieval Europe,* ed. R. MCKITTERICK (Cambridge, 1990), pp. 297-318.

[31] V. 114: "*umbra prior quarum causaque posterior*".

and we, with our hearts, speak to him. The fourth part (ll. 177-200) reminds the king that it was wisdom that made Solomon rich, and therefore led him to understand that cultural power comes before political power, with ascetic recommendations about monastic spirituality and a final prayer for the king.

The short poem recalls the precedents of Alcuin and Theodulf through textual elements that I have analysed elsewhere,[32] but it reveals a less ordered and schematic structure. It thus develops the Theodulfian model that led to meditative amplifications, above all showing that it was conditioned by the physical and symbolic presence of the royal addressee to whom the codex was offered, which turns this introduction into an instance of micro-*speculum principis* by a court dignitary who in this context represents monastic culture and its power in the Carolingian system. We shall see that this approach remains evident also in the miniature captions.

I will not attempt an analysis that is also linguistic and stylistic here. However, I cannot neglect to mention that, placed in contrast to the topical declaration in the *modicus et rusticus* style (l. 88), is a complex management of the sentences, with frequent enjambments that indicate planning prior to the writing of the line, with a density of archaisms and Graecisms, and with different absolute hapaxes and a clausula ("*versificalis apex*", l. 188, glossed as "*laus*"), which is found again only in a preface to Donatus's commentary: the text is filled with biblical annotations written by Abbot Smaragdus of Saint-Mihiel at the beginning of the century (1, 10, 14: *c.* 805)). The largely Theodulfian model is broken down into the different topoi that make up the scheme – carried out here with a terse conventionality, there with innovative modifications and personal additions – but it remains dominated by an osmosis between the concrete occasion of presentation to the king and the cultural and exegetical subjects of the *laus bibliothecae*, on behalf of the petitions that called for the autonomy of the ecclesiastical and monastic class and the primacy of the intellectuals over politics. This would seem to be confirmed by the comparative analysis between image and text that Kessler does of the page with the presentation of the book to the king, where the commissioner Vivian is almost confined to the margins of an operation that seeks primarily to draw attention to the monks.[33]

---

[32] STELLA, *Poesia carolingia latina*, pp. 81-91.

[33] H.L. KESSLER, "A lay abbot as patron: Count Vivian and the First Bible of Charles the Bald", in: *Committenti e produzione artistico-letteraria nell'alto medioevo occidentale*, 2 vols. (Spoleto, 1992: *Settimane di studio del Centro Italiano di Studi sull'Alto Medioevo* 39), 2, pp. 647-675.

Versus ad picturas *in the Carolingian Era*

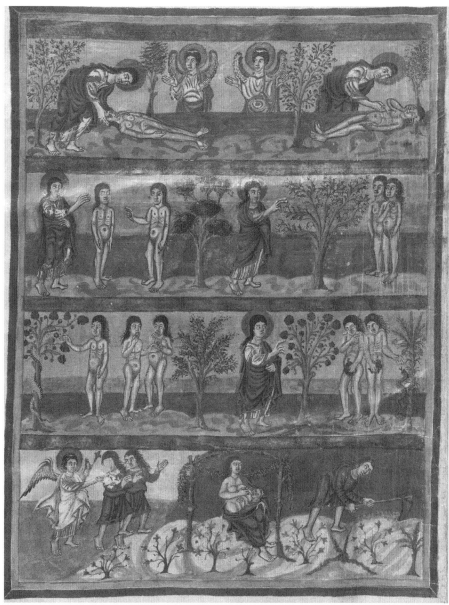

Fig. 9   MS London, British Library, Add. 10546, f. 5v.

The seven series of *tituli* introduce a complex stratification: four of them are in fact copied exactly from the Bible of Tours, called the Moutier-Grandval Bible (MS London, British Library, Add. 10546), like the related miniatures. They are the ones on Genesis, Exodus, *Maiestas Domini*, and the Revelation. Three more were added in a style that instead recalls that of the general preface: the frontispiece of Jerome (f. 3v), as well as those of the Psalms (f. 215v) and Saint Paul's letters (f. 386v).

The first series (cf. Fig. 9) which can be read in the upper bands of each book, is characterised by an entirely unexpected metrical variation: "*Adam primus uti fingitur istic / cuius costa sacrae carpitur Evae*" are in Terentian verse, according to the scheme – – – ⏑⏑ x ⏑⏑ – x, so named because it was found for the first time in Terentianus Maurus (around 180 CE), and in the early Middle Ages it was used by an anonymous Italian from the fifth century, in a hymn mentioned by Bede ("*squalent arva soli*"), by Martianus Capella and Boethius, two authors whom we will encounter again, and in the Carolingian era by Hrabanus Maurus, Candidus, Wandalbert of Prüm, Sedulius Scotus, Hucbald of Saint-Amand, and many others. We may note that *fingitur* shows that these lines were written for an illustration; and that *istic*, the deictic typical of *tituli*, confirms that this is a line for an illustration that was supposed to be juxtaposed and coexistent. *Sacrae Evae* is a sort of dative of advantage. The appellative *sacra* is an unusual one for Eve,[34] which seems to appear only in this epigram. The couplet that follows is instead in trochaic septenaries, also widespread in the early medieval period (think of Venantius Fortunatus's *Pange lingua*, which had entered the liturgy):[35] "*Christus Evam ducit Adae, quam vocat viraginem. / Ast edant ne poma vitae prohibet ipse conditor*" ("Christ presents to Adam Eve, whom he calls '*virago*', but the creator forbids eating the fruits of life"). Here, too, there are many theological and linguistic observations to be made, starting with the presence of Christ at the creation up to the epithet *virago*, here etymologised narratively (*virago* comes from *vir*, just as Eve comes from Adam), while the second line, which corresponds to the figure only in the Moutier-Grandval Bible and not in the Vivian Bible, was interpreted as one of the proofs of the latter's dependence on the former. It was not noted that the upper *tituli* on Vivian's page were slightly mismatched, not

---

[34] The closest example is Sedulius, *Carmen Paschale* 2, 18, ed. J. HUEMER (Vienna, 1885: CSEL 10), pp. 1-146, at p. 45: "*Sic Evae de stirpe sacra veniente Maria*".

[35] Here with a short two-syllable substitution, also attested in other Carolingian poets (KLOPSCH, *Einführung in die mittellateinische Verslehre*, p. 18, and NORBERG, *Introduction à la versification latine médiévale*, pp. 112 ff.).

Versus ad picturas *in the Carolingian Era* 193

Fig. 10   MS Paris, Bibliothèque nationale de France, latin 1, f. 27v.

on a coloured background like the ones after, perhaps one more piece of evidence for the absence of a coordinated development of *tituli* and illustrations in the Vivian Bible.

The next epigraph, "*suadet nuper creatae / anguis dolo puellae / post haec amoena lustrans / Adam vocat redemptor*" ("the serpent persuades the newly created girl with trickery, and afterwards while exploring the garden [the Lord] calls Adam"), further changes the metre, which escaped the editor of the *Monumenta* who printed the lines alongside the ones before: those, however, were trochaic septenaries, while these are catalectic iambic dimeters like those found in Prudentius (*Liber cathemerium* VI) or in Mozarabic hymns (*Analecta Hymnica* 27, 72 *Assunt tenebrae primae* and 27, 73 *Quieti tempus adest*), with the use of poetic language (*amoena lustrans*) and great theological anticipation, which is why the one who summons Adam is not God the Father but Christ the Redeemer. Kessler has noted that this image fuses two different models of the protoplast, while the *titulus* refers to one of the two, but this is inevitable from the moment that not the models but the (single) image that results from them need to be explained. If anything, we should observe that the texts adds a kind of short backstory, *amoena lustrans*, which the images do not describe and which finds a parallel only in a poem by Sedulius Scotus (II 41, 113: "*nonque superbus equo lustrabat amoena virecta*"). The following "*uterque ab umbris pellitur inde sacris / et iam labori rubra colunt habiti*" is a metrical enigma that the Dutton edition did not even address and that Arnulf decoded as two apparent pentameters ($\smile\smile x\_ \mid -\smile\smile-\smile\smile-$), composed from the beginning of an Alcaic line (two iambs and one long syllable, or an iamb and a bacchius) and a hemiepes, i.e. a half-line of a pentameter: a reworking of the Horatian iambelegus (*Epode* 13: $x\_ \smile-^{x}-\smile- \mid -\smile\smile-\smile\smile-$) that has parallels only in a lyric by Luxorius for the Vandal nobleman Fridamal, preserved in the *Anthologia Latina* (No. 305: "*Felix marinis alitibus Fridamal / felix iuvenis, prosperior genio*").[36] I would tend to believe that they are iambic tetrameters, with an undue substitution in the eighth syllable of the first, rather than forms of iambelegus (iambic dimeter + dactylic trimeter) as in Horace's first *Epode*.[37] We should recall, however, that knowledge of the Horatian metres was not at all common

---

[36] A recent edition by H. HAPP, *Luxurius: Text und Untersuchungen* (Stuttgart, 1986). Translation by M. ROSENBLUM, *Luxorius: A Poet among the Vandals* (New York and London, 1961).

[37] E.g. Aelius Festus Aphthonius = (Ps.-) Marius Victorinus, *De metris Horatianis*, ed. in: *Grammatici Latini* 6, ed. H. KEIL (Leipzig, 1874), pp. 174-184, Ode 1, vv. 1-2, p. 182: "*Ibis Liburnis inter alta navium, / Amice, propugnacula*".

in the Carolingian era, and that it only began to spread with the arrival of the second generation of Irish scholars, such as Sedulius Scotus himself.

A metrical curiosity also surfaces in the *titulus* on Exodus (Fig. 10), which is in Sapphic strophe, a metrical form that was relatively widespread in the Carolingian era, especially in the *speculum principis* of Sedulius Scotus, and closely and extensively studied in a masterly book by Peter Stotz,[38] but which had escaped the attentions of art historians and was first noted by Arnulf. He in turn did not realise that the depiction of Moses as Paul is not "*rhetorisch ein Anachronismus*"[39] but rather a typological representation, which characterises Moses as St. Paul (and Kessler also shows this with figurative comparisons) to the point of describing him in the act of preaching not to the Jewish people but to the Christians: rhetorically speaking, the author does not contrast type and anti-type, but merges them directly by using the face of the *antitypus* Paul in the context of the *typus* Moses. Intertextually speaking, *dextra* and *corusca* are found close together, but not as a compound term, in Vulfinus of Die's contemporary *Vita Marcelli* 241: "*praesul signa crucis dextra subeunte corusca*". *Dextra regis* is found before this only in Paulinus of Périgueux 3, 79, and then in Hrotsvita *Iohannes* 6, while *Christi populus* is a relatively common expression, from Ps.-Tertullian (twice), to Prudentius *Peristefanon* 7, 33, Prosper *De ingratis* 1, 251, Bede *Hymn*. 2, 478 and *carmen* 1, 40, Alcuin 109, 24, 16 and *Carm. Nyn*. 64, Florus of Lyon 10, 45, and once again Sedulius Scotus. The Adonic *nectare sancto*, however, seems to be an isolated formulation, a variation of *sacro nectare* that already appeared in Statius *Sylv*. 4, 2, 54 and especially in John Scotus Eriugena 7, 1, 1, in the famous expression "*sacro Graecorum nectare*", which was adopted as a symbol of the cultural leanings of Eriugena, an Irish theologian. It is found later in the *Vita Clementis* of Carus, another Irish monk from the eleventh century.

The following *titulus* is found only in the Vivian Bible and concerns the Psalms (Fig. 11): "*Psalmificus David respendet et ordo peritus / Eius opus canere musica ab arte bene*" ("David psalm-singer will shine with the group of experts (singers) in the perfect intonation for musical art").[40] Metrically speaking it is a banal elegiac couplet, but in this form it uses an adjective, *psalmificus*, in reference to David, which is not found in other texts but resembles the

---

[38] P. STOTZ, *Sonderformen der sapphischen Dichtung: Ein Beitrag zur Erforschung der sapphischen Dichtung des lateinischen Mittelalters* (Munich, 1982).
[39] ARNULF, *Versus ad picturas*, p. 185.
[40] *Carmina Bibliothecarum* 3, 5.

Fig. 11   MS Paris, Bibliothèque nationale de France, latin 1, f. 215v.

hymnificus in the prologue to the Vivian Bible, a rather rare adjective (only in Commodianus). *Ordo peritus* refers to the order of the singers, while Dutton translates "the company is well trained in the art of music": an expression curiously taken up again only in Ricardus, *Passio Catharinae* 1, 346 "*sacrorum ritus, quem predicat ordo peritus*", while Traube's hypothesis – according to which *ab arte* would be a classical or late antique expression, though being used in Bernowin, Theodulf, and Hrabanus *De imagine Caesaris* – leads nowhere. The four virtues in the corners of the miniature are emphasised consistently also in the prologue (I 165-166) as the forces that pull men to heaven, and taken up again in the dedication to Charles (10, 29), as Dutton has observed.[41] Thus, they are included in a coherent ideological plan, whereas the *tituli* taken up in the Moutier-Grandval Bible seem to remain outside of it: one proof of this is the contradiction between the interpretation of Creation, given by *tituli* and miniatures, as the work of Christ, and that of the summary of biblical content in the prologue of the Vivian Bible, which on ll. 159-160 distinguishes the role of the creator from the role of the Son.

Folio 422 recto presents a short poem of 44 lines, elegiac couplets, still a commentary on the Psalms, that addresses Charles as David, painted in this miniature with exceptional artistry, "*pictus es hic studio artis ab eximio*", which finds its value only in the correspondence of the image to reality. This is another point of discussion of the text / image relationship, here in an encomiastic sense, which until then had not often been taken into account in studies of the subject: "*sed quia tam haec rutilans species it, non nisi fecit / vera tui, omnis cui cedit imago viri*". A phrase composed in the intricate, ambitious, and slightly awkward style typical of the third Carolingian generation, which Dutton translates as "coloring these things so, an outline emerges, but not unless it represents true aspects of you, to whom every image of a man is inferior" and which I would interpret rather as "but this image appears so splendid because it represents only your true aspect, to which any other image of man is inferior". The following lines confirm this: "*es prior effigie, sensu prior, artibus, odis: / his prior aut illis? Restat in ambiguis*" ("you are more important in image, meaning, arts, song; more important than these or those? remains uncertain"), where King David's precedence is both ontological and due to his own excellence, an excellence justified by his human and artistic abilities, by his virtues, and above all by his support for the Church, expressed with the usual formulae, "*ecclesie fotor*" ("supporter of the Church"), "*cleris populisque*

---

[41] DUTTON and KESSLER, *The Poetry and the Paintings*, p. 59.

Fig. 12   MS Paris, Bibliothèque nationale de France, latin 1, f. 329v.

levamen" ("relief of the clergy and people") – formulae that apply praise typically reserved for ecclesiastical authorities to political authority (Alcuin 1, 1399, "*catholicae fidei fautor, praeceptor, amator, ecclesiae rector*" ("supporter of the Catholic faith, teacher, lover and governor of the Church"), said of Aelbert; Hibernicus Exul 12, 11 "*ecclesiae cultor, fautor peregrum, altor egentum*" ("curator of the Church, supporter of pilgrims, feeder of the needy"), said of Fulrad of Saint-Denis); nor does the rhetorical structure spare allusions to political difficulties, such as the Breton rebellion (35: "*ante Brito stabilis fiet vel musio muri / pax bona, quam nomen desit honosque tuum*" – "the Briton will stabilize and the cat will make peace with the mouse before your name and honour disappear"), used as adynatons of praise that employ rare terms once again derived from Theodulf (25, 164 "*aut timido muri musio terga dabit*" – "or the cat will turn its back on the scary mouse"; *musio* also in Ermoldus, *Carmen in laudem Pippini* 2, 80 and 2, 94).

The illustration of the *Maiestas* (Fig. 12) is accompanied by, exceptionally, by two different *tituli*. First there is an elegiac couplet characterised by an atypical use of *micare*, referring to the king, and the adverb *condigne*, which is used in the same metrical placement by Eugenius 22, 11, Bede, *Hymni* 2, 125, 386, and in the Codex Sangallensis app. 8, 17, and clearly makes reference to the image thanks to the deictic *hic*. There is additionally a short poem in 30 lines, also couplets, which dedicates the text of the Gospels to the king, involving him in a renewed meditative display – in the micro-*speculum principis* style – of the ideology of clerical privilege and exaltation of civil power as a supporter of the Church ("*gloria cleri, eclesiae fautor*", ll. 3-4) that also makes stylistic use, heavily indebted to Theodulf, of many expressions shared by the author of the prologue. Some of these, such as *sensu parili* ("with the same meaning; 1, 92 and 6, 16) also appear, exclusively, in other poetic texts of a codicological nature, such as the dedication to the life of Saint Maximin written by Bertold of Saint Maximin of Trier for Jonas of Orléans,[42] l. 10 "*sed sensum paene repperies parilem*" ("but you will find almost the same meaning"), and in a sacramentary of Fulda published in the *Carmina in miniaturis* from the Ottonian age, No. 3, 2 "*missas cum sensu conficiunt parili*", and transmitted by MS Berlin, Staatsbibliothek, Theol. Lat. Fol. 192 (tenth century), and MS Düsseldorf, Universitätsbibliothek D 2 (also from the tenth century).

---

[42] Bertold of Saint Maximin of Trier, *Versus Bertoldi*, ed. in: *Versus libris adiectis*, ed. K. STRECKER, in: *PLAC* 4.3, p. 1060 (after J. MABILLON, *AASS OSB*, 1, p. 591).

Fig. 13   MS Paris, Bibliothèque nationale de France, latin 1, f. 415v.

This revival is one of the many signs of the creation of a catalogue of metrical *tituli* with a biblical theme, not limited to the formulaic epithets of the evangelists, along a path that leads at least from Theodulf, and before him Eugenius of Toledo and Isidore of Seville, to the eleventh century. Given this, the poet, whom Dutton identifies as Audradus Modicus, might have been composing a kind of response to the earlier miniature that he had already found in the model.

There has also been much discussion about the interpretation of the miniature of the Revelation (Fig. 13), also derived from the Moutier-Grandval Bible. The matters debated have been both the image in the upper band of the closed book between a lion and a lamb, with the evangelists in the corners, to whom in the sole Vivian Bible a knight is added, and the one in the lower band with the figure of the old man who is lifting the veil above his head, a character variously interpreted as God, John, the Son of man, and – in my opinion the most likely reading – Moses.[43] This is usually explained as an illustration of Revelation 5, with the opening of the book's seals by the lamb, a symbol of Christ just as the lion would also be, according to Victorinus of Pettau's commentary, to which Köhler refers;[44] although we might also see an opposition between the lion of Judah and the Christian lamb, a contrast first 'sealed' in the closed book and then 'released' or revealed by the lifting of the veil. Here the epigraph, two iambic trimeters – a measure never used for *tituli* – plus three

---

[43] A list of the opinions is found in KESSLER, "'*Facies bibliothecae revelata*'", pp. 564-565. The key to the image is identified by Kessler in the incipit of Jerome's prologue to the Revelation (Jerome, *Epistolae, Epistola ad Paulinum* 53, 4, ed. I. HILBERG, 3 vols. (Vienna, 1910-1918: CSEL 54-56), 1, p. 450), which reads: "*Lex enim spiritalis est et revelatione indiget ut intellegatur, ac revelata facie Dei gloriam contemplemur*". Cf. also Ambrosius Autpertus, *Expositionis in Apocalypsim libri I-V*, 3, 4, ed. R. WEBER, 2 vols. (Turnhout, 1975: CCCM 27-27A), 1, p. 222: "*cui* (the four living creatures in Revelation) *recte humana facies adscribitur, non autem illa quae Moysi velamine tegitur, sed illa quae in Apostolis revelata gloriam Domini speculatur*".

[44] Victorinus of Pettau, *In Apocalypsin*, ed. in: *Victorini episcopi Petavionensis Opera*, ed. J. HAUSSLEITER (Vienna, 1916: CSEL 49), pp. 44-64, esp. "*Ecce vidit leo de tribu Iuda, radix David. Hunc leonem de tribu Iuda vicisse in Genesi legimus, ubi Iacob patriarcha ait : Iuda te laudabunt fratres tui: recubuisti et dormisti et surrexisti tamquam leo et tamquam catulus leonis. Ad devincendum enim mortem leo dictus est, ad patiendum vero pro hominibus tamquam agnus ad occisionem ductus est. Hic ergo aperit et resignat, quod ipse signaverat testamentum. Hoc significans Moses legislatur, quod oportebat esse signatum et celatum usque ad adventum passionis eius, velavit faciem suam et sic est populum locutus (…). Ideo modo merito signatur per agnum occisum, qui tamquam leo confregit mortem, et quae de eo praenuntiata fuerant replevit ... Merito ergo facies Mosi aperitur et revelatur; ideoque Apocalypsis, Revelatio, dicitur*"; cf. ARNULF, *Versus ad picturas*, pp. 185-186.

medieval Phalaecean hendecasyllables,[45] limits itself to highlighting the *modi miri* with which the innocent lamb explains the laws of the Father signed with seven seals. *Modi miri* may allude to typological exegesis, but the lifting of the veil is clearly interpreted as an unveiling, and as a reversal of the short line quoted by Victorinus, by Köhler, and by Arnulf: Exodus 34, 33 "*impletisque sermonibus [Moses] posuit velamen super faciem suam*" ("in fulfilling the texts Moses placed the veil on his face"). Arnulf refers to studies, such as that of C. Davis-Weyer[46], which reject these links and propose other exegetical sources: commentaries on the Revelation were in fact attested in the Carolingian and pre-Carolingian eras by Alcuin, Haimo, Bede, and Ps.-Isidore, as well as by the famous Beatus of Liébana. As far as this discussion is concerned, the five lines nonetheless show a word placement disposed to *traiectio*, hyperbaton, and the crossover of compound terms that is typical of the Irish, also in hymns: see *modis... miris* in two different lines, *leges ... novellae*, the inversion of *veteris*, etc. The expressive texture does not, however, help to identify origins, because it makes use of common *iuncturae*, with the exception of *almis pectoribus*, which despite appearing entirely ordinary has no equivalent elsewhere.

Deserving of much more attention is the text accompanying the book's presentation miniature (Fig. 14), which Paul Zumthor called "*le plus ancien tableau connu inspiré par un evénément actuel*",[47] and which depicts Abbot Vivian, referred to as *heros*, along with priest Aregarius, caretaker of the monastery (to the left of the *pater*, in grey and blue) and the canons Sigualdus (in blue) and Tesmundus (in vermillion), plus variously identified figures, while the poet follows fourth, in salmon pink. The miniature was closely studied by

---

[45] An excellent explanation by ARNULF, *Versus ad picturas*, pp. 190-191, who recalls Bede's definition in *De arte metrica* 1, 17, ed. C.B. KENDALL and M.H. KING, in: *Beda Venerabilis, Opera didascalia*, 1 (Turnhout, 1975: CCSL 123A), pp. 82-141, p. 132 (based on Mallius Theodorus, *De metris*, ed. in: *Grammatici Latini*, ed. H. KEIL, 7 vols. (Leipzig, 1857-1880), 6, p. 590, ll. 21-22): "*est igitur metrum dactylicum Falleucium pentametrum, quod constat ex spondeo et dactylo et tribus trocheis. Huius exemplo 'Contentus Domino Deoque nostro / cui gloria cum honore pollens* '", interpreting the line as a sequence consisting of a spondee, a dactyl, and three trochees, which corresponds to the line of the Carolingian bibles that diverges only on the last syllable of the second line.

[46] C. DAVIS-WEYER, "*Aperit quod ipse signaverat testamentum*: Lamm und Löwe im Apokalypsebild der Grandval-Bibel", in: *Studien zur mittelalterlichen Kunst 800-1250: Festschrift für Florentine Mütherich zum 70. Geburtstag*, ed. K. BIERBRAUER *et al.* (Munich, 1985), pp. 67-74.

[47] P. ZUMTHOR, *Charles le Chauve* (Paris, 1957), p. 89; cf. DUTTON and KESSLER, *The Poetry and the Paintings of the First Bible of Charles the Bald*, p. 72.

Fig. 14 MS Paris, Bibliothèque nationale de France, latin 1, f. 423v.

Fig. 15 MS Paris, Bibliothèque nationale de France, latin 1, ff. 1v-2r.

many specialists, particularly Köhler and Kessler, who proposed the attribution of texts and paintings to the very same Audradus who in his *Revelationes* would be the spokesperson for the need for restoration of ecclesiastical power and proto-Carolingian ideology in the empire of Charles the Bald. I cannot linger on the text as much as I would like to, but my impression, as editor of his *Fons vitae*,[48] is that Audradus's style is too different from that of Vivian's *tituli*, and that the linguistic evidence brought forward by Dutton is in large part overvalued, while the attribution of the *tituli* of the Moutier-Grandval Bible taken up again in the Vivian Bible should in my opinion be directed at an Irish author, due both to its metrical as well as its rhetorical and linguistic characteristics. Hypotheses about this may vary, although the arrival of John Scotus and Sedulius Scotus in France seems to be documented only in the second half of the 840s, a decade later than the likely period of composition of the *tituli*. It is curious that the only attestation of the substantive *veneratus* in poetry, other than in Flodoard, is this short poem and the dedication of a famous evangelistary (MS Paris, Bibliothèque nationale de France, latin 266, from Saint Martin of Tours, later at Metz) by someone called Sigilaus to Em-

---

[48] Audradus of Sens, *Il fonte della vita,* ed. F. STELLA (Florence, 1991).

peror Lothair before 851, and therefore during the same years as the codex: there, too, is a reference to an image of the emperor's face (Fig. 15), "*pictus habetur ob hoc necnon rex pagina in ista, / ut quisquis vultum Augusti hic conspexerit umquam / supplex ipse 'deo' dicat 'laus cunctipotenti'*" ("There is therefore a character painted on this page who is also king, so that anyone who ever wants to see the face of Augustus says as a supplication 'Praise to Almighty God'"), followed by the final prayer. And even the term *renovatio*, before Marbod and Baldric, is only found in poetry, here and in a *carmen intextum* from Hrabanus Maurus's *De laudibus sanctae crucis* (1 fig. III 6).[49] There are many indications, therefore, that lead us to identify, alongside the Tours and Reims schools of paintings studied by Köhler and Mütherich, a poetic school of Tours, and specifically a catalogue from Tours for the poetic *tituli*, with its own models, formulae, and style, within a broader but to my mind still circumscribable language of Latin poetry about images. It is an important field, which deserves to be explored analytically for the benefit of the history of poetry but also the histories of art and political institutions. Here I have tried to propose a sample investigation, but many tasks await anyone who might wish to take on this challenge: identifying the author of the *tituli* of the Bible of San Paolo fuori le Mura; studying the close relationship and the different text / image language in the *tituli* of that same bible, known as the third bible of Charles the Bald; comparatively analysing the style of the wall painting epigraphs that have been preserved, such as those at Reichenau-Oberzell, or not, such as the *Versus Wissenburgenses* and the *Carmina Sangallensia*; and, based on that, formulating better-substantiated hypotheses about the possible reading level of these cycles by the different sections of the public, but also following the entire birth and evolution of a descriptive and narrative way of writing with its own specific characteristics. Here, the communicative relationship was not established as usual between an author and one or more readers, but between a narrator and an iconographic figure, or between a character and an observer-reader,[50] in a multiplication of the levels of expression that went

---

[49] *Mutatio* (in l. 31) was used in the Carolingian era only by Milo of Saint-Amand and Heiric of Auxerre, just as *nocivus* (in l. 34) was used in this period only by Walahfrid, Ermoldus Nigellus, Milo, Gottschalk, and Heiric. See passages in *Poetria Nova*.

[50] Think for example of the sixth epigraph of Weissenburg, ed. as: *Versus Wissemburgenses* 6, ed. in: PLAC 4.2-3, ed. K. STRECKER, pp. 1047-1050, at p. 1049, where the scene is described by the main character Tabitha-Dorcas, not by the honoured saint (Peter) or the author: "*hinc gressu repetita volebat visere tecta, / atque propinquantes donantur gaudio gentes, / hymnorum fusis implebant cantbus auras*".

beyond the common relational framework and introduced new registers to medieval Latin poetry. These ranged from the expressionistic one, which dramatised – sometimes even disjointedly – biblical narration for a more effective and incisive presentation, to what I would call the pragmatic one, moulded from the contrasting constraints of the image and its official explanation. In my opinion, the Carolingian laboratory introduced the birth of a genre of textuality with a capacity for linguistic innovation that we are only able to comprehend and study fully today, due to our familiarity with comics, cinema, and television.

Appendix

Vivian's Bible, poetic captions (selection)
(ed. L. TRAUBE, in: *PLAC* 3, pp. 248-249)

    3.

Adam primus uti fingitur istic,
Cuius costa sacrae carpitur Euae.
Christus Euam ducit Adae, Suadet nuper creatae
Quam uocat uiraginem. Anguis dolo puellae.
5 *Ast edant ne poma uitae, Post haec amoena lustrans*
Prohibet ipse conditor. Adam uocat redemptor.
Vterque ab umbria pellitur inde sacris
Et iam labori rura colunt habiti.

    4.

Suscipit legem Moyses corusca
Regis e dextra superi, sed infra
Iam docet Christi populum repletus
Nectare sancto.

    5.

Psalmificus Dauid resplendet et ordo peritus
   Eius opus canere musica ab arte bene.

6.

Exulta, laetare satis, rex inclite Dauid,
   Egregii uoti compos ubique tui.
Carle, decus regni, fax cosmi, gloria cleri,
   Eclesiae fautor militiaeque decor,
5 *En iam lecta tibi series transacta uetusta,*
   Sed noua rite sequens ista legenda patet,
Cuius in initio clare primordia clara
   Mattheus domini concinit ex genesi.
Ceu leo per deserta fremit deserta minando
10   *Vox tua, Marce, suo fulta perenne deo.*
Mystica sacra sacre partis per quattuor orbis
   Fert studium Lucae lucis ab arce piae.
Ad genitum patria super aethera, celse Iohannes,
   Scandis et ex uerbo uerba colenda canis.
15 *Eximii hi iaciunt late mysteria Christi,*
   In sensu parili conueniuntque sibi.
Plusue minusue uel aequa boant, sua sicque dehiscunt,
   Attamen effectus unus utrinque nouus.
Hoc euangelium sanat blanditur honorat
20   *Castigat reficit munit honestat alit.*
Hic modus effandi, hic uirtus, hic actio munda,
   Hic cibus, hic potus, hic benedicta salus,
Hic uita caritas uia spes uerumque fidesque
   Seu bona cuncta simul consociata uigent:
25 *His assuesce, diu haec meditare, haec dilige siue*
   In sermone, opere haec habitare stude.
Rex bone, rex sapiens, rex prudens, rex uenerande,
   Rex Carole alme, uale cum pietatis ope.
Det tibi sceptra patris Iesus, confirmet, adunet,
30   *Proemia sanctorum ut merearis. Amen.*

7.

Rex micat aethereus condigne siue prophetae
   Hic, euangelicae quattuor atque tubae.

8.

Hic Saulum dominus caecat, hinc fundit in imam
    Terram, post trahitur caecus, ut ire queat.
Alloquitur Sabaoth Annaniam quaerere Saulum,
    Reddit et en olli lumina adempta sibi.
5 *Quam bene, sancte, doces uitalia dogmata, Paule,*
    Ex serie prisca caelitus atque noua.

9.

Septem sigillis agnus innocens modis
Signata miris iussa disserit patris.
Leges e ueteris sinu nouellae
Almis pectoribus liquantur ecce,
5 *Quae lucem populis dedere multis.*

Chapter 9

Verse Historiography in the Carolingian Era: The Political Typology of the Ingelheim Paintings

The Studies

The idea of 'typology', at least in the early Middle Ages, seems to be specific to exegesis but absent from historiography. In the texts of pre-Carolingian or Carolingian historians no passage makes explicit reference to 'typology': strictly speaking, this method was a necessary way for Christian exegetes of the Bible to connect a character, event, or object from the Old Testament with a character, event, or object from the New Testament, thus creating a focussed direction for the story of salvation. Of course we often find applications of the typological method to the interpretation of the historical books of the Bible: one example, among others, is Hrabanus Maurus's commentary on the Book of Judith,[1] which is characterised by the continued use of typology. But the consultation of digital archives relating to Carolingian writers confirms that no use of *typicus* or *typice* is found explicitly with reference to historical facts.

To find typological processes in historiography, at least during the early Middle Ages, it is therefore necessary to adopt an extended meaning of the lexeme 'typology-typological', that of 'secondary significance' and 'projection of biblical elements on a historical event' or 'valorisation of a character or historical fact through a parallel or a model drawn from the Bible'.

---

[1] *Expositio in librum Judith*, ed. in: *PL* 109, cols. 539-92; also edited as: Rabano Mauro, *Commentario al libro di Giuditta*, ed. A. SIMONETTI (Florence, 2008).

During the *Settimana di Studio* of the Centro di Studi sull'Alto Medioevo held in Spoleto in 1961, dedicated to none other than the Bible in the early Middle Ages and including lectures assigned to giants of medieval studies such as Leclercq and Daniélou, Ganshof and Monteverdi, Hubert and Fichtenau, Paul Lehmann offered a contribution called "Der Einfluss der Bibel auf frühmittelalterliche Geschichtsschreiber",[2] where he recalled the vast biblical section that Gregory of Tours places in the prologue to his *Libri Historiarum*, discovering that Gregory expands this biblical tone to the other books of his *History*, even when he does not quote from biblical texts. Lehmann also observes that there are not many traces of the Bible in Bede's *History*, nor in Paul the Deacon and Einhard, who uses the Bible only ten times in his *Vita Karoli* – and even reverses Waitz's[3] remark that Erchempert imitated the Bible more than these authors. In contrast, the Bible had a wide influence on the language of Thegan, Freculf of Lisieux, and the biographies of the abbots of Cluny in the tenth and eleventh centuries, as well as on that of the ecclesiastical historiography of Adam of Bremen. But Lehmann's investigation stopped at the linguistic surface, not addressing the more subtle question of allegorical or typological interpretation. The content of Lehmann's paper was taken up and extended to the eleventh and twelfth centuries in 1996 by Mauro Donnini in the chapter "Bibbia e storiografia" of the volume *La Bibbia nel medioevo*,[4] remaining within the framework of a rapid enumeration and adding comparisons of kings and authorities with biblical characters and their political implications in letters, laws, and treaties.

In 1984, Pierre Riché contributed to the volume *Le Moyen Âge et la Bible* with a short but very sophisticated essay on "La Bible et la politique carolingienne",[5] which was very clear about what could be presented here as a use of typology in historiography.

---

[2] P. LEHMANN, "Der Einfluß der Bibel auf frühmittelalterliche Geschichtsschreiber", in: *La bibbia nell'alto medioevo* (Spoleto, 1963: *Settimane di studio del Centro Italiano di Studi sull'Alto Medioevo* 10), pp. 129-140.

[3] G. WAITZ, Introduction to the edition of Erchempert of Monte Cassino, *Historia Langobardorum Beneventanorum*, ed. G. WAITZ, in: *MGH SS rerum Langobardorum et Italicorum* 1, ed. G. WAITZ et al. (Hanover, 1878), pp. 231-264, at p. 232.

[4] M. DONNINI, "Bibbia e storiografia", in: *La Bibbia nel medioevo*, ed. G. CREMASCOLI (Bologna, 1996), pp. 313-326.

[5] P. RICHÉ, "La Bible et la vie politique carolingienne", in: *Le Moyen Âge et la Bible*, ed. P. RICHÉ and G. LOBRICHON (Paris, 1984), pp. 388-400.

The Political Use of Biblical References

What marks the beginning of the biblicisation of the symbolism of the Frankish monarchy is the crowning of Pippin in 751 by the pope, who anointed him just as Samuel did Saul and David: he is the son of Charles Martel, who in turn is compared to Joshua[6] and who "may owe his nickname to a rapprochement with Judas Maccabeus".[7] Pippin himself insists on this point,[8] and in the letter sent by Pope Stephen II,[9] the enemies of the Franks are compared to the enemies of Israel, like new incarnations of Jeroboam and Ahab. Riché correctly points out that the commentaries on the Books of Kings by Bede and Gregory may have legitimised this parallel. Whenever medieval Latin literature offers a revival of the paratextual writings or reworkings of this book, especially versifications and comments, it is – both at the beginning of the Carolingian monarchy and at the beginning of the Capetian monarchy and during the conflict between Church and Empire – during a time of new religious investiture of the monarchy, which starts from the king's interest in presenting himself as chosen by the Lord, a powerful figure accepted by the Church, and especially from the interest of the clerics in reiterating that the source of their own legitimisation, and of the legitimisation of power, comes from religion and cannot be exercised without its approval and machineries. This is not the place to recall all the letters, poems, manuscript illuminations, and documents where Charlemagne is represented as, compared to, or called David, who plays the triple role of conqueror, missionary, and preacher, and at the same time singer – that is, lover and defender – of letters and scholars: the most extensive text on this point is undoubtedly Alcuin's letter 41. Riché remarks that this text was written shortly after the Council of Frankfurt, during which Charlemagne was called *rex* and *sacerdos*,[10] but also recalls, taking up Fichtenau, that David was

---

[6] E. EWIG, "Zum christlichen Königsgedanken im Frühmittelalter", in: ID., *Spätantikes und fränkisches Gallien: Gesammelte Schriften*, ed. H. ATSMA (Munich, 1976-1979), 1, pp. 3-71, at p. 41.

[7] RICHÉ, "La Bible", p. 388; cf. L. HALPHEN, *Charlemagne et l'Empire carolingien* (Paris, 1947); M. BLOCH, *Les rois thaumaturges: Étude sur le caractère surnaturel attribué à la puissance royale particulièrement en France et en Angleterre* (Paris, 1983²).

[8] HALPHEN, *Charlemagne*, pp. 23, 75.

[9] *Codex Carolinus*, 10, ed. W. GUNDLACH, in: *Epistolae Merowingici et Karolini aevi* 1, ed. W. GUNDLACH, E. DÜMMLER et al. (Berlin, 1892: *MGH Epp.* 3), pp. 501-503, at p. 503.

[10] RICHÉ, 'La Bible', p. 389. He writes, without referring to a specific passage, that in Paulinus of Aquileia "he is a king in his power, a priest in his sermons". On this point Ph. DEPREUX, "La *pietas* comme principe de gouvernement d'après le Poème sur Louis le Pieux

not a priest-king, a role that the Old Testament attributes only to Melchizedek. I therefore think, after intensive frequentation of Carolingian poetry, that the main connotation of the nickname 'David', borrowed from the king composer of Psalms and lyre player, is his interest in culture, represented by its pinnacle, poetry. Charlemagne was also compared to Solomon for his sense of justice, and the *Admonitio generalis*[11] compares himself to Josiah, who had the temple restored and reformed the priestly class (2 Kings, 22-23). The intellectual king is a figure that also belonged to the symbolic system of Charles the Bald, both in dedications to treatises on theology[12] and in manuscript paintings: exemplary in this sense is the Bible of San Paolo fuori le Mura, which includes a miniature with Nathan's anointing of Solomon. This parallelism, which becomes structural, is also evoked by the liturgy: Ewig[13] has documented it in the *Missa pro principe* of the Bobbio Missal, which invokes Joshua and David for the benediction of kings, in the palimpsest from Reichenau mentioning the Maccabees (2 Mac 1, 24-25),[14] and in the *Benedictio super principes* of the sacramen-

---

d'Ermold le Noir", in: *The Community, the Family and the Saint: Patterns of Power in Early Medieval Europe: Selected Proceedings of the International Medieval Congress, University of Leeds, 4-7 July 1994, 10-13 July 1995*, ed. J. HILL and M. SWAN (Turnhout, 1998), pp. 201-224, at pp. 217-219, with a focus on the lines by Ermoldus Nigellus, *Carmen elegiacum in honorem Hludowici caesaris*, 3, 1248-1249, ed. in: *Ermold le Noir, Poème sur Louis le Pieux et Épitres au roi Pépin*, ed. E. FARAL (Paris, 1932: *Les classiques de l'histoire de France au Moyen Âge*), pp. 2-200, at p. 96, that present Louis as emperor and abbot: "*Namque idem Benedictus erat pater illius aedis / Et Hludowicus adest Caesar et abba simul*" (here, however, I believe that *abba* refers to Benedict), and the passage from the *Vita Benedicti abbatis Ananiensis et Indensi auctore Ardone*, c. 42, ed. G. WAITZ, in: MGH SS 15.1, ed. G. WAITZ, W. WATTENBACH, *et al.* (Hanover, 1887), pp. 198-220, at p. 219, where it is recalled that upon Benedict's death Louis took on the abbot's role himself: "*et post eius discessum actenus abbatem se monasterii illius palam esse profitetur*". In the Carolingian period, of course, the title of 'abbot' was not necessarily an ecclesiastical one (see the case of Einhard).

[11] *Admonitio generalis*, Preface, ed. as: *Die Admonitio generalis Karls des Großen*, ed. H. MORDEK, K. ZECHIEL-ECKES, and M. GLATTHAAR (Wiesbaden, 2013: MGH *Fontes iuris Germanici antiqui in usum scholarum separatim editi* 16), p. 182: "We have after all read in the Book of Kings how the saint Josiah endeavours to bring his kingdom to worship the true God, and how to that end he traversed, admonished, and corrected it, not that I wish to equate myself with his holiness, but we must always follow the example of the saints and reunite all those we can in the effort for a holy life".

[12] F. STELLA, "Poesia e teologia: L'età carolingia: Predestinazione, culto delle immagini, poesia della conoscenza e dell'esegesi", in: *Figure del pensiero medievale*, ed. I. BIFFI and C. MARABELLI, 6 vols. (Milan 2008-2010), 3, *Il mondo delle scuole monastiche* (2010), pp. 466-614, at p. 469.

[13] EWIG, "Zum christlichen Königsgedanken", p. 20.

[14] RICHÉ, "La Bible", p. 390.

tary of Angoulême, from the end of the eighth century. Here the symbolic objects of royal power – such as the sword, the sceptre, or the crown – are described using the words of the Psalms.[15] The throne in the chapel of Aachen, with its six steps and its armrests on each side, resembles the throne of Solomon described in Book of Kings (1 Kings 10, 18), and the imperial palace described by Walahfrid Strabo in his *De imagine Tetrici* is an image of the heavenly Jerusalem, just as the heavenly Jerusalem is the model for the Castle of Paradise in the *Visio Wettini* by the same author.

Many other uses of biblical references in legislation and in the public texts of the Carolingian period have been noted and studied, and they are very prevalent in the literature of *specula principum*. In this genre, which relates political instruction and Christian morality, intellectuals close to the ruler give him advice on Christian government and propose a model of behaviour inspired by biblical heroes such as Samson, Gideon, David, Joshua, and Judas Maccabee, but also, for the family, Joseph or Job, and many others. As Hans Hubert Anton[16] has shown, the prevalence of references to the Old Testament "is explained by the fact that the Franks regarded themselves as the 'new chosen people', and therefore as the direct heirs of the Jews of the Old Testament".[17] In the *De institutioe laicali* addressed by Jonas of Orléans to Count Matfrid of Orléans, as in Smaragdus of Saint-Mihiel's *Via regia* for Louis the Pious, in Hincmar's *De regis persona*, and in Sedulius Scotus's *De regimine christiano*, quotations and biblical references are used in several ways. They make up the backbone of the moral argument for the justification of war as the defence of the Christian people, the background of each social discourse aimed primarily at the protection of the Church and activities such as school or religious practice, and finally the narrative horizon that is a model for how to describe the exploits of Frankish kings. This repertoire of figures, this background of idealities personified in a history, was reflected in epitaphs and inscriptions – that is,

---

[15] Psalm 44, 4: "*accingere gladio tuo super femur tuum*"; Psalm 2, 9: "*reges eos in virga ferrea*"; cf. Wisdom 6, 22 and Jesus Sirach 45, 14: "*corona aurea super mitram eius (i.e. Aaron)*", to be compared with Is 62: 3 and Jeremiah 13, 18.

[16] H.H. ANTON, *Fürstenspiegel und Herrscherethos in der Karolingerzeit* (Bonn, 1968: *Bonner Historische Forschungen* 32).

[17] A. KNAEPEN, "L'histoire gréco-romaine dans les sources littéraires latines de la première moitié du IXe siècle: Quelques conclusions provisoires", *Revue belge de philologie et d'histoire* 79 (2001), pp. 341-372, at p. 356; cf. also J.L. NELSON, "Translating images of authority: The Christian Roman emperors in the Carolingian world", in: *Images of Authority: Papers presented to Joyce Reynolds on the Occasion of her 70th Birthday*, ed. M.M. MCKENZIE and C. ROUECHÉ (Cambridge, 1996), pp. 194-205.

in writings on display to the public – that contributed to the formation and spreading of the system of values used to justify the balance of powers or one of its interpretations. It would also be in use during the investiture controversy and in pamphlets for the pope or the emperor, who in both cases relied on biblical quotations and their patristic authority: suffice it to recall the theory of the two swords based on Luke 22, 38. Similarly, it is undeniable that some biblical models contributed not exactly to the birth of the chivalric ideal, as Pierre Riché writes, but rather to its legitimisation, as in the case of the Crusades.

Riché clearly succeeds in proving that with Louis the Pious the biblical paradigm changed: at the time of the conflict with the episcopate, when Louis presented a programme of reforms to the Council of Paris in 829, "they evoke[d] the spectre of Saul, from whom the kingdom was taken away due to his disobedience, only to be given to David", "they sp[oke] about Heli and his sons, whose negligence earned them the loss of the Ark" (my translation), and during the crisis that led to Louis's deposition at Saint-Médard re-readings of the Books of Kings[18] were multiplied, while the resumption of relations between the episcopate and the king was marked by an increase in quotations of Proverbs relating to the concept of fraternity (Proverbs 18, 19: "The brother helped by his brother is like a strong city"; 11, 14: "Where there are no leaders the people collapse"). Hincmar especially, who was politically active with different rulers, often resorted to scholarly variations of biblical quotations to indicate examples, support his arguments, present his identifications, and accredit or discredit royal interlocutors. The Bible, or rather the projection onto a biblical background, of movements of positions of power and their ideological and cultural support, was the communication code of the ruling class. Slippage from one reference, for example David, to another, say Solomon, translated a political or moral choice in narrative and mythological terms. And we can see the traces of this in all kinds of expressions, be they figurative, literary, or legislative.

But let us return to historiography. Does this 'genre' contain examples of 'typology'? Here and there, there are signs of it: commenting on the Book of Lamentations, Paschasius Radbertus draws a parallel between the devastation of Jerusalem by the Babylonians (whose prophet – who as we now know is not Jeremiah – attributes it to the sins of his people) and the devastation by the Normans in France of his time. By the same process, Notker from Saint Gall in

---

[18] RICHÉ, "La Bible", p. 394, based on HALPHEN, *Charlemagne*, pp. 201-202.

the *Gesta Caroli* 2, 19 connects the triumphs of Charles and his son over the Normans to the victories of David and Solomon over the pagans. Hincmar compares the reconstitution of the Church of Reims by Pippin with the collection of books of Holy Scripture by Ezra. And of course the revolt of the sons of Louis the Pious is represented by Hrabanus Maurus[19] in real time, as they say, comparing it to the rebellion of Absalom, who was trying to seize the kingdom of his father David: in this context, all intellectuals involved in the debate, Agobard as well as Florus of Lyon,[20] Amalarius, and Paschasius, use biblical paradigms as projections or announcements of the characters involved. This is the case for Achitophel, who incited Absalom and was the *typus* or *figura* of the bad counsellor, as shown by G. Bidault;[21] similarly, Empress Judith's critical views of Lothair lead the latter's supporters to compare her to the queen mother Athaliah or to less noble women like Jezebel or Delilah.[22]

With this in mind, I have tried to examine the situation of Carolingian historiographical poems. I have focussed my research mainly on the Poeta Saxo's poem dedicated to Charlemagne and on Ermold the Black's poem on the history of Louis the Pious, because they present a retrospective symbolic conception of the Carolingian empire's place in history that, by associating it 'typologically' with other empires, gives it a defined ideological meaning.

---

[19] Hrabanus Maurus, *Liber de reverentia filiorum erga patres et erga reges*, ed. in: *Hrabani (Mauri) abbatis Fuldensis et archiepiscopi Moguntiacensis epistolae*, ed. E. DÜMMLER, in: *Epistolae Karolini aevi* 3, ed. E. DÜMMLER, K. HAMPE, *et al.* (Berlin, 1898-1899: MGH *Epist.* 5), pp. 403-415; cf. *Dhuoda, Manuel pour mon fils*, ed. P. RICHÉ (Paris, 1975: Sources Chrétiennes 225), pp. 1 and 137.

[20] Florus of Lyon, *Querela de divisione imperii*, ed. in: *Flori Lugdunensis carmina*, ed. E. DÜMMLER, in: PLAC 2, pp. 507-566, at pp. 559-564, citing Ez.13: 10 and Amos 8 to announce the disasters threatening the empire.

[21] G. BIDAULT, "Achitophel conseiller de la dissidence", *Revue du Moyen Âge Latin* 1 (1945), pp. 57-60.

[22] Paschasius Radbertus, *Epitaphium Arsenii*, ed. in PL; better edition: ed. E. DÜMMLER, in: *Abhandlungen der Preußischen Akademie der Wissenschaften, Philologisch-historische Klasse* (1900), 2, pp. 18-98; Agobard of Lyon, *Liber Apologeticus*, ed. in: PL 104, cols. 307-320. [See also M. DE JONG, "Jeremiah, Job, Terence and Paschasius Radbertus: Political rhetoric and biblical authority in the Epitaphium Arsenii", in: *Reading the Bible in the Middle Ages*, ed. J. NELSON and D. KEMPF (London, 2015), pp. 57-76, and EAD., *Epitaph for an Era: Politics and Rhetoric in the Carolingian World* (Cambridge, 2019).]

The Poeta Saxo

The *Annales de gestis Caroli Magni imperatoris*[23] is a long poem in five books of 2963 lines (hexameters and couplets) composed for Arnulf of Carinthia before 891. Its subject is the history of Charlemagne and the submission of the Saxon people; and the anonymous author was a Saxon and probably a monk from Corvey, who was grateful to the ruler for giving him the chance to learn to write and pass down the memory of these events. The first books (three and a half) are based on the *Einhardi Annales*, the rest on other annalistic sources, only partially known; the poem itself was used as a historical source by the *Annales* of Quedlinburg. The last book is devoted to the welcoming of Charlemagne in the afterlife, where he is accompanied by those Apostles who, like him, converted pagan peoples: Peter, Paul, Andrew, Matthew, and Thomas. Bischoff[24] wrote that the model for this interpretation was a sermon by Gregory the Great,[25] but Gregory did not know Charlemagne; what interests us here is the emperor's place in the gallery of biblical characters with which he is associated, and how this relationship can be interpreted typologically. Already in book IV the poet could not help renouncing the parallel between David, who passed on the throne to Solomon, and Charles, who incorporated Louis in the imperial office, while in ll. 140 ff. the blessing of Charlemagne's ancestor Arnulf is compared to that of Jacob blessing Judah, by which he indicated to him that he would carry the sceptre. But the most important passage can be read in ll. 655-656 of the fifth book: the poet urges readers to stop admiring the stories of the ancients. Neither the Decii nor the Scipions, Camillus, Cato, nor even Caesar, he says, were greater than him; Pompey or the Fabii family, who sacrificed themselves for their country, have now been surpassed by him. Perhaps they had a similar reputation on earth, but now Charles is at the pinnacle of celestial glory. He is found there with Constantine and Theodosius thanks to the virtues exemplified by David. The latter rejoices at having

---

[23] Ed. P. VON WINTERFELD, in: *PLAC* 4, pp.1-71; Italian translation by A. ISOLA, *Poeta Sassone: Le gesta dell'imperatore Carlo Magno* (Milan, 1987); bibliography, with translation and commentary of an excerpt, in *La poesia carolingia*, ed. F. STELLA (Florence, 1995), pp. 111-112, 332-335 and 485-486.

[24] B. BISCHOFF, "Das Thema des Poeta Saxo", in: *Speculum historiale: Geschichte im Spiegel von Geschichtsschreibung und Geschichtsdeutung: Johannes Spörl aus Anlass seines sechzigsten Geburtstages dargebracht von Weggenossen, Freunden umd Schülern*, ed. C. BAUER, L. BOEHM, and M. MÜLLER (Freiburg im Breisgau and Munich, 1965), pp. 198-203.

[25] Gregory the Great, *Homiliae XL in Evangelia* 1, 17, 17, ed. in: *PL* 76, cols. 1075-1312, at col. 1148 B-C.

defeated the ancient Enemy, rescuing many people from his traps; and Constantine and Theodosius rejoice because, by the grace of God, thousands of souls have been saved. In the same way Charles has saved many Saxons, and when it is time for the Last Judgment, he will be able to demonstrate how he has made use of his talents. At that moment no one will be closer to him than the group of the Apostles, when Peter will walk followed by a group of Jews, Paul will be followed by nations around the world saved by his message of faith, Andrew by the Greeks, John by the communities of Asia, and Matthew by Ethiopians bleached (sic!) by baptism, when Thomas will lead the crowds of the Indians to heaven, and the Saxons will follow Charles. In conclusion, the poet wishes to join this troop and to save himself thanks to his songs of praise. This seems to be the first time that Charlemagne was inserted in such a precise and articulate eschatological framework, considering that the anonymous Carolingian visions of the afterlife and that of Walahfrid placed him – because of his sexual sins – in a provisional hell, almost a purgatory, long before the birth of Purgatory as described by Jacques Le Goff. But we will see that the general meaning of the place thus attributed to him goes hand in hand with the celebratory intention that is documented by other poetic testimonies.

Ermold

The second case I would like to examine is the poem *In honorem Hludowici* by Ermold the Black (Ermoldus Nigellus).[26] A monk or cleric from a Frankish family, he frequented the court of Pippin of Aquitaine by following him

---

[26] *Ermold le Noir, Poème sur Louis le Pieux et Épîtres au roi Pépin*, ed. and trans. E. FARAL (Paris, 1932). Bibliography, with translation and commentary of an excerpt, in: *La poesia carolingia*, ed. STELLA, pp. 98, 324-331, 482; among the recent contributions see C.D. FLEINER, *In Honor of Louis the Pious, a Verse Biography by Ermoldus Nigellus (826): An Annotated Translation*, PhD thesis University of Virginia, 1996; A. ENCUENTRA ORTEGA, "Luis el Piadoso, un Eneas cristiano en el poema laudatorio de Ermoldo", *Latomus* 64 (2005) pp. 445-455; M. DONNINI, "L'*ars narrandi* nel *Carmen in honorem Hludowici* di Ermoldo Nigello", *Studi medievali* 47 (2006), pp. 111-176. On my point: Ch. RATKOWITSCH, "Die Fresken im Palast Ludwigs des Frommen in Ingelheim (Ermold., Hlud. 4, 181 ff.): Realität oder poetische Fiktion?", *Wiener Studien* 107-108 (1994-1995), pp. 553-581; and DEPREUX, "La *pietas*". I was unable to consult A. DUBREUCQ, "Les peintures murales du palais carolingien d'Ingelheim et l'idéologie impériale carolingienne", *Hortus Artium Medievalium* 16 (2010), pp. 27-38. [Ch. VEYRARD-COSME, "Du *Pius Aeneas* à Louis le Pieux: Ermold le Noir et l'influence virgilienne", in: *Virgiliennes: Hommages à Philippe Heuzé*, ed. J. PIGEAUD (Paris, 2016), pp. 209-226.]

against the Bretons, but was exiled in 825 to Strasbourg. There he wrote two elegiac epistles to plead for his return and, around the years 826-828, an encomiastic poem in four books of 2649 lines (couplets), in a Vergilian language filtered by late antique and proto-Carolingian poetry – especially by *Karolus Magnus et Leo papa*, which celebrated the Paderborn meeting of 799. Ermold's poem is characterised by a certain precision in its historical details, confirmed by Faral's and Geuenich's studies, but also by an irony that is not all that typical of epic poems. It is the first complete medieval secular epos that has reached us, except maybe for *Beowulf*, and it represents, so to speak, the most important political poem in what has been called a 'classicising' era: it recounts the enterprises of Louis the Pious before and after his ascension to the throne: his expedition to Barcelona, his foundation of Conques, prophecies about his succeeding Charlemagne, his conversion of the Danes, and his campaign against the Bretons. Scholars' opinions on the poem's literary value vary widely, but in this case aesthetic taste is not relevant: I have commented on the different critical positions in my anthology of Carolingian poetry, but I believe that this classicism was a dead end for Carolingian poetry and prevented the expression of more authentic values of this culture.

However, in this poem, and generally in Ermold's poetry, there are unique pieces that seem to have no parallels or models in other texts. One of the most famous is the description, in ll. 179 ff. of the fourth book, of the murals of the palace of Ingelheim near Mainz, where Louis welcomed the Danish King Harold, who had just been baptised. The first note on this palace is in Einhard's *Vita Karoli*, in chapter 17, where he describes the palaces and churches built by Charlemagne and, referring to the year 787, writes: "*Inchoavit and palatia operis egregii, unum haud longe in Mogontiaco civitate, iuxta villam cui vocabulum is Ingilenheim, alterum Noviomagi super Vahalem fluvium*" ("He also began the construction of two magnificent palaces: one not far from the city of Mainz, near the township called Ingelheim, and the other at Nijmegen, on the River Waal").[27] After this passage, the palace is mentioned in the *Annales Fuldenses* and by sources from the time of Louis, when the palace was the seat of royal assemblies: the *Annales Regni Francorum*,[28] the *Annales Altahen-*

---

[27] Einhard, *Vita Karoli Magni*, c. 17, ed. O. HOLDER-EGGER (Hanover and Leipzig, 1911: MGH SRG *in usum scholarum* 25), p. 20; trans. in: *Einhard and Notker the Stammerer: Two Lives of Charlemagne*, trans. L. THORPE (Harmondsworth, 1969), p. 71.

[28] *Annales regni Francorum inde ab a. 741 usque ad a. 829, qui dicuntur Annales Laurissenses maiores et Einhardi*, ed. F. KURZE (Hanover, 1895: MGH SRG *in usum scholarum separatim editi* 6), p. 169.

ses (from Niederaltaich),[29] and Thegan's *Gesta Hludowici imperatoris*.[30] One document even establishes the appointment of an "*exactor palatii Ingelenheim*" called Agano. After the Carolingians, especially among the Ottonians and the Salians, the palace became the centre of many imperial meetings. The building and its location have frequently been examined in studies of the imperial palaces, which flourished at least since the time of Percy Ernst Schramm,[31] Karl Schumacher, Walter Schlesinger,[32] Hermann Heimpel,[33] Peter Classen,[34] and, more recently, Holger Grewe[35] and Jean-Pierre Caillet.[36] Many excavation campaigns were led by Christian Rauch from 1909 to 1919, then by Adolf Zeller,[37] Walter Sage,[38] and Uta Weimann[39] during the sixties, and by Holger

[29] *Annales Altahenses maiores*, ed. E. VON OEFELE (Hanover, 1881: MGH SRG *in usum scholarum separatim editi* 4).

[30] Ed. in: *Thegan, Die Taten Kaiser Ludwigs (Gesta Hludowici imperatoris) – Astronomus, Das Leben Kaiser Ludwigs (Vita Hludowici imperatoris)*, ed. and trans. E. TREMP (Hanover, 1995: MGH SRG *in usum scholarum separatim editi* 64), pp. 167-277, at pp. 214, 220.

[31] P.E. SCHRAMM, *Die zeitgenössischen Bildnisse Karls des Grossen: Mit einem Anhang über die Metallbullen der Karolinger* (Leipzig, 1928).

[32] W. SCHLESINGER, "Die Pfalzen im Rhein-Main Gebiet: Percy Ernst Schramm zum siebzigsten Geburststag", *Geschichte in Wissenschaft und Unterricht* 16 (1965), pp. 487-504, at pp. 487-489.

[33] H. HEIMPEL, "Bisherige und künftige Erforschung deutscher Königspfalzen: Zugleich Bericht über Arbeiten des Max-Planck-Instituts für Geschichte zur Pfalzenforschung", *Geschichte in Wissenschaft und Unterricht* 16 (1965), pp. 461-487.

[34] P. CLASSEN, "Die Geschichte der Königspfalz Ingelheim bis zur Verpfändung an Kurpfalz 1375", in: *Ingelheim am Rhein: Forschungen und Studien zur Geschichte Ingelheims*, ed. J. AUTENRIETH (Stuttgart, 1964), pp. 87-146; see also H. SCHMITZ, *Pfalz und Fiskus Ingelheim* (PhD thesis, Frankfurt, 1967).

[35] H. GREWE, "Die Königspfalz zu Ingelheim am Rhein", in: *799: Kunst und Kultur der Karolingerzeit: Karl der Grosse und Papst Leo III. in Paderborn*, ed. Ch. STIEGEMANN and M. WEMHOFF (Mainz, 1999), 3, *Beiträge zum Katalog der Ausstellung Paderborn 1999*, pp. 142-151; H. GREWE, "Die Ausgrabungen in der Königspfalz zu Ingelheim am Rhein", in: *Deutsche Königspfalzen: Beiträge zu ihrer historischen und archäologischen Erforschung*, ed. L. FENSKE, J. JARNUT, and M. WEMHOFF (Göttingen, 2001: *Splendor palatii: Neue Forschungen zu Paderborn und anderen Pfalzen der Karolingerzeit* 5), pp. 155-174.

[36] J.-P. CAILLET, "Prééminence dans la menée des desseins de Dieu: Configuration et décor des salles d'audience carolingiennes et pontificales", in: *L'audience: Rituels et cadres spatiaux dans l'Antiquité et le haut Moyen Âge*, ed. J.-P. CAILLET and M. SOT (Paris, 2007), pp. 291-302.

[37] A. ZELLER, *Die Auswertung des Befundes früherer Bauanlagen im Saale in Ingelheim: Reichssaal und Kaiserwohnung* (Berlin, 1935).

[38] W. SAGE, "Zur archäologischen und baugeschichtlichen Erforschung der Ingelheimer Pfalz in Ingelheim am Rhein", in: *Ingelheim am Rhein*, pp. 65-86.

[39] H. AMENT, W. SAGE, and U. WEIMANN, "Die Ausgrabungen in der Pfalz zu Ingelheim am Rhein in den Jahren 1963 und 1965", *Germania* 46 (1968), pp. 291-312.

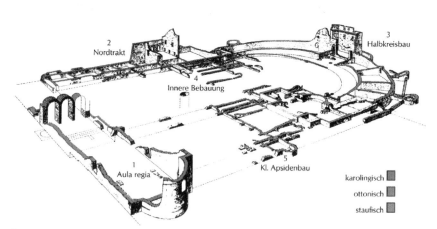

Fig. 16   Ingelheim, isometric representation of the remains of the palace, with indication of the building preiods. After <http://www.kaiserpfalz-ingel heim.de>.

Grewe and others[40] after 1993: on this topic see the publications listed on the website *Kaiserpfalz Ingelheim*,[41] which also provides attempts at virtual reconstruction. It has been confirmed that the *aula* had only one nave and not three, but it was discovered that the aisleless church (*Saalkirche*), which was considered Carolingian, actually dated from middle of the tenth century, and that in Ottonian times many structural changes were made to the Carolingian founda-

---

[40]   See the website <http://www.kaiserpfalz-ingelheim.de>.
[41]   H. GREWE, "Geschichte und Neubeginn der archäologischen Forschung in der Königspfalz zu Ingelheim am Rhein", *Acta Praehistorica et Archaeologica* 30 (1998), pp. 177-184; ID., "Forschen, Erschließen, Bewahren: Ein Zwischenbericht über die Kaiserpfalz Ingelheim", *Baudenkmäler in Rheinland Pfalz* 59 (2004), pp. 54-60; ID., "Die bauliche Entwicklung der Pfalz Ingelheim im Hochmittelalter: Architekturbefunde und Schriftquellen des 10. und 11. Jahrhunderts", in: *Zentren herrschaftlicher Repräsentation im Hochmittelalter: Geschichte, Architektur, und Zeremoniell*, ed. C. EHLERS, J. JARNUT, and M. WEMHOFF (Göttingen, 2007: *Deutsche Königspfalzen: Beiträge zu ihrer historischen und archäologischen Erforschung* 7), pp. 101-120; ID., "Visualisierung von Herrschaft in der Architektur: Die Pfalz Ingelheim als Bedeutungsträger im 12. und 13. Jahrhundert", in: *Staufisches Kaisertum im 12. Jahrhundert: Konzepte, Netzwerke, Politische Praxis*, ed. S. BURKHARDT (Regensburg, 2010), pp. 383-403; ID., "Palast, Ruine, Denkmal: Konzeptionelle Grundsätze für das Erforschen, Bewahren und Erschließen der Kaiserpfalz Ingelheim", in: *Schutzbauten und Rekonstruktionen in der Archäologie*, ed. M. MÜLLER, T. OTTEN, and U. WULF-RHEIDT (Mainz, 2011), pp. 305-328. See also <http://www.kaiserpfalz-ingelheim.de>.

Fig. 17 Ingelheim, reconstruction of the Aula Regia. After <http://www.kaiserpfalz-ingelheim.de>.

tions: the *aula regia* is in any case datable to 807 at the latest, but we know that the palace had already hosted official meetings in 787 and 788[42] (Fig.16).

At a textual level, however, it turns out that the most detailed source on this palace is Ermold's poem, which must have been written between the autumn of 826 and the spring of 828. It had always been believed that his verse offered a reliable enough description of paintings, but Christine Ratkowitsch sought to demonstrate that Ermold selected paintings in order to develop a set to highlight the *clementia* ('clemency') and *pietas* ('mercifulness') of Louis, who he hoped would end his exile.[43] In 2001 Knaepen accepted this hypothesis, yet completely ignored the results of excavations and other studies that leave no room for the assumption according to which there would have been many more painted scenes than those Ermold described, and according to which, as a result, Ermold would have been modifying reality to put together a virtual

[42] W. LAMMERS, "Ein karolingisches Bildprogramm in der Aula Regia von Ingelheim", in: ID., *Vestigia mediaevalia: Ausgewählte Aufsätze zur mittelalterlichen Historiographie, Landes- und Kirchengeschichte* (Wiesbaden, 1979), pp. 219-283, at p. 227, n. 33.

[43] RATKOWITSCH, "Die Fresken im Palast Ludwigs des Frommen in Ingelheim".

cycle intended to exalt implicitly a sovereign who is not represented or compared to other figures, or even mentioned in Ermold's verse.

Ermold begins his description by introducing the place according to the clichés of the digression:

> *Engilin – ipse pius placido tunc tramite – heim*
> *advolat induperans coniuge cum, sobole.*
> *Is locus ille situs rapidi flumina Rheni,*
> *ornatus variis cultibus and dapibus*, etc.

> The pious emperor goes on a happy journey with his wife and children to Ingelheim. This place is near the fast-flowing Rhine, in the middle of lands with rich and varied cultures, etc.

This is a very generic description, which researchers consider symbolic (I would say 'hyperbolic', without overestimating the poet), intended to give the impression of a labyrinthine, monumental ensemble of buildings. The archaeological reality – which can be found in Ament, Sage and Weimann's plan, and in Grewe's virtual reconstruction (Fig. 17) – shows a straight room, whose longest axis from north to south (about 40 metres, or 120 Carolingian feet), ends in a semicircular apse which was later elevated, with doorways in the middle of the two long walls and probably decorative paintings, of which remnants have been found.[44] All of this also shows a kinship with the palace at Aachen, which however, was larger and had lateral apses.

The Biblical Cycle

In Ermold's poem, the generic presentation of the palace is immediately followed by the much more detailed and realistic description of a church or several churches:

> The temple [the temples?] of God is built of hard stone, with a large door lined with bronze and a small one covered with gold. There you can read, recalled by beautiful paintings, the sublime works of God and the story of long generations of men.[45]

---

[44] LAMMERS, "Ein karolingisches Bildprogramm", p. 230.
[45] *Ermold le Noir, Poème sur Louis le Pieux et Épîtres au roi Pépin*, ed. and trans. FARAL,

Unfortunately there is no space here for a thorough discussion of the church's identification, which is nonetheless a fascinating subject. It will suffice to recall that Ernst Dümmler, the poem's editor in volume 2 of the *Poetae Latini aevi Carolini*, thought of the basilica of Sankt Alban in Mainz, while Faral, responsible for the second critical edition, proposed Saint Rémi at Ingelheim, which is 500 metres from the palace and was the seat of a meeting of Frankish and German bishops in 948.[46] Walther Lammers, who dedicated a more careful study to Ermold's composition, left the question open. However, if I understand correctly, the excavations proved – as has happened for Homer and for other texts – that the poet was a rather reliable source: in Ingelheim there was a small Carolingian church, which served the religious needs of the court.[47]

The first series (ll. 2072-2123) of paintings concerns sacred history:

ut primo, ponente Deo, pars laeva recenset,
Incolitant homines te, paradise, novi ...

On the left it is explained how God placed the first men to live in you, paradise ...

So on the left side the Old Testament is represented "*per innumeros sequaces*" and each scene is introduced into the poem with *ut*: paradise, temptation, fig leaves, Cain's murder of Abel with his bare hands,[48] the flood, the ark with the raven and the dove, the story of Abraham and his descendants, of Joseph and his brothers, of Pharaoh. We can see how Moses delivered his people from the Egyptian yoke, and how the Egyptians perished in the waters while Israel escaped, we see the law dictated by God and inscribed on the two tablets, the water that sprang from the rock, the food that flies,[49] the promised land, the power of Joshua. Then we can admire the series of prophets and kings, with David, Solomon, and the temple, and then the Hebrew leaders ("*inde duces*

---

ll. 2068-70: "*Templa Dei summi constant operata metallo, / Aerati postes aurea hostiola, / Inclita gesta Dei, series memoranda virorum, / Pictura insigni quo relegenda patent*". My translation.

[46] LAMMERS, "Ein karolingisches Bildprogramm", p. 243, n. 81.

[47] The plan of the church is online at <http://www.kaiserpfalz-ingelheim.de/archaeologie_pfalz_der_ottonen_02.php>. See, besides the archaeological bibliography, CAILLET, "Prééminence", p. 293.

[48] In contrast to the precedent from Prudentius, *Hamartigenia*, Praef., v. 16, ed. in: Prudentius, *Carmina*, ed. M.P. CUNNINGHAM (Turnhout, 1960: CCSL 126), p. 116: "*germana curvo colla frangit sarculo*".

[49] "*Volucre cibum*", "food flying from the sky", refers to the *coturnices* ('quails') of Exodus 16, 13.

populi quales quantum fuere") and the priests with the heroes ("*atque sacerdotum culmina seu procerum*") if the latter addition is not synonymous, that is, if 'priests and heroes' are not the same as 'prophets and kings'. Lammers divided this series in 24 scenes forming six groups (Paradise, Expulsion and Flood, from Abraham to Joseph, Moses, Kings, gallery of priests and chiefs).

On the right side we can admire the life-giving story of Jesus: "*altera pars retinet Christi vitalia gesta*", writes Ermold (l. 2100), reusing the famous clausula of the poem of Juvencus on the Gospel (*Evangeliorum libri IV*, Praef. 19), which was read in schools and was well known to all readers. The annunciation, the acceptance of Mary, the nativity of Christ announced by the prophets, the shepherds, and the three wise men, Herod, the flight to Egypt, the return and Jesus's submission to the Law – or rather, if we correct the translation of Faral, his presentation in the Temple –, the baptism of God who came to save mankind, his long fasts and his fight against the Tempter, his teaching and the healings that he performed, resurrections and exorcism, betrayal of a disciple and of the people, the death and the apparitions after his resurrection, and finally the ascension, all perfectly painted by an exceptional artist. Here Lammers only counts 16 scenes, and these can be subdivided into three groups: Birth and Childhood; Activity of Christ; and Death and Resurrection. Carolingian poetry has preserved many series of *tituli* for miniature cycles in the famous Bibles of Tours and of Charles the Bald, or for murals or frescoes that have only been passed down to us in the case of Sankt Georg in Reichenau-Oberzell. We possess the *tituli* for the cycle of Bernowin perhaps for Saint-Alyre in Clermont; the inscriptions of Gorze by Alcuin; the Genesis of the pseudo-Alcuinian *carmen* 115; the *Versus Wissenburgenses*; the *Carmina Sangallensia*; a few *Carmina Centulensia* for Saint-Riquier; and even Sedulius Scotus's lines for a sundial and for Empress Ermengarde's silk coat. I studied these texts in a chapter of my 1993 book, and Arwed Arnulf dedicated the volume *Versus ad picturas* to them in 1997.[50] I shall therefore not linger on the subject, but we can place this passage of Ermold in this tradition.

It would be tempting to put the two series in typological parallel and perhaps some or many of them suggest this relationship. For example, the flood and the baptism are two paintings traditionally in a typological relationship; the murder of Abel with the massacre of the Innocents; the proto-parents with the

---

[50] F. STELLA, *La poesia Carolingia latina a tema biblico* (Spoleto, 1993), pp. 172-207. A. ARNULF, *Versus ad Picturas: Studien zur Titulusdichtung als Quellengattung der Kunstgeschichte von der Antike bis zum Hochmittelalter* (Munich, 1997).

holy family; Eve with Mary; the miracles of Moses with the miracles of Jesus; and even the Hebrew kings with the three Kings. However, this arrangement is not certain, because Ermold gives a rather unsystematic description, and, although as such it is reliable because it is not artificial, it is not very useful for a precise reconstruction. In any case, it would be in the realm of traditional – that is to say, intra-biblical – typology, without any noteworthy novelties at the exegetical level. Comparable texts are numerous and go back to the *Dittochaeon* composed by Prudentius in the fourth century, where two series of *tituli* in metric quatrains correspond perfectly, and to the hymn of Sedulius in the fifth century in epanaleptic couplets, taken up again and integrated by Hrabanus Maurus in the ninth century in his *carmen* 39. There are also many artistic parallels, even if they are more frequent in the central Middle Ages than in the Carolingian period, of which we have few remnants; but the impressive frescoes of Müstair, Saint-Benoît de Mals (Sankt Benedikt in Mals, Vinschgau), of Sankt Georg of Reichenau-Oberzell, and the missing paintings that were described by the series of *tituli* that I have mentioned, are just evidence for the realism of this description.

The Cycle of Power

In the *domus regia*, which is now identified as the *aula regia* of the excavations, Ermold describes "sculptures" (which will be interpreted rather as 'reliefs') that tell ("sing", in the language of the poem) the most important deeds of heroes, "*maxima gesta virum*". We start with Cyrus, king of the Persians: recalling his canalisation of the River Gyndes, today's Diyala, accomplished to avenge the drowning of his favorite horse, and his death, with his head cut off and thrown into a wineskin of blood by order of a woman – here the queen of the Scythians, Tomyris – whose kingdom he had invaded, a dramatic narrative told by Justin and the subject of many modern paintings.[51] We next see the founder of Nineveh, Ninus, the first great king of the Assyrians, of whom the numerous wars and cruelties are mentioned generically here ("*proelia multimoda duraque facta nimis*", l. 2129).

Each character appears in a couplet, in the form of a *titulus*: "*hic videas*", etc.; but it is interesting that the alternative verb is used in synonymy with

---

[51] Herodotus, *Histories* 1, 205 ff.; Pompeius Trogus, *Historiae Philippicae*, in: Justinus 1, 8. Other versions in Ctesias, *Persika* 2 and in Xenophon, *Cyropaedia*, book 7.

either *videre* or *canere*, 'to sing', which creates a symmetry between visual communication and poetic communication and produces a parallel monumentalisation of content. Ermold alludes to the significant details of history with adjectives that are more affective than picturesque: for example *carus*, applied to the horse, refers to the fact that the horse was Cyrus's favourite, *infelix* announces the tragedy that threatens the king. The *exempla* of the paintings of Ingelheim continue with the episode of the bull of Phalaris, the tyrant of Sicily in the sixth century BCE, who killed the builder Beryl, here named Pyrillus (classical form: Perillus): four couplets are dedicated to him, which make this little story the most extended development of this pagan gallery. It is followed by sketches of the story of Romulus and Remus, the battles and the partial blindness (or death) of Hannibal,[52] the world conquests of Alexander, and the power of the Romans. These last, who could presumably have been represented by one emperor, perhaps Augustus, reached heaven: "*usque polum*" (l. 2147).

After the series of seven powerful pagans, a second series of portraits dedicated to Christian rulers and Carolingians begins "*alia parte tecti*", that is to say on another wall of the room or, as Faral correctly interprets, in another part of the palace:

gesta paterna
piae fidei proximiora magis.
Caesarei actis Romanae sedis opimae
Iunguntur Franci gestaque mira simul

ll. 2148-2149: "in another part of the palace we can admire the exploits of ancestors closer to the Christian spirit. The actions of the Roman Caesars mingle with the the heroic deeds of the Franks".[53]

---

[52] *Ermold le Noir, Poème sur Louis le Pieux et Épîtres au roi Pépin*, ed. and trans. FARAL, ll. 2144-2145: "*Hannibal ut bellis semper persuetus iniquis, / Lumine privatus ut fuit ipse suo*". Faral translates "et comment lui-même périt"; I believe in contrast that the line refers to sight, as this is frequent with *lumen*.

[53] Faral remarks that this preoccupation about relating the history of the Franks to that of the Roman Empire is found in lines 718-719 (2, 66-7) : "*Caesareum primus Francorum nomen adeptus / Francis Romuleum nomen habere dedi*" and 1077 (2, 423-4, the coronation): "*Roma tibi, Caesar, transmittit munera Petri / Digna satis digno, conveniensque decus*" and in the second Epistle to Pepin (159-160): "*Iam venit armipotens Carolus Pippinea proles, / Romuleum Francis praestitit imperium*". This comment has been ignored by other researchers.

Verse Historiography in the Carolingian Era 227

First Constantine, who leaves Rome "out of love" and founds Constantinople, then *felix* Theodosius, 'happy' in the sense of 'successful', 'lucky' in his endeavours, and finally the royal house: Charles Martel the master of war ("*Marte magister*") and conqueror of the Frisians (around 730), Pippin, who subdues the Aquitanians (several times until 768) and reassigns them to his kingdom, and finally Charles the scholar, *Carolus sapiens* whose face is radiant – a detail that confirms the attentive examination of paintings by the poet or by his source – and whose head is crowned, who faces the Saxons and subdues them. Here ends the decoration, which nourishes the eyesight and makes resplendent the place where the emperor pronounces his acts of law and governs.

The Meaning of the Paintings

What is the meaning of this gallery? Did it really exist? Publishers, art historians, and historians have devoted much interpretative effort to this poetic passage. We have discussed and confirmed Ermold's credibility due to the iconographic parallels that we have mentioned; and we have identified the source of the references to Assyrian, Persian, Greek, and Roman history, Orosius's *Historia adversus paganos*, characterised by an ideological opposition that presents the biographies of pagan sovereigns with unfortunate traits and negative destinies. Jean-Pierre Caillet would have identified the source of the layout of the paintings that characterise the Carolingian dynasty by its military conquests rather than by conversions to Christianity or by cultural policy in Ps.-Fredegarius (an author of Burgundian origin who would have written in Austrasia around the years 658-660), but without textual evidence and while failing to explain, but not to notice, Ermold's omissions of the Merovingians and of the link with the Trojans. Orosius would therefore explain the relief dedicated to relatively secondary figures such as Phalaris and Tomyris, and even the choice of the details about Hannibal. In the early Middle Ages, after Orosius, the bull of Phalaris is mentioned almost only after the ninth century, by Ekkehard of Saint Gall's *Chronicon*, which explicitly quotes Orosius,[54] and later by Otto of Freising,[55] Conrad de Mure,[56] and Lucas de Tuy.[57] In the ninth

---

[54] *Ekkehardi Chronicon universale*, ed. G. WAITZ, in: *Chronica et annales aevi Salici*, ed. G.H. PERTZ et al. (Hanover, 1844), pp. 33-231, at p. 49.

[55] *Ottonis episcopi Frisingensis Chronica sive Historia*, 2, 5, ed. A. HOFMEISTER (Hanover,

century we find this story in the *Chronicon* by Freculf of Lisieux,[58] a pupil of Helisachar, who was Louis the Pious's chancellor and was often cited by Ermold as an important figure and master-dedicatee of the poem.[59] Helisachar then, as Lammers proposed in a valuable note[60] which has escaped the researchers, could also be the inspiration for the cycle of paintings of Ingelheim, if it is dated to the time of Louis and not before. We would thus reconstruct a cultural historiographico-poetico-pictorial system that shares common views and values the same sources. If Orosius, through Freculf or Helisachar, is the source of the paintings on the kings of Antiquity, the common thread – the meaning – of the gallery is the demonstration of the negative destiny of the stories of pagan sovereigns, which was at the basis of Orosius's and Freculf's work, as it was for Lactantius. The same meaning could extend to more recent times, where the action of Theodosius and the Carolingians is characterised by the same military victories as that of their pagan predecessors, while their missionary work, since it was in the Poeta Saxo's eschatological setting, remains implied or obscure. From this perspective – except for the insertion of Phalaris, which is due exclusively to moral reasons – the choice of characters points to Oriosius's four universal monarchies, *die vier Weltreiche*: Babylon, Macedonia, Carthage, and Rome, which represent, according to Lammers – but we can doubt this geographical interpretation – East, North, South, and West.

The 'modern' part of the gallery may thus reflect a dynastic and imperial vision rather than a religious one. This is why the Merovingians, devoid of victories, are not there, and also why the papal coronations of Pippin and Char-

---

1912: MGH SRG *in usum scholarum separatim editi* 45), p. 73.

[56] Conradus de Mure, *Fabularius*, Lexicon P, ed. T. VAN DE LOO (Turnhout, 2006: CCCM 210), p. 418.

[57] Lucas Tudensis, *Chronicon Mundi* 1, 30, ed. E. FALQUE REY (Turnhout, 2003: CCCM 74), p. 35.

[58] Freculf of Lisieux, *Chronicon*, I, 3, 11, ed. M.I. ALLEN, 2 vols. (Turnhout, 2002: CCCM 169-169a), 1, p. 173.

[59] On Helisachar, see: E. BISHOP, "Ein Schreiben des Abts Helisachar", *Neues Archiv der Gesellschaft für ältere deutsche Geschichtskunde* 11 (1886), pp. 564-568; G. MORIN, "Une rédaction inédite de la préface au supplément du Comes d'Alcuin", *Revue bénédictine* 29 (1912), pp. 341-348; E. BISHOP, "A letter of Abbot Helisachar", in: ID., *Liturgica historica: Papers on the Liturgy and Religious Life of the Western Church* (Oxford, 1918), pp. 333-338; M. HUGLO, "D'Helisachar à Abbon de Fleury", *Revue bénédictine* 104 (1994), pp. 204-230.

[60] LAMMERS, "Ein karolingisches Bildprogramm", p. 247, n. 100. Lammers also recognised the presence of *Perillus* in Freculf even though in his time he only had available the PL edition, where we read *per illos* (two words), now corrected in the CCCM edition of Allen, vol. 1 (Pars I, book 3, chapter 11).

lemagne are missing. The pagan political paintings are therefore associated from a military point of view. The victories of the pagans were the signs of a cruelty that would later be punished; would the victories of the Carolingians then be a sign of the triumph of the 'good' side over other peoples? But not only pagan nations are considered here, because the Aquitanians subdued by Pippin were already Christians.

So the 'hypersign' of the whole gallery is imperial and ethnic rather than ideological, and this is justified very well, not, as Ratkowitsch proposes, in reference to the pious and merciful image of Louis, but by his image as a military leader who nevertheless knows how to impose himself without bloodshed, an image celebrated throughout the epic poem through his enterprises against the Bretons, in Barcelona, and in Denmark. We must remember that this description sets up the baptismal ceremony of Harold, who will offer Christianity and the Empire a new people. The Romans, Constantine and Theodosius, mark a chronological threshold – before or after Christ – rather than a specifically ideal or religious one. If we assume the typological meaning – of a secular typology – of the series of paintings, that is to say, if we accept the correspondence between old paintings and modern paintings, then Charlemagne, who alone bears the crown and who is the fifth, just as Hannibal is the fifth pagan, is not the new Constantine, as he was called by Pope Hadrian I,[61] but the last conqueror, and the first true Carolingian king. This is why the gallery ignores the coronation by the pope, but highlights the trend – which emerges in the *Annales Mettenses*, which are very close to the royal house – of starting the Carolingian reign and sometimes even the empire with Pippin.[62]

This interpretation, which is based on the typological parallelism of the series, seems confirmed by the choice of the enterprise that characterises Constantine: it is not his openness to the Christian religion, as could be expected, but the movement of the imperial seat to Constantinople. From then on, the Empire was no longer in Rome, but with Louis, in Ingelheim. Walter Schle-

---

[61] Letter from 778, in: *Codex Carolinus*, ed. W. GUNDLACH, in: *Epistolae Merowingici et Karolini aevi* 1, ed. W. GUNDLACH, E. DÜMMLER *et al.* (Berlin, 1892: MGH *Epp.* 3), p. 587.

[62] LAMMERS, "Ein karolingisches Bildprogramm", p. 270, n. 191; H. LÖWE, "Von Theoderich der Grosse zu Karl der Grosse: Das Werden des Abendlands im Geschichtsbild des frühen Mittelalters", *Deutsches Archiv* 9 (1952), pp. 353-410, at p. 391, n. 145; SCHLESINGER, "Die Pfalzen", p. 221; Ermoldus writes in his second elegy to Pippin writes (2, ll. 147-50): "*Primus adest Pippin, Caroli pater ecce potentis, / Rex bonus et sapiens ecclesiamque colens, / Francia gens nimium cuius virtute secunda / crevit et ecce suum claret in orbe decus*" ("first here is Pepin, the father of the powerful Charles, a good and wise king who honours the Church, with whose value the Frankish people grew much, and now his honour shines in the world").

singer and other historians have established that the same, so to speak 'autonomist', attitude is in the non-papal version of the *Divisio regnorum* of 806, where Charlemagne disagrees with the concept of attribution of imperial dignity by the pope, but presents it instead as a transfer by the Roman people, *renovatio imperii Romani*.[63] The implicit message in the omission of the coronation is so strong that some scholars[64] have tried to date the paintings before 800, but the depiction of Charles with the crown and especially the archaeological data contradict this hypothesis.

If we accept these remarks, the interpretations[62] that try to establish a precise correspondence between the biblical series and the political series on the basis of the tripartition *ante legem*, *sub lege*, and *sub gratia* – that is to say, before the establishment of the Hebrew religion, under that religion, and after Christ – appear very forced and less supported by the facts.

Whatever the interpretation, it is still the application of interpretive and representative processes of biblical typology in miniatures and paintings of the time that allow us to read the political message of Ingelheim's 'historical' cycle. Unlike other scholars, I think that we cannot connect the historical series to the strictly biblical series that decorates the church, or the palace chapel.

---

[63] I. HASELBACH, *Aufstieg und Herrschaft der Karolinger in der Darstellung der sogenannten Annales Mettenses priores: Ein Beitrag zur Geschichte der politischen Ideen im Reiche Karls des Grossen* (Hamburg, 1970).

[64] Notably W. Jacobsen: see CAILLET, "Prééminence", pp. 294-295.

[62] According to KNAEPEN, "L'histoire gréco-romaine", p. 361, who, however, does not seem to be familiar with the studies on this subject, Ratkowitsch "*a tout d'abord prouvé que les quelques vers consacrés aux peintures du palais d'Ingelheim (qui représentent des* gesta virum) *ne pouvaient être étudiés séparément de ceux dévoués aux fresques de l'église du même lieu (qui représentent des* gesta Dei*). Elle a montré ensuite que les deux textes suivaient une structure ternaire identique, évoquant successivement des événements représentatifs des époques* ante legem *(de la création du monde au Déluge),* sub lege *(du Déluge à l'avènement du Christ) et* sub gratia *(de l'avènement du Christ à nos jours). Enfin, elle a mis en évidence que les tableaux décrits par Ermold le Noir avaient fait l'objet d'un choix étudié: leur succession permet en effet de retracer quelques étapes de l'évolution de l'humanité, caractérisée au départ par une impiété et une* ὕβρις *sans bornes, vers la piété et l'humilité parfaites, atteintes sous le règne du* pius Louis". But we can easily see that the same interpretation would also and especially be applicable to other Carolingian sovereigns; on the contrary, the poet does not say a word about Louis, and Louis is not even depicted in the paintings, nor is he contrasted to his predecessors in any passage. The only form of contrast is envisaged by Ratkowitsch and Knaepen in the fact that Ermold is the only one who specifies that the crown from Louis's coronation was the same as the one from Constantine's coronation by Pope Sylvester, but this would be a strongly mediated and absolutely imperceptible contrast from an isolated episode. [A. DUBREUCQ, "Les peintures murales du palais carolingien d'Ingelheim", defends Ratkowitsch's point.]

The biblical paintings probably have an internal semiotic link, albeit one that is sometimes flexible and blurry, between the Old Testament part and the New Testament part, but they have little or nothing to do with the 'political' series – aside from the fact that they share the same matching technique, either binary or plural, from one tableau to another and from one figure to another, and above all the same dynamic of progressive construction of meaning by the sequence of paintings and their points of correspondence. The paintings of Ingelheim, as can be reconstructed from Ermold's verse and thanks to parallels with other palaces and other churches of the time, therefore offer a multiform (and propagandistic) but systematic communication, which translates into figures and a graphic layout of a conception of power and political relations from examples that integrate the conception of the historiographical sources of late Antiquity and their Carolingian continuations. Later, in texts from the end of the ninth century, the image of the Carolingians that imposed itself would no longer be that of Ingelheim, of the *Annales Mettenses priores* and the *Divisio regnorum prior*, but that of the Poeta Saxo and the *Sacrum Romanum Imperium*, that is, of the missionary symmetry Constantine-Charlemagne, which Ermold himself helped to form. Ingelheim remains the testimony of a grandiose but aborted self-representation – the last failure of Charlemagne.

Chapter 10

The Sense of Time in Carolingian Poetry: *Horologium nocturnum* and the Christian Zodiac in Pacificus of Verona

Let us imagine a bright night in the year 830: at a window of Verona Cathedral's bell tower (later destroyed by an earthquake in 1117) a clerk is observing the sky with a kind of telescope without lenses (an optical tube). After finding Ursa Minor, he moves the larger pointer on a timetable disk along the axis of the tube towards Polaris and the smaller pointer towards a lateral star called *computatrix*.

Where the tip of the pointer meets the disk, he reads the time of night. He has been testing this tool for days. It was built according to instructions from an unknown source. Now he finally understands: it seems that the mechanism works day after day and could help the monks and clerks to manage the succession of their offices and to count with precision the time between sunset and dawn, weather permitting. So he celebrates his success with a little poem[1] explaining the working of the tool, or *horologium nocturnum*, later called the 'night clock' or 'star clock' (*nocturlabium*). He uses the rhythmical versification[2] currently popular in Verona, Corbie, and Saint Gall and soon to conquer Europe.

---

[1] *Rhythmus* 116, ed. K. STRECKER, in: *PLAC* 4.2, p. 692. See below.

Fig. 18　MS Venice, Biblioteca Nazionale Marciana, lat. VIII. 22 (= 2760) (s. XII-XIII), f. 1r, photo F. STELLA.[3]

Joachim Wiesenbach[4] identified this clock as the night-time forerunner of the astrolabe of Gerbert of Aurillac, or at least of the star clock that Gerbert built for Otto III in Magdeburg in 997.[5] On the contrary, in histories of the measurement of time, on the Internet and Wikipedia, the first iconographical witnesses of the *nocturlabium* are dated to the twelfth century[6] and its European diffusion to the fifteenth century. In some sources this invention is attrib-

---

[2] See the bibliography of *Corpus Rhythmorum Musicum* in Chapter Seven, pp. 147-174.

[3] A discussion on other attempts to represent this figure and his tool in other manuscripts can be found in F. STELLA, "Poesie computistiche e meraviglie astronomiche: Sull'*horologium nocturnum* di Pacifico", in: *Mirabilia: Gli effetti speciali nelle letterature del Medioevo: Atti delle IV Giornate internazionali interdisciplinari di Studio sul Medioevo (Torino, 10-12 Aprile 2013)*, ed. F. MOSETTI CASARETTO and R. CIOCCA (Alessandria, 2014), pp. 181-206, some parts of which are necessarily repeated here, in translation.

[4] J. WIESENBACH, "Pacificus von Verona als Erfinder einer Sternenuhr", in: *Science in Western and Eastern Civilization in Carolingian Times*, ed. P.L. BUTZER and D. LOHRMANN (Basel, Boston, MA, and Berlin, 1993), pp. 229-250, and ID., "Der Mönch mit dem Sehrohr: Die Bedeutung der Miniatur Codex Sangallensis 18", *Schweizerische Zeitschrift für Geschichte – Revue suisse d'histoire – Rivista storica svizzera* 44 (1994), pp. 367-388.

[5] Thietmar of Merseburg, *Chronicon*, VI, 100, ed. *Die Chronik des Bischoffs Thietmar von Merseburg und ihre Korveier Überarbeitung (Thietmari Merseburgensis episcopi Chronicon)*, ed. R. HOLTZMANN (Hanover, 1935: MGH SRG Nova series 9, p. 392: "*et cum eo* [scil. *Imperatori*] *diu conversatus in Magadaburg oralogium fecit, illud recte constituens, considerata per fistulam quadam stella nautarum duce*" ("and after having stayed with him [that is with the emperor] in Magdeburg for a long time he built a clock, setting it correctly on the basis of the observation, through a tube, of a certain star that acts as a guide for mariners"). Wiesenbach does not believe that this tool was a real astrolabe, like Bubnov and Schramm, because it is not hooked to a ring and because the astrolabe does not include a tube *(fistula).* It would seem more credible (according to E. POULLE, "L'astronomie de Gerbert", in: *Gerberto: Scienza, storia e mito: Atti del Gerberti symposium* (Bobbio, 1985: *Archivum Bobiense: Studia* 2), pp. 597-617, esp. pp. 607-609) that Gerbert's object is an *horologium nocturnum*. In a letter to Constantine of Fleury, Gerbert explains the construction of a *sphaera,* an instrument which represented the parallel circles of the sky (a kind of armilla?) and included an optical tube to be pointed towards the Pole: "*Si autem de polo dubitas, unam fistulam tali loco constitue, ut non moveatur tota nocte, et per eam stellam suspice, quam credis esse polum, et si polus est, eam tota nocte poteris suspicere, sin alia, mutando loca non occurrit visui paulo post per fistulam*" ("If you have doubts about the Pole, put a tube in that place so that you do not move it all night and through it observe the star that you think is the Polar and if it is, you can see it all night; if instead it is another, changing position shortly thereafter will no longer offer sight through the tube"; Gerbert, Letter to Constantine of Fleury, ed. in: Gerbert d'Aurillac, *Correspondance*, ed. and trans. P. RICHÉ and J.P. CALLU, 2 vols. (Paris, 1993: *Les classiques de l'hisoire de France* 35-36), 2, pp. 680-687, at p. 684); quoted by J. WIESENBACH, "Pacificus von Verona", p. 245, n. 39, after *Gerberti Opera Mathematica*, ed. N. BUBNOV (Berlin, 1899, repr. Hildesheim, 1963), p. 28.

[6] See E. FARRE I OLIVE, "La Sphaera Horarum Noctis de Ramon Llull', *La Busca de Paper* 22 (1996), pp. 3-12, and <https://en.wikipedia.org/wiki/Nocturnal_(instrument)>.

Fig. 19 Pacificus's Epitaphs in Verona (photo C. Savini).

uted to the Arabs and dates to the time of the earliest Latin translations of Eastern treatises.[7] But as Adorno wrote, "the forms of art count the history of mankind more exactly than do documents themselves",[8] and in this case poetry allows us to move the date for the knowledge and use of a technical invention of some historical importance back by four centuries. So who was this clerk and what was his poem?

The Inscription of Verona

The lintel of the door to the sacristy of Verona Cathedral bears an inscription that has been dated to different times, ranging from the ninth to the twelfth

---

[7] The website <http://gerlos.altervista.org/notturnale>, published 2008, is no longer available. B.S. EASTWOOD, *La scienza bizantina e Latina prima dell'influsso della scienza araba: Astronomia, computo e astrologia*, <http://treccani.it/enciclopedia/la-scienza-bizantina-e-latina-prima-dell-influsso-della-scienza-araba-astronomia-computo-e-astrologia_%28Storia-della-Scienza%29/>, correctly attributes the *nocturlabe* to Pacificus.

[8] Th.W. ADORNO, *Philosophy of Modern Music*, trans. A.G. MITCHELL and W.V. BLOMSTER (New York, 1984), p. 43.

century. The inscription mentions the death of the archdeacon Pacificus, a personality of enormous initiative who passed away in 844 (Fig. 19). Tradition attributes much to him: the foundation or restoration of the seven most beautiful churches of Verona, certain artistic decorations, the transcription of 218 manuscripts of the capitular scriptorium, the editing of biblical commentaries, and unending manifestations of prodigious cultural activity and versatile technical curiosity.

The epigraph, clearly reassembled after displacement, presents a double block: a rhythmic text praising the enterprises of Pacificus, and a metrical epitaph with a more funerary content, recycling and adapting the self-epitaph attributed to Alcuin of York, who died in 804.[9] A lively dispute concerning the interpretation and attribution of these texts has arisen: however, they voice what at least part of the Veronese community acknowledged as a historical fact in the Middle Ages.[10]

---

[9] Alcuin, *Carmen* 123, ed. *Alcuini Carmina*, ed. E. DÜMMLER, in: *PLAC* 1, pp. 169-351, at p. 350. Both texts can be read in the Appendix.

[10] An attempt to demythicise his biography is C. LA ROCCA, *Pacifico di Verona: Il passato carolingio nella costruzione della memoria urbana* (Rome, 1995), later summarised as "A man for all seasons: Pacificus of Verona and the creation of a local Carolingian past", in: *The Uses of the Past in the Early Middle Ages*, ed. Y. HEN and M. INNES (Cambridge, 2000), pp. 250-277. She tried to demonstrate that the two epigraphs in Verona cathedral were put together and possibly composed in twelfth century, dedicated to a Carolingian inventor, architect, director of the scriptorium, and sculptor, a myth which served as an ideal reference for Bishop Theobald and for rebuilding the cathedral. Some of the formal and stylistic arguments put forward in her study have been rebutted, or even reversed by specialists of medieval Latin poetry, such as Gabriel Silagi (review in *Deutsches Archiv* 52 (1996), pp. 349-350), or of Veronese history, such as Gian Paolo Marchi (G.P. MARCHI, "Per un restauro della biografia di Pacifico, humilis levita Christi", in: *Scripturus vitam: Lateinische Biographie van der Antike bis in die Gegenwart: Festgabe fur Walter Berschin zum 65. Geburtstag*, ed. D. WALZ (Heidelberg, 2002), pp. 379-392) and M.G. Di Pasquale *(Rivista di storia della Chiesa in Italia* 51 (1997), pp. 549-555). From my perspective, the main point is that La Rocca's reconstruction, based mostly on archival documents, neglected or underestimated the exegetical and poetic evidence of Pacificus, which clearly must be dated to the ninth and not to the twelfth century, thus linking it to other evidence of Pacificus's activity, as identified and dated by Adda and Meersemann *(Manuale di computo con ritmo mnemotecnico dell'arcidiacono Pacifico di Verona († 844)*, ed. G.G. MEERSSEMAN and E. ADDA (Padua, 1966) and G.G. MEERSSEMAN, E. ADDA, and J. DESHUSSES, *L'Orazionale dell' arcidiacono Pacifico e il carpsum del cantore Stefano: Studi e testi sulla liturgia del Duomo di Verona dal IX all'XI sec.* (Fribourg (Suisse), 1974); R. AVESANI, review in *Studi medievali* 8 (1967), pp. 913-920; A. CAMPANA, "Veronensia", in: *Miscellanea Giovanni Mercati*, 6 vols. (Città del Vaticano, 1946: *Studi e testi* 121-126), 2, pp. 57-91 and ID., "Il carteggio di Vitale e Pacifico di Verona col monaco Ildemaro sulla sorte eterna di Adamo", in: *Atti del Congresso internazionale di diritto romano e di storia del diritto (Verona 27-29 Settembre 1948)*, 1 (Milan, 1951), pp. 393-404, and to new possible attributions (see below). Of course, this figure may have

Among the achievements listed in the epigraphic aretalogy of Pacificus, we find a "*horologium nocturnum*" that "*nullus ante viderat*" and a "*horologioque carmen sperae caeli*". For a long time no one understood what the former was, and the books of Veronese history and of histories of the clock hold the most varied opinions, including one that Pacificus invented the compass.[11] Few scholars noticed the latter – that is, the poem – since the existing edition by Karl Strecker (which is also found in the Appendix) is purely textual and aniconic, and is neither useful for understanding the content nor based on a collation of the manuscripts suitable for the dissemination of the text.

The Horologium Nocturnum

The poem about the *horologium nocturnum* is indeed poem No. 116 of volume 4.2 of the MGH *Poetae latini aevi Carolini* and can be dated to the early ninth century. The bases of the attribution of the texts to Pacificus are the explicit mention of the *horologium* in the cathedral's epitaph and its linguistic and prosodic similarity (together with frequent contiguity, and even continuity, in manuscript transmission) to another rhythmic poem 'signed' by Pacificus, No. 117 of the Strecker edition, which we will read later. The text, probably incomplete or corrupted in its current form, can be translated as follows:

> As the sphere turns through the twenty-four hours, all the fixed stars, which go around with the sphere, make smaller circles around the pipe. Therefore the star that seems closer to the Pole has the brightest radiance and is called the *calculator* of the night hours. Here is the system: if you trace a straight line opposite the turning pivot with your eyes, you will be able to tell the hours of the night without the

been turned into a legend in order to strengthen Veronese identity in the twelfth century and modern times, but it is also likely that contemporary social history tends to overvalue the weight that such propaganda could have had in the past. [New remarks concerning La Rocca by G.P. MARCHI, "Ancora sull'arcidiacono Pacifico di Verona", *Studi Medievali e Umanistici* 7 (2009, publ. 2012), pp. 356-380. Cristina La Rocca repeated her conjectures in "Pacifico di Verona", in: *Dizionario Biografico degli Italiani* 80 (online in 2014), again without any mention of the poetical works, the exegetical and theological positions, or with any account of the criticism her arguments received. So the history of Pacificus and his activity has to be still written. A first critical edition of his work is announced in the *Edizioni Nazionali dei Testi Mediolatini d'Italia* (published in Florence by SISMEL).]

[11] S. MAFFEI, *Verona illustrata*, 4 vols. (Verona, 1731), 2, pp. 61-62. A. SPAGNOLO, "L'arcidiacono Pacifico di Verona inventore della bussola", *Nuovo Archivio Veneto*, n.s 8 (1904), pp. 39-62, refers to the hypotheses on the compass.

crowing of the cock. Oh, what a lovely image is held in this clock of the fixed wheel by the driving of the nails of the cross of Christ, where he hung in his own flesh for the salvation of mankind! At different times the calculating star always keeps to the right, the left, the abyss, and then the heavens, marking equinox and solstices. If some curious fellow wishes to look through the tube, he will find the spring equinox on the left and the autumn equinox on the right. The solstices are distributed in two stages: the summer solstice is the upper ray that leads to heaven, the lower ray leads to the winter solstice.

The poem describes a spherical table for determining the hours by focussing the telescope on Polaris and orienting the pointer to a reference star, which Joachim Wiesenbach identifies as Camelopardalis 32 H, in the Giraffe constellation:[12] Pacificus calls it *computatrix*, a word not found prior to him, which can be read later in texts and captions apparently independent of his poem, like MS Avranches, Bibliothèque Municipale, 235 (Fig. 20) and MS Paris, Bibliothèque nationale de France, latin 12117 (Fig. 24), where it is linked to the hemisphere of Gerbert. The method, mentioned on line 3, 1 of the *argumentum*, as is usual in the computistical tradition and of Pacificus in particular,[13] is not clearly explained in the poem, which contains apparent inconsistencies. It seems to describe two steps: first, draw a straight line along the axial pipe towards the star nearest to the Pole, then compare it with the direction of the *computatrix*, tracing a vector or radius that indicates the hour on the disk: here a cross in a circle splits the space into four quarters corresponding to the four seasons, which indicate equinoxes and solstices.

How could this technically and poetically significant innovation have emerged in Verona before the mid-ninth century? The answer to this question would require research that has not yet been done. During the discussion of a paper of mine at a Turin conference,[14] a colleague conjectured that the name Pacificus, equivalent to the biblical Solomon, hid a possible Hebrew origin and therefore contact with Eastern science. Indeed, previous evidence of the name *horologium nocturnum* leads us back in time to the East, as in the story of the

---

[12] WIESENBACH, "Pacificus von Verona", pp. 242-244.

[13] Ps.-Dionysius, *Anni domini notantur*, ed. among the *Dubia* of Bede, in: PL 94, col. 637-642, as Anonymus, *Anni domini notantur*; new edn. of 2020 in the *Corpus Rhythmorum Musicum* <www.corimu.unisi.it>; Manfredus, *Carmina* 21, 2 (still among the *Dubia* of Beda, in: PL 94, 651C); *Rhythm. Comput.*, ed. in: *Rhythmi*, ed. STRECKER, No. 113 (pp. 673-682), 25, 2; No. 115 (pp. 687-692), 20, 1 and 37, 1; *De ratione temporum* 861, ed. K. STRECKER and O. SCHUMANN, in: PLAC 6.1, pp. 188-189; all of this besides the prose treatises.

[14] See *supra*, n. 3.

gift sent by Caliph Harun al Rashid to Charlemagne. But in that case it was about a mechanical water clock, an imperfect legacy of Greek and Roman science, with which Pope Paul I had already paid homage in 757 to King Pippin I and which the *quaestor sacri palatii* Cassiodorus described in the period of Ostrogoth occupation of Italy.[15] In a wonderful letter sent in 507 to Boethius in the name of Theoderic, he remarked that the water clock – which for the Roman court was a rather ordinary fact[16] – was considered a wonder by the Burgundians, and indeed it was a great achievement of civilisation, a product of mathematical disciplines and mechanical techniques that testified to the dignity of man through his ability of intellectual conception more than his skill in material realisation. Therefore it was not the *horologium nocturnum* of Pacificus, and this could not have been how it came to Verona. So we cannot exclude the third hypothesis, to which the epitaph refers: that with his wide-ranging ingenuity Pacificus actually invented the nocturlabe and did not merely praise it in verse. Be that as it may, this poem was edited by Strecker just over a century ago on the sole basis of the tenth- to eleventh-century MS Vatican, Vat. Lat. 644, but is transmitted in many other manuscripts, some of which (including the Vaticanus) illustrate the text with drawings which help to understand its content.[17] The plan for a new edition, which seems necessary in the light of so much new data, will contribute to a new chapter in the history of science and the measurement of time, despite starting from a poem.

---

[15] Cassiodore, *Variae* I, 45, ed. Th. MOMMSEN (Hanover, 1894: *MGH AA* 12), pp. 39-41; *Annales Fuldenses* a. 807, ed. *Annales Fuldenses sive Annales regni Francorum orientalis*, ed. F. KURZE (Hanover, 1891: *MGH SRG in usum scholarum separatim editi* 7), p. 16 lin. 30; *Annales Lobienses*, ed. G. WAITZ, in: [*Supplementa tomorum 1-12, pars 1*], ed. G. WAITZ et al. (Hanover, 1887: *MGH SS* 13), pp. 224-235, at p. 231 lin. 13; *Annales Regni Francorum* a. 807, ed. *Annales regni Francorum inde ab a. 741 usque ad a. 829, qui dicuntur Annales Laurissenses maiores et Einghardi*, ed. F. KURZE (Hanover, 1895: *MGH SRG in usum scholarum separatim editi* 6), p. 123. See E. KROTZ, "Remigius von Auxerre und die Ars Prisciani", *Archivum Latinitatis Medii Aevi* 72 (2014), pp. 21-82, esp. p. 66.

[16] The tool was known since Ctesibius (second century BCE) to Heron of Alexandria and Vitruvius.

[17] MS Padua, Biblioteca Antoniana 27 (s. IX^{ex}), f. 96r, from Verona; MS Vatican, Biblioteca Apostolica Vaticana, Reg. lat. 309, f. 128r (s. XI, illuminated); MS Paris, Bibliothèque nationale de France, latin 12117, f. 130v (s. XI, with illuminations); a humanistic manuscript owned by L.P. Daverio, Milan, from Tortona, f. 126r (without illustrations); MS Vatican, Biblioteca Apostolica Vaticana, Vat. lat. 644 (s. X), f. 76r (with figure); MS Cava dei Tirreni, 3, f. 203rv (s. XI, with image); MS Venice, Biblioteca Nazionale Marciana, lat. VIII.22 (s. XII-XIII), f. 1r (illuminated).

The Sense of Time in Carolingian Poetry 241

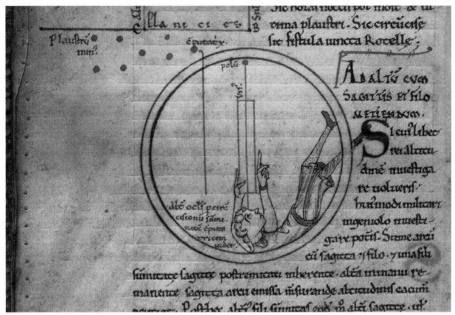

Fig. 20 MS Avranches, Bibliothèque Municipale, 235, f. 32v (detail).

Sequens figura docet emycyclum fieri et in eum fistulam mitti, per quam polus possit videri et ultima stella minoris arcturi, ad cognoscendas horas noctis, que omnia per astrolapsum probare poteris. Sic horas noctis polus indit et ultima plaustri. Sic circumcise sit fistula iuncta rotellae.

The following figure explains how the semicircle is made and a tube is inserted, through which you can see the Polar star and the last star of the constellation Arthur minor to identify the hours of the night, that you can all test with the astrolabe. So the Polar star and the last of the Chariot indicate the hours of he night. So the tube is etched to be joined to the wheel.

Avranches

In the figure taken from Avranches 235 (Fig. 20), a manuscript comprising geological, meteorological, and climatic treatises (including *De utilitatibus astrolabii*), we clearly read the words *computatrix* and *plaustrum minus* (little plough or little bear), followed by the gloss to the image:

The description does not perfectly match what we see in Fig. 20, where the observer is incorporated into the sphere and holds the spyglass in his left hand, whereas originally he would probably have been in front of the wheel and the tube would have been inserted into the wheel itself.

In the illustration another caption appears, stating that "*alter oculus per circumcisionum summitatem computatricem videt*" ("the other eye sees the calculating star through the edge of the cut part"), but this explanation, according to Wiesenbach, seems to require the observer to watch two stars simultaneously. I find this criticism too strict: perhaps he watched the second star at a different time, possibly aided by a mark on the disc or its edge, and this is depicted primitively, as if each eye were looking at a different thing. A doubt therefore remains about the function of this tool: according to Poulle[18] it is a *nocturlabium*, a night clock like those still built today.[19] On the contrary, Wiesenbach maintains that it is not a night clock because there is only one disc (although I suppose it could perform the functions of both support and indicator) and the nocturlabe has no floor stand, and finally because the *computatrix* in the Avranches manuscript is the Polaris (which around the year 1000 was actually near the Pole), which is visible without any tube. Here again I think the tube served to frame the star, not just to find and see it, given that lenses were not invented until the fifteenth or sixteenth century. So, in my opinion, the tool represented in the Avranches manuscript is indeed a *nocturlabium*.

Chartres

The illustrations of MS London, British library, Old Royal 15.B.IX, f. 76v, containing the caption "*fistula per medium rotelle fixa*", MS Chartres, Bibliothèque Municipale, 214,[20] and MS Paris, Bibliothèque nationale de France, latin 7412, f. 15r, are all dated to around the eleventh century; they are not linked to Pacificus, but to the nocturlabe.

They depict a small wheel and a tube pointed at the pole star, with the figure of the star *computatrix* in the Little Bear. In the Chartrensis, destroyed in 1944 like almost all of that abbey's treasury (here we show a drawing from a nineteenth century reproduction), the small wheel has four rings, the second and fourth of which are split into 24 sections, while the third is split in two,

---

[18] POULLE, "L'astronomie de Gerbert".
[19] An example can be found at: <http://www.iisgalileiartiglio.gov.it/artiglio-almanacco/quaderni/www/notturlabio/WITN_notturlb.htm>.
[20] WIESENBACH, "Pacificus von Verona", p. 236.

The Sense of Time in Carolingian Poetry 243

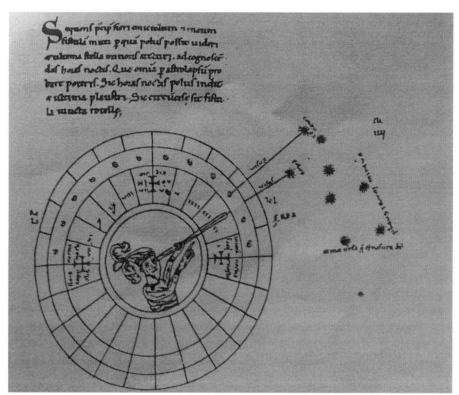

Fig. 21   Detail of MS Chartres, Bibliothèque Municipale, 214 (now lost), in WIESEN-
BACH 1993.

one of which is divided into 12 cells with openings for observation (Fig. 21). One of these is crossed by the optical tube pointed at the *computatrix*, here again the main star of the Little Bear: that is, Polaris. A second ray emerging from the small wheel points to an isolated star called *polus*. The cells of the third ring in the upper part are marked with numbers from I to XII. Crosses mark the beginning, the middle and the end (which reminds one of the *carmina*). The caption reads: "*inicium noctis seu aequinoctis; media nox; finis noctis aequinoctialis*".

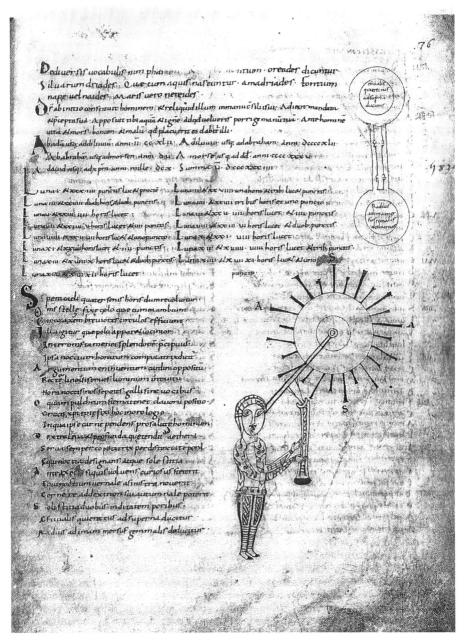

Fig. 22   MS Vatican, Biblioteca Apostolica Vaticana, Vat. lat. 644, f. 76r.

The Sense of Time in Carolingian Poetry 245

Fig. 23   MS Cava dei Terreni, Archivio e Biblioteca della Badia, 3, f. 203r.

Vatican

The Vatican illustration (Fig. 22) is like that of the Marciana, differing only in that the stand does not rest on the floor but is held by the observer, the marks on the outer circle number 24 instead of 12, and 2A and 2S are inscribed at the four hinges. Wiesenbach does not decipher these signs, but I propose that A indicates *aequinoctium* and S *solstitium*, corresponding to line 5, 3 of Pacificus's text.

In the Cava manuscript (Fig. 23), here reproduced for the first time, the tube and stand are missing, while the wheel contains three concentric circles and 25 cells instead of 24, by mistake. In the left part of the illustration a group of people is holding a scroll and looking upwards, at a double semicircle that suggests a sphere. A master with long hair indicates with his right hand the top. The writing reads: "*Abraham astronomiam discipulos Egyptios informat*". The figure is accompanied by other astronomical illustrations.

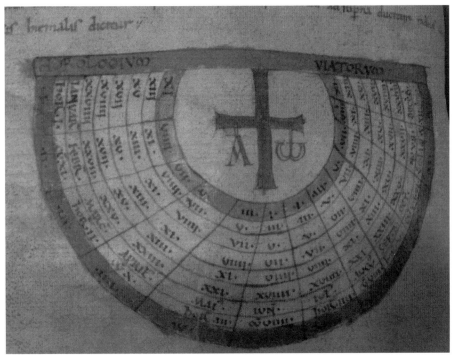

Fig. 24 MS Paris, Bibliothèque nationale de France, latin 12117 (detail).

Another manuscript, famous but not associated with Pacificus, shows a device similar to the one depicted in the Vatican and Marciana manuscripts: the palimpsest MS Saint Gall, Stiftsbibliothek 18, f. 45, written around the year 1000.[21]

Is the device depicted in the manuscripts of Vatican, Cava, Avranches, Paris, and Chartres the same as the one described in Pacificus's poem? Wiesenbach is sceptical, because he clearly distinguishes astrolabes from nocturlabes, always referring to their latest forms, and does not suspect they could have had intermediate or mixed forms during their evolution. And yet the manuscripts themselves prove this fluidity, since the captions in the Avranches manuscript speak about an astrolabe that reads the hours instead of geographical position. So, on the contrary, we believe it impossible to avoid identifying Pacificus's tool with something like what is depicted in these manuscripts, because the

---

[21] See WIESENBACH, "Der Mönch mit dem Sehrohr", and D. GANZ, "Der lineare Blick: Geometrie und Körperwelt in mittelalterlichen Bildern der Himmelsschau", in: *Sehen und Sakralität in der Vormoderne*, ed. D. GANZ et al. (Berlin, 2011), pp. 266-291.

poem clearly mentions equinoxes and solstices, a wheel and a tube (if *axis* is a tube), and two reference stars for positioning the needle or arrow.

Paris 12117 and the Link with the Astrolabe

A last puzzle is offered (and solved) by MS Paris, Bibliothèque nationale de France, latin 12117, which at f. 130v includes the text of Pacificus's rhythmic poem illustrated by a half-circle split into twelve sections (corresponding to the months) around a cross, topped by a bar with the inscription *horologium viatorum*, the same as the one we find in a manuscript of Hermannus the Cripple's *De utilitate astrolabii*.[22] This may be evidence of a link between *nocturlabium* and *astrolabium*, at least on the iconographic level.

But how did the device work? How was the time read? How was the tube positioned?

When the first star began to shine, we suppose that Polaris could be seen through the first hole. Due to the position of the holes in the middle of the hour sections, Polaris indicated the first hour of night. Then the position of the disc was fixed and the ring with notches 1-12 was aligned with Polaris's axis. Every time the observer saw Polaris at a new mark, one hour had passed. In other models of night clock, the notches on the edge of the wheel were replaced by more precise holes.[23]

---

[22] See W. BERSCHIN, *Hermann der Lahme: Gelehrter und Dichter (1013-1054)* (Heidelberg, 2013), p. 29.

[23] There are still some doubts about how the tool worked. How were hours read in the *horologium*? What was positioned and towards what object? Perhaps the rotation point of the disk towards the sky pole, or the rotation point towards the edge of the disk? Wiesenbach states that, on the basis of the Chartres manuscript, the process required permanent pointing of the tube at what was then Polaris (in the present Giraffe): after the sunset, as soon as the first stars began to shine, the observer could see Polaris through the first hole. Using the position of the holes at the centre of the hours sectors, this indicated the first hour of the night. Then the disk was kept still and the ring with holes I-XII was aligned with the path of Polaris. The observer *only* had to pay attention to the rotation of the starry sky behind the disk. Every time Polaris appeared in the next hole (a movement of 15 degrees) one hour had passed. So Polaris was the *computatrix*. Actually, Pacificus's tool lacked hole-sights, which were merely signs on the edge of the disk, like in the Avranches illustration. WIESENBACH, "Pacificus von Verona", pp. 246-247, specifies that the Chartres wheel was only fit for spring and autumn, when day and night are more or less the same length and one night hour corresponds to a rotation of 15 degrees. In summer and winter, other wheels were needed, with larger or smaller hour-gaps.

Fig. 25 Night clock (s. XVI) with Zodiac from the Museo della Scienza Galileo Galilei, Florence.

We can better understand what Pacificus meant by examining how a modern night clock works (Fig. 25).[24] The month ring is on the outside in brass. The inner disk shows the time and bears an indicator on its edge. By setting the indicator to the month and day (in this case a few days into October), centring Polaris in the hole in the middle, and rotating the pointer attached to the centre to a specific circumpolar star, the arm indicates the time (8 p.m. in the figure).

Today the reference stars are called 'pointers'. The ones in the Great Bear or Big Dipper are Duhbe and Merak, permanently in line with Polaris, forming a kind of astronomical pointer (needle), which on the cardboard or tin disc is represented by the watch hand, called *alidada*, from the Arabic.[25]

---

[24] G. OESTMANN, "On the history of the nocturnal", *Bulletin of the Scientific Instrument Society* 69 (2001), pp. 5-9.

[25] A series of images of ancient and modern nocturlabes, with a link to an animation showing how they worked, can be found on the website of the Museo della Scienza Galileo Galilei di Firenze: <http://brunelleschi.imss.fi.it/museum/esim.asp?c=500044>. After Wiesenbach, Pacificus's clock drew the attention of many scholars, but this literature escaped the medievalists' notice: see E. DEKKER, *Illustrating the Phenomena in Antiquity and the Middle Ages* (Oxford, 2012), pp. 160, 196, 458, with further particulars; S.C. MCCLUSKEY, *Astronomies and Cultures in Early Medieval Europe* (Cambridge, 2000), p. 112: "Pacificus of Verona described a simple instrument to determine the time of the night by watching the rotation of the bright star in the handle of the little dipper (Polaris, Ursa [sic!] minoris) around a faint fifth-magnitude star that marked the pole at the year 800. This instrument's demonstration of the turning of the stars around the geometric axis of the world, and the use of classical constellation names (*plaustrum minus* and *arctos minor*) in the texts that describe it, bring elements from the astronomy of the liberal arts into the tradition of nocturnal timekeeping": see D. PRATT, "Persuasion and invention at the court of King Alfred the Great", in: *Court Culture in the Early Middle Ages: Proceedings of the First Alcuin Conference*, ed. C. CUBITT (Turnhout, 2003), pp. 189-221, at p. 205; D. WOODWARD, *The History of Cartography*, 3.1, *Cartography in the European Renaissance* (Chicago, 2007), pp. 101, 121; J.J. HAMBURGER, "Idol curiosity", in: *Curiositas: Welterfahrung und ästhetische Neugierde in Mittelalter und früher Neuzeit*, ed. K. KRÜGER (Göttingen 2002: *Göttinger Gespräche zur Geschichtswissenschaft* 15), pp. 19-58, esp. pp. 43-44, mentioning the

Sense of Time and Stellar Observation in the Middle Ages

In addition to marking the importance of this technical-astronomical creation, the little poem is the first sign of the second innovation linked to Pacificus: the attempt at a *poetic* – and therefore didactic – Christianisation both of the zodiac signs – that is, the symbols of the distribution of the segments of the sun's orbit in time –, and of the technical system, as he draws a cross on the disk to create belts matching the four seasons, in reference to the religious horizon that gives meaning to the determination of time.

The traditional connection of the measurement of time with astronomical observation became increasingly important in the Middle Ages until mechanical clocks become more widespread. In the years when Cassiodorus described the Burgundians' astonishment at the water clock, in his *De cursu stellarum* Gregory of Tours oriented astronomy towards chronometrics, stating that the course of time itself was a divine miracle. He laid the foundations for a religious transcoding of astronomy, which studies the stars in relation to the deeds of Jewish-Christian history or the moments of the liturgy of the monastic hours. Even Cassianus in *De institutis coenobiorum* 2, 17 reminds the monk entrusted with waking his brothers for night prayers to observe the stars.[26] And Bede in his *De temporum ratione* 30 attests that it is possible to calculate the date of Easter "*sicut non solum auctoritate paterna sed et horologica consideratione docemur*" ("as we learn not only from the authority of the fathers but also from the observation of the clock"): this means that *horologium* was also a device (a timetable) for teaching and taking note of the seasons and their

---

poem; A. WIECZOREK, and H.-M. HINZ, *Europe's Centre Around* A.D. *1000*, 3 vols. (Stuttgart, 2000), 1, p. 7; Ph. DUTARTE, *Les instruments de l'astronomie ancienne de l'Antiquité à la Renaissance* (Paris, 2006), p. 294; Th. FLURY, *Frauen im Galluskloster: Katalog zur Ausstellung in der Stiftsbibliothek St. Gallen (20. Marz-12. November 2006)* (Saint Gall, 2006), p. 128; G. SIGISMONDI, "Gerberto e le fistulae: tubi acustici ed astronomici", in: *Atti dell'XI Convegno SIA (Società Italiana di Archeoastronomia)* [Bologna and Marzabotto, 2011 published 2012], <http://arxiv.org/ftp/arxiv/papers/1211/1211.0448.pdf>, and ID., "Gerbert of Aurillac: Astronomy and geometry in tenth century Europe", *International Journal of Modern Physics: Conference Series* 23 (2013), pp. 467-471, discusses Gerbert's texts.

[26] "*Is autem, cui religiosi conventus commonitio vel synaxeos cura committur... quamvis eum consuetudo diurna hora solita evigilare conpellat, tamen sollicite frequenterque stellarum cursu praestitutum congregationis tempus explorans ad orationum eos invitat officium*" (Johannes Cassianus, *Les institutions cinobitiques*, ed. J.-C. GUY (Paris, 2001: Sources Chrétiennes 109).

boundaries. The same word means a disc used for didactic purposes in learning *computus*, of which we find many examples in the computistical manuscripts.[27]

Until the Lyon conference on *Time in the Middle Ages*, the history of the sense of time in the Middle Ages has hardly been the subject of global research based on a significant quantity of textual and iconographic documentation. As late as 2005, Jean-Claude Schmitt defined the sense of time as the "*impensé de l'histoire*", something not yet conceived as an object of history.[28] Even in the much celebrated 2012 volume by Rosenberg and Grafton on the history of chronometrics and chronographics, the part on the Middle Ages is limited and superficial.[29] In specialist research less influenced by clichés and biases about the presumed lack of scientific knowledge in the early Middle Ages, a series of studies, editions, and conferences has lately opened[30] a new field burgeoning with evidence of lively interest and debate on astronomical, computistical, geometrical, and arithmetical questions at the Carolingian court, sometimes even identified in poetic production. Some of these texts still await their first critical editions and raise enigmatic philological questions, such as the *Carmina computistica* cycle of a scholar known as Manfred, the attribution of which incredibly ranges between the seventh and fifteenth centuries.[31]

---

[27] Just one example at <http://digital.library.mcgill.ca/ms-17/apparatus.php?>.

[28] J.-C. SCHMITT, "Le Temps: Impensé de l'histoire ou double objet de l'historien?", *Cahiers de Civilisation Médiévale* 48 (2005), pp. 31-52.

[29] D. ROSENBERG and A. GRAFTON, *Cartographies of Time: A History of the Timeline* (Princeton, 2010); trans. *Cartografie del tempo: Una storia della linea del tempo* (Turin, 2012).

[30] See A. CORDOLIANI, "Contribution à la littérature du comput ecclésiastique au Moyen Age", *Studi Medievali* 1 (1960), pp. 107-137 and 2 (1961), pp. 169-208, and the many contributions by Arno Borst (A. BORST, *Computus: Zeit und Zahl in der Geschichte Europas* (Berlin, 2004), trans. *Computus: Tempo e numero nella storia d'Europa* (Genoa, 1997); ID., *Wie kam die arabische Sternkunde ins Kloster Reichenau?* (Konstanz, 1988); ID., *Schriften zur Komputistik im Frankenreich* (Munich, 2006)); W.M. STEVENS, "Astronomy in Carolingian schools", in: *Karl der Grosse und sein Nachwirken: 1200 Jahre Kultur und Wissenschaft in Europa*, ed. P.L. BUTZER, W. OBERSCHELP, and H. JONGEN, 2 vols. (Turnhout, 1997-1998), 2, pp. 417-487; P.L. BUTZER, "Mathematics and astronomy at the court school of Charlemagne and its Mediterranean roots", CRM: *Cahiers de recherches médiévales (XIIIe-XIVe siècles)* 5 (1998), pp. 203-244; D. LOHRMANN, "Alcuins Korrespondenz mit Karl dem Grossen über Kalender und Astronomie", in: *Science in Western and Eastern Civilization in Carolingian Times*, pp. 90-92; M. LEJBOWICZ, "Le nombre et le temps altimedievaux", in: *Le Temps, sa mesure et sa perception au Moyen Âge: Actes du Colloque (Orléans, 12-13 Avril 1991)*, ed. B. RIBEMONT (Caen, 1992), pp. 151-187; J. CONTRENI, "Counting, calendars, and cosmology: Numeracy in the early Middle Ages", in: *Word, Image, Number: Communication in the Middle Ages*, ed. J. CONTRENI (Florence and Turnhout, 2002), pp. 43-83, and many others.

[31] BORST, *Schriften zur Komputistik im Frankenreich*, introduction.

According to what until now was the most famous and oft-cited reflection on the topic, the chapter "What is time?" in *The Categories of Medieval Culture* by Aaron Gurevich,[32] the sense of time in the Middle Ages was structured around a double confrontation between natural cyclic rhythms (the agricultural calendar and the alternation of the seasons) and religious and therefore narrative-dramatic rhythms. According to Gurevich, there are three relevant aspects: the agricultural calendar, with its variability; the astronomical calendar, with its ancient roots and its Christian transformations; and the liturgical calendar, a profound representation of time combined with social prescription – feasts and prayers, hagiographical commemoration, and ritual celebrations – to an ultra-temporal horizon where each of these sequences is cast and from which they acquire their meaning.

Computistical Verse

The theories and practices used to make the different sequences and conceptions of time compatible with each other are expounded in what medieval culture called *computus*, the science of the measurement of time. Many disciplines come under the umbrella of *computus*, which Charlemagne in chapter 72 of the *Admonitio generalis* included among the compulsory subjects of his school programme. These included astronomy, with particular reference to the sun and moon cycles and their interferences and overlaps; equinoxes and solstices; the calculation of shadows at various latitudes; the description of the belts of the Earth; the partition of ordinary and leap years; the articulation of the hours of day and night; the doctrine of the relationships between seasons, elements, and humours having the *quaternitas* in common; astrology; digital (i.e. finger) calculation; and the science and history of the civil and religious (i.e. hagiographical) calendar in general. The computation of time became the core of global knowledge of the structure of the universe and the phases of daily life. According to recent studies, it was a hallmark of Carolingian culture, which more and more, as previously unknown texts are being published, proves to have been interested in the natural science, and especially in astronomy.

---

[32] A.J. GUREVIČ, *Le categorie della cultura medievale*, ed. C. CASTELLI (Turin, 1983, reprint 2007), Italian trans. of the first edn. (Moscow, 1972).

Computus was learnt and taught in schools via treatises and handbooks, such as Bede's *De computo* or *De temporum ratione*,[33] the content of which was summarised in poems that were widely circulated. This *computus* poetry also included astronomical poetry. Classical and especially late antique poetry, even apart from Aratus, Germanicus, and Manilius, had already produced a minor but enduring thread of compositions on the sequence of the months and the zodiac signs: for example, the ninth eclogue of Ausonius and the *Anthologia Latina* (Nos. 615-626, 679, 490a, 761, etc.) are clearly linked to the didactic exercise involving the poetic paraphrasis of basic astronomical knowledge. The early Middle Ages inherited and developed this practice but articulated its production with new content that included elements of *computus*. Poems of this kind are sometimes metrical, such as the ones by Walahfrid Strabo (*carmen* 89) or Agius of Corvey,[34] or Wandalbert of Prüm's martyrological cycle; more often they are rhythmic, such as the series published in 1923 by Strecker in volume 4.3 of *Poetae latini aevi Carolini*, Nos. 108-121.[35] Alfred Cordoliani found many others and gathered evidence of their impressive manuscript transmission.[36] Wolfgang Irtenkauf's discovery, developed by the research team of the *Corpus Rhythmorum*,[37] that such compositions were set to music in the manuscripts, reveals that they were probably sung at school to memorise their content.

Three such rhythmic poems have been traced back to Pacificus of Verona. One is none other than the rhythmic poem on the night clock. The second text, the attribution of which is still disputed, is *Anni Domini notantur*, Strecker No. 113, an abridgement of *computus* theories about to be published for the *Corpus Rhythmorum* by Chiara Savini, on the basis of many more manuscripts than previously published by other editors.[38] The third is Strecker No. 117, *Spera*

---

[33] Ed. *Beda venerabilis, Opera didascalia*, 2, *De temporum ratione*, ed. C.W. JONES (Turnhout, 1977: CCSL 123B).

[34] E. KONSGEN, "Eine neue komputistische Dichtung des *Agius von Corvey*", *Mittellateinisches Jahrbuch* 14 (1979), pp. 66-75.

[35] *Rhythmi computistici*, in: *Rhythmi aevi Merovingici et Carolini*, ed. STRECKER, in: PLAC 4.2-3, pp. 667-702.

[36] CORDOLIANI, "Contribution à la littérature du comput ecclésiastique".

[37] See M.G. DI PASQUALE, "Versi computistici: Proposte per una nuova edizione", in: Poetry of the Early Medieval Europe, pp. 171-181.

[38] C. SAVINI, *Il ritmo 'Anni domini notantur' nella tradizione computistica medievale)* (Tesi di laurea magistrale dell'Universita di Siena, Facolta di Lettere e Filosofia di Arezzo, rel. F. STELLA, anno accademico 2010-2011). [A first draft of the new edition is already online in the web site of the Corpus.]

celi duodenis (see the Appendix), structured in 21 tercets of rhythmic verse of 15 syllables, signed by a certain "*humilis levita Christi Hirenicus*", the Greek translation of *Pacificus*, who also signed other writing with "*humilis levita*".[39] It is a poem about the zodiac, like antecedents in the *Anthologia Latina* and many in later medieval manuscripts,[40] walls, and stones, often decorated or illustrated with the zodiac and / or allegorical figures representing the months. It draws its inspiration from a short sermon by Zeno of Verona,[41] which was analysed in depth by Wolfgang Hübner in an article in 1975[42] and is the earliest of a series of treatises, frequently anonymous, of Christian astrology, published in academic journals or in the appendix of Hübner's *Zodiacus christianus*.[43] Thus Pacificus's poem, neglected by Hübner's essays, is the earliest poem with a summary of a Christian translation of the astrological system. The homiletic source was identified by Bernhard Bischoff, but here it is adapted to oppose the pagan interpretation more strongly.

The re-semantisation offered by Zeno and versified by Pacificus is based on the principle of cultural neutrality of the signs but not of their meanings, and is developed from a contention against paganism: according to Pacificus, the names of the twelve signs derive from the "*fabulae gentilium*" (1, 3), thereby testifying the "*seva dementia*" of the pagans, who placed so many animals in heaven, while Olympus was inhabited by cohorts of angels. Drawing on Zeno, Pacificus interprets them afresh one by one: the Bull is not the one in whose form Jupiter abducted Europe, but the symbol of Christ, which Luke's Gospel 15, 23 describes as a calf fattened for the sacrifice,[44] a meaning analogous to that of the Lamb (corresponding to the Ram, with which the zodiac formally starts): it is therefore not grim and haughty, not threatening like a bull, but sweet and meek as a calf. This Bull urges us with merciful zeal to submit to the yoke of Christ in order to plough the field of vices and sow his precepts.

---

[39] CAMPANA, "Veronensia".

[40] See B. OBRIST, "La représentation carolingienne du zodiaque: A propos du manuscrit de Bâle, Universitätsbibliothek, F III 15", *Cahiers de Civilisation Médiévale* 44 (2001), pp. 3-33.

[41] Zeno of Verona, *Tractatus*, XLIII, *Ad Neophytos post baptisma*, IV, *De duodecim signis*, ed. B. LÖFSTEDT (Turnhout, 1971: CCSL 22), replacing PL 11, cols. 493-496.

[42] W. HÜBNER, "Das Horoskop der Christen (Zeno, 1, 38 L.)", *Vigiliae Christianae* 29 (1975), pp.120-137.

[43] W. HÜBNER, Zodiacus Christianus: *Judisch-christliche Adaptationen des Tierkreises von der Antike bis zur Gegenwart* (Meisenheim, 1983).

[44] *Rhythmus* 117, 7, 1, ed. in: *Rhythmi aevi Merovingici et Carolini*, ed. STRECKER, pp. 693-695, at p. 694: "*Saginatus vitulus: Christus saginatus vitulus*" (MS Saint-Omer, Bibliothèque Municipale, 351 (or. Saint- Bertin), f. 16v (STRECKER app.)).

The reversal of the meaning of a symbol of time is extended to a global reinterpretation at an allegorical level. This contrasts with Zeno and the chapter (III, 71) that Isidore's *Etymologiae* dedicate to the zodiac, both of which preserve the sequence Ram-Bull, that is the present one, rather than the sequence Bull-Ram that we find in the poem, and which may be due to a reversal during textual transmission. The reference to Europe is found only in Isidore.[45] In the same way, Gemini are the two Testaments; Cancer the vice of greed to avoid; Leo is Christ sleeping in death and awoken for victory; Virgo is the sixth sign of the zodiac, just as Christ was born of a Virgin in the sixth age of the world, bringing the Libra of God's justice. If we approach Him with a pure heart, we need not fear Scorpio's venom or Sagittarius's arrows – symbols of the devil –, and terrible Capricorn will drive other people, but not Christians, to murder or adultery. Innocent Aquarius will wash away all the misdeeds – be they spontaneous or inspired by the devil – of the converted, while the two Pisces represent the Jewish and Christian peoples, who are called to salvation through baptism.

The circular survey, which becomes a kind of narration by symbols, ends up inviting Christians to abandon the madness of believing that mortals live in heaven and of worshipping empty signs of animals burdened by the weight of flesh; they should understand that the mediator between God and mankind is in heaven together with the souls of the blessed.

The last strophe closes with a computistical datum inconsistent with the zodiac theme, saying that Pacificus composed as many strophes ("*totidem versiculos*"[46]) as the years (19) that the moon takes to return to the same point of its orbit, thus creating a philological problem due to the presence of two more strophes (Nos. 20 and 21), perhaps supernumerary, perhaps interpolated.[47] A closer reading reveals further problems: some references, for example, are not explained by known sources: the association of Christ with the sixth age is absent in Isidore and Zeno's zodiac pieces, even if it is traditional in patristic writings, and the idea that Capricorn causes madness derives from Zeno, but it is not clear whence Zeno drew it: even Hübner does not clarify this point in his commentary.

---

[45] Isidore of Seville, *Etymologiae*, 3, 71, 22 ff., ed. W.M. LINDSAY, 2 vols. (Oxford, 1911), 1, without pagination

[46] Same meaning of *versiculus* in *Rhythmus* 81, 46, 2, ed. in: *Rhythmi aevi Merovingici et Carolini*, ed. STRECKER, p. 629.

[47] Indeed, these two strophes, together with the first, make up an extremely reduced version of that poem in MS Rome, Biblioteca Angelica, 123.

On this basis other attributions flourished: Wolfgang Hübner[48] also proposed acknowledging Pacificus as the author of certain rhythmic glosses to some zodiac verses by Alexander of Villadei, discovered in 1991 by Martínez Gazquez in a Girona manuscript.[49] However, these have no Christian interpretation, and simply testify the vast heritage of unpublished computistical verse still to be explored.

The collation of manuscripts transmitting computistical 'rhythms', which we are editing for the *Corpus Rhythmorum,* reveals that this zodiac poem is interlaced with the computistical rhythmic digest *Anni domini notantur*, which is attributed in some manuscripts – and also in some modern digital archives – to Pacificus or to Bede or to Dionysius Exiguus, depending on the version. This overlap between *computus* and Christian zodiac – strictly related to the link between time-measuring devices and Christian symbolism – confirms that at least in some cases cultural and religious interpretation followed the technical progress of the calculation system.

The sacralisation of the zodiac achieved in Pacificus's verse is not yet comparable to the link established in classical culture between mythology and astrology, but nevertheless shows second-degree processing of scholastic learning. It bears witness to a need, which, as we have seen, began to materialise with Gregory of Tours's *De cursu stellarum* and has been systematically coded as an intellectual initiative, outside the classicist mainstream, which emerges in a series of anonymous treatises in both Greek and Latin. Many of these were edited in the appendix of Hübner's 1983 book but never studied in detail, while a more systematic but mysterious *De astronomia more christiano*, written at Corbie in Carolingian times, possibly by Paschasius Radbertus, was published by Hubert Les Bourdellès as late as 1991.[50] This attribution, largely conjectural, has been called into question by David Ganz[51] but has been accepted in recent studies, such as Ramirez-Weavier's dissertation (2008),[52] which

---

[48] W. Hübner, "Une glose a la 'massa Compoti' d'Alexandre de Villedieu contenant des vers sur le zodiaque", in: *Science antique science médiévale (autour d'Avranches 25): Actes du colloque international (Mont Saint-Michel, 4-7 Septembre 1998)*, ed. L. Callebat and O. Desbordes (Hildesheim, Zurich, and New York, 2000), pp. 373-389.

[49] J. Martinez Gazquez, "La glosa a los signos del zodíaco en la 'Massa compoti' del ms. 91 del A.C. de Girona", *Annals de l'Institut d'Estudis Gironins* 31 (1990-1991), pp. 31-40.

[50] *De Astronomia more Christiano*, ed. H. Le Bourdellès, "De Astronomia more Christiano", *Studi medievali* 32 (1991), pp. 385-444.

[51] Ganz, "Der lineare Blick".

[52] E.M. Ramirez-Weaver, *Carolingian Innovation and Observation in the Paintings and Star Catalogs of Madrid, Biblioteca Nacional, Ms. 3307*, PhD New York University, 2008, pp.

contextualises the diffusion of such astronomy, also finding figurative evidence of it in manuscript illuminations (MS Madrid, Biblioteca Nacional 3307). He links the process to the theological conception of the neutrality of images and names, theorised during the iconoclastic debate in the *Opus Caroli* and celebrated in Theodulf's verses on the liberal arts. Textual and iconographic evidence therefore documents the de-activation of the pagan cultural heritage that was potentially connected to the maintenance of the names of the zodiac signs; this method was clearly theorised in the introduction to the anonymous *De astronomia*[53] and was fulfilled by the de- and re-semantisation of names and icons following the preparation of the huge scientific handbook compiled by a Carolingian ' on of which was published by Arno Borst in 2006 and has not yet been explored.[54]

So besides the branch of late antique poetic zodiology inaugurated by Ausonius and developed in the diverse sources of the *Anthologia Latina* between the fourth and fifth centuries, and also very productive in the Middle Ages, a minor branch of Christian poetic zodiology has been discovered, which is frequently contrastive but nevertheless innovative, and according to the Augustinian and in a sense post-modern orientation of Carolingian hermeneutics, indefinitely open to new meanings.

Pacificus's rhythmic poetry, which can now be interpreted as a small but consistent original corpus, turns out to be an unexpected forerunner in this process, which is also part of a wider Carolingian interest in science, and surprisingly leads us to hitherto unknown scientific and technical innovations.

[Addendum: As this book goes to print, we learn of the existence of a further eleventh-century manuscript of the poem *Spera caeli*, MS New York, Pierpont Morgan Library, M. 925, whose first collation seems to confirm the hypotheses set out here about the transmission of text and image together.]

330-331.

[53] LE BOURDELLÈS, "De Astronomia more Christiano", p. 410: "*Quia ex his est indagata disciplina, usurpantur et nomina, nec propterea christiani sensibus, ea quae sunt necessaria, debentur videri indigna, quia non obest conspectui, quod non inest sensui*" ("Since from these [i.e. the ancients] [astronomical] science has been studied, from them also derive the names, which are not for this reason to be considered unworthy of Christian ideas, at least those that are necessary, since what does not touch the thought does not damage the sight").

[54] A. BORST, "Die Aachener Enzyklopädie von 809 (*Lib. Comp.*), in: ID., *Schriften zur Komputistik im Frankenreich von 721 bis 818*, 3 vols. (Hanover, 2006), 3, pp. 1054-1334, at p. 1054: "*erstes Teamwork der europäischen Wissenschaftsgeschichte*".

Appendix

Pacificus's Epitaph (PLAC 2, pp. 846-847)

Archidiaconus quiescit hic vero Pacificus,
sapientia preclarus et forma prefulgida.
Nullus talis est inventus nostris in temporibus.
Quod nec ullum advenire umquam talem credimus.
Ecclesiarum fundator, renovator optimus
Zenonis, Proculi, Viti, Petri et Laurentii.
Dei quoque genitricis, necnon et Georgii.
Quicquid auro vel argento et metallis ceteris,
Quicquid lignis ex diversis et marmore candido,
Nullus unquam sic peritus in tantis operibus.
Bis centenos terque senos codicesque fecerat.
Horologium nocturnum nullus ante viderat,
En invenit argumentum et primum fundaverat.
Glosam veteris et novi testamenti posuit
Horologioque carmen sperae caeli optimum,
Plura alia grafiaque prudens inveniet.
Tres et decem vixit lustra, trinos annos amplius.
Quadraginta et tres annos fuit archidiaconus.
Septimo vicesimo [aetatis] anno Cesaris Lotharii
Mole carnis est solutus, perrexit ad dominum.
Nono sane Kalendarum obiit Decembrium,
Nocte santa, que vocatur a nobis dominica.
Lugent quoque sacerdotes et ministri optimi,
Eius mortem nempe dolet infinitus populus.
Vestros pedes quasi tenens vosque precor cernuus,
O lectores, exorare queso pro Pacifico.

Hic, rogo, pauxillum veniens subsiste, viator.
    Et mea scrutare pectore dicta tuo.
Quod nunc es, fueram, famosus in orbe, viator.
    Et quod nunc ego sum, tuque futurus eris.
Dilicias mundi pravo sectabar amore,
    Nunc cinis et pulvis, vermibus atque cibus.
Quapropter potius animam curare memento,
    Quam carnem, quoniam haec manet, illa perit.
Cur tibi plura paras? quam parvo cernis in antro
    Me tenet hic requies: sic tua parva fiet.

Ut flores pereunt vento veniente minaci,
  Sic tua namque caro, gloria tota, perit.
Tu mihi redde vicem, lector, rogo carminis huius
  Et dic: 'da veniam, Christe, tuo famulo'.
Pacificus Salomon nihi nomen atque Ireneus,
  Pro quo funde preces mente legens titulum.
Obsecro, nulla manus violet pia iura sepulcri,
  Personet angelica donec ab arce tuba:
qui iaces in tumulo terrae de pulvere surge,
  Magnus adest iudex milibus innumeris.
Tolle hic segnitiem, pone fastidia mentis,
  Crede mihi, frater, doctior hinc redies.

ANNO DOMINICE INCARNATIONIS DCCCXLVI, INDICT.E

Rhythmus 116 (PLAC 4, p. 692)

1 *Spera caeli quater senis horis dum reuoluitur,*
   Omnes stellę fixę cęlo, quae cum ea ambiunt,
   Circa axem breuiores circulos efficiunt.
2 *Illa igitur, quae polo apparet vicinior,*
   Inter omnes tamen ei splendor est precipuus,
   Ipsa noccium horarum computatrix dicitur.
3 *Argumentum en inuentum: cardini oppositum*
   Recta linea si serves luminum intuitu,
   Horas noctis nosse potes galli sine vocibus.
4 *O quam pulchrum stemma tenet clavorum positio*
   Crucis Christi rotę fixę hoc in orologio,
   In qua ipse carne pendens pro salute hominum!
5 *Dextra, leva et profunda, quae tendit ad aethera,*
   Seruat semper computatrix per distincta tempora
   Ęquinoctia designans atque solestitia.
6 *Ante axem siquis volvens curiosus steterit,*
   Aequinoctium vernale a sinistra noverit,
   Cernere ad dextram sui autumnale poterit.
7 *Solistitia duobus indita temporibus:*
   Ęstiualis, qui erectus ad superna ducitur,
   Radius, ad ima mersus hiemalis dicitur.

Rhythmus 117 (*ibidem*, pp. 693-695)

1   *Spera cęli duodenis signis circumvoluitur,*
    Exornata mire tantis candidis sideribus,
    Quibus nomina dedere fabulę gentilium.
2   *Unumquodque tamen signum sol tricenis diebus*
    Denis horis atque semis illustrare dicitur,
    Unius sic anni complens zodiaci circulum.
3   *Mira prorsus paganorum et seva dementia,*
    Qui in caelo transtulerunt tam diversas bestias,
    Cum Olimpo constet esse angelorum agmina.
4   *Illi Taurum radiare dicunt inter sidera,*
    Qui in bovem uersum Iovem fabulis adseverant;
    Ad Italiam transuexit Agenoris filiam.
5   *Habet fides Christiana signorum memoriam,*
    Primum agni, qui in cęlo maiestate fulgida
    Regnat unicus cum patre per immensa secula.
6   *Igitur non torvus fronte uel cervice tumidus*
    Noster taurus est putandus, non minax, sed optimus,
    Dulcis, blandus atque mitis atque suavis vitulus:
7   *Ipse ergo est credendus saginatus vitulus,*
    Cuius caro immolata in crucis patibulo
    Nos cruore suo tulit de mortis periculo.
8   *Hic non cessat nos hortari pietate sedula,*
    Iugo Christi nos submitti, exarare vicia,
    Divinorum preceptorum reportare semina.
9   *Prosequentibus hortatur testamentum Geminis*
    Idolatriam calcare, deum solum colere,
    Auaritiam uitare, Cancrum incurabilem.
10 *Leo noster obdormivit, ut in morte vinceret,*
    Ideo evigilavit, ut possemus surgere
    Et, quas iuste merebamur, a penis eriperet.
11 *Virginis hoc sextum signum competenter sequitur:*
    Sexta mundi iam aetate venit dei filius,
    Equitatis Libram tenens, deus iure dicitur.
12 *Huic puro si quis corde bene ministraverit,*
    Iam securus non timebit venenum pestiferi,
    Conculcare tuta planta Scorpionem poterit.
13 *Scuto fidei protectus sevum Sagittarium*
    Deformatum non pavebit cum equinis cruribus,
    Ipsum quoque superabit nefandum diabolum.

14 *Capricornus ac deformis, vultu despicabilis,*
   Alios amentes facit, alios sacrilegos,
   Homicidas furiosos, alios adulteros.
15 *Sed his omnibus conversis atque bene flentibus*
   Tergere de fronte solet candidus Aquarius
   Crimina, quę sponte fiunt uel instinctu demonum.
16 *Duo Pisces, qui sequuntur, uno signo editi,*
   Duos populos figurant vocatos per gratiam
   Baptismatis unda lotos soli deo credere.
17 *Insanire iam illorum desinat dementia,*
   Qui in cęlo esse credunt aliqua mortalia,
   Cassa spernat, illa credat, que dei ecclesia.
18 *Animalia pusilla magna et reptilia*
   Carnis pondere gravata non petunt celestia,
   Sed cum carne horum credant interire animas.
19 *Ubi hominum et dei mediator fuerit,*
   Esse ibi electorum credimus et animas.
   Hęc daturum se promisit infinita bonitas.
20 *Vnumquodque signum luna tantum binis diebus*
   Senis horis atque besse peragrare creditur.
   Sic per singula discurrens ad primum revertitur.
21 *Post novenos atque denos annos luna circuli*
   Ad priorem redit cursum: totidem versiculos
   Humilis levita Christi edidit Hirenicus.

Chapter 11

Everyday Life in the Literary Inscriptions of the Carolingian Monastery

The Matter of Poetic Epigraphy

In a culture like the Carolingian one, whose driving force in comparison to the preceding decades was primarily the exponential multiplication of means of communication, attention paid to public writings inevitably takes on a central role: the old, rather persistent image of a literary rebirth primarily characterised by an imitative revival of ancient literature is not helpful to an exploration of the many paraliterary expressions that are proof of the extraordinary vitality of this communicative impulse. According to my own reading experience, Carolingian poetry is entirely dictated by a concrete relationship with social reality, and it is difficult to find Carolingian poems that cannot be traced back to an at least seemingly concrete motivation, to a real context rather than an imaginary or fantastical one, to an actual goal for which writing is an expression or tool. Literary epigraphy – that is, epigraphy handed down primarily through manuscripts – is in fact one of the manifestations in which the functional nature of Carolingian literature becomes more explicit. This is precisely why, like the other expressive forms of this vast poetic corpus, it can never be reduced to simple imitation or rewriting: because we have at least the partial possibility of reconstructing the environment in which it was really located. And even when we are uncertain whether all the epigraphs attested in the manuscripts were actually used or not, about which physical spaces may have held them, it still seems clear that – aside from the exceptions that we can identify – we are nevertheless looking at texts that were composed to be read by others, and not simply for practice or imitation. Luce Pietri clearly showed that from Paulinus of Nola to Ambrosius, to Paulinus of Périgueux and Venantius Fortunatus, a genuine genre of epigraphs in verse, written by poets on secular or ecclesiastical commission, was being developed; and that in Cimitile, Milan, and Tours attestations in later documents and the results of archaeological excavations have confirmed the actual use of those compositions, already widely demonstrated by internal evidence like the authors' concern for location, the dimensions of the support, and even the colour of the letters of the epigraphs and cartouches, or by specific texts such as Paulinus of Nola's letter 32 *De aedificiis*.[1] Pietri's arguments were revived at a conference in Spoleto by Guglielmo Cavallo,[2] who, in referring to the Augustinian expression "*versus publice scripti*" (*Sermones* 319, 8) reminded us that opportunities to avail oneself of these inscriptions – which were also challenging in a literary sense – included, for the *illitterati* but not only for them, reading and explanation by an inside guide, typically provided by the *aedituus* or *ostiarius*, as several texts by Gregory of Tours also confirm.[3] In a masterful essay from 2012,[4] Peter Stotz, investigating a number of verse inscriptions on plates, reliquaries, crosses, and chalices from medieval Germany and Finland, sets out about a dozen sample categories of the way in which inscriptions, not so much those on stone as those on artefacts, communicate cultural elements or poetic form – such as rhythmic contrafactum, quotation, fortuitous textual coincidence, reuse of common poetic formulas, reflection of scholarly readings, the specific format of a type of inscription, deixis, typological interpretation of the painted figure or shape of the artefact, first person form that recalls the riddle scheme,

---

[1] L. PIETRI, *Pagina in pariete reserata: Epigraphie et architecture religieuse*, in: *La terza età dell'epigrafia, Colloquio AIEGL-Borghesi, Bologna, October 1986*, ed. A. DONATI (Faenza, 1998), pp. 137-157. [See also A. ARNULF, *Versus ad picturas: Studien zur Titulusdichtung als Quellengattung der Kunstgeschichte von der Antike bis zum Hochmittelalter* (Munich, 1997).]

[2] G. CAVALLO, "Testo e immagine: Una frontiera ambigua", in: *Testo e immagine nell'alto Medioevo*, 2 vols. (Spoleto, 1994: *Settimane di Studio del Centro Italiano di Studi sull'Alto Medioevo* 41), 1, pp. 31-62.

[3] Gregory of Tours, *De passione et virtutibus Juliani martyris*, 2, ed. in: *Gregorii Turonensis Opera*, 2, *Miracula et opera minora*, ed. B. KRUSCH, 2nd edn. (Hanover, 1885: MGH SRM 1.2), pp. 112-134, at p. 263; ID., *De virtutibus Martini* II, 14, ed. *ibid.*, pp. 134-211, p. 163; II, 29, p. 170; II, 49, p. 176; and I, 2, p. 138.

[4] P. STOTZ, "Beobachtungen zu metrischen Inschriften auf Werken der Schatzkunst: Formen, Gehalte, Traditionen", originally presented at a conference in Halberstadt in 2004 ('Inschriften und Europäische Schatzkunst'), whose proceedings were never published. It can be read in: ID., *Alte Sprache – Neues Lied: Kleine Schriftem zur christlichen Dichtung des lateinischen Mittelalters* (Florence, 2012), pp. 279-305, with 3 plates.

epigraphic appeal to a passer-by, apostrophe to or among depicted figures, simple caption, correction, reflection dictated by an image, and wordplay with signifiers – often identifying intertextual relationships as incontestable as they are unlikely and coming to the conclusion that the driving force was always an "*überpersönliche, allenfalls kanoniserte Formulierungstradition*", if not "*Zufall*",[5] which makes analyses of purely textual links unsupported by other evidence seem dubious.

Rosamond McKitterick omitted inscriptions from the attestations examined in her overview of writing in the Carolingian period.[6] They were partially taken into consideration only in a recent essay from 2015, in which Florian Hartmann asserts the influence of the Lombards' (in particular Liutprand's) strategy of epigraphic propaganda over the Carolingians.[7]

Robert Favreau showed that the engraving of these poems is in some cases still demonstrable: regardless of archdeacon Pacificus's controversial epitaph, this is true at least for an Alcuinian line that is found in a good six ecclesiastical inscriptions,[8] for an epigram by Theodulf for Germigny-des-Prés, for Al

---

[5] Stotz, "Beobachtungen zu metrischen Inschriften", p. 290.

[6] R. McKitterick, *The Carolingians and the Written Word* (Cambridge, 1989), p. 271: "I have also had to leave for treatment or fuller discussion another time, and by others, many more kinds of evidence and other contexts and manifestations of literacy ... One obvious omission is, of course, the evidence of inscriptions. Thanks to the new project for publishing the inscriptions for mediaeval Gaul, we may soon be in a position to assess his evidence".

[7] F. Hartmann, "Karolingische Gelehrte als Dichter und der Wissenstransfer am Beispiel der Epigraphik", in: *Karolingische Klöster: Wissenstransfer und kulturelle Innovation* ed. J. Becker, T. Licht, and S. Weinfurter (Berlin, 2015), pp. 255-274. One opportunity for this influence would have been Charlemagne's stays in Italy in 774 and 781, the authorial vessel, through the good offices of Adalard of Corbie in Italy under the regent Pippin, being Paulus Diaconus, passionate transcriber of epigraphs also of Anglo-Saxon kings in his *Historia Langobardorum*, composer of epigraphs for the Lombard kings, and author of the epigraphs of Hildegard, as well as of two of Charles's daughters and two of his sisters. After him, other fellow countrymen wrote them: Paulinus of Aquileia, Fardulf, and Peter of Pisa. Alcuin began to compose them only after these figures had left court. Adalhard would also be behind the Corbie manuscript (De Rossi No. 76, pp. 168-169), which gathered models of epigraphs from Italy and was transcribed from the *Sylloge Centulensis*, ed. in: *Inscriptiones Christianae urbis Romae septimo saeculo antiquiores*, 2.1, *Series codicum in quibus veteres inscriptiones christianae praesertim urbis Romae sive solae sive ethnicis admixtae descriptae sunt ante saeculum XVI*, ed. G.B. de Rossi (Rome, 1888), pp. 72-94), an antigraph from St Riquier, a monastery headed by Angilbert, poet chancellor of the Italian court from 781, which nonetheless ends with a composition by the *scotus* monk Caidoc, which reuses Alcuinian models. The role of Alcuin, which Hartmann wishes to minimise somewhat, therefore comes back into play.

[8] *Hic decus ecclesiae promptus in omne bonum*, written for Saint-Denis (Liegi 1037, Toul 1126, Saint-Denis 1140, Beauvais 1283, Rouen 1110, Grandmont 1209): R. Favreau, "Les

cuin's epitaph for Pope Hadrian I,[9] for Hincmar's inscriptions whose usage is attested by Flodoard of Reims, and for Sedulius Scotus's epitaph for Hildebert, archbishop of Cologne, in 862. But this list could be further updated to include examples such as the *Versus Augienses*, that is the 'Reichenau verses', which were published in the *Poetae* of the *Monumenta* and later on in other places, but which we can also read under the frescoes at Sankt Georg in Oberzell, Reichenau.[10] The list would become enormous if we considered *tituli librarii*, which I have had the chance to examine already elsewhere. But while the question of their actual usage, from Edmond Le Blant[11] and Giovanni Battista de Rossi[12] onwards, has provoked some uneasiness among epigraphists, who are justifiably concerned about defining the limits of the material available to them, this remains a secondary concern for a literary scholar who can be equally interested in these texts whether the engraving's support is preserved or not.

---

inscriptions médiévales – Reflet d'une culture et d'une foi", in: *Epigraphik 1988: Fachtagung für mittelalterliche und neuzeitliche Epigraphik, Graz, 10.-14. Mai 1988*, ed. W. KOCH (Vienna, 1990), pp. 57-89, at p. 77; see also A. PETRUCCI, "Scrittura e figura nella memoria funeraria", in: *Testo e immagine nell'alto Medioevo*, pp. 277-296.

[9] On which see L. WALLACH, *Alcuin and Charlemagne: Studies in Carolingian History and Literature* (Ithaca, NY, 1959), pp. 178-97, and S. SCHOLZ, "Karl der Große und das 'Epitaphium Adriani': Ein Beitrag zum Gebetsgedenken der Karolinger", in: *Das Frankfurter Konzil von 749: Kristallisationspunkt karolingischer Kultur: Akten zweier Symposien (vom 23. bis 27. Februar und vom 13. bis zum 15. Oktober 1994) anläßlich der 1200-Jahrfeier der Stadt Frankfurt am Main*, 1, *Politik und Kirche*, ed. R. BERNDT (Mainz, 1997), pp. 373-394.

[10] These have developed an impressive bibliography: see K. KOSHI, "Die Buchmalerei der Reichenau zwischen Ost und West: Ikonographie anhand von den Wandbildern der Wunder Christi in St. Georg zu Reichenau-Oberzell", in: *Testo e immagine nell'alto Medioevo*, pp. 595-629; W. BERSCHIN, "Die Tituli der Wandbilder von Reichenau-Oberzell St. Georg", *Mittellateinisches Jahrbuch* 29.2 (1994), pp. 3-17, reprinted in: ID., *Mittellateinische Studien* (Heidelberg, 2005), pp. 215-228; and *Reichenauer Waldmalerei 840-1120: Goldbach – Reichenau-Oberzell St. Georg – Reichenau-Niederzell St. Peter und Paul*, ed. W. BERSCHIN and U. KUDER (Heidelberg, 2012).

[11] E. LE BLANT, *Inscriptions chrétiennes de la Gaule antérieures au VIIIe siècle*, 1, *Provinces gallicanes* (Paris, 1856), pp. 4 ff.

[12] *Inscriptiones Christianae urbis Romae septimo saeculo antiquiores*, ed. DE ROSSI, 2.1, pp. XLVIII-XLIX. Camille Julian (*Inscriptions romaines de Bordeaux*, ed. C. JULLIAN, 2 vols. (Bordeaux, 1887-1890), 2), also includes texts by Venantius, as do Franz Xaver Kraus for Mainz (*Die christlichen Inschriften der Rheinlande*, ed. F.X. KRAUS, 2 vols. (Freiburg im Breisgau, 1890-1894)), and Emile Hübner (*Inscriptiones Hispaniae christianae*, ed. E. HÜBNER (Berlin, 1871) and *Supplementum* (Berlin, 1900)) and José Vivès for Spain (*Inscripciones cristianas de la España romana y visigoda*, ed. J. VIVÈS, 2nd edn. (Barcelona, 1969: Biblioteca histórica de la biblioteca Balmes, 2nd series 18): R. FAVREAU, "Fortunat et l'épigraphie", in: *Venanzio Fortunato tra Italia e Francia: Atti del convegno internazionale di studi, Valdobbiadene, 17 maggio 1990 – Treviso 18-19 maggio 1990*, ed. T. RAGUSA (Treviso, 1993), pp. 161-173, at p. 162.

Sometimes history takes it upon itself to contradict our most rational expectations: one of Venantius Fortunatus's inscriptions, whose use on stone is demonstrable or at least highly probable, is in fact one of the lengthiest and most clearly anti-epigraphic pieces that the poet composed.[13] Moreover, who would believe in the actual engraving of Pope Hadrian's epitaph could we not see it for ourselves at Saint Peter's basilica in the Vatican?

Carolingian Monastic Epigraphy: Saint-Riquier

The Carolingian monasteries that may be considered the most important centres of this kind of literary production are chiefly Tours, Fulda, Saint Gall, Reichenau, Saint-Amand, and most of all Saint-Riquier, although a significant number of other sites may be included due to individual cases or small groups of texts.

The least studied of these *corpora* is certainly Saint-Riquier's, about which we have only a few – albeit analytical and precise – pages by Günter Bernt, the author in 1968 of the only volume dedicated to early medieval Latin epigrams.[14] The Centula abbey was subject to detailed archaeological reconstructions, also following recent excavations,[15] but not much attention was paid to

---

[13] Glastonbury 700, on behalf of King Ine of Wessex: FAVREAU, "Fortunat et l'epigraphie", p. 165, from William CAMDEN, *Britannia sive florentissimorum regnorum Angliae, Scotiae, Hiberniae et insularum adiacentium* (London, 1607), p. 165; see LE BLANT, *Inscriptions chrétiennes de la Gaule*, pp. 261-264 and 295-300.

[14] G. BERNT, *Das lateinische Epigramm im Übergang von der Spätantike zum frühen Mittelalter* (Munich, 1968), pp. 295-305. Giuseppe Scalia does not go into this genre, which he calls "epigrammatic literature", in G. SCALIA, "Le epigrafi", in: *Lo spazio letterario del Medioevo*, 1, *Il medioevo latino*, ed. G. CAVALLO, C. LEONARDI and E. MENESTÒ, 3 vols. (Rome, 1992-1994), 3, *La circolazione del testo*, pp. 409-441, esp. p. 410 n. 3 (much less the manuals of 'classic' epigraphy such as R.M. KLOOS, *Einführung in die Epigraphik des Mittelalters und der frühen Neuzeit* (Darmstadt, 1980) and the overview by R. FAVREAU, *Les inscriptions médiévales* (Turnhout, 1979: *L'atelier du médiéviste* 5). I dedicated chapter 1 of the first part of F. STELLA, *La poesia carolingia latina a tema biblico* (Spoleto, 1993), pp. 27-210, to poetic Carolingian epigraphs with a biblical theme. [Two exemplary explorations of local production are F.E. CONSOLINO, "La poesia epigrafica a Pavia longobarda nell'VIII secolo", in: *Storia di Pavia*, 2, *L'alto medioevo* (Pavia, 1987), pp. 159-176, and M. PETOLETTI, "Poesia epigrafica pavese di età longobarda: Le iscrizioni sui monumenti", *Italia Medioevale e Umanistica* 60 (2019) pp. 1-32.]

[15] H. BERNARD, "Premières fouilles à Saint-Riquier", in: *Karl der Grosse: Lebenswerk und Nachleben*, ed. W. BRAUNFELS *et al.*, 5 vols. (Düsseldorf, 1966-1968), 3, *Karolingische Kunst*, pp. 369-374; ID., "Une restitution nouvelle de la basilique d'Angilbert", *Revue du Nord* 71 (1989), pp. 307-361; ID., "L'abbaye de Saint-Riquier: Evolution des bâtiments monastiques du

Fig. 26 Saint-Riquier. Engraving of 1612 after a (now destroyed) miniature of the eleventh century.

its literature – if we exclude the hagiographies of St. Richarius and the reformer Angilbert and works by him (such as the *De ecclesia Centulensi*)[16] and Hariulf (*Chronica* III, 3),[17] which help us to reconstruct the abbey's appearance and history. The Saint-Riquier *corpus* consists of a collection of poems that Traube titled the *Carmina Centulensia*. These preserve a substantial number of epigraphs, handed down by a codex from Gembloux, now in MSS Brussels, Bibliothèque Royale, 10470-473 and 10859. The first group (IV-XV) appears in the series attributed to Micon, a monk and deacon who also compiled a famous prosodic florilegium. It consists of engravings from the church of the Virgin Mary – one of the three poles of the famous triangular cloister at Centula – such as *carmen* 4, which a colophon clarifies is about individuals who are "*Zonatim picti discipulique sui*", whom Hubert attributed to the altars of the Apostles arranged in a group around the altar of the Virgin, or from the *scriptorium* (where as usual the difficulty of the scribe's work was lamented

---

IXe au XVIIIe siècle", in: *Sous la règle de saint Benoît: Structures monastiques et sociétés en France du Moyen Âge à l'époque moderne, Abbaye bénédictine Sainte-Marie de Paris, 23-25 October 1980* (Geneva, 1982), pp. 499-526; a fine description, with a reproduction of the Parisian print of 1612, in J. HUBERT, J. PORCHER, and W.F. VOLBACH, *L'empire carolingien* (Paris, 1968), trans. *L'impero carolingio* (Milan, 1981²); and J. HUBERT, "Saint-Riquier et le monachisme bénédictin en Gaule à l'époque carolingienne", in: *Il monachesimo nell'alto medioevo e la formazione della civiltà occidentale* (Spoleto, 1957: *Settimane di studio del Centro Italiano di Studi sull'Alto Medioevo* 4), pp. 293-309; B. DELMAIRE, "Saint-Riquier", in: *LMA*, ed. N. ANGERMANN *et al.* 7.6 (Munich, 1995), col. 1198.

[16] Angilbert, *De ecclesia Centulensi libellus*, ed. in: *Hariulf, Chronique de l'abbaye de Saint-Riquier*, ed. F. LOT (Paris, 1894: *Collection de textes pour servir à l'étude ... de l'histoire* 17), pp. 296-306.

[17] Hariulf, *Chronicon Centulense*, ed. in: *Hariulf, Chronique de l'abbaye de Saint-Riquier*, ed. F. LOT (Paris, 1894), pp. 1-286.

Epitaphs

A second group consists of epitaphs of figures such as Nithard (No. 33) – this text refers to a tomb painting[18] – or Angilbert himself, which are characterised by precise information such as the names of the deceased and the days of their demise. These unveil a style that is rather more casual than the standard Carolingian one, as can be seen in the poetry by Micon himself or his confrère Fredegard (from No. 68 on), "*procurator pauperum*" in around 866. No. 34 recalls, for instance, the "*flaccentia membra*" of Ermenrich, "*callenti more catorum*",[19] rather bluntly commended for skills he acquired by dint of practice rather than through specialist expertise: "*quamvis arte carens, tamen usu iure calebat: / praecipuus scriba, vivax lector fuit atque / insuper occentor nec non numerator opimus*" ("although lacking in technical expertise, nonetheless he distinguished himself for practice: he was an excellent scribe, lively reader and also a brilliant singer and calculator"); No. 36, those of the monk *geometricus* Donadeus, "*mechanica doctus in arte*"; and No. 40, the foreigner Israhel. For more or less all of these deceased men, the epitaph, which in No. 42 is self-proclaimed a *titulus*, urges the reader to pray, in keeping with the typical forms of the genre; and for many of them we encounter the tradition of versifying the date of death. A kind of internal formulary is also created, which sees the recurrence of attributes such as *veridicus* and identifications such as *astu pollebat* at the beginning of the poem, and not only in the typical locations of the 'here lies' or the appeal to the reader. But elements of social customs also emerge, such as clapping at the funeral (No. 43, 7: "*et manibus plausis flebat tunc contio praesens*"), which allows us to locate the composition of the *titulus* at a point in time after the funerary rites. It is almost never the deceased who speaks: exceptions in this regard are the epitaphs of Godelenda (No. 47) and Gervide (No. 65), both in first person.[20] In some instances, allusions are made

---

[18] "*Hic rutilat species Nithardi picta sagacis*".

[19] *Cattus* is a 'cat', before attested only in the *Anthologia Latina* (375, 1, and 181, 3); *catus* is already documented in classical Latin and means 'acute'.

[20] The suspicion that these are exercises emerges when doubles of epitaphs are found for the same person: 64 is also for Godelenda. But it is also possible that they are inscriptions on different sides or surfaces of the same tomb.

to the hope of resurrection in original ways, such as in No. 59, for Adalelm, who is wished a tranquil interment ("*donec / accensus redeat corporis ad speciem*" – "until he ignites to return to the beauty of the body", or "until he returns in the form of a flame to the beauty of the body"), or unusual circumlocutions are invented to describe permanence on earth, as in No. 100 for Magenard, who "*desivit in hac <c>nephosa caligine mundi*" ("he stopped living in this dark fog of the world"), with interference of the Greek that recalls the Paschal hymns of John Scotus Eriugena. Others are copies of inscriptions with one section in prose, with personal information, and another in verse, a homage to and prayer for the deceased (Nos. 93, 94, 96, 98, 99, 100, 110). In one of these cases (No. 100), sceptics were proven wrong, as it enabled the finding of the engraved plate, along with others, in the Carolingian cemetery discovered by accident during construction works on the abbey in 1693. It was conveniently transcribed by a correspondent of Mabillon, whose letters are still to be found in the Bibliothèque nationale de France in Paris.[21] However, the two texts do not correspond perfectly, which can help us to understand that inscribed poetic epigraphy and literary poetic epigraphy are often unfaithful adaptations of each other.

History and life at court surface, such as in the epitaph to Nithard, in No. 122, which recalls Eridadus killed by Danish arrows, or in No. 141 for Rudolf, likened to a candle in Charles's candelabra (in the year 866), whose following inscription introduces us to the emperor's *auletas*. A borderline case, where we may perhaps speak accurately of pseudoepigraphy, is *carmen* 166, which Micon writes in the form of an epitaph to an ostiary, who – as was the case in the monasteries – was also in charge of the wardrobe and furnishings. "*Hic quidam levita cubat sub tegmine ponti / custos ecclesiae fidus ubique bene, / sunt cui commissae vestes ac vasa sacrata*" ("Here a deacon rests, covered by the sea [?], who has always and everywhere been a good faithful caretaker of the church, to whom sacred vestments and furnishings were entrusted"). Following this is a prayer to the custodian priest not to let too many people in, so as to not "*sanctam commaculare larem*" ("to stain the holy house"). It is important for the place where the Lord's body is broken to stay as clean as possible. Then he asks, in return for these lines, for a *cuppa* ('cup') and "*nec non

---

[21] No. 100 for Hildeland, Carte Grenier XXVIII, f. 134: see L. DELISLE, *Le cabinet des manuscrits de la Bibliothèque Impériale: Étude sur la formation de ce dépôt comprenant les éléments d'une histoire de la calligraphie, de la miniature, de la reliure, et du commerce des livres à Paris avant l'invention de l'imprimerie*, 4 vols. (Paris, 1868-1881), 2, p. 332.

copello[22] *desuper imposito*", promising to "fight against" ("*contra certare parabo*": against intruders, we imagine) if the request is granted, and to worry less ("*stat mihi cura levis*") in case of refusal. The epitaph has a joking tone that does not easily permit serious interpretation, although it is possible that here, too, we are being sidetracked by preconceptions and it could be more easily understood if instead of considering it an epitaph, as Traube did, we interpret it as a plate of residence, similar to those for the abbot's house, obviously understanding *cubat* in the sense of 'rest' and not 'death'.

Vestments and Furniture

Other inscriptions refer instead to items of clothing, like the belt: these are Nos. 50 and 52, which ask God for a check, close-fitting as a belt, on the vices of the wearer, and which in the commentary that I prepared for the 1995 anthology I realised I could use as evidence not so much of – as Bernt proposes – a "good luck" ("*guter Wunsch*") as a relationship with reality that always keeps in mind the double terrestrial and spiritual dimension of all objects. And if each object finds a balance between its immediate function and that of its *signum*, in Christianised medieval culture this link to the hidden dimension also absorbs the magical properties generally associated with everyday matter, and in any case with the inscriptions that introduced them and communicated their *virtus* to their users and the general public. Other texts in this category concern furniture: on the bed (Nos. 54), where Christ is called on to chase away the deceitful devil, "*zabulus lubricus*"; on the dining table – where the consumption of food is constantly associated with the nourishment and purification of the soul – with the corresponding blessing of foods and beverages; or on the washbasin, where it is hoped that by washing one's face heavenly Grace washes the soul. Another double couplet on the bath (*Super lavacro*), or more likely on the washbasin (No. 86), instead focusses on the filthiness of the devil, who must not sully the purity of God's creation; No. 70 on the lantern reminds the 'bearer' (*gestator*) of the evangelical precept to not hide the light shut away in one's soul. Ten technically elaborate lines on the hourglass praise its maker, who constructed it thinking of lessening his brethren's labour. Again, in No. 134 *In quodam gestatorio*, an everyday object appears, a kind of sedan-chair

---

[22] Usually *copellum* is a measure of grain, but in texts from much later (thirteenth century); here it is probably a diminutive of *cuppa*.

where people sat, whose ability to shelter the user from bad weather is praised: "*decutit ardorem solis pluviamque ferenti / hoc tegmen capitis tempore disparili*" ("it repels the heat of the sun and the rain and for the wearer it offers this protection from unequal weather"). And the final adjective, used only very rarely and never in similar contexts, confirms that even the humblest and most ordinary of occasions were felt to be a chance for expressive experiment and stylistic risk-taking. No. 135 is carved or painted on a *muscarium*, a 'fly-swatter'[23] whose twofold use is celebrated: swatting flies and giving shade ("*nam muscas pellit umbraculumque facit*"), or rather making the user cool by fanning "*ferventi tempore*", when the air is muggy. Talking objects also include the little bed in No. 144 (where there is a prayer to banish the devil, whose influence on nocturnal dreams is clearly feared), the chalice of No. 129, which speaks in first person to remind us of its ability to quench thirst, the lamp made by the Abbess Hruodona (867), and again the lantern of No. 147, made of horn so that it will not break easily if dropped. Here, too, we see the emergence of a continuity of expressive schemes dating back to the riddle and already canonised, following Symphosius, as of the insular collections of early medieval *Aenigmata* and then of Alcuin.[24] But the recourse to poetic tradition as expressive repertoire should not make us think – as Bernt suggests – that these are variations on exactly the same subject: I think it more reasonable to hypothesise different inscriptions for objects that are different, though of the same type. It is typical of our literary, serial mentality to think that two texts about a lamp are two poetic variations on the same object. But it would be hoped that a monastery the size of Saint-Riquier had more than one lamp, each perhaps with its own personalised inscription, just as its cemetery housed many dead, each with a different epitaph. Even when different epitaphs are found for the same person, as transpires for Rudolf (Nos. 141, 142, and 143 on his lamp), it is highly possible that these are inscriptions engraved on different sides of the same tomb.[25] The use of the first person, which on the part of the object recalls the techniques used in riddles, is sometimes employed by the author of the *titulus*, who flaunts his own restoration work, such as No. 127, in which Odulf attests that he recovered a ciborium that was formerly "*manibus ... vastatus iniquis /*

---

[23] An everyday Latin term already used by Martial and Petronius.

[24] In particular, the self-description in the first person, and with a focus on the uses of the object: see STOTZ, "Beobachtungen zu metrischen Inschriften", p. 292.

[25] BERNT, *Das lateinische Epigramm*, p. 299 is of the same opinion.

nec non foedatus turpiter heu nimium" ("ruined and horribly devastated by wicked hands").

Locales

One of the most interesting roles of these epigraphic collections is that of a guide to the monastery premises, which the inscriptions allow us to walk through with a certain amount of detail, and not only in the spaces designated for sacred ceremonies, which are described by Angilbert in *De ecclesia Centulensi*. Apart from the locations of crypts and altars, discussed in depth by Bernard and Hubert, we find instead, in No. 88, one of the few attributed to the hospital worker Fredegard, three couplets *In sessione peregrinorum*, in which Christ is described as one of the seated strangers. It refers to the "*domus peregrinorum et pauperum*", an accommodation consisting – as set out by the famous Plan of Saint Gall – of a great hall with benches, sleeping quarters, and annexes with furnaces and pantries, very distinct from the *hospitale* for the rich who passed through, which was necessarily fitted with heating, rooms for servants, and stables. The same place, the hospital for the poor, is referred to in No. 119, which introduces a structural innovation to the epigraphic schemes in these collections: the dialogical epigraph. Here, the first speaker calls on the porter to give as much as he can, and Christ answers, seated in human aspect and foreign attire as in 88, blessing the cohort of brethren that serves him and hopes for the flight of the great Enemy. The dialogical scheme is highlighted with some refinement by the adoption of the epanaleptic couplet, in which the first half of the first hemistich is repeated in the second half of the second. In the form of a dialogue, this time with the Muse, an epitaph – or possibly an epicedium – is even introduced: No. 32 for young Leutgaudus, a student at the school. In fact, the initial couplet invites the *Fistula*, as the muse of song is often metonymised in this collection, to tell us the facts, the *causa*, of the young man. And the Muse, thus indicated by the manuscript, replies. She mourns for the youth's metric ability, which rivalled Porphyrion's (a choice indicative of a kind of education), and his goodness of spirit, and summarises his biographical information: born across the Seine, buried in this world on the calends of May in his eighteenth year. His soul entered Olympus, assisted by the merits of the saints to whom he often addressed prayers, which are referred to here with the Commodian formula *suppetia*.[26] The closing, with its appeal to the reader and call to prayer, seems to suggest a concrete destination for this epitaph, despite the originality of its approach.

Also dedicated to pilgrims and foreigners is No. 136 on a *domus peregrinis adtitulata*: "*illis ostensa qua manet humanitas*", a line that can be interpreted not so much in a social sense, as might be misunderstood by a modern reading that sees the stranger as the place where the very heart of humanity resides, but perhaps evangelically and theologically as the guise in which the humanity of Christ manifests itself most clearly – also through a coordinated reading with the other two inscriptions. This attention to *humanitas*, this time in a more cultural sense, moreover shines through to some degree in the epitaph of Flodegerus (No. 146), about whom it is remembered that "*humanis floruit eloquiis*".

No. 114 *In quadam mansione* brings us to a *domuncula*, also attested at Saint Gall, where the brethren who were gravely ill – today we would say terminal – withdrew to render their "*extremos spiritus*" unto Christ, assisted by the angel Gabriel who preserved them for heaven, where they were awaited by the *messores clypeati* (an imaginative metaphor for the Apostles[27] interested in their souls): this is the place that the Plan of Saint Gall also allocates to the seriously ill.[28]

One plaque even gives a warning on the use of a fruit cellar (No. 78 *In domo pomorum*). A curse *In mansione cuiusdam* (No. 70) wishes for any trespasser in the residence to turn deaf and mute, but also wishes for the resident to remain silent about all that he hears here.

No. 13, which the manuscript titles *Item similiter de prosperitate*, and which follows a couplet for a cross, is correctly attributed by Traube to a map divided into continents, which was probably found in the *scriptorium*:

hic mundi species perituri picta videtur,
partibus in ternis qui spatiatus inest,
quarum Asia primumque locum hinc Europa secundum
possidet extremum Africa deinde suum.

---

[26] Classical Latin *suppetiae*. *Carmina Centulensia* 32, 12, ed. L. TRAUBE, in: *PLAC* 3, pp. 265-368, at p. 310: "(*sanctorum*) *quorum etiam supplex suppetia saepe petebat*".

[27] From St. Augustine, *Sermones* 101, 3, ed. in: *PL* 38, col. 605 (evangelical image).

[28] P. RICHÉ, *La vie quotidienne dans l'empire carolingien* (Paris, 1975), trans. *La vita quotidiana nell'impero carolingio* (Rome, 1994), p. 230.

here we see the look of the transient world painted, the extension of which consists of three parts, of which Asia occupies the first place, then Europe the second and finally Africa has its own.

More conventional are the epigraph for the *scriptorium* (No. 5, *In domo scriptorum*, cited earlier), and also No. 15, which as usual laments the difficulty of the task of transcription, unknown to those who do not practice it:

Scribentis labor ignaris nimium levis extat,
sed durus notis sat manet atque gravis.

The effort of the writer seems light to those who do not know it, but for those who know, it remains hard and heavy.

No. 6 *In lectrico*, or 'On the lectern', according to the title corrected by Traube in a way that to me seems debatable and unnecessary;[29] and No. 111, *In quodam oratorio*, which again takes up the Alcuinian topos of slumber to be chased away on dark nights, cleansing the eyes from the gloomy haze of tiredness:

noctibus in furvis pulso iam corpore somno
et geminis detersa oculis caligine tetra,
quo sol iustitiae lucem tribuat renitentem
gratis in hac servis parva vigilantibus aede
(...)

in the dark nights, when sleep is rejected from the body and the dark mist has been washed from your eyes, so that the sun of justice grants it the riotous light, you serve for free in this little house of keepers

It is these very epigraphs, like many others, that lead us back to the transmission of a topical catalogue that falls into the category of 'monastic literary epig-

---

[29] The manuscript has "*In setico*", which Traube deleted and substituted: but *seticus* or *seticum*, attested from this era (*Recueil des actes de Charles II le Chauve, Roi de France*, ed. G. TESSIER *et al.*, 3 vols. (Paris, 1943-1955), 1, No. 58 p. 165 a. 844), means 'rural abode', as well as 'urban site', 'emplacement by water of a mill' (or of a brewery or furnace), in any case a workshop and warehouse. *Lectricum*, however, means 'lectern' and is completely inappropriate for the text's description: "*Hic quidam residet calamis ornatus honestis / cum quibus assidue haud laborare piget*" ("Here resides one adorned with decorous quills, with which he does not mind working assiduously").

raphy': the constant association of specific poetic motifs in specific spaces of the monastic site constitutes none other than the topical structure of a genre in the making. We cannot, in this instance, avoid thinking of Alcuin's inscription No. 98 IIII: "*discute torpentes, frater, tibi pollice somnos, / et contende prior tecta subire dei*" ("push away the torpor of sleep with your thumbs, brothers, and strive to enter the house of God first"). In Alcuin, the motif is also used in *carmen* 97, a beautiful lyric on slumber and its temptations, which prevent us from contemplating the lights of the stars, and urges the young monk to make use of "*collyrium salutis*" to win this difficult battle.

The Role of Alcuin

Alcuin of York, whom we find at the root of many patterns of Carolingian and medieval culture, is also the father of the Carolingian literary epigraph, as well as the public figure who most successfully managed to operate a fruitful osmosis between the motifs and styles of his epigraphic output and the generative nuclei of his intellectual and poetic world. His production of literary inscriptions includes dozens of pieces, which underlie all the other Carolingian collections – those of Hrabanus Maurus for Fulda and other locations, widely inspired by Alcuinian models, the one from Saint-Riquier, which even ends with an imitation of Alcuin, etc. – just as his biblical *titulus* (that is, a poem summarising the Bible) scheme was imitated, altered, and reproduced for centuries in competition with Theodulf's. In the Dümmler edition of Alcuin's *Carmina*, the epigraphs comprise Nos. 86-115, excluding the scriptural *tituli*, but many numbers contain several inscriptions (up to eighteen), and others are even scattered among the earlier nuclei of the edition (e.g. No. 64, *Fornax*), for a total of about 170 pieces, still excluding the *tituli librarii*, that is, the headlines of texts in manuscripts. The study of this material was brilliantly initiated by Luitpold Wallach in two chapters of *Alcuin and Charlemagne*, and by Günter Bernt on pages 194-202 of his monograph *Das lateinische Epigramm* (1968), but it still awaits special attention.[30]

We are all aware that there were important precedents before Alcuin. These include, on the one hand, the poetic models from the tradition that con-

---

[30] [A significant contribution has has been dedicated to this aspect of Alcuinian production by C. Treffort, "La place d'Alcuin dans la rédaction épigraphique carolingienne", *Annales de Bretagne et des Pays de l'Ouest* 111.3 (2004), pp. 353-369.]

nects Paulinus of Nola, and even before him, Damasus, the most imitated,[31] to Venantius Fortunatus; and on the other, the epigraphic compilations studied by Silvagni: the *Cantabrigiensis*, *Laureshamensis*,[32] and *Cantuariensis*, in addition to what is known as the *Martinellus* of Tours – handed down by a good 90 witnesses[33] – and to collections that are not specifically epigraphic, among them MS Paris, Bibliothèque nationale de France, latin 8071, almost all from the Carolingian period,[34] which proves the existence of an intense and widespread impulse to commission epigraphic apparatus. Some of these collections have been transmitted in manuscripts that also contain Alcuinian poems[35] and certainly served as models for epigraphic composition, as demonstrated by Bischoff's discovery in 1984 of a formulary for epitaphs by abbesses in the eighth century, drawn from royal inscriptions.[36] The driving force behind their composition were undoubtedly the royal commissions of various monasteries,

---

[31] According to HARTMANN, "Karolingische Gelehrte als Dichter und der Wissenstransfer am Beispiel der Epigraphik", p. 267, these imitations were mainly based on mnemonic processes. On this subject, see M. MASKARINEC, "The Carolingian afterlife of the Damasan inscriptions", *Early Medieval Europe* 23 (2015), pp. 129-160.

[32] MS Vatican, Bibliotheca Apostolica Vaticana, Pal. Lat. 833, which DE ROSSI, *Inscriptiones Christianae urbis Romae*, pp. 36-37, 95-07, 124-125, 142-143, 158-160, considers to be a merge of four different sources (one from Saint Peter between the seventh and eighth centuries; one North Italian from the end of the eighth century; one with parts from Rome, Ravenna, and Spoleto from the seventh century; one Roman, datable to between 821 and 846) and is traceable, according to H. FICHTENAU, "Karl der Große und das Kaisertum", *Mitteilungen des Instituts für Österreichische Geschichtsforschung* 61 (1953), pp. 257-334, at pp. 300-301, to Ricbod, the abbot of Lorsch, and according to B. BISCHOFF, *Die Abtei Lorsch im Spiegel seiner Handschriften* (Lorsch, 1989), p. 99, n. 52, to his successor Adalung and his journey to Rome in 823. Nick Everett wrote on the subject with new arguments (N. EVERETT, *Literacy in Lombard Italy 568-774* (Cambridge, 2003: *Cambridge Studies in Medieval Life and Thought*, 4th series 52), p. 243, and more specifically C. VIRCILLO FRANKLIN, "The epigraphic syllogae of BAV, Palatinus Latinus 833", in: *Roma, magistra mundi: Itineraria culturae medievalis: Mélanges offerts au Père L.E. Boyle à l'occasion de son 75e anniversaire*, ed. J. HAMESSE (Louvain-la-Neuve, 1998), pp. 975-990.

[33] Edition: F.J. GILARDI, *The Sylloge Epigraphica Turonensis de S. Martino*, PhD thesis Catholic University of America, Washington 1983, on which see L. PIETRI, "Une nouvelle édition de la Sylloge Martinienne de Tours", *Francia* 12 (1985), pp. 621-631.

[34] On these collections see BERNT, *Das lateinische Epigramm*, p. 196.

[35] *Inscriptiones christianase urbis Romae septimo saeculo antiquiores: Colligere coepit Iohannes Baptista De Rossi, complevit edidtque Angelus Silvagni: Nova series*, 1, *Inscriptiones incertae originis*, ed. A. SILVAGNI (Rome, 1922), pp. XVIII-XX: in particular the lost codices of St. Bertin and Regensburg, in addition to MS Munich, Bayerische Staatsbibliothek, Clm. 19140 (s. IX) (No. 21 of Silvagni). [On this, see now TREFFORT, "La place d'Alcuin", pp. 360-361.]

[36] B. BISCHOFF, "Epitaphienforme für Äbtissinen (Achtes Jahrhunderts)", in ID., *Anecdota novissima: Texte des 4. bis 16. Jahrhundert* (Stuttgart, 1984), pp. 150-153.

sometimes also confirmed by epistolary documentation.[37] As said in Chapter Six, Alcuin wrote for Saint-Amand, for Saint-Vaast, for Saint-Denis, definitely for Tours, for Fleury and Metz, for St. Avold,[38] for Corméry, for Nouaillé (Vienne, Nobilicum), for Sankt Peter in Salzburg, for Cologne, for Jumièges (Gemeticum), for Rome, for Gorze, and for other churches whose identities cannot be confirmed. This wide dissemination of poetic and epigraphic forms of communication extended his influence for a very long time across many genres: the *tituli librarii*, for one. And Cécile Treffort has shown that the models for the Alcuinian epigraphs came most of all from Alcuin's own *carmina*.[39]

A recurring setting, which obviously gives rise to iterated formulas, is the restoration of a sacred place, church, or altar, by an abbot or another commissioner who wishes to leave a record of the project.[40] Alcuin's poetic inscriptions introduce a gallery of founders and restorers, which makes up both a kind of prosopography of the revival – the twenty-seven cathedrals, the forty-seven and possibly more monasteries[41] of which the sources speak – as well as a geography of ecclesiastical commissioning. The most typical example of this subgenre, on which we will not linger, is No. 89,[42] *In ecclesia sancti Vedasti in pariete scribendum*, which describes, with devoted care, the restoration completed by Abbot Radon in around 790 after the monastery fire. Alcuin's gaze

---

[37] The monks of Saint-Vaast, e.g. (*Alcuini Carmina*, 88 [*recte* 89], ed. E. DÜMMLER, in: *PLAC* 1, pp. 169-351, at pp. 308-313, with p. 308, n. 1 referring to *Alcuini Epistolae*, 296, ed. E. DÜMMLER, in: *Epistolae Karolini aevi* 2, ed. E. DÜMMLER *et al.* (Berlin, 1895: *MGH EPP* 4), pp. 18-481, at pp. 454-455; but see also the marginal notes on ff. 85 and 87ff. of MS Douai, Bibliothèque municipale, 753 (s. XII). [On is, see TREFFORT, "La place d'Alcuin", pp. 360-361.]

[38] On the river Moselle, not far from Saarbrücken.

[39] C. TREFFORT, *Mémoires carolingiennes: L'épitaphe entre célébration mémorielle, genre littéraire et manifeste politique (milieu VIIIe-début XIe siècle)* (Rennes, 2007), p. 150. Of the same opinion is Robert Favreau, in a discussion quoted by HARTMANN, "Karolingische Gelehrte als Dichter und der Wissenstransfer am Beispiel der Epigraphik", p. 265, n. 60.

[40] It is interesting that this activity of architectural renovation is associated with the cultural entrepreneurship of the first decades of Charlemagne, and remains a sign of this effort in many ways—from the transcription of codices to the renovation of a crypt, to the repair of a lamp, to the reinstatement of Latin orthography, and all the way to the reorganisation of the garden at Reichenau, which Walahfrid Strabo would then describe as a long and involved process, "*stirpibus antiquis priscae renovare iuventae* [...] *culturae impulsus amore*" (*Hortulus*, ed. E. DÜMMLER, in: *PLAC* 2, p. 337, vv. 52 and 55). A formulaic epithet that seems made precisely to seal the great effort of the Carolingian century and summarises its unique impetus.

[41] J. CONTRENI, "The Carolingian Renaissance", in: *Renaissances before the Renaissance: Cultural Revivals of Late Antiquity and the Middle Ages*, ed. W.T. TREADGOLD (Stanford, 1984), pp. 56-74, at p. 65.

[42] Erroneously 88 in: *Alcuini Carmina*, ed. DÜMMLER.

brushes over the gates, the altars covered in precious metals, the *pallia* hung on the walls, and the lamps, the sacred silver furnishings, even the beautiful paraments for the priests, because that kind of decorum and beauty – which confers dignity on the offering of faith and the institution that mediates it – must exist everywhere, in each aspect and element of the surroundings. A historian would find materials and inspiration for socio-archaeological itineraries here; a hagiologist would identify sets and subsets of recurring saints or isolated cults. A scholar of literature, if able to look past the repetitiveness of these schemes, which were later adopted in a reductive and obsessive manner by Hrabanus Maurus, could find a gateway to the relationship of writing with everyday reality, whose fading from the literature of the period is often lamented. Alcuin, who reveals an unexpected richness of spirit – in all senses of the word – to those who spend time with him, does not disappoint. Moreover, even studies of the schemes would provide literary material: to give just one example, the identification of the Hieronymian formulaic epithet which is almost always used to designate the apostle John in his epigraphs, *symmista*, or 'initiated into the same mysteries',[43] helps us to see which, of the many possibilities, was the primary image that this St. Alcuin and his imitators were proposing to the public, to the reader who was regularly addressed and often involved in the act of worship. And even the title *In pariete scribendum* reveals the stage at which these epigraphs were recorded in the manuscript: before being engraved on stone and wood or painted on a wall and fabrics, that is, according to the author's own written template, as we can see from the use of the gerundive, frequent in these formulas. But much more compelling are the free or unexpected interpretations, such as No. 92, that we also mentioned in Chapter Six, which seems to be an inscription for individual bathing in a wooden washtub: the text seems initially to hide the riddle structure, both because of the first person approach and the actual recall of an epigram-riddle by Symphosius, thus present in Alcuin's poetic memory:[44]

Nudus erat hospes, placeat cui ludere mecum
atque fovere meo corpora fonte sua.

---

[43] *Alcuini Carmina*, 90, 19; 109, III, 9; and 110, V, ed. DÜMMLER, pp. 327, 335, and 341; Hrabanus Maurus, *Carmina,* 42, I, 5, ed. E. DÜMMLER, in: *PLAC* 2, p. 209.

[44] Symphosius, *Aenigmata*, 90, 3, in: CCSL 133A, ed. F. GLORIE (Turnhout, 1968), p. 711: "*Non est nuda domus, sed nudus convenit hospes*" (the famous riddle quoted in the *Historia Apollonii regis Tyri*, c. 42 and *Gesta Romanorum*, c. 153). Symphosius, for example, was clearly inspired by No. 64, for a furnace, which speaks in first person without naming itself.

*Qui pisces quondam gelidis generavit in undis,
nunc calidus homini forte minister erit
(...).*

The guest was naked, who likes to play with me and warm his body to my spring. What once spawned fish in freezing waters may now be a warm servant to that man (...).

But the recollection of what once carried the wood, that is: boats, and is now in turn poured into the wood, that is: the tub, and earlier flowed over meadows and is now shut in at home, is an elegiac reproduction of a play on the typical ambivalence of riddles. While the prayer to distract the eyes from what the hand of the first man was covering is a call to modesty, for the poem's addressee, whom we discover only on the last line to be the *puer*, the serving boy. This appeal, as usual, brings the reading of medieval Latin lines back to its double horizon, but without the use of doctrinaire devices, and instead with an entirely Alcuinian lightness: "*hoc natura docet, hoc et persuasit honestas*" ("this teaches nature, this has convinced us to do modesty").[45] At Saint-Denis and Corbie, there is a record of baths located near the cloister, whose use must have been overseen by the abbot, as required by the monastic regulations of 817;[46] and in Murbach it seems that the statutes ultimately called for the substitution of the communal bath with an individual one, of which the privileged Alcuin is evidently speaking.

Similarly distinctive – and I would say elegant – touches can be found in No. 93, the *titulus* of a place, perhaps an oratorium where youths were invited to learn songs of praise from the voice of a master and, more generally, to dedicate themselves to studying while they were young, because

nec bene namque senex poterit vel discere, postquam

---

[45] In the well-received P. RICHÉ, *La vie quotidienne dans l'empire carolingien* (Paris, 1973), p. 200-201, Pierre Riché, who nonetheless does not use epigraphic material, pauses to remind us that, contrary to popular belief, the bath was a well-established medieval habit, especially on Saturdays, at least for the Germanic peoples.

[46] RICHÉ, *La vie quotidienne, ibid.*; specifics on the monastic setting: H. ATSMA, "Die christlichen Inschriften aus Gallien als Quelle für Kloster und Klosterbewohner bis zum Ende des VI. Jahrhunderts", *Francia* 4 (1976), pp. 1-57, and A. DAVRIL and E. PALAZZO, *La vie des moines au temps des grandes abbayes, Xe-XIIIe siècles* (Paris, 2000); these two contributions nonetheless entirely omit the period from the seventh to the ninth centuries that we are considering from their examination.

tondenti[47] *in gremium* [sic!] *candida barba cadit*

not even the old man will be able to learn it well, after the white beard has fallen on his lap while he shaves it.

This suddenly presents us with a scene from a Carolingian barber's, but continues in a game of exhortations crossed with images of old age and youth, which in my opinion indicates the loss of a couplet, just as on l. 11 there is a mechanical lacuna, and which above all introduces us to one of the liveliest emotional currents in Alcuinian poetics.

A similar gap, if it is one, concerns epigraph No. 105, part V, which in the text conspicuously repeats, among others, several passages of No. 104 IV, where the brethren are invited to enter singing, but with a drastic distinction between the "*amicus ovans*", the only one authorised to enter, and the stranger, here qualified with adjectives describing the devil: *fur, falsiloquus, alienus*.[48] The youths must hurry ("*currite, vos, iuvenes, Christi properantes ad aulam*", l. 10) and not let themselves be taken in by the pleasure of jest, carnal love, play, *petulantia*,[49] or laughter, dedicating themselves to sacred knowledge until they have come of age, an obsession that anyone perusing Alcuin's poetry will discover recurs like a leitmotif of his internal elegy. But the titbits of the Alcuinian catalogue – which is familiar with serial production, when necessary, but if desired can deploy unexpected creativity – reveal, as in the case of the washtub, poetry dedicated to spaces of everyday use. No. 96, for example, is divided into two parts. The first focusses on the dormitory (*In dormiturio*), which is formally an invocation so that the one who subdues the force of the winds and waves grants the brethren sweet rest, and appeases the fears awakened by the black power of the devil:

et quos inmittit somno vis nigra timores
conpescat clemens domini, rogo, dextra potentis.

and I pray that the lenient hand of the mighty Lord will repress the fears that the black force inserts into sleep.

---

[47] I am using the lesson from the codex: the edition of Du Chesne has *tondentem* instead.

[48] But not identifiable simply as the devil because of an indefinite pronoun on l. 5: "*non fur, falsiloquus quisquam, non mente maligna*".

[49] 'Impudence': Gregory the Great, *Homiliae in euangelia*, 9, 1, ed. R. ÉTAIX (Turnhout, 1999: CCSL 141), p. 59: "*se a carnis petulantia ... custodiunt*".

But the most curious section is the second part, on the toilet (*In latrinio*), which urges the reader to refrain from the sin of gluttony due to the unpleasant results that this vice may provoke. This is far from being, as some have written, an expression of a proximity to life that borders on the grotesque, and that cannot escape a comic – though unintended[50] – effect. It is an essentially exceptional example in ancient and medieval epigrams – with the possible exception of three brutally moralistic texts by Agathias (*Anthologia Palatina* IX, 642-644), written to celebrate the construction of a public latrine in Myrina[51] – that I believe demonstrates how Alcuin, with the same ease with which he confronted all aspects of reality, managed to put his own Christian culture on the line, understanding it not as a doctrine but as a hermeneutical resource, by reading a transcendent meaning into all elements – even the humblest – of life, and by reconstructing a way of being, a behaviour that this acknowledgement entailed. Paradoxically, the most realistic point of Alcuinian poetry actually becomes its most allegorical manifestation, just like, less daringly, Micon's inscriptions on the belt. Particularly as this kind of focus is not an isolated incident in the author's consciousness, but finds at least one parallel in a letter from the abbot to his protégé Dadon,[52] where he returns to the subject with the same thought: "*quod comedisti et bibisti hodie stercus est, quod non dico tangere, sed etiam horrescis videre*" ("what you have eaten and drunk today is dung, which I do not say to touch, but it disgusts even to see"). The moral that was, however, obtained from the epigram was not understood so much as a statement on the insignificance of the body, in the Neoplatonic sense that is reflected in the expressionistic violence of Dante's *Inferno* 28, 26-27, but as an exhortation to sobriety, analogous to the original use of the motif in Cynic-Stoic reasoning.

---

[50] BERNT, *Das lateinische Epigramm*, p. 200.
[51] *Anthologia Palatina*, ed. H. BECKBY, 4 vols. (Munich, 1965²), 3, pp. 384-386. The content of 642 can be summarised thus: 'all the luxury of mortals and their costly nutrients excreted here have lost the charm that they had shortly before. Pheasants and fish, meats ground in a mortar, a throng of mixed foods that seduce the palate, everything here becomes filth, the stomach expels everything that the famished gullet has received. It is too late for everyone to recognise that by glorifying their senseless humours they have purchased mud for the price of gold'. 643: Stomach ache for gluttony. 644: Macarismos for the frugal countryman, little fed but quick of limb and able to defecate rapidly. Unhappy are the rich, who live in plenty and prefer feasts to health.
[52] *Alcuini Epistolae*, 65, ed. E. DÜMMLER, in: *Epistolae Karolini aevi* 2, ed. E. DÜMMLER *et al.* (Berlin, 1895: MGH EPP 4), pp. 18-481, at pp. 107-109, in particular p. 108.

A similar, although milder, warmth is found also in some of the epigrams composed for the monastery of Fleury, among them No. 101 II, for the *mansa* ('house') bought by Abbot Magulfus, a church dedicated to St. Peter and St. Benedict. Here we find a note to the reader – inserted, as is often the case, during the call to the dedicatory prayer – that introduces us to the ways in which one might avail oneself of epigraphic texts, in other words reading out loud: "*Tu quoque, qui titulum recitas, rogitare memento, / obsecro pro patre Magulfo, lector amice*" ("You too, who read this inscription aloud, remember to pray please for Father Magulfus, friend reader").

The joking side of Alcuin's personality and of a certain tone of Carolingian poetry resurfaces in another epigraph from or for Fleury (No. 105 II), a multi-assonant couplet, probably inspired by Anglo-Saxon traditions, which also presents us with a lexical *hapax*:

semper in aeternum faciat haec clocula tantum
carmina, sed resonet nobis bona clocca cocorum.

always, forever this bell only be chanting chants, but let the good bell of the cooks ring for us.

In question here is the hand bell, since if *clocca* has meant 'bell' as far back as the letters of Boniface and Lullus,[53] according to Erhardt-Siebold[54] *clocula* is not just a random diminutive but specifically suggests the *Klosterglocke*, called upon to make songs (sacred hymns, we imagine) ring out forever, and likened rather unsuccessfully to the apparently just as appreciated serving bell, the *clocca cocorum* or *Speiseglocke*.[55]

We are presented with the very same choice between stomach and spirit in No. 111, which sources transmit with texts about the church of Sankt Peter in Salzburg, but which the editor rightly separated from the group:[56] here Alcuin

---

[53] Boniface, *Epistulae*, 76 and 116, ed. in: *Die Briefe des Heiligen Bonifatius und Lullus*, ed. M. TANGL (Berlin, 1916: MGH *Epistolae selectae* 1), pp. 158-159, at p. 159 and pp. 250-252 at p. 251; see also Willibald, *Vita Bonifacii*, c. 8, ed. in: *Vitae Sancti Bonifatii Archiepiscopi Moguntine*, ed. W. LEVISON (Hanover and Leipzig, 1905: MGH SS *rerum Germanicarum in usum scholarum*), p. 53, and *Alcuini Epistolae*, 226, ed. DÜMMLER, p. 370.

[54] E. EHRHARDT-SIEBOLD, *Die lateinischen Rätsel der Angelsachsen: Ein Beitrag zur Kulturgeschichte Altenglands* (Heidelberg, 1925), p. 138.

[55] EHRHARDT-SIEBOLD, *Die lateinischen Rätsel*, p. 133, No. 285.

[56] *Alcuini Carmina*, 111, ed. DÜMMLER, p. 343: "*Hic tu per stratam pergens subsiste, uiator, / Versiculos paucos studiosa perlege mente. / Inuia, quam cernis, duplici ditatur honore:*

places the *viator* who passes *per stratam* at a crossroads that is not the one between rhetoric and philosophy, but rather between the tavern and the library, as we understand from the text, although it is missing a line. Alcuin leaves the reader with a free choice between "*aut potare merum sacros aut discere libros*", drinking wine or reading books (holy, of course), "*elige quod placeat*" ("choose what you like"). But know that if you wish to drink, you will pay, while if you wish to learn, you will not spend a penny: "*gratis quod quaeris habebis*". And this should not surprise us either: at Saint-Riquier, which due to its extension actually resembled something closer to a village than an abbey, the 2500 individual houses were grouped into neighbourhoods, called *vici*, specialised according to trade as in medieval cities (founders, blacksmiths, shoemakers, tanners, cellarmen, cobblers, etc.[57]) and one of them was appointed the *vicus cauponum*. But taverns were also reported at Saint-Vaast and Saint-Philibert-de-Granlieu, and also at Compiègne: it is just that we were used to thinking of them as destinations for pilgrims and merchants, particularly during the abbey market, and not as an alternative option for uncertain monks.[58] Speaking in No. 112 of an "*aula pulchra*", whose owner he addresses, Alcuin invites the "*viator praegelidus*", paralysed by the cold but nonetheless *ovans*, 'elated' (usually 'singing'), as all the figures of this Alcuinian Christmas crib necessarily are – to "*sua membra fovere*", to warm himself in a house protected by the cross but where the door is always open to friends seeking the heart of the father, "*haec pateat caris iam ianua semper amicis / qui laeto quaerant pectore namque patrem*". And this reminds us of the existence of a calefactory, called the *pisalis*, adjacent to the medieval cloisters, which receives the heat from an underlying *hypocaustum*, as at Saint Gall.[59]

Of course, this geography of taverns and washtubs, kitchens and toilets, flyswatters and warming rooms, is not part of the mental imagery that we typically associate with noble Carolingian culture. However, out of these marginal categories, this paratextual literature, an everyday landscape emerges that the generation's grandiose intellectualism tends to obscure from sight. What we

---

/ *Haec ad cauponem ducit potare uolentem.* / 5 *Elige quod placeat tibi nunc iter, ecce uiator,* / *Aut potare merum, sacros aut discere libros.* / *Si potare uelis, nummos praestare debebis,* / *Discere si cupias. Gratis, quod quaeris habebis*".

[57] RICHÉ, *La vie quotidienne*, p. 51.

[58] E. LESNE, *Histoire de la propriété ecclésiastique en France*, 6 vols. (Lille, 1910-1943), 6, *Les Églises et les monastères, centres d'accueil, d'exploitation et de peuplement*, pp. 391 and 414.

[59] RICHÉ, *La vie quotidienne*, p. 201.

needed to discover was Alcuin's warmth, first imitated and then parodied in the *Carmina Centulensia*.

What might be the apex of this interpenetration between the requirements of the local setting, Alcuin's expressive repertoire, and the liveliest currents of his poetry is perhaps glimpsed in No. VI of series 104, dedicated to the hermitage of Corméry (Cormaricum), near his locale of Tours – eight miles from Saint-Martin to be precise, as Alcuin specifies in a letter to Archbishop Arno.[60] Here, the author contrasts the *cellula* built in the hermitage in the forest (*"silvestri... in heremo"*) with the *"nova culmina"* ("new roofs") that arise in the *"urbes egregiae"* ("magnificent towns"), in the cities that were already sung of in the books of the ancient bards but were clearly undergoing expansion or re-urbanisation during the years of the Carolingian impetus. Alcuin, without lingering on the contrast, pauses to celebrate the peace of the cloister where the *"theosophica iura"*, the sacred studies, flourish and where the *"clancula dicta senum"*, the mysterious words of the ancients, are contemplated. While in the city schools – and this seems to be a portrait of the twelfth century – they sell and turn over thousands of lies, also from the ancients and created to trick their fellow men, here religious research is done, *"quaeritur hic verum ... sacrum"*, and done through a *"famen pacificum"* ("peaceful speech"), where even the tone of the message hints at the option of a radical and perfect life, and the monastery becomes a school of the arts, *"syllogistica claustra"*. While the big cities are dominated by a drunkenness that drowns intelligence, and the servant barely manages to carry his master back in his arms (a painting worthy of Bruegel), in the woodland hermitage long fasts continue until evening, and only sacred foods nourish the hearts of the scholars.[61]

Given this epigraph, it is hard not to think of Alcuin's famous ode to his *cella*, which Waddell called "the loveliest" lyric of the medieval period, the abbot's farewell to an unspecified monastery, perhaps the one where he spent his youth, his *"sacra iuventus"*. Appearing both there and here, for those who still had doubts about the author of the texts, are the same positive terminology (*sophia, sacri libri*) and above all the same tone of voice: *"pacificis sonuit vocibus atque animis"* ("the place resounded with peaceful words and minds", with a lovely zeugma) in the abandoned monastery, the sign of an irretrievable age, and *"famine pacifico"* in our epigraph from Corméry. It is the formulation of a monastic ideal deeply rooted in a rural context and in the model of a com-

---

[60] *Alcuini Epistolae*, 184, ed. DÜMMLER, pp. 308-310, at p. 309.
[61] I take up and repeat some passages from Chapter Six, pp. 138-139.

munity of studying, a school, that small sacred city that finds one of its most unexpected expressions in the affection with which the poetic inscriptions – a sample of which we have leafed through here – guide us through the spaces of that existential model. These epigraphs leave behind a trace that, much more than the treatises or theological and political output that until now have attracted so much interest, restores to us the lives of men who dwelt in the silent corners of history; it helps us reconstruct the link that unites the conditions of material life with their echoes on the spiritual plain and in the individual states of mind of figures who seem so far away. The entry of poetic motifs into epigraphic composition corresponds somehow to the very same cultural impetus that attests, through graphic evolution, to the influence of literary standards on the epigraphic writing of the period, consistent with the direction common to all Carolingian movement: on the one hand, the recovery of writing as a public form of communication and privileged instrument for the acquisition and sharing of knowledge, and on the other, its reflection in the concept of reality as writing, which we may find our way around only insofar as it is translated into a linguistic sign.

Chapter 12

New Forms of Verse Collections in the Carolingian Laboratory

In the nineties the matter of the poetic collection was much debated, especially in Italy and France. During this period entire books and conferences were dedicated to lyric anthologies, to *canzonieri* ('songbooks'), and anything that fits into the category of *macrotesto*. Inspired by Gérard Genot in 1972[1] and created by Maria Corti 1975,[2] this was a privileged conceptual tool for depicting the cultural outline and literary canons of a time or setting. It was researched, in relation to medieval Latin studies, by Peter Dronke[3], Pascale Bourgain,[4] Michele Camillo Ferrari,[5] Jean-Yves Tilliette,[6] Sam Barrett,[7] A.G.

---

[1] G. GENOT, "Strutture narrative della poesia lirica", *Paragone* 18 (1967), pp. 35-52.

[2] M. CORTI, "Testi o macrotesto? I racconti di *Marcovaldo*", *Strumenti critici* 27 (1975), pp. 182-197. The whole story in A. VITI, "Macrotesto: Original conceptualization and possible extensions", in: *Cycles, Recueils, Macrotexts: The Short Story Collection in Theory and Practice*, ed. E. D'HOKER and B. VAN DEN BOSSCHE = *Interférences littéraires / Literaire interferenties* 12 (2014), pp. 105-117.

[3] P. DRONKE, "Le antologie liriche del Medioevo latino", *Critica del testo* 2.1 (1999), pp. 101-117.

[4] P. BOURGAIN, "Les chansonniers lyriques latins", in: *Lyrique romane médiévale: La tradition des chansonniers: Actes du Colloque de Liège, Liège-Bibliothèque de la Faculté de Philosophie et Lettres*, ed. M. TYSSENS (Liège, 1991), pp. 61-84; EAD., "Les recueils carolingiens de poésie rythmique", in: *De Tertullien aux mozarabes: Mélanges offerts à J. Fontaine*, ed. L. HOLTZ and J. FREDOUILLE (Paris, 1992), pp. 119-127. The best publication on songbooks is: *'Liber', 'Fragmenta', 'Libellus' prima e dopo Petrarca: In ricordo di d'Arco Silvio Avalle, Seminario Internazionale di Studi, Bergamo, 23-25 October 2003*, ed. F. LO MONACO, L.C. ROSSI, and N. SCAFFAI (Florence, 2006). See also *Convivio: estudios sobre la poesía de cancionero*, ed. V. BELTRÁN, V. BELTRÁN PEPIÓ, and J. PAREDES NÚÑEZ (Granada, 2006).

[5] M.C. FERRARI, *Il 'Liber sanctae crucis' di Rabano Mauro: Testo – immagine – contesto*,

Rigg[8] and a few others. In the late nineties I had the opportunity to work for about a decade on Carolingian collections of rhythmic poetry,[9] after which my interest shifted to twelfth-century anthologies.[10]

Late Antiquity

We are usually told that the early Middle Ages is marked by school collections such as the *Anthologia Latina*, best represented in the *codex Salmasianus* (MS Paris, Bibliothèque nationale de France, latin 10318).[11] This gathering of 380 epigraphs, riddles, ekphraseis, rhetorical exercises, love poems, and mythological poems, which originated from fifth century Africa, would influence all subsequent poetry. To this, we can add authors' collections such as Venantius Fortunatus's in Merovingian Gaul and Eugenius of Toledo's in Visigothic Spain. On the other hand, Bede's *Liber hymnorum* and *Liber epigrammaton* are lost.[12]

---

with a preface by C. LEONARDI (Berne etc., 1999), pp. 101-127 and 167-227.

[6] J.-Y. TILLIETTE, "Le sens et la composition du florilège de Zürich", in: *Non recedet memoria eius: Beiträge zur lateinischen Philologie des Mittelalters im Gedenken an Jakob Werner (1861-1944): Akten der wissenschaftlichen Tagung vom 9-10 September 1994 am Mittellateinischen Seminar der Universität Zürich*, ed. P. STOTZ and M.C. FERRARI (Berne etc., 1995), pp. 147-167.

[7] S. BARRETT, "Music and writing: On the compilation of Paris Bibliothèque Nationale lat. 1154", *Early Music History* 16 (1997), pp. 55-96.

[8] A.G. RIGG, "Medieval poetic anthologies I", *Medieval Studies* 39 (1977), pp. 281-330; II, *ibid*. 40 (1978), pp. 387-407; III, *ibid*. 41 (1979) pp. 468-505. [See now G. DINKOVA-BRUUN, "Latin poetic anthologies from the later Middle Ages", in: *Collecting, Organizing and Transmitting Knowledge: Miscellanies in Late Medieval Europe*, ed. S. CORBELLINI, G. MURANO, and G. SIGNORE (Turnhout, 2018), pp. 39-49.]

[9] F. STELLA, "Le raccolte di ritmi precarolingi e la tradizione manoscritta di Paolino d'Aquileia: Nuclei testuali e rapport di trasmissione", *Studi medievali* 39 (1998), pp. 809-832. I apologise for the frequent references to my own contributions on such topics.

[10] F. STELLA and A. ISCARO, "Estratti poetici di nuova identificazione nel ms. Zürich, C 58/275: Parte I: *Carmina Rivipullensia*, Alberto Stadense, Abelardo *Carmen in Astralabium*, Enrico di Augsburg e altro", in: *Le rigueur et la passion: Mélanges en l'honneur de Pascale Bourgain*, ed. C. GIRAUD and D. POIREL (Turhout, 2016), pp. 381-396.

[11] A vast literature exists on this collection. See, e.g. L. ZURLI, *The Manuscript Transmission of the 'Anthologia Latina'* (Hildesheim, 2017); a dedicated journal called *AL: Rivista di studi sull'Anthologia Latina* has been published since 2010.

[12] [The latest reconstruction in *Bede's Latin Poetry*, ed. M. LAPIDGE (Oxford, 2019).]

The Carolingian Age: Authors' Collections

In the Carolingian age, the typology of verse collections was much richer and more varied than has been previously described. We often read that collections made by authors are relatively infrequent, and this reminds us of the anachronism of reading early medieval texts according to the romantic, modern category of the author. Nevertheless, the idea of a total absence of authors' collections in Carolingian times derives more from the loss of crucial witnesses than from an objective census. In the first generation, that of Charlemagne, Alcuin's verses were probably collected after his death in the codex of Saint-Bertin, now lost, but transcribed by André Du Chesne in 1617, and were anthologised, perhaps by his pupil Arno, bishop of Salzburg, in another lost manuscript from Regensburg, which Frobenius was still able to read in 1816.[13]

Although many manuscripts[14] contain series of poems by Theodulf of Orléans, there are no anthologies or complete collections. We should also mention that a complete collection by this poet, whose work was much less homogenous than Alcuin's, would have made little sense given the wide difference of genres as well as the use and destination of his *carmina*. Yet some traces have been left of *Carmina Theodulphi continua serie*.[15]

The manuscript transmission of Paul the Deacon[16] and Paulinus of Aquileia[17] was very fragmented and was carried out according to destination or occasional criteria, because much of their verse consisted of relational or contextual compositions such as epigraphs, letters, and so on. But even in that case, sequences of more texts exist in poetical mixed anthologies such as MS Leipzig, Universitätsbibliothek, Rep. I 74, from the tenth century, which gathered together poetry from Ovid to Carolingians, and MS Paris, Bibliothèque nationale de France, latin 528, from the ninth century, often in a grammatical

---

[13] D. BULLOUGH, "Alcuin's cultural influence: The evidence of the manuscripts", in: *Alcuin of York: Scholar at the Carolingian Court: Proceedings of the Third Germania Latina Conference held at the University of Groningen, May 1995*, ed. L.A.J.R. HOUWEN and A.A. MACDONALD (Groningen, 1998), pp. 1-26.

[14] See *Theodulfi Carmina*, in: PLAC 1, ed. E. DÜMMLER, pp. 437 ff.

[15] *Theodulfi Carmina* 2, ed. DÜMMLER, p. 452, vv.1-12 (cited by FERRARI, *Il 'liber sanctae crucis'*, p. 175).

[16] I am obliged to refer to my census in F. STELLA, "La poesia di Paolo Diacono: Nuovi manoscritti e attribuzioni incerte", in: *Paolo Diacono: Uno scrittore fra tradizione longobarda e rinnovamento carolingio: Atti del convegno internazionale Cividale del Friuli-Udine 6-9 maggio 1999*, ed. P. CHIESA (Udine, 2000), pp. 551-574.

[17] STELLA, "Le raccolte di ritmi precarolingi".

context. Yet Moduin of Autun (*Eclogues* Praef. 5) speaks explicitly of two *libelli* comprising his eclogues, and this publication by *libelli* would be, together with the sending of individual letters, the most common way of transmitting poetry in the Middle Ages.[18]

Evidence of general collections occurs more often for the second generation, in the time of Louis the Pious. These collections were put together shortly after the death of their authors, probably by their collaborators or pupils. For example, the elegant verses of Walahfrid Strabo are transmitted on a large scale in MS Saint Gall, Stiftsbibliothek 869, which includes the opera omnia except the *Hortulus*, and may have been commissioned for the Aachen court, and in MS Saint Gall, Stiftsbibliothek 899.[19] Another collection, coming from Fulda, the abbey where Walahfrid continued his studies, was transmitted in MS Vatican, Reg. lat. 469. The Sangallensis 869, dated a few decades after the author's death, may have been close to an authorial project.

Two collections of Hrabanus Maurus remain, besides the iconopoetic *Liber de laudibus sanctae crucis*: one from Fulda, probably drawn up in the monastic school where Hrabanus was abbot and still read by Christopher Brower in 1617, and another copied in MS Einsiedeln, Stiftsbibliothek 266, which is incomplete.[20] For Hrabanus, as for Alcuin, the original impetus for the assembly of a collection came from his school.

In the third generation, that of Lothair and Charles the Bald, the collections start matching real self-fashioned projects promoted by the living authors. This was the case for Wandalbert of Prüm, who died in about 870, and dedicated to the clerk Otricus of Cologne a poetical *libellus* about structures of time in different metres, consisting of a *martyrologium* (liturgical time), a poem about the months (astronomical time), and an *hexameron* (biblical time), whose parts were also handed down separately. The primary dedication is significant, because it introduces a paratext articulated in *invocatio*, *allocutio*, *commendatio*, and *propositio*. In this case, according to Ferrari,[21] the lack of a title shows that

---

[18] Some hints in *La poesia carolingia*, ed. F. STELLA (Florence, 1995), pp. 386-390. [For the bibliography on the numerous manuscripts we will deal with, we refer to the indications of Mirabile Web (<mirabileweb.it>), avoiding accumulating titles that would quickly need to be inegrated and updated.]

[19] On both codices, see the updated literature to be found on the Mirabile website: <http://sip.mirabileweb.it/manuscript/sankt-gallen-stiftsbibliothek-869-manuscript/3511> and <http:// sip.mirabileweb.it/manuscript/sankt-gallen-stiftsbibliothek-899-manuscript/99>.

[20] See FERRARI, *Il 'liber sanctae crucis'*, pp. 179 ff.

[21] FERRARI, *Il 'liber sanctae crucis'*, pp. 197-198.

the author did not make distinctions between text and manuscript, but in my opinion the relevant fact is the consistent organisation of the whole, which reveals a significant cultural project edited by the author himself.[22]

In those same years the great philosopher John Scotus Eriugena gathered, presumably in chronological order, according to Michael Herren,[23] a series of theological Greco-Latin poems whose main manuscript date from his lifetime (MSS Vatican, Reg. lat. 1587 and 1709).

Simultaneously, Audradus Modicus, a suffragan of Sens famous for his political visions, gathered together his poetical production in a thirteen-book work brought to Pope Leo IV (894) to support his bishopric's cause against Hincmar. It consisted of hagiographical and theological poems with an original narrative thread.[24] As for Wandalbert, here too the presence of *seuils*, or 'paratexts', displays a comprehensive plan. But its audience did not prove ready to receive this kind of codicological self-monumentalisation, since the poems, though jointly collected, were then transmitted in groups or single texts in different manuscripts, exactly as was the case for the poets of the first generation.

Towards the end of the Carolingian age, Notker the Stammerer, who died in 912, published his *liber ymnorum*. This collection featured a new poetic form, the *sequentia*, whose graphical achievement, independent of the versification system, is evident in MS Einsiedeln, Stiftsbibliothek 121 (tenth century). This example allows us to see the formation process: the texts were first written *in rotulas*, that is in loose sheets, and were then put together in a *codicellus* by master Marcel for the students of the school. The liturgical genre itself lies beyond our interests, but the method described could be analogous to the one used for non-liturgical collections.[25]

---

[22] Literature and description in *La poesia carolingia*, ed. F. STELLA, pp. 120-121 and 441-442.

[23] *Johannis Scotti Eriugenae Carmina,* ed. M.W. HERREN (Dublin, 1993: *Scriptores Latini Hiberniae* 12).

[24] Analysis of the manuscript transmission in Audrado Modico, *Il fonte della vita*, ed. F. STELLA (Florence, 1991), pp. 65-72.

[25] W. VON DEN STEINEN, *Notker der Dichter und seine geistige Welt* (Berne, 1948); M. HUGLO, *Les sources du plain-chant et de la musique médiévale* (London, 2014), pp. 20 and 84; and A.E. PLANCHAT, *Embellishing the Liturgy: Tropes and Polyphony* (London and New York, 2017), p. 87.

Local Collections

In late Carolingian times a new kind of anthology appeared: the homogenous anthology compiled as a collective work by different poets from the same area, which therefore gave voice to a community of authors and readers. The *Carmina Centulensia*, 170 poems from the monastery of Saint-Riquier, not yet studied by scholars, are preserved in MS Brussels, Bibliothèque Royale 10470-73 (from Gembloux) and partially in MS Brussels, Bibliothèque Royale 10859, both having once formed part of a single manuscript. The project seems to be composed of four sections: two, not in succession and dated between 825 and 853, by Mico; one by Fredegard, *procurator pauperum* (that is, 'procurator of the poor') of the abbey between 861 and 871; and one by the *ostiarius* ('janitor') Odulf, 864-866. According to Ferrari[26] there is no clear order, such as in the collections of Hrabanus from Fulda, which are organised according to ecclesiastical hierarchy, but rather a creative chaos, slightly moderated by thematic arrangements, such as in the *Anthologia Latina*. Yet I suspect that this disorder is more a dismissive definition induced by lack of analysis than a reality. The origin and the context are surely scholastic, not because the manuscript includes a *glossarium*, a prosodic treatise, and a prosodic *florilegium*, but because the school is the setting and the constant reference of all the texts. The content, still unexplored,[27] mixes epitaphs and other *tituli*, poems for the abbot, requests for books, odes to identified persons, school memories, dialogues with the Muse, confessions, invitations, prayers, apologues, and jokes (even rude ones): I translated and commented on some pieces in my Carolingian anthology from 1995.[28] It is striking how deeply such collections can plunge us into the daily life of a Carolingian town like Saint-Riquier. In such cases, the anthology becomes a guide to a lost place and a means of bringing it back to life.

Epigraphic Collections

Another kind of verse anthology that is typically Carolingian is the epigraphic collection, which served as a model for announcements, notices, and

---

[26] FERRARI, *Il 'liber sanctae crucis'*, pp. 186-191.
[27] See *supra*, Chapter Eleven.
[28] STELLA, *La poesia carolingia*, Nos. 7 and 52. There are a limited number of studies on the *florilegium*, but none on the poetry collection.

inscriptions that covered the walls and the doors of every monastery, as documented by John Mitchell. The first ones were, after Pope Damasus († 384), martyrial compositions collected in the seventh century by Anglo-Saxon compilers; the series by Alcuin and Hrabanus, who wrote hundreds of metrical epigraphs; then the Lorsch Sylloge including northern Italian inscriptions; the Milred Sylloge edited by a bishop of Worcester between 743 and 775 and studied by Michael Lapidge; the Tours collection called Martinellus (90 manuscripts); the Cantabrigiensis; the Cantuariennsis; and a few others. Such manuscripts, often including common nuclei of Roman origin with local extensions, have been well studied by Silvagni and De Rossi, but many mixed anthologies of poems include large sections of epigraphs, such as Alcuin's, which features 170 inscriptions, Hrabanus, and the *Carmina Centulensia*.[29]

Biblical Anthologies

A relevant production which is never taken into consideration in studies of poetical collections concerns the anthologies of biblical poetry, comprising the four authors of the late antique canon (Juvencus, Sedulius, Avitus, and Arator), the extra-canonical biblical poets such as Proba, Marius Victorius, and Dracontius, and the pseudo-epigraphical poems and centos attributed to some pre-Ambrosian fathers of the Church. The most important examples are the twin MSS Laon, Bibliothèque Municipale 279[30] and 273,[31] MS Vatican, Reg. lat.

---

[29] I am obliged to refer to Chapter Eleven in this book, with the relevant bibliography.

[30] See B. BISCHOFF, *Katalog der festländischen Handschriften des neunten Jahrhunderts*, 2, *Laon-Paderborn*, ed. B. EBERTSPERGER (Wiesbaden, 2004), No. 2100: "Zahlreiche (wohl Reimser) Mgg. (hinter 'Nota'); J. CONTRENI, *[The] Cathedral School [of Laon from 850 to 930: Its Manuscripts and Masters* (Munich, 1978)], p. 45. Wahrscheinlich Westdeutschland, IX. Jh., 1./2. Viertel". Updated description in M. GORMAN, "The encyclopedic commentary on Genesis prepared for Charlemagne by Wigbod", *Recherches augustiniennes et patristiques* 17 (1982), pp. 173-201, at p. 198, and CONTRENI, *The Cathedral School of Laon*, p. 68.

[31] Bischoff, *Katalog*, ibid., No. 2099: "s. IX/X Bernardus und Adelelmus an Laon, Kathedrale. Von Martinus Scotus zahlreiche Mgg. Chresimon". Updated description in GORMAN, "The encyclopedic commentary", pp. 198-199, and CONTRENI, *The Cathedral School of Laon*, p. 68. The content of 279 is *Genesis ciprianea*, Avitus book 5 (Exodus), and the other parts of *Heptateucus*, while in the 273 Genesis and *Exodus* by Ps.-Cyprian are absent. According to R. HERZOG, *Die Bibelepik der lateinischen Spätantike: Geschichte einer erbaulichen Gattung* (Munich, 1975), 1, p. XXX, n. 85, this means that 273 was perceived as the closest to the prose Bible text and occurred only with somehow lacking biblical poetry in a subsidiary role ("*trat nur bei etwa fehlender sonstiger Bibeldichtung subsidiär ein*").

582,[32] and MS Paris, Bibliothèque nationale de France, latin 2772,[33] all from the ninth century. Those agglomerates build *corpora* of metrical bibles, which are typical of the Carolingian times, when the complete bible, including paratexts and interpretative apparatus, became a codicological and cultural, if not an ideological, model. We can find the same structure even in later poetic bibles, both Latin and vernacular ones such as the Vorauer Bible (twelfth century), the Millstädter and others. This project of supplemented narrative is frequently organised thematically, what Reinhart Herzog called "*stoffliche Koupierung*". The integrated model was recovered in the twelfth and thirteenth centuries, as the analysis of the biblical anthologies by Greti Dinkova Bruun demonstrated, on the basis of Alexander of Ashby's manuscript transmission.[34] The fact itself that the thirteenth-century MS Paris, Bibliothèque nationale de France, latin 14758 replicates the content of the two Laon manuscripts, also adding new poetic material from the twelfth century, confirms the hypothesis that after the Gregorian reform the project of metrical rewriting of the Bible resurfaced, especially in France, as a didactic-theological counterpoint to the classicist renaissance of that time.

---

[32] Bibliography in K. POLLMANN, *Das Carmen adversus Marcionitas* (Göttingen, 1991), pp. 12-13; M. BAZIL, *"Centones christiani": Métamorphoses d'une forme intertextuelle dans la poésie latine chrétienne de l'Antiquité tardive* (Paris and Turnhout, 2009); and C. MICAELLI, "'Carmen adversus Marcionitas': Ispirazione biblica e sua ripresa nei centoni 'De lege' e 'De nativitate'", in: *La poesia tardoantica e medievale: Atti del I Convegno internazionale di studi, Macerata, 4-5 maggio 1998*, ed. M. SALVADORE (Alessandria, 2001), pp. 171-198.

[33] Bibliothèque Nationale, *Catalogue générale des manuscrits latins* 3, ed. J. PORCHER (Paris, 1952), pp. 68-71: dated to the ninth century; content: Prosper of Aquitaine, *Epigrammatum Liber*; Quintus Serenus, *Liber Medicinalis*; *Carmina duodecim sapientium*; *Epistolae Senecae ad Paulum et Pauli ad Senecam*; Tiberianus; Cyprianus Gallus, *Carmen ad quendam senatorem*; *Carmen Sibyllae Erythraeae*; Ovidius, *Argumenta*; Phocas, *Carmen Octaviani Caesaris de Vergilio*; Hilarius, *De martyrio Macchabaeorum*; [Cyprianus Gallus,] *De Sodoma*; Ausonius, Dialogue on grammar; Paulinus of Nola, *Carmina* XVII, IX, and VII; Cato, *Disticha*; St. Martin of Braga, *Formula vitae honestae*; Ps.-Caecilius Balbus, *Sententiae Philosophorum*; *Praecepta Pythagorae*; moral *Sententiae*; *Disputatio Pippini*; Ausonius, *De signis et mensibus XII*; Boethius, *Consolatio Philosophiae*, metrum II 5.

[34] Alexander Essebiensis, *Opera omnia*, 2, *Opera poetica,* ed. G. DINKOVA-BRUUN (Turnhout, 2004: CCSM 188A).

Poetic Anthologies

If we speak about real lyrical anthologies in the modern sense of the term, the major and newest collections are the ones that include rhythmic poetry. A reconstruction of the processes that led to the formation of such collections is fundamental, because they single out rhythmic poetry, which would become the form of versification in modern literatures, as an autonomous genre, even if originally connected to oral performance and music, with a specific poetic register that could then be imitated and reproduced.

I have had the opportunity to research such anthologies since 1998, when, together with some other scholars, I edited the first volume and CD-ROM of the *Corpus Rhythmorum Musicum*, published in 2007.[35] That edition was transferred and updated in 2011 on the website <www.corimu.unisi.it>. This was the first critical edition, prepared over three conferences under the European programme TMR, of the earliest medieval texts set to music, and it provides the critically reconstructed text, the apparatus of variants and *loci similes*, all scribal versions with photographic reproductions of every manuscript, linguistic and statistical analysis, and palaeographical and musical commentary. It includes prayers, riddles, biblical narrations, confessions, moral poems, and *planctus*, such as the one for Charlemagne's death. The main manuscripts of the 80 used for the edition are MSS Verona, Biblioteca Capitolare, 88 and 90; MS Paris, Bibliothèque nationale de France, latin 1154 from Limoges; MS Brussels, Bibliothèque Royale, 8860-67; MS Berne, Burgerbibliothek, B 455; and MS Leiden, Universiteitsbibliotheek, Voss. Lat. Qu. 69. I will summarise the most relevant features of their content, referring to Pascale Bourgain for an initial inquiry into the role of such manuscripts[36] and to Patrizia Stoppacci, in *Corpus Rhythmorum Musicum* I, for a codicological description and a vast bibliography, updated to 2007.[37]

> Berne 455 (here Be), dated to the ninth century, comes from the Parisian area, according to Bischoff – or from Laon, according to Hagen, or from Tours, according to Contreni. It contains hymns and poems both religious and profane, if this kind of modern distinction can be applied to the ninth century, including 25 *rhythmi* (or *versus*, as musicologists prefer to say). Among them are compositions by Paulinus of Aquileia with music, and also metrical pieces by Boethius and

---

[35] *CRM* 1 <www.corimu.unisi.it>.
[36] BOURGAIN, "Les chansonniers lyriques latins".
[37] P. STOPPACCI, "I manoscritti", in: *CRM* 1, pp. LIII-CLXXXIV.

Prudentius inside a prosodic *florilegium*, followed by a section of musical anthems, which suggests liturgical use, while Barrett labels it an "educational anthology".[38]

The small Bruxellensis (B), with 76 folios, has been dated to the beginning of the tenth century, then led back to the third quarter of the ninth century, and is one of the key witnesses of this panorama. It comprises 58 poems, including 41 *rhythmi* and 17 *abecedarii*, and generally follows liturgical guidelines or rather, according to Barrett,[39] a coherent design that features a structural group (of alphabetical *versus*) in biblical order, and a thematic group of Christ and saints in hierarchical order. Its origin, long said to be Saint Gall, was traced by Bischoff to a northern French scriptorium in the area of Arras, between Corbie and Amiens. Yet the presence of a very ancient poem in medieval German – *Hirsch und Hinde* – in a Saint Gall text proves that, wherever it may have be composed, it was brought to Saint Gall in the tenth century, that is, a few decades after it was written.

The lost Fuldensis (F) is the one we mentioned *à propos de* Hrabanus Maurus: appearing in the middle of his *carmina minora* are rhythmic poems with biblical content by Paulinus of Aquileia, and others by Theofrid of Corbie (seventh century), in addition to another copy of Charlemagne's *planctus*. According to Ferrari there is no doubt that the original was done in a setting near the main author, Hrabanus, given the presence of author's variants and local *tituli*, and following his death (856), given that it contains also non-Hrabanian texts and the epitaph to Hrabanus engraved in the cathedral of Sankt Alban of Mainz. The sequence of epitaphs follows a hierarchical criterion: first bishops and abbots, then priests and monks, then laymen, in the same way that Venantius arranged the fourth book of his *Carmina* and the hymnic section of the Bruxellensis.

The Leidensis (L), of 54 folios, also little enough, is dated with certainty to before 800 and is located in Saint Gall. It too comprises, besides a series of *rhythmi abecedarii* including some Ps.-Hrabanian ones (like the Fuldensis) and one by Theofrid of Corbie, metrical texts by Eugenius and Prudentius as in the Bernensis, school texts such as a glossary and a letter about the Septuagesima. Once again, we are looking at an educational tool of a religious type. Traces of Irish chronology in a poem confirm the well-known Irish influence on the abbey of Corbie.

MS Paris, Bibliothèque nationale de France, latin 1154 (Pa), to whom Chailley devoted a monograph in 1960 and Barrett a thorough essay in 1997, comes from the abbey of Saint Martial in Limoges, and is dated by Strecker to the ninth cen-

---

[38] S. BARRETT, "Music and writing: On the compilation of Paris Bibliothèque Nationale lat. 1154", *Early Music History* 16 (1997), pp. 55-96.

[39] BARRETT, "Music and writing", p. 66.

tury, and by Chailley and Bourgain to the end of the tenth. Its format is only slightly larger than the others, but it is much thicker (145 folios) and with more decoration and colours. It contains prayers and psalms, Isidore's *Synonima*, hymns, a series of metrical poems (Boethius, Fortunatus, etc.) and 23 *rhythmi*, including Paulinus with the *planctus* for Abbot Hugh and Duke Heric, the *planctus* for Charlemagne, the *planctus* for the battle of Fontenoy, Gottschalk, and other pieces, supplied with neumes. The final part presents a *confessio*, also perfectly compatible with the penitential design of the selection,[40] and computistic notes, which refer again to a scholastic setting, distinguished by a specific musical mark.

The Verona manuscripts too, especially Verona XC (85), deserved a monograph, this time by Meersemann (1975). Verona LXXXVIII (83), small like the Leiden manuscript (150 × 118 mm, 141 ff.), is dated to the middle of the ninth century, contains 80 folios, and has been traced to Saint-Denis, whose Abbot Waldo (806) had also been abbot of Saint Gall and Reichenau. After some litanies on the saints, an antiphonary, and a lectionary, it includes Paulinus's *rhythmi* and some *responsoria*. Some texts have a lay character, for example the riddles, and some are written in parts of the folios that were left blank, so they were not part of the original liturgical project. Five poems recur in the *Carmina Cantabrigiensia*.

Verona 90 (V1) is slightly bigger (150 × 188 mm) and its content is completely different, being defined as a collective manuscript, drawn up by six or seven different hands on a partially palimpsest base, which was used as a draft sheet by the junior canons of Verona, but contains a liturgical calendar from Monza. It includes prayers, *sententiae*, and sermons by Augustine, hymns and *rhythmi*, such as, again, Charlemagne's *planctus*, some compositions by Paulinus, and parodies of religious persons, confessions, Bede's martyrology, a computistic treatise, and a medical treatise.

The relationships between the manuscripts have been disputed for at least a century, not so much for the philological purpose of reconstructing the texts, as for the literary aim of identifying the source of the extraordinary innovation that is rhythmic poetry, the birth of modern versification.

At the beginning of the 1900s Von Winterfeld connected this literary production to the *sequentiae* of Limoges, because some of them seem to be transmitted only in manuscripts from Limoges and Verona, where they had arrived from France, and yet he did not necessarily assume the same route for the *rhythmi*. A few years later (1909), Strecker, the first editor of the *Rhythmi Mero-*

---

[40] J. CHAILLEY, *L'école musicale de Saint-Martial de Limoges jusqu'à la fin du XIe siècle* (Paris, 1960), p. 73: "*un penitentiel completé par un florilège de pénitence et de lamentations*".

wingici et Carolingi aevi, proposed a more systematic argument, by analysing the relationships between the main collections.[41] The corresponding table is reproduced in the Appendix. Strecker's analysis, based on a one-by-one comparison, leads to an initial nucleus of metrical and rhythmic poems produced at Saint Gall with material of diverse origins, even French, later circulated in different directions (Verona, Limoges) with the accidental separation of small fragments (as in the Clairmont manuscript).[42]

Here I summarise his proofs and extend them with my own remarks.

1. F includes poems present only in manuscripts from Saint Gall or inspired by poems from there.
2. L, written at Saint Gall, includes poems present only in Codices Sangallenses.
3. B contains a sequence of 17 *rhythmi abecedarii* (while L has 9) and shares a common nucleus with F. Therefore it is connected to Saint Gall.
4. Be shares a series of texts, metrical and rhythmic, with F. So even the source common to Be+F was in Saint Gall and included metrical texts.
5. In the manuscripts from Saint Gall and Verona there are some poems by Theofrid, a monk at Luxeuil and later abbot of Corbie in 657, and others that are even older, such as *Angelus venit* and *Ama puer*, together with the Ps.-Hrabanian *Gratuletur*.
6. The *abecedarii* of L may come from or be otherwise related to Luxeuil.
7. V1 has the *planctus* for Charlemagne which is transmitted only by Saint Gall manuscripts (B, P, F). Besides, the rhythmic story of St. Eustachius, transmitted only in V1, is largely mentioned in a *Life of St. Eustachius,* which was written at Saint Gall (561, tenth-eleventh century) but presents a text better than V1: therefore, the two witnesses are independent and we can suppose that in Saint Gall there was some material, later lost, which was transmitted to Verona, where some additions were supplied, such as the *rhythmus* of St. Zeno present only in V1 P, B, and Be share texts missing from V1 (*Christus rex vita, Qui de morte, Tristis venit, Mecum Timavi, Ad caeli clara*).

Fifty years later, Dag Norberg criticised Strecker's reconstruction by suggesting that "*Pour Strecker, c'était un axiome qu'il y avait un archétype dont tous les recueils étaient provenus*".[43] On the contrary, Strecker spoke about a common source of a recurrent nucleus, specifying that it was "*nicht eine Hand-*

---

[41] P. VON WINTERFELD, "Zur Geschichte der rhythmischen Dichtung", *Neues Archiv* 30 (1900), pp. 379-408.

[42] Here I summarise some arguments I examined in more detail in STELLA, "Le raccolte", where you can also find all references to the mentioned literature.

[43] D. NORBERG *La poésie latine rythmique du haut moyen âge* (Stockholm, 1954), p. 113.

schrift".[44] According to Norberg, at any rate, rhythmic chants were composed here and there, their movements cannot be better reconstructed, and the archetype "*est une chimère*", but Verona is an older centre of original production.

Our analysis in 1998 of the relationships between the manuscripts and of the distribution of the texts showed that Norberg's arguments were weak or erroneous, and that the Saint Gall nucleus (witnessed only in manuscripts connected to Saint Gall and absent in Verona) reveals a certain consistency. Moreover, no text shared by the two Veronenses is witnessed just in them, and a significant portion of the texts included in a manuscript from Verona do not even come from Italy.

Indeed, after Norberg's book new data emerged that shed a completely different light on the situation.

First, there was the surfacing of a codex from Naples, Biblioteca Nazionale, IV.G.68 (N), which included, in addition to Boethius, Lupus of Ferrières on Boethius's metres, Prudentius, and Martianus Capella, grammatical and mathematical treatises, and a miscellany of texts known as of 1934 just as "liturgical fragments". The earliest research on this manuscript was published only in 1964 by Schaller,[45] who identifies in it the *Ante saecula et mundi principium* of Theofrid, the *Gratuletur*, 42 *Audite omnes*, 20 *Alma vera ac praeclara*, and the beginning of *Tercio in flore*, now attributed to Paulinus of Aquileia. The first four texts are in the same sequence as in L. Strecker was of course unable to use this manuscript in his edition, yet it comes from Saint Gall itself and contributes further strong evidence to his argument. The main feature we acknowledge for the Naples manuscript is one we find again in MS Cambridge, University Library, G.g.5, of the *Carmina Cantabrigiensia*: that is, the rhythmic poems are not transcribed in their entirety; instead, only the first strophe is provided, along with music. The Saint Gall users would have known these songs by heart, and the text simply served to remind them of the music.

A second example of the findings that came to light after Norberg's book is MS Paris, Bibliothèque nationale de France, latin 12161, a palimpsest from the seventh to eighth century, written in northern France and preserved first at Corbie: it includes the very old *rhythmus* 82 by Theofrid, which was said to be

---

[44] K. STRECKER, "Zu den karolingischen Rhythmen", *Neues Archiv* 34 (1908), pp. 601-561, at p. 641.

[45] D. SCHALLER, "Frühmittelalterliche lateinische Dichtung in einer ehemals St. Galler Handschrift", *Zeitschrift für deutsches Altertum und deutsche Literatur* 93 (1964), pp. 272-291, reprinted in: ID., *Studien zur lateinischen Dichtung des Frühmittelalters* (Stuttgart, 1995), pp. 27-46, with additions at pp. 404-406.

attested only in MS Paris, Bibliothèque nationale de France, latin 17655, again from Corbie.

A third discovery was the attribution by Schaller to Paulinus of Aquileia of the Easter rhythmic chant *Regi regum*, MS Paris, Bibliothèque nationale de France, latin 13027, from Corbie, with a kind of versification that Schaller considered influenced by Irish poetry. There was moreover the publication of a *rhythmus* in praise of God, in rhyming decapentasyllable, which Schaller also attributed to Paulinus or his circle, again transmitted in a manuscript from St. Petersburg, originally from Corbie.[46]

So the new acquisitions seemed to indicate that Corbie was a centre for the initial gathering of rhythmic Latin poems from England, Ireland, or Italy, produced in Corbie itself, and later attested at Saint Gall.

A fourth finding worth mentioning, not used enough in the reconstruction of the itineraries of the texts, is their imitative relationship. Working along two lines of hierarchy I developed the following diagram:

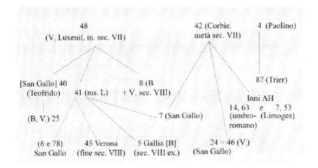

Rhythmus 48 *Ama puer castitatem*, prior to Theofrid of Corbie and probably from Luxeuil, transmitted in V1, was imitated by No. 40 *Ante saecula et mundi* of Theofrid (Sang. 2, L, N, F), by No. 41 *Angelus venit de caelo*, from the Leidensis, and by No. 8 *Alta prolis sanctissime*, witnessed both in Saint Gall (B) and V1.

No. 40 in turn is surely used by No. 25 *Ante saecula et tempora*, transmitted again by B and V1; No. 41 by No. 6 *Angelus domini Mariae* (B+L), by No. 78 *Angelus domini venit ad virginem* in the Fuldensis, both from Saint Gall, by

---

[46] D. SCHALLER, "Ein übersehenes karolingisches Gebets-Canticum in einer St. Petersburger Handschrift: '... *ne dimittas nos intrare in hanc pestilentiam*'", *Filologia Mediolatina* 3 (1996), pp. 160-162.

No. 45 (the only Veronese *rhythmus* on Christmas), by No. 7 *A superna caeli parte* transmitted by manuscripts from the Saint Gall area (B, L, and MS Saint Gall, Stiftsbibliothek 1395), and by No. 5 *De diebus tredecim* from B. Even the only Veronese text, the *rhythmus* on Christmas, imitates texts from Saint Gall. This chain further weakens Norberg's hypothesis about the role of Verona in the production of the earliest *rhythmi*, confirming that V1 contains ancient, but foreign, material.

The second tree represents the hypotextual influxes or refractions of *rhythmus* 42 from Corbie (Leiden + Naples) *Audite omnes canticum*, imitated by the aforementioned *rhythmus* 7; by No. 28 *Gratuletur omnis caro*, also very ancient even if erroneously attributed to Hrabanus; by the hymns *Analecta Hymnica* 14, 63 from the Umbro-Roman hymnary; by the *sequentia O beata et venerabilis*; and by *rhythmus* 24 *Surrexit Christus*, transmitted in B and F and in V1. This is another text from Corbie and imitated in Verona but witnessed in Saint Gall: this seems to be the most typical order of transmission, in different time periods. Luxeuil in the seventh century, then Corbie and Saint Gall in the eighth century, Verona in the ninth, and finally the *sequentiae*.

The combination of codicological data, new attributions, and textual imitations gives the following results:

1. At the source of the most ancient thread, except for the metrical texts, we find the models used *by* Theofrid of Corbie, maybe from Luxeuil (such as *rhythmus* 48); those, together with Theofrid's compositions, creates a first set, homogeneous culturally speaking, written by authors from the same background who applied the same procedures, techniques, language, and content: long, often alphabetical, poems about biblical topics that included dense exegetical interpretations (Nos. 48, 42, 81). So, a nucleus from Corbie.

2. The presence of some texts from Luxeuil or Corbie only in Saint Gall and some others only in Verona proves that neither of those two centres alone represent an old enough phase of rhythmic tradition. An imitation or reduction of poems from Saint Gall can be showed in manuscripts from Verona (Nos. 45, 46). So it is probable that in Verona a kind of sylloge from Saint Gall that included *rhythmi* was read and transcribed, as well as some compositions of Merovingian origin that did not pass through Saint Gall. Verona 1 was, in fact, a collection of external material supplemented by local grafts. Perhaps some manuscripts were brought there for a short time: think of the exchanges with the Bodensee area through the Verona bishops Regino and Ratold, both from the Reichenau, at the end of the eighth and beginning of the ninth centuries, confirmed by the presence of *Tercio in Flore* in N,

from Saint Gall, close to Reichenau, and of the well-documented exchanges of Verona with Corbie and other Irish settings.[47]

Such remarks do not, of course, cover all possible options for the origins of rhythmic innovation. Ancient poems such as Strecker Nos. 98, 101, and 102, according to Traube from Rome and transmitted by manuscripts other than the ones we have mentioned, are evidence of an educational praxis of rhythmic versification that followed schemes not so different from the ones used at Corbie and Saint Gall, but adapted to rather different topics. A further source could have been the rhythmic versification of Ambrosian hymns diffused in Gallican and later Irish hymnals. Even the popular practice of psalms and recitations or acting of poems (for example, *rhythmus* 42) may have been a source of rhythmic production.

We still do not have access to all the evidence we need to establish a general history of the origins of rhythmic versification. In any case, as far as we can imagine it, its evolution as a genre and many of the formal structures that characterise it (syllabo-tonic patterns, alphabetical incipits, rhyme, refrain, formularity, mix of stories and exegesis, performative orientation) were polygenetic and felt the effects of an external, maybe Irish and Anglo-Latin, development of late antique precedents (*Psalmus responsorius*, Augustine, Fulgentius) and Roman para-liturgical practices. It is likely that small nuclei of rhythmic sequences formed in various monasteries of Irish foundation (Luxeuil, Corbie, Reichenau-Saint Gall), where they were supplemented and transmitted to northern Italy and southwestern France (Limoges, Clermont). There, those nuclei produced many different kinds of original fusions with elements of local culture (*laudes civitatis* and literature on Zeno in Verona, musical experiences at Limoges).

In conclusion, with regard to the history of poetry collections as well as in other areas of cultural history, the Carolingian age introduced multiple innovations that can be called "*traditionbildend*", in addition to some experiments which remained isolated, and each one of them satisfied a specific demand. The most significant typologies are the biblical-exegetical anthology, which corresponds to the new production of complete bibles promoted by the court; the collective poetry-book of Saint Riquier, designed as a kind of community journal; the authorial collections, which were on the one hand structured by 'environmental' gathering, as in the case of Alcuin and Hrabanus, and on the

---

[47] Evidence in STELLA, "Le raccolte".

other hand were manifestations of an impulse to self-fashion projects, as for Wandalbert and Audradus; and lastly, the scholastic or para-scholastic anthologies of performable rhythmic poems, mostly with religious content, but in forms that could vary from the Veronese scribbling-pad for seven hands to the musical songbooks of Naples and Limoges, which paved the way for the *Carmina Cantabrigiensia* and other texts. Even from this perspective, the Carolingian period was far from being an age of classical recovery, and rather a time of vibrant experimentation.

Appendix

The following list gives the number of the *Rhythmi* in the edition of Strecker in *PLAC* 4.2, followed by the incipit, and by the sigla of the manuscripts containing the main collections of *rhythmi*, i.e.

B MS Brussels, Bibliothèque Royale, 8860-67.
Be MS Berne, Burgerbibliothek, 455.
F MS Fuldensis (lost).
L MS Leiden, Universiteitsbibliotheek, Voss. Lat. Qu. 69.
P MS Paris, Bibliothèque natinale de France, latin 1154.
R MS Berlin, Staatsbibliothek zu Berlin – Preussischer Kulturbesitz, lat. 4° 676 (*olim* Cheltenham 18908).
V^1 MS Verona, Biblioteca Capitolare, XC.
V^2 MS Verona, Biblioteca Capitolare, 88.
X Other manuscripts.

The *rhythmi* are presented in the groups in which they occur in two or more manuscripts / collections.

1   *Anno tertio in regno* B+V^2+P
2   *Tertio in flore mundus* B+V^2+Be+F
4   *Angelus domini Maria* B+L
5   *A superna caeli parte* B+L
11 *A solis ortu cardine* B+P
16 *Apparebit repentina* B+P
18 *Alma fulget in caelesti* B+V^1
19 *Alma vera ac praeclara* B+L+Be

22 *Quique de morte* B+P
23 *Qui cupis esse bonus* B+Be
24 *O mortalis homo* B+Be
25 *Surrexit Christus a sopore* B+F
27 *Ante saecula et tempora* B+V^2
28 *Congregavit nos in unum* B+V^1+X
30 *Gratuletur omnis caro* B+V^1+F+X
31 *Cantemus socii domino* B+V^2+P
33 *Refulget omnis* B+V^1+V^2+P+X
34 *Gloriam deo* B+V^1+V^2+P+F+R+X
35 *Tristis venit ad Pilatum* B+P
36 *Aspera conditio* B+V^1+V^2+Be
37 *Fuit domini dilectus* B+V^1+V^2+P+X
38 *Christus rex noster* B+P
39 *Apostolorum gloria* B+X
40 *Homo quidam erat* B+V^1+L+P
43 *Audite versus parabole* V^1+C
46 *Apostolorum passio* V^1+Be
47 *Aterna Christi munera* V^1+Be
53 *Beatus homo est* V^1+P
54 *Deus orbis reparator* V^1+F
59 *Placidas fuit dictus* V^1+X
61 *Sancte Paule pastor bone* V^1+P
66 *Asia ab oriente* L+X+S
67 *Ante saecula et mundi* L+S+F
72 *Ad caeli clara* P, Be, C, R, X

89 *Cantemus socii* V^2+Be
91 *Quamvis se tyrio* V^2+Be
93 *O crucifer bone* V^2+Be

1   *Anno tertio in regno* B+P +V^2
11 *A solis ortu cardine* B+P
16 *Apparebit repentina* B+P
22 *Quique de morte* B+P
31 *Cantemus socii domino* B+ P+V^2
80 *Qui se volet esse potentem* V^2+P

2   *Tertio in flore mundus* B+Be+V^2+F+N
23 *Qui cupis esse bonus* B+Be
24 *O mortalis homo* B+Be

36 *Aspera conditio* B+Be +V^1+V^2

4   *Angelus domini Maria* B+L
5   *A superna caeli parte* B+L
19 *Alma vera ac praeclara* B+L+Be+N

33 *Refulget omnis* B+P +V^1+V^2 +X
34 *Gloriam deo* B+P +V^1+V^2 +F+R+X
37 *Fuit domini dilectus* B +P+V^1+V^2+X
40 *Homo quidam erat* B+P +V^1+L
35 *Tristis venit ad Pilatum* B+P
38 *Christus rex noster* B+P
18 *Alma fulget in caelesti* B+V^1
28 *Congregavit nos in unum* B+V^1+X
30 *Gratuletur omnis caro* B+V^1+F+X

72 *Ad caeli clara* P+Be+C+R+X
77 *Mecum Timavi* P+Be+X
78 *O stelliferi conditor orbis* P+Be
79 *Bella bis quinis operatus* P+Be

89 *Cantemus socii* V^2+Be
91 *Quamvis se tyrio* V^2+Be
93 *O crucifer bone* V^2+Be

83 *Quod chorus vatum venerandus* Be+F
84 *Fit porta Christi pervia* Be+F
86 *Area luce et decore* Be+F

46 *Apostolorum passio* V^1+Be
47 *Aterna Christi munera* V^1+Be

66 *Asia ab oriente* L+S+X
67 *Ante saecula et mundi* L+S+F+N

53 *Beatus homo est* V^1+P
61 *Sancte Paule pastor bone* V^1+P

25 *Surrexit Christus a sopore* B+F
27 *Ante saecula et tempora* B+V^2
39 *Apostolorum gloria* B+X

43 *Audite versus parabole* V¹+C
54 *Deus orbis reparator* V¹+F
59 *Placidas fuit dictus* V¹+X

Chapter 13

The Modern Success and Medieval Marginality of Modoin of Autun's *Karolus Magnus et Leo Papa*

The Meaning of Anonymity

The concept of 'anonymity' is a modern one. *Anonymus* is a term that is never found in Latin, except in three or four cases: in Pliny, to denote a plant without a specific name (27, 31, but with uncertain meaning), in Cassiodorus (*Inst.* 1, 8, 2) and Ambrose (*In Psalmum CXVIII*, 5, 11: "*in tempore illo anonymo*") as a synonym of 'unspecified'. The first and only passage in which *anonymus* indicates a work without an author's name is again Cassiodorus, *Inst.* 26, 16, where we also find an attempt at attribution based on style: "*quidam etiam est -us, ex cuius stilo beatum esse suspicamur Hilarium*".[1] The juxtaposition of the author and the anonymous individual is clearly derived from the interest of romantic aesthetics in the figure of the author, today further emphasised by the media's idolatry of the person compared to the interest in his or her work. We should remember that one of the first informal seminars organised at the newly created Fondazione Franceschini by Claudio Leonardi with his Florentine students, also at the behest of Francesco Santi, was dedicated to none other than the concept of 'author' in the medieval period, behind the enthusiasm for reading Foucault. And after many years, during which Alistair Minnis dedicated a study fundamental for the concept of author in the

---

[1] In *Institutiones* 1, 8, 2, Cassiodore uses the term in reference to a manuscript: "*quendam anonymum codicem subnotatum divina repperi provisione collatum*" (*Cassiodori Senatoris Institutiones*, ed. R.A.B. Mynors (Oxford, 1937; 1961²), p. 30).

Middle Ages,[2] a large number of the reports at Benevento's medieval Latin conference *Auctor et auctoritas*[3] again directed the attention of the medieval studies community to the question of authorship. At that forum, I myself, on the basis of Bonaventure's famous distinction, proposed an extension of the role of 'author', introducing the concept of heterography to epistolary literature.[4] But here there is another problem at hand: we are in fact wondering how to evaluate the *authority* of important but anonymous texts, as in anepigraphs, which were transmitted without any indication of author and have so far remained without certain attributions, highlighting the paradoxical fact that a text with no indication of author has become authoritative in some circles of readers. In reality, the paradox of an authority without an author is based on semantic and chronological slippage: what it means to be *auctor* in the Middle Ages has been explained well by Curtius and Munk Olsen, Kristeller and Minnis, Zumthor and Barthes. In his *Dialogus super auctores*, Conrad of Hirsau lists 21 authors, no anonymous work. Of the 37 listed by Eberhard the German, the only anonymous works are the *Pamphilus*, the *Ilias Latina*, and the *Solinarius*, a forgotten epic poem on the crusades, while of the 100 of Hugo von Trimberg, at the threshold of the pre-humanistic fourteenth century, there are many texts without authors, such as, again, the *Pamphilus*, the *gesta metrica* of several saints, collections of fables, and the *Liber genealogus* which is called an *anagraphus* (l. 555) but whose inclusion Hugo apologises for because authors should not be anonymous: "*Liber Genealogus his annumeretur, / quamvis is anagraphus esse comprobetur*" ("The *Liber Genealogus* is included here, although it is demonstrably anonymous").[5]

None of the works being discussed at the conference *Anonimi autorevoli* (2015),[6] had ever entered the circle of *auctores* as the medieval school would

---

[2] A. MINNIS, *Medieval Theory of Authorship: Scholastic Literary Attitudes in the Later Middle Ages* (London, 1984; 1988²).

[3] *Auctor et auctoritas in latinis medii aevi litteris – Author and Authorship in Medieval Latin Literature: Proceedings of the VIth Congress of the International Medieval Latin Committee (Benevento-Naples, November 9-13, 2010)*, ed. E. D'ANGELO and J. ZIOLKOWSKI (Florence, 2014).

[4] F. STELLA, "Chi scrive le mie lettere? La funzione-autore e l'eterografia nei modelli epistolari del XII secolo", in: *Auctor et auctoritas*, pp. 1070-1095.

[5] Others include *De virgula et flore*, two *libelli de sacramentis*, a *Liber de miraculo virginis Marie*, several *gesta metrica quorundam sanctorum*, and later a *Fabularius, Lapidarius*, etc.

[6] *Anonimi autorevoli: Un canone di anonimi nella letteratura latina medievale: XVIII Convegno annuale della Società Internazionale per lo Studio del Medioevo Latino, Firenze 27 marzo 2015*; the proceedings in *Filologia mediolatina* 23 (2016).

have defined them, although we are well aware that in the Middle Ages all written sources were credited with some kind of reliability just by virtue of the fact that they were written. The authority of the texts discussed at this conference has been a prevalently modern authority. Or rather, if we wish to be precise in our use of the word, it is above all the modern reception or success of medieval texts for which we do not know the authors and of which the Middle Ages in many cases had only limited knowledge.

Karolus Magnus et Leo Papa (KMLP)

I will address what is called the *Karolus Magnus et Leo papa*, a short poem or a passage from a longer poem, which I had the chance to analyse sixteen years ago, at the request of Jörg Jarnut and Peter Godman, for the anniversary of the event that the poem describes: the meeting of Charlemagne and Pope Leo III in Paderborn in 799.[7] It has not be easy for me to readdress such a tricky problem, which I had not revisited later.

For those who do not remember its contents, the text – in 536 well-crafted hexameters – announces a desire to reattempt the dangerous journey across the sea *for the third time*, which suggests that it may have been the third book of a longer poem. The wind now brings the ship to a place where the lighthouse of Europe shines: in other words, King Charles, compared to a Sun never obscured by clouds and a King David incapable of sin. A long encomiastic portrait of the king ends with the description of the feverish construction of Aachen, the second Rome, which Charles follows and controls from on high, like Dido in Carthage. The description also includes elements of Rome not related to Aachen, such as the port and the theatre. Not far from the site of these activities are a forest and a park inhabited by lovely animals, where Charles often comes hunting with his court of followers, women included, which the poet describes with manneristic accuracy from the moment that the king solemnly exits the city walls until the killing of the wild boar, lingering in particular detail on the vestment of each knight and the trappings of each horse. Once they have returned home, the Carolingians celebrate with a lavish banquet, but

---

[7] F. STELLA, "Autore e attribuzioni del 'Karolus Magnus et Leo papa'", in: *Am Vorabend der Kaiserkrönung: Das Epos 'Karolus Magnus et Leo papa' und der Papstbesuch in Paderborn 799*, ed. P. GODMAN, J. JARNUT, and P. JOHANEK (Berlin, 2002), pp. 19-33. German version: "Autor und Zuschreibungen des sog. Karolus Magnus et Leo papa", in: *Nova de veteribus: Festschrift P.G. Schmidt* (Berlin, 2004), pp. 155-175.

that night Charles dreams of Pope Leo crying, with his eyes bloodied and sorely wounded. He then sends messengers to Rome to check what is happening and goes to Saxony for the war underway there. The delegates arrive in Rome, and see the model for what is being reproduced in Aachen, and they discover that the pope had been blinded and stripped of his tongue because of an ambush near San Lorenzo. But a doctor had cured him and he had fled to Spoleto, where he was welcomed by Duke Winiges, who had also learned that Frankish ambassadors had come to Rome but had refused to convey their greetings to the Roman people because of what had happened. The pope has them summoned, hoping for the protection of Charles, by whose messengers he asks to be accompanied. Germar answers for all of them and accepts the request. Thus, the pope sets off, arriving amid the rejoicing and gathering of the crowd. Meanwhile, Charles crosses the Rhine and arrives in Paderborn. A messenger tells him the news, announcing the arrival of the pope. Charles remembers his dream and sends Pippin to him with 100 soldiers. The pope opens his arms to him, and the army prostrates itself before the pope, who then invites Pippin to a private meeting. In the meantime, King Charles speaks to the people, inviting the armed noblemen to run to meet the pope, preceded by the company of priests. The entire scene of the meeting is described, up to the religious ceremony and the banquet in the palace. The poem ends with the exchange of goods and the return of Leo to his own camp and of Charles to his private rooms.

The text is transmitted in a single manuscript, MS Zurich, Zentralbibliothek, C. 78, in one part that goes back to the late ninth century, originally from Saint Gall, where it remained until 1712, as demonstrated by several notes of ownership on folios 7r and 50v. It contains didactic materials and textual evidence of different authors, partially identifiable also in MSS Saint Gall, Stiftsbibliothek 397 and 147, which earned it the name *St. Galler Anthologie* in Bernhard Bischoff's study.[8] In turn, the manuscript has been shown to have been used as an apograph of several texts traceable to other manuscripts from Saint Gall but also from the Vatican.[9] A unique transmission, other than this poem, are the glosses to the *Liber medicinalis* of Quintus Serenus written or

---

[8] B. BISCHOFF, "Bücher am Hofe Ludwigs des Deutschen und die Privatbibliothek des Kanzlers Grimalt", in: ID., *Mittelalterliche Studien: Ausgewählte Aufsätze zur Schriftkunde und Literaturgeschichte* 3 (Stuttgart, 1981), pp. 187-212, at p. 210.

[9] Description and bibliography in H.W. STORK, *Die Sammel-Handschrift Zürich, Zentralbibliothek, C 78, in De Karolo rege et Leone papa*, ed. W. HENTZE, with an introduction by L.E. VON PADBERG and a facsimile of the manuscript (Paderborn, 1999), pp. 105-118, at p. 108.

transcribed by a certain Jacobus, and the *De mundi transitu* of Colombanus. The complete description of the content, which follows from that of Leo Cunibert Mohlberg in 1952, is found in the Hans-Walter Stork volume accompanying the reprinting of the Franz Brunhölzl edition edited by Wilhelm Hentze in 1999. As we cannot reproduce it here in detail, it should suffice to remember that included in the two ninth-century sections are also the *De virtutibus et vitiis* and a letter from Alcuin to Dafni, the *De civitate Dei*, a rhythmic hymn to Mary from the patriarch of Constantinople, Saint Germanus, the *Versus de evangelio ad picturam* (a series of epigraphs for frescos that I had the chance to examine in a volume on Carolingian biblical poetry),[10] rules for the iconography of the saints, legal forms, the *Confessio* of Pelagius, the riddles of Boniface, the *carmina* of Theodulf and Moduin's response to him, the *Disticha Catonis*, scattered lines and *conflictus* that include two bits of bucolic verse, a letter attributed to Bede, and scholastic writings by Laurentius Scottus, a unique version of Priscian's translation of *Dionysius Periegetes*, the *In mulieres* and the *Mundus iste* attributed to Colombanus (the latter later copied from here in another codex from Saint Gall, today MS Vatican, Reg. lat. 421), Silvius's lines on the names of the Saviour, and the *Sententiae* of Publilius Syrus.

The text of the poem, which recent criticism suggests calling *De Carolo rege et Leone papa*, according to the *epitheta* used in the poem, and not *Karolus Magnus et Leo papa*, as it was entitled in the past without a clear textual basis, is found on folios 103v-114v and does not seem very far from the original. It contains several obvious errors, thanks to which we can exclude the idea of it being an original. The edition in common use, which is nonetheless neither the most recent nor the best, that of Ernst Dümmler, does not include these errors in the critical apparatus, thereby confirming that printed editions are an irresistible temptation to falsify data, even unwittingly. But it is these very errors, which you can find listed in the Appendix, that would demonstrate the use of an antigraph in pre-Caroline orthography, which would confirm the dating to close to the date of the event and not later, as claimed in the past by some scholars, including Dieter Schaller. The reviser's hand, which is very distinct from the scribe's, at times intervenes in orthographic matters.

---

[10] Cf. *supra*, Chapter Eight.

Editions and Studies

No further medieval copies have been found, although the manuscript contains traces of markings in preparation for copying, or at least of an arrangement for a new transcription, which you can find in the Appendix. The *editio princeps* was prepared by Canisius in 1604,[11] obviously from this same codex, which had at least one documentable reader in Melchior Goldast (1576-1635), and this edition was revived by Quercetanus[12] in his editions of Alcuin's works and of French historical documents, therefore by Frobenius,[13] still as Alcuin's work, by Bouquet,[14] and finally in the *Monumenta* by Pertz[15] and in the *Patrologia Latina*.[16] These editions largely consist of reprintings or revisions of the original edition. A second genuine critical edition was edited by Orelli in 1832,[17] who called it *Helperici sive ut alii arbitrantur Angilberti Karolus magnus et Leo papa*, with reference to the name to which a second hand of the manuscript seems to attribute the poem, *Helpericus*, as you can see in the reproductions in the Appendix. Today the standard edition is that of Ernst Dümmler (1881), in the first volume of the *Poetae Latini*, found among Angilbert's *Carmina dubia*, without any explanation for the attribution. Franz Brunhölzl finally edited an edition with Joseph Brockmann in 1966[18] with a translation that has remained almost unknown, reprinted in 1999 as an annex to the volume *De Karolo rege et Leone papa*, edited by Wilhelm Hentze in Paderborn. The text published is Brunhölzl's,[19] accompanied by the reproduction of

---

[11] H. CANISIUS, *Antiquae Lectiones, seu antiqua monumenta ad historiam mediae aetatis illustrandam*, 6 (Ingolstadt, 1604), pp. 521-535.

[12] *Alcuini Opera*, ed. A. DUCHESNE [Quercetanus] (Paris, 1617), pp. 451-456; A. DUCHESNE, *Historie Francorum Scriptores* 2 (Paris, 1636), pp. 188-197.

[13] *Alcuini Opera* (Sankt Emmeram, 1777), pp. 1747-1756.

[14] *Recueil des historiens de la Gaule et de la France*, 24 vols. (Paris, 1738-1904), 5 (1744), pp. 388-397.

[15] MGH SS 2 (Hanover, 1829), pp. 391-403.

[16] PL 99, cols. 849-854.

[17] I.C. ORELLI, *Helperici [...] Karolus magnus et Leo papa* (Zürich, 1832).

[18] *Karolus magnus et Leo papa: Ein Paderborner Epos vom Jahre 799*, ed. J. BROCKMANN (Paderborn, 1966), re-edited by F. BRUNHÖLZL in: *De Karolo rege et Leone papa: Ein Paderborner Epos vom Jahre 799*, ed. H. BEUMANN, F. BRUNHÖLZL, and W. WINKELMANN (Paderborn, 1966; 2nd edn. 1999).

[19] In the prefatory note to the 1999 edition Brunhölzl reaffirms, in contrast to what Von Padberg writes in the introduction to the Hentze edition, that in his opinion the text is not fragmentary by nature but is a complete account composed soon after the events it describes, that is, in 799. The author would not be Einhard or Angilbert but one of the Irish authors who

the manuscript, a careful description, and an introduction that is based instead on the works of Dieter Schaller. It would be advisable to make an edition with an Italian translation, but an adequate commentary would require the resolution of an imposing number of historical and interpretative problems.

The history of the studies of the poem is in fact very eventful, chaotic, and dynamic. It began in 1872 with an article by Bernhard Simson, who claims with incredible prescience that *"die Discussion über diese Frage werde fast nothwendig fruchtlos bleiben"*.[20] Barely ten years later, in 1883, Ausfeld called *Karolus Magnus et Leo Papa* (henceforth KMLP)[21] *"das schon oft besprochene Gedicht"*,[22] a poem that has already been often discussed. But philological critics were not deterred by this scepticism; they continued to analyse every detail of the poem for the duration of the following century with dozens of essays and contributions that could not be covered in an entire university course, also because almost all the major scholars have changed their mind about their original remarks.[23]

It is worthwhile to recall just a few turning points here: Carl Erdmann's essay written in 1943 but released only in 1951, *Forschungen zur politischen Ideenwelt des Frühmittelalters*,[24] relaunched the investigation on the text as the primary witness of an Aachen conception (*Aachener Kaiseridee*) of the empire. This was explored by the prominent historian Helmut Beumann,[25] who in 1966 considered the poem as a complete work, written by an eyewitness between

---

frequented Charles's Court. In this study I do not intend to tackle the matters of dating the text (see note 6), but insofar as the readings carried out allow, I believe we can agree with Brunhölzl's opinion, in the absence of material evidence for the existence of other cantos and in consideration of the fact that the dating after 800 is based on none other than the fragmentary nature of the poem (which would explain the absence of reference to Luitgard's death). On the author, see *infra*.

[20] B. SIMSON, "Über das Gedicht von der Zusammenkunft Karls des Großen und Papst Leos III. in Paderborn", *Forschungen zur deutschen Geschichte* 12 (1872), pp. 567-590, at p. 588.

[21] For the sake of convenience I use the title chosen by the first editors (up to E. DÜMMLER, in: *PLAC* 1, pp. 366-379) because, in the absence of indications from the only manuscript (MS Zürich, Zentralbibliothek, C 78) each title has an element of arbitrariness (even those that claim to reflect the text). On this matter see D. SCHALLER, "Interpretationsprobleme im Aachener Karlsepos", *Rheinische Vierteljahrsblätter* 41 (1977), pp. 160-179, at p. 160.

[22] E. AUSFELD, "Zur Frage nach dem Verfasser des Epos 'Carolus Magnus et Leo Papa'", *Forschungen zur deutschen Geschichte* 23 (1883), pp. 609-615, at p. 609.

[23] Doxography in A. EBENBAUER, *Carmen historicum: Untersuchungen zur historischen Dichtung im karolingischen Europa* (Vienna, 1978), pp. 39 ff., and in the HENTZE edition, p. 69.

[24] C. ERDMANN, *Forschungen zur politischen Ideenwelt des Frühmittelalters* (Berlin, 1951).

[25] H. BEUMANN, "Die Kaiserfrage bei den Paderborner Verhandlungen von 799", in: *Das erste Jahrtausend: Kultur und Kunst im werdenden Abendland an Rhein und Ruhr*, ed. V. EBERN, 3 vols. (Düsseldorf, 1962-1964), 1, pp. 296-317, at pp. 296 and 316.

July and August 799, during the presence of the pope in Paderborn, leading to the renaming of the *Karolus Magnus et Leo papa* as *Paderborner Epos*. Reactions to this came in 1970 with Karl Hauck,[26] who postulated that the epos was written before Leo's arrival by order of Charles as a "salutatory panegyric" (*"Begrüssungspanegyricus"*) and double encomium of both figures, and in 1978 with Alfred Ebenbauer,[27] who even supposed a staging (*"Aufführung"*) of the text in the summer or in December of 800, an anticipated celebration of the coronation. In those years Dieter Schaller began to work on the text; I wish to recognise him for the generosity with which, despite not agreeing with me on some interpretations, he accepted to reread and correct the commentary to my 1995 Carolingian anthology, which benefited greatly. With him the poem's title became *Aachener Epos*,[28] and the work was understood as part of a celebratory poem in honour of Charles, the rest of which would have been lost, composed in the first decade of the ninth century. In later contributions from the seventies and eighties,[29] Schaller clarified his ideas, referring to *Karlsepos*, the first epic poem of the new Western culture beginning at the end of late Antiquity, a milestone of Western literary history. In the nineties, Hans Hubert Anton called the poem an attempt by the Frankish royal circle to propagandise imperial dignity in the Roman sense, also with respect to the rivalry with Byzantium.[30] This is the source of the repeated accentuation of the European-wide sovereignty of Charles. 'European' in what sense? A question just as topical and pivotal then as it is today, and on which I had the chance to reflect just a few weeks ago while reviewing the latest book by Chris Wickham,[31] who in his

---

[26] K. HAUCK, "Die Ausbreitung des Glaubens in Sachsen und die Verteidigung der römischen Kirche als konkurrierende Herrscheraufgaben Karls des Grossen", *Frühmittelalterliche Studien* 4 (1970) pp. 138-172.

[27] EBENBAUER, *Carmen historicum*.

[28] D. SCHALLER, "Das Aachener Epos für Karl den Kaiser", *Frühmittelalterliche Studien* 10 (1976), pp. 134-168.

[29] D. SCHALLER, "Interpretationsprobleme"; ID., "De Karolo rege et Leone papa (Aachener Karlsepos)", in: *Die deutsche Literatur des Mittelalters: Verfasserlexikon*, 2nd. edn., ed. K. RUH et al. (Berlin and New York, 1977-), 4 (1983), pp. 1041-1045; ID., "Frühkarolingische Corippus-Rezeption", *Wiener Studien* 105 (1992), pp. 173-187, all (except the second) were later republished with brief updates in ID., *Studien zur lateinischen Dichtung des Frühmittelalters* (Stuttgart, 1995).

[30] H.H. ANTON, "Beobachtungen zum fränkisch-byzantinischen Verhältnis in karolingischer Zeit", in: *Beiträge zur Geschichte des Regnum Francorum:Wissenschaftliches Colloquium zum 75. Geburtstag von Eugen Ewig*, ed. R. SCHIEFFER (Sigmaringen, 1990), pp. 97-119, at p. 115.

[31] Ch. WICKHAM, *The Inheritance of Rome: A History of Europe from 400 to 1000* (London, 2009); trans.: *L'eredità di Roma: Storia d'Europa dal 400 al 1000* (Rome and Bari, 2014).

introduction emphatically denies the possibility of tracing the roots of Europe back to the early Middle Ages, a stance that earned him the sensationalistic attention of many journals, while the actual content of his essay continuously contradicts this assertion and brings up substantial counter-evidence of structures, concepts, and institutions founded between the sixth and tenth centuries that later became characteristic features of modern Europe. In this respect the poem is worthy of special attention, because, in naming Europe a good four times, it points decisively at the assignment to Charles of the role of representative of the West. But in the flood of historical reconstructions about the identitarian awareness tied to this term, scholars overlooked the fact that, outside of this poem, we find attestations of Charles's European dimension also in an ode by Theodulf to Charles, *carmen* 39, 5, in Ermoldus Nigellus's poem for Louis the Pious (3, 267) and in a poem by Sedulius Scotus for Louis *decus* of Europe (2, 14, 8 and 2, 28, 2). The epithetic *decus Europae* was later transferred to Henry II.[32] These could be made the subject of an investigation on European self-awareness in celebratory political poems, which so far has not been attempted.

In 1999, the celebrations of the meeting that was the subject of the poem took place, among other events, at an exhibition of manuscripts and artistic and archaeological material that required an enormous three-volume catalogue,[33] and at the conference *Am Vorabend der Kaiserkrönung*, organised by Peter Godman, Jörg Jarnut, and Peter Johanek, from which my own interest in the text dates: apart from, obviously, my own, the 20 contributions, published in the proceedings from 2002, make up the foremost point of research on the subject to date. In the last ten years there have been another twenty or so papers published on the *KMLP*, often summaries of common knowledge, for the most part updated to reflect the *status quaestionis* prior to the conference in Paderborn and therefore curiously foreign to the discussion in which they purported to participate. Some of these concentrated on the historical and especially the socio-literary analysis of two of the poem's main scenes: the construction of the royal palace, which was compared with the other known descriptions by Gemma Gandino,[34] and the hunt scene, which Godman, Helena

---

[32] Inscription on a casula in the Bamberg Domschatz, ed. K. STRECKER and N. FICKERMANN in *PLAC* 5.1.2, p. 362.

[33] *Kunst und Kultur der Karolingerzeit: Karl der Grosse und Papst Leo III. in Paderborn: Katalog der Austellung Paderborn 1999*, ed. Ch. STIEGEMANN and M. WEMHOFF, 3 vols. (Mainz, 1999).

[34] G. GANDINO, "Il 'palatium' e l'immagine della casa del padre: L'evoluzione di un

de Carlos,[35] and others have studied at length due to the historical importance of this theme, a favourite in early medieval literature.

The modern authority of the text, namely its reception as a text of cultural interest, was therefore attested primarily between the end of the nineteenth and the end of the twentieth century, and largely in a philological context, due to curiosity about the name of the author, and a historical one, and thus more as a witness of information not found in other sources than as a literary work. The text was not authoritative, but the source was precious.

The Problem of Dating and Completeness

Naturally, key to understanding the text also from a historiographical perspective are the definition of its completeness, its chronological position, and the attribution of authorship.

As regards completeness, there are two crucial elements: the prologue and the final couplet. The latter (*"Cum tali a Karolo Leo fit susceptus honore, / Romanos fugiens propriisque repulsus ab oris"* – "When Leo [III], who fled from the Romans and had been expelled from his land, was welcomed by Charles with honour") seems to summarise the subject of the poem and so it has been interpreted as a sign of closure by those who thought that the poem was whole, for example Brunhölzl, or as an addition by a reader by those who believed the poem continued. In my opinion this hypothesis, defended by Schaller, remains fanciful until there is proof that the couplet is false or interpolated: the time has passed when the parts of a text that do not agree with the interpreter's hypotheses are expunged without evidence. However, the *incipit*,

> *Rursus in ambiguos gravis ammonet anchora calles*
> *Tela dare, incertis classem concredere ventis;*
> *Languida quae geminas superarunt membra procellas,*

modello nel mondo franco", *Studi medievali* 50 (2009), pp. 75-104.

[35] P. GODMAN, "The poetic hunt: From Saint Martin to Charlemagne's heir", in: *Charlemagne's Heir*, ed. P. GODMAN and R. COLLINS (Oxford, 1990), pp. 565-589; H. DE CARLOS VILLAMARÍN, "Una escena de caza en la 'Epistola ad Hugonem' de Godofredo de Reims", in: *Poesía latina medieval (siglos V-XV): Actas del IV Congreso del 'Internationales Mittellateinerkomitee' (Santiago de Compostela, 12-15 septiembre de 2002)*, ed. M.C. DÍAZ Y DÍAZ and J.M. DÍAZ DE BUSTAMANTE (Florence, 2005), pp. 233-243. [See now P. GALLONI, "Un gioco che non è un gioco: La caccia altomedievale", in: *Il gioco nella società e nella cultura dell'Alto Medioevo*, 2 vols. (Spoleto, 2018: *Settimane di Studio del CISAM* 65), pp. 531-570.]

Ad nova bella iubet lassos reparare lacertos,

> Again the heavy anchor invites me to set sails on uncertain routes, entrusting the ship to erratic winds; he orders me to recover for new battles the tired muscles and the weak limbs that survived two storms,

makes clear reference to two earlier poems or, according to Schaller, to two earlier books of the very same poem. Schaller even launches into creative conjecture about the lost content, which in his opinion contained, respectively, the celebration of Charles's ancestors and the first wars, while a fourth book would have described the coronation. But he himself called these ideas *"pure Spekulation"*.[36] The fact remains that *the poem was preceded by another two by the same author*. And this remains a substantial clue also as to the attribution of the work, as we shall see. In the context of this analysis I believe it may be of some importance that the manuscript contains a subdivision into chapters, whose divisions are indicated by blank lines, showing a reading of the text as a completed work.

The dating is conditioned by the presence of the attribute *augustus*, which led Schaller to a hypothesis of after Christmas of 800:[37] in reality Charles was awarded this title also in poems from twenty years before the coronation, for example by Hibernicus Exul and Angilbert, as well as by Moduin.[38] More compelling seems the fact that the poem mentions neither the resettlement of Leo in Rome nor, moreover, the death of Queen Liutgard, who died in June 800 but is one of the characters in the poem.

One element of Schaller's evidence in favour of a dating after the coronation was the fact that in the poem there are long portions of text (listed in the Appendix) that coincide with passages of the two eclogues of Moduin of Autun, the correspondent of Theodulf, perhaps Alcuin's student, whose poetic abilites are praised by many of his contemporaries and whose passion for the classics was denounced in one of the various metrical letters that Florus of Lyon addressed to him[39] and that studies tend to ignore. Given that in Schaller's time these eclogues were dated to between 804 and 814, it was assumed that Moduin was the one who quoted the *KMLP*, and that therefore the date of

---

[36] SCHALLER, "Das Aachener Epos", p. 163.
[37] *Ibid.*
[38] Hibernicus Exul, *carmen* 5, 17, ed. E. DÜMMLER in: *PLAC* 1, p. 401; or Angilbert, *carmen* 5, 1, 9, ed. E. DÜMMLER, in: *PLAC* 1, p. 365; Modoin, *Eclogues* 2, 10, ed. *ibid.*, p. 391.
[39] In particular Florus of Lyon, *carmen* 25, ed. E. DÜMMLER, in: *PLAC* 2, pp. 553-554.

composition must have been between 801 and 804. The dating of these eclogues has, however, changed considerably in recent research, and this radically alters things also with regard to the KMLP.

The Author

The hypotheses about attribution proposed over time have taken into consideration almost the entire poetic fauna of the first Carolingian court – the Irish exile who authored the panegyric for the victory over the Bavarians in 787; the court chaplain Angilbert, called Homer; Archbishop Ricolf of Mainz; Moduin of Autun, called Naso (i.e. Ovid); Theodulf of Orléans; and Alcuin – until Schaller even suggested Einhard, based on the fact that his contemporaries praised him as a poet, although none of his poetry except the lyric on the translation of Marcellinus and Peter has been handed down to us. But Schaller had the sense of humour to present the hypothesis, already attempted by Buchner in 1922 and scornfully rejected by Strecker in 1926, as a possible "*Tollkünheit oder Torheit*".[40] And yet for a little while this name was repeated in works summarising the literature of that time (e.g. by Godman[41]), as if it were an accepted fact.

The very first hypothesis, the only one supported by the manuscript, makes reference to a certain Helperic, based on the note added several times in the bottom margin of the folio by a later hand, but the only person we know of with this name was an author from Auxerre dated to the end of the century, who left behind only a computational treatise[42] and is therefore evidently unlikely. No one, however, has been able to explain why the manuscript attributes it to him or whether this name conceals a more believable candidate.

When Dieter Schaller began to tackle the question of authorship, his initial assessment was rather disappointing: "*Die Suche nach dem Person des Verfasser gilt heute fast als aussichtslos*",[43] because

---

[40] SCHALLER, "Das Aachener Epos", p. 165.
[41] P. GODMAN, *Poetry of the Carolingian Renaissance* (Oxford, 1985), and ID., *Poets and Emperors: Frankish Politics and Carolingian Poetry* (Oxford, 1987), pp. 49, 82 ff., 111-112, 120 ff., 173.
[42] Helperic of Auxerre, *Liber de computo*, ed. in: PL 137, cols. 19-48.
[43] SCHALLER, "Das Aachener Epos", p. 163.

man hat die Reihe der bekannten Dichter schon des öfteren Revue passieren lassen und einen nach dem anderen wieder verworfen: Theodulf, Alcuin, Angilbert, Hibernicus Exul, Naso – ihre Produktionen sind vom dichterischen Stil, von formalen Gesichtspunkte her zu verschieden von unserem Epos – es gibt sehr handfeste Argumente![44]

But if then we go to check this,[45] the *"sehr handfeste Argumente"* are reduced to very debatable observations. To give one example, Max Manitius[46] formerly supported Angilbert's authorship, citing a dozen stylistic coincidences – among them rather banal details such as the use of the term *decus*, the verb *mirari*, and the verb *rutilare* – and clausulae derived from Vergil or Lucan. Elements that are found in dozens of authors. The scholar, who had already expressed awareness of the controvertibility of this evidence:

Es sind dies sprachliche Anklänge, welche durchaus nicht auf directe Benutzung von Angilberts Gedichten deuten, indem sie sich mehr auf einzelne Worte und auf Gedanken beziehen, während (...) andere Dichter, denen Angilberts Gedichte vorlagen, ganze Verse oder Sätze abschreiben[47]

published a retraction the following year, but based on arguments that were not much more compelling: *"Eine intensivere Beschäftigung mit dem Gebiete der*

---

[44] *Ibid.*, p. 164. Inevitably recalling in these pages several excerpts of what was already published in STELLA, "Autore e attribuzioni".

[45] Schaller cites on this point M. MANITIUS, "Das Epos Karolus Magnus et Leo Papa", *Neues Archiv* 8 (1883), pp. 9-45, at pp. 11-14 and 34-45; AUSFELD, "Zur Frage nach dem Verfasser des Carolus Magnus et Leo papa"; K. STRECKER, "Studien zu den Karolingischen Dichtern", *Neues Archiv* 44 (1922), pp. 209-251, at p. 221; W. WATTENBACH, *Deutschlands Geschichtsquellen im Mittelalter: Vorzeit und Karolinger*, ed. W. LEVISON and H. LÖWE, Heft 2 (Weimar, 1953), pp. 241 and 245; O. SCHUMANN, "Angilbert", in: *Die deutsche Literatur des Mittelalters: Verfasserlexikon*, ed. W. STAMMLER and K. LANGOSCH, 5 vols. (Berlin and Leipzig, 1933-1955), 1, coll. 83-84; and BEUMANN, "Die Kaiserfrage", pp. 296 and 316.

[46] MANITIUS, "Das Epos", pp. 38-39.

[47] Manitius would later resolve the problem of the difference of prosody and of *dispositio verborum* between the poem and the authentic poetry of Angilbert with a different anagraphic time of composition: at least three years passed between the enduring poems of Angilbert (796) and the KMLP, given that the poem refers to the meeting between Charles and Leo III that happened in July 799 and the dating of the text oscillates between 799 and 814. The matter is summarised well by C. RATKOWITSCH, *Karolus Magnus – alter Aeneas, alter Martinus, alter Iustinus: Zur Intention und Datierung des Aachener Karlsepos* (Vienna, 1997), pp. 60-63.

karolingischen Dichtkunst hat mich von der Schwierigkeit, derartige Fragen zu entscheiden, überzeugt".[48] Sometime later he made a further declaration:

> *ich möchte diese meine frühere Ansicht nicht mehr festhalten; der genaue Einblick in die Hofverhältnisse könnte zu dieser Ansicht wohl führen, aber gerade Angilbert hatte doch wenig Veranlassung, mancherlei geradezu auf den Kopf zu stellen, wie das Mißgeschick Leos und das Verhältnis Karls zum Papste. Auch die größere grammatische und prosodische Schulung in dem Epos spricht gegen Angilberts Autorschaft.*[49]

It is thought that, in the 1950s, an Italian Latinist rejected the Alcuin hypothesis, advanced by Fichtenau[50] following the old editors, Canisius, Frobenius, and Monnier, with the argument that "the pious monk would not have indulged with such delight (…) in the hunt".[51] These arguments are similar to those according to which Heloise could not have written her letters because they were too 'modern' for the twelfth century: a logical fallacy known as *petitio principii*.

In recent times, almost a century after the first studies cited, an authoritative literary history[52] upheld, albeit with some reservations, the attribution of the poem – already attempted and failed by Simson – to the mysterious Hibernicus Exul, the author of the epic fragment on Tassilo and of a few courtly *carmina*, based on the following arguments:

1. both speak of contemporary events and satisfactorily arrange the material;
2. both adopt a philo-Frankish point of view;
3. both have the tone of a panegyric;
4. formal parallels.[53]

---

[48] M. MANITIUS, "Zu dem Epos 'Karolus magnus et Leo papa'", *Neues Archiv* 9 (1884), pp. 614-619, at p. 616.

[49] M. MANITIUS, *Geschichte der lateinischen literatur des Mittelalters*, 3 vols. (Munich, 1911-1931), 1, p. 547.

[50] H. FICHTENAU, "Byzanz und die Pfalz zu Aachen", *Mitteilungen des Instituts für Österreichische Geschichtsforschung* 59 (1951), pp. 1-54, at p. 29.

[51] N. SCIVOLETTO, "Angilberto abate di S. Riquier e l'humanitas carolingia", *Giornale Italiano di Filologia* 5 (1952), pp. 298-303.

[52] F. BRUNHÖLZL, *Geschichte der lateinischen Literatur des Mittelalters*, 1 (Munich, 1975), p. 62.

[53] BRUNHÖLZL, *Geschichte*, 1, pp. 303-304: "*Behandlung zeitgeschichtlicher Ereignisse in angemessener Verteilung des Stoffes, der dezidiert fränkische Standpunkt in beiden Stücken, der panegyrische Ton und sogar formale Ähnlichkeiten*".

Considerations of this kind could also be true for other authors: certainly for the author of the *Carmen de Conversione Saxonum*, but also Alcuin, Theodulf, Moduin, and Einhard, if not other court poets from the eighth to the ninth centuries.

The last monograph on the poem before the celebrations of 1999, written by Christine Ratkowitsch and appearing in 1997, presented contributions related to the text's literary relationships. The matter of the author only takes up part of a footnote where, on the subject of the attribution to Angilbert, it is said:

> *Diese Zuweisung ist allerdings schon allein aus stilistischen Gründen ebenso unwahrscheinlich wie die von P. Dronke versuchte an Modoin in seiner Rezension von D. Korzeniewski. Für die von Schaller vorgeschlagene Zuweisung an Einhard spricht einiges, sie ließ sich allerdings bis jetzt nicht beweisen.*[54]

What the stylistic reasons so often called on are, is hardly ever explained, and often we find ourselves dealing with apodictic claims unsupported by evidence, based on impressions that would make good arguments if they were not subject to the problem common to all arguments of authority and already discovered by Abelard, which is that each authority conflicts with other authorities and therefore is insufficient as evidence. The "*sehr handfeste Argumente*" are thus revealed to be frequently inconsistent. The latest idea, submitted by Helene Scheck in 2012,[55] is that the author was a woman, specifically Charles's cousin Gundrada, because of the importance given to female figures in the poem, especially in the hunt scene with women, an *unicum* in medieval literature.

---

[54] RATKOWITSCH, *Karolus Magnus*, p. 10, n. 4. In the introduction to the Paderborn edition Von Padberg simply reiterates that "*Da (...) keine weiteren Vorschläge aufge- kommen sind, wird man bei aller gebotenen Zurückhaltung Einhards Verfasserschaft erwägen müssen*".

[55] H.E. SCHECK, "Nuns on parade: Memorializing women in 'Karolus Magnus et Leo papa'", in: *Reading Memory and Identity in the Texts of Medieval European Holy Women*, ed. M. COTTER-LYNCH and B. HERZOG (New York, 2012), pp. 13-38.

New Developments in the Research[56]

1. In recent years a series of new results from the research has completely changed the terms of the problem. The works of Korzeniewski[57] and Green[58] on the Carolingian eclogues, and in particular on those by Moduin, have rebutted, based on a simple syntactic analysis, the dating of these eclogues to after 801, via a reinterpretation of the passage on which the old dating was based.[59] Green's article in the *Mittellateinisches Jahrbuch* of 1981 confirmed the new dating[60] and overturned the chronological terms of their relationship with the *KMLP*: it is no longer Moduin who is imitating the poem, but the reverse. Through further analysis, Christine Ratkowitsch's work has also led to new arguments in favour of Moduin's antecedence, showing that the imitator is the author of the poem and that his connection with Moduin is surprisingly strong on matters that are surprisingly central. As you can see in the Appendix, these are not simply echoes or allusions but large-scale revivals of entire lines and of complex and elaborate motifs, like that of the *nova Roma* or of the comparison between Charles and the Sun, or of rare expressions such as *Sophocleo coturno*, which was found only in Moduin and in this poem in the medieval period before John of Garland. This single chronological and exegetical element alone implies a chain of determinative historical-literary consequences, because a series of inferences that are now no longer sustainable were based on this dat-

---

[56] A panorama of the progress of the research, in particular from a historical perspective, is provided by the edition of Hentze, with an extensive introduction by Lutz von Padberg and a new apparatus of *loci similes* edited by Johannes Schwind.

[57] D. KORZENIEWSKI, *Hirtengedichte aus spätrömischer und karolingischer Zeit* (Darmstadt, 1976).

[58] R.P.H. GREEN, "Modoin's Eclogues and the Paderborn epic", *Mittellateinisches Jahrbuch* 16 (1981), pp. 43-53. See notes 65 and 67.

[59] Modoin, *Ecloga*, 1, 85-93, ed. E. DÜMMLER, in: *PLAC* 1, p. 387: "*Nam meus ecce solet magno facundus Homerus / carminibus Carolo studiosis saepe placere. / Ni Flaccus calamo modulari carmina nosset, / non tot praesentis tenuisset praemia vitae. / Theodulfus gracili iam dudum lusit avena, / plurima cantando meruit commertia rerum. / Aonias avide solitus recitare camenas / Nardhus ovans summo praesenti pollet honore*". The problem of dating is linked to the interpretation of the adjective *praesens* and of the pluperfect subjunctive in comparison to Alcuin; if it was intended as the past, Alcuin would have been dead at the time of the text's composition, and its dating should consequently be moved to after 804.

[60] Green shows that the past tense can refer to the present. His demonstration is not agreed on by Godman (GODMAN, *Poetry of the Carolingian Renaissance*, p. 162: "the crucial point at vv. 87-8 is not the tense but the mood (...). Given Carolingian poetic freedom with tense and mood, no argument based upon these criteria can be decisive") and by Schaller (SCHALLER, "Frühkarolingische Corippus-Rezeption", pp. 181-182), without further arguments.

ing.[61] For example Schaller's attribution to Einhard,[62] cited earlier, was also based on the passages in which Moduin's eclogues and a letter by Alcuin call him a connoisseur of Vergil[63] and one of the most prominent poets of his time.[64] But Alcuin's letter, dated 796, is from *before* the date of the poem and therefore cannot be alluding to the poem. If Moduin's eclogue is also dated prior to 801, then the eulogies of Einhard cannot refer to the poem.[65] In this way the only element in favour of Einhard collapses, even if this does not categorically exclude its theoretical possibility. The other arguments adopted, such as the scant presence of theological culture, may perhaps contribute to eliminating Alcuin or Theodulf, already excluded due to their absence from Aachen during the event and for other reasons, but they could also apply to Hibernicus Exul and Moduin.[66] Stronger are the findings, opposing the Einhard hypothesis, of an extremely different attitude about Charles from that of the *Vita Karoli*,[67] of the different weight of political culture in the two works, and the almost complete lack of other documentation of the historian's poetic abilities.[68] Not

---

[61] The entire reconstruction that Manitius proposes for the chronological relationships between the poem, Angilbert, Hibernicus Exul, and Moduin, is based on the old dating of the latter. Now this entire literary genealogy, also repeated in modern literary histories, has lost its primary foundation.

[62] Already attempted, however, by M. BUCHNER, *Einhards Künstler und Gelehrtenleben: Ein Kulturbild aus der Zeit Karls des Großen und Ludwigs des Frommen* (Leipzig, 1922), pp. 39 ff. and initially also by MANITIUS, "Das Epos Karolus Magnus et Leo Papa".

[63] Alcuin, *carmen* 26, a. 796.

[64] Moduin, *Ecloga* 1, 92. The extremely low presence of poetic memory in the *Vita Karoli* is justified by Schaller as a difference of literary genre.

[65] The hypothesis that Moduin is celebrating the poetic excellence of Einhard on the basis of unpublished versions of the poem heard during court performances (RATKOWITSCH, *Karolus Magnus*, p. 76) seems frankly unlikely, because – if we accept the plausible conclusions of Green and Ratkowitsch about the imitative relationship between the two texts – it presumes an author (the author of *KMLP*) who was imitating his model (Moduin's *Eclogues*) before it was written!

[66] In my opinion the interest of *KMLP* in building activities cannot be considered a strong argument – according to SCHALLER, "Das Aachener Epos", p. 167, this would lead us back to the architect's functions that Einhard performed – also because all the elements of this description come from Vergil and do not demonstrate personal skill.

[67] Although in this regard it is necessary to keep in mind the substantial difference between a panegyric written *in praesentia* and a *post mortem* biography.

[68] In his nod to the content of the poem *In honorem Hludowici pii*, which nonetheless, due to its epic stylisation, depends entirely and continuously draws on the model of *KMLP*, Ermoldus Nigellus does not mention Einhard as coming before him or as the singer of imperial feats, but as a royal counsellor (*Ermold le Noir*, ed. FARAL, ll. 682-685, p. 54 = ed. DÜMMLER, in: *PLAC* 2, 2, 31-35, p. 25: "*Tunc Heinardus erat Caroli dilectus amore, / ingenioque sagax et bonitate vigens, / hic cadit ante pedes, vestigia basiat alma, / doctus consiliis incipit ista prior*".

to mention the fact that Einhard does not speak of this episode in the *Vita Karoli*, nor does he write of ever having treated it.[69]

2. Schaller's latest contribution[70] identified the presence of an imitation of Corippus, throughout the entire Carolingian age, only in our poem, in Theodulf, and in Moduin, a combination that will re-emerge in this survey; and Ratkowitsch's book investigated the importance knowingly conferred on the poet's text, structurally inspired by the Vergilian ethic of the state, by the national sanctity of Venantius Fortunatus's *Vita Sancti Martini*, and by the imperial predominance of Corippus's poems.

3. The later statistics about metrical phenomena in work by Jean-Yves Tilliette[71] and especially by Edoardo D'Angelo,[72] together with the work of Strecker and Manitius, provided data useful for an objective comparison. In my work in 2002 I tried to make good use of these and other metrical-stylistic information, together with the new discoveries cited above, exploring several of the consequences of those discoveries in relation to the matter of the author of the poem, with results that I will not repeat here (for some important data see the Appendix).

Essentially, in addition to the Vergilian model, that of Venantius Fortunatus, the *De virginitate* almost more than the *Vita Martini*, and Corippus's panegyric for Justin has clearly emerged. The presence of contemporaries, however, is scarce, with the exception of the very rare echoes of Alcuin (whose *De sanctis Euboricensis ecclesiae*[73] and the *Vita Willibrordi*,[74] the two real epic poems

---

Walahfrid, in *De imagine Tetrici*, also only calls him a famous architect (ed. DÜMMLER, in: *PLAC* 2, ll. 221-226 (*De Einharto magno*), p. 377): "*Nec minor est magni reverentia patris habenda / Beseleel, fabre primum qui percipit omne / artificum praecautus opus: sic denique summus / ipse legens infirma deus, sic fortia temnit. / Magnorum quis enim maiora receperat umquam, / quam radiare brevi nimium miramur homullo?*". This is true for other famous quotations: no testimony on Einhard is therefore applicable to *KMLP*.

[69] More recently, Zwierlein's research demonstrated the purpose of the imitation of Vergil, understood to set up the figure of Charles based on the model of Aeneas: O. ZWIERLEIN, "Karolus Magnus – alter Aeneas", in: *Literatur und Sprache im europäischen Mittelalter: Festschrift für K. Langosch*, ed. A. ÖNNERFORS, J. RATHOFER, and F. WAGNER (Darmstadt, 1973), pp. 44-52.

[70] SCHALLER, "Die frühkarolingische Corippus-Rezeption".

[71] J.-Y. TILLIETTE, "Métrique carolingienne et métrique auxerroise: Quelques réflexions sur la Vita sancti Germani d'Heiric d'Auxerre", in: *L'Ecole carolingienne d'Auxerre: De Muretach à Remi, 830-908*, ed. D. IOGNA-PRAT, C. JEUDY, and G. LOBRICHON (Paris, 1991), pp. 313-327.

[72] E. D'ANGELO, *Indagini sulla tecnica versificatoria nell'esametro del Waltharius* (Catania, 1992), based on the continuous comparison with Carolingian metre.

[73] *Per colla lapillis*, cf. Alcuin, *De sanctis Eboracensis Ecclesiae* (ed. E. DÜMMLER, in: *PLAC* 1, pp. 169-206), l. 1501; *KMLP* l. 286: *exercitus omnis* (repeated in ll. 429, 440, 455, 476,

of the time, are perhaps imitated in a few passages[75]), Hibernicus Exul, and Angilbert[76] (with whom it coincides – aside from the instances traceable to classical models – in a few expressions[77]). With Moduin, however, as we have seen, the poem shares not only expressions, formulae, *iuncturae*, and topical combinations, but fundamental characteristics at both an ideological level, such as faith in the *nova Roma*, and a structural one, such as the mention of two books in the preface, the simile of the king and the sun and that of the workers constructing Aachen with the industriousness of bees, the *affectatio modestiae* in controversy with older poets, and many expressions, even rare ones. The metrical statistical data also seem to head in the same direction, excluding other interpretations:[78]

Dactyl in the first foot: *KMLP* 72.6%, Naso 77.5%, Hibernicus Exul 52.4%
Anomalous clauses: *KMLP* 0.5%, Naso 0.5%, Hibernicus Exul 0%
Feminine caesuras: *KMLP* 35%, Naso 36.5%, Hibernicus Exul 3.9%
Leonine rhyme: *KMLP* 18.2%, Naso 17.5%, Hibernicus Exul 32%

501), cf. Alcuin, *De sanctis*, 1, l, 252 (the only non-clause precedent); *KMLP* l. 402 *venerandus (...) sacerdos* l. 1, 846 (and 106 III. 1), *ibid*. p. 333.

[74] On *KMLP* l. 402 *pastor apostolicus* cf. Alcuin, *Vita Willibrordi* (ed. W. LEVISON, in: *MGH SRM* 7, pp. 113-141), 3, 6; 522 *rite peractis* cf. Alcuin, *Vita Willibrordi*, 18, 2 (and before this already Cyprianus Gallus, *Heptateuchus*, ed. R. PEIPER (Vienna, 1881: *CSEL* 23), Exodus, 705; Eugenius of Toledo, *Carmina*, ed. F. VOLLMER, in: *MGH AA* 14.1 (Berlin, 1905), *carmen* 37, 7; and *Anthologia Latina*, ed. A. RIESE, 2 vols. (Leipzig, 1894-1906), 16, 51). The clause *carmina laudum* from l. 514 is very frequent in Alcuin, *Carmina* (ed. DÜMMLER, in: *PLAC* 1): 7, 2; 8, 25; 54, 2; 95, 3. It is also found in Angilbert, *Carmina* (ed. DÜMMLER, in: *PLAC* 1), 2, 81.

[75] This is the opinion expressed also by Peter Godman in his edition of the text (*Alcuin, The Bishops, Kings and Saints of York*, ed. P. GODMAN (Oxford, 1992), p. XCI). Contra D. SCHALLER, "Vergil und die Wiederentdeckung des Epos im frühen Mittelalter", *Medioevo e Rinascimento* 1 (1987), pp. 75-100, at p. 85, with reference to Aristotelian poetics.

[76] Already indicated by MANITIUS, "Das Epos".

[77] The *transnavigat amnem* of l. 415, which recalls Hibernicus Exul, *carmen* 2, 80 (ed. DÜMMLER in: *PLAC* 1, p. 398), is important; the verb has no other Carolingian attestations, but comes from *Aen.* 6, 671 *transnavimus amnes*. For *ambiguos calles* cf. Angilbert, *Carmina* (ed. DÜMMLER, in *PLAC* 1) 1, 16 and 178, 4; *KMLP* 30 *duces (...) comites*; and cf. Angilbert 1, 58.

[78] These statistics, together with other elements, seem to definitively exclude Hibernicus Exul, defended by Brunhölzl. Manitius eliminated him from the list of possible authors based on his dissimilar metrical skill; but in reality it is possible for the style of an author to have evolved over ten or eleven years (787-799), as Schaller also upheld in relation to the attribution to Einhard, to justify the differences from the *Vita Karoli*; and thus it is possible that Hibernicus Exul (Dungal) could have ironed out his visible prosodic shortcomings. But it is less likely that he would have modified the metrical structure of his verse so drastically, moving from specific characteristics of rhyme or caesura (not errors, but stylistic choices) to completely opposite ones.

Rhyme in the *KMLP*: double frequency compared to Angilbert (Strecker)
Elision: 28.7%, Naso 22%, Hibernicus Exul 24.2%
Trochee in the first foot: *KMLP* more than 20%, Naso 26.5%, Hibernicus Exul 1.9%
Dactyl/spondee ratio: *KMLP* 1.1%, Nose 1.1%, Angilbert 1.5%, Alcuin 0.9%, Theodulf of Orléans 0.8%, Hibernicus Exul 0.4%

Hypotheses about the Author

Limiting ourselves to the usual positive proofs, the research has therefore led to significant coincidences – thematic, stylistic, and metrical – with Moduin, the author of the two *Eclogues* and of a poetic exchange with Theodulf, so powerful that it seems improbable that they can be explained by a simple imitative relationship. Green had already identified 17 parallels between Moduin's texts and the *KMLP*,[79] and Christine Ratkowitsch, while objecting to some, convincingly affirmed Moduin's precedence: surely a relationship of such great dependence in a sort of cento that, all things considered, barely imitates its contemporaries needs some justification. Imitating Moduin so heavily is not like imitating Vergil or Venantius. On the other hand, regardless of stylistic considerations, it seems difficult to use the category of imitation to explain the profound, multiple, and continuous similarities with Moduin in the interpretation of the *nova Roma*, in the emphasis of the emperor through the simile with the sun (even if this was drawn from Corippus), in the Ovidian reinterpretation of Vergil, in many – I would say too many – poetic expressions, including those of topical passages such as the preface and the *affectatio modestiae*, or the comparison of writing to navigation. What is really striking is the presence, both in Moduin's eclogues and in the *KMLP*, and *only* in these two works, of the declaration of modesty, expressed not only in the same Ovidian terms (*arte rudis, sermone rudi*), but in polemic with the *senes vates*, characterised in both places with the curious connotation of victors (89-90: "*quisve putat sermone rudi se pincipis acta / posse referre, senes cum vincant omnia vates?*" – "who believes that in such crude language they can tell the deeds of the prince, since the old poets win everything?"), which belongs more to a socio-cultural dialectic within the Carolingian court than to a literary conven-

---

[79] See note 54. Of Ratkowitsch see RATKOWITSCH, *Karolus Magnus*, pp. 65-66, to which I refer for its list and analysis of individual passages. SCHALLER. "Das Aachener Epos", p. 151, emphasises that "*der Epilog [der Eklogen Modoins] (in der Funktion der an Karl gerichteten "dedication") hat also genau die gleiche Kombination von Benennungen Karls wie unser Epos!*".

tion. There are hints in the two passages of the very same sense of exclusion from the clique of intellectuals who are already enjoying Charles's esteem and the concrete benefits that this esteem brings. The aspiration to *publica carmina* (Modoin, *Ecloga* 1, 33: "*publica nulla canis, nulli tua carmina digna*" – "you do not sing of public events, your poems are not worthy for anyone") also returns in the exaltation of "*publica gesta*" in l. 201 of the poem: this reflects an ambition that seems to be a concern of Moduin's, a tool that permits one to enter the dominant group. Other scholars have examined these passages to establish who the imitator was. But why would one imitate a passage like this, unless one completely shared Moduin's condition and spirit, and who else would nurture social feelings so similar to those that the *puer Modoinus* so often displays?[80]

Added to these observations are now two factors that I had not considered in my article from 2002-2004. The first was already intuited by Dronke in his critical revision of Korzeniewski:[81] the so-called eclogues of Moduin are actually called *libri* by the manuscript tradition and *gemini libelli* by Moduin himself,[82] and the second *libellus* finishes by hoping that Charles, to whom he addresses the two *carmina*, welcomes them generously. If this happens, Moduin will dedicate himself to recounting Charles's feats: "*ordine cuncta volo gesta referre tua*" ("I want to tell all your deeds in one story"). But the execu-

---

[80] The same devotion to Alcuin, and the isoglosses with his student Ethelwulf, would be explained well by the disciple relationship that united Moduin with the master from York, as shown by Alcuin's *carmen* 32, l. 31 (ed. DÜMMLER, in: *PLAC* 1, p. 250) which refers to a poet, *Naso* (Moduin's nickname at court), of whom he quotes a line that is definitely not Ovidian. According to Ebert this Naso coincides with the student whose departure Alcuin laments, indicated in the *carmen* with the name Corydon, a *rusticus* and *presbyter* intellectual who nonetheless in Alcuin's school had already proven himself capable of *superare senes*: the same expression, the very same dialectic so dear to our poet. The Theodulfian isoglosses fit well into the friendly relationship reflected by the poetic letters exchanged between Theodulf and Moduin known to us: a token of an esteem that led Theodulf and later Florus and even Walahfrid to salute Moduin as a great poet, and Moduin to respond with the same expressions of *rusticitas* and *ruditas artis* that we find again in his other works (cf. A. EBERT, *Allgemeine Geschichte der Literatur des Mittelalters im Abendlande*, 3 vols. (Leipzig 1874-1887), 2, p. 31; ID., "Naso, Angilbert und der Conflictus veris et hiemis", *Zeitschrift für das deutsches Altertum und deutsche Literatur* 22 (1878), pp. 328-335; and see also A. EBENBAUER, "Nasos Ekloge", *Mittellateinisches Jahrbuch* 11 (1976), pp. 13-27, at p. 13, note 3.

[81] P. DRONKE, [Review of: D. KORZENIEWSKI, *Hirtengedichte aus spätrömischer und karolingischer Zeit* (Darmstadt, 1976)], *Cahiers de Civilisation Classique et Médiévale* 23 (1980), pp. 61-63.

[82] Modoin, *Ecloga* (ed. E. DÜMMLER, in: *PLAC* 1, pp. 384-391), *Praef.* l. 5: "*Istis in geminis legitur tua fama libellis*".

tion of this project has not reached us, unless it is the KMLP. The KMLP in turn begins with "*Rursus in ambiguos gravis ammonet anchora calles*", which is far too reminiscent of "*Rursus in antiquos mutataque saecula mores*" in Moduin 1, 26. And he continues by saying that he wants to take on the sea once more, after having survived two storms, in other words after having written two books. The only two *libri* in honour of Charles of which we are now aware are those of Moduin, called eclogues.

The second factor is that the Zurich manuscript also preserves the correspondence between Moduin and Theodulf, or rather a poem by Theodulf and a response from Moduin. The only other witness is copied from this one. Thus, the Saint Gall antigraph of Zurich in all probability had both the Theodulf-Moduin correspondence (or at least Moduin's response) and the KMLP. But who would have had access to a correspondence between two people – that is, a letter and its reply – if not one of the individuals involved?

The idea of Moduin's authorship is not at all new, and had already been aired briefly by Beumann in a note in his 1962 essay[83] and then occasionally had been taken up again by Dronke,[84] as I have mentioned. Some objections to this hypothesis have come up: the most serious ones, put forward once again by Beumann,[85] concerned always and above all the fact that in the eclogues, which then were believed to have come after the poem, Moduin called himself a poet who had not yet become an epic storyteller. And obviously he would not have done so if he had been the author of the earlier KMLP. But also in this case the new dating of the eclogues brings Moduin back into play: it was the eclogues that came first and expressed that very desire for *epos* that, with the extended use of imitation *en bloc* so consistent with Moduin's manner of composition,[86] the KMLP managed to fulfil. The new dating further weakens the hypotheses of Einhard and of anyone who did not wish to contrast themselves with the *senes* because they already belonged to that group: Alcuin and Theodulf, who more-

---

[83] BEUMANN, "Die Kaiserfrage", p. 316.

[84] DRONKE, [Review].

[85] Apart from those based on the different quality of the two works, which are extremely questionable.

[86] R.P.H. GREEN, *Seven versions of Carolingian Pastoral* (Reading, 1980), p. 65, observes in Moduin's eclogues "an amazing frequency of classical reminiscences, a feature they share with *Karolus Magnus et Leo papa*". As for the stylistic differences between Moduin and the 'poem' (explainable, in my opinion, as differences of genre and model), Green's observation about the differences between the two eclogues can be considered illustrative of such variation: "The difference between the two poems in imaginative quality and in their realisation is a surprising fact".

over were not at Paderborn in 799, but also once again Hibernicus Exul, who in 799 would have been at least 25-30 years old, and Angilbert who, if the eclogues came earlier, had already been gratified with the material rewards that the poet of the *KMLP* still seems to be waiting to receive. Alternative interpretations and obstacles of detail undoubtedly remain.

Of course, we cannot conclusively eliminate all the hypotheses that, while they cannot be proven, also cannot be refuted, in other words those that lack textual comparisons: first of all Helperic (of Auxerre?), whose name can be read in a corner of the manuscript and which it has not be possible to trace to any plausible candidate; secondly Fardulf of Saint-Denis, who accompanied Charles on his expedition to Saxony and whose very few lines contain two coincidences with the poem;[87] and finally Grimald, an extremely young attendee of the court school and later chancellor and chaplain until his abbacy at Saint Gall, where the codex was written. But of all the hypotheses that have the support of textual evidence, that of Moduin undoubtedly remains the strongest, as Rosamond McKitterick also seems to recognise in her last book on Charlemagne.[88]

Medieval Authority

The *KMLP* is a poem whose author its contemporaries did not even bother to identify and into which modern readers, in search of novel information about the history of power, have put a great deal of thought. So, what kind of reading did this poem experience in its own period? Could it be called influential? Did it have readers? Was it commented on and imitated? As I have mentioned, the poem was transmitted in a single codex and we know of no copies or commentaries, although the codex is not the original. The only certain reader is the corrector of the Zurich manuscript. In his poem in honour of Louis the Pious, the only of Charles's sons unnamed in the *KMLP*, Ermoldus Nigellus revives the hunt scene from the poem and imitates many other passages of it, which Manitius had already identified, albeit perhaps with excessive generosity, in 1883.[89] The set of models that Ermoldus had before him also includes Theodulf

---

[87] Fardulfus, *Carmina* (ed. E. DÜMMLER, in: *PLAC* 1, pp. 353-354), 2, l. 5 *pulcherrimus heros*; cf. *KMLP* ll. 63, 149, 337, 431, 468, 482 *et al.*

[88] R. McKITTERICK, *Charlemagne:The Formation of a European Identity* (Cambridge, 2014), p. 140, note 9.

[89] MANITIUS, "Das Epos", p. 44.

and Moduin's correspondence, and therefore seems to come from a specific setting, which could be Lyon, where Moduin and Theodulf may have crossed paths and where Ermoldus, who was Aquitanian in origin, might have had the chance to pass by, or – at this point already at the first level of manuscript transmission – the Saint Gall area, possibly with the mediation of Bishop Bernold, who studied at Reichenau and welcomed Ermoldus to Strasbourg at the time of his exile.

Helena de Carlos Villamarin believed she had found echoes of the same *KMLP* hunting scene in the *Epistola ad Hugonem* of Godfrey of Reims, but a careful check reveals that these parallels can be explained by their common Vergilian source. The immediate success of the so-called *KMLP* seems therefore to be documented only in the context of composition, as a product of the court, without any recognition as an epic capable of representing a national identity or an otherwise collective feeling.

The constantly and heavily Vergilian inspiration for the *KMLP* was long considered an element of favourable evaluation, as if it were a merit in itself.[90] My opinion, like Florus of Lyon's, is a little different, and it led me to exclude the text from my anthology of Carolingian poetry:[91] *KMLP* fails in its epic intent and therefore its aesthetic result, because it is inspired by a model, the classical panegyric epic, which is not suited to the new culture whose values a new epos must be able to represent, and reduces its own operation to an archaeological recovery. From this point of view, the *KMLP* carries out a function of self-representation of power rather than the function, essential to epic, of mythicisation of collective identities – a function better fulfilled by hagiography and by poems such as Alcuin's *De sanctis Euboricensis ecclesiae*. The *KMLP* was therefore consigned to exclusive appreciation by modern readers, both because of its prioritised attention to facts and characters not from literature but from institutional history, in other words figures of power, which continues to condition our approaches and scale of values, and also due to its strong classicist quality, which has made it a text that is recognisable and appreciated by the dominant criteria of philological humanism.

---

[90] "*Es macht unstreitig einen Vorzug des Karolus Magnus et Leo papa aus, daß der Dichter es sich nicht wie andere genügen ließ, seine Verse mit antiken Floskeln afzuputzen, sondern daß es ihm gelungen ist, in bewußter Imitation antiker epischer Dichtung das Ganze in eine antikisch anmutende Atmosphäre zu versetzen, dem ganzen Werk ein antikisierendes Kolorit zu verleihen*" (BRUNHÖLZL, *Geschichte*, p. 302).

[91] *La poesia carolingia*, ed. F. STELLA (Florence, 1995).

Appendix

1. Author's indications, subdivision into books and copying process (MS Zurich, Zentralbibliothek, C 78; after <http://e-codices.ch/de/searchresult/list/one/zbz/C0078>).

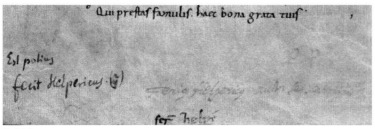

f. 103v

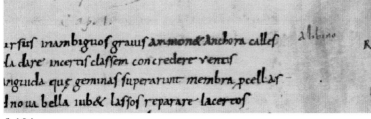

f. 104r

f. 107v

f. 110r

Tunc karolus prędā pcerēs partī
Spolūs onerat grauidīs sociosq;

Cap. III.

nde reflectit iter campū. repe
Frondosum lucū natulīs fontesc

f. 113r

Hortā iñplexuque oīm placida osculalibens
Tcomes & suprasē confert vertice toto
Pippīnus variās miscent semone loquellas
Inque vice diuersā leuant pro blepsinnatiubo

Cap. IIII.

Ex pius Interea solīū conscendit &omnem
Alloquitr populū karolus venerabilīs heros
Ergo agite o pceres inquit quibs; induīte arma

f. 114v

Rex & apostolicus repetit quoq; castrū suorū
Cīvitali a karolo leo fit susceptus honore
Romanos fugiens ppriūsq; repulsus aboris

usq; huc

Cap. I. Septennodiū dicimus herbā cuius radices in septēnodīs uidē

2. 'Pre-Caroline' orthographic peculiarities eliminated in the edition

37 *imponet* for *imponit*
209 *murmoris*
284 *vidit* for *videt*
448 *ibit* for *ivit*
490 *praecepit* with a short syllable for *praecipit*

3. Corrections

105 *inclaudunt*
403 *volotas*

4. Author's vulgarisms or barbarisms (Brünholzl)

246 *dependunt*
286 *acra* (*proelia*)
436 *recensat*
447 *facessans*
533 *revisat* for *revisit*
384 *ut* ending with future ind.
338 relative phrase, partly in the indicative (390 *vindicat*, 391 *allevat*), partly in the subjunctive (*examinet*)

5. The *Karolus Magnus et Leo papa* compared to Moduin's *Eclogae*

The third of two books and writing as navigation

KMLP

1   *Rursus in ambiguos* gravis ammonet anchora calles
        Tela dare, incertis classem concredere ventis;
    Languida quae *geminas* superarunt membra procellas,
        Ad nova bella iubet lassos reparare lacertos,

    cf. Venant. *Mart.* 3, 11 s.

    Quos ego sub geminis claudo pede curro libellis,
        Infimus egregii contexens gesta patroni;

Eclogae	
1, 26	*Rursus in antiquos* mutataque secula mores.
1 Praef.	Caesareis Carolus sapiens hec auribus hauri
	Carmina, que nulla sunt peritura die,
	Dum rapidis sol currit equis, vibramine terras
	Inlustrat, gelidis dum *mare* fervet aquis,
5	*Istis in geminis legitur tua fama libellis*
	Carmine velato cum seniore viro.
2nd	Dilectus domini David benedictus in aevum,
	Suscipe nunc famuli munera parva tui.
	Ille ego Naso tuus tibi carmina mitto pusillus,
	Quem sua paupertas vix sinet arcta loqui.
5	Haec tu si capias animo vultuque sereno,
	Ordine cuncta volo gesta referre tua.

10 Vela movet *placidus* tremulis cita *flatibus Eurus*,

    2, 26   *molliter adspirans... flatibus Eurus*

Georg. 2, 339 Orbis, et hibernis parcebant *flatibus Euri*
Coripp. *Iust.* 2, 321 *placidis bene flantibus Euris*

Charles is compared to the Sun

KMLP

    Sol nitet ecce suis radiis: sic denique David
15 Inlustrat magno pietatis lumine terras.
    Res tamen una duos variando separat istos,
    Et vice disiuncti mutata saepe feruntur:
    Illum aliquando tegunt nimboso *nubila tractu*,
    Hunc ullae numquam possunt variare *procellae*;
20 Ille caret proprio bissenis lumine horis,
    Iste suam *aeterno conservat sidere lucem*;
    Pace nitet laeta, pariter pietate redundans

Nescit habere pio lapsurum lumine casum.
Vultu hilari, ore nitet, semper quoque fronte serena
25 Fulget et aeterno pietatis lumine Phoebum
Vincit, ab occasu dispergens nomen in ortum.

       Eclogae

    II, 69 ff.   Aureus in medio rutilans sol emicat orbe,

    70   Inque plagas mundi radios protendit in omnes,
        Aestuat in totas placido vibramine partes,
        Cedere nulla valent cui nusquam *nubila vultu*,
        Ora neque imbrifera obscurantur nube serena, *Perpetuoque suam conservat sidere lucem.*
    75   Mitigat ille notho saevas surgente *procellas*:

    cf. Corippus, *Iust.* 2, 148-58

    Astitit in clipeo princeps fortissimus illo
    Solis habens speciem. Lux altera fulsit ab urbe.
150   Mirata est pariter geminos consurgere soles
    Vna fauens eademque dies. mea carmina numne
    Mensuram transgressa suam? Mirabere forsan,
    Quod dixi geminos pariter consurgere soles,
    Nec uacuis uerbis nec inanibus ista figuris
155   Ore feres prolata meo, si dicta rependis.
    Mens iusti plus sole nitet. Non mergitur undis,
    Non cedit tenebris, non fusca obtexitur umbra.
    Lux operum aeterno lucet splendore bonorum.

    Venantius, *Carm.* 3, 23a, 1-6

    Phoebus ut elatum suspendit in aethera currum
        Purus et igniferum spargit ubique iubar,
    Effusis radiis totum sibi uindicat orbem,
        Montes, plana replens ima uel alta tenet.

    5   Sic, praesul, splendore animi cum sole coruscas:
        Ille suis radiis fulget et ipse tuis.

39 *Impia colla premit rigidis constricta catenis,*

> II 87 *Improba colla gemunt duris constricta catenis*
>
> cf. Lucan. 4, 421 constricta catenis

74 Atque suis dictis *facundus* cedit *Homerus,*

> I 85 *facundus Homerus*
>
> cf. Iuv. 7, 38 atque uni cedit Homero

The 'ancient' poets

KMLP

89f. Quisve putat sermone *rudi* se principis acta
90   Posse referre, *senes* cum vincant omnia *vates*?

> *Eclogae*
>
> Prol. 12 "Cur haec presumpsit arte referre *rudis*?"
> 1, 1   Tu frondosa, *senex vates*, protectus opaca
>
> cf. Venant. *Carm.* 8, 3, 133 senum vatum (the 24 elders in Revelation)
>
> In Moduin this is the central theme of the two *libelli*.

Second Rome

KMLP

98 Stat pius arce procul Karolus loca singula signans,
    *Alta*que disponens *venturae moenia Romae.*

> *Eclogae*
>
> I 31   Quae fuit *alta novae* cernendi *moenia Romae*?
>   cf. Verg. *Aen.* 1, 7 atque altae moenia Romae

Simile with bees

KMLP

      Fervet opus; velutique solent aestate, futurae,
      Pulchra, hiemis non inmemores, alimenta ciborum
      Cum facere, *ore legunt* carpentes *floscula* apesque
130 Per latices, *per thima volant stridentibus alis*;
      Floribus insidunt aliae, praedaque redire
      Accepta studeant, redolentia castra revisant;
      Aut foetus aliae certant educere adultos,
      Aut cum nectareas componunt ordine *cellas*,
135 Roscida stipantes sinuoso poplite *mella*:
      Haud aliter lata Franci spatiantur in urbe.

          Eclogae

II, 9 ff. *Ore legunt flores*, lentis *stridentibus alis*
10   *Per tima summa volant*, apibus populatur agellus,
         His mixtis pariter nam murmurat ore susurro.

      cf. Verg. *Georg.* 4, 200-01

      Verum ipsae e foliis natos, e suauibus herbis
      Ore legunt,

Aen., 1, 430-436

      Qualis apes aestate noua per florea rura
      Exercet sub sole labor, cum gentis adultos
      Educunt fetus, aut cum liquentia mella
      Stipant et dulci distendunt nectare *cellas*,
      Aut onera accipiunt uenientum, aut agmine facto
435 Ignauum fucos pecus a praesepibus arcent;
      Feruet opus redolentque *thymo* fragrantia *mella*.

Ov. *Ars* 1, 96 *per flores et thyma summa volant* [*apes*]

Corippus *Iust.* 4, 27-33

      More apium, quas uer tepidum noua condere castra
      Et munire fauos ceris iubet. aethere capto

30   Densa per herbosos errant examina campos,
        Floribus insidunt (Aen. 6, 708) uariis, roremque madentem
        Ore legunt onerantque umeros, cerasque liquentes
        Conficiunt, dulcesque lares in pumice figunt.

Other iuncturae

KMLP

121 Plaustraque dant sonitum; *vastus fragor* aethera pulsat;

  Eclogae

  II, 56 Conclamat nemus, it *vastus fragor* undique, pacem Convocat

  cf. Paul. Petr. *Mart.* 3, 10 fragor undique vastus

  Only known attestation of such *iunctura*.

147 f. *Fronde retecta* vacat; passim genus omne ferarum
  His latet in silvis.

  II, 45 Quoque ferat se quisque, latet *sub fronde retectus*

201 Restaurat proprii qui *publica gesta* parentis,
  I, 33 *Publica* nulla canis, nulli tua carmina digna

257 Clara *Sophocleoqu*e ornatur virgo *coturno*.

  II, 60 Scripta *Sophocleo* cum sint memoranda *coturno* (only known attestations between the sixth and twelfth centuries, from Verg. *Ecl.* 8, 10 *sola Sophocleo tua carmina digna coturno* and Ov. *Am.* 1, 15 *Nulla Sophocleo ueniet iactura cothurno*)

The Modern Success and Medieval Marginality

Other elements

Knowledge and revival of Corippus in the Carolingian age: only Theodulf, Moduin, *Karolus Magnus et Leo papa*	Zürich, Zentralbibliothek, C 78: it contains the correspondence between Theodulf and Moduin and the KMLP
Enjambment: more than 10%	Hibernicus Exul: 4.47%; Moduin: 15.75%. Theodulf and Alcuin much lower.
Frequency of the enclitic -que in the first foot	Frequent in Moduin, absent in HE, rare in Alcuin, Theodulf, Angilbert.
Irregular clauses: 0.5%	Moduin 0.5%; other poets: lower.
Feminine cesuras: 35%	Moduin 36%, Hibernicus Exul 3.9%
Leonine rhyme: 17.5%	Moduin: 17.5%, Hibernicus Exul 32%
Ratio dactyls/spondees: 1.1%	Moduin: 1.1% (Angilbert 1.5%, Alcuin 0.9%, Theodulf 0.8%)
Dactyls in the first foot: 72.6%	Moduin 77.5%, Hibernicus Exul 52.4%
Stylometric data, e.g.: use of the nexus *iam dudum* more than once	Only Theodulf and Moduin

Chapter 14

A 'Post-Colonial' Approach to Medieval Latin Literature?

The language I have learn'd these forty years
My native English, now I must forego,
And now my tongue's use is to me no more
Than an unstringed viol or a harp
Or like a cunning instrument cas'd up
Or, being open, put into his hands
that knows no touch to tune the harmony.
Within my mouth you have engaol'd my tongue,
Doubly portcullis'd with my teeth and lips,
And dull, unfeeling, barren ignorance
Is made my gaoler to attend on me.
I am too old to fawn upon a nurse,
Too far in years to be a pupil now.

(*Richard II*, Act 1, scene 3).

The words above are adapted from the speech by Thomas Mowbray, Duke of Norfolk, in Shakespeare's play *Richard II*, after King Richard has banished him from England to France. In these words, as Seliger and Shohamy point out, "We find the common fears experienced by someone who must leave his native language and culture, adjust to new surroundings, and acquire a new language".[1] Second-language learning occurs all over the world

---

[1] H.W. SELIGER and E. SHOHAMY, *Second Language Research Methods* (Oxford, 1989), p. 22.

and has occurred throughout history "for a variety of reasons such as immigration, the demands of commerce and science, and requirements of education". Therefore this lament could be interpreted not only as a symbol of my situation as an Italian-speaking author, but an epigraphic allegory of a situation involving the whole of medieval Latin literature, that can become an opportunity for new surveys aiming at a post-colonial observation of medieval Latin texts.

In her *Medieval Literature and Postcolonial Studies*,[2] Lisa Lampert-Weissig examines "how post-colonial theory has influenced the reading of medieval texts and contexts", "how medievalists have provided important critiques of key terms and concepts in post-colonial studies, including Orientalism, colonialism and nationalism", and "the development of medieval studies in the contexts of the rise of European nationalism and colonialism", or regarding concepts such as race or civilisation. So it seems that there are three main reasons for exploring a post-colonial approach to medieval studies: one oriented towards medieval texts as research object, one towards the theory itself, and one towards the contribution of medieval studies to modern history and culture. Two of the three are also subordinated to issues of modern studies, and indeed, part of Lampert-Weissig's introduction is dedicated to the history of the difficulties this approach has raised and discovered among specialists of post-colonial studies. The implicit presupposition is that to employ this method would offer a wider appeal and a noble licence to studies which need a kind of approval by the circles in which we would like to take part. The concern of the editor is that "postcolonial medieval studies" is "still viewed with scepticism by non-medievalists", as demonstrated by the position adopted by Gabrielle Spiegel in 2000, who argues against "superimposing contemporary theories, including postcolonial theory, on periods and persons for which they were never designed".[3] Lampert-Weissig's account of the debate is generally correct, even though strictly limited to the fields of Romance and Germanic literatures and above all to historiographic issues, almost entirely excluding the immense domain of Latin texts. But the very point at stake is the *opportunity* of such an approach and the necessity of its acknowledgment by both modernists and medievalists. In the same way, projects like the *Global Middle Ages Project*, founded by Geraldine Heng and web-based but idle until 2008, or indeed *Interfaces* (promoted by the Centre for Medieval Literature, based in Odense and York), which links themes and texts of Latin and non-Latin literature with one

---

[2] L. LAMPERT-WEISSIG, *Medieval Literature and Postcolonial Studies* (Edinburgh, 2010).
[3] G. SPIEGEL, "Épater les médiévistes", *History and Theory* 39 (2000), pp. 243-250.

another, or publications such as *Premodern Places: Calais to Surinam, Chaucer to Aphra Behn* by David Wallace[4] and the many essays on the medieval roots of contemporary problems such as the clash of civilisations, the conflict between lay authorities and the Catholic Church, or the perception of the Orient, show their main concern to be the compatibility of medieval research with modern issues or issues that are expected to be an object of interest for today's readers.

The miscellany *The Postcolonial Middle Ages*, edited in 2000 by Jeffrey Jerome Cohen,[5] already included chapters on Orientalism, on oriental elements in Dante's *Commedia*, on Chaucer as a post-colonial author, on the monsters of Gerald of Wales, on imperialism and racism in the novels of Walter Scott, and on the conflict of civilisations as represented by the legend of Prester John among the natives: almost all of these are the same subjects that are addressed in Lampert-Weissig's book. This gives the impression that a fixed repertoire has been created of favoured topics for a post-colonial approach to the Middle Ages. Moreover, the foreword by Cohen explicitly selects (pp. 6-7) a set of objectives for enquiry, namely:

1. "Rethinking the keywords of post-colonial theory's collective discourse by insisting on cultural, historical, even textual specificity";
2. "Rethink history as effective history, history that intervenes within the disciplinisation of knowledge to loosen its sedimentation";
3. "Destabilise hegemonic identities (racial sexual, ethnic, religious, class, age)";
4. "Displace the domination of Christianity";
5. "Decenter Europe".

These objectives do not primarily concern the cultural history of the Middle Ages as much as the medieval foundations of modern issues and contemporary behaviours that should be corrected or condemned.

Thus, current post-colonial approaches to medieval literature not only refer mainly to the antecedents of modernity in any form they can be presented, but

---

[4] D. WALLACE, *Premodern Places: Calais to Surinam, Chaucer to Aphra Behn* (Chichester and Malden, MA, 2004). According to L. LAMPERT-WEISSIG, *Medieval Literature and Postcolonial Studies*, p. 7, Wallace "weaves a narrative that brings together Calais, Flanders, Somerset, Genoa, the Canary Islands, Surinam, and Guyana through attention to significant moments of cultural hybridity". [This perspective has been later developed in *Europe: A Literary History, 1348-1418*, ed. D. WALLACE, 2 vols. (Oxford, 2015). See also *Postcolonial Approaches to the European Middle Ages*, ed. A.J. KABIR and D. WILLIAMS (Cambridge, 2005).]

[5] *The Postcolonial Middle Ages*, ed. J.J. COHEN (New York, 2001).

the research focusses, and should focus, on topics that are deemed acceptable and appreciable according to the current set of values and priorities, whether or not they are suited to medieval issues, and whether or not they are central to medieval documentation and to the actual medieval way of life. In this view, medievalist questions are frequently tackled with the aim of correcting Eurocentric developments of modern literary outlines, for example, or mistaken perceptions of Orientalism, or to free ourselves from the guilt complex derived from the chivalric roots of English colonialism or from the alleged medieval (and, much more, Graeco-Roman) origins of modern racism, with results that certainly are motivated by noble impulses, but could appear weak or irrelevant for current medieval studies and that are still affected by moralism and ideology, and therefore are non-scientific by definition.

The research on medieval literature has suffered greatly, from the creation of the name 'Middle Ages' itself onwards, from being constantly analysed according to references outside its own field: usually, and first of all, with the afterlife of its classical ancestors and the transmission of manuscripts or the literary rewriting of Roman texts, then with the birth or formation of political or ideological developments in modern history or modern culture. While admitting that these could be plausible and praiseworthy remote reasons for a moral or institutional justification of the interest in medieval texts that make it acceptable to contemporary eyes, it would be dangerous or naive for research itself to be admittedly conditioned by external criteria. *Extimité,* as Jeffrey Cohen writes (p. 6), "is the guarantee that only a localising, perspectivist epistemology can hope to do justice to the heterogeneity of the past, refusing to bend it to some master narrative of progress and complete differentiation".

In my opinion, other ways could be found of rethinking medieval literature in the light of post-colonial interests – given that so far, no single or major post-colonial theory exists – that would activate a different type of analysis and shed new light on medieval texts, applying categories derived from intercultural analysis or post-colonial theories without exploiting this approach by drawing on modern issues, moral judgements, or political contrapositions in the belief that this will increase the appeal of the research. The most promising methods are, in my view, the studies on migration literature and the hybridisation, following Homi Bhabha's idea of "mutually constructed discourse",[6] in a linguistic version that analyses the layers of the texts as cultural layers. I have had the chance to experiment with such typologies of textual interrogation in

---

[6] See LAMPERT-WEISSIG, *Medieval Literature and Postcolonial Studies,* p. 55.

a series of seminars organised some years ago, with European funding, by the comparative literature journal of which I am editor, on 'other language' topics, the so-called second-language literature.[7] This is a problem that involves both post-colonial literature, in the strict sense of the term, an historically determined phenomenon that Spivak[8] defined in 1987 as finished, and migration literature, which is the real current issue of the former post-colonial theories. We invited writers from all over the world, writing in a language different from their mother tongues, to explore and define the feelings they had with the language they were currently using and the consequences this condition exerted on their literary technique, text production, and way of thinking. Most of these cases were Anglo-Indians, Anglo-Africans, francophone Arabs, Slavo-Americans and migrants to Italy from different linguistic areas, but we tried to extend the scope of the observation to an initial investigation of ancient textual constellations, such as late Latin and medieval biblical poems, that proved to be a field of cultural interplay generating stylistic innovations and linguistic changes. We learned that many forms of influence and a rich repertoire of metaphorical representations are generated by this experience, and I was able to appreciate how much contemporary migration literature shares with all second-language literature of the past. In a later issue of the same journal we tried to examine the positions that post-colonial literature has developed about 'western'-tagged metrical forms such as the sonnet, collecting contributions from specialists or poets from different cultural traditions.[9]

Carolingian Cases

Such an approach could easily be applied to what we would today define as international environments: for example the Carolingian court and its intellectuals, who came from Ireland, England, Germany, France, Italy, Spain, and, occasionally and to a lesser extent, from elsewhere. Important figures included the Anglo-Saxon Alcuin of York, sponsor and ideologist of the whole Carolingian 'revolution'; the 'Italian' Peter of Pisa, the first master of grammar at the

---

[7] *La lingua assente: Autrotraduzione e interculturalità nella poesia europea*, ed. F. STELLA (Florence, 2001 = *Semicerchio: Rivista di poesia comparata* 20-21).

[8] G.C. SPIVAK, *Decolonizing the Mind: The Politics of Language in African Literature* (London, 1986), and ID. *In Other Worlds: Writing, History and the West* (New York and London, 1987).

[9] *Antropologia del sonetto* (= *Semicerchio: Rivista di poesia comparata* 23 (2002)).

Carolingian court; the Spanish-Visigoth Theodulf, later bishop of Orléans, a great poet and author of the *Opus Caroli* on the iconoclastic issue; the German Hrabanus, later abbot of Fulda and author of one of the most widely circulated medieval encyclopaedias; and many other protagonists of Carolingian culture, including Irishmen and Franks. All of them communicated with each other in Latin and developed a literature that shared common features, increasingly enhanced by the standardisation favoured by orthographical reforms, but also revealing individual differences and peculiarities that could be interpreted as national or cultural, and that acted beneath the surface not only at a syntactic, morphologic, and lexical level, but also in the selection of the genre, the modes of expression, and their chosen topics. These cultural tags changed time after time, influencing each other and helping to forge the innovations of medieval literature. For example, the Debate between Spring and Winter (*Conflictus veris et hiemis*) by Alcuin, and a few decades later Sedulius Scotus's Debate (*tenson*) between the Lily and the Rose, are the first attested cases of an immense chain of *altercationes* studied by Hans Walther and Paul Gerhard Schmidt, and completely different from the alleged post-classical forerunners such as Vespa's *Altercatio coci et pistoris* or some bucolic dialogues. Although an alternative hypothesis exists that ascribes their origin to rhetorical exercises, these are examples of the Latinisation of folklore themes that emerge only much later in vernacular literature. For the first time, these topics find their way into the writing of, and are circulated among, the higher milieus, revealing the specific form that proved to be the most appropriate in the Latin system: that is, the bucolic debate, where Vergilian formulae and motifs that have become a common heritage of the European 'imperial' education intersect with folkloric elements rooted in individual cultures, such as the symbolic meanings of the cuckoo, or treasure hidden in a cave, giving a Roman face to Germanic, Celtic, or English customs. René Martin has studied these phenomena in a paper titled "Au confluent des traditions antique, germanique et chrétienne",[10] but if we extend this type of investigation to all of Carolingian and pre- or post-Carolingian Latin literature, we can find this overlapping, intersecting, and re-lexicalisation of *Realien* from an oral culture to the Latin-literate culture everywhere. Another example familiar to me is the poem *De fonte vitae*, 'The Source of Life', by the visionary Audradus of Sens. This is a strange account from the middle of the ninth century about an initiation into the ecclesiastical

---

[10] R. MARTIN, "Au confluent des traditions antique, germanique et chrétienne", *Revue des Études Latines* 72 (1994), pp. 177-191.

life, narrated as a search for a sacred cup whose recovery depended – according to the instructions of a high priest or magician named Hincmar, like the archbishop of Reims – on acquaintance with the knowledge of the Easter Computus and of a concise account of the sacred history as narrated by the devil in a kind of combat. The surfacing of such a narrative transformation of a symbol, completely unknown to Latin literature and still isolated until Chrétien de Troyes and Robert de Boron, probably depended on the conversion of a Celtic common archetype into a Christian Latin literarisation, but was overlooked by Marx[11] and by later writers during their investigations into the origins of the narrative and symbols of the Grail. It is not an example of textual influence, at least if we take 'text' to mean a written chain of signs, nor can we define it as an example of 'interfaces', the circulation of motifs among contiguous text-groups in different languages that shared common topics. It is an example that is better analysed with the tools typical of post-colonial or migration literature theories such as hybridisation, transculturation, or representation of subalternity.

Extensions

Similarly, folklore material also rises to the surface in medieval Latin writing. A few well-known examples of this include: the *Riddles* by Aldhelm of Malmesbury, Eusebius, Tatuinus, and other Anglo-Latin collections comparable to the Anglo-Saxon *Exeter Riddles*; the Latinised Germanic epics of *Waltharius* in tenth and *Ruodlieb* in the eleventh century, and the tales and fairy tales narrated in twelfth- and thirteenth-century England and France and included in the *De nugis curialium* of Walter Map, who retold Welsh folk tales from the oral tradition in Latin, or in the *Otia imperialia* of Gervais of Tilbury, who writes about typically English *grants* and Provençal witches; and the character of the wild magician from the Welsh 'kingdom' depicted in the *Vita Merlini* by Geoffrey of Monmouth; not to mention proper accounts of national stories such as, besides Geoffrey's own *Historia Regum Britanniae*, the *Gesta Danorum* by Saxo Grammaticus and the *Gesta episcoporum Hammaburgen-*

---

[11] J. MARX, *La légende arthurienne et le Graal* (Paris, 1952). See now J. GOERING, *The Virgin and the Grail: Origins of a Legend* (New Haven, 2005); *The Grail, the Quest and the World of Arthur*, ed. N.J. LACY (Woodbridge, 2008: *Arthurian Studies* 72); and J. CAREY *Ireland and the Grail* (Aberystwyth, 2007).

sium by Adam of Bremen, as well as many other instances of folkloric material in the Latin novelistic production of the high Middle Ages. Hundreds of medieval Latin texts, possibly the entire medieval Latin heritage, can be interpreted in the light of second-language creation as an interaction of oral cultures and written repertoire, itself carrying implicit cultural assumptions.

Some of these works have been analysed from time to time in contributions to comparative studies that have suggested the possibility of founding what has been called *Mediävistische Komparatistik*,[12] characterised by a horizontal comparison instead of the great diachronic comparisons represented by Curtius, Auerbach, and Spitzer, a study of the synchronic interconnections previously launched in 1972 by Jean Frappier[13] in the *Grundriss der romanischen Literaturen des Mittelalters* that so far has never achieved the grand narrative that is necessary at a foundational stage.

Second-language Analysis

Adopting this approach in a wider sense, we could apply research methods that are typical of SLA (second language acquisition), a research field that has seen impressive growth in recent decades, generating hundreds of books, specialised journals, scientific societies, and yearly conferences dedicated to this topic. Such methods are almost exclusively employed in studies about the learning process in modern times and today, but could find an interesting field of investigation in literary texts produced in a second language. Studies of SLA have generated categories such as "interlanguage pragmatics" (Cenoz)[14], or "multi-competence" (Cook)[15] or "intercultural style hypothesis" (Blum-Kulka),[16] and even real integrated models such as the SMM (dynamic model of

---

[12] See *Mediävistische Komparatistik: Festschrift für Franz-Josef Worstbrock zum 60. Geburtstag*, ed. W. HARMS and J.-D. MÜLLER (Stuttgart and Leipzig, 1997).

[13] J. FRAPPIER, "Littérature médiévale et littérature comparée", in: *Grundriß der romanischen Literaturen des Mittelalters* 1, ed. H.R. JAUß (Heidelberg 1972), pp. 139-162. A revival of this perspective in F. STELLA, "Eteroglossia del testo e comparazione interculturale", in: *Interculturalità: Società, religioni, letterature* (= *Testimonianze* 384-385 (1996)), pp. 99-122; modified version in *Semicerchio: Rivista di poesia comparata* 14 (1996), pp. 2-14.

[14] J. CENOZ and J.F. VALENCIA, "Cross-cultural communication and interlanguage pragmatics: American vs. European requests", *Pragmatics and Language Learning* 7 (1996), pp. 41-54.

[15] V. COOK, "Evidence for multi-competence", *Language learning* 42 (1992), pp. 557-591.

[16] S. BLUM-KULKA, "Interlanguage pragmatics: The case of requests", in: *Foreign / Second*

multilingualism, Herdina and Jessner).[17] Most of these new models appreciate the fact that bi- or multilingual competence is not comparable to monolingual competence in either language, and I think the same remark can be developed with regard to cultural interferences, as Jury Lotman stated in his essays on the semiosphere about the dynamics of the interactions of cultures and their consequences for the development of a specific culture in a context of multiple influences. Many features of multilingual activity can be transferred to the analysis of multicultural literary production, which is what medieval literature is: retardation, fossilisation, code-switching, interference, language attrition and loss, regression, and many phenomena that have been observed in linguistic contexts but are absolutely active and detectable in a literary context provided with 'post-colonial' features – that is, the context of authors writing in a second language coming from first languages that are, or could be, exclusively oral. We would assign concepts such as 'pidgin' or 'creole', 'migration literature' and 'dominancy' to literary texts, thus developing a method or at least a critical attitude that could be quite profitable for medieval literature (and specifically for medieval Latin literature as a second-language literature). Just a few months before I wrote this paper, David Ian Hanauer published a volume on *Poetry as Research: Exploring Second Language Poetry Writing*,[18] seemingly on the same topics as the *Semicerchio* issue I edited in 1998, devoted to the mechanisms and procedure of poetry writing in a second language as a method for understanding the process of second-language acquisition and with reference to actual linguistic or creative writing rather than to historical texts. Hanauer's work considers some characteristics of "second language poetry"[19] and raises the question of the so-called "poetic identity" as an experimental

---

Language Pedagogy Research, ed. R. PHILLIPSON, E. KELLERMAN, L. SELINKER, M. SHARWOOD SMITH, and M. SWAIN (Clevedon, 1991), 255-272.

[17] P. HERDINA and U. JESSNER, *A Dynamic Model of Multilingualism* (Clevedon, 2001). According to U. JESSNER, "A dynamic approach to language attrition in multilingual systems", in: *Effects of the Second Language on the First*, ed. V. COOK (Clevedon, 2003), pp. 234-246, at p. 235, this is a psycholinguistic model that "studies the complex relationships in multilingualism by focusing on the description of time-dependent changes in the psycholinguistic system, such as the change of dominance in a bilingual system".

[18] D.I. HANAUER, *Poetry as Research: Exploring Second Language Poetry Writing* (Amsterdam etc., 2010).

[19] HANAUER, *Poetry as Research*, pp. 38-53.

tool for linguistic research.[20] I propose to reverse the relationship and to adopt linguistic tools as literary research methods.

The specificity of medieval Latin literature is that it produces thousands of texts in a second language that is not the first language of any people or country, a no-land's language whose country is a time, not a space, whose country is the past. This specificity requires a methodological innovation that combines intercultural analysis with intertextual background and checks the influence of the latter on the former.

In adopting this model, we should be ready to pay attention to the directions and decay, not to say distortions, that this process conveys and at the same time to the cultural enrichment that contributions from oral cultures made to the development of Latin culture, which was the common European culture from 500 BCE to 1100 CE, if we are considering literature, or from 500 BCE to the nineteenth century, if we are referring to official political documents or scientific treatises.

In my opinion, the qualms expressed about the legitimacy of applying postcolonial approaches to medieval literature – that is, to literature that predates the concept – are justifiable but not historically grounded. Indeed, many theorists[21] have come to accept the idea that, if the word 'colonial' is intended in its true historical meaning, such an approach can be validly extended to the colonies of Ancient Greece and particularly to what we may call the colonies of the Roman Empire or of the Holy Roman Empire. From this perspective, research studies on the hybridisation of cultures that were subdued by Roman culture and found expression, for centuries, by and in the Latin language and were influenced by Latin culture even after the birth of vernacular texts, are in fact post-colonial, whether they are labelled and accepted as such or not.

An interesting example of this approach in a wider sense is the book by Catherine E. Léglu, *Multilingualism and Mother Tongue in Medieval French, Occitan, and Catalan Narratives*,[22] in which she speaks of a "dynamic intercultural exchange rather than colonised defeat" in relation to Occitan, which she

---

[20] Y.M. LOTMAN, *Universe of the Mind: A Semiotic Theory of Culture*, trans. A. SHUKMAN (London and New York, 1990). See also ID., " Una teoria del rapporto reciproco tra le culture (da un punto di vista semiotico)", in: *La semiosfera: Asimmetria e dialogo fra le strutture pensanti* (Venice, 1983), pp. 113-130; trans. "On the semiosphere", *Sign Systems Studies* 33.1 (2005), pp. 205-226.

[21] M. MELLINO, *La critica postcoloniale* (Rome, 2005), p. 21.

[22] C.E. LÉGLU, *Multilingualism and Mother Tongue in Medieval French, Occitan, and Catalan Narratives* (University Park, PA, 2010).

does not accept as defining a "politically oppressed minority language", probably ironising on the commonplaces of political correctness. Léglu, as Michelle Warren points out in *The Medieval Review*,[23] analyses texts written in multiple languages such as the *Girart de Roussillon*, texts that refer to multilingual interactions or monolingual texts produced in multilingual environments, thus defying the assumptions made by language-based definitions of community. Her goal is to explore the intercultural polyphony that constructs the texts both in the nature of the narrative and in the metaphorical texture, where the languages are images of motherness or otherness, social alienation or Pentecostal reconciliation. Léglu creates the category of *entredeux* or 'in-between', or better 'abroad at home', which is remarkably appropriate for describing Latin authors throughout the Middle Ages, introducing a series of remarks, in Lacanian terms, on the psychoanalytical distance between self and language.[24] The translation of this approach into post-colonial terms is self-aware in Léglu and draws on Homi Bhabha's theory of the "third space", a borderline where multilingual texts can find their voice,[25] and on Lawrence Venuti's translation theory that contrasts domesticating versus foreignising translations. A final suggestion that, according to Léglu, could also be transferred to medieval Latin literature is Derrida's[26] emphasis on the 'otherness' of the maternal language, the discovery of the mother tongue as an illusion and a nostalgic symbol of lost pre-Babelian communication.[27] A medieval-Latinist could compare this imagery with the representation of medieval Latin as 'father-tongue' developed by Ludwig Traube, the great Munich palaeographer who is considered the father, to remain in the same parental allegory, of Medieval Latin literature studies.[28]

At a methodological level, carrying out such research presents problems generated by the difficulty of access to documentation about the oral elements transformed and re-semanticised into Latin forms, because the Latin texts are frequently the first evidence of these elements before the much later vernacular texts. Thus, we are obliged to extract and reconstruct from the comparison between early Latin disguises and later vernacular testimonies of a motif, sym-

---

[23] <https://scholarworks.iu.edu/journals/index.php/tmr/article/view/17162>.

[24] LÉGLU, *Multilingualism*, p. 113.

[25] J. RUTHERFORD, "The third space: Interview with Homi Bhabha", in: *Identity, Community, Culture, Difference*, ed. J. RUTHERFORD (London, 1990), pp. 207-221.

[26] J. DERRIDA, *Le monolinguisme de l'autre ou la prothèse d'origine* (Paris, 1996), and ID., "Des tours de Babel", in: *Poststructuralism as Exegesis* (Atlanta, GA, 1991), p. 3.

[27] LÉGLU, *Multilingualism*, pp. 141, 193.

[28] Cf. J. LEONHARDT, *Latin: Story of a World Language* (Cambridge, MA, 2013).

bol, or character, the possible and yet only virtual 'ethnic' shape of such a motif, symbol, or character. A typical manifestation of this process of inverse and tautological demonstration is what we have of original Irish culture, as confirmed during the Spoleto *Settimana di studio* in 2009.[29] In Audradus's case, the mythology of the cauldron of wisdom that would have influenced the symbology of the *scyphus* or cup in the ninth century Latin text is documented only by much later Irish or French narratives, and yet we must presuppose its influence in order to explain the presence of cultural signs extraneous to the Roman system also in its late antique and early medieval texts.

In any case, it seems necessary to accept and respect such shifting and sliding in the chronology of the historical documentation of different cultures, which we cannot change except in the event of the discovery of new manuscripts, and to use this virtual reconstruction as the basis for a field of research that links texts from diverse European and non-European traditions. This same assumption functions on a linguistic level: the African Latin writers have a different style from French or Irish Latin texts, so we must presuppose the influence of what are called *adstrata*, local linguistic layers contiguous to major official languages. These often lack documentation until after the time of the Latin evidence itself, and yet we have to explain and justify the differences that are common to writers of a determined area.

The tools and methods of post-colonial linguistics, or second-language linguistics, could help us to create a new perspective in studies on medieval Latin literature, if we can agree that the Roman and, to an even greater extent, medieval Latin language functioned as an international, or imperial, second or 'father tongue'.

---

[29] *L'Irlanda e gli irlandesi nell'alto medioevo* (Spoleto, 2009: *Settimane di studio del Centro Italiano di Studi sull'Alto Medioevo* 57).

Bibliography

Sources

Abelard, *Commentaria in Epistolam Pauli ad Romanos*, ed. in: Petrus Abaelardus, *Opera theologica*, 1, ed. E.M. BUYTAERT (Turnhout 1969: CCCM 11).

Abelard, *Theologia Christiana*, ed. in: Petrus Abaelardus, *Opera theologica* 2, E.M. BUYTAERT (Turnhout, 1969: CCCM 12), pp. 71-372.

Accessus ad auctores: Bernard d'Utrecht, Conrad d'Hirsau: Dialogus super auctores, ed. R.B.C. HUYGENS (Leiden, 1970).

Acronis et Porphyrii Commentarii in Q. Horatium Flaccum, ed. F. HAUTHAL, 2 vols. (Berlin, 1864; reprinted Amsterdam, 1966).

Admonitio generalis, ed. as: *Die Admonitio generalis Karls des Großen*, ed. H. MORDEK, K. ZECHIEL-ECKES, and M. GLATTHAAR (Wiesbaden, 2013: MGH Fontes iuris Germanici antiqui in usum scholarum separatim editi 16).

Aelius Festus Aphthonius, *De arte metrica*, ed. in: *Grammatici Latini* 6, ed. KEIL (as part of Marius Victorinus, *Ars grammatica* – q.v.).

Aenigmata Anglica or *Laureshamensia*, ed. F. GLORIE in: CCSL 133 (Turnhout, 1968), pp. 347-358.

Agius of Corvey, *Dialogus Agii*, ed. L. TRAUBE, in: PLAC 3, pp. 372-388.

Agius von Corvey, See: E. KÖNSGEN, "Eine neue komputistische Dichtung des *Agius von Corvey*", *Mittellateinisches Jahrbuch* 14 (1979), pp. 66-75.

Agobard of Lyon, *Liber Apologeticus*, ed. in: PL 104, cols. 307-320.

Alain de Lille, *Theologicae Regulae* and *Quoniam homines*, ed. P. GLORIEUX, "La somme 'Quoniam homines' d'Alain de Lille", *Archives d'Histoire Doctrinale et Littéraire du Moyen Âge* 20 (1953), pp. 113-369.

Albertino Mussato, *Écérinide: Épîtres métriques sur la poésie: Songe*, ed. J.-F. CHEVALIER (Paris, 2000).

Albertus Magnus, *Summa theologiae*, in: *Beati Alberti Magni, Ratisbonensis episcopi, Ordinis Praedicatorum, Opera quae hactenus haberi potuerunt*, ed. T. TURCO et al., 21 vols. (Lyon, 1651), 17.

Alcimus Ecdicius Avitus, *De consolatoria castitatis laude* [= *De virginitate*], ed. as: Avit de Vienne, *Éloge consolatoire de la chasteté (sur la virginité)*, ed. N. HECQUET-NOTI (Paris, 2011: SC 546).

Alcimus Ecdicius Avitus, *De virginitate*, ed. R. PEIPER (Hanover, 1883: MGH AA 6.2), pp. 275-294.

Alcimus Ecdicius Avitus, *De spiritalis historiae gestis, Buch 3*, ed. M. HOFFMANN (Berlin, 2005).

Alcuin, *Carmina*, ed. E. Dümmler, in: PLAC 1, pp. 169-351.

Alcuin, *De patribus, regibus et sanctis Euboricensis ecclesiae*, ed. as: *The Bishops, Kings and Saints of York*, ed. P. GODMAN (Oxford, 1982).

Alcuin, *Epistolae*, ed. as: *Alcuini sive Albini Epistolae*, ed. E. DÜMMLER, in: *Epistolae Karolini aevi* 1, ed. E. DÜMMLER *et al.* (Berlin, 1895: MGH EPP 4), pp. 1-481.

Alcuin, *Epistolae*, ed. E. DÜMMLER, in: *Epistolae Karolini Aevi*, 4, ed. E. DÜMMLER, E. PERELS, *et al.* (Berlin, 1902-1925: MGH EPP 4), pp. 18-481.

Alcuin, *Nauta rudis pelagi*, ed. in: *La poesia carolingia*, ed. F. STELLA (Florence, 1995), No. 37, pp. 266-267.

Alcuin (?), *Summi regis archangele*, ed. in: Alcuin, *Carmina*, ed. E. DÜMMLER, in: PLAC 1, pp. 348-349.

Alcuin, *Vita Willibrordi*, ed. W. LEVISON, in: MGH SRM 7, pp. 113-141.

Alcuin, *Vitae Willibrordi, Vedasti, Richarii*, ed. in: C. VEYRARD-COSME *L'oeuvre hagiographique en prose d'Alcuin:* Vitae Willibrordi, Vedasti, Richarii*: Edition, traduction, études narratologiques* (Florence, 2003).

Alcuin, see also: *Monumenta Alcuiniana* and *Alcuini Opera*.

Alcuini Opera (Sankt Emmeram, 1777), pp. 1747-1756.

Alcuini Opera, ed. A. DUCHESNE [Quercetanus] (Paris, 1617).

Aldhelm of Malmesbury, *Aldhelm: The Poetic Works*, ed. and trans. M. LAPIDGE and J.L. ROSIER (Cambridge, 1985).

Aldhelm of Malmesbury, *Aldhelmi opera*, ed. R. EHWALD (Berlin, 1913-1919: MGH AA 15).

Aldhelm of Malmesbury, *De Laudibus Virginitatis* (in prose), ed. in: *Aldhelmi Opera*, ed. R. EHWALD (Berlin, 1913-1919: MGH AA 15), pp. 226-323.

Aldhelm of Malmesbury, *De Laudibus Virginitatis* (metrical), ed. in: *Aldhelmi Opera*, ed. R. EHWALD (Berlin, 1913-1919: MGH AA 15), pp. 350-471.

Aldhelm of Malmesbury, *Prosa de virginitate cum glosa Latina atque Anglosaxonica*, ed. S. GWARA (Turnhout, 2001: CCSL 124).

Alexander of Ashby [Essebiensis], *Opera omnia*, 2, *Opera poetica,* ed. G. DINKOVA-BRUUN (Turnhout, 2004: CCSM 188A).

Alexander Halensis, *Summa theologiae*, ed. Collegium S. Bonaventurae, 4 vols. (Quaracchi, 1924-1948).

Ambrosius Autpertus, *Expositionis in Apocalypsim libri I-V*, ed. R. WEBER, 2 vols. (Turnhout, 1975: CCCM 27-27A).

Angilbert, *Carmina*, ed. E. DÜMMLER, in: *PLAC* 1, pp. 358-381.
Angilbert, *De ecclesia Centulensi libellus*, ed. in: *Hariulf, Chronique de l'abbaye de Saint-Riquier*, ed. F. LOT (Paris, 1894), pp. 296-306.
Annales Altahenses maiores, ed. E. VON OEFELE (Hanover, 1881: *MGH SRG in usum scholarum separatim editi* 4).
Annales de gestis Caroli Magni imperatoris, trans. A. ISOLA, *Poeta Sassone: Le gesta dell'imperatore Carlo Magno* (Milan, 1987).
Annales de gestis Caroli Magni imperatoris, ed. P. VON WINTERFELD, in: *PLAC* 4.1, pp.1-71.
Annales Fuldenses sive Annales regni Francorum orientalis, ed. F. KURZE (Hanover, 1891: *MGH SRG in usum scholarum separatim editi* 7).
Annales Lobienses, ed. G. WAITZ, in: [*Supplementa tomorum 1-12, pars 1*], ed. G. WAITZ et al. (Hanover, 1887: *MGH SS* 13), pp. 224-235.
Annales regni Francorum inde ab a. 741 usque ad a. 829, qui dicuntur Annales Laurissenses maiores et Einhardi, ed. F. KURZE (Hanover, 1895: *MGH SRG in usum scholarum separatim editi* 6).
Anni domini notantur, ed. in: C. SAVINI, *Il ritmo 'Anni domini notantur' nella tradizione computistica medievale* (Tesi di laurea magistrale dell'Università di Siena, Facolta di Lettere e Filosofia di Arezzo, rel. F. STELLA, anno accademico 2010-2011).
Anthologia Latina, ed. A. RIESE, 2 vols. (Leipzig, 1894-1906).
Anthologia Palatina, ed. H. BECKBY, 4 vols. (Munich, 1965²).
Arator, *Actus Apostolorum*, ed. A.P. MCKINLAY (Vienna, 1951: *CSEL* 72).
Ardo, see: *Vita Benedicti abbatis Ananiensis et Indensi auctore Ardone.*
Arnold of Bonneval, *Commentarius in Psalmum* CXXXII, ed. in: *PL* 189, cols . 1569-1590.
Ars Palaemonis de metrica institutione, ed. in: *Grammatici latini*, 6, *Scriptores artis metricae*, ed. H. KEIL (Leipzig, 1874), pp. 206-215.
Atilius Fortunatianus, *Ars metrica*, ed. in: *Grammatici latini* 6, *Scriptores artis metricae*, ed. H. KEIL (Leipzig, 1874), pp. 279-304.
Audax, *De Scauri et Palladii libris excerpta*, in: *Grammatici latini*, 7, *Scriptores de orthographia*, ed. H. KEIL (Leipzig, 1880), pp. 320-362.
Audradus of Sens, *Il fonte della vita,* ed. F. STELLA (Florence, 1991).
Augustine, *De doctrina christiana*, ed. J. MARTIN in: *CCSL* 32, ed. K.-D. DAUR and J. MARTIN (Turnhout, 1962), pp. 1-167, replacing *PL* 34, cols. 15-122.
Augustine, De *musica*, ed. M. JACOBSSON with L. J. DORFBAUER (Vienna, 2017: *CSEL* 102), replacing *PL* 32, cols. 1079-1194.
Augustine, *Enarrationes in Psalmos*, ed. E. DEKKERS and J. FRAIPONT, 2nd edn. (Turnhout, 1990: *CCSL* 38-40), replacing *PL* 37-38.
Augustine, *Retractationes libri II*, ed. A. MUTZENBECHER (Turnhout, 1984: *CCSL* 57), replacing *PL* 32, cols. 581-656.

Augustine, *Sermones*, ed. in: PL 38-39, and *Supplementum* 3, cols. 417-840.
Avitus, see: Alcimus [Ecdicius] Avitus.
BATTIATO, Franco, *Bandiera bianca*, from *La voce del Padrone* (EMI Italiana, 1981).
Bede, *Computus*, see: Bede, *De temporum ratione*.
Bede, *De arte metrica*, ed. C.B. KENDALL and M.H. KING, in: *Beda Venerabilis, Opera didascalia*, 1 (Turnhout, 1975: CCSL 123A), pp. 82-141.
Bede, *De temporum ratione*, ed. *Beda venerabilis, Opera didascalia*, 2, *De temporum ratione*, ed. C.W. JONES (Turnhout, 1977: CCSL 123B).
Bede, *Historia Ecclesiastica Gentis Anglorum*, ed. B. COLGRAVE and R.A.B. MYNORS (Oxford, 1969).
Bede, *Libri II De arte metrica et De schematibus et tropis*, ed. and trans. C.B. KENDALL (Saarbrücken, 1991).
Bede's Latin Poetry, ed. M. LAPIDGE (Oxford, 2019).
BENNATO, Edoardo, *Cantautore*, released as a single (Ricordi, 1976).
BENNATO, Edoardo, *Sono solo canzonette*, from the album of that name (Ricordi, 1980).
BERTÉ, Loredana, *Traslocando* (CDG, 1982).
Bertold of Saint Maximin of Trier, *Versus Bertoldi*, ed. in: *Versus libris adiecti*, ed. K. STRECKER, in: PLAC 4.3, p. 1060.
Bible, The: Authorized Version (Oxford, s.a.).
Biblia sacra iuxta vulgatam versionem, ed. R. WEBER, 2 vols. (Stuttgart, 1969; revised edn. R. GRYSON 1994).
Bibliothecarum et psalteriorum versus, ed. L. TRAUBE, in: PLAC 3, pp. 241-264.
Boccaccio, Giovanni, see: Giovanni Boccaccio.
Boniface, *Epistulae*, ed. as: *Die Briefe des Heiligen Bonifatius und Lullus*, ed. M. TANGL (Berlin, 1916: MGH Epistolae selectae 1).
Bucolicon Carmen, see: *Il Bucolicon Carmen e i suoi commenti inediti*.
CARBONI, Luca, *Persone silenziose*, from the album of the same name (BMG Ariola 1989).
Carmina Bibliothecarum, see: *Bibliothecarum et psalteriorum versus*.
Carmina Centulensia, ed. L. TRAUBE, in: PLAC 3, pp. 265-368.
Cassiodore, *Expositio Psalmorum*, ed. M. ADRIAEN, 2 vols. (Turnhout, 1958: CCSL 97-98), replacing PL 70, cols. 9-1056.
Cassiodore, *Variae*, ed. Th. MOMMSEN (Hanover, 1894: MGH AA 12).
Codex Carolinus, ed. W. GUNDLACH, in: *Epistolae Merowingici et Karolini aevi* 1, ed. W. GUNDLACH, E. DÜMMLER *et al.* (Berlin, 1892: MGH Epp. 3), pp. 469-657.
Coluccio Salutati, *De laboribus Hercolis*, ed. B.L. ULLMAN (Zurich, 1951).
Columella, *De re rustica*, ed. R. H. RODGERS (Oxford, 2010).
CONCATO, Fabio, *Guido piano*, in: *Fabio Concato* (Polygram, 1984).
Concilia aevi Karolini [742-842], ed. A. WERMINGHOFF, 2 parts (Hanover and Leipzig, 1906-1908: MGH Conc. 2.1-2).

Conrad of Hirsau, *Dialogus super auctores*, ed. in: *Accessus ad auctores*, ed. R.B.C. HUYGENS (Leiden, 1970), pp. 71-131.

Conradus de Mure, *Fabularius*, Lexicon *P*, ed. T. VAN DE LOO (Turnhout, 2006: CCCM 210).

Corpus Rhythmorum Musicum saec. IV-IX, 1, *Songs in Non-Liturgical Sources*, 1, *Lyrics*, ed. F. STELLA, S. BARRETT, *et al.* (Florence, 2007).

Corpus Scriptorum Muzarabicorum, ed. I. GIL (Madrid, 1973).

Cyprianus Gallus, *Heptateuchus*, ed. R. PEIPER (Vienna, 1881: CSEL 23).

DE ANDRÉ, Fabrizio, *Marinella* (Karim, 1964).

De Astronomia more Christiano, ed. H. LE BOURDELLÈS, "De Astronomia more Christiano", *Studi medievali* 32 (1991), pp. 385-444.

De beato Alcuino Caroli Magni praeceptore Testimonia veterum et quorundam recentiorum scriptorum, ed. in: *PL* 100, cols. 121-134.

De ratione temporum, ed. K. STRECKER and O. SCHUMANN, in: *PLAC* 6.1, pp. 188-189.

Der Liber benedictionum Ekkeharts IV.: Nebst kleineren Dichtungen aus dem Codex Sangallensis 393, ed. J. EGLI (St. Gall, 1909).

Dhuoda, Manuel pour mon fils, ed. P. RICHÉ (Paris, 1975: *Sources Chrétiennes* 225).

Die christlichen Inschriften der Rheinlande, ed. F.X. KRAUS, 2 vols. (Freiburg im Breisgau, 1890-1894).

Die Gedichte des Gottschalk von Orbais, ed. M.-L. WEBER (Frankfurt am Main, etc., 1992).

Dionysius, see: Ps.-Dionysius.

Donato Acciaioli, *Vita Caroli Magni*, ed. W. STROBL (Berlin, 2019).

Dracontius, *De laudibus Dei*, ed. F. VOLLMER in: *MGH AA* 14 (Berlin, 1905), pp. 23-113.

Dracontius, *De laudibus Dei*, ed. as: *Blossii Aemili Dracontii, De laudibus Dei libri tres*, ed. F. CORSARO (Catania, 1962).

Dracontius, *Louanges de Dieu*, 3, *Répartition*, in: Dracontius, *Oeuvres,* ed. C. MOUSSY, 4 vols. (Paris, 1985-1996), 2.

Einhard, *Vita Karoli Magni*, ed. O. HOLDER-EGGER (Hanover and Leipzig, 1911: *MGH SRG in usum scholarum* 25).

Einhard, *Vita Karoli Magni*, trans. in: *Einhard and Notker the Stammerer: Two Lives of Charlemagne*, trans. L. THORPE (Harmondsworth, 1969), pp. 49-90.

Ekkehard IV of Saint Gall, ["Captions for Saint Gall frescoes"], ed. K. STRECKER, with N. FICKERMANN, in: *PLAC* 5.1-2, pp. 540-546.

Ekkehard IV of Saint Gall, see also: *Der Liber benedictionum Ecckehards IV.*

Ekkehard of Aura, *Ekkehardi Chronicon universale*, ed. G. WAITZ, in: *Chronica et annales aevi Salici*, ed. G.H. PERTZ *et al.* (Hanover, 1844), pp. 33-267.

Emonis et Menkonis Werumensium chronicon, Continuatio, ed. L. WEILAND, in: *[Chronica aevi Suevici]*, ed. G.H. PERTZ *et al.* (Hanover, 1874: *MGH SS* 23), pp. 465-572.

Epistolae selectae pontificum Romanorum Carolo Magno et Ludowico Pio regnantibus scriptae, ed. K. HAMPE, in: *Epistolae Karolini aevi* 3, ed. E. DÜMMLER, K. HAMPE, et al. (Berlin, 1898-1899: *MGH Epp.* 5).

"Epitaphienforme für Äbtissinen (Achtes Jahrhunderts)", ed. B. BISCHOFF, in: ID., *Anecdota novissima: Texte des 4. bis 16. Jahrhundert* (Stuttgart, 1984), pp. 150-153.

Erchempert of Monte Cassino, *Historia Langobardorum Beneventanorum*, ed. G. WAITZ, in: *MGH SS rerum Langobardorum et Italicorum* 1, ed. G. WAITZ et al. (Hanover, 1878), pp. 231-264.

Eriugena, see: John Scotus Eriugena.

Ermoldus Nigellus [Ermold the Black], *Carmen elegiacum in honorem Hludowici caesaris*, ed. as: *Ermold le Noir, Poème sur Louis le Pieux et Épitres au roi Pépin*, ed. E. FARAL (Paris, 1932), pp. 2-200.

Eugenius of Toledo, *Carmina*, ed. F. VOLLMER, in: *MGH AA* 14.1 (Berlin, 1905); more recent edition in: Eugenius Toletanus, *Opera omnia*, ed. P.F. ALBERTO (Turnhout, 2006: *CCSL* 114).

Fardulfus, *Carmina*, ed. E. DÜMMLER, in: *PLAC* 1, pp. 353-354.

Florus of Lyon, *Carmina*, ed. E. DÜMMLER, in: *PLAC* 2, pp. 507-566.

Florus of Lyon, *Querela de divisione imperii*, ed. E. DÜMMLER, in: *PLAC* 2, pp. 559-564.

FOSSATI, Ivano, *E di nuovo cambio casa* (from *Le Città di frontiera* (CBS 1983).

Francesco Petrarca, *Epistolae familiares*, ed. V. ROSSI and U. BOSCO (Florence, 1933-1942); *Letters on Familiar Matters (Rerum familiarium libri)*, trans. A.S. BERNARDO, 3 vols. (New York, 2005).

Franco of Cologne, *Ars cantus mensurabilis*, ed. G. REANEY and A. GILLES (s.l., 1974).

Freculf of Lisieux, *Chronicon*, ed. M.I. ALLEN, 2 vols. (Turnhout, 2002: *CCCM* 169-169a).

Gerbert of Aurillac, *Epistolae*, ed. as: Gerbert d'Aurillac, *Correspondance*, ed. and trans. P. RICHÉ and J.P. CALLU, 2 vols. (Paris, 1993).

Gerbert of Aurillac, *Gerberti Opera Mathematica*, ed. N. BUBNOV (Berlin, 1899, repr. Hildesheim, 1963).

Gesta Apollonii, ed. E. DÜMMLER, in: *PLAC* 2, pp. 483-506.

Gesta Romanorum, ed. H. OESTERLEY (Berlin, 1872).

Giovanni Boccaccio, *Genealogie deorum gentilium*, ed. V. ZACCARIA, in: *Tutte le opere di Giovanni Boccaccio*, 7, 2 vols. (Milan, 1998).

Giovanni Boccaccio, *Genealogie deorum gentilium*, trans. *Genealogy of the Pagan Gods*, trans. J. SOLOMON, 3 vols. planned; vol. 1 (Cambridge, MA, 2011) and vol. 2 (Cambridge, MA, 2017) published to date.

Giovanni Dominici, *Lucula noctis*, ed. E. HUNT (Notre Dame, 1960).

Gregory of Tours, *De passione et virtutibus Iuliani martyris*, ed. in: *Gregorii Turonensis Opera*, 2, *Miracula et opera minora*, ed. B. KRUSCH, 2nd edn. (Hanover, 1885: MGH SRM 1.2), pp. 112-134.
Gregory of Tours, *De virtutibus Martini*, ed. in: *Gregorii Turonensis Opera*, 2, *Miracula et opera minora*, ed. B. KRUSCH, 2nd edn. (Hanover, 1885: MGH SRM 1.2), pp. 134-211.
Gregory of Tours, *Historia Francorum*, ed. B. KRUSCH (Hanover and Leipzig, 1937-1951: MGH SRM 1.1).
Gregory the Great, *Epistolae*, ed. D. NORBERG, 2 vols. (Turnhout, 1982: CSEL 140-140A).
Gregory the Great, *Homiliae in euangelia*, ed. R. ÉTAIX (Turnhout, 1999: CCSL 141).
Gregory the Great, *Homiliae XL in Evangelia*, ed. in: PL 76, cols. 1075-1312.
Hariulfus Alenburgensis, *Chronicon Centulense,* ed. in: *Hariulf, Chronique de l'abbaye de Saint-Riquier*, ed. F. LOT (Paris, 1894: *Collection de textes pour servir à l'étude ... de l'histoire* 17), pp. 1-286, replacing PL 174, cols. 1213-1366.
Helperic of Auxerre, *Liber de computo*, ed. in: PL 137, cols. 19-48.
Helperici [...] Karolus magnus et Leo papa, ed. I.C. ORELLI (Zürich, 1832).
Heriger of Lobbes, *Vita Ursmari*, ed. K. STRECKER, in: PLAC 5.1, pp. 178-210.
Hibernicus Exul, *Carmina*, ed. E. DÜMMLER in: PLAC 1, pp. 396-413.
Hieronymus, *Epistolae*, ed. I. HILBERG, 3 vols. (Vienna, 1910-1918: CSEL 54-56).
Hieronymus, *Tractatus in psalmos*, ed. G. MORIN, in: Hieronymus, *Tractatus sive homiliae in Psalmos – in Marci evangelium – Alia varia argumenta*, ed. G. MORIN, B. CAPELLE, and J. FRAIPONT (Turnhout, 1958: CCSL 78), pp. 353-447.
Hieronymus, see also: Ps.-Hieronymus.
Hincmar of Reims, *Coronationes Regiae*, ed. in: PL 125, cols. 803-818.
Historia Apollonii Regis Tyrii, ed. A. RIESE, 2nd edn. (Leipzig, 1893); new edn. *Storia di Apollonio re di Tiro*, ed. G. VANNINI (Milan, 2018).
Honorius Augustudonensis, *Expositio in Psalmos*, ed. in: PL 172, cols. 269-312.
Horace, *Epistolae*, ed. as: Orazio, *Epistole*, ed. M. BECK (Milan, 1997).
Hrabanus Maurus, *Carmina*, ed. E. DÜMMLER, in: PLAC, 2, pp. 159-244.
Hrabanus Maurus, *Commentaria in libros Iudicum*, ed. in: PL 108, cols. 1111-1200.
Hrabanus Maurus, *De clericorum institutione*, ed. in: PL 107, cols. 293-420.
Hrabanus Maurus, *De rerum naturis seu De universo*, ed. A. KNÖPFLER, in: *Veröffentlichungen aus dem Kirchenhistorischen Seminar München* 5 (1900).
Hrabanus Maurus, *Expositio in librum Judith*, ed. as: Rabano Mauro, *Commentario al libro di Giuditta*, ed. A. SIMONETTI (Florence, 2008).
Hrabanus Maurus, *Expositio in librum Judith*, ed. in: PL 109, cols. 539-592.
Hrabanus Maurus, *Liber de reverentia filiorum erga patres et erga reges*, ed. in: *Hrabani (Mauri) abbatis Fuldensis et archiepiscopi Moguntiacensis epistolae*, ed. E. DÜMMLER, in: *Epistolae Karolini aevi* 3, ed. E. DÜMMLER, K. HAMPE, *et al.* (Berlin, 1898-1899: MGH Epist. 5), pp. 403-415.

Hrabanus Maurus and Iohannes Hymonides: Rabano Mauro, Giovani Immonide, *La Cena di Cipriano*, ed. E. ROSATI and F. MOSETTI CASARETTO (Alessandria, 2002).
Hugh of St. Victor (attr.), *Sermo XLIX: In circumcisione Domini*, ed. in: PL 177, cols. 1034-1039.
Il Bucolicon Carmen e i suoi commenti inediti, ed. A. AVENA (Padua, 1906).
Il pensiero pedagogico dell'umanesimo, ed. E. GARIN (Florence, 1958).
Inscripciones cristianas de la España romana y visigoda, ed. J. VIVÈS, 2nd edn. (Barcelona, 1969: *Biblioteca histórica de la biblioteca Balmes*, 2nd series 18).
Inscriptiones christianae urbis Romae septimo saeculo antiquiores: Colligere coepit Iohannes Baptista De Rossi, complevit ediditque Angelus Silvagni: Nova series, 1, *Inscriptiones incertae originis*, ed. A. SILVAGNI (Rome, 1922).
Inscriptiones christianae urbis Romae septimo saeculo antiquiores, 2, *Pars prima: Series codicum in quibus veteres inscriptiones christianae praesertim urbis Romae sive solae sive ethnicis admixtae descriptae sunte ante saeculum XVI*, ed. J.-B. DE ROSSI (Rome, 1888).
Inscriptiones Hispaniae christianae, ed. E. HÜBNER (Berlin, 1871) and *Supplementum* (Berlin, 1900).
Inscriptions chrétiennes de la Gaule antérieures au VIIIe siècle, ed. E. LE BLANT, 1, *Provinces gallicanes* (Paris, 1856).
Inscriptions romaines de Bordeaux, 2 vols., ed. C. JULLIAN (Bordeaux, 1887-1890).
Iohannes Cassianus, *Les institutions cenobitiques*, ed. J.-C. GUY (Paris, 2001: *Sources Chrétiennes* 109).
Iohannes Scotus Eriugena, *Expositiones super Ierarchiam Caelestem Sancti Dionysii*, ed. J. BARBET (Turnhout, 1975: CCCM 31), superseding PL 122, col. 125-266.
[Iohannes Scotus Eriugena,] *Iohannis Scotti Eriugenae Carmina*, ed. M.W. HERREN (Dublin, 1993: *Scriptores Latini Hiberniae* 12).
Ionas Aurelianensis, *De cultu imaginum*, ed. in: PL 106, cols. 305-387.
Isidore of Seville, *Allegoriae*, ed. in PL 83, cols. 97-130.
Isidore of Sevilla, *Etymologiae*, ed. W.M. LINDSAY, 2 vols. (Oxford, 1911), replacing PL 82, cols. 73-728.
Jerome, see: Hieronymus.
John of Salisbury, *Metalogicon*, ed. C.Ch.J. WEBB (Oxford, 1929).
John Scotus Eriugena, see: Iohannes Scotus Eriugena.
Jonas of Orléans, see: Ionas Aurelianensis
Julian of Toledo, ed. as: *Sancti Iuliani Toletanae sedis episcopi Opera* 1, ed. J.N. HILLGARTH, with W. LEVISON and B. BISCHOFF (Turnhout, 1976: CCSL 115).
Karolus magnus et Leo papa, ed. as: *De Karolo rege et Leone papa*, ed. L.E. VON PADBERG (Paderborn, 1999).
Karolus magnus et Leo papa: Ein Paderborner Epos vom Jahre 799, ed. J. BROCKMANN (Paderborn, 1966), re-edited by F. BRUNHÖLZL as: *De Karolo rege et Leone*

papa: Ein Paderborner Epos vom Jahre 799, ed. H. BEUMANN, F. BRUNHÖLZL, and W. WINKELMANN (Paderborn, 1999).

Karolus magnus et Leo papa, see also: *Helperici* [...] *Karolus magnus et Leo papa*.

La poesia carolingia, ed. F. STELLA (Florence, 1995).

Libri Karolini, see: *Opus Caroli regis contra synodum*.

Lucas Tudensis [Lucas de Tuy], *Chronicon Mundi*, ed. E. FALQUE REY (Turnhout, 2003: *CCCM* 74).

Luxurius, ed. in: H. HAPP, *Luxurius: Text und Untersuchungen* (Stuttgart, 1986).

Luxurius, trans. M. ROSENBLUM, *Luxorius: A Poet among the Vandals* (New York and London, 1961).

Mallius Theodorus, *De metris*, ed. in: *Grammatici Latini*, 6, *Scriptores artis metricae*, ed. H. KEIL (Leipzig, 1874), pp. 585-601.

Manfredus, *Carmina*, ed. in: *PL* 94, cols. 641-655.

Marbod of Rennes, *Liber decem capitulorum*, ed. W. BULST (Heidelberg, 1947: *Editiones Heidelbergenses* 8).

Marcus Plotius Sacerdos, *Ars Grammatica*, ed. in: *Grammatici Latini* 6, *Scriptores artis metricae*, ed. H. KEIL (Leipzig, 1874), pp. 427-546.

Marius Victorinus, *Ars grammatica*, ed. in: *Grammatici Latini*, 6, *Scriptores artis metricae*, ed. H. KEIL (Leipzig, 1874), pp. 3-215.

Martianus Capella, *De nuptiis Mercurii et Philologiae*, ed. A. DICK with corrections by J. PRÉAUX (Stuttgart, 1969).

Martianus Capella, *Les Noces de Philologie et de Mercure*, IX, *L'Harmonie*, ed. and trans. J.-Y. GUILLAUMIN (Paris, 2011).

Martinellus of Tours, ed. F.J. GILARDI, *The Sylloge Epigraphica Turonensis de S. Martino* (PhD thesis Catholic University of America, Washington 1983).

Matthew of Vendôme, *Tobias*, ed. in: *Mathei Vindocinensis Opera*, ed. F. MUNARI (Rome, 1977), pp. 161-255.

Maurus Servius Honoratus, *In Vergilii Georgicon librum secundum commentarius*, ed. in: *Servii Grammatici qui feruntur in Vergilii carmina commentarii* 3.1, *Bucolica et Georgica*, ed. G. THILO (Leipzig, 1887).

Messale Romano (Turin and Rome, 1933).

Milo of Saint-Amand, *Carmen de sobrietate*, ed. L. TRAUBE, in: *PLAC* 3, pp. 612-675.

Milo of Saint-Amand, *Carmina*, ed. L. TRAUBE, in: *PLAC* 3, pp. 569-609.

Milo of Saint-Amand, *Vita S. Amandi*, ed. L. TRAUBE, in: *PLAC* 3, pp. 561-609.

Modoin, *Carmina*, ed. E. DÜMMLER, in: *PLAC* 1, pp. 384-391, 569-573.

Monumenta Alcuiniana, ed. W. WATTENBACH and E. DÜMMLER (Berlin, 1873: *Bibliotheca Rerum Germanicarum* 6).

Opus Caroli regis contra synodum [Libri Carolini], ed. A. FREEMAN, with P. MEYVAERT (Munich, 1998: *Concilia aevi Karolini: Supplementum* 1).

Otloh of St. Emmeram, *De doctrina spirituali*, ed. in: *PL* 146, cols. 29-434.

Otto of Freising, *Ottonis episcopi Frisingensis Chronica sive Historia*, ed. A. HOFMEISTER (Hanover, 1912: *MGH SRG in usum scholarum separatim editi* 45).

Pacificus of Verona, *Manuale di computo con ritmo mnemotecnico dell'arcidiacono Pacifico di Verona († 844),* ed. G.G. MEERSSEMAN and E. ADDA (Padua, 1966).

Palaemon, ed. as: *Rhemnius Palaemon de summa grammatices* (Basel, 1527).

PAOLI, Gino, *La gatta* (Ricordi, 1960).

Paschasius Radbertus, *Ecloga duarum sanctimonialium*, ed. L. TRAUBE, in: *PLAC* 3, pp. 45-51.

Paschasius Radbertus, *Epitaphium Arsenii*, ed. E. DÜMMLER, in: *Abhandlungen der Preußischen Akademie der Wissenschaften, Philologisch-historisch Klasse* (1900), 2, pp. 18-98.

Paulinus of Nola, *Carmina*, edited as: *Sancti Pontii Meropii Paulini Nolani Carmina*, ed. W. HARTEL (Vienna, 1894: *CSEL* 30).

Paulinus of Nola, *Carmina*, trans. as: *The Poems of St. Paulinus of Nola*, trans. P.G. WALSH (New York, 1975).

Paulus Alvarus, *Carmina*, ed. in: *Corpus Scriptorum Muzarabicorum*, ed. I. GIL (Madrid, 1973); best edn.: ed. L. TRAUBE, in: *PLAC* 3, pp. 126-142, replacing *PL* 121, cols. 555-566, replacing in turn ed. E. FLÓREZ, in: *España sagrada* 11 (Madrid, 1753), pp. 275-290.

Peter Lombard, *Collectanea in Paulum: Epistola II ad Timotheum*, ed. in: *PL* 192, cols. 363-384.

Petrarch, see: Francesco Petrarca.

Peter Abelard, see: Abelard.

Poeta Saxo, *Annales de gestis Caroli Magni*, ed. P. VON WINTERFELD, in: *PLAC* 4.1, pp. 1-71.

Poeta Saxo, *Annales de gestis Caroli Magni*, ed. as: Poeta Saxo, *Le gesta dell'imperatore Carlo Magno*, ed. A. ISOLA (Milan, 1988).

Poeta Saxo, see also: *Annales de gestis Caroli Magni imperatoris*.

Poetria Nova 2: A CD-ROM of Medieval Latin Poetry (650-1250 A.D., with a Gateway to Classical and Late Antique Texts, ed. P. MASTANDREA and L. TESSAROLO (Florence, 2010).

Polydore Vergil, *Historia Anglica* (Basel, 1570).

Prudentius, *Psychomachia*, ed. in: Prudentius, *Carmina*, ed. M.P. CUNNINGHAM (Turnhout, 1966: *CCSL* 126), pp. 149-181.

Prudentius, *Psychomachia*, ed. and trans. H.J. THOMSON in: *Prudentius*, 1 (Cambridge, MA, 1949: *Loeb Classical Library*), pp. 274-343.

Ps.-Dionysius, *Anni domini notantur*, ed. among the *Dubia* of Bede, ed. in: *PL* 94, col. 637-642, as Anonymus, *Anni domini notantur*; new edn. of 2020 in the *Corpus Rhythmorum Musicum* <www.corimu.unisi.it>.

Ps.-Hieronymus, *Sermo in Psalmum XLI ad neophitos*, ed. in: *PL* 40, col. 1203-1206.

Quintilian, *Institutiones oratoriae libri duodecim*, ed. M. WINTERBOTTOM, 2 vols. (Oxford, 1970).
RAMAZZOTTI, Eros, *Non c'è più fantasia*, from the album *Tutte storie* (Sony BMG, 1993).
Recueil des actes de Charles II le Chauve, Roi de France, ed. G. TESSIER *et al.*, 3 vols. (Paris, 1943-1955).
Recueil des historiens de la Gaule et de la France, 24 vols. (Paris, 1738-1904).
Remigius of Auxerre, *Commentum in Martianum Capellam*, ed. C.E. LUTZ, 2 vols. (Leiden, 1962-1965).
Remigius of Auxerre, *Remigii Musica = Commentum in Martianum Capellam*, IX (q.v.), ed. in: *PL* 131, cols. 939-964.
Rhythmi aevi Merovingici et Carolini, ed. K. STRECKER, in: *PLAC* 4.2-3 (Berlin, 1914), pp. 447-900.
Rhythmi computistici, in: *Rhythmi aevi Merovingici et Carolini*, ed. STRECKER, in: *PLAC* 4.2-3, pp. 667-702.
Rhythmi ex variis codicibus collecti, ed. K. STRECKER, in: *PLAC* 4.2-3, p. 614-666.
Rhythmi syllogae Sangellensis, ed. K. STRECKER, in: *PLAC* 4.2-3, pp. 447-613.
Roman Missal, see: *Messale Romano*.
Saxo Grammaticus, *Gesta Danorum*, ed. K. FRIIS-JENSEN, trans. P. FISHER, 2 vols. (Oxford, 2015).
Saxo Grammaticus, *Gesta Danorum*, trans. as: Sassone Grammatico, *Gesta dei re e degli eroi danesi*, trans. L. KOCH (Turin, 1993).
SCALIGER, J.J., *Declamatio contra poetices calumniatores* (Leiden, 1600).
Schriften zur Komputistik im Frankenreich von 712 bis 818, ed. A. BORST, 1 (Hanover, 2006: *MGH Quellen zur Geistesgeschichte des Mittelalters* 21.1).
Sedulius, *Carmen Paschale*, in: *Sedulii Opera omnia*, ed. J. HUEMER (Vienna, 1885: *CSEL* 10), pp. 1-154.
Sedulius, *Collatio*, in: *Sedulii Opera omnia*, ed. J. HUEMER (Vienna, 1885: *CSEL* 10), pp. 155-162.
Seneca, *De ira* (Pisa, 1981).
Sextus Amarcius, *Sermones*, ed. K. MANITIUS (Weimar, 1969).
Sidonius Apollinaris, *Carmina*, trans. W.B. ANDERSON, in: Sidonius, *Poems* (Cambridge, MA, 1936: *Loeb Classical Library*), pp. 243.
Smaragdus of Saint-Mihiel, *Liber in partibus Donati*, ed. B. LÖFSTEDT, L. HOLTZ, and A. KIBRE Turnhout, 1986: *CCCM* 68).
Symphosius, *Aenigmata*, in: *CCSL* 133A, ed. F. GLORIE (Turnhout, 1968), pp. 611-722.
Thegan, *Gesta Hludowici imperatoris*, ed. in: *Thegan, Die Taten Kaiser Ludwigs (Gesta Hludowici imperatoris) – Astronomus, Das Leben Kaiser Ludwigs (Vita Hludowici imperatoris)*, ed. and trans. E. TREMP (Hanover, 1995: *MGH SRG in usum scholarum separatim editi* 64), pp. 167-277.
Theodulf of Orléans, *Carmina*, ed. E. DÜMMLER, in: *PLAC* 1, pp. 445-581.

Thietmar of Merseburg, *Chronicon*, ed. as: *Die Chronik des Bischoffs Thietmar von Merseburg und ihre Korveier Überarbeitung (Thietmari Merseburgensis episcopi Chronicon)*, ed. R. HOLTZMANN (Hanover, 1935: MGH SRG Nova series 9).

Thomas Aquinas, *Quaestiones de quolibet*, ed. in: Sancti Thomae de Aquino *Opera omnia* 25, *Quaestiones de quolibet*, 1 (Rome and Paris, 1996).

Thomas Aquinas, *Summa Theologiae*, ed. R. SPIAZZI (Turin, 1956).

Thomas Aquinas, *Super Sententias [Petri Lombardi]*, ed. as: S. Tommaso d'Aquino, *Commento alle Sentenze di Pietro Lombardo* (Bologna, 2001).

Thomas Aquinas, *Super Sententias [Petri Lombardi]*, ed. R. BUSA (Stuttgart-Bad Cannstatt, 1980).

Vergil, *The Works of Virgil*, ed. J. CONINGTON, fifth edn., revised by H. NETTLESHIP and F. HAVERFIELD, 2 vols. (London, 1898).

"Verse in Miniaturenhandschriften", ed. K. STRECKER, in: *PLAC*, 5.1-2, pp. 415-463, at pp. 452-453.

Versus libris adiecti, ed. K. STRECKER, in: *PLAC* 4.2-3, pp. 1056-1072.

Versus libris saeculi VIII adiectis, ed. E. DÜMMLER, in: *PLAC* 1, pp. 86-968.

Versus Wissemburgenses, ed. in: *PLAC* 4.2-3, ed. K. STRECKER, pp. 1047-1050.

Victorinus of Pettau, *In Apocalypsin*, ed. in: *Victorini episcopi Petavionensis Opera*, ed. J. HAUSSLEITER (Vienna, 1916: CSEL 49), pp. 44-64.

Vincent of Beauvais, *Speculum historiale* (Strasbourg, 1473-1476).

Vincent of Beauvais, *Speculum historiale* (Douai, 1624).

Virgilius Maro Grammaticus, *Epitomi ed epistole*, ed. G. POLARA (Naples, 1979).

Vita Benedicti abbatis Ananiensis et Indensi auctore Ardone, ed. G. WAITZ, in: *MGH SS* 15.1, ed. G. WAITZ, W. WATTENBACH, *et al.* (Hanover, 1887), pp. 198-220.

Vivian's Bible, [poetic captions], ed. L. TRAUBE, in: *PLAC* 3, pp. 248-249.

Walahfrid Strabo, *Carmina*, ed. E. DÜMMLER, in: *PLAC* 2, pp. 259-423.

Walahfrid Strabo, *De imagine Tetrici*, ed. in: M. HERREN, "The *De imagine Tetrici* of Walahfrid Strabo: Edition and translation", *Journal of Medieval Latin* 1 (1991), pp. 118-139.

Walahfrid Strabo, *Hortulus*, see: Walahfrid Strabo, *Carmina*, at pp. 335-350.

Walahfrid Strabo, *Libellus de exordiis et incrementis quarundam in observationibus ecclesiasticis rerum*, ed. and trans. A.L. HARTING-CORREA (Leiden, 1996), replacing *PL* 114, cols. 919-966.

Walahfrid Strabo, *Libellus De exordiis et incrementis quarundam in observationibus ecclesiasticis rerum*, ed. in: *Capitularia regum Francorum*, 2, ed. A. BORETIUS and V. KRAUSE (Hanover, 1890-1897: MGH *Capitularia* 2), pp. 473-516.

Walther of Speyer, *Scolasticus*, ed. K. STRECKER, in: *PLAC* 5.1, pp. 11-61.

William of Saint-Thierry, *Expositio in Epistolam ad Romanos*, ed. in: *PL* 180, cols. 547-694.

Willibald, *Vita Bonifatii*, ed. in: *Vitae Sancti Bonifatii Archiepiscopi Moguntine*, ed. W. LEVISON (Hanover and Leipzig, 1905: MGH SS rerum Germanicarum in usum scholarum), pp. 1-58.
Winithar, ed. in: *Subscriptiones librorum saeculi VIII*, ed. E. DÜMMLER, in: PLAC 1, pp. 89-90.
Zeno of Verona, *Tractatus*, ed. B. LÖFSTEDT (Turnhout, 1971: CCSL 22), replacing PL 11, cols. 253-528.
Zucchero, *Donne*, from *Zucchero & the Randy Jackson Band* (Polydor, 1985).

Literature

ADORNO, Th.W., *Philosophy of Modern Music*, trans. A.G. MITCHELL and W.V. BLOMSTER (New York, 1984).
AL: Rivista di studi sull'Anthologia Latina 1- (2010-).
ALTER, R., *The Art of Biblical Narrative* (New York, 1981).
AMENT, H., W. SAGE, and U. WEIMANN, "Die Ausgrabungen in der Pfalz zu Ingelheim am Rhein in den Jahren 1963 und 1965", *Germania* 46 (1968), pp. 291-312.
ANGELUCCI, P., *Centralità della chiesa e primato romano in Aratore* (Rome, 1990).
ANGELUCCI, P., *La tecnica poetica di Aratore* (Rome, 1990).
Anonimi autorevoli: Un canone di anonimi nella letteratura latina medievale: XVIII Convegno annuale della Società Internazionale per lo Studio del Medioevo Latino, Firenze 27 marzo 2015 = Filologia mediolatina 23 (2016).
ANTON, H.H., "Beobachtungen zum fränkisch-byzantinischen Verhältnis in karolingischer Zeit", in: *Beiträge zur Geschichte des Regnum Francorum: Wissenschaftliches Colloquium zum 75. Geburtstag von Eugen Ewig*, ed. R. SCHIEFFER (Sigmaringen, 1990), pp. 97-119.
ANTON, H.H., *Fürstenspiegel und Herrscherethos in der Karolingerzeit* (Bonn, 1968: Bonner Historische Forschungen 32).
Antropologia del sonnetto (= *Semicerchio: Rivista di poesia comparata* 23 (2002)).
APEL, W., *Gregorian Chant* (Bloomington, 1958).
APPLEBY, D., "Instruction and inspiration through images in the Carolingian period", in: *Word, Image, Number: Communication in the Middle Ages*, ed. J.J. CONTRENI and S. CASCIANI (Florence, 2002), pp. 85-111.
ARNULF, A., *Versus ad picturas: Studien zur Titulusdichtung als Quellengattung der Kunstgeschichte von der Antike bis zum Hochmittelalter* (Munich, 1997).
ARWEILER, A., *Die Imitation antiker und spätantiker Literatur in der Dichtung "De spiritalis historiae gestis" des Alcimus Avitus: Mit einem Kommentar zu Avit. Carm. 4, 429-540 und 5, 526-703* (Berlin, 1999).
ATSMA, H., "Die christlichen Inschriften aus Galliens als Quelle für Kloster und Klosterbewohner bis zum Ende des VI. Jahrhunderts", *Francia* 4 (1976), pp. 1-57.

Auctor et auctoritas in latinis medii aevi litteris – Author and Authorship in Medieval Latin Literature: Proceedings of the VIth Congress of the International Medieval Latin Committee (Benevento-Naples, November 9-13, 2010), ed. E. D'ANGELO and J. ZIOLKOWSKI (Florence, 2014).

AUERBACH, E., *Mimesis: Dargestellte Wirklichkeit in der abendländischen Literatur* (Berne, 1946); trans. *Mimesis: The Representation of Reality in Western Literature*, trans. W.R. TRASK (Princeton, NJ, 1953).

AUSFELD, E., "Zur Frage nach dem Verfasser des Epos 'Carolus Magnus et Leo Papa'", *Forschungen zur deutschen Geschichte* 23 (1883), pp. 609-615.

AVESANI, R., [review of *Manuale di computo con ritmo mnemotecnico dell'arcidiacono Pacifico di Verona († 844)*, ed. G.G. MEERSSEMAN and E. ADDA (Padua, 1966)], *Studi medievali* 8 (1967), pp. 913-920.

Bakhtin and the Classics, ed. R.B. BRANHAM (Evanston, IL, 2002).

BAKHTIN, M., *Slovo v romane* (1934-1935) partially published in *Voprosy literatury* 6 (1972), then in: ID., *Voprosy literatury i estetiki* (Moscow, 1975), trans. C. STRADA JANOVIČ, *Estetica e romanzo* (Turin, 1979), pp. 83-108.

BALE, J. *Scriptorum illustrium maioris Brytanniae catalogus*, 2 vols. (Basel, 1557-1559).

BANDINI, F., "Una lingua poetica di consumo", in: *Poetica e stile: Saggi su opsis e lexis*, ed. L. RENZI and F. DONADI (Padua, 1976), pp. 191-200.

BARCHIESI, A., "Cento bocche: Narratività e valutazione nello studio dell'epica romana", in: *Reges et proelia: Orizzonti e atteggiamenti dell'epica antica, Pavia 17 marzo 1994* (Como, 1994), pp. 45-71.

BARCHIESI, A., "The crossing", in: *Texts, Ideas and the Classics*, ed. S.J. HARRISON (Oxford, 2001), pp. 142-163.

BARRETT, S., "Music and writing: On the compilation of Paris Bibliothèque Nationale lat. 1154", *Early Music History* 16 (1997), pp. 55-96.

BARTHES, R., "La lutte avec l'ange: Analyse textuelle de Genèse 32. 23-33", in: ID., *Analyse structurale et exégèse biblique: Essais d'interprétation* (Neuchâtel, 1971), pp. 27-39.

BASSETTI, M., "Le Bibbie imperiali d'età carolingia ed ottoniana", in: *Forme e modelli della tradizione manoscritta della Bibbia,* ed. P. CHERUBINI (Vatican City, 2005), pp. 175-265.

BAZIL, M., *"Centones christiani": Métamorphoses d'une forme intertextuelle dans la poésie latine chrétienne de l'Antiquité tardive* (Paris and Turnhout, 2009).

BERNARD, H., "L'abbaye de Saint-Riquier: Evolution des bâtiments monastiques du IXe au XVIIIe siècle", in: *Sous la règle de saint Benoît: Structures monastiques et sociétés en France du Moyen Âge à l'époque moderne, Abbaye bénédictine Sainte-Marie de Paris, 23-25 October 1980* (Geneva, 1982), pp. 499-526.

BERNARD, H., "Premières fouilles à Saint-Riquier", in: *Karl der Grosse: Lebenswerk und Nachleben*, ed. W. BRAUNFELS *et al.*, 5 vols. (Düsseldorf, 1966-1968), 3, *Karolingische Kunst*, pp. 369-374.

BERNARD, H., "Une restitution nouvelle de la basilique d'Angilbert", *Revue du Nord* 71 (1989), pp. 307-361.

BERNT, G., *Das lateinische Epigramm im Übergang von der Spätantike zum frühen Mittelalter* (Munich, 1968).

BERSCHIN, W., "Die Tituli der Wandbilder von Reichenau-Oberzell St. Georg", *Mittellateinisches Jahrbuch* 29.2 (1994), pp. 3-17, reprinted in: ID., *Mittellateinische Studien* (Heidelberg, 2005), pp. 215-228.

BERSCHIN, W., *Hermann der Lahme: Gelehrter und Dichter (1013-1054)* (Heidelberg, 2013).

BERTONI, A., "La musicalità della poesia", *Argo: Rivista ufficiale del Collegium Scribarum Histrionumque*, 1, *Musica e poesia* (Nov. 2000: <https://www.argonline.it/argo/argo-n-1/argo-n-1_alberto-bertoni-musicalita-poesia/>).

BEUMANN, H., "Die Kaiserfrage bei den Paderborner Verhandlungen von 799", in: *Das erste Jahrtausend: Kultur und Kunst im werdenden Abendland an Rhein und Ruhr*, ed. V. EBERN, 3 vols. (Düsseldorf, 1962-1964), 1, pp. 296-317.

BIDAULT, G., "Achitophel conseiller de la dissidence", *Revue du Moyen Âge Latin* 1 (1945), pp. 57-60.

BISCHOFF, B., "Bücher am Hofe Ludwigs des Deutschen und die Privatbibliothek des Kanzlers Grimalt", in: ID., *Mittelalterliche Studien: Ausgewählte Aufsätze zur Schriftkunde und Literaturgeschichte* 3 (Stuttgart, 1981), pp. 187-212.

BISCHOFF, B., "Das Thema des Poeta Saxo", in: *Speculum historiale: Geschichte im Spiegel von Geschichtsschreibung und Geschichtsdeutung: Johannes Spörl aus Anlass seines sechzigsten Geburtstages dargebracht von Weggenossen, Freunden umd Schülern*, ed. C. BAUER, L. BOEHM, and M. MÜLLER (Freiburg im Breisgau and Munich, 1965), pp. 198-203.

BISCHOFF, B., *Die Abtei Lorsch im Spiegel seiner Handschriften* (Lorsch, 1989).

BISCHOFF, B., *Katalog der festländischen Handschriften des neunten Jahrhunderts*, ed. B. EBERTSPERGER, 4 vols. (Wiesbaden, 1998-2017).

BISHOP, E., "A letter of Abbot Helisachar", in: ID., *Liturgica historica: Papers on the Liturgy and Religious Life of the Western Church* (Oxford, 1918), pp. 333-338.

BISHOP, E., "Ein Schreiben des Abts Helisachar", *Neues Archiv der Gesellschaft für ältere deutsche Geschichtskunde* 11 (1886), pp. 564-568.

BLOCH, M., *Les rois thaumaturges: Étude sur le caractère surnaturel attribué à la puissance royale particulièrement en France et en Angleterre* (Paris, 1983^2).

BLOOM, H., *Ruin the Sacred Truths: Poetry and Belief from the Bible to the Present* (Cambridge, MA, etc., 1989); trans. *Rovinare le sacre verità: Poesia e fede dalla Bibbia a oggi* (Milan, 1992).

BLUM-KULKA, S., "Interlanguage pragmatics: The case of requests", in: *Foreign / Second Language Pedagogy Research*, ed. R. PHILLIPSON, E. KELLERMAN, L. SELINKER, M. SHARWOOD SMITH, and M. SWAIN (Clevedon, 1991), 255-272.
BLUMENBERG, H., *Die Legitimität der Neuzeit* (Frankfurt am Main, 1966).
BOITANI, P., *Ri-scritture* Bologna, 1997).
BORGNA, G., *Storia della canzone italiana*, 2nd edn. (Milan, 1992).
BORI, P.C., *L'interpretazione infinita: L'ermeneutica cristiana antica e le sue trasformazioni* (Bologna, 1987).
BORST, A., *Computus: Zeit und Zahl in der Geschichte Europas* (Berlin, 2004), trans. *Computus: Tempo e numero nella storia d'Europa* (Genoa, 1997).
BORST, A., *Wie kam die arabische Sternkunde ins Kloster Reichenau?* (Konstanz, 1988).
BOURGAIN, P., "Les chansonniers lyriques latins", in: *Lyrique romane médiévale: La tradition des chansonniers: Actes du Colloque de Liège, Liège-Bibliothèque de la Faculté de Philosophie et Lettres*, ed. M. TYSSENS (Liège, 1991), pp. 61-84.
BOURGAIN, P., "Les recueils carolingiens de poésie rythmique", in: *De Tertullien aux Mozarabes: Mélanges offerts à Jacques Fontaine à l'occasion de son 70e anniversaire*, 2, *Antiquité tardive et christianisme ancien (VIe-IXe siècles)*, ed. L. HOLTZ (Paris, 1992), pp. 117-127.
BOURGAIN, P., "Les théories du passage du mètre au rythme d'après les textes", in: *Poesia dell'alto Medioevo europeo: Manoscritti, lingua e musica dei ritmi latini*, ed. F. STELLA (Florence, 2000), pp. 25-42.
BRAGUE, R., *Il futuro dell'Occidente: Nel modello romano la salvezza dell'Europa*, trans. A. SOLDATI and A.M. LORUSSO (Milan, 2005).
BRENK, B., "Schriftlichkeit und Bildlichkeit in der Hofschule Karls d. Gr.", in: *Testo e immagine nell'alto medioevo*, 2 vols. (Spoleto, 1994: *Settimane di Studio del Centro Italiano di Studi sull'Alto Medioevo* 41), 2, pp. 631-691.
BRIGHT, D.F., *The Miniature Epic in Vandal Africa* (Norman and London 1987).
BROWN, P., *The Rise of Western Christendom: Triumph and Diversity 200-1000 AD* (Malden, MA, etc., 1996).
BRUNHÖLZL, F., *Geschichte der lateinischen Literatur des Mittelalters*, 1 (Munich, 1975).
BUCHNER, M., *Einhards Künstler und Gelehrtenleben: Ein Kulturbild aus der Zeit Karls des Großen und Ludwigs des Frommen* (Leipzig, 1922).
BULLOUGH, D., *Alcuin: Achievement and Reputation: Being Part of the Ford Lectures Delivered in Oxford in Hilary Term 1980* (Leiden and Boston, 2004).
BULLOUGH, D., "Alcuin's cultural influence: The evidence of the manuscripts", in: *Alcuin of York: Scholar at the Carolingian Court: Proceedings of the Third Germania Latina Conference held at the University of Groningen, May 1995*, ed. L.A.J.R. HOUWEN and A.A. MACDONALD (Groningen, 1998), pp. 1-26.

BULLOUGH, D., "Hagiography as patriotism: Alcuin's 'York Poem' and early Northumbrian vitae sanctorum" in: *Hagiographie, cultures et sociétés IVe-XIIe siècles* (Paris, 1981), pp. 339-359.

BURCH BROWN, F., *Religious Aesthetics: A Theological Study of Making and Meaning* (Basingstoke and London, 1990).

BUREAU, I., *Lettre et sens mystique dans l'"Historia Apostolorum" d'Arator: Exégèse et épopée* (Paris, 1997).

BURGER, M., *Recherches sur la structure et l'origine des vers romans* (Genève, 1957).

BURGHARDT, H.D., *Philologische Untersuchungen zu den Gedichten Alkuins* (unpublished Diss. Phil. Heidelberg, 1960).

BUTZER, P.L., "Mathematics and astronomy at the court school of Charlemagne and its Mediterranean roots", *CRM: Cahiers de recherches médiévales (XIIIe-XIVe siècles)* 5 (1998), pp. 203-244.

CAFFARELLI, E., G. D'ACUNTI, and A. RICCI, "Neri a metà: Blues, rhythm & blues, funky e fusion", in: *Versi rock: La lingua della canzone italiana negli anni '80 e '90*, ed. Accademia degli Scrausi (Milan, 1996), pp. 251-262.

CAILLET, J.-P., "Prééminence dans la menée des desseins de Dieu: Configuration et décor des salles d'audience carolingiennes et pontificales", in: *L'audience: Rituels et cadres spatiaux dans l'Antiquité et le haut Moyen Âge*, ed. J.-P. CAILLET and M. SOT (Paris, 2007), pp. 291-302.

CAMDEN, W., *Britannia sive florentissimorum regnorum Angliae, Scotiae, Hiberniae et insularum adiacentium* (London, 1607).

CAMERON, A., *Continuity and Change in Sixth-Century Byzantium* (London, 1981).

CAMES, G., *Allégories et symboles dans l'Hortus deliciarum* (Leiden, 1971).

CAMPANA, A., "Il carteggio di Vitale e Pacifico di Verona col monaco Ildemaro sulla sorte eterna di Adamo", in: *Atti del Congresso internazionale di diritto romano e di storia del diritto (Verona 27-29 Settembre 1948)*, 1 (Milan, 1951), pp. 393-404.

CAMPANA, A., "Veronensia", in: *Miscellanea Giovanni Mercati*, 6 vols. (Città del Vaticano, 1946: *Studi e testi* 121-126), 2, pp. 57-91.

CAMPANALE, M.I., "Il *De Virginitate* di Venanzio Fortunato (*carm.* 8, 3 Leo): Un epitalamio mistico", *Invigilata Lucernis* 2 (1980), pp. 75-128.

CANISIUS, H., *Antiquae Lectiones, seu antiqua monumenta ad historiam mediae aetatis illustrandam*, 6 (Ingolstadt, 1604).

CAREY, J., *Ireland and the Grail* (Aberystwyth, 2007).

CASTAGNA, L., *Studi draconziani (1912-1996)* (Naples, 1997).

CAVALLO, G., "Scrivere leggere memorizzare le sacre scritture", in: *Morfologie sociali e culturali in Europa fra tarda antichità e alto medioevo*, 2 vols. (Spoleto, 1998: *Settimane di Studio del Centro Italiano di Studi sull'Alto Medioevo* 45), 2, pp. 987-1008.

CAVALLO, G., "Testo e immagine: Una frontiera ambigua", in: *Testo e immagine nell'alto Medioevo*, 2 vols. (Spoleto, 1994: *Settimane di Studio del Centro Italiano di Studi sull'Alto Medioevo* 41), 1, pp. 31-62.

CENOZ, J., and J.F. VALENCIA, "Cross-cultural communication and interlanguage pragmatics: American vs. European requests", *Pragmatics and Language Learning* 7 (1996), pp. 41-54.

CEREDA, L., G. MEACCI, and F. SERAFINI, "Ci ragiono e canto: la canzone d'autore", in: *Versi rock: La lingua della canzone italiana negli anni '80 e '90*, ed. Accademia degli Scrausi (Milan, 1996), pp. 27-143.

CESERANI, R., "Brevi appunti sulla riscoperta della Bibbia come grande testo letterario", in: *La Scrittura infinita: Bibbia e poesia in età romantica e contemporanea*, ed. F. STELLA (Florence, 1999), pp. 19-38.

CHAILLEY, J., *L'école musicale de Saint-Martial de Limoges jusqu'à la fin du XIe siècle* (Paris, 1960).

CHATILLON, J., "La Bible dans les écoles du XIIe siècle", in: *Le Moyen Âge et la Bible*, ed. P. RICHÉ and G. LOBRICHON (Paris, 1984), pp. 163-197.

CLASSEN, P., "Die Geschichte der Königspfalz Ingelheim bis zur Verpfändung an Kurpfalz 1375", in: *Ingelheim am Rhein: Forschungen und Studien zur Geschichte Ingelheims*, ed. J. AUTENRIETH (Stuttgart, 1964), pp. 87-146.

Clavis des auteurs latins du Moyen Âge: Territoire français 735-987, 2, *Alcuin*, ed. M.-H. JULLIEN and L. PERELMAN (Turnhout, 1999).

CLAYTON, M., "Aelfric's *Esther*: A *speculum reginae*?", in: *Text and Gloss: Studies in Insular Learning and Literature Presented to Joseph Donovan Pheifer*, ed. H. CONRAD-O'BRIAIN, V.J. SCATTERGOOD, and A.M. D'ARCY (Dublin, 1999), pp. 89-101.

COLISH, M.L., "Rethinking lying in the twelfth century," in: *Virtue and Ethics in the Twelfth Century*, ed. I.P. BEJCZY and R.G. NEWHAUSER (Leiden, 2005), pp. 155-173.

CONSOLINO, F.E., "La poesia epigrafica a Pavia longobarda nell'VIII secolo", in: *Storia di Pavia*, 2, *L'alto medioevo* (Pavia, 1987), pp. 159-176.

Continuity and Change: The Harvest of Late Medieval and Reformation History: Essays Presented to Heiko A. Oberman on His 70th Birthday, ed. R.J. BAST and A.C. GOW (Leiden and Boston, 2000).

CONTRENI, J., "Carolingian Renaissance: Education and literary culture", in: *The New Cambridge Medieval History*, 2, *c. 700-c.900*, ed. R. MCKITTERICK (Cambridge, 1995), pp. 709-757.

CONTRENI, J., "Counting, calendars, and cosmology: Numeracy in the early Middle Ages", in: *Word, Image, Number: Communication in the Middle Ages*, ed. J. CONTRENI (Florence and Turnhout, 2002), pp. 43-83.

CONTRENI, J., "The Carolingian Renaissance", in: *Renaissances before the Renaissance: Cultural Revivals of Late Antiquity and the Middle Ages*, ed. W.T. TREADGOLD (Stanford, 1984), pp. 56-74.
CONTRENI, J., *The Cathedral School of Laon from 850 to 930: Its Manuscripts and Masters* (Munich, 1978).
Convivio: estudios sobre la poesía de cancionero, ed. V. BELTRÁN, V. BELTRÁN PEPIÓ, and J. PAREDES NÚÑEZ (Granada, 2006).
COOK, V., "Evidence for multi-competence", *Language learning* 42 (1992), pp. 557-591.
CORDOLIANI, A., "Contribution à la littérature du comput ecclésiastique au Moyen Âge", *Studi Medievali* 1 (1960), pp. 107-137 and 2 (1961), pp. 169-208.
CORTI, M., "Testi o macrotesto? I racconti di *Marcovaldo*", *Strumenti critici* 27 (1975), pp. 182-197.
COURCELLE, P., "Le cliché virgilien des cent bouches", *Revue des Études Latines* 33 (1955), pp. 231-240.
COURCELLE, P., "Les pères de l'Église devant les enfers virgiliens", *Archives d'histoire doctinale et littéraire du moyen âge* 30 (1955), pp. 5-74.
COUSSY, C., *La figure de Judith dans l'Occident médiéval (V^e-XVe siècles)*, 2 vols. (Limoges, 2004).
CURTIUS, E.R., *Europäische Literatur und lateinisches Mittelalter* (Berne, 1948); trans. *European Literature and the Latin Middle Ages* (London, 1953).
D'ANGELO, E., *Indagini sulla tecnica versificatoria nell'esametro del Waltharius* (Catania, 1992).
D'ARCO SILVIO AVALLE, A., "Dalla metrica alla ritmica", in: *Lo spazio letterario del Medioevo*, 1, *Il medioevo latino*, 1, *La produzione*, ed. G. CAVALLO, C. LEONARDI, and E. MENESTÒ (Rome, 1992), pp. 391-476.
D'IMPERIO, F.S., *Alcuino di York, Expositio in Ecclesiasten: Studio della tradizione manoscritta* (PhD thesis, Florence, 2004).
DATURI, E.L., *Représentations d'Esther entre écritures et images* (Berne, 2004).
DAVIS-WEYER, C., "*Aperit quod ipse signaverat testamentum*: Lamm und Löwe im Apokalypsebild der Grandval-Bibel", in: *Studien zur mittelalterlichen Kunst 800-1250: Festschrift für Florentine Mütherich zum 70. Geburtstag*, ed. K. BIERBRAUER *et al.* (Munich, 1985), pp. 67-74.
DAVRIL, A., and E. PALAZZO, *La vie des moines au temps des grandes abbayes, Xe-XIIIe siècles* (Paris, 2000).
DAWSON, J.D., *Christian Figural Reading and the Fashioning of Identity* (Berkeley, CA, 2002).
DE ANGELIS, E., "Nota", in: *Il suono e l'inchiostro: poesia e canzone nell'Italia contemporanea* (Milan, 2009), pp. 249-251.
DE CARLOS VILLAMARÍN, H., "Una escena de caza en la 'Epistola ad Hugonem' de Godofredo de Reims", in: *Poesía latina medieval (siglos V-XV): Actas del IV*

Congreso del 'Internationales Mittellateinerkomitee' (Santiago de Compostela, 12-15 septiembre de 2002), ed. M.C. DÍAZ Y DÍAZ and J.M. DÍAZ DE BUSTAMANTE (Florence, 2005), pp. 233-243.

DE GAETANO, M., *Scuola e potere in Draconzio* (Alessandria, 2009).

DE JONG, M., *Epitaph for an Era: Politics and Rhetoric in the Carolingian World* (Cambridge, 2019).

DE JONG, M., "Jeremiah, Job, Terence and Paschasius Radbertus: Political rhetoric and biblical authority in the Epitaphium Arsenii", in: *Reading the Bible in the Middle Ages*, ed. J. NELSON and D. KEMPF (London, 2015), pp. 57-76.

DE JONG, M.B., "The empire as ecclesia: Hrabanus Maurus and biblical *Historia* for rulers," in: *The Uses of the Past in the Early Middle Ages*, ed. Y. HEN and M. INNES (Cambridge, 2000), pp. 191-226.

DE MAN, P., *Allegories of reading: Figural Language in Rousseau, Nietzsche, Rilke and Proust* (New Haven, 1979); trans. *Allegorie della critica: Strategie della decostruzione nella critica americana*, ed. M. AJAZZI MANCINI and F. BAGATTI, (Naples, 1987).

DE MARGERIE, B., *Introduction à l'histoire de l'exégèse*, 3, *Saint Augustin* (Paris, 1983).

DEKKER, E., *Illustrating the Phenomena in Antiquity and the Middle Ages* (Oxford, 2012).

DELISLE, L., *Le cabinet des manuscrits de la Bibliothèque Impériale: Étude sur la formation de ce dépôt comprenant les éléments d'une histoire de la calligraphie, de la miniature, de la reliure, et du commerce des livres à Paris avant l'invention de l'imprimerie*, 4 vols. (Paris, 1868-1881).

DELMAIRE, B., "Saint-Riquier", in: *LdM* 7.6 (Munich, 1995), col. 1198.

DEMPSEY, G.T., "Aldhelm of Malmesbury's social theology: The barbaric heroic ideal christianised", *Peritia* 15 (2001), pp. 58-80.

DEPREUX, Ph., "La *pietas* comme principe de gouvernement d'après le Poème sur Louis le Pieux d'Ermold le Noir", in: *The Community, the Family and the Saint: Patterns of Power in Early Medieval Europe: Selected Proceedings of the International Medieval Congress, University of Leeds, 4-7 July 1994, 10-13 July 1995*, ed. J. HILL and M. SWAN (Turnhout, 1998), pp. 201-224.

DEPROOST, P.A., "L'épopée biblique en langue latine: Essai de définition d'un genre littéraire", *Latomus* 56.1 (1997), pp. 15-39.

DERRIDA, J., "Des tours de Babel", in: *Poststructuralism as Exegesis* (Atlanta, GA, 1991), p. 3.

DERRIDA, J., *L'écriture et la différence* (Paris, 1967); trans. *Writing and Difference*, trans. A. BASS (Chicago,1978).

DERRIDA, J., *Le monolinguisme de l'autre ou la prothèse d'origine* (Paris, 1996).

DEUG-SU, I., *L'opera agiografica di Alcuino* (Spoleto, 1983).

DI GIROLAMO, C., "Regole dell'anisosillabismo", in: ID., *Teoria e prassi della versificazione* (Bologna, 1976; 2nd edn. 1983), pp. 119-135.

DI PASQUALE, M.G., "Versi computistici: Proposte per una nuova edizione", in: *Poetry of the Early Medieval Europe: Manuscripts, Language and Music of the Rhythmical Latin Texts: III Euroconference for the Digital Edition of the "Corpus of Latin Rhythmical Texts 4th-9th Century"*, ed. E. D'ANGELO and F. STELLA (Florence, 2003), pp. 171-181.

DI PASQUALE, M.G., [review of C. LA ROCCA, *Pacifico di Verona: Il passato carolingio nella costruzione della memoria urbana* (Rome, 1995)], *Rivista di storia della Chiesa in Italia* 51 (1997), pp. 549-555.

Die Verschriftlichung der Welt: Bild, Text und Zahl in der Kultur des Mittelalters und der frühen Neuzeit, ed. H. WENZEL, W. SEIPEL, and G. WUNBERG (Vienna and Milan, 2000).

DINKOVA-BRUUN, G., "Latin poetic anthologies from the later Middle Ages", in: *Collecting, Organizing and Transmitting Knowledge: Miscellanies in Late Medieval Europe*, ed. S. CORBELLINI, G. MURANO, and G. SIGNORE (Turnhout, 2018), pp. 39-49.

DOLEŽALOVA, L., *Reception and its Varieties: Reading, Re-Writing, and Understanding "Cena Cypriani" in the Middle Ages* (Trier, 2007).

DONNINI, M., "Bibbia e storiografia", in: *La Bibbia nel medioevo*, ed. G. CREMASCOLI (Bologna, 1996), pp. 313-326.

DONNINI, M., "L'*ars narrandi* nel *Carmen in honorem Hludowici* di Ermoldo Nigello", *Studi medievali* 47 (2006), pp. 111-176.

DRONKE, P., "Le antologie liriche del Medioevo latino", *Critica del testo* 2.1 (1999), pp. 101-117.

DRONKE, P., [Review of: D. KORZENIEWSKI, *Hirtengedichte aus spätrömischer und karolingischer Zeit* (Darmstadt, 1976)], *Cahiers de Civilisation Classique et Médiévale* 23 (1980), pp. 61-63.

DUBREUCQ, A., "Les peintures murales du palais carolingien d'Ingelheim et l'idéologie impériale carolingienne", *Hortus Artium Medievalium* 16 (2010), pp. 27-38.

DUCHESNE, A., *Historie Francorum Scriptores* 2 (Paris, 1636).

DÜMMLER, E., "Die handschriftliche Überlieferung der lateinischen Dichtungen aus der Zeit der Karolinger", *Neues Archiv* 5 (1879), pp. 89-159.

DUTARTE, Ph., *Les instruments de l'astronomie ancienne de l'Antiquité à la Renaissance* (Paris, 2006).

DUTTON, P.E., and H.L. KESSLER, *The Poetry and the Paintings of the First Bible of Charles the Bald* (Ann Arbor, 1997).

EASTWOOD, B.S., *La scienza bizantina e Latina prima dell'influsso della scienza araba: Astronomia, computo e astrologia*, in: *Storia della scienza Treccani* (2001), online at: <https://www.treccani.it/enciclopedia/la-scienza-bizantina-e-latina-prima-

dell-influsso-della-scienza-araba-scienze-della-vita-e-medicina_%28Storia-della-Scienza%29/>.
EBENBAUER, A., "Nasos Ekloge", *Mittellateinisches Jahrbuch* 11 (1976), pp. 13-27.
EBENBAUER, A., *Carmen historicum: Untersuchungen zur historischen Dichtung im karolingischen Europa* (Vienna, 1978).
EBERT, A., "Naso, Angilbert und der Conflictus veris et hiemis", *Zeitschrift für das deutsches Altertum und deutsche Literatur* 22 (1878), pp. 328-335.
EBERT, A., *Allgemeine Geschichte der Literatur des Mittelalters im Abendlande*, 3 vols. (Leipzig 1874-1887).
ECO, U., *Apocalittici e integrati: Comunicazioni di massa e teorie della cultura di massa* (Milan, 1964).
ECO, U., *Arte e bellezza nell'estetica medievale* (Milan, 1988).
EDMUNDS, L., *Intertextuality and the Reading of Roman Poetry* (Baltimore, MD, 2001).
EHRHARDT-SIEBOLD, E., *Die lateinischen Rätsel der Angelsachsen: Ein Beitrag zur Kulturgeschichte Altenglands* (Heidelberg, 1925).
ELSNER, J., "Late antique art: The problem of the concept and the cumulative aesthetic", in: *Approaching Late Antiquity: The Transformation from Early to Late Empire*, ed. S. SWAIN and M. EDWARDS (Oxford, 2004), pp. 271-304.
ENCUENTRA ORTEGA, A., "Luis el Piadoso, un Eneas cristiano en el poema laudatorio de Ermoldo", *Latomus* 64 (2005) pp. 445-455.
Epochenschwelle und Epochenbewusstsein, ed. R. HERZOG and R. KOSELLECK (Munich, 1987).
ERDMANN, C., *Forschungen zur politischen Ideenwelt des Frühmittelalters* (Berlin, 1951).
ERKENS, F.-R., "*Sicut Esther Regina*: Die westfränkische Königin als *consors regni*", *Francia* 20 (1993), pp. 15-38.
ERNST, U., *Carmen figuratum: Geschichte des Figurengedichts von den antiken Ursprüngen bis zum Ausgang des Mittelalters* (Vienna etc., 1991).
Europe: A Literary History, 1348-1418, ed. D. WALLACE, 2 vols. (Oxford, 2015).
EVANS, G., *The Language and Logic of the Bible: The Earlier Middle Ages* (Cambridge, 1984).
EVERETT, N., *Literacy in Lombard Italy 568-774* (Cambridge, 2003: *Cambridge Studies in Medieval Life and Thought*, 4th series 52).
EWIG, E., "Zum christlichen Königsgedanken im Frühmittelalter", in: ID., *Spätantikes und fränkisches Gallien: Gesammelte Schriften*, ed. H. ATSMA (Munich, 1976-1979), 1, pp. 3-71.
FARRE I OLIVE, E., "La Sphaera Horarum Noctis de Ramon Llull', *La Busca de Paper* 22 (1996), pp. 3-12.

FAVREAU, R., "Fortunat et l'épigraphie", in: *Venanzio Fortunato tra Italia e Francia: Atti del convegno internazionale di studi, Valdobbiadene, 17 maggio 1990 – Treviso 18-19 maggio 1990*, ed. T. RAGUSA (Treviso, 1993), pp. 161-173.
FAVREAU, R., *Les inscriptions médiévales* (Turnhout, 1979: *L'atelier du médiéviste* 5).
FAVREAU, R., "Les inscriptions médiévales – Reflet d'une culture et d'une foi", in: *Epigraphik 1988: Fachtagung für mittelalterliche und neuzeitliche Epigraphik, Graz, 10.-14. Mai 1988*, ed. W. KOCH (Vienna, 1990), pp. 57-89.
FERRARI, M.C. "'Dum profluit est lutulentus': Thiofrido, Alcuino e la metrica della 'Vita S. Willibrordi'", in: *Gli umanesimi medievali: Atti del II Congresso dell' 'Internationales Mittellateinerkomitee', Firenze, Certosa del Galluzzo, 11-15 settembre 1993*, ed. C. LEONARDI (Florence, 1998), pp. 129-140.
FERRARI, M.C., *Il "Liber sanctae crucis" di Rabano Mauro: Testo – immagine – contesto*, with a preface by C. LEONARDI (Berne etc., 1999).
FICHTENAU, H., "Byzanz und die Pfalz zu Aachen", *Mitteilungen des Instituts für Österreichische Geschichtsforschung* 59 (1951), pp. 1-54.
FICHTENAU, H., "Karl der Große und das Kaisertum", *Mitteilungen des Instituts für Österreichische Geschichtsforschung* 61 (1953), pp. 257-334.
FICHTNER, R., *Taufe und Versuchung Jesu in den Evangeliorum libri quatuor des Bibeldichter Juvencus* (Stuttgart and Leipzig, 1994).
FLEINER, C.D., *In Honor of Louis the Pious, a Verse Biography by Ermoldus Nigellus (826): An Annotated Translation* (PhD thesis University of Virginia, 1996).
FLIEGER, M., *Interpretationen zum Bibeldichter Iuvencus* (Stuttgart, 1993).
FLURY, Th., *Frauen im Galluskloster: Katalog zur Ausstellung in der Stiftsbibliothek St. Gallen (20. Marz-12. November 2006)* (Saint Gall, 2006).
FRANKE, B., *Assuerus und Esther am Burgunderhof: Zur Rezeption des Buches Esther in den Niederlanden (1450-1530)* (Berlin, 1998).
FRAPPIER, J., "Littérature médiévale et littérature comparée", in: *Grundriß der romanischen Literaturen des Mittelalters* 1, ed. H.R. JAUß (Heidelberg 1972), pp. 139-162.
FRYE, N., *The Great Code: The Bible and Literature* (New York, 1982).
GAEHDE, J.E., *The Painters of the Carolingian Bible Manuscript of San Paolo Fuori le Mura in Rome* (Ann Arbor, 1993).
GALLONI, P., "Un gioco che non è un gioco: La caccia altomedievale", in: *Il gioco nella società e nella cultura dell'Alto Medioevo*, 2 vols. (Spoleto, 2018: *Settimane di Studio del CISAM* 65), pp. 531-570.
GANDINO, G., "Il 'palatium' e l'immagine della casa del padre: L'evoluzione di un modello nel mondo franco", *Studi medievali* 50 (2009), pp. 75-104.
GANZ, D., "Der lineare Blick: Geometrie und Körperwelt in mittelalterlichen Bildern der Himmelsschau", in: *Sehen und Sakralität in der Vormoderne*, ed. D. GANZ et al. (Berlin, 2011), pp. 266-291.

GANZ, D., "*Pando quod ignoro*: In search of Carolingian artistic experience", in: *Intellectual Life in the Middle Ages: Essays Presented to Margaret Gibson*, ed. L. SMITH and B. WARD (London, 1992), pp. 25-32.

GARGAN, L., *Dante, la sua biblioteca e lo Studio di Bologna* (Rome and Padua, 2014).

GARRISON, M., "Alcuin, 'Carmen IX' and Hrabanus, 'Ad Bonosum': A teacher and his pupil write consolation", in: *Poetry and Philosophy in the Middle Ages: A Festschrift for Peter Dronke*, ed. J. MARENBON (Leiden, Boston, and Cologne, 2001), pp. 63-78.

GARRISON, M., "Send more socks: On mentality and the preservation context of medieval letters", in: *New Approaches to Medieval Communication*, ed. M. MOSTERT (Turnhout, 1999: *Utrecht Studies in Medieval Literacy* 1), pp. 69-99.

GARRISON, M.B., *Alcuin's World through his Letters and Verse* (unpublished PhD thesis, University of Cambridge, Christ's College and Corpus Christi College, 1995, 1995) [to be found on <academia.edu>].

GASPAROV, M.L., *Storia del verso europeo*, trans. S. GARZONIO (Bologna, 1993).

GENETTE, G., *Seuils* (Paris, 1987); trans. *Soglie: I dintorni del testo* (Turin, 1989).

GENOT, G., "Strutture narrative della poesia lirica", *Paragone* 18 (1967), pp. 35-52.

GILLEN, O., *Herrad von Landsberg, Hortus Deliciarum* (Neustadt, 1979).

GIUNTA, C., *Versi a un destinatario* (Bologna, 2002).

GIVONE, S., "Poesia e interpretazione della Bibbia", *Annali di Storia dell'Esegesi* 3 (1988), pp. 7-17.

GNÄDINGER, L., "Esther: Eine Skizze," *Zeitschrift für deutsche Philologie* 113 (1994), pp. 31-62.

GODMAN, P., *Poetry of the Carolingian Renaissance* (Oxford, 1985).

GODMAN, P., *Poets and Emperors: Frankish Politics and Carolingian Poetry* (Oxford, 1987).

GODMAN, P., "The poetic hunt: From Saint Martin to Charlemagne's heir", in: *Charlemagne's Heir*, ed. P. GODMAN and R. COLLINS (Oxford, 1990), pp. 565-589.

GOERING, J., *The Virgin and the Grail: Origins of a Legend* (New Haven, 2005).

GOMPE, L., "Figmenta poetarum", in: *Literatur und Sprache im europäischen Mittelalter: Festschrift für Karl Langosch* (Darmstadt, 1973), pp. 53-62.

GORMAN, M., "The encyclopedic commentary on Genesis prepared for Charlemagne by Wigbod", *Recherches augustiniennes et patristiques* 17 (1982), pp. 173-201.

GRABMANN, M., *Gentile da Cingoli, ein italienischer Aristoteleserklärer aus der Zeit Dantes* (Munich, 1940: *Sitzungsberichte der Bayerischen Akademie der Wissenschaften*).

GREEN, R., *Herrad of Hohenbourg, "Hortus deliciarum"*, 1, *Commentary*, 2, *Reconstruction* (Leiden, 1979).

GREEN, R.P.H., "Modoin's Eclogues and the Paderborn epic", *Mittellateinisches Jahrbuch* 16 (1981), pp. 43-53.

GREEN, R.P.H., *Seven versions of Carolingian Pastoral* (Reading, 1980).

Bibliography

GREENFIELD, C.C., *Humanistic and Scholastic Poetics, 1250-1550* (London and Toronto, 1981).

GREWE, H., "Die Ausgrabungen in der Königspfalz zu Ingelheim am Rhein", in: *Deutsche Königspfalzen: Beiträge zu ihrer historischen und archäologischen Erforschung*, ed. L. FENSKE, J. JARNUT, and M. WEMHOFF (Göttingen, 2001: *Splendor palatii: Neue Forschungen zu Paderborn und anderen Pfalzen der Karolingerzeit* 5), pp. 155-174.

GREWE, H., "Die bauliche Entwicklung der Pfalz Ingelheim im Hochmittelalter: Architekturbefunde und Schriftquellen des 10. und 11. Jahrhunderts", in: *Zentren herrschaftlicher Repräsentation im Hochmittelalter: Geschichte, Architektur, und Zeremoniell*, ed. C. EHLERS, J. JARNUT, and M. WEMHOFF (Göttingen, 2007: *Deutsche Königspfalzen: Beiträge zu ihrer historischen und archäologischen Erforschung* 7), pp. 101-120.

GREWE, H., "Die Königspfalz zu Ingelheim am Rhein", in: *799: Kunst und Kultur der Karolingerzeit: Karl der Grosse und Papst Leo III. in Paderborn*, ed. Ch. STIEGEMANN and M. WEMHOFF (Mainz, 1999), 3, *Beiträge zum Katalog der Ausstellung Paderborn 1999*, pp. 142-151.

GREWE, H., "Forschen, Erschließen, Bewahren: Ein Zwischenbericht über die Kaiserpfalz Ingelheim", *Baudenkmäler in Rheinland Pfalz* 59 (2004), pp. 54-60.

GREWE, H., "Geschichte und Neubeginn der archäologischen Forschung in der Königspfalz zu Ingelheim am Rhein", *Acta Praehistorica et Archaeologica* 30 (1998), pp. 177-184.

GREWE, H., "Palast, Ruine, Denkmal: Konzeptionelle Grundsätze für das Erforschen, Bewahren und Erschließen der Kaiserpfalz Ingelheim", in: *Schutzbauten und Rekonstruktionen in der Archäologie*, ed. M. MÜLLER, T. OTTEN, and U. WULF-RHEIDT (Mainz, 2011), pp. 305-328.

GREWE, H., "Visualisierung von Herrschaft in der Architektur: Die Pfalz Ingelheim als Bedeutungsträger im 12. und 13. Jahrhundert", in: *Staufisches Kaisertum im 12. Jahrhundert: Konzepte, Netzwerke, Politische Praxis*, ed. S. BURKHARDT (Regensburg, 2010), pp. 383-403.

GUREVIČ [GUREVICH], A.J., *Le categorie della cultura medievale*, ed. C. CASTELLI (Turin, 1983, reprint 2007), Italian trans. of the first edn. (Moscow, 1972).

HAEFELE, H., "*Decerpsi pollice flores*: Aus Hrabans Vermischten Gedichten", in: *Tradition und Wertung: Festschrift Franz Brunhölzl zum 65. Geburtstag*, ed. G. BERNT, F. RÄDLE, and G. SILAGI (Sigmaringen, 1989), pp. 59-74.

HAGENDAHL, H., "Methods of citation in postclassical Latin", *Eranos* 45 (1947), pp. 114-128.

HALPHEN, L., *Charlemagne et l'Empire carolingien* (Paris, 1947).

HAMBURGER, J.J., "Idol curiosity", in: *Curiositas: Welterfahrung und ästhetische Neugierde in Mittelalter und früher Neuzeit*, ed. K. KRÜGER (Göttingen 2002: *Göttinger Gespräche zur Geschichtswissenschaft* 15), pp. 19-58.

HANAUER, D.I., *Poetry as Research: Exploring Second Language Poetry Writing* (Amsterdam etc., 2010).
HARRIES, R., *Art and the Beauty of God* (London and New York, 1993).
HARTMANN, F., "Karolingische Gelehrte als Dichter und der Wissenstransfer am Beispiel der Epigraphik", in: *Karolingische Klöster: Wissenstransfer und kulturelle Innovation* ed. J. BECKER, T. LICHT, and S. WEINFURTER (Berlin, 2015), pp. 255-274.
HASELBACH, I., *Aufstieg und Herrschaft der Karolinger in der Darstellung der sogenannten Annales Mettenses priores: Ein Beitrag zur Geschichte der politischen Ideen im Reiche Karls des Grossen* (Hamburg, 1970).
HAUCK, K., "Die Ausbreitung des Glaubens in Sachsen und die Verteidigung der römischen Kirche als konkurrierende Herrscheraufgaben Karls des Grossen", *Frühmittelalterliche Studien* 4 (1970) pp. 138-172.
HEIMPEL, H., "Bisherige und künftige Erforschung deutscher Königspfalzen: Zugleich Bericht über Arbeiten des Max-Planck-Instituts für Geschichte zur Pfalzenforschung", *Geschichte in Wissenschaft und Unterricht* 16 (1965), pp. 461-487.
HERDINA, P., and U. JESSNER, *A Dynamic Model of Multilingualism* (Clevedon, 2001).
HERZOG, R., *Die Bibelepik der lateinischen Spätantike: Geschichte einer erbaulichen Gattung* (Munich, 1975).
HILLIER, R., *Arator on the Acts of the Apostles: A Baptismal Commentary* (Oxford, 1993).
HINDS, S., *Allusion and Intertext: Dynamics of Appropriation in Roman Poetry* (Cambridge, 1998).
HÖLSCHER, U., *Die Odyssee: Epos zwischen Märchen und Roman* (Munich, 1988).
HUBERT, J., "Saint-Riquier et le monachisme bénédictin en Gaule à l'époque carolingienne", in: *Il monachesimo nell'alto medioevo e la formazione della civiltà occidentale* (Spoleto, 1957: *Settimane di studio del Centro Italiano di Studi sull'Alto Medioevo* 4), pp. 293-309.
HUBERT, J., J. PORCHER, and W.F. VOLBACH, *L'empire carolingien* (Paris, 1968); trans. *L'impero carolingio* (Milan, 1981).
HÜBNER, W., "Das Horoskop der Christen (Zeno, 1, 38 L.)", *Vigiliae Christianae* 29 (1975), pp.120-137.
HÜBNER, W., "Une glose a la 'massa Compoti' d'Alexandre de Villedieu contenant des vers sur le zodiaque", in: *Science antique science médiévale (autour d'Avranches 25): Actes du colloque international (Mont Saint-Michel, 4-7 Septembre 1998)*, ed. L. CALLEBAT and O. DESBORDES (Hildesheim, Zurich, and New York, 2000), pp. 373-389.
HÜBNER, W., *Zodiacus Christianus: Judisch-christliche Adaptationen des Tierkreises von der Antike bis zur Gegenwart* (Meisenheim, 1983).
HUEMER, J., *Untersuchungen über die ältesten lateinisch-christlichen Rhythmen* (Vienna, 1879).

HUGLO, M., "D'Helisachar à Abbon de Fleury", *Revue bénédictine* 104 (1994), pp. 204-230.
HUGLO, M., *Les sources du plain-chant et de la musique médiévale* (London, 2014).
HUNEYCUTT, L.L., "Intercession and the high-medieval queen: The Esther topos", in: *Power of the Weak: Studies on Medieval Women*, ed. J. CARPENTER and S.-B. MACLEAN (Urbana, IL, 1995), pp. 126-146.
ILLICH, I., *In the Vineyard of the Text: A Commentary to Hugh's* Didascalicon (Chicago, 1993); trans. *Nella vigna del testo: Per una etologia della lettura* (Milan, 1994).
INGRAFFIA, B.D., *Postmodern Theory and Biblical Theology: Vanquishing God's Shadow* (Cambridge, 1995).
IRVINE, M., *The Making of Textual Culture: "Grammatica" and Literary Theory, 350-1100* (Cambridge, 1994).
JACHIA, P., *La canzone d'autore italiana 1958-1997: Avventure della parola cantata* (Milan, 1998).
JACOB, D., "Poésie rythmique et 'traditions discursives'", in: *Poetry of the Early Medieval Europe: Manuscripts, Language and Music of the Rhythmical Latin texts: III Euroconference for the Digital Edition of the "Corpus Rhythmorum", Munich 2-4 november 2000*, ed. E. D'ANGELO and F. STELLA (Florence, 2003), pp. 267-289.
JAKOBSON, R., "Linguistics and poetics," in: *Style in Language*, ed. Th. SEBEOK (Cambridge, MA, 1960), pp. 350-377.
JAUSS, H.R., *Literaturgeschichte als Provokation der Literaturwissenschaft* (Konstanz, 1967); trans. *Perché la storia della letteratura?*, trans. A. VARVARO (Naples, 1970).
JEAUNEAU, E., "L'usage de la notion d'integumentum à travers les gloses de Guillaume de Conches", *Archives d'histoire doctrinale et littéraire du Moyen Âge* 32 (1957), pp. 35-100.
JESSNER, U., "A dynamic approach to language attrition in multilingual systems", in: *Effects of the Second Language on the First*, ed. V. COOK (Clevedon, 2003), pp. 234-246.
KARTSCHOKE, D., *Bibeldichtung: Studien zur Geschichte der epischen Bibelparaphrase von Juvencus bis Otfrid von Weissenburg* (Munich, 1975).
KELLER, H., "Vom heiligen Buch zur Buchführung: Lebensfunktionen der Schrift im Mittelalter", *Frühmittelalterliche Studien* 26 (1992), pp. 1-31.
KESSLER, H.L., "A lay abbot as patron: Count Vivian and the First Bible of Charles the Bald", in: *Committenti e produzione artistico-letteraria nell'alto medioevo occidentale*, 2 vols. (Spoleto, 1992: *Settimane di studio del Centro Italiano di Studi sull'Alto Medioevo* 39), 2, pp. 647-675.
KESSLER, H.L., "'*Facies bibliothecae revelata*': Carolingian art as spiritual seeing", in: *Testo e immagine nell'alto medioevo*, 2 vols. (Spoleto, 1994: *Settimane di studio del Centro italiano di studi sull'alto Medioevo* 41), 2, pp. 533-594.

KESSLER, H.L., *The Cotton Genesis: British Library, Codex Cotton, Otho B. VI* (with K. WEITZMANN) (Princeton, 1986).

KESSLER, H.L., *The Illustrated Bibles from Tours* (Princeton, 1977).

KIRSCH, W., "Alkuins York-Gedicht (C. 1) als Kunstwerk", in: *Gli umanesimi medievali*, ed. C. LEONARDI (Florence, 1998), pp. 283-295.

KLEIN, S.S., *Ruling Women: Queenship and Gender in Anglo-Saxon Literature* (Notre Dame, 2006).

KLOOS, R.M., *Einführung in die Epigraphik des Mittelalters und der frühen Neuzeit* (Darmstadt, 1980).

KLOPSCH, P., *Einführung in die mittellateinische Verslehre* (Darmstadt, 1972).

KNAEPEN, A., "L'histoire gréco-romaine dans les sources littéraires latines de la première moitié du IXe siècle: Quelques conclusions provisoires", *Revue belge de philologie et d'histoire* 79 (2001), pp. 341-372.

KOCH, P., and W. OESTERREICHER, "Langage parlé et langage écrit", in: *Lexikon der Romanistischen Linguistik*, ed. G. HOLTUS *et al.*, 8 vols. (Tübingen, 2001-2005), 1.2, pp. 584-627.

KOHLER, W., *Die karolingische Miniaturen*, 1, *Die Schule von Tours*; 2, *Die Bilder* (Berlin, 1933).

Kontinuität – Diskontinuität in der Geisteswissenschaft, ed. H. TRÜMPY (Darmstadt, 1973).

Kontinuität – Wandel: kulturwissenschaftliche Versuche über ein schwieriges Verhältnis, ed. N. LANGREITER (Vienna, 2002).

KORZENIEWSKI, D., *Hirtengedichte aus spätrömischer und karolingischer Zeit* (Darmstadt, 1976).

KOSHI, K., "Die Buchmalerei der Reichenau zwischen Ost und West: Ikonographie anhand von den Wandbildern der Wunder Christi in St. Georg zu Reichenau-Oberzell", in: *Testo e immagine nell'alto Medioevo*, 2 vols. (Spoleto, 1994: *Settimane di Studio del Centro Italiano di Studi sull'Alto Medioevo* 41), 2, pp. 595-629.

KROTZ, E., "Remigius von Auxerre und die Ars Prisciani", *Archivum Latinitatis Medii Aevi* 72 (2014), pp. 21-82.

Kulturbruch oder Kulturkontinuität im Übergang von der Antike zum Mittelalter, ed. P.E. HUBINGER (Darmstadt, 1968).

KÜNG, H., and W. JENSEN, *Dichtung und Religion: Pascal, Gryphius, Lessing, Hölderlin, Novalis, Kierkegaard, Dostojewski, Kafka* (Munich and Zurich, 1988^2).

Kunst und Kultur der Karolingerzeit: Karl der Grosse und Papst Leo III. in Paderborn: Katalog der Austellung Paderborn 1999, ed. Ch. STIEGEMANN and M. WEMHOFF, 3 vols. (Mainz, 1999).

KUSCH, H., *Einführung in das lateinische Mittelalter*, 1, *Dichtung* (Darmstadt, 1957).

L'Irlanda e gli irlandesi nell'alto medioevo (Spoleto, 2009: *Settimane di studio del Centro Italiano di Studi sull'Alto Medioevo* 57).

La Bible et la littérature: Actes du colloque international de Metz, ed. P.-M. BEAUDE (Paris, 1987).
La lingua assente: Autrotraduzione e interculturalità nella poesia europea, ed. F. STELLA (Florence, 2001 = *Semicerchio: Rivista di poesia comparata* 20-21).
La lingua cantata: L'italiano nella canzone dagli anni Trenta ad oggi, ed. G. BORGNA and L. SERIANNI (Rome, 1994).
La poesia tardoantica e medievale: *Atti del I convegno internazionale di studi, Macerata 4-5 maggio 1998*, ed. M. SALVADORE (Alessandria, 2001).
LA ROCCA, C., "A man for all seasons: Pacificus of Verona and the creation of a local Carolingian past", in: *The Uses of the Past in the Early Middle Ages,* ed. Y. HEN and M. INNES (Cambridge, 2000), pp. 250-277.
LA ROCCA, C., "Pacifico di Verona", in: *Dizionario Biografico degli Italiani* 80 (online in 2014).
LA ROCCA, C., *Pacifico di Verona: Il passato carolingio nella costruzione della memoria urbana* (Rome, 1995).
La Scrittura infinita: Bibbia e poesia in età medievale e umanistica , ed. F. STELLA (Florence, 2001).
La Scrittura infinita: Bibbia e poesia in età romantica e contemporanea, ed. F. STELLA (Florence, 1999).
LA VIA, S., *Poesia per musica e musica per poesia: Dai trovatori a Paolo Conte* (Rome, 2006).
LAMMERS, W., "Ein karolingisches Bildprogramm in der Aula Regia von Ingelheim", in: ID., *Vestigia mediaevalia: Ausgewählte Aufsätze zur mittelalterlichen Historiographie, Landes- und Kirchengeschichte* (Wiesbaden, 1979), pp. 219-283.
LAMPERT-WEISSIG, L., *Medieval Literature and Postcolonial Studies* (Edinburgh, 2010).
LAPIDGE , M., "Il secolo VIII", in: *Letteratura latina medievale*, ed. C. LEONARDI (Florence, 2003; reprinted 2004), pp. 41-73.
LÉGLU, C.E., *Multilingualism and Mother Tongue in Medieval French, Occitan, and Catalan Narratives* (University Park, PA, 2010).
LEHMANN, P., "Das Problem der karolingischen Renaissance", in: *I problemi della civiltà carolingia* (Spoleto, 1954: Settimane di Studio del Centro Italiano di Studi sull'Alto Medioevo 1), pp. 309-358, reprinted in ID., *Erforschung des Mittelalters: Ausgewählte Abhandlungen und Aufsätze*, 5 vols. (Leipzig and Stuttgart, 1941-1962), 2, pp. 109-138.
LEHMANN, P., "Der Einfluß der Bibel auf frühmittelalterliche Geschichtsschreiber", in: *La bibbia nell'alto medioevo* (Spoleto, 1963: Settimane di studio del Centro Italiano di Studi sull'Alto Medioevo 10), pp. 129-140.
LEJBOVICZ, M., "Le nombre et le temps altimedievaux", in: *Le Temps, sa mesure et sa perception au Moyen Âge: Actes du Colloque (Orléans, 12-13 Avril 1991)*, ed. B. RIBEMONT (Caen, 1992), pp. 151-187.

LELAND, J., *Commentarii de scriptoribus Britannicis*, ed. A. HALL (Oxford, 1709).
LEMOINE, M., *Intorno a Chartres: Naturalismo platonico nella tradizione cristiana del XII secolo*, Italian trans. (Milan, 1998).
LEONARDI, C., "L'intellettuale nell'Altomedioevo", in: *Il comportamento intellettuale nella società antica* (Genoa, 1980), pp. 119-139; , reprinted in ID., *Medioevo Latino: La cultura dell'Europa cristiana* (Florence, 2004), pp. 3-21.
LEONHARDT, J., *Latin: Story of a World Language* (Cambridge, MA, 2013).
LESNE, E., *Histoire de la propriété ecclésiastique en France*, 6 vols. (Lille, 1910-1943), 6, *Les Églises et les monastères, centres d'accueil, d'exploitation et de peuplement* (1943).
LEWIS, C.S., "Is theology poetry?", Presented to the Oxford University Socratic Club, November 6, 1944, in: ID., *The Weight of Glory and Other Addresses*, ed. W. HOOPER (New York, 1980).
Lezioni di poesia, ed. A. FRANCINI, P.F. IACUZZI, and F. STELLA (Florence, 2000).
'Liber', 'Fragmenta', 'Libellus' prima e dopo Petrarca: In ricordo di d'Arco Silvio Avalle, Seminario Internazionale di Studi, Bergamo, 23-25 October 2003, ed. F. LO MONACO, L.C. ROSSI, and N. SCAFFAI (Florence, 2006).
Literary Theory and Biblical Hermeneutics: Proceedings of the International Conference: 'Reading Scripture – Literary Criticism and Biblical Hermeneutics': Pannonhalma, Hungary, 4th-6th July 1991, ed. T. FABINY (Szeged, 1992).
Littérature et histoire, ed. C. JOUHAUD (= *Annales E.S.C.* 49.2 (1994)).
LOBRICHON, G., "Le texte des bibles alcuiniennes", in: *Alcuin, de York à Tours: Écriture, pouvoir et réseaux dans l'Europe du haut Moyen Âge*, ed. P. DEPREUX and B. JUDIC (Rennes, 2004 = *Annales de Bretagne et des Pays de l'Ouest* 111 (2004)) pp. 209-219.
LOHRMANN, D., "Alcuins Korrespondenz mit Karl dem Grossen über Kalender und Astronomie", in: *Science in Western and Eastern Civilization in Carolingian Times*, ed. P.L. BUTZER and D. LOHRMANN (Basel, Boston, MA, and Berlin, 1993), pp. 79-114..
LOTMAN, Y.M., " Una teoria del rapporto reciproco tra le culture (da un punto di vista semiotico)", in: *La semiosfera: Asimmetria e dialogo fra le strutture pensanti* (Venice, 1983), pp. 113-130; English trans. "On the semiosphere", *Sign Systems Studies* 33.1 (2005), pp. 205-226.
LOTMAN, Y.M., *Universe of the Mind: A Semiotic Theory of Culture*, trans. A. SHUKMAN (London and New York, 1990).
LOUVEL, L., *The Poetics of the Iconotext* (Franham and Burlington, Vermont, 2011).
LÖWE, H., "Von Theoderich der Grosse zu Karl der Grosse: Das Werden des Abendlands im Geschichtsbild des frühen Mittelalters", *Deutsches Archiv* 9 (1952), pp. 353-410.
LUHMANN, N., "Das Problem der Epochenbildung und die Evolutionstheorie", in: *Epochenschwellen und Epochenstrukturen im Diskurs der Literatur- und Sprach-*

theorie, ed. H.U. GUMBERT and U. LINK-HEER (Frankfurt am Main, 1985), pp. 11-33.
LUKÁCS, G., *Estetica*, Italian trans. (Turin, 1970).
MAFFEI, S., *Verona illustrata*, 4 vols. (Verona, 1731).
MALSBARY, G., "Epic exegesis and the use of Vergil in the early biblical poets", *Florilegium* 7 (1985), pp. 53-83.
MANITIUS, M., "Das Epos Karolus Magnus et Leo Papa", *Neues Archiv* 8 (1883), pp. 9-45.
MANITIUS, M., *Geschichte der lateinischen literatur des Mittelalters*, 3 vols. (Munich, 1911-1931).
MANITIUS, M., "Zu dem Epos 'Karolus magnus et Leo papa", *Neues Archiv* 9 (1884), pp. 614-619.
MARCHI, G.P., "Ancora sull'arcidiacono Pacifico di Verona", *Studi Medievali e Umanistici* 7 (2009, publ. 2012), pp. 356-380.
MARCHI, G.P., "Per un restauro della biografia di Pacifico, humilis levita Christi", in: *Scripturus vitam: Lateinische Biographie van der Antike bis in die Gegenwart: Festgabe fur Walter Berschin zum 65. Geburtstag,* ed. D. WALZ (Heidelberg, 2002), pp. 379-392.
MARTIN, R., "Au confluent des traditions antique, germanique et chrétienne", *Revue des Études Latines* 72 (1994), pp. 177-191.
MARTINEZ GAZQUEZ, J., "La glosa a los signos del zodíaco en la 'Massa compoti' del ms. 91 del A.C. de Girona", *Annals de l'Institut d'Estudis Gironins* 31 (1990-1991), pp. 31-40.
MARX, J., *La légende arthurienne et le Graal* (Paris, 1952).
MASKARINEC, M., "The Carolingian afterlife of the Damasan inscriptions", *Early Medieval Europe* 23 (2015), pp. 129-160.
MCCARTNEY, E.S., "Vivid ways of indicating uncountable numbers", *Classical Philology* 55 (1960), pp. 79-89.
MCCLUSKEY, S.C., *Astronomies and Cultures in Early Medieval Europe* (Cambridge, 2000).
MCKITTERICK, R., *Charlemagne: The Formation of a European Identity* (Cambridge, 2014).
MCKITTERICK, R., "Text and image in the Carolingian world", in: *The Uses of Literacy in Early Medieval Europe,* ed. R. MCKITTERICK (Cambridge, 1990), pp. 297-318.
MCKITTERICK, R., *The Carolingians and the Written Word* (Cambridge, 1989).
Mediävistische Komparatistik: Festschrift für Franz-Josef Worstbrock zum 60. Geburtstag, ed. W. HARMS and J.-D. MÜLLER (Stuttgart and Leipzig, 1997).
Medieval Memory: Image and Text, ed. F. WILLAERT *et al.* (Turnhout, 2004).
MEERSSEMAN, G.G., E. ADDA, and J. DESHUSSES, *L'Orazionale dell' arcidiacono Pacifico e il carpsum del cantore Stefano: Studi e testi sulla liturgia del Duomo di Verona dal IX all'XI sec.* (Fribourg (Suisse), 1974).

MELLINO, M., *La critica postcoloniale* (Rome, 2005).
MERKLE, S., "Die Ambrosianische Tituli: Eine literarhistorische-archäologische Studie: Mit einer Ausgabe der Tituli als Anhang", *Römische Quartalschrift* 10 (1896), pp. 181-222.
MÉSONIAT, C., *Poetica Theologia: La «Lucula noctis» di Giovanni Dominici e le dispute letterarie tra '300 e '400* (Rome, 1984).
MEYER, W., "Anfang und Ursprung der lateinischen und griechischen rythmischen Dichtung", in: ID., *Gesammelte Abhandlungen zur mittellateinischen Rythmik*, 3 vols. (Berlin, 1905-1936), 2, pp. 1-202.
MICAELLI, C., "'Carmen adversus Marcionitas': Ispirazione biblica e sua ripresa nei centoni 'De lege' e 'De nativitate'", in: *La poesia tardoantica e medievale: Atti del I Convegno internazionale di studi, Macerata, 4-5 maggio 1998*, ed. M. SALVADORE (Alessandria, 2001), pp. 171-198.
Midrash and Literature, ed. G. HARTMAN and S. BUDICK (New Haven, 1986).
MINNIS, A., *Medieval Theory of Authorship: Scholastic Literary Attitudes in the Later Middle Ages* (London, 1984; 1988[2]).
MITCHELL, J., "Literacy displayed: The use of the inscriptions at the monastery of San Vincenzo al Volturno in the early ninth century", in: *The Uses of Literacy in Early Medieval Europe*, ed. R. MCKITTERICK (Cambridge, 1990; reprint 1992), pp. 186-225.
MOMIGLIANO, A., *Alien Wisdom: The Limits of Hellenization* (Cambridge, 1975).
MORIN, G., "Une rédaction inédite de la préface au supplément du Comes d'Alcuin", *Revue bénédictine* 29 (1912), pp. 341-348.
MOSTERT, M., "A bibliography of works on medieval communication", in: *New Approaches to Medieval Communication*, ed. M. MOSTERT (Turnhout, 1999: *Utrecht Studies in Medieval Literacy* 1), pp. 193-318.
MOSTERT, M., *A Bibliography of Works on Medieval Communication* (Turnhout, 2012: *Utrecht Studies in Medieval Literacy* 2).
MÜLLER, S., "Paradigmenwechsel und Epochenwandel: Zur Struktur wissenschaftshistorischer und geschichtlicher Mobilität bei Thomas S. Kuhn, Hans Blumenberg und Hans Freyer", *Saeculum* 32 (1981), pp. 1-30.
MUNZI, L., "Compilazione e riuso in età carolingia: Il prologo poetico di Wigbodo", *RomanoBarbarica* 12 (1992-1993), pp. 189-210.
NELSON, J.L., "Translating images of authority: The Christian Roman emperors in the Carolingian world", in: *Images of Authority: Papers presented to Joyce Reynolds on the Occasion of her 70th Birthday*, ed. M.M. MCKENZIE and C. ROUECHÉ (Cambridge, 1996), pp. 194-205.
NICOLAU, M.G., "Les deux sources de la versification latine accentuelle", *Archivum Latinitatis Medii Aevi* 9 (1934), pp. 55-87.
NOBLE, T., *Images, Iconoclasm, and the Carolingians* (Philadelphia, 2009).

NORBERG, D., *Introduction à la versification latine médiévale* (Stockholm, 1958), trans. G.C. ROTI and J. DE LA CHAPELLE SKUBLY, ed. J.M. ZIOLKOWSKI, *An Introduction to the Study of Medieval Latin Versification* (Washington, DC, 2004).
NORBERG, D., *L'oeuvre poétique de Paulin d'Aquilée* (Stockholm, 1975).
NORBERG, D., "La poésie du roi Chilperic", in: ID., *La Poésie latine rythmique du Haut Moyen Âge* (Stockholm, 1954), pp. 31-54.
NORBERG, D., *La Poésie latine rythmique du Haut Moyen Âge* (Stockholm, 1954).
NORBERG, D., "Mètre et rythme entre le bas-empire et le haut moyen âge", in: *La cultura in Italia fra tardo antico e alto Medioevo: Atti del convegno tenuto a Roma, Consiglio nazionale delle ricerche, dal 12 al 16 novembre 1979*, 2 vols. (Rome, 1981), 1, pp. 357-372.
NORTON, D., *A History of the Bible as Literature*, 2 vols. (Cambridge, 1993).
OBRIST, B., "La représentation carolingienne du zodiaque: A propos du manuscrit de Bâle, Universitätsbibliothek, F III 15", *Cahiers de Civilisation Médiévale* 44 (2001), pp. 3-33.
OESTMANN, G., "On the history of the nocturnal", *Bulletin of the Scientific Instrument Society* 69 (2001), pp. 5-9.
ORCHARD, A., *The Poetic Art of Aldhelm* (Cambridge, 1994).
PAGANI, I., "La critica letteraria", in: *Lo spazio letterario del Medioevo*, 1, *Il medioevo latino*, ed. G. CAVALLO, C. LEONARDI and E. MENESTÒ, 3 vols. (Rome, 1992-1994), 3, *La circolazione del testo*, pp. 113-162.
PAGNINI, M., *Lingua e musica: Proposta per un'indagine strutturalistico-semiotica* (Bologna, 1974).
PARIS, G., "Lettre à Léon Gautier sur la versification latine rythmique", *Bibliothèque de l'École des Chartes* 27 (1866), pp. 578-610.
Parole in musica: Lingua e poesia nella canzone d'autore italiana, ed. L. COVERI (Novara, 1996).
PASCUCCI, G., "Ennio, Ann. 561-562 V. e un tipico procedimento di auxesis nella poesia latina", in: ID., *Scritti scelti* 2 (Florence, 1983), pp. 575-597.
PAVESE, E., "Situare lo stile nel suono di De André", in: *Il suono e l'inchiostro: poesia e canzone nell'Italia contemporanea* (Milan, 2009), pp. 221-249.
PETOLETTI, M., "Poesia epigrafica pavese di età longobarda: Le iscrizioni sui monumenti", *Italia Medioevale e Umanistica* 60 (2019) pp. 1-32.
PETRUCCI, A., "Scrittura e figura nella memoria funeraria", in: *Testo e immagine nell'alto Medioevo*, 2 vols. (Spoleto, 1994: *Settimane di Studio del Centro Italiano di Studi sull'Alto Medioevo* 41), 1, pp. 277-296.
PETTIT, E., "Holiness and masculinity in Aldhelm's opus geminatum De Virginitate", in: *Holiness and Masculinity in the Middle Ages*, ed. P.H. CULLUM and K.J. LEWIS (Cardiff, 2004), pp. 8-23.
PIACENTINI, A., "Riflessioni a partire da un recente libro sulla biblioteca e le Ecloghe di Dante", *Rivista di Studi Danteschi* 15 (2015), pp. 144-165.

PIETRI, L., "Pagina in pariete reserata: Epigraphie et architecture religieuse", in: *La terza età dell'epigrafia, Colloquio AIEGL-Borghesi, Bologna, October 1986*, ed. A. DONATI (Faenza, 1998), pp. 137-157.

PIETRI, L., "Une nouvelle édition de la Sylloge Martinienne de Tours", *Francia* 12 (1985), pp. 621-631.

PLANCHAT, A.E., *Embellishing the Liturgy: Tropes and Polyphony* (London and New York, 2017).

Poesia europea dell'alto medioevo latino: Manoscritti, lingua e musica dei ritmi latini IV-IX secolo:. Atti delle Euroconferenze per il Corpus dei ritmi latini (IV-IX sec.), Arezzo 6-7 novembre 1998 e Ravello 9-12 settembre 1999, ed. F. STELLA (Florence, 2000).

Poesis et pictura: Studien zum Verhältnis von Text und Bild in Handschriften und alten Drucken: Festschrift für Dieter Wüttke zum 60. Geburtstag, ed. S. FUSSEL and J. KNAPE (Baden Baden, 1989).

Poetry of the Early Medieval Europe: Manuscripts, Language and Music of the Rhythmical Latin Texts: III Euroconference for the Digital Edition of the "Corpus of Latin Rhythmical Texts 4th-9th Century", ed. E. D'ANGELO and F. STELLA (Florence, 2003).

PÖGGELER, O., "Dichtungstheorie und Toposforschung", in: *Toposforschung*, ed. M. BÄUMER (Darmstadt, 1973), pp. 22-135.

POLLMANN, K., "Das lateinische Epos in der Spätantike", in: *Von Göttern und Menschen erzählen: Formkonstanzen und Funktionswandeln vormoderner Epik*, ed. J. RÜPKE (Stuttgart, 2001), pp. 93-129.

POLLMANN, K., *Das Carmen adversus Marcionitas* (Göttingen, 1991).

Postcolonial Approaches to the European Middle Ages, ed. A.J. KABIR and D. WILLIAMS (Cambridge, 2005).

POULLE, E., "L'astronomie de Gerbert", in: *Gerberto: Scienza, storia e mito: Atti del Gerberti symposium* (Bobbio, 1985: *Archivum Bobiense: Studia* 2), pp. 597-617.

PRATT, D., "Persuasion and invention at the court of King Alfred the Great", in: *Court Culture in the Early Middle Ages: Proceedings of the First Alcuin Conference*, ed. C. CUBITT (Turnhout, 2003), pp. 189-221.

PRICKETT, S., *Words and 'The Word': Language, Poetics and Biblical Interpretation* (Cambridge, 1986).

PULGRAM, E., "Latin-Romance metrics: A linguistic view", in: *Metrik und Medienwechsel – Metrics and Media*, ed. H.L.C. TRISTRAM (Tübingen, 1991), pp. 53-80.

QUACQUARELLI, A., *Reazione pagana e trasformazione della cultura (fine IV secolo d.C.)* (Bari, 1986).

QUENTIN, H., *Biblia sacra iuxta vulgatam versionem*, 1, *Librum Genesis* (Rome, 1926).

RABY, F.J.E., *A History of Christian Latin Poetry* (Oxford, 1924).

RÄDLE, F., "Eigil", in: *LdM* 3, coll. 1725-1726.

RAHNER, K., "Priest and poet", in: *The Word: Readings in Theology*, ed. R.A.F. MAC-KENZIE (New York, 1964), pp. 3-26.

RAMIREZ-WEAVIER, E.M., *Carolingian Innovation and Observation in the Paintings and Star Catalogs of Madrid, Biblioteca Nacional, Ms. 3307* (PhD New York University, 2008).

RANKIN, S., "Carolingian Music", in: *Carolingian Culture: Emulation and Innovation*, ed. R. MCKITTERICK (Cambridge, 1994), pp. 274-316.

RATKOWITSCH, C., *Karolus Magnus – alter Aeneas, alter Martinus, alter Iustinus: Zur Intention und Datierung des Aachener Karlsepos* (Vienna, 1997).

RATKOWITSCH, Ch., "Die Fresken im Palast Ludwigs des Frommen in Ingelheim (Ermold., Hlud. 4, 181 ff.): Realität oder poetische Fiktion?", *Wiener Studien* 107-108 (1994-1995), pp. 553-581.

Reading the Text: Biblical Criticism and Literary Theory, ed. S. PRICKETT (Oxford and Cambridge, MA, 1991).

Reichenauer Waldmalerei 840-1120: Goldbach – Reichenau-Oberzell St. Georg – Reichenau-Niederzell St. Peter und Paul, ed. W. BERSCHIN and U. KUDER (Heidelberg, 2012).

Rezeption und Identität: die kulturelle Auseinandersetzung Roms mit Griechenland als europäisches Paradigma, ed. G. VOGT-SPIRA and B. ROMMEL (Stuttgart 1999).

RHU, L.F., *The Genesis of Tasso's Narrative Theory: English Translations of the Early Poetics and a Comparative Study of Their Significance* (Detroit, 1993), pp. 99-153.

RICHÉ, P., *Écoles et enseignement dans le Haut Moyen Âge* (Paris, 1979), p. 326; trans. *Le scuole e l'insegnamento nell'Occidente cristiano dalla fine del V secolo alla metà dell'XI secolo* (Rome, 1984).

RICHÉ, P., "La Bible et la vie politique carolingienne", in: *Le Moyen Âge et la Bible*, ed. P. RICHÉ and G. LOBRICHON (Paris, 1984), pp. 388-400.

RICHÉ, P., *La vie quotidienne dans l'empire carolingienne* (Paris, 1973), trans. *La vita quotidiana nell'impero carolingio* (Rome, 1994).

RICHÉ, P., *The Carolingians: A Family Who Forged Europe*, trans. (Philadelphia, 1993).

RICOEUR,P., *Biblical Hermeneutics* (Missoula, 1975).

RIGG, A.G., "Medieval poetic anthologies I", *Medieval Studies* 39 (1977), pp. 281-330; II, *ibid.* 40 (1978), pp. 387-407; III, *ibid.* 41 (1979) pp. 468-505.

ROBERTS, M., *Biblical Epic and Rhetorical Paraphrase in Late Antiquity* (Liverpool, 1985).

ROBERTS, M., *The Jeweled Style: Poetry and Poetics in Late Antiquity* (Ithaca and London, 1989).

RONCONI, G., *Le origini delle dispute umanistiche sulla poesia (Mussato e Petrarca)* (Rome, 1976).

ROSENBERG, D., and A. GRAFTON, *Cartographies of Time: A History of the Timeline* (Princeton, 2010); trans. *Cartografie del tempo: Una storia della linea del tempo* (Turin, 2012).

RUTHERFORD, J., "The third space: Interview with Homi Bhabha", in: *Identity, Community, Culture, Difference*, ed. J. RUTHERFORD (London, 1990), pp. 207-221.

RYKEN, L., "Literature and the Bible", in: *Oxford Companion to the Bible*, ed. B.M. METZGER and M.D. COOGAN (New York and Oxford, 1993), pp. 438-463.

SAGE, W., "Zur archäologischen und baugeschichtlichen Erforschung der Ingelheimer Pfalz in Ingelheim am Rhein", in: *Ingelheim am Rhein: Forschungen und Studien zur Geschichte Ingelheims*, ed. J. AUTENRIETH (Stuttgart, 1964), pp. 65-86.

SANTINI, G., *Inter iura poeta: Ricerche sul lessico giuridico in Draconzio* (Rome, 2006).

SCALIA, G., "Le epigrafi", in: *Lo spazio letterario del Medioevo*, 1, *Il medioevo latino*, ed. G. CAVALLO, C. LEONARDI and E. MENESTÒ, 3 vols. (Rome, 1992-1994), 3, *La circolazione del testo*, pp. 409-441.

SCHALLER, D., "Alkuin", in: *Die deutsche Literatur des Mittelalters: Verfasserlexikon*, 2nd. edn., ed. K. RUH *et al.* (Berlin and New York, 1977-), 1.1, cols. 241-243.

SCHALLER, D., "Das Aachener Epos für Karl den Kaiser", *Frühmittelalterliche Studien* 10 (1976), pp. 134-168.

SCHALLER, D., "De Karolo rege et Leone papa (Aachener Karlsepos)", in: *Die deutsche Literatur des Mittelalters: Verfasserlexikon*, 2nd. edn., ed. K. RUH *et al.* (Berlin and New York, 1977-), 4 (1983), pp. 1041-1045.

SCHALLER, D., "Ein übersehenes karolingisches Gebets-Canticum in einer St. Petersburger Handschrift: '... ne dimittas nos intrare in hanc pestilentiam'", *Filologia Mediolatina* 3 (1996), pp. 160-162.

SCHALLER, D., "Frühkarolingische Corippus-Rezeption", *Wiener Studien* 105 (1992), pp. 173-187.

SCHALLER, D., "Frühmittelalterliche lateinische Dichtung in einer ehemals St. Galler Handschrift", *Zeitschrift für deutsches Altertum und deutsche Literatur* 93 (1964), pp. 272-291, reprinted in: ID., *Studien zur lateinischen Dichtung des Frühmittelalters* (Stuttgart, 1995), pp. 27-46, with additions at pp. 404-406.

SCHALLER, D., "Interpretationsprobleme im Aachener Karlsepos", *Rheinische Vierteljahrsblätter* 41 (1977), pp. 160-179.

SCHALLER, D., *Studien zur lateinischen Dichtung des Frühmittelalters* (Stuttgart, 1995).

SCHALLER, D., "Vergil und die Wiederentdeckung des Epos im frühen Mittelalter", *Medioevo e Rinascimento* 1 (1987), pp. 75-100.

SCHAUWECKER, H., *Otloh von St. Emmeram: Ein Beitrag zur Bildungs- und Frömmigkeitsgeschichte des 11. Jahrhunderts* (Munich, 1964).

SCHECK, H.E., "Nuns on parade: Memorializing women in 'Karolus Magnus et Leo papa'", in: *Reading Memory and Identity in the Texts of Medieval European Holy Women*, ed. M. COTTER-LYNCH and B. HERZOG (New York, 2012), pp. 13-38.

SCHLESINGER, W., "Die Pfalzen im Rhein-Main Gebiet: Percy Ernst Schramm zum siebzigsten Geburststag", *Geschichte in Wissenschaft und Unterricht* 16 (1965), pp. 487-504.

SCHLICHER, J.J., *The Origin of Rhythmical Verse in Late Latin* (PhD diss., University of Chicago, 1900).

SCHMID, W., "Tityrus christianus", *Rheinisches Museum* 96 (1953), pp. 101-165, reprinted in: *Europäische Bukolik und Georgik*, ed. K. GAMBER (Darmstadt, 1976), pp. 44-121.

SCHMITT, J.-C., "Le Temps: Impensé de l'histoire ou double objet de l'historien?", *Cahiers de Civilisation Médiévale* 48 (2005), pp. 31-52.

SCHMITZ, H., *Pfalz und Fiskus Ingelheim*, PhD thesis, Frankfurt, 1967.

SCHOLZ, S., "Karl der Große und das 'Epitaphium Adriani': Ein Beitrag zum Gebetsgedenken der Karolinger", in: *Das Frankfurter Konzil von 749: Kristallisationspunkt karolingischer Kultur: Akten zweier Symposien (vom 23. bis 27. Februar und vom 13. bis zum 15. Oktober 1994) anläßlich der 1200-Jahrfeier der Stadt Frankfurt am Main*, 1, *Politik und Kirche*, ed. R. BERNDT (Mainz, 1997), pp. 373-394.

SCHRAMM, P.E., *Die zeitgenössischen Bildnisse Karls des Grossen: Mit einem Anhang über die Metallbullen der Karolinger* (Leipzig, 1928).

SCHUMANN, O., "Angilbert", in: *Die deutsche Literatur des Mittelalters: Verfasserlexikon*, ed. W. STAMMLER and K. LANGOSCH, 5 vols. (Berlin and Leipzig, 1933-1955), 1, coll. 83-84.

SCHWIND, J., *Arator-Studien* (Göttingen, 1990).

SCHWIND, J., *Sprachliche und Exegetische Beobachtungen zu Arator* (Stuttgart, 1995).

SCIVOLETTO, N., "Angilberto abate di S. Riquier e l'humanitas carolingia", *Giornale Italiano di Filologia* 5 (1952), pp. 298-303.

SEGAL, C., "Classics and comparative culture", *Materiali e discussioni* 19 (1984), pp. 9-21.

SELIGER, H.W., and E. SHOHAMY, *Second Language Research Methods* (Oxford, 1989).

Semicerchio: Rivista di poesia comparata, 1- (1989-).

SIGISMONDI, G., "Gerbert of Aurillac: Astronomy and geometry in tenth century Europe", *International Journal of Modern Physics: Conference Series* 23 (2013), pp. 467-471.

SIGISMONDI, G., "Gerberto e le fistulae: tubi acustici ed astronomici", in: *Atti dell'XI Convegno SIA (Società Italiana di Archeoastronomia) (Bologna and Marzabotto, 2011 published 2012)*, <http:// arxiv.org/ftp/arxiv/papers/1211/1211.0448.pdf>.

SILAGI, G., [review of C. LA ROCCA, *Pacifico di Verona: Il passato carolingio nella costruzione della memoria urbana* (Rome, 1995)], *Deutsches Archiv* 52 (1996), pp. 349-350.

SIMSON, B., "Über das Gedicht von der Zusammenkunft Karls des Großen und Papst Leos III. in Paderborn", *Forschungen zur deutschen Geschichte* 12 (1872), pp. 567-590.

SITI, W., "An American gnosis: Appunti su critica e religione in margine all'opera di Harold Bloom", *Rivista di Letteratura Italiana* 3 (1985), pp. 147-170.

SMOLAK, K., "Die Bibeldichtung als 'verfehlte Gattung'", in: *La Scrittura infinita: Bibbia e poesia in età medievale e umanistica*, ed. F. STELLA (Florence, 2006), pp. 14-29.

SPAGGIARI, B., "Parità sillabica a oltranza nella metrica neolatina delle origini", *Metrica* 3 (1982), pp. 15-105.

SPAGNOLO, A., "L'arcidiacono Pacifico di Verona inventore della bussola", *Nuovo Archivio Veneta,* n.s 8 (1904), pp. 39-62.

SPIEGEL, G., "Épater les médiévistes", *History and Theory* 39 (2000), pp. 243-250.

SPIVAK, G.C., *Decolonizing the Mind: The Politics of Language in African Literature* (London, 1986).

SPIVAK, G.C., *In Other Worlds: Writing, History and the West* (New York and London, 1987).

STELLA, F., "Ad cantandum carmina: Testo e musica nel Corpus di ritmi latini musicati", in: *La poesia tardoantica e medievale, IV Convegno internazionale di studi, Perugia, 15-17 novembre 2007*, ed. C. BURINI DE LORENZI and M. DE GAETANO (Alessandria, 2010), pp. 333-354.

STELLA, F., "Antichità Europee", in: *Letteratura comparata*, ed. A. GNISCI (Milan, 2002), pp. 31-61; a Spanish version in: *Introducción a la literatura comparada* (Barcelona, 2002), pp. 71-127.

STELLA, F., "Autore e attribuzioni del 'Karolus Magnus et Leo papa'", in: *Am Vorabend der Kaiserkrönung: Das Epos 'Karolus Magnus et Leo papa' und der Papstbesuch in Paderborn 799*, ed. P. GODMAN, J. JARNUT, and P. JOHANEK (Berlin, 2002), pp. 19-33; German version: "Autor und Zuschreibungen des sog. Karolus Magnus et Leo papa", in: *Nova de veteribus*: *Festschrift P.G. Schmidt* (Berlin, 2004), pp. 155-175.

STELLA, F., "Chi scrive le mie lettere? La funzione-autore e l'eterografia nei modelli epistolari del XII secolo", in: *Auctor et auctoritas in latinis medii aevi litteris – Author and Authorship in Medieval Latin Literature: Proceedings of the VIth Congress of the International Medieval Latin Committee (Benevento-Naples, November 9-13, 2010)*, ed. E. D'ANGELO and J. ZIOLKOWSKI (Florence, 2014), pp. 1070-1095.

STELLA, F., "Condanna e difesa della poesia: Dalla Scolastica all'Umanesimo", in: *Figure del pensiero medievale*, 6, *La via moderna: XIV e inizi del XV secolo* (Milan, 2010), pp. 251-328, 350-357.

STELLA, F., "Epigrafia letteraria e topografia della vita quotidiana dei monasteri carolingi", in: *Le scritture dei monasteri: Atti del II seminario internazionale di studio 'I monasteri nell'alto medioevo': Roma 9-10 maggio 2002,* ed. F. DE RUBEIS and W. POHL (Rome, 2003), pp. 123-144.

STELLA, F., "Epiteti di Dio in Draconzio fra tradizione classica e cristiana", *Civiltà Classica e Cristiani* 8 (1987), pp. 601-633.

STELLA, F., "Eteroglossia del testo e comparazione interculturale", in *Interculturalità: Antropologia Religioni Letteratura* (= *Testimonianze* 384-385 (1995)) pp. 99-122; reprinted in: *Semicerchio: Rivista di poesia comparata* 14 (1996), pp. 2-14.

STELLA, F., "Fra retorica e innografia: Sul genere letterario delle 'Laudes Dei' di Draconzio," *Philologus* 132 (1988), pp. 213-245.

STELLA, F., "Gotescalco, la 'scuola' di Reims e l'origine della rima mediolatina", in: *Il verso europeo: Atti del seminario di metrica comparata (4 maggio 1994),* ed. F. STELLA (Florence, 1995), pp. 159-165.

STELLA, F., "Innovazioni lessicali delle *Laudes Dei* di Draconzio fra latinità tardoantica e medievale," *Invigilata Lucernis* 21 (1999), pp. 417-444.

STELLA, F., *Il senso dell'immagine: Fonti testuali dell'arte medievale* (Milan, 2020).

STELLA, F., "La comunicazione nella poesia carolingia", in: *Comunicazione e significazione nell'alto medioevo*, 2 vols. (Spoleto, 2005: *Settimane di studio del Centro italiano di studi sull'alto Medioevo* 52), 2, pp. 615-652.

STELLA, F., "La poesia biblica come problema interculturale: Saggi sulle creazioni di Eva", *Semicerchio: Rivista di poesia comparata* 20-21 (1999), pp. 28-32.

STELLA, F., "La poesia di Paolo Diacono: Nuovi manoscritti e attribuzioni incerte", in: *Paolo Diacono: Uno scrittore fra tradizione longobarda e rinnovamento carolingio: Atti del convegno internazionale Cividale del Friuli-Udine 6-9 maggio 1999*, ed. P. CHIESA (Udine, 2000), pp. 551-574.

STELLA, F., "La trasmissione letteraria: la poesia", in: *La Bibbia nel Medioevo*, ed. G. CREMASCOLI and C. LEONARDI (Bologna, 1996), pp. 40-63.

STELLA, F., "Le raccolte di ritmi precarolingi e la tradizione manoscritta di Paolino d'Aquileia: Nuclei testuali e rapport di trasmissione", *Studi medievali*, 3a serie 39 (1998), pp. 809-832.

STELLA, F., "Per una teoria dell'imitazione poetica cristiana: Saggio di analisi sulle *Laudes Dei* di Draconzio," *Invigilata Lucernis* 7-8 (1985-1986), pp. 193-224.

STELLA, F., *Poesia carolingia latina a tema biblico* (Spoleto, 1993).

STELLA, F., "Poesia e teologia: L'età carolingia: Predestinazione, culto delle immagini, poesia della conoscenza e dell'esegesi", in: *Figure del pensiero medievale*, ed. I. BIFFI and C. MARABELLI, 6 vols. (Milan 2008-2010), 3, *Il mondo delle scuole monastiche* (2010), pp. 466-614.

STELLA, F., *Poesia e teologia: L'Occidente latino tra IV e VIII secolo* (Milan, 2001).
STELLA, F., "Poesia e teologia III. Condanna e difesa della poesia dalla Scolastica all'Umanesimo", in: *Figure del pensiero medievale: VI "La via moderna": XIV e inizi del XV secolo* (Milan, 2010), pp. 251-328, 350-357.
STELLA, F., "Poesie computistiche e meraviglie astronomiche: Sull'*horologium nocturnum* di Pacifico", in: *Mirabilia: Gli effetti speciali nelle letterature del Medioevo: Atti delle IV Giornate internazionali interdisciplinari di Studio sul Medioevo (Torino, 10-12 Aprile 2013)*, ed. F. MOSETTI CASARETTO and R. CIOCCA (Alessandria, 2014), pp. 181-206.
STELLA, F., "Ristrutturazione topica ed estensione metaforica nella poesia cristiana: Da spunti draconziani," *Wiener Studien* 102 (1989), pp. 213-245.
STELLA, F., "Tra retorica e innografia", *Philologus* 132 (1989), pp. 258-274.
STELLA, F., "Variazioni stemmatiche e note testuali alle *Laudes Dei* di Draconzio: Con edizione del florilegio Paris, *B.N.*, Lat. 8093, f. 15^v (sec. VIII-IX)," *Filologia Mediolatina* 3 (1996), pp. 1-34.
STELLA and A. ISCARO, F., "Estratti poetici di nuova identificazione nel ms. Zürich, C 58/275: Parte I: *Carmina Rivipullensia*, Alberto Stadense, Abelardo *Carmen in Astralabium*, Enrico di Augsburg e altro", in: *Le rigueur et la passion: Mélanges en l'honneur de Pascale Bourgain*, ed. C. GIRAUD and D. POIREL (Turnhout, 2016), pp. 381-396.
STEVENS, W.M., "Astronomy in Carolingian schools", in: *Karl der Grosse und sein Nachwirken: 1200 Jahre Kultur und Wissenschaft in Europa,* ed. P.L. BUTZER, W. OBERSCHELP, and H. JONGEN, 2 vols. (Turnhout, 1997-1998), 2, pp. 417-487.
STOPPACCI, P., "I manoscritti", in: *Corpus Rhythmorum Musicum saec. IV-IX*, 1, *Songs in Non-Liturgical Sources*, 1, *Lyrics*, ed. F. STELLA, S. BARRETT, *et al.* (Florence, 2007), pp. LIII-CLXXXIV.
STORK, H.W., *Die Sammel-Handschrift Zürich, Zentralbibliothek, C 78, in De Karolo rege et Leone papa*, ed. W. HENTZE, with an introduction by L.E. VON PADBERG and a facsimile of the manuscript (Paderborn, 1999), pp. 105-118.
STOTZ, P., "Beobachtungen zu metrischen Inschriften auf Werken der Schatzkunst: Formen, Gehalte, Traditionen", in: ID., *Alte Sprache – Neues Lied: Kleine Schriftem zur christlichen Dichtung des lateinischen Mittelalters* (Florence, 2012), pp. 279-305.
STOTZ, P., *Sonderformen der sapphischen Dichtung: Ein Beitrag zur Erforschung der sapphischen Dichtung des lateinischen Mittelalters* (Munich, 1982).
STRECKER, K., "Studien zu den Karolingischen Dichtern", *Neues Archiv* 44 (1922), pp. 209-251.
STRECKER, K., "Zu den karolingischen Rhythmen", *Neues Archiv* 34 (1908), pp. 601-561.
TAGG, P., *Popular music, da Kojak al Rave: Analisi e interpretazioni,* ed. R. DE AGOSTINI and L. MARCONI (Bologna, 1994).

Testo e immagine nel medioevo germanico: Atti del 26. Convegno dell'Associazione Italiana di Filologia Germanica [Venice 26-28 May 1999], ed. M.G. SAIBENE and M. BUZZONI (Milan, 2001).
Testo e immagine nell'Alto medioevo, 2 vols. (Spoleto, 1994: *Settimane di Studi* 41).
Text – Bild – Kommunikation / Bild – Text – Kommunikation, ed. E. STRASSNER (Tübingen, 2002).
Text und Bild: Aspekte des Zusammenwirkens zweier Kunste im Mittelalter und früher Neuzeit, ed. C. MEIER-STAUBACH and U. RUBERG (Wiesbaden, 1980).
Text und Bild: Text-Bild-Kommunikationen aus sprachwissenschaftlicer Sicht, ed. M. MUCKENHAUPT (Tübingen, 1986).
THAYER, A.T., "Judith and Mary: Hélinand's sermon for the Assumption", in: *Medieval Sermon and Society: Cloister, City, University: Proceedings of International Symposia at Kalamazoo and New York*, ed. J. HAMESSE et al. (Louvain-la-Neuve, 1998), pp. 63-75.
The Grail, the Quest and the World of Arthur, ed. N.J. LACY (Woodbridge, 2008: *Arthurian Studies* 72).
The Literary Guide to the Bible, ed. R. ALTER and F. KERMODE (Cambridge, MA, 1987).
The Postcolonial Middle Ages, ed. J.J. COHEN (New York, 2001).
Thesaurus Linguae Latinae, 1- (Leipzig, 1900-).
THRAEDE, K., "Epos", in: *Reallexikon für Antike und Christentum: Sachwörterbuch zur Auseinandersetzung des Christentums mit der antiken Welt* 5 (Stuttgart, 1960), pp. 1034-1041.
THRAEDE, K., "Untersuchungen zur Ursprung und zur Geschichte der christlichen Poesie", *Jahrbuch für Antike und Christentum* 4 (1961), pp. 108-127; 5 (1962), pp. 125-157; 6 (1963), pp. 101-111.
TILLIETTE, J.-Y., "Le sens et la composition du florilège de Zürich", in: *Non recedet memoria eius: Beiträge zur lateinischen Philologie des Mittelalters im Gedenken an Jakob Werner (1861-1944): Akten der wissenschaftlichen Tagung vom 9-10 September 1994 am Mittellateinischen Seminar der Universität Zürich*, ed. P. STOTZ and M.C. FERRARI (Bern etc., 1995), pp. 147-167.
TILLIETTE, J.-Y., "Métrique carolingienne et métrique auxerroise: Quelques réflexions sur la Vita sancti Germani d'Heiric d'Auxerre", in: *L'Ecole carolingienne d'Auxerre: De Muretach à Remi, 830-908*, ed. D. IOGNA-PRAT, C. JEUDY, and G. LOBRICHON (Paris, 1991), pp. 313-327.
TRAUBE, L., *Karolingische Dichtungen* (Berlin, 1888).
TREFFORT, C., "La place d'Alcuin dans la rédaction épigraphique carolingienne", in: *Alcuin, de York à Tours: Écriture, pouvoir et réseaux dans l'Europe du haut Moyen Âge*, ed. P. DEPREUX and B. JUDIC (Rennes, 2004 = *Annales de Bretagne et des Pays de l'Ouest* 111 (2004)), pp. 353-360.

TREFFORT, C., *Mémoires carolingiennes: L'épitaphe entre célébration mémorielle, genre littéraire et manifeste politique (milieu VIIIe-début XIe siècle)* (Rennes, 2007).
ULLMAN, B.L., *The Humanism of Coluccio Salutati* (Padua, 1963).
VEIT, W., "Toposforschung: Ein Forschungsbericht", in: *Toposforschung*, ed. M. BÄUMER (Darmstadt, 1973), pp. 136-210.
VERDIER, P., "L'iconographie des arts libéraux dans l'art du Moyen Âge jusqu'à la fin du quinzième siècle", in: *Arts libéraux et philosophie au moyen âge: Actes du quatrième congrès international de philosophie médiévale Université de Montréal, Montréal, Canada, 27 août-2 septembre 1967* (Montréal and Paris, 1969), pp. 305-355.
VERONESI, S., [Preface to] *Versi rock: La lingua della canzone italiana negli anni '80 e '90*, ed. Accademia degli Scrausi (Milan, 1996), p. 7-19.
Versi rock: La lingua della canzone italiana negli anni '80 e '90, ed. Accademia degli Scrausi (Milan, 1996).
VEYRARD-COSME, Ch., "Du *Pius Aeneas* à Louis le Pieux: Ermold le Noir et l'influence virgilienne", in: *Virgiliennes: Hommages à Philippe Heuzé*, ed. J. PIGEAUD (Paris, 2016), pp. 209-226.
VIARRE, S., "Les Carmina d'Alcuin et la réception de la tradition chrétienne dans les formes antiques", in: *Lateinische Kultur im VIII. Jahrhundert*, (St. Ottilien, 1989), pp. 217-241.
VINAY, G., *Alto medioevo: Conversazioni e no* (Naples, 1978).
VIRCILLO FRANKLIN, C., "The epigraphic syllogae of BAV, Palatinus Latinus 833", in: *Roma, magistra mundi: Itineraria culturae medievalis: Mélanges offerts au Père L.E. Boyle à l'occasion de son 75e anniversaire*, ed. J. HAMESSE (Louvain-la-Neuve, 1998), pp. 975-990.
VIRCILLO FRANKLIN, C., "Words as food: Figuring the Bible in the early Middle Ages", in: *Comunicare e significare nell'alto medioevo*, 2 vols. (Spoleto, 2005: *Settimane di studio della Fondazione Centro italiano di Studi sull'alto medioevo* 52), 2, pp. 733-764.
VITI, A., "Macrotesto: Original conceptualization and possible extensions", in: *Cycles, Recueils, Macrotexts: The Short Story Collection in Theory and Practice*, ed. E. D'HOKER and B. VAN DEN BOSSCHE = *Interférences littéraires / Literaire interferenties* 12 (2014), pp. 105-117.
VON BALTHASAR, U., *Gloria: Una estetica teologica* (Milan, 1975).
VON DEN STEINEN, W., *Notker der Dichter und seine geistige Welt* (Berne, 1948).
VON MOOS, P., *Consolatio: Studien zur mittellateinischen Trostliteratur über den Tod und zum Problem der christlichen Trauer*, 4 vols. (Munich, 1971-1972).
VON MOOS, P., "La retorica del Medioevo", in: *Lo spazio letterario del Medioevo*, 1, *Il medioevo latino*, ed. G. CAVALLO, C. LEONARDI and E. MENESTÒ, 3 vols. (Rome, 1992-1994), 2, *La circolazione del testo*, pp. 231-272.

VON PETRIKOVITS, H., *Der diachorische Aspekt der Kontinuität von der Spätantike zum frühen Mittelalter* (Göttingen, 1982: Nachrichten der Akademie der Wissenschaften in Göttingen, Philologisch-Historische Klasse).
VON WINTERFELD, P., "Zur Geschichte der rhythmischen Dichtung", *Neues Archiv* 30 (1900), pp. 379-408.
VROOM, H.B., *Le Psaume abécédaire de saint Augustin et la poésie latine rythmique* (Nijmegen, 1933).
WALLACE, D., *Premodern Places: Calais to Surinam, Chaucer to Aphra Behn* (Chichester and Malden, MA, 2004).
WALLACH, L., *Alcuin and Charlemagne: Studies in Carolingian History and Literature* (Ithaca, NY, 1959).
WALLACH, L., "Libri Carolini sive Opus Caroli Magni Contra Synodum auctore Alcuino", *Illinois Classical Studies* 42.2 (2017), pp. 319-468.
WATTENBACH, W., *Das Schriftwesen im Mittelalter* (Leipzig, 1896; reprint Graz, 1958).
WATTENBACH, W., *Deutschlands Geschichtsquellen im Mittelalter: Vorzeit und Karolinger*, ed. W. LEVISON and H. LÖWE, 2 (Weimar, 1953).
WEHRLI, M., "Sacra Poesis: Bibelepik als europäische Tradition", in: ID., *Formen mittelalterlicher Erzählung* (Zurich and Freiburg im Breisgau, 1969), pp. 51-71.
WENDOR, R., *Zeit und Kultur: Geschichte des Zeitbewusstseins in Europa* (Opladen, 1980^2).
WEST, M., *The East Face of Helicon: West Asiatic Elements in Greek Poetry and Myth* (Oxford, 1997).
WICKHAM, Ch., *The Inheritance of Rome: A History of Europe from 400 to 1000* (London, 2009); trans. *L'eredità di Roma: Storia d'Europa dal 400 al 1000* (Rome and Bari, 2014).
WIECZOREK, A., and H.-M. HINZ, *Europe's Centre Around A.D. 1000*, 3 vols. (Stuttgart, 2000).
WIESENBACH, J., "Der Mönch mit dem Sehrohr: Die Bedeutung der Miniatur Codex Sangallensis 18", *Schweizerische Zeitschrift für Geschichte – Revue suisse d'histoire – Rivista storica svizzera* 44 (1994), pp. 367-388.
WIESENBACH, J., "Pacificus von Verona als Erfinder einer Sternenuhr", in: *Science in Western and Eastern Civilization in Carolingian Times*, ed. P.L. BUTZER and D. LOHRMANN (Basel, Boston, MA, and Berlin, 1993), pp. 229-250.
WOODWARD, D., *The History of Cartography*, 3.1, *Cartography in the European Renaissance* (Chicago, 2007).
Wort – Bild – Text: Studien zur Medialität des Literarischen im Hochmittelalter und früher Neuzeit (Baden Baden, 2007).
ZELLER, A., *Die Auswertung des Befundes früherer Bauanlagen im Saale in Ingelheim: Reichssaal und Kaiserwohnung* (Berlin, 1935).
ZUMTHOR, P., *Charles le Chauve* (Paris, 1957).

ZUMTHOR, P., *La Lettre et la voix: De la "littérature" médiévale* (Paris, 1987).
Zur Frage der Periodengrenze zwischen Altertum und Mittelalter, ed. P.E. HUBINGER (Darmstadt, 1969).
ZURLI, L., *The Manuscript Transmission of the 'Anthologia Latina'* (Hildesheim, 2017).
ZWIERLEIN, O., "Karolus Magnus – alter Aeneas", in: *Literatur und Sprache im europäischen Mittelalter: Festschrift für K. Langosch*, ed. A. ÖNNERFORS, J. RATHOFER, and F. WAGNER (Darmstadt, 1973), pp. 44-52.

Indices[*]

Manuscripts

Alençon, Bibliothèque Municipale
   14: 135
Avranches, Bibliothèque Municipale
   235: 239, 241
Bamberg, Staatsbibliothek
   Hist. 161 (E.III.1): 188
Berlin, Staatsbibliothek zu Berlin – Preussischer Kulturbesitz
   lat. 4° 676 (*olim* Cheltenham 18908): 301
   Theol. Lat. Fol. 192: 199
Bern, Burgerbibliothek
   455: 163, 301
   B 455: 293
Brussels, Bibliothèque Royale
   8860-67: 45, 168, 172, 293
   10470-73: 266, 290
   10859: 266, 291
Cambridge, Trinity College
   O.2.26: 130
Cambridge, University Library
   G.g.5: 297
Cava dei Terreni, Archivio e Biblioteca della Badia
   3: 240, 245
Chartres, Bibliothèque Municipale
   214: 242, 243

Cologne, Erzbischöfliche Diözesan- und Dombibliothek
   212: 170
Cordoba
   Archicanon: 111
Darmstadt, Hessische Landes- und Hochschulbibliothek
   3303: 115
Douai, Bibliothèque Municipale
   302: 127
   753: 137, 276
Düsseldorf, Universitätsbibliothek
   D 2: 199
Einsiedeln, Stiftsbibliothek
   121: 289
   266: 288
Fulda, Hessische Landesbibliothek
   Aa 62: 164, 165
Ghent, Centrale Bibliotheek der Rijksuniversiteit
   169: 118
Gotha, Forschungs- und Landesbibliothek
   Chart A. 117: 151
Göttweig, Stiftsbibliothek
   429: 127
   430: 127
Kremsmünster, Stiftsbibliothek

---

[*] Prepared by Ophelia Norris.

14614: 127
Laon, Bibliothèque Municipale
   273: 291
   279: 291
Leiden, Universiteitsbibliotheek
   Voss. Lat. Qu. 69: 172, 293, 301
Leipzig, Universitätsbibliothek
   Rep. I 74: 287
London, British Library
   Add. 10546: 191, 192
   Add. 19768: 164, 165
   Cotton Vitellius A. XV: 47
   Harley 3091: 106
   Harley 3685: 133
   Old Royal 15.B.IX: 242
Lyon, Bibliothèque Municipale
   425: 170
Madrid, Biblioteca Nacional
   3307: 256
Milan, L.P. Daverio
   s.n.: 240
Modena, Archivio storico diocesano
   O.1.4: 163
Munich, Bayerische Staatsbibliothek
   Clm. 14478: 127
   Clm. 14614: 127
   Clm. 19140: 275
Naples, Biblioteca Nazionale
   IV. G. 68: 161
New York, Pierpont Morgan Library
   M. 925: 256
Padua, Biblioteca Antoniana
   27: 240
Paris, Bibliothèque nationale de France
   latin 1: 185, 187, 193, 196, 198, 200, 203, 204
   latin 266: 204
   latin 528: 287
   latin 1121: 168
   latin 1154: 45, 172, 293, 294, 301
   latin 2772: 292
   latin 2846: 106
   latin 7412: 242
   latin 7559: 151
   latin 8071: 275
   latin 10318: 286
   latin 12117: 239, 240, 246, 247
   latin 12161: 297
   latin 13027: 298
   latin 14758: 292
   latin 17655: 298
   n.a.l. 1203: 105
Paris, Bibliothèque Sainte-Geneviève
   80: 127
Rome, Biblioteca Angelica
   123: 161, 162, 163, 254
Saint Gall, Stiftsbibliothek
   18: 246
   147: 308
   393: 175
   397: 308
   565: 135
   869: 288
   1395: 299
Saint-Omer, Bibliothèque Municipale
   351: 253
Stuttgart, Württembergische Landesbibliothek
   G 38: 135
Trier, Stadtbibliothek
   23: 188
   1285: 128
Valenciennes, Bibliothèque Municipale
   149: 127
Vatican, Bibliotheca Apostolica Vaticana
   Pal. Lat. 833: 275
   Pal. Lat. 1753: 100
   Reg. lat. 192: 106
   Reg. lat. 309: 240
   Reg. lat. 421: 309
   Reg. lat. 469: 288
   Reg. lat. 582: 291-292
   Reg. lat. 1587: 289
   Reg. lat. 1709: 289
   Vat. lat. 644: 240
Venice, Biblioteca Nazionale Marciana

Indices

lat. VII. 22 (= 2760): 234, 240
Verona, Biblioteca Capitolare
  88 (83): 45-46, 293, 301
  XC (85): 45, 46, 172, 293, 301
Vienna, Österreichische Nationalbibliothek
  743: 98

lat. 808: 135
lat. 1888: 165
Wolfenbüttel, Herzog Augustbibliothek
  Weiss. 26: 188
Zurich, Zentralbibliothek
  C. 78: 98, 308, 311, 329

Websites

<academia.edu>: 133
<http://apps.brepolis.net/BrepolisPortal/default.aspx>: 126
<http://arxiv.org/ftp/arxiv/papers/1211/1211.0448.pdf>: 249
<http://brunelleschi.imss.fi.it/museum/esim.asp?c=500044>: 248
<http://digital.library.mcgill.ca/ms-17/apparatus.php?>: 250
<http://e-codices.ch/de/searchresult/list/one/zbz/C0078>: 329
<http://gerlos.altervista.org/notturnale>: 236
<http://sip.mirabileweb.it/manuscript/sankt-gallen-stiftsbibliothek-869-manuscript/ 3511>: 288
<http://sip.mirabileweb.it/manuscript/sankt-gallen-stiftsbibliothek-899-manuscript/99>: 288
<http://treccani.it/enciclopedia/la-scienza-bizantina-e-latina-prima-dell-influsso-della-scienza-araba-astronomia-computo-e-astrologia_%28Storia-della-Scienza%29>: 236
<http://woerterbuchnetz.de/cgi-bin/WBNetz/wbgui_py?sigle=MLW&lemid=NA00001&mode=Vernetzung&hitlist=&patternlist=&mainmode=Quellenverzeichnis>: 6
<https://www.argonline.it/argo/argo-n-1/argo-n-1_alberto-bertoni-musicalita-poesia/>: 160
<http://www.bibliotecaitaliana.it/xtf/view?docId=bibit000478/bibit000478.xml>: 76
<http://www.iisgalileiartiglio.gov.it/artiglio-almanacco/quaderni/www/notturlabio/WITN_notturlb.htm>: 242
<http://www.kaiserpfalz-ingelheim.de>: 220, 221
<http://www.kaiserpfalz-ingelheim.de/archaeologie_pfalz_der_ottonen_02.php>: 223
<http://www.uni-mannheim.de/mateo/itali/scaliger2/jpg/s409.html>: 76
<https://archive.org/stream/summatheologicao011thom/summatheologicao011thom_djvu.txt>:66
<https://archive.org/stream/summatheologicao011thom/summatheologicao011 thom_djvu.txt>: 80

<https://clavis.brepols.net/clacla/Default.aspx>: 6
<https://en.wikipedia.org/wiki/Nocturnal_(instrument)>: 235
<https://scholarworks.iu.edu/journals/index.php/tmr/article/view/17162>: 349
<https://www.ourladyswarriors.org/saints/augcon12.htm>: 60
<mirabileweb.it>: 288
<www.corimu.unisi.it>: 114, 149, 156, 239, 293

General Index

50 Cent, rapper 169
A solis ortu 157, 167, 173
Aachen 31, 139, 213, 222, 288, 307, 308, 311, 321, 323; chapel of 213
Aachener Epos 312
Abelard, Peter, 52, 56, 61, 63, 66, 78, 79 n. 19, 319; *Commentary on the Letter to the Romans* 56; *Sic et non* 61
Abraham 21, 36, 223, 224, 245; and Isaac 36
Absalom 215; rebellion 215
Abyssus 110
accubitor 84-85
Achilles, shield 176
Achitophel 215
Adalelm 268
Adam and Eve 15, 16, 85, 87 n. 42, 158, 192, 194; *rhythmus* 158
Adam of Bremen 210; *Gesta episcoporum Hammaburgensium* 345-346
Admonitio generalis, see: Charlemagne
Adorno, Theodor 3, 236
Aelbert of York 130, 131, 199
Aenigmata 3, 270
Aesop 93
Æthelthryth (Adaltrude) Queen 132
Agano 219
Agathias 137, 280
Agius of Corvey 30-31, 113, 252; *planctus* for Hatumoda, abbess of Gandersheim 113
Agnes, abbess of the convent of the Holy Cross 30
Agobard of Lyon 215
Ahab 211
Aileran 188
Aiminus of Saint-Amand 118-120
Alain de Lille 25, 79, 83; *Regulae Theologicae* 64-65
Albertino Mussato 55, 65, 75, 94
Albertus Magnus 75
Alcimus Avitus, see: Avitus
Alcmena with Hercules 182
Alcuin of York 1, 10, 101, 108, 118, 121-146, 183, 186, 189-190, 195, 199, 202, 211, 224, 237, 263-264, 287-288, 291, 316, 318, 319, 321, 322, 326, 343; abbacy 186; *carmina* 119; *carmen* to Paulinus of Aquileia 119; *Conflictus veris et hiemis* 344; *De orthographia* 2; *De sanctis Euboricensis ecclesiae* 3, 328; *De scribis* 100; 'Flaccus' 121-146; Forster and Migne collection of Alcuin's *testimonia* 122; *In ecclesia sancti Vedasti in pariete scribendum* 276; *In Latrino* 137; inscription 118; letter to Dado 138; letter to Dafni 309; muse Thalia 131; *Opus Caroli* 3; *tituli* 184; *Vita Willibrordi* 322 *De virtutibus et vitiis* 309; pseudo-Alcuin, *carmina* 188, 224
Aldhelm of Malmesbury 40, 41, 48; *Riddles* 345
Alcestis 33

Indices

Alexander of Ashby 292
Alexander of Hales 77
Alexander of Villadei 255
Alexander the Great 226
Alter, Robert 82
Amalarius of Metz 123, 215
Ambrose 30, 44, 52, 159, 176, 201, 262, 300, 305; *De Helia et ieiunia* 44
Ambrosian hymns 300
Ament, Hermann 222
Amiatine Bible of the Biblioteca Laurenziana, Florence 186
Amiens 294
anagraphus 306
Andreas Sunesen 55
Andrew, Saint 216, 217
Andromache with Astyanax 182
Agnellus, *Liber pontificalis ecclesiae Ravennatis* 176
Angelomus of Luxeuil 3
Angers 32
Angilbert 142, 144, 266, 267, 315-317, 319, 323; *Carmina dubia* 310; *De ecclesia Centulensi* 266, 271
Angoulême, sacramentary of 212-213
Anna, prophetess, mother of Samuel 30, 32, 51
Annales Altahenses 218-219
Annales Fuldenses 218
Annales Mettenses 229
Annales Mettenses priores 231
Annales Regni Francorum 218
Anni Domini notantur 252, 255
anonymus 305
Anselm of Laon 78
Ante saecula 162, 163
Anthologia Latina 85, 252, 253, 256, 267, 280, 286, 290
Anton, Hans Hubert 213, 312
Appius Claudius 36
Apthonius 153
Apuleius 1
Arator, subdeacon, 11, 12, 25 n. 49, 52, 81, 82, 87, 88, 94 n. 58, 95, 291; *De actibus apostolorum* 87
Aratus 252
Aregarius, priest 202
Arevalo, Faustino 22
Aribo, bishop 175
Arno, bishop of Salzburg 142, 283, 287
Arnold of Bonneval, abbot 65
Arnulf of Carinthia 188, 194, 202, 216
Arnulf, Arwed 177, 178, 183, 188, 224
Arras 294
Ars Palaemonis 150, 152
Arthurian romance 132
Arweiler, Alexander 86
Athaliah 215
Atkinson, Charles 5
Auerbach, Erich 11, 25, 67, 69, 82, 116, 346
Auden, Wynstan Hugh 53
Audradus Modicus of Sens 129, 201, 204, 289, 301, 344, 350; *Fons vitae* 68; *Revelationes* 204
Augustine, 2, 3, 11, 12, 17, 29, 30 n. 2, 33, 60, 61, 152, 159, 205, 226, 262, 295, 300; *Confessions* 59; *Contra Faustum* 62; *De civitate Dei* 36, 39, 309; *De doctrina christiana* 59; *De natura et gratia* 29; *Enarrationes in Psalmos* 63; *oculi* in *rhythmus* 167; Platonism 64; *Psalmus* 173; *Psalmus contra Donatistas* 147, 150, 156; *Retractiones* 150
Ausfeld, Eduard 311
Ausonius 14, 252, 256
Auxerre 316
Avalle, A. D'Arco Silvio 148
Averroes 80
Avianus 93
Avitus, Alcimus, archbishop of Vienne 11, 12, 30, 33, 34, 35, 39, 40, 42, 81, 86, 87, 88, 92, 291; *De spiritalis historiae gestis* 86; *De virginitate* 33; sister 35

Avold, St. 276
Babylon 228; Babylonians 214
Baglioni, Claudio 166
Baker, Anita 169
Baker, Deirdre F. 55
Bakhtin, Mikhail 12, 15; Bachtinian 10
Baldric of Bourgueil 176, 205
Bale, John, *Scriptores Britannici* 124
Barcelona 218, 229
Barcelona Papyrus, *Psalmus responsorius* 147, 156
Barchiesi, Alessandro 19
Barking, monastic community 40
Barrett, Sam 156, 161, 164, 285, 294
Barthes, Roland 54, 306
Battiato, Franco 170
Battisti, Lucio 166, 167 n. 69
Baudelaire, Charles 25
Beatus of Liébana 202
Bede 78, 127 n. 15, 131-135, 158, 192, 202, 211, 255, 309; *Apparebit repentina* 166; *carmen* 195; *De arte metrica* 152; *De computo* 252; *De temporum ratione* 249, 252; *docta* 158; *Liber hymnorum* 286; *Liber epigrammaton* 286; martyrology 295; *Historia ecclesiastica* 132-133, circulation at Charlemagne's court 133; *Hymni* 195, 199,
Benedictine *Rule* 267
Beornrad, archbishop of Sens and abbot of Echternach 134
Beowulf 47, 218
Bernard, Honoré 271
Bernard of Morlaix 50
Bernold, archbishop of Strasbourg 328
Bernowin of Clermont 184, 197, 224
Bernt, Günter 118, 136, 177, 265, 269, 270, 274
Bertold of Saint Maximin of Trier 199
Bethleem 162
Beumann, Helmet 311, 326
Bhabha, Homi 342, 349

Bibliae pauperum 177
Bidault, G. 215
Bischoff, Bernhard 216, 253, 275, 293, 294, 308
Blake, William 53, 66, 76, 81
Bloom, Harold 57
Blumenberg, Hans 9
Blum-Kulka, Shoshana 346
Bobbio Missal 212
Boccaccio 55, 76
Boethius 192, 240, 295, 297; *Consolatio Philosophiae* 89
Boitani, Piero 82
Bonaventure of Bagnoregio 306
Boniface, Saint 281, riddles 309
Borges, Jorge Luis 171
Borst, Arno 256; *Karolingische Enzyklopädie* 3
Bouquet 310
Bourgain, Pascale 148, 285, 293, 295
Brague, Remi 10
Brassens, Georges 154
Bretons 199, 217, 229
Brinkmann, Hennig 68, 82
Brockmann, Joseph 310
Brower, Christopher 288
Brown, Raymond 62
Bruegel, Pieter 139, 283
Brunhölzl, Franz 139, 309, 310, 314
Bullough, Donald A. 128
Burghardt, Jacob 122, 126
Caesar, Julius 216
Caillet, Jean-Pierre 219, 227
Cain and Abel 223, 224
Camillus, Marcus Furius 216
Campanale, Maria I. 30
Candidus of Fulda 192
Canisius, Peter 310, 318
Canticle of Canticles 170
Capella, Martianus 192, 297
Carmen de Conversione Saxonum 319
Carmina Burana 172
Carmina Cantabrigensia 172, 291, 297,

Indices 401

301
Carmina Cenomanensia 172
Carmina Centulensia 3, 118, 224, 266, 283, 290, 291
Carmina computistica 250
Carmina Sangallensia 205, 224
Caroline minuscule 2, 4
Carthage 228
Carus, *Vita Clementis* 195
Cassianus, *De institutis coenobiorum* 249
Cassiodorus 66 n. 51, 110 n. 36, 186, 240, 249, 305, ideology 100
Cato 93, 216
Catullus 21
Cena Cypriani 153
Ceolfrith, king 186
Ceserani, Remo 82
Chailley, Jacques 294-295
Charlemagne 2, 98, 100, 122, 133, 141, 157, 167, 173, 183, 197, 211, 212, 215, 216, 218, 227, 228-229, 230, 231, 240, 268, 287, 293, 296, 307, 308, 312-315, 320-321, 325-326, 327; *Admonitio generalis* 2, 116, 212, 251; *planctus* 295
Charles Martel 211, 227
Charles the Bald 3, 31, 45, 106, 109, 133, 183, 185, 186, 189, 204, 205, 212, 224, 288; visit to Rome 45
Chartres, school of 64, 75, 79
Chaucer 341
Chilperic, King, hymn to St. Medard 152
Chrétien de Troyes 345
Cimitile 262
Classen, Peter 219
Claudian (Pseudo-), *Miracula Christi* 176
Clavis clavium 6
clementia 221
Clermont, church of Saint Alyre 184
Clermont 300
clocca cocorum 138
clocula 281
Cluny, abbots of 210
Codex Aureus of Sankt Emmeram 189

Codex Bertinianus 176
Codex Salmasianus 286
Codrus 36
Cohen, Jeffrey Jerome 341, 342
Cohen, Leonard 154
Colbert, Jean-Baptiste 189
Camus, Colette 17
Cologne 137, 276
Colombanus, *De mundi transitu* 309; *In mulieres* 209; *Mundus iste* 209
Coluccio Salutati 55, 76
Commodianus 52, *Apologeticum* 17, *Carmen de duobus populis* 17
Compiègne 282
computatrix 233, 239, 241
computus 251-252, 255 ; Easter computus 345
conflictus 3
Conques 218
Conrad of Mure 227
Conrad of Hirsau, *Dialogus super auctores* 306, 93-94
Consolino, Franca Ela 5
Constantine 81, 216-217, 227, 229, 231
Constantinople 227, 309
Conte, Gian Biagio 18
Contreni, John 118
Cook, Vivian 346
Corbie 115, 171, 233, 255, 294, 298-300
Cordoliani, Alfred 252
Corippus 322, 324
Corméry 137, 139, 276, 282
Corpus Rhythmorum Musicum 5, 114, 148, 156-158, 160, 161, 162, 252, 255, 293
Corti, Maria 285
Corvey 216
Courcelle, Pierre 18, 19
Coussy, Cécile 47
Curtius, Ernst Robert 11, 19, 53, 54, 67, 70, 76, 77, 82, 104, 306, 346
Cuthbert, saint 132
Cynic-Stoic reasoning 280

Cyprianus "Gallus" the poet 12, 14, 51, 52; *Exodus* 15; *Genesis* 18, 52; *Heptateuchos* 15
Cypselus, tyrant of Corinth 175
Cyrus, Persian king 225, 226
Cyzicus, temple of Apollo 176
Dadon 280
Damasus, pope 136, 275, 291
Daniel 34
Daniele, Pino 171
Daniélou, Jean 210
Dante 55, 89; *Commedia* 341; *Inferno* 280
Daub, Susanne 56
David 170, 189, 195, 197, 211, 212, 213, 214, 215, 216, 223, 307
Davis-Weyer, Cecilia 202
De André, Fabrizio, *Canzone di Marinella* 161
De astronomia more christiano 255-256
Deborah 31, 33, 52
De Bruyne, Edgar 82, 89, 186
De Carlos Villamarin, Helena 313-314, 328
Decii 216
De creatione mundi 55
Delilah 215
De Lubac, Henri-Marie 25
De Man, Paul 57, 64, 76
Denmark 229
Denys the Areopagite 77, *Celestial Hierarchy* 77-78
De Rossi, Giovanni Battista 264, 291
Derrida, Jacques 53, 58, 60, 62, 64, 349
Dido 38, in Carthage 307
Dinkova-Bruun, Greti 292
Dionysius Exiguus 255
Disticha Catonis 309
Domenicus Gundisalvo (Gundissalinus) 80
Dominici, Giovanni 67, 94, 95
domus regia 225
Donadeus 267
Donatism 150

Donatus 106
Donizo of Canossa, *Vita Mathildis* 50
Donnini, Mauro 210
Dracontius of Carthage 12, 16, 17, 18, 19, 21-23, 41, 43, 66, 81, 291; *De laudibus Dei* 15, 16, 17, 19-20, 35, 37-39; Lazarus 35; *Medea* 37; *Orestis Tragoedia* 37; *Satisfactio* to Vandal King 35
Dronke, Peter 285, 319, 325, 326
Dryhthelm 132
Du Chesne (Duchesne), André [Andreas Quercetanus] 126, 127, 136, 176, 287, 310
dulcis amor 143
Dümmler, Ernst 47, 126, 127, 128, 136, 188, 223, 274, 309, 310
Dutton, Paul, 185, 197, 201, 204
D'Angelo, Edoardo 162, 164, 322
Eagles, The, *Hotel California* 167
Ebbesen, Sten 55
Ebenbauer, Alfred 312
Eberhard the German 306
Ecgfrith, king 131n24, 132
Eco, Umberto 82, 90, 154, 155 n. 36
Edward the Confessor 50; his queen Edith 50
Egbert, archbishop of York 131
Egli, Johannes 175
Einhard 58, 316, 319, 321, 322, 326, *Vita Karoli* 3, 210, 218, 321-322
Einhardi Annales 216
Ekkehard IV of Saint Gall, 175, 176, *Chronicon* 227, *tituli* for life of Saint Gall 175
Elio e le Storie Tese, *Cateto* 167
Eliot, Thomas Stearns 11
Elsner, Jas 24
Eminem 169
England, mission of 132
Epistola de litteris colendis 2
Epithalamium 30, 51
Erdmann, Carl 311
Erhardt-Siebold, Erika von 281

Indices

Eridadus 268
Eriugena, John Scotus 3, 25, 64, 66, 75, 78, 83, 195, 204, 289; *De praedestinatione* 77; Paschal hymns 268; symbolism of 77
Ermenrich 267
Ermengarde, wife of Lothair I and empress 47, 48, 49, 184, 224
Ermold the Black (Nigellus), 215, 217-231, 313, 327, 328; exile to Strasbourg 218; *In honorem Hludowici* 217
Ernst, Ulrich 185
Esther 30, 32, 34, 44, 45, 49, 51, 52
Eugenia of Rome 34
Eugenius of Toledo 42, 186, 199, 201, 286, 294
Eugenius Vulgarius 184
Eulalia, Saint 170
Eurasian Latin Archive 6
Eusebius 345
Eustachius, Life of St. 296
Evadne 38
Evangeliary of London 68
Evans, Gillian 65
Eve 16, 24, 225
Ewig, Eugen 212
Exeter Riddles 345
extimité 342
Exodus 192, 202
Ezekiel 89
Ezra 215
Fabiny, Tibor 58, 62
Fabricius, Georg 176
Faral, Edmond 218, 223, 224, 226,
Fardulf of Saint-Denis 327
Favreau, Robert 263
Felix, saint in Nola 176
Ferradini, Marco, *Lupo solitario* 163
Ferrari, Michele Camillo 124, 185, 285, 288, 290, 294
Fichtenau, Heinrich 210, 318
Fichtner, Rudolf 54
Finland 262

Fleury, 276, 281; abbey church 177; inscription on bell 138
Flieger, Manfred 54
Flodegerus 271
Flodoard of Reims 204, 264; *De triumphis Christi* 88
Florence 4, 81
Florus of Lyon 68, 84, 117, 129, 195, 215, 315, 328
Fontenoy, battle 295
Formgeschichtliche readings 14
Forster, Frobenius 122, 126, 127, 287, 310, 318
Fossati, Ivano 167
Foucault, Michel 305
Frankfurt, Council of 211
Frappier, Jean 346
Freculf of Lisieux 210, 228
Fredegard 267, 271, 280
Fredegarius (pseudo-) 227
Freeman, Ann 178, 179
Fridugisus of Tours 189
Friesland, mission of 132
Frye, Northrop 57, 62, 63, 82
Fulda, abbey 47, 61, 265, 274, 288; sacramentary 199; scriptorium 100
Fulgentius 300; *Psalmus* 148
Fulrad of Saint-Denis 199
Fuscina (sister of Avitus) 33
Gabriel, angel 271
Gaehde, Joachim E. 185
Gall, St., see: Saint Gall
Gandino, Gemma 313
Ganshof, François Louis 210
Ganz, David 255
Gasparov, Michail 148
Gembloux 290
Genette, Gérard 99, 144
Genot, Gérard 285
Gentile, Giovanni 1
Gentile da Cingoli 77
Geoffrey of Monmouth, *Historia Regum Britanniae* 345; *Vita Merlini* 345

Gerald of Wales 341
Gerbert of Aurillac 235, 239
Germanicus 252
Germanus, Saint patriarch 309
Germar 308
Gershwin, Ira, and George Gershwin, *The Man I Love* 173
Gervais of Tilbury, *Otia imperialia* 345
Gervide 267
Geuenich, Dieter 218
Gideon 213
Gisla, Psalter for 117
giullaresco poetry 160
Givone, Sergio 57
Glorieux, Palémon 65
Glunz, Hans Hermann 82
Godelenda 267
Godfrey of Reims 328
Godman, Peter 117, 124, 132, 307, 313, 316
Goldast, Melchior 310
Goliath 33
Gorze 137, 224, 276
Gottschalk, gospel of 105
Gottschalk the Saxon 119-120, 154, 157, 158, 295
Grafton, Anthony 250
Grail, legend of 89
Grammarians 149
Gratianus, *Decretum* 75
Green, Roger P.H 320
Gregory I, pope 89, 179, 216; Anglo-Saxon mission 131 n. 24
Gregory of Tours 211, 262; *De cursu stellarum* 249, 255; *Libri Historiarum* 210
Gregory the Great, see: Gregory I
Grewe, Holger 219, 222
Grimald of Weissenburg 327
Gundrada, Charlemagne's cousin 319
Gurevich, Aaron 251
Hadrian I, pope 129, 136, 183, 229, 264-265

Haimo of Auxerre 202
Haman 44
Hamann, Georg 57
Hanauer, David Ian 347
Hannibal 226, 227, 229
Harald, king of Denmark 218
Hariulf of Saint Riquier 123; *Chronica* 266
Harthgrepa 107
Hartman, Florian 263
Hartman, Geoffrey 57, 119
Harun al Rashid, Caliph 240
Hatumoda, abbess of Gandersheim 30, 113
Hauck, Karl 312
Heimpel, Hermann 219
Helinand of Froidmont 50
Helisachar, abbot 228
Heloise 318
Helperic (of Auxerre) 310, 316, 327
Heng, Geraldine 340
Henry II 313
Hentze, Wilhelm 309, 310
Herdina, Philip 347
Heric, duke 295
Hermannus the Cripple, *De utilitate astrolabii* 247
Herod 224
Herrad of Landsberg, *Hortus Deliciarum* 73-75
Herren, Michael 289
Herrin, Judith 5
Herzog, Reinhart 13-15, 54, 67, 68, 81, 292
Hibernicus Exul 113, 130, 199, 315, 318, 321, 323, 327
Higbald, abbot 133
Hilarius of Poitiers 52
Hildebert of Cologne 264
Hildebert of Lavardin, 50, 84, 134, 176-177; *Carmina minora* 55; *De ordine mundi* 50; *In libros Regum* 51
Hilduin, abbot of Saint-Denis 77

Indices 405

Hincmar, archbishop of Reims 214, 215, 264, 289, 345; *De regis persona* 213
Hinds, Stephen E. 19
Holiday, Billie 173
Holofernes 43, 45
Homer 22, 67, 223, 316; narrative strategies 11, 12
Homo quidam 164, 173
Honorius of Autun 153
Horace, *Epodes* 194; Horatian poets 70
Hrabanus Maurus abbot of Fulda and archbishop of Mainz 3, 46, 47, 49, 60-61, 68, 70, 85, 180-181, 185, 192, 209, 225, 274, 277, 288, 291, 294, 299, 344; *carmina* 129; *Collatio* 111; *De clericorum institutione* 60; *De imagine Caesaris* 197; *De laudibus sanctae crucis* 48, 185, 205; *De natura rerum* 51; *In Iudices* 44; to Atto 102, 180; to Eigil 102; pseudo-Hrabanus 294, 296
Hrotsvita, *Iohannes* 195
Hruodona, abbess 270
Hubert, Jean 210, 266, 271
Hübner, Wolfgang 253-255
Hucbald of Saint-Amand 192
Huemer, Johann 168
Hugh, abbot of SaintQuentin (Charroux) 295
Hugh of Saint Victor 105, 153
Hugo von Trimberg 70, 306
Huldah, prophetess 31-32
Hygbald, Abbot 1
Iacobus, scribe 309
Ilias Latina 306
Illich, Ivan 105
Imma 132
Ingelheim 218-221, 223, 226, 228, 229-231, cycle of paintings 228
Ingobert 68, 109-110, 184, 186, 188, *tituli* 184
Innocents, massacre of 224
Irish hymnals 300
Irtenkauf, Wolfgang 252

Irvine, Martin 116
Isaac, sacrifice of 11
Isaiah 24
Isidore of Seville 186, 201, *Etymologiae* 254, *Sententiae* 80, *Synonima* 295; Pseudo-Isidore 202
Israhel 267
iudicium aurium 114, 150, 153
Jacob, Daniel 114, 159
Jacob 18
Jael 33, 43
Jagger, Mick 167
Jakobson, Roman 24, 154
Jarnut, Jörg 307, 313
Jauss, Hans Robert 10, 24-25, 70, 83; Jaussian hermeneutics 82
Jeremiah 214
Jeroboam 211
Jerome 11, 30, 51, 81, 189, 192, 277; *Epistola* 29; Pseudo-Jerome 89, 109n36
Jerusalem 213, 214
Jessner, Ulrike 347
Jezebel 52, 215
Job 213
Joel, King, in Cana 45
Johanek, Peter 313
Johannes Hymmonides, *Cena Cypriani* 45
Johannes Trithemius 124
John, the Evangelist 85, 217, 201
John, Prester 341
John of Garland 50, 320
John of Salisbury, *Metalogicon* 79; *Policraticus* 50
John Scotus, see: Eriugena
John the Baptist 45
John the Deacon, *Cena Cipriani* 115
John the Saracen 77
Jonas of Orléans 2-3, 199; *De institutione laicali* 213
Joseph 34, 41, 50, 213, 223, 224; and his brothers 158; resists advances of Potiphar's wide 34

Joseph Scotus 184
Joshua 211, 212, 213, 223
Josiah 212
Judah 201
Judas Maccabeus 211, 213
Judith, Book of 209
Judith, Empress 215
Judith 30-32, 34, 37, 39-52
Julian of Toledo 152, letter to Modoenus 151
Jumièges 137, 276
Justin, Emperor 322
Justin, historian 225
Juvenal 18, 36
Juvencus 11, 12, 14, 15, 53, 66, 291; *Benedictus* 15; *Evangeliorum libri* 27, 81, 224
Karolus Magnus et Leo papa 5, 130, 218, 307-337; editions and studies 310-314; dating and completeness 314-316; author 316-319
Kartschoke, Dieter 54, 81
Keller, Haagen 104
Kermode, Frank 56, 82
Kessler, Herbert 185, 188, 190, 194, 204
Kierkegaard, Søren Aabye 53
Kings, Books of 211, 213, 214, 224
Kirsch, Wolfgang 19
Klopsch, Paul 165
Klopstock, Friedrich Gottlieb 53, 81
Koch, Ludovica 107
Köhler, Wilhelm Reinhold Walter 185, 188, 201, 202, 204, 205
Korzeniewski, Dieter 320, 325
Kristeller, Paul Oskar 306
Kuhn, Thomas S. 9
Lactantius 228
Lamentations, Book of 214
Lammers, Walther 223, 224, 228
Lampert-Weissig, Lisa 340, 341
Laon 292
Lapidge, Michael 124, 125, 128, 291
Laurence of Durham 56

Laurentius Scottus 309
La Via, Stefano 166
Lazarus 158
Leah 52
Le Blant, Edmond 264
Leclerq, Jean 210
Léglu, Catherine E. 348, 349
Le Goff, Jacques 217
Lehmann, Paul 3, 121, 210
Leiden 295, 299
Leo III, pope 307, 308, 312, 315
Leo IV, pope 289
Leonardi, Claudio 68, 110, 124, 305
Leonidas 36
Leovigildus, Bible of 111
Les Bourdellès, Hubert 255
Leutgaudus 271
Lévi-Strauss, Claude 58
Lewis, Clive Staples 53, 82
Liber genealogus 306
Libri Carolini, see: *Opus Caroli regis contra Synodum*
Life of Gauzlinus 177
Limoges 295, 300-301
Lindisfarne 1, 133, 140, destroyed by Danes 133
Lisbon 6
Literary epigraphy 261, 267-269
Littera antiqua 4
Little Bear (constellation) 242-243
Liutgard, queen 315
Liuvigild 186
Lobrichon, Guy 186
Lombard, Peter 124
Lorsch Sylloge 291
Lothair, Emperor 204, 215, 288
Lotman, Jury 347
Louis the Pious 31, 106, 213, 214, 215, 216, 218, 221, 228, 229, 288, 313, 327
Louis XVI 189
Lucan 316
Lucas de Tuy 227
Lucius Junius Brutus 36

Indices 407

Lucretia 33, 38
Luhmann, Niklas 9
Lukács, György 56
Luke 253
Lupus of Ferrières 123, 297
Luxeuil 298-300
Luxorius 14, for Fridamal 194
Lyon 5
Mabillon, Jean 268
Maccabees 212
Macedonia 228
Maecenas 98
Magdeburg 235
Magenard 268
Magulfus 281
Maiestas Domini 192
Mainz 218; cathedral of 175
Manilius 252
Manitius, Max 316, 322, 327
Manlius Curtius 36
Marbod of Rennes 32, 33, 50, 84, 176, 205; *Liber decem capitulorum* 32, 50
Marcel, master 289
Marcellinus, Saint 316
Marius Victor, *Alethia* 12, 15, 51, 81, 114, 291
Martha 35
Martial 186
Martianus Capella, s. Capella
Martin, René 344
Martinez Gázquez, José 255
Marvell, Andrew 53
Marx, Jean 345
Mary 24, 30, 32, 32, 33, 35, 224, 225, 266, 309; medieval devotion to 50
Mathilda of France 52
Matthew 216, 217
Matthew of Vendôme 55, 70, 92; *Tobias* 51, 66, 69, 91
Maximin, St. 199
McKitterick, Rosamond 188-189, 263, 327
Melchizedek 212
Menoeceus 36

Mésoniat, Claudio 55
Metz 137, 276; cathedral 189
Meyer, Wilhelm 147
Micon of Saint-Riquier 129, 266, 267, 268, 280
Migne, Jacques Paul 122, 126
Milan 262
Millstädter Bibel 292
Milo of Saint-Amand 42, 45, 51; *De sobrietate* 42; presents *Vita Amandi* to Aiminus 118-120; *Vita Amandi* 135
Milred Sylloge 291
Milton, John 53, 81
Minerva 37
Minnis, Alastair J. 305, 306
Miriam, prophetess 40
Mitchell, John 118, 183, 91
Modenese sentinels, *O tu qui servas* 163
modicus et rusticus 190
Moduin, bishop of Autun 123, 288, 309, 315, 316, 319-321, 322, 323-324, 326, 328; *Ecloga* 325
modulatio 151
modus symbolicus 81, 83
Mogol (Giulio Rapetti) 166
Mohlberg, Leo Cumbert 309
Momigliano, Arnaldo 10
Monnier, Francis 318
Monteverdi, Angelo 210
Monza 295
Mortensen, Lars Boje 55
Mostert, Marco 97
Moses 59, 189, 195, 201, 202, 223, 224, 225
motus corporis 114
Moussy, Claude 17, 37
Moutier-Grandval Bible 185, 192, 197, 201, 204
Mowbray, Thomas, Duke of Norfolk 339
Mozarabic Andalusia 152
Mozarabic hymns, 194
Munari, Franco 55
Munk Olsen, Birger 306

Mussato, Albertino see Albertino
Müstair 225
Mütherich, Florentine 205
Nabal 41
Naomi 30, 32, 51
Naples 299, 301
Narcissus 16
Nicaea, council of 178
Nicolau, Mathieu G. 148
Niederaltaich 219
Nijmegen 218
Nineveh 225
Ninus, first Assyrian king 225
Nithard 267, 268
nocturlabium 233, 235, 242
Nonnos of Panopolis 11
Norberg, Dag 148, 149, 153, 165, 166, 167, 296-298
Notker of Saint Gall (Notker the Stammerer) 2, 119, 214, 289; *Gesta Caroli* 215
Nouaillé 137, 276
Novalis 76
nova Roma 320, 323-324
Numantia 36
Odulf of Saint-Riquier 270, 290
officium linguae 120
Olympus 253, 271
Opus Caroli (*Karoli*) regis *contra Synodum* 178, 182 ; see also Theodulf of Orléans
Orelli, Johann Kaspar von 310
Orosius 228, *Historia adversus paganos* 227
Oswald, king 132
Oswi 132
Otfrid, *Evangelienbuch* 3
Othlo of St. Emmeram, *De doctrina spiritualis* 90, 91
Otricus of Cologne 288
Otto III 235
Otto of Freising 227
Ovid 23, 132, 37, 85, 287, 316, 324, *Metamorphoses* 37; Ovidian structure 84
Pacificus of Verona 5, 129, 236-240, 245-249, 252-260, 263, epitaphs in Verona 236; *horologium nocturnum* 238-241
Paderborn 307, 308, 312, 327, 799 meeting 218
Palestine, landscape 15
Pamphilus 306
Panella, Pasquale 166
Paradise, Expulsion and Flood 224
Paris, 829 council 182, 214
Paris, Gaston 147, 148
Paris, University of 123
Paschasius Radbertus 120 n. 61, 214, 215, 255
Pascoli, Giovanni 141
Pascucci, Giovanni 19
Pasolini, Pier Paolo 154, 158
Paul the Apostle 109, 195, 216, 217, conversion of 189, letters of 192
Paul I, pope 240
Paul the Deacon 130, 210, 287; *Gesta episcoporum Mettensium* 3
Paulinus of Aquileia 3, 119, 134, 142, 149, 152, 158, 162, 287, 293-295, 297-298; biblical narrative *rhythmi* 115; *De Lazaro* 173; epitaph for Cimitile 136; *Fuit domini*; Lazarus 158; *Gloriam Deo* hymn 162, 163; *Tertio in flore*; Joseph and his brothers 158; *Regula fidei* 106
Paulinus of Nola 38, 39, 52, 136, 176, 183, 262, 275; *Epistola* to Nicetas 176; *Regula Fidei* 106
Paulinus of Périgueux 195, 262
Paulus Alvarus 68, 109, 186; *carmina* 111-114; life of Eulogius 152
Pausanias, *Descriptio Greciae* 175
Péguy, Charles 11, 53, 67
Pelagius, *Confessio* 309
Penda, King 132
Perkins, David, 9
Pertz, Georg Heinrich 310
Peter, Saint 216, 217, 316

Indices

Peter of Pisa 343
Petrarch 55, 76, 81, 120
Phalaris 226, 227
Pharaoh 223
Philaeni 36
Philip of Harvengt, *Commentaria in Cantica Canticorum* 63
pietas 221
Pietri, Luce 262
Pippin I of Aquitaine, 215, 217, 227, 228-229, 308; crowning of 211
pius 131
planctus, regularity of structure 117
Plato 75
Pliny the Elder 305
Poeta Saxo 98, 215, 216-217, 228, 231; *Gesta Karoli Magni* 2
Poetria Nova 6
Polaris (Star) 233, 242-243, 247-248
Pompeii, House of Epigrams 176
Porphyrion 271
Poulle, Emmanuel 242
Prickett, Stephen 57, 64
Primuliacum, basilica of 176
Priscian, translation of *Dionysius Periegetes* 309
Proba 15, 18, 291
Prosper of Aquitaine, *De ingratis* 195
Prudentius (the poet) 33, 41, 42, 87, 97, 170, 176, 225, 294, 297; *Contra Symmachum* 16; *Dittochaeon* 176 ; *Liber cathemerinon* VI 192, 194; *Peristefanon* 170, 195; *Psychomachia* 39, 41, 42
Prudentius of Troyes 188
Psalms 192, 195, 197, 212, 213
Psalmus Responsorius 12, 300
Publilius Syrus, *Sententiae* 309
Pulgram, Ernst 148
Pyrillus (Perillus), tyrant of Sicily 226
Quedlinburg, *Annales* of 216
Quintus Serenus, *Liber medicinalis* 308
Raby, Frederic James Edward 124
Rachel 30, 32, 52

Radegund 30, 49
Ramazzotti, Eros 160, 170; *Libertà* 167
Ramirez-Weavier, Eric 255
Randon, abbot 276
Rankin, Susan 161
Ratkowitsch, Christine 221, 229, 319, 320, 322, 324
Rauch, Christian 219
Ravenna 31
Rebecca, mother of Isaac 30, 32, 52
Red Sea 33, 86
Regensburg 287
Regulus (Marcus Atilius) 36
Reichenau, 212, 265, 295, 300, 328; *tituli* 186; verses 264
Reichenau-Oberzell 205; inscriptions 184
Reims 133, 205; church of 215; Bible of 188
renovatio 205
Revelation 189, 192, 201
Rhine 308
Rhythmi Merowingici et Carolini aevi 295-296
rhythmus 159
Ricardus, *Passio Catharinae* 197
Richard of Lorsch 142
Richarius, saint 266
Riché, Pierre 210, 211, 214
Ricoeur, Paul 54, 57, 58, 65, 69, 76, 82; *Biblical Hermeneutics* 65
Ricolf, archbishop of Mainz 316
Rigg, Arthur George 55, 285-286
Robert de Boron 345
Roberts, Michael 24, 54
Roca-Puig, Ramon 12
Rolling Stones, The, *Paint it Black* 167
Romanisierung 15
Rome 137, 228, 276, 300, 307-308, 315
Romulus and Remus 226
Ronconi, Giorgio 55
Rosenburg 250
Rudolf 268, 270
Ruodlieb 345

Rusticius Elpidius 177; *Tristicha* 176
Ruth 31, 32, 34
Sacerdos, grammarian 165
Sacrum Romanum Imperium 231
Sage, Walter 219
Saguntum 36
Saint-Alyre in Clermont 184, 224
Saint-Amand 137, 265, 276
Saint-Avold 137
Saint-Benoît de Mals 225
Saint-Bertin 127
Saint-Denis 137, 276, 295
Saint Gall 98, 115, 138, 171, 172, 184, 233, 265, 282, 271, 294-300, 308, 309, 326, 328; copyists Winitharius and Jacob 98; inscriptions 184; Plan of 271-272
Saint-Martial in Limoges 172, 294
Saint-Médard, Louis's deposition at 214
Saint Peter in the Vatican 183, 265
Saint-Philibert-de-Granlieu 282
Saint Rémi 223
Saint-Riquier 129, 138, 265, 266, 274, 282, 290
Saint-Vaast 137, 276, 282
Salutati, Coluccio see Coluccio
Salzburg 126, 127
Samson 213
Samuel 211
San Paolo Fuori-le-Mura, Bible 109, 185, 205 212
Sankt Alban in Mainz 223, 294
Sankt Georg in Reichenau-Oberzell 224, 225, 264
Sankt Peter in Salzburg 137, 138, 276, 281
Santagata, Toni 167
santautore 160
Santi, Francesco 305
Sapphic strophe 195; (pseudo-), strophe 148
Sappho 32
Sarah 30, 32

Saturnian metre 150
Saul 211, 214
Savini, Chiara 252
Saxo Grammaticus 98, 100, 107, 116; *Gesta Danorum* 345
Saxony 308
Scaliger, Josephus Justus 76
Schaller, Dieter 297, 298, 309, 311, 312, 314-316, 322
Scheck, Helene 319
Schlesinger, Walter 219, 229-230
Schmid, Wolfgang *Tityrus christianus* 14
Schmidt, Paul Gerhard 344
Schmitt, Jean-Claude 250
schola palatina 2
Schramm, Percy Ernst 219
Schumacher, Karl 219
Scipions 216
Scotland, mission of 132
Scott, Alexander Brian 55
Scott, Walter 341
Second language, acquisition 6, 343; analysis 346
Sedulius Caelius, 3, 11, 12, 21-22, 66, 70, 81, 85, 93, 95, 111, 135, 170, 225, 291; *Carmen Paschale* 16, 21; *Collatio* 68, 85; poetics 88
Sedulius Scotus, 129, 184, 192, 194, 195, 204, 213, 224, 264, 313, 344; *De regimine christiano* 213
Seine river 271
Seliger, Herbert W. 339
Semiramis 38
sensus literalis 80
Sequence of Eulalia 3
Serment de Strasbourg 3
Servius 150, 152; *ad Aeneidem* 16; *ad rhythmum* 151
Severus of Malaga 55
Shakespeare, William 339; *Richard II*, 339
Shohamy, Elana 339
Sidonius Apollinaris 33, 40; *libellus* in

Indices 411

carmen 144
Siegfried 171
Sigfried of Corbie 68
Sigilaus 204
Sigualdus, canon 202
Silius, *Punica* 17
Silvagni, Angelo 275, 291
Silvius 309
Simeon of Durham, *Historiae* 1
Simonetti, Adele 47
Simon Magus, baptism 88
Simson, Bernhard 311, 318
Sinatra, Frank 169
Sisara, leader of the Canaanites 3344
Smaragdus, abbot of Saint-Mihiel-sur-Meuse 3, 108, 186, 190; commentary on Donatus 106; *tituli* 184; *Via regia* 213
Solinarius 306
Solomon 212, 214, 215, 216, 223, 239; Nathan's anointing of 212; son of 52
specula principum 213
Spiegel, Gabrielle 340
Spitzer, Leo 346
Spivak, Gayatri Chakravorty 343
Statius, *Thebais* 37
Stephen II, pope 211
Stoppacci, Patrizia 293
Stork, Hans-Walter 309
Stotz, Peter 148, 195, 262
Strasbourg 328
Streker, Karl 238, 240, 252, 294, 295, 296, 316, 322; *De laude dei* 170
Suger of Saint-Denis 177
Sulpicius Severus 176, 183
Supplement 58, *Supplementum* 62
Susanna, wife of Joachim 31, 34, 52
Symphosius 270, 277
Tassilo III, Duke of Bavaria 318
Tasso, Torquato 53, 67
Tatarkiewicz, Władysław 82
Tatuinus 345
Terentianus Maurus 192
Tertullian 11, *Ad martyras* 36; Pseudo-Tertullian 195
Tesmundus, canon 202
Thegan 210, *Gesta Hludowici imperatoris* 219
Theoderic (Theodoric), King 31, 240
Theodosius 216-217, 227, 228, 229
Theodulf of Orléans 3, 22, 42, 104, 108-109, 110, 123, 141, 178, 182, 183, 186, 189-190, 197, 199, 201, 256, 274, 287, 313, 315, 316, 319, 321, 326, 327-328, 344; *carmina* 109, 188, 309; epigram for Germigny-des-Prés 263; *Opus Caroli* 3, 256, 344: Psalter for Gisla 117
Theofrid of Corbie 171, 294, 296-298
Thiofrid of Echternach 124, 129
Thomas Aquinas 75, 77; *Summa Theologiae* 80; Thomism 76, 79, 80
Thomas 216, 217
Thomism, see: Thomas Aquinas
Thomson, Henry John 39
Thraede, Klaus 13, 18, 54
Thrasea 33
Tilliette, Jean-Yves 285, 322
Times New Roman 4
Tomyris, Scythian queen 38, 225, 227
Toulouse 151
Tours 126, 137, 205, 262, 265, 276, 283; Bible of Tours 188, 192, 224; Cycles of the Bibles of Tours 188-206 *Martinellus* 275, 291; *scriptorium* 186
Tozzi, Umberto, *Gloria* 163
traditionbildend 300
translatio studiorum 123
Traube, Ludwig 266, 300
Treffort, Cécile 136, 276
typicus 209
typology 209, 214-215, 287
Ulysses 11
Ursa Minor 233
Vatican 308
Vaughan, Sarah 173
Venantius Fortunatus 30-31, 33, 40, 44, 49, 136, 142, 177, 192, 262, 265, 275,

286, 294, 295, 324; *De virginitate* 29, 33, 40, 322; *Vita Sancti Martini* 144, 322
Venus with Aeneas 182
Venuti, Lawrence 349
Vergil, 21, 132, 150, 316, 321, 322, 324; *Aeneid* 14, 16, 18; post-Vergilian epic 12; post-Vergilian legacy 13; Vergilian poetry 80
Verginius and Verginia 36
Verona 171, 233, 238, 239, 295, 296, 297, 299-301; cathedral 233, 236; churches 237
Veronesi, Sandro, *Versi rock* 167
Versus ad picturas 175-208; *Bibliae pauperum* 177; typological explanation 183
Versus de Bibliotheca 186
Versus de evangelio ad picturam 309
versus quadrati 147
Versus Sangallenses 188
Versus Wissenburgenses 205, 224
Vespa, *Altercatio coci et pistoris* 344
Vestiments and furniture 269-271
Victorinus of Pettau 201, 202
Vienne 276
Vigilius, Pope 88
Vikings (TV series) 1
Vinay, Gustavo 91, 97
Virgil the Grammarian, *Epitome* 151
Virgin Mary, see: Mary
Vita Eduardi 50
Vivarium 186
Vivian, Abbot 186, 190, 202, 204
Vivian Bible 118, 185, 188, 189, 192, 194, 195, 197, 201, 204, 206-208
Von Moos, Peter 55, 56, 65, 66, 114
Von Schlosser, Julius 177
Von Winterfeld, Paul 295
Vorauer Bible 292
Vroom, Hermann Bernard 148
Vulfinus of Die, *Vita Marcelli* 195
Waal, river 218
Waddell, Helen 124, 139, 283

Walahfrid Stabo of Reichenau 31, 42, 51, 119, 182, 217, 252, 288; *De imagine Tetrici* 31, 213; *Visio Wettini* 213
Waldo, abbot 295
Wallace, David 341
Wallach, Luitpold 274
Walter Map, *De nugis curialium* 345
Walter of Châtillon 50
Waltharius 345
Walther, Hans 344
Walther of Speyer, *Scolasticus* 50
Wandalbert of Prüm 68, 192, 252, 288, 289, 301
Warren, Michelle 349
Wattenbach, Wilhelm 99
Wearmouth-Jarrow 186
Wehrli, Max 54, 68
Weimann, Uta 219
Weissenburg, inscriptions 184
Wickham, Chris 312
Wiesenbach, Joachim 235, 239, 242, 245, 247 n. 23
Wigbod 42
Wilfrid, bishop 131 n. 24
William of Conches 79
William of Saint-Thierry 62
Willibrord, on his father, Wilgisus 135; *Vita metrica* 134
Winiges, duke 308
Women of the Old Testament 30-52
Worcester 291
Xerxes, King 44
Yale, deconstructionist school 57
York, 139, 140, 141, 340; Church of 127, 130, 132; history of 143-144; library of 131
Zeller, Adolf 219
Zeno of Verona 253-254, 296, 300
Zodiology, Christian 254-256
Zumthor, Paul 114, 128, 159, 202, 306
Zurich 5, 326